Custom Edition Prepared for
Education Foundations, Law, and Ethics
80-205

Beyond the Art of Teaching

FOUNDATIONS, POLICIES, AND PRACTICES

Faculty of Education, University of Windsor
Instructors: Dr. Yvette Daniel and Dr. Benedicta Egbo

Excerpts taken from:

Becoming a Teacher, Second Canadian Edition
by Forrest W. Parkay, Beverly Hardcastle Stanford, John P. Vaillancourt, and Heather C. Stephens

Classroom Management for Elementary Teachers, Seventh Edition
by Carolyn M. Evertson, Edmund T. Emmer, and Murray E. Worsham

Curriculum and Instruction for Becoming a Teacher
by Forrest W. Parkay

Your First Year of Teaching and Beyond, Fourth Edition
by Ellen L. Kronowitz

Principles of Classroom Management: A Professional Decision-Making Model, Canadian Edition
by James Levin, James F. Nolan, James W. Kerr, and Anne E. Elliott

Classroom Management for Middle and High School Teachers, Seventh Edition
by Edmund T. Emmer, Carolyn M. Evertson, and Murray E. Worsham

PEARSON

Custom
Publishing

Cover Art: *July Morning,* by William Padien.

Excerpts taken from:

Becoming a Teacher, Second Canadian Edition
by Forrest W. Parkay, Beverly Hardcastle Stanford, John
P. Vaillancourt, and Heather C. Stephens
Copyright © 2005, 1996 by Pearson Education Canada
Inc., Toronto, Ontario
Published by Allyn and Bacon
Boston, Massachusetts 02116

Classroom Management for Elementary Teachers,
Seventh Edition
by Carolyn M. Evertson, Edmund T. Emmer, and
Murray E. Worsham
Copyright © 2006, 2003, 2000, 1997, 1994, 1989, 1984 by
Pearson Education
Published by Allyn and Bacon

Curriculum and Instruction for Becoming a Teacher
by Forrest W. Parkay
Copyright © 2006 by Pearson Education
Published by Allyn and Bacon

Your First Year of Teaching and Beyond, Fourth Edition
by Ellen L. Kronowitz
Copyright © 2004 by Pearson Education
Published by Allyn and Bacon

*Principles of Classroom Management: A Professional Deci-
sion-Making Model,* Canadian Edition
by James Levin, James F. Nolan, James W. Kerr, and
Anne E. Elliott
Copyright © 2005 by Pearson Education Canada Inc.,
Toronto, Ontario
Published by Allyn and Bacon

Classroom Management for Middle and High School Teachers,
Seventh Edition
by Edmund T. Emmer, Carolyn M. Evertson, and
Murray E. Worsham
Copyright © 2006, 2003, 2000, 1997, 1994, 1989, 1984
by Pearson Education
Published by Allyn and Bacon

Printed in Canada

10 9 8 7 6 5 4 3 2

ISBN 0-536-43662-2

2007220105

ED/MJ

Please visit our web site at *www.pearsoncustom.com*

PEARSON CUSTOM PUBLISHING
501 Boylston Street, Suite 900, Boston, MA 02116
A Pearson Education Company

Brief Table of Contents

The Teaching Profession

1

My Pedagogic Creed

John Dewey

Article I—What Education Is

I believe that

- all education proceeds by the participation of the individual in the social consciousness of the race. This process begins unconsciously almost at birth, and is continually shaping the individual's powers, saturating his consciousness, forming his habits, training his ideas, and arousing his feelings and emotions. Through this unconscious education the individual gradually comes to share in the intellectual and moral resources which humanity has succeeded in getting together. He becomes an inheritor of the funded capital of civilization. The most formal and technical education in the world cannot safely depart from this general process. It can only organize it or differentiate it in some particular direction.

- the only true education comes through the stimulation of the child's powers by the demands of the social situations in which he finds himself. Through these demands he is stimulated to act as a member of a unity, to emerge from his original narrowness of action and feeling, and to conceive of himself from the standpoint of the welfare of the group to which he belongs. Through the responses which others make to his own activities he comes to know what these mean in social terms. The value which they have is reflected back into them. For instance, through the response which is made to the child's instinctive babblings the child comes to know what those babblings mean; they are transformed into articulate language, and thus the child is introduced into the consolidated wealth of ideas and emotions which are now summed up in language.

John Dewey was a philosopher and educator; he founded the progressive education movement. This article was published originally as a pamphlet by E. L. Kellogg and Co., 1897.

- this educational process has two sides—one psychological and one sociological—and that neither can be subordinated to the other, or neglected, without evil results following. Of these two sides, the psychological is the basis. The child's own instincts and powers furnish the material and give the starting-point for all education. Save as the efforts of the educator connect with some activity which the child is carrying on of his own initiative independent of the educator, education becomes reduced to a pressure from without. It may, indeed, give certain external results, but cannot truly be called educative. Without insight into the psychological structure and activities of the individual the educative process will, therefore, be haphazard and arbitrary. If it chances to coincide with the child's activity it will get a leverage; if it does not, it will result in friction, or disintegration, or arrest of the child-nature.

- knowledge of social conditions, of the present state of civilization, is necessary in order properly to interpret the child's powers. The child has his own instincts and tendencies, but we do not know what these mean until we can translate them into their social equivalents. We must be able to carry them back into a social past and see them as the inheritance of previous race activities. We must also be able to project them into the future to see what their outcome and end will be. In the illustration just used, it is the ability to see in the child's babblings the promise and potency of a future social intercourse and conversation which enables one to deal in the proper way with that instinct.

- the psychological and social sides are organically related, and that education cannot be regarded as a compromise between the two, or a superimposition of one upon the other. We are told that the psychological definition of education is barren and formal—that it gives us only the idea of a development of all the mental powers without giving us any idea of the use to which these powers are put. On the other hand, it is urged that the social definition of education, as getting adjusted to civilization, makes of it a forced and external process, and results in subordinating the freedom of the individual to a preconceived social and political status.

- each of these objections is true when urged against one side isolated from the other. In order to know what a power really is we must know what its end, use, or function is, and this we cannot know save as we conceive of the individual as active in social relationships. But, on the other hand, the only possible adjustment which we can give to the child under existing conditions is that which arises through putting him in complete possession of all his powers. With the advent of democracy and modern industrial conditions, it is impossible to foretell definitely just what civilization will be twenty years from now. Hence it is impossible to prepare the child for any precise set of conditions. To prepare him for the future life means to give him command of himself; it means so to train him that he will have the full and ready use of all his capacities; that his eye and ear and hand may be tools ready to command, that his judgment may be capable of grasping the conditions under which it has to work, and the executive forces be trained to act economically and efficiently. It is impossible to reach this sort of adjustment save as constant regard is had to the individual's own powers, tastes, and interests—that is, as education is continually converted into psychological terms.

In sum, I believe that the individual who is to be educated is a social individual, and that society is an organic union of individuals. If we eliminate the social factor from the child we are left only with an abstraction; if we eliminate the individual factor from society, we are left only with an inert and lifeless mass. Education, therefore, must begin with a psychological insight into the child's capacities, interests, and habits. It must be controlled at every point by reference to these same considerations. These powers, interests, and habits must be continually interpreted—we must know what they mean. They must be translated into terms of their social equivalents—into terms of what they are capable of in the way of social service.

Article II—What the School Is

I believe that

- the school is primarily a social institution. Education being a social process, the school is simply that form of community life in which all those agencies are concentrated that will be most effective in bringing the child to share in the inherited resources of the race, and to use his own powers for social ends.
- education, therefore, is a process of living and not a preparation for future living.
- the school must represent present life—life as real and vital to the child as that which he carries on in the home, in the neighborhood, or on the playground.
- that education which does not occur through forms of life, forms that are worth living for their own sake, is always a poor substitute for the genuine reality, and tends to cramp and to deaden.
- the school, as an institution, should simplify existing social life; should reduce it, as it were, to an embryonic form. Existing life is so complex that the child cannot be brought into contact with it without either confusion or distraction; he is either overwhelmed by the multiplicity of activities which are going on, so that he loses his own power of orderly reaction, or he is so stimulated by these various activities that his powers are prematurely called into play and he becomes either unduly specialized or else disintegrated.
- as such simplified social life, the school life should grow gradually out of the home life; that it should take up and continue the activities with which the child is already familiar in the home.
- it should exhibit these activities to the child, and reproduce them in such ways that the child will gradually learn the meaning of them, and be capable of playing his own part in relation to them.
- this is a psychological necessity, because it is the only way of securing continuity in the child's growth, the only way of giving a background of past experience to the new ideas given in school.
- it is also a social necessity because the home is the form of social life in which the child has been nurtured and in connection with which he has had his moral training. It is the business of the school to deepen and extend his sense of the values bound up in his home life.
- much of the present education fails because it neglects this fundamental principle of the school as a form of community life. It conceives the school as a place where certain information is to be given, where certain lessons are to be learned, or where certain habits are to be formed. The value of these is conceived as lying largely in the remote future; the child must do these things for the sake of something else he is to do; they are mere preparations. As a result they do not become a part of the life experience of the child and so are not truly educative.
- the moral education centers upon this conception of the school as a mode of social life, that the best and deepest moral training is precisely that which one gets through having to enter into proper relations with others in a unity of work and thought. The present educational systems, so far as they destroy or neglect this unity, render it difficult or impossible to get any genuine, regular moral training.

- the child should be stimulated and controlled in his work through the life of the community.
- under existing conditions far too much of the stimulus and control proceeds from the teacher, because of neglect of the idea of the school as a form of social life.
- the teacher's place and work in the school is to be interpreted from this same basis. The teacher is not in the school to impose certain ideas or to form certain habits in the child, but is there as a member of the community to select the influences which shall affect the child and to assist him in properly responding to these influences.
- the discipline of the school should proceed from the life of the school as a whole and not directly from the teacher.
- the teacher's business is simply to determine, on the basis of larger experience and riper wisdom, how the discipline of life shall come to the child.
- all questions of the grading of the child and his promotion should be determined by reference to the same standard. Examinations are of use only so far as they test the child's fitness for social life and reveal the place in which he can be of the most service and where he can receive the most help.

Article III—The Subject-Matter of Education

I believe that

- the social life of the child is the basis of concentration, or correlation, in all his training or growth. The social life gives the unconscious the unity and the background of all his efforts and of all his attainments.
- the subject-matter of the school curriculum should mark a gradual differentiation out of the primitive unconscious unity of social life.
- we violate the child's nature and render difficult the best ethical results by introducing the child too abruptly to a number of special studies, of reading, writing, geography, etc., out of relation to this social life.
- the true center of correlation on the school subjects is not science, nor literature, nor history, nor geography, but the child's own social activities.
- education cannot be unified in the study of science, or so-called nature study, because apart from human activity, nature itself is not a unity; nature in itself is a number of diverse objects in space and time, and to attempt to make it the center of work by itself is to introduce a principle of radiation rather than one of concentration.
- literature is the reflex expression and interpretation of social experience; that hence it must follow upon and not precede such experience. It, therefore, cannot be made the basis, although it may be made the summary of unification.
- history is of educative value in so far as it presents phases of social life and growth. It must be controlled by reference to social life. When taken simply as history it is thrown into the distant past and becomes dead and inert. Taken as the record of man's social life and progress it becomes full of meaning. I believe, however, that it cannot be so taken excepting as the child is also introduced directly into social life.
- the primary basis of education is in the child's powers at work along the same general constructive lines as those which have brought civilization into being.

- the only way to make the child conscious of his social heritage is to enable him to perform those fundamental types of activity which make civilization what it is.
- the so-called expressive or constructive activities are the center of correlation.
- this gives the standard for the place of cooking, sewing, manual training, etc., in the school.
- they are not special studies which are to be introduced over and above a lot of others in the way of relaxation or relief, or as additional accomplishments. I believe rather that they represent, as types, fundamental forms of social activity, and that it is possible and desirable that the child's introduction into the more formal subjects of the curriculum be through the medium of these activities.
- the study of science is educational in so far as it brings out the materials and processes which make social life what it is.
- one of the greatest difficulties in the present teaching of science is that the material is presented in purely objective form, or is treated as a new peculiar kind of experience which the child can add to that which he has already had. In reality, science is of value because it gives the ability to interpret and control the experience already had. It should be introduced, not as so much new subject-matter, but as showing the factors already involved in previous experience and as furnishing tools by which that experience can be more easily and effectively regulated.
- at present we lose much of the value of literature and language studies because of our elimination of the social element. Language is almost always treated in the books of pedagogy simply as the expression of thought. It is true that language is a logical instrument, but it is fundamentally and primarily a social instrument. Language is the device for communication; it is the tool through which one individual comes to share the ideas and feelings of others. When treated simply as a way of getting individual information, or as a means of showing off what one had learned, it loses its social motive and end.
- there is, therefore, no succession of studies in the ideal school curriculum. If education is life, all life has, from the outset, a scientific aspect, an aspect of art and culture, and an aspect of communication. It cannot, therefore, be true that the proper studies for one grade are mere reading and writing, and that at a later grade, reading, or literature, or science, may be introduced. The progress is not in the succession of studies, but in the development of new attitudes towards, and new interests in, experience.
- education must be conceived as a continuing reconstruction of experience; that the process and the goal of education are one and the same thing.
- to set up any end outside of education, as furnishing its goal and standard, is to deprive the educational process of much of its meaning, and tends to make us rely upon false and external stimuli in dealing with the child.

Article IV—The Nature of Method

I believe that

- the question of method is ultimately reducible to the question of the order of development of the child's powers and interests. The law for presenting and treating material is the law implicit within the child's own nature. Because this is so I believe the following statements are of supreme importance as determining the spirit in which education is carried on:

- the active side precedes the passive in the development of the child-nature; that expression comes before conscious impression; that the muscular development precedes the sensory; that movements come before conscious sensation; I believe that consciousness is essentially motor or impulsive; that conscious states tend to project themselves in action.
- the neglect of this principle is the cause of a large part of the waste of time and strength in school work. The child is thrown into a passive, receptive, or absorbing attitude. The conditions are such that he is not permitted to follow the law of nature; the result is friction and waste.
- ideas (intellectual and rational processes) also result from action and devolve for the sake of the better control of action. What we term reason is primarily the law of orderly and effective action. To attempt to develop the reasoning powers, the powers of judgment, without reference to the selection and arrangement of means in action, is the fundamental fallacy in our present methods of dealing with this matter. As a result we present the child with arbitrary symbols. Symbols are a necessity in mental development, but they have their place as tools for economizing effort; presented by themselves they are a mass of meaningless and arbitrary ideas imposed from without.
- the image is the great instrument of instruction. What a child gets out of any subject presented to him is simply the images which he himself forms with regard to it.
- if nine-tenths of the energy at present directed towards making the child learn certain things were spent in seeing to it that the child was forming proper images, the work of instruction would be indefinitely facilitated.
- much of the time and attention now given to the preparation and presentation of lessons might be more wisely and profitably expended in training the child's power of imagery and in seeing to it that he was continually forming definite, vivid, and growing images of the various subjects with which he comes in contact in his experience.
- interests are the signs and symptoms of growing power. I believe that they represent dawning capacities. Accordingly the constant and careful observation of interests is of the utmost importance for the educator.
- these interests are to be observed as showing the state development which the child has reached.
- they prophesy the stage upon which he is about to enter.
- Only through the continual and sympathetic observation of childhood's interests can the adult enter into the child's life and see what it is ready for, and upon what material it could work most readily and fruitfully.
- these interests are neither to be humored nor repressed. To repress interest is to substitute the adult for the child, and so to weaken intellectual curiosity and alertness, to suppress initiative, and to deaden interest. To humor the interests is to substitute the transient for the permanent. The interest is always the sign of some power below; the important thing is to discover this power. To humor the interest is to fail to penetrate below the surface, and its sure result is to substitute caprice and whim for genuine interest.
- the emotions are the reflex of actions.
- to endeavor to stimulate or arouse the emotions apart from their corresponding activities is to introduce an unhealthy and morbid state of mind.
- if we can only secure right habits of action and thought, with reference to the good, the true, and the beautiful, the emotions will for the most part take care of themselves.

- next to deadness and dullness, formalism and routine, our education is threatened with no greater evil than sentimentalism.
- this sentimentalism is the necessary result of the attempt to divorce feeling from action.

Article V—The School and Social Progress

I believe that

- education is the fundamental method of social progress and reform.
- all reforms which rest simply upon enactment of law, or the threatening of certain penalties, or upon changes in mechanical or outward arrangements, are transitory and futile.
- education is a regulation of the process of coming to share in the social consciousness; and that the adjustment of individual activity on the basis of this social consciousness is the only sure method of social reconstruction.
- this conception has due regard for both the individualistic and socialistic ideals. It is duly individual because it recognizes the formation of a certain character as the only genuine basis of right living. It is socialistic because it recognizes that this right character is not to be formed by merely individual precept, example, or exhortation, but rather by the influence of a certain form of institutional or community life upon the individual, and that the social organism through the school, as its organ, may determine ethical results.
- in the ideal school we have the reconciliation of the individualistic and the institutional ideals
- the community's duty to education is, therefore, its paramount moral duty. By law and punishment, by social agitation and discussion, society can regulate and form itself in a more or less haphazard and chance way. But through education society can formulate its own purposes, can organize its own means and resources, and thus shape itself with definiteness and economy in the direction in which it wishes to move.
- when society once recognizes the possibilities in this direction, and the obligations which these possibilities impose, it is impossible to conceive of the resources of time, attention, and money which will be put at the disposal of the educator.
- it is the business of every one interested in education to insist upon the school as the primary and most effective interest of social progress and reform in order that society may be awakened to realize what the school stands for, and aroused to the necessity of endowing the educator with sufficient equipment properly to perform his task.
- education thus conceived marks the most perfect and intimate union of science and art conceivable in human experience.
- the art of thus giving shape to human powers and adapting them to social service is the supreme art; one calling into its service the best of artists; that no insight, sympathy, tact, executive power, is too great for such service.
- with the growth of psychological service, giving added insight into individual structure and laws of growth; and with growth of social science, adding to our knowledge of the right organization of individuals, all scientific resources can be utilized for the purpose of education.

- when science and art thus join hands the most commanding motive for human action will be reached, the most genuine springs of human conduct aroused, and the best service that human nature is capable of guaranteed.
- the teacher is engaged, not simply in the training of individuals, but in the formation of the proper social life.
- every teacher should realize the dignity of his calling; that he is a social servant set apart for the maintenance of proper social order and the securing of the right social growth.
- in this way the teacher always is the prophet of the true God and the usherer in of the true kingdom of God.

POST NOTE

John Dewey, the father of progressivism, was the most influential educational thinker of the last 100 years. Many of the beliefs expressed in this article (originally published in 1897) have greatly affected educational practice in America. What we find most curious is how current some of these statements still are. On the other hand, many seem dated and clearly from another era. Those that appeal to altruism and idealism have a particularly old-fashioned ring to them. The question remains, however: Which is "out of sync"— the times or the appeals to idealism and altruism?

2

Teaching: Your Chosen Profession

The best part of teaching is being a "learning catalyst." I love it when I can introduce my students to a project or concept and then "take the ball and run with it." My goal is accomplished when they go beyond what I know and I start learning from them.

—Sonya Vanderhoeden-Bracken
Teacher of Senior Mathematics
Laurentian Regional High School
Lachute, Quebec

Taken from *Becoming a Teacher,* Second Canadian Edition, by Forrest W. Parkay, Beverly Hardcastle Stanford, John P. Vaillancourt, and Heather C. Stephens.

Your first interview for a job as a teacher is today, and you can hardly believe that it was only two years ago that you began to take courses to become a teacher. Several questions about your readiness for teaching occupy your mind while you walk from the staff parking lot toward the school, which is one of the newer educational facilities in the province and is recognized as a technologically innovative school. "Am I ready? Do I have what it takes to become a good teacher? Can I handle the stress? Do I have sufficient skills to use educational technology in my classroom?"

Approaching the main entrance, you look at the dozens of students playing on the open field next to the building. Their joyful, exuberant sounds this warm early September morning remind you of your own school days. Some children are moving constantly, running in tight circles and zigzags as they yell and motion to friends who are also on the move. Others stand near the entrance in groups of two or three, talking and milling about as they wait for the bell signalling the start of the first day of school.

At the bottom of the long stairs leading up to a row of green metal doors, you overhear the conversation of three students.

"It's such a great movie. What time do you want to meet?" the taller of two girls asks. Before her friends can respond, she adds, "My aunt's going to pick me up at four o'clock, so I should be home by four-thirty."

"Let's meet at five o'clock," the other girl says. "I can be ready by then."

You notice a young man in a wheelchair appear from around a corner; he jokes and laughs with two other students about skipping classes on this first day of school. As more students arrive, it is obvious that adolescents with special needs are integrated into the student body in a seamless way. Reaching the top of the stairs, you open a door and walk through the entrance out into a brightly lit hallway.

A large permanent sign asks all visitors to report to the main office and you realize that the main office is directly in front of you. To the right of the office door is a bulletin board proclaiming in large red block letters, "Welcome back, students!" Beneath that greeting, in smaller black letters, is another message: "It's going to be a great year!"

Inside the office, you approach the counter on which sits a plastic sign that says "Welcome" in four languages: English, French, Arabic, and Chinese. You introduce yourself to the school's head secretary. He remains seated behind a grey steel desk covered with loose papers.

"I have an appointment with Ms Carmichael," you inform him. "It's about a replacement for Mr. Medina."

"Good. She's expecting you. Why don't you have a seat over there?" He motions for you to sit on the couch across from the teachers' mailboxes. "She's working with some teachers on setting up a meeting of our School Advisory Council. She should be finished in just a few minutes."

While waiting for Ms Carmichael, you think about questions you might be asked. Why did you choose to become a teacher? What is your philosophy of education? How would you integrate technology into your curriculum? What is your approach to classroom management? How would you meet the needs of students from different cultural and linguistic backgrounds? How would you set up a program in your major content area? How familiar are you with provincial curriculum documents? What experience do you have in working with students with special needs? In what extracurricular areas could you make contributions? How would you involve parents in the classroom? What are your strengths? Why should the district hire you?

Reflecting on these questions, you admit they are actually quite difficult. Your answers, you realize, could determine whether or not you get the job.

Though predictable, the interview questions just posed are surprisingly challenging. Why did you decide to become a teacher? How will you meet the needs of all students? What do you have to offer students? The answers to these and similar questions depend on the personality and experiences of the person responding. However, they are questions that professional teachers recognize as important and worthy of careful consideration.

The primary purpose of this book is to orient you within the world of education and to help you begin to formulate answers to such questions. In addition, this book will help you answer your own questions about the career you have chosen. What is teaching really like? What are the trends and issues in the profession? What problems can you expect to encounter in the classroom? What kind of rewards do teachers experience?

We begin this book by asking you to examine why you want to become a teacher because we believe that "good teachers select themselves" (Carmichael, 1981, 113). They know why they want to teach and what subjects and ages they want to teach. They are active in the choosing process, aware of the options, informed about the attractions and obstacles in the field, and anxious to make their contributions to the profession.

Figure 2.1

Why do teachers enter the profession?

Source: Based on a survey by Environics for the Canadian Teachers' Federation. Canadian Teachers' Federation June 2001 Workplace Survey.

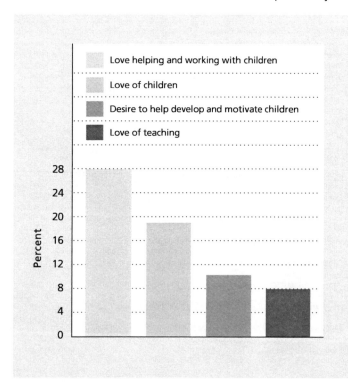

Why Do You Want to Teach?

People are drawn to teaching for many reasons. For some, the desire to teach emerges early and is nurtured by positive experiences with teachers during the formative years of childhood. For others, teaching is seen as a way of making a significant contribution to the world and experiencing the joy of helping others grow and develop. And for others, life as a teacher is attractive because it is exciting, varied, and stimulating.

Desire to Work with Children and Young People

Though the conditions under which teachers work may be challenging, their salaries modest, and members of their communities unsupportive, most teach simply because they care about students. Figure 2.1, based on the Canadian Teachers' Federation (CTF) Workplace Survey (2001), indicates that the most important factor influencing teachers' choice of profession is related to the love of children and teaching.

The day-to-day interactions between teachers and students build strong bonds. Daily contact also enables teachers to become familiar with the personal as well as the academic needs of their students, and this concern for students' welfare and growth outweighs the difficulties and frustrations of teaching. Like the following teachers, they know they can make a difference in students' lives:

> When I was struggling as a kid, one of my teachers was really there for me. She listened to me and supported me when nobody else believed in me. I want to pay her back by helping others like me (Zehm and Kottler 1993, 35).

> [Students] need someone to recognize their uniqueness and specialness and respect it and nurture it (Hansen 1995, 132).

Others, no doubt, love students because they appreciate the unique qualities of youth. They enjoy the liveliness, curiosity, freshness, openness, and trust of young children; or the abilities, wit, spirit, independence, and idealism of adolescents. Like the following teacher, they want to be connected to their students: "... I now know that I teach so I can be involved in my students' lives, in their real life stories" (Henry et al. 1995, 69).

Teachers also derive significant rewards from meeting the needs of diverse learners. Canadian classrooms include 10 to 15 percent of students who have special educational needs, and another 25 percent who arrive with problems and needs arising from their socio-economic background or from a lack of proficiency in English or French (CTF 2003). While Canadian students come from increasingly diverse racial and ethnic backgrounds and those with special needs are increasing in number, effective teachers recognize that their classrooms are enriched by the varied backgrounds of students. To enable you to experience the satisfaction of helping all students learn, significant portions of this book are devoted to **student variability** (differences among students in regard to their developmental needs, interests, abilities, and disabilities) and **student diversity** (differences among students in regard to gender, race, ethnicity, culture, and socioeconomic status). An appreciation for such diversity will help you to experience the rewards that come from enabling each student to make his or her unique contribution to classroom life.

The opportunity to work with young people, whatever their stage of development and whatever their life circumstances, is a key reason people are drawn to teaching and remain in the profession.

Love of Teaching

The CTF Workplace Survey asked teachers why they remained in teaching. The results indicate that for four in ten teachers, the most important factor influencing their decision is that they love helping and working with children (2001). Why do teachers find teaching so satisfying? What does it mean to *love* teaching?

Love of Subject

Some teachers who expressed a love of teaching may have meant that they love teaching in their discipline. The opportunity to continually learn more in one's profession and to share that knowledge with students is a definite attraction. Most of us can recall teachers who were so excited about their subjects that they were surprised when students were not equally enthusiastic. The affinity of such teachers toward their subjects was so great that we tended to see the two as inseparable—saying, for instance, "Ms Gilbert the French teacher" or "Mr Montgomery the math teacher." Though other factors may draw teachers to their work, a love of subject is clearly one of them.

Love of the Teaching Life

For those teachers who always enjoyed school, it is often the life of a teacher that has appeal—to be in an environment that encourages a high regard for education and the life of the mind, and to have daily opportunities to see students become excited about learning. Albert Einstein, for example, regretted that he did not devote his career to the teaching life:

> Believe it or not, one of my deepest regrets [is that I didn't teach]. I regret this because I would have liked to have had more contact with children. There has always been something about the innocence and freshness of young children that appeals to me and brings me great enjoyment to be with them. And they are so open to knowledge. I have never really found it difficult to explain basic laws of nature to children. When you reach them at their level, you can read in their eyes their genuine interest and appreciation (quoted in Bucky 1992, 99).

Love of the Teaching–Learning Process

To love teaching can also mean to love the act of teaching and the learning that can follow. Many teachers, like the following high school special education teacher, focus on the process rather than on the subject or even the students: "I enjoy what I do.... I've been teaching long enough that when the fun stops ... I'll get out. But it hasn't stopped yet, after 34 years. Every day is different. Every day is interesting" (Godar 1990, 244). Persons with this orientation are attracted by the live, spontaneous aspects of teaching and are invigorated by the need to think on their feet and to capitalize on teachable moments when they occur. "[T]hey possess a variety of schemata for seeing what is important, [and they] have a broad repertoire of moves with which to quickly and gracefully act on the situation that they see" (Eisner 1998, 200).

Influence of Teachers

It seems reasonable to assume that the process of becoming a teacher begins early in life. In fact, a Metropolitan Life Survey of 1002 graduates who began teaching in a public school in 1990–91 reported that 52 percent decided to become teachers before college (Louis Harris and Associates 1990). Although it is not true that some people are born teachers, their early life experiences often encourage them to move in that direction. A teacher's influence during the formative years may have been the catalyst. In most cases, the adults who have the greatest influence on children—beyond their parents or guardians—are their teachers.

Evidence also suggests that those who become teachers are often more influenced by their teachers as people than as subject-matter experts. "It is the human dimension that gives all teachers ... their power as professional influencers" (Zehm and Kottler 1993, 2). Behind the decision to become a teacher is often the inspirational memory of earlier teachers to whom one continues to feel connected in a way that goes beyond the subjects they taught.

Table 2.1 lists the minimum requirements for individuals to enter the teaching profession in Canada. General requirements for entrance into the teaching profession in most Canadian provinces is a Grade 12 high school diploma and four years of post-secondary education. Exceptions to this rule are Ontario, Quebec, and Nova Scotia. In addition to the academic requirements, teacher education programs frequently interview candidates to determine their suitability for the teaching profession. Positive qualities for prospective teacher education candidates include a good command of French or English, good health, emotional stability, enthusiasm, and an interest in and enjoyment of children and youth (CTF 1999). In most programs, this interview is the

Table 2.1

Minimum requirements to enter the teaching profession and lowest entry salaries (last updated August 1999)

Province or Territory	Last Year of Secondary Education	Minimum Years of Post-Secondary	Lowest Entry Designation	Lowest Entry-Level Salary	Requirements
NF	Grade 12	4	Certificate Level IV	$26 487 (Provincial)	A four-year (120 credit hours) degree in education. Restrictions are in place regarding content of the degree.
PE	Grade 12	4	Certificate Level IV	$26 958 (Provincial)	A Bachelor of Education with a minimum of four years university training.
NS	Grade 12	4	Class 5	$31 135 (Provincial)	An undergraduate degree (minimum three years) and a Bachelor of Education.
NB	Grade 12	4	Certificate 4	$29 562 (Provincial)	An approved four-year New Brunswick university degree, including teacher education or equivalent.
QC	Grade12	4	17 years of age	$30 222 (Provincial)	Graduation from the two year CEGEP program after Grade 11, plus a four-year Teacher Education degree.
ON	Grade 12	4	Category A1	$33 421 (Ottawa/ Carleton) $29 835 (Thames Valley) $31 445 (Toronto)	Generally, requirements include an acceptable three- or four-year university degree and at least the equivalent of one full year of teacher college acceptable to the Ontario College of Teachers.
NB	Grade 12	4	Class 4	$33 366 (Winnipeg)	Senior matriculation or equivalent, plus five years of study in a degree program, including at least one year of professional study. An undergraduate Bachelor's degree or equivalent is required.
SK	Grade 12	4	Class IV	$30 588 (Provincial)	A minimum of four years of recognized post-secondary education, and: a Professional "A" Certificate or a Professional "B" Certificate; or Vocational Teacher's Certificate, or Technical Teacher's Certificate, and additional training so that only one year of university education is required to complete a four-year degree.
AB	Grade12	4	Category 4	$33 188 (Edmonton Public) $32 676 (Calgary Public)	A four-year Bachelor of Education degree or four years of university education and one year of professional teacher education from an institution acceptable to the Alberta Minister of Education.

Table 2.1 (continued)

Province or Territory	Last Year of Secondary Education	Minimum Years of Post-Secondary	Lowest Entry Designation	Lowest Entry-Level Salary	Requirements
BC	Grade12	4	Category 4	$35 409 (Vancouver)	Completion of a minimum four-year program, or equivalent, of post-secondary professional and academic or specialist studies beyond 12, or equivalent, including appropriate basic teacher education acceptable to the College of Teachers.
YK	Grade 12	4	Category IV	$43 727 (Territorial)	Four years post-secondary education.
NT	Grade 12	4	Level 5	$46 226 (Territorial)	Junior matriculation (Grade 11) plus five years of teacher education or Senior matriculation plus four years of teacher education.

Source: Canadian Teachers' Federation. "Becoming a Teacher." Retrieved January 18, 2003 from www.ctf-fce.ca/E/TIC/becoming.htm

sole means of screening out mentally unhealthy people. Should formal psychological assessments be used to further assist in the screening process? Would using such tests lead to lawsuits against the colleges and universities that conduct them? Can a psychological instrument measure who is likely to be a good or poor teacher?

Desire to Serve

Many choose to teach because they want to serve others; they want the results of their labor to extend beyond themselves and their families. Some decide to select another program or leave teaching in order to earn more money elsewhere, only to return to teaching, confiding that they found the other program or work lacking in meaning or significance. Being involved in a service profession is their draw to the field. Twenty-nine percent of Canadian teachers surveyed reported the major factors for remaining in education to be the love of the profession and job satisfaction, followed by the desire to make a difference (15 percent) (CTF 2001).

For many teachers, the decision to serve through teaching was influenced by their experiences as volunteers. During admission interviews, teacher education program applicants often cite their volunteer work in Boy Scouts, Girl Guides, summer camps, church activities, and other child and youth organizations as influential in their decision to enter the teaching profession.

Explore more deeply your reasons for becoming a teacher. The Professional Reflection feature on page 13 focuses on several characteristics that may indicate your probable satisfaction with teaching as a career.

Should psychological assessments be used to identify students who should not become teachers?

Psychological assessments should be used to identify students who should not become teachers.

With our increasing knowledge about how the brain develops and its responsiveness to stimuli in the environment, especially for the young, we realize the power that teachers have to impact students' cognitive and emotional development for good or ill. Teachers who appear threatening to students can impact their learning as well as their sense of emotional well-being. A teacher who has problems with authority, a quick temper, insensitivity to the feelings of others, or poorly-defined personal boundaries, can be a menace to children and youth. Psychological assessments should be used to screen out teacher education candidates with these characteristics.

Just as extra psychological screening is needed for pilots and air traffic controllers, so too is it needed for people who work with the minds of our children and youth. In all three groups, if the individuals in positions of power fail to live up to their responsibilities or make mistakes, the consequences can be serious. The substitute teacher who exposed himself to a class of Grade Twos, the physical education teacher who had sexual relations with students, and the Grade 5 teacher who regularly ridiculed and humiliated students in class should not have been permitted to teach in the first place. Psychological assessments of them would have revealed their mental health problems and prevented them from entering the profession.

Psychological assessments should not be used to disqualify students who want to become teachers.

Psychological assessments should not be used to disqualify prospective teachers because they could screen out potentially superb teachers and could admit others likely to fail in a classroom. How can an assessment measure something that years of education research have failed to determine, the ingredients of a good teacher? If psychological assessments are used, will teachers begin to look alike, measured against a narrowly defined profile? How can instruments measure the rich array of personalities that motivate students to learn and love learning?

Psychological assessments are costly in terms of both money and personnel time. Evaluators who interview teacher education program candidates require extensive and expensive training. Not many colleges and universities can afford such a time- and cost-intensive approach.

The legalities of screening out candidates on the basis of a psychological assessment is another obvious concern. Could teacher education institutions be sued by people who believe that they were denied admission to their programs on false grounds?

An assessment instrument or process is not able to measure the psychological dimension that encompasses what today's teachers need: "interpersonal skills, willingness to confront and deal with social and cultural complexity, self-awareness and disposition toward reflection, cosmopolitanism, and a well-developed social conscience" (Griffin 1999, 10). An interview process similar to that proposed by Martin Haberman is more likely to get us closer to the mark. In attempting to predict the best candidates for teaching successfully in urban schools, Haberman (1996) proposes asking questions that address classroom situations and test character traits such as perseverance, resourcefulness, and ability to tolerate ambiguities. For instance, candidates are asked what they would do if a student didn't turn in his or her homework. Then they are asked, "What if that didn't work?" After a reply, again, "What if that didn't work either?" Such an approach is more likely to identify who should not be in a classroom than a psychological assessment.

Where do you stand on this issue?

1. What support can you give for your position?

2. How would you measure up in the homework question exercise?

3. What other situational and character-trait testing questions can you suggest to someone wanting to use Haberman's evaluation approach?

4. What legal challenges might be raised about psychological assessments for teacher candidates? What ethical challenges might be raised?

Recommended Sources

Beauchamp, L. & Parsons, J. (2000). *Teaching from the inside out.* Edmonton, AB: Duval House Publishing.

Dolmage, W.R. (1996). *So you want to be a teacher: The guide to teaching as a career choice in Canada.* Toronto, ON: Harcourt Brace and Company, Canada.

Griffin, G. A. (1999). Changes in teacher education: looking to the future. In G. A. Griffin (Ed). *The education of teachers: ninety-eighth yearbook of the National Society for the Study of Education.* Chicago: The University of Chicago Press.

Professional Reflection — Assessing your reasons for choosing to teach

For each of the following characteristics, indicate on a scale from 1 to 5 the extent to which it applies to you.

	Very applicable			Not at all applicable	
1. Love of learning	1	2	3	4	5
2. Success as a student	1	2	3	4	5
3. Good sense of humour	1	2	3	4	5
4. Positive attitudes toward students	1	2	3	4	5
5. Tolerance toward others	1	2	3	4	5
6. Patience	1	2	3	4	5
7. Good verbal and writing skills	1	2	3	4	5
8. Appreciation for the arts	1	2	3	4	5
9. Experiences working with children (camp, church, tutoring, etc.)	1	2	3	4	5
10. Other teachers in family	1	2	3	4	5
11. Encouragement from family to enter teaching	1	2	3	4	5
12. Desire to serve	1	2	3	4	5

Total score

Now that you have completed the self-assessment, calculate your total score; the highest score = 60, the lowest = 12. Interpret the results of your self-assessment with caution. A high score does not necessarily mean that you will be dissatisfied as a teacher, nor does a low score mean that you will be highly satisfied.

Practical Benefits of Teaching

Not to be overlooked as attractions to teaching are its practical benefits. Teachers' hours and vacations are widely recognized as benefits. Though the number of hours most teachers devote to their work goes far beyond the number of hours they actually spend at school, their schedules do afford them a measure of flexibility not found in other professions. For example, teachers with school age children can often be at home when their children are not in school, and nearly all teachers, regardless of their years of experience, receive the same generous vacation time: holiday breaks and a long summer vacation. For Canadian teachers, the official classroom day usually runs from 8:30 or 9:00 AM to 3:30 or 4:00 PM. Weekends and statutory holidays are free, and vacations usually include a Christmas and spring break of a week or more, and eight weeks in the summer.

Salaries and Benefits

Although intangible rewards represent a significant attraction to teaching, teachers are demanding that the public acknowledge the value and professional standing of teaching by supporting higher salaries. Though there is still a general consensus that teachers are underpaid, teacher salaries are becoming more competitive with other occupations; in fact, salaries are becoming one of the attractions for the profession.

In seven Canadian provinces and the territories, basic salary scales and fringe benefits are established through negotiations between teacher associations or unions and the governments. In many areas, further bargaining concerning **fringe benefits** and work conditions takes place at the individual board level. The CTF "Salaries and Fringe Benefits" document states that all negotiations take place at the board level in Alberta, Manitoba, and Ontario (2002).

Canadian salary schedules are frequently based on a combination of years of service and level of post-secondary education, with additional allowances paid for those in administrative positions. "For 2001–2002, the minimum salary for a teacher with one university degree, including teacher training (Grade 12 plus four years post-secondary education) ranges from approximately $28 000 to $50 000 annually, depending upon the jurisdiction and experience. The maximum salary for the same level of training ranges from $38 000 to $70 000 (CTF 2002)."

Fringe benefits negotiated in collective agreements may include the following:

- Compassionate leave
- Supplementary medical insurance
- Cumulative sick leave
- Long term disability insurance
- Maternity leave
- Sabbatical and study leave
- Life insurance
- Dental insurance (CTF 2002).

Canadian Teacher Supply and Demand

The Survey of Canadian School Boards, conducted by Vector Research for the CTF in July 2000, showed that 51 percent of Canadian school boards surveyed indicated that they found it increasingly difficult to attract qualified candidates for full-time teaching jobs, with rural areas most affected. Two-thirds of the boards anticipated difficulty in hiring teachers in the next year. The top three factors contributing to this situation were teacher retirement, increased number of students with special needs, and fewer teacher education program graduates. Additional key findings included the following:

- Teacher shortages in science, French, technology, and mathematics.
- Difficulty recruiting and retaining beginning teachers in Northwest Territories and Ontario school boards.

- Problems attracting and keeping a pool of qualified substitute teachers.
- Hiring difficulties anticipated by 100 percent of school boards in Newfoundland and Labrador and the Territories for 2001.

Across Canada, research is taking place to improve understanding of demographic patterns that will affect teacher supply and demand. Examples include "Nova Scotia Public Education Teacher Demand and Supply," a research paper released by the Nova Scotia Department of Education in January 2000; and "Teacher Supply/Demand in Newfoundland and Labrador: 1998–2010," completed in 1998 by Dr. Robert Crocker of the Faculty of Education at Memorial University of Newfoundland.

Job Opportunities for Teachers from Diverse Groups

During the first part of the twenty-first century, there will be exceptional job opportunities for teachers from diverse racial and ethnic backgrounds and for teachers with disabilities. The changing Canadian demographics will be increasingly reflected in the student population. There are current projected increases in Aboriginal students in the western provinces and the territories and growing diversity in Canada's urban areas. For example, there is a growing Aboriginal student population in Saskatchewan that will provide challenges for staffing First Nations and public schools. For a society to understand cultural and ethnic diversity, teachers need to reflect that diversity. The CTF admits that there is a dearth of information available on how the diversity of the Canadian teaching force reflects the diversity of the student population (2002). However, it is known that visible minorities and people of Aboriginal heritage are under-represented as teachers and administrators in Canadian schools (Canadian Coalition for the Rights of Children 1999). Clearly, students from diverse racial, ethnic, and cultural backgrounds and students with disabilities benefit from having role models with whom they can easily identify. In addition, teachers from diverse groups and teachers with disabilities may have, in some instances, an enhanced understanding of student diversity and student variability that they can share with other teachers (CTF 2000).

What Are the Challenges of Teaching?

Like all professions, teaching has undesirable or difficult aspects. As one high school social studies teacher put it: "Teaching is not terrible. It's great. I love it. It just feels terrible sometimes" (Henry et al. 1995, 119).

Prospective teachers need to consider the problems as well as the pleasures they are likely to encounter. You need to be informed about what to expect if you are to make the most of your professional preparation program. With greater awareness of the realities of teaching, you can more purposefully and meaningfully (1) reflect on and refine your personal philosophy of education, (2) acquire teaching strategies and leadership techniques, and (3) develop a knowledge base of research and theory to guide your actions. In this manner, you can become a true professional—free to savour the joys and satisfactions of teaching and confident of your ability to deal with its frustrations and challenges. Table 2.2 shows that teachers must deal with a variety of problems in the schools.

Classroom Management and Increasing Violence

For three of the five years from 1994 to 1998, the public ranked lack of discipline as the most important problem facing the schools in the annual Gallup Polls of the Public's

Attitudes toward the Public Schools. For the other two years, the public ranked fighting, violence, and gangs as the most important. Not surprisingly, discipline and increased crime and violence among youth are strong concerns for teacher education students. Before teachers can teach they must manage their classrooms effectively. Even when parents and the school community are supportive and problems are relatively minor, dealing with discipline can be a disturbing, emotionally draining aspect of teaching. Moreover, the last few years of the 1990s were marked by frequent reports of random, horrific violence in and around schools. Thirty-six percent of parents in 1998 feared for their oldest child's safety while at school; in 1977, only 25 percent of parents had such fears (Rose and Gallup 1998). Several communities previously immune to such tragedies were recently thrust into the national spotlight as a result of violent incidents: Littleton, Colorado; Paducah, Kentucky; and Taber, Alberta to name a few. Though such acts of violence in schools are rare, the possibility of experiencing such events can cause additional job-related stress for teachers.

In addition, many schools have high **teacher–student ratios**, which can make classroom management more difficult. Feeling the press of overcrowding and valiantly resisting the realization that they cannot meet the needs of all their students, teachers may try to work faster and longer to give their students the best possible education. All too often, however, they learn to put off, overlook, or otherwise attend inadequately to many students each day. The Workplace Survey (CTF 2001) reports that 14 percent of teachers surveyed felt that class size and being overworked were among the most stressful parts of their job. The problem of high teacher–student ratios becomes even more acute when complicated by the high **student-mobility rates** in many schools. In such situations, teachers have trouble not only in meeting students' needs but also in recognizing students and remembering their names! As you will see, developing a leadership plan, a learning environment, and communication skills will help you face the challenges of classroom management.

Social Problems That Impact Students

Many social problems affect the lives and learning of many children and youth, such as substance abuse, teen pregnancy, homelessness, poverty, family distress, child abuse and neglect, violence and crime, suicide, and health problems such as HIV/AIDS and fetal alcohol syndrome. The social problems that place students at risk of school failure are not always easy to detect. Students' low productivity, learning difficulties, and attitude problems demand teacher attention; yet teachers may be unaware of the source of those difficulties. Even when teachers do recognize the source of a problem, they may lack the resources or expertise to offer help. Teachers feel frustrated by the wasted potential they observe in their students. In addition, when the public calls for schools to curb or correct social problems, that expectation can increase the stress teachers experience. The Workplace Survey reports that six in ten teachers surveyed felt that their job was more stressful than two years before, and student behaviour and discipline issues were the most stressful parts of their work. Further, 56 percent of teachers reported an increase in the amount of time they spend dealing with the "personal, non-academic problems of their students" (CTF 2001).

Canada's Rural and Urban Challenges

Teacher education programs are working to better prepare education students for the challenges they will face in rural and urban schools.

Table 2.2

Teacher's perceptions of the frequency of discipline problems

About how often do each of the problems listed occur at the school where you teach?

Most of the Time/Fairly Often

	All Teachers			Elementary Teachers			High School Teachers		
	1997	1989	1984	1997	1989	1984	1997	1989	1984
	%	%	%	%	%	%	%	%	%
Schoolwork/homework assignments not completed	71	79	76	68	76	73	78	85	80
Behaviour that disrupts class	58	87	47	65	60	48	45	50	47
Talking back to, disobeying teachers	50	45	43	54	45	42	43	44	43
Truancy/being absent from school	41	45	47	35	32	29	57	67	62
Sloppy or inappropriate dress	40	45	37	36	43	33	51	49	41
Cheating on tests	27	45	40	19	33	29	47	64	51
Stealing money or personal property belonging to other students, teachers, or staff	21	21	32	21	26	25	25	40	39
Vandalizing school property	20	25	29	18	20	22	25	34	35
Skipping classes	18	29	35	9	18	16	41	59	57
Using drugs at school	15	14	17	5	5	6	39	30	29
Theft of school property	14	15	23	13	13	18	15	19	29
Selling drugs at school	9	14	13	3	1	4	26	32	24
Racial fights	6	6	4	5	5	3	6	9	5
Carrying of knives, firearms, or other weapons at school	5	4	8	3	3	5	7	8	10
Drinking alcoholic beverages at school	4	6	10	1	1	2	10	14	17
Sexual activity at school	4	6	8	1	1	3	8	13	12
Taking money or property by force, using weapons or threats	2	2	2	2	2	2	2	2	2
Physical attacks on teachers or staff	2	2	1	2	2	1	2	2	1

Note: Figures add to more than 100 percent because of multiple answers.

Source: From Carol A. Langdon, "The Fourth Phi Delta Kappa Poll of Teachers' Attitudes toward the Public Schools," *Phi Delta Kappan,* November 1997, p. 213. Used by permission of the author and publisher. Copyright 1997, Phi Delta Kappa.

Data from the Canadian Youth in Transition Survey (Statistics Canada 2002) found that students from urban schools in Canada performed significantly better in reading than students from rural schools. Rural students were more likely to come from families with lower socio-economic backgrounds, and the parents tended to be less educated and less likely to be employed in professional occupations. The study shows that the difference between rural and urban reading performance is most strongly related to community differences. Compared to the urban communities, rural communities are characterized by lower levels of education, fewer jobs, and jobs that were, on average, lower earning and less likely to require a university degree (Statistics Canada 2002). Inner city schools also place special demands on teachers, especially in the area of teaching literacy.

Urban schools need resources to support the large number of children that come from impoverished circumstances. Toronto, for example, has nearly twice as many families with incomes under $10 000 compared to other Ontario cities. Not only that, its high rents force tenants to spend almost twice as much of their income on housing. As such, there is a large troubled student sector that requires extensive professional and paraprofessional services from the school board. These include assistance of youth counsellors, halls monitors, and attendance counsellors.

The publication *Every Kid Counts* (2001), an initiative of the Vancouver Elementary School Teachers' Association, details efforts of inner city activists and provides advocacy materials and guidance strategies to schools and community groups in Vancouver and beyond.

Schools in inner city areas must have teachers who care about children living in poverty and who are willing to make the extra efforts to meet their diverse needs. Many teachers and administrators leave these schools after a year or two because of the immense pressure of the social and educational environment. Beginning teachers need to become familiar with the literature on family literacy of children in poverty. In addition, teacher education programs need to emphasize the importance of developing school-family-community partnerships for student success.

Aboriginal Education in Inner Cities

Aboriginal Education in Winnipeg Inner City High Schools (2002) describes the life experiences and cultural values of many Aboriginal students and their families as very different from those they experience in schools, which are run largely by non-Aboriginal, middle class people. The report discusses the marginalization of Aboriginal students through curriculum that does not reflect their cultural values or daily realities. Incidences of racism—both overt (name-calling and stereotyping) and institutional—are prevalent. There are few Aboriginal teachers, and little Aboriginal content in the curriculum. Many Aboriginal students resist and reject this middle-class, non-Aboriginal curriculum. The paper states, "What Aboriginal people have said to us about the educational system is not that Aboriginal people should be forced to change in order to fit into and succeed in school, but rather that the educational system needs to change" (p. 3).

Canada's Sprawling Geography

Canada's large land mass provides challenges in terms of furnishing equitable educational services to small and isolated communities, especially those in the north. Northern and geographically isolated school boards have difficulty attracting and maintaining staff, and providing appropriate educational experiences is costly. The educational systems of these regions must be developed to meet the needs of the students in the context of their communities. The culture of the local communities must be valued and should shape the curriculum. Teachers need to be prepared to meet the special challenges of these regions. Initiatives that encourage young people to become teachers and to remain in their home communities are important. One example of a small school in Fort Providence, Northwest Territories, is the Déh Gah Elementary and Secondary School. Déh Gah is "committed to provide a balanced educational experience; one that is academically strong while incorporating traditional values." It is important to maintain community schools, as in the case of the Charles Yohin School in Nahanni Butte, also in the Northwest Territories. Built of logs with two large classrooms and a mezzanine, the school currently has an enrollment of 18 students, from Kindergarten to Grade 10.

In recent years, technology has had a positive effect on the ability of such schools to communicate and reach out to other areas of the country. Joseph Burr Tyrell School, located in remote Fort Smith, NT, is one such school that has used technology to increase contact with its Canadian peers. The school is working to bridge the distance gap and communicate with such schools as Harry Camsell School in Hay River, NT. Grade 6 students at the school are working on a "Frontier Earth" project, in which they research the effects of global warming and share their findings with students at Harry Camsell. Grade 4 students are now interested in accessing the "Space" project databases Harry Camsell students have already created. Technology will continue to assist schools in isolated areas to make important connections.

Diverse Populations

Canada is becoming increasingly diverse in its population, and such diversity enriches the school systems as well as providing challenges. Large urban areas, such as Vancouver and Toronto, have large populations of immigrants from Asia, Africa, and Latin America that have joined the more established populations with European roots, as well as Aboriginal people. The report on the future of education in Ontario, *The Schools We Need: A New Blueprint for Ontario* (Leithwood, Fullan, & Watson 2003), contends that 59 percent of immigrants to Canada moved to Ontario in 2001, and the vast majority of these settled in the Toronto area. The report argues that the Toronto student population is one of the most diverse found anywhere in the world.

The *Response to the Education Tax Credit* (2001) report, by the Toronto District School Board (TDSB) states the following:

- Approximately 53 percent of TDSB secondary students do not speak English as their first language. In elementary schools, 41 percent of students have a language other than English as their first language.
- More than 80 languages are represented in TDSB schools. Languages from all over the world, such as Urdu, Serbian, Spanish, Swahili, and Cantonese, are spoken by TDSB students.
- More than 47 000 (24 percent) of elementary students were born outside of Canada, in more than 175 different countries.
- More than 11 500 (12 percent) of secondary students have been in Canada for three years or less.

Immigrant students need intake workers and translation services, and their families need school community advisors. It is the public school's responsibility to support the diversity of cultures and tradition; the curriculum and the teaching staff need to address the cognitive and social needs of all learners. (Toronto Parent Network 2001).

Need for Family and Community Support

Support from parents and the community can make a significant difference in the teacher's effectiveness in the classroom. Increasingly, there has been a realization that school, parents, and community must work together so that children and youth develop to their maximum potential academically, socially, emotionally, and physically. Parents who talk with their children, help with homework, read to them, monitor their television viewing, and attend meetings of the Parent Teacher Organization (PTO) and school open houses can enhance their children's ability to succeed in school (Henry 1996; Moore 1992; Fuligni and Stevenson 1995). Similarly, communities can support schools by providing essential social, vocational, recreational, and health support services to students and their families. The CTF Workplace Survey reveals that stress and workload related issues are the most frequently stated reasons that influence Canadian teachers' decisions to leave the profession (CTF 2001).

A low rate of parental participation in their children's schooling is reflected in the 1994 Gallup Poll of the Public's Attitudes toward the Public Schools, which reported that less than 50 percent of the parents of public school students attended a PTA (Parent-Teacher Association) meeting during the academic year, and in the 1995 poll, which reported that only 38 percent of parents attended a school board meeting during the past school year. Nevertheless, the 1997 poll revealed that 69 percent of the public would be willing to work as an unpaid volunteer in local schools—a significant increase compared to 1992, when 59 percent indicated their willingness to volunteer. In Canada, demographic information states that teachers have the confidence of 80 percent of the population (CTF 2000).

Long Working Hours and Job Stress

The official working hours for teachers are attractive, but the real working hours are another matter. Not built into contracts are the after-hours or extra assignments found at all levels of teaching—from recess duty and parent conferences, to high school club advisorships and coaching. Also not obvious are the hours of preparation that occur before and after school—frequently late into the night and over the weekend. Over 90 percent of teachers work more than 40 h per week, with the largest percentage working more than 55 h per week (Louis Harris and Associates 1995).

The need to complete copious amounts of paperwork, including record keeping, may be the most burdensome of the teacher's non-teaching tasks. On average, teachers spend ten hours per week on school-related responsibilities not directly related to teaching (Louis Harris and Associates 1995, 68). Other non-teaching tasks include supervising student behaviour on the playground, at extracurricular events, and in the halls, study halls, and lunchrooms; attending faculty meetings, parent conferences, and open houses; and taking tickets or selling at concessions for athletic events. Individually, such assignments and responsibilities may be enjoyable; too many of them at once, however, become a burden and consume the teacher's valuable time.

In addition to long working hours, factors such as students' lack of interest, conflicts with administrators, public criticism, overcrowded classrooms, lack of resources, and isolation from other adults cause some teachers to experience high levels of stress. Unchecked, acute levels of stress can lead to job dissatisfaction, emotional and physical exhaustion, and an inability to cope effectively—all classic symptoms of teacher **burnout**. To cope with stress and avoid burnout, teachers report that activities in seven areas are beneficial: social support, physical fitness, intellectual stimulation, entertainment, personal hobbies, self-management, and supportive attitudes (Gmelch and Parkay 1995, 46–65).

Gaining Professional Empowerment

In an interview with journalist Bill Moyers, noted Harvard educator Sara Lawrence Lightfoot eloquently describes why teachers desire **professional empowerment**:

Will I be prepared to teach in a digital age?

One of the challenges of teaching in the 21st century will be to keep abreast of new technologies that can enhance students' learning. Therefore, it will be important throughout your teacher education program to evaluate your ability to use newly emerging technology. Most colleges and universities offer a wide range of courses and training in the use of technology. To make a self-assessment of your current level of technological literacy, compare your skills with those highlighted in the following case illustration of a teacher education student at Acadia University in Wolfville, Nova Scotia, Canada.

A Day in the Life of ...

Jude wakes up in the morning, turns on his laptop computer, sends an email to his parents, checks the sports scores from last night to find that the university basketball team won their game, accesses his group discussion topic for the first class of the day from the virtual bulletin board, adds his thoughts to the ongoing electronic exchanges, and grabs his CD-ROM of readings for the course.

He arrives at his first class, Reading in the Content Areas, finds a seat at one of the tables, takes out his laptop, and connects to the internet. The professor for the course circulates among the students, her computer docked into the teaching station. On a large projection screen is a Microsoft PowerPoint slide that features the topic for the day, the use of web quests as a teaching tool in secondary classrooms. The URL

for a website for this topic has been sent to students prior to the class so Jude quickly brings up the site. After the professor explains the history and philosophy behind web quests, small groups form according to content areas. Groups then choose a web quest in their content area and critique it as a possible teaching resource according to a set of criteria. The group discussions are animated and the professor circulates around the room to facilitate the group work. During the class, the professor switches the computer docking station to show a video about reading strategies and the use of technology in the process. After class, groups will be required to continue their critique and to send their completed assignment via an email attachment. The professor reminds the group that the multimedia project is due for next class.

After lunch, Jude goes to his Education Issues class where the professor discusses the electronic case study discussion on censorship. The discussion focuses on several key points. One of Jude's classmates wonders which books are most frequently censored in schools, and the professor asks someone in the class to find that information. An internet search takes Jude to the National Council of Teachers of English (NCTE) site that lists the most frequently banned books and offers guidelines on this issue to educators.

At four o'clock, Jude returns to his room, connects to the internet, checks email, and orders two online articles from the library. He then attaches his contribution to a group project and sends it to the other group

[Teachers are] saying, "I haven't had the opportunity to participate fully in this enterprise." Some teachers are speaking about the politics of teachers' voice. They're saying, "We want more control over our lives in this school." Some of them are making an even more subtle point—they're talking about voice as knowledge. "We know things about this enterprise that researchers and policy makers can never know. We have engaged in this intimate experience, and we have things to tell you if you'd only learn how to ask, and if you'd only learn how to listen" (Moyers 1989, 161).

Although some teachers may experience frustration in their efforts to gain professional empowerment, efforts to empower teachers and to "professionalize" teaching are leading to unprecedented opportunities for today's teachers to extend their leadership roles beyond the classroom.

members for feedback. He goes off to the dining hall where his student card is electronically swiped before he picks up his meal.

After dinner, Jude logs on to the internet again, and sends his unit lesson plans to his cooperating teacher at the school where he starts his field experience next week. He is proud of the learning object he has designed for one of the lessons. For his final task of the evening, he goes to a URL where he views some scenes from a Virtual Learning Environment that simulate the experience of a Grade 7 teacher. Jude emails home, checks the online edition of the local paper, and logs off for the night.

The task for the next day is to complete the electronic portfolio CD-ROM for use when applying for teaching positions.

Acadia University is an example of an innovative and technologically advanced Canadian school. All students enrolled at Acadia University lease an IBM ThinkPad, which they are allowed to take anywhere with them—from the classroom, to residence, or home for vacations. In addition, each student is provided with an email account. The university campus has over 5200 on-campus data connections; students can connect from classrooms, residences, and other locations throughout the campus and off-campus students use a dial-up service. The students and faculty use the technology in a number of ways from classroom applications, to out-of-class communication and instant messaging. Professors may put class notes on Microsoft PowerPoint and post course materials on the Automated Courseware Management Environment (ACME). Email is used to communicate outside class, set up appointments, post announcements, and exchange files. The university promises, "You will learn to access the world's knowledge, use today's technology, and develop the advanced technological skills you will need to adapt to ever-changing study and work environments." (Irwin 2003)

In universities across Canada, teachers of tomorrow are being prepared in a similar way for the technology-laden future by learning to keep abreast of change. Canadian teacher-training programs recognize the challenges future teachers face and they are focusing on preparing future educators to use and integrate technology into their curriculum in a meaningful way.

What Is Teaching Really Like?

In this section we examine six basic **realities of teaching** that illustrate why teaching is so demanding and why it can be so exciting, rewarding, and uplifting. And when we say that teaching is demanding, we mean more than the fact that Ms Masih's third-period math students just can't seem to learn how to compute the area of a triangle; or that Mr. LeBlanc's Grade 6 English class can't remember whether to use *there* or *their*; or even that 35 percent of teachers in 1995 reported they were "under great stress" almost every day or several days a week (Louis Harris and Associates 1995, 55). Although there are many frustrating, stressful events with which teachers must cope, the difficulty of teaching goes much further, or deeper, than these examples suggest.

Reality 1: The Unpredictability of Outcomes

The outcomes of teaching, even in the best of circumstances, are neither predictable nor consistent. Any teacher, beginner or veteran, can give countless examples of how the outcomes of teaching are often unpredictable and inconsistent. Life in most classrooms usually proceeds on a fairly even keel—with teachers able to predict, fairly accurately, how their students will respond to lessons. Adherence to the best laid lesson plans, however, may be accompanied by students' blank stares, yawns of boredom, hostile acting out, or expressions of befuddlement. On the other hand, lack of preparation on the teacher's part does not necessarily rule out the possibility of a thoroughly exciting class discussion, a real breakthrough in understanding for an individual student or the entire class, or simply a good, fast-paced review of previously learned material. In short, teachers are often surprised at students' reactions to classroom activities.

Students' Responses

Contrary to the popular notion that teaching consists entirely of specific competencies or observable behaviours that have predetermined effects on students, the reactions of students to any given activity cannot be guaranteed. Furthermore, teachers, unlike other professionals, cannot control all the results of their efforts.

One example of the unpredictability of teaching is given in a teacher intern's description of setting up an independent reading program in his middle-school classroom. Here we see how careful room arrangement and organization of materials do not ensure desired outcomes, and how a teacher learned to adjust to one reality of teaching.

> I wanted everything looking perfect. For two more hours, I placed this here and stuffed that in there.... There were stacks of brand-new books sitting on three odd shelves and a metal display rack.... I coded the books and arranged them neatly on the shelves. I displayed their glossy covers as if the room was a [chain bookstore].

A few weeks after setting up the reading program, however, this teacher observes that

> The orderly environment I thought I had conceived was fraught with complications. For example, the back rows of the classroom were inaccessible regions from which paper and pencil pieces were hurled at vulnerable victims, and there were zones where, apparently, no teacher's voice could be heard.... The books ... remained in chaos. Novels turned up behind shelves, on the sidewalks outside, and in the trash can. And still, at least once a week, I dutifully arranged them until I was satisfied. But something was happening. It was taking less and less for me to be satisfied.... [I] loosened up (Henry et al. 1995, 73–76).

Contrary to the preceding example, unpredictability in the classroom is not always bad. Another teacher intern describes her unexpected success at setting up a writing workshop at an urban middle school with a large population of at-risk students. One day she began by telling her students that

> "We're going to be starting something new these six weeks.... We will be transforming this classroom into a writing workshop." What was I trying to do here? They're not writers.... Raymond stared down at *Where's Waldo*. Michael was engrossed in an elaborate pencil drum solo. Edwina powdered her nose and under her eyes.

"Listen to me, you guys," I said, trying not to lose it before we even started. "We're starting something completely different, something you never get a chance to do in your other classes."

A few heads turned to face me. Veronica slugged Edwina, and Edwina slid her compact into her back pocket.

"What, Miss ... chew gum?"

In spite of her initial reservations, this teacher made the following observations the next day—the first day of the writing workshop.

Today, it's all clicking.

"Aw, man, I told you I don't understand that part. Why does that guy in your story ... Chris ... say that it's too early to rob the store?" David pleads. "It doesn't make sense."

Raymond tips his desk forward and smiles. "It's too early because they want to wait until the store's almost closed."

"Well, then, you've got to say that. Right, Miss?"

I lean against the door frame and try not to laugh. I listen to the conversations around me. Yes, they're loud and they're talking and they're laughing. But they're learning. My students are involved in their writing, I say to myself and shake my head (Henry et al. 1995, 54–55).

Philip Jackson describes the unpredictability of teaching in his well-known book *Life in Classrooms:* "[As] typically conducted, teaching is an opportunistic process.... Neither teacher nor students can predict with any certainty exactly what will happen next. Plans are forever going awry and unexpected opportunities for the attainment of educational goals are constantly emerging" (Jackson 1990, 166).

In what ways must this classroom teacher face the reality of unpredictable outcomes? What are five other basic realities that all teachers face in their work?

Results in the Future

Teachers strive to effect changes in their students for the future as well as for the here and now. In *Life in Classrooms*, Jackson labels this the preparatory aspect of teaching. In addition to having students perform better on next Monday's unit exam or on a criterion-referenced test mandated by the province, teachers expect students to apply their newly acquired skills and knowledge at some indeterminate, usually distant, point in the future.

Just as months or years may pass before the results of teaching become clear, teachers may wait a long time before receiving positive feedback from students. The following comment by a Kindergarten teacher illustrates the delayed satisfaction that can characterize teaching:

> About a month ago I had a 22-year-old boy knock on the door. He said, "Miss R?" I said, "Yes." He is now in England, an architect; he's married and has a little girl. I thought, "This is not happening to me. I had you in Kindergarten." If you teach high school and a kid comes back and he's married in two or three years, that's expected, but 16 years or 18 years—first year in Kindergarten. It's rewarding ... be it one year, or ten years down the road.... There are daily satisfactions—"She got it!"—that's a reward in itself, but I think it's a little bit down the road that you get your satisfaction (Cohn and Kottkamp 1993, 42–43).

Reality 2: The Difficulty of Assessing Students' Learning

It is difficult to assess what students learn as a result of being taught. The ultimate purpose of teaching is to lead the student to a greater understanding of the things and ideas of this world. But, as even the most casual appraisal of human nature will confirm, it is very difficult, perhaps impossible, to determine precisely what another human being does or does not understand. Although the aims or intentions of teaching may be specified with exacting detail, one of the realities of teaching, as the following junior high school teacher points out, is that some of what students learn may be indeterminate and beyond direct measurement:

There is no clear end result.... That frustrates me. I want so badly for my joy [of teaching] to be neatly tied up so that I can look at it admiringly.... I want so badly to *see* my successes—I don't know, give me certificates or badges or jelly beans. Then I can stack them up, count them, and rate myself as a teacher (Henry et al. 1995, 68–69).

Advocates of national testing stress the need for objective measurement of school and student performance. Proponents of national testing stress that it is an accurate measure of Canada's public school system and a valuable method to compare results across schools, school boards, provinces or territories, and nations. Teachers' concerns about national testing include the interpretation of results, and the areas of learning that cannot be measured by such tests. (CTF n.d.)

We have miles of computer printouts with test data but very little knowledge of what lies behind a child's written response, little understanding of how the child experiences the curriculum. As one educational researcher concludes: "The inaccessibility of data is similar both in science and in learning. We cannot directly 'see' subatomic particles, nor can we 'see' the inner-workings of the mind and emotions of the child. Both are inferential: both are subject to human interpretation" (Costa 1984, 202).

On the one hand, then, teachers must recognize their limited ability to determine what students actually learn; on the other, they must continuously work to become aware of the latest approaches to assessing students' learning. Figure 2.2 presents a set of guiding principles for teachers to follow in developing a student-centred approach to classroom assessment.

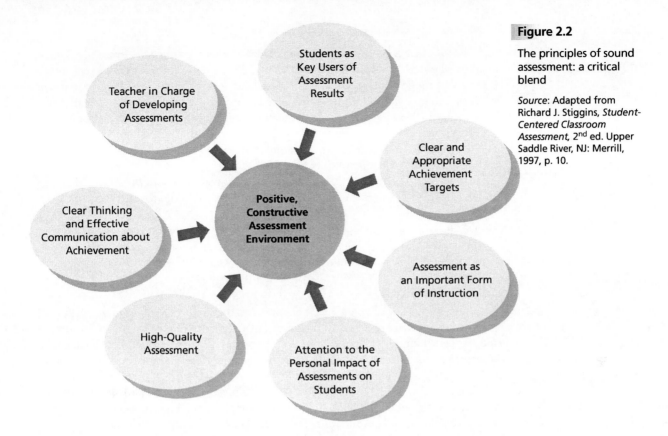

Figure 2.2

The principles of sound assessment: a critical blend

Source: Adapted from Richard J. Stiggins, *Student-Centered Classroom Assessment*, 2nd ed. Upper Saddle River, NJ: Merrill, 1997, p. 10.

Reality 3: The Need for Student-Teacher Partnership

The teacher's ability to influence student behaviour is actually quite limited. The very fact that we refer to the teaching–learning process indicates the extent to which classroom events are "jointly produced" (Doyle 1986, 395) and depend upon a teacher–student partnership. According to Arthur Combs (1979, 234–35) in a book aptly titled *Myths in Education: Beliefs That Hinder Progress and Their Alternatives*:

> A teacher's influence on all but the simplest, most primitive forms of student behaviour, even in that teacher's own classroom, cannot be clearly established. The older children get, the less teachers can influence even those few, primitive forms of behaviour. The attempt to hold teachers responsible for what students do is, for all practical purposes, well nigh impossible.

At best, a teacher tries to influence students so that they make internal decisions to behave in the desired manner—whether it be reading the first chapter of *The Shipping News* by Friday or solving ten addition problems during a mathematics lesson. Teaching is a uniquely demanding profession, therefore, because the work of teachers is evaluated not in terms of what teachers do but in terms of their ability "to help the students become more effective as learners," to "become active seekers after new development" (Joyce and Weil 2000, 408, 399).

This reality underscores the need for a partnership between teacher and learners, including learners who are culturally diverse.

Reality 4: The Impact of Teachers' Attitudes

With the role of teacher also comes the power to influence others by example. Educational psychologist Anita E. Woolfolk (1998, 223) states that "teachers serve as models for a vast range of behaviours, from pronouncing vocabulary words, to reacting to the seizure of an epileptic student, to being enthusiastic about learning." Clearly, students learn much by imitation, and teachers are models for students. In the primary grades, teachers are idolized by their young students. At the high school level, teachers have the potential to inspire students' emulation and establish the classroom tone by modelling expected attitudes and behaviours.

In *The Tact of Teaching: The Meaning of Pedagogical Thoughtfulness*, Max van Manen (1991, 167) states the importance of teachers' attitudes toward students:

> An educator needs to believe in children. Specifically, he or she needs to believe in the possibilities and goodness of the particular children for whom he or she has responsibility. My belief in a child strengthens that child—provided of course that the child experiences my trust as something real and as something positive.

A high school social studies teacher expresses the same idea in this manner: "[The] relationship between teachers and students is becoming one of the most important aspects of teaching. [In] a world of broken homes and violence, the encouragement of their teachers may be the only thing students can hold onto that makes them feel good about themselves" (Henry et al. 1995, 127).

Teachers also model attitudes toward the subjects they teach and show students, through their example that learning is an ongoing, life-enriching process that does not end with diplomas and graduations. Their example confirms the timeless message of Sir Rabindranath Tagore that is inscribed above the doorway of a public building in India: "A teacher can never truly teach unless he is still learning himself. A lamp can never light another lamp unless it continues to burn its own flame."

How do teacher's attitudes affect students' learning? In what ways are teachers significant role models for students?

Reality 5: The Drama and Immediacy of Teaching

Interactive teaching is characterized by events that are rapid-changing, multidimensional, and irregular. We have already discussed how the outcomes of teaching are unpredictable and inconsistent. Yet the challenges of teaching go beyond this. The face-to-face interactions teachers have with students—what Jackson (1990, 152) has termed **interactive teaching**—are themselves rapid-changing, multidimensional, and irregular. "Day in and day out, teachers spend much of their lives 'on stage' before audiences that are not always receptive ... teachers must orchestrate a daunting array of interpersonal interactions and build a cohesive, positive climate for learning" (Gmelch and Parkay 1995, 47).

When teachers are in the **preactive teaching** stages of their work—preparing to teach or reflecting on previous teaching—they can afford to be consistently deliberate and rational. Planning for lessons, grading papers, reflecting on the misbehaviour of a student—such activities are usually done alone and lack the immediacy and sense of urgency that characterize interactive teaching. While actually working with students, however, you must be able to think on your feet and respond appropriately to complex, ever-changing situations. You must be flexible and ready to deal with the unexpected. During a discussion, for example, you must operate on at least two levels. On one level, you respond appropriately to students' comments, monitor other students for signs of confusion or comprehension, formulate the next comment or question, and be alert for signs of misbehaviour. On another level, you ensure that participation is evenly distributed among students, evaluate the content and quality of students' contributions, keep the discussion focused and moving ahead, and emphasize major content areas.

During interactive teaching, the awareness that you are responsible for the forward movement of the group never lets up. Teachers are the only professionals who practice their craft almost exclusively under the direct, continuous gaze of up to 30 or 40 clients. Jackson (1990, 119) sums up the experience: "The *immediacy* of classroom events is something that anyone who has ever been in charge of a roomful of students can never forget."

Reality 6: The Uniqueness of the Teaching Experience

Teaching involves a unique mode of being between teacher and student—a mode of being that can be experienced but not fully defined or described. On your journey to become a teacher, you will gradually develop your capacity to listen to students and to convey an authentic sense of concern for their learning. Unfortunately, there is no precise, easy-to-follow formula for demonstrating this to students. You will have to take into account your personality and special gifts to discover your own best way for showing this concern.

One reason it is difficult to describe teaching is that an important domain of teaching, **teachers' thought processes**, including professional reflection, cannot be observed directly. Figure 2.3 shows how the unobservable domain of the teacher's "interior reflective thinking" interacts with and is influenced by the observable domain of the teacher's "exterior reflective action." Teachers' thought processes include their theories and beliefs about students and how they learn, their plans for teaching, and the decisions they make while teaching. Thought processes and actions can be constrained by the physical setting of the classroom or external factors such as the curriculum, the principal, or the community. On the other hand, teachers' thought processes and actions may be influenced by unique opportunities, such as the chance to engage in curriculum reform or school governance. The model also illustrates a further complexity of teaching—namely, that the relationships between teacher behaviour, student behaviour, and student achievement are reciprocal. What teachers do is influenced not only by their thought processes before, during, and after teaching but also by student behaviour and student achievement. This complexity contributes to the uniqueness of the teaching experience.

What Does Society Expect of Teachers?

The prevailing view within our society is that teachers are public servants accountable to the people. As a result, society has high expectations of teachers—some would say too high. Entrusted with our nation's most precious resource, its children and youth, today's teachers are expected to have advanced knowledge and skills and

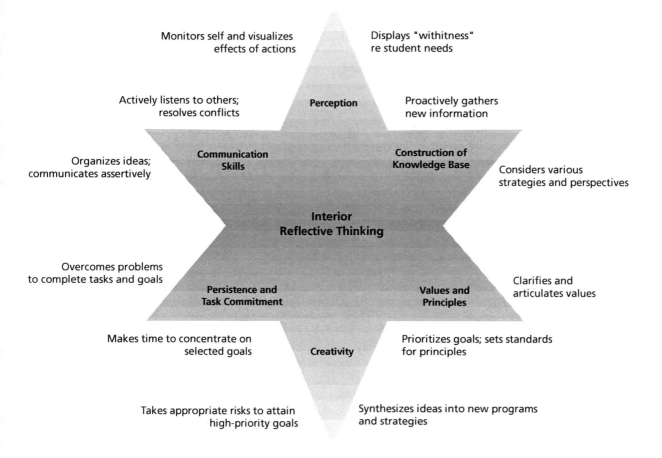

Teacher observes
a class event or
student behaviour

Monitors self and visualizes
effects of actions

Displays "withitness"
re student needs

Actively listens to others;
resolves conflicts

Perception

Proactively gathers
new information

Organizes ideas;
communicates assertively

**Communication
Skills**

**Construction of
Knowledge Base**

Considers various
strategies and perspectives

**Interior
Reflective Thinking**

Overcomes problems
to complete tasks and goals

**Persistence and
Task Commitment**

**Values and
Principles**

Clarifies and
articulates values

Makes time to concentrate on
selected goals

Creativity

Prioritizes goals; sets standards
for principles

Takes appropriate risks to attain
high-priority goals

Synthesizes ideas into new programs
and strategies

**Exterior
Reflective Action**

Figure 2.3

A model of reflective
action in teaching

Source: Judy W. Eby,
*Reflective Planning,
Teaching, and Evaluation:
K–12,* 2nd ed. Upper Saddle
River, NJ: Merrill, 1996,
p. 14. © 1996. Reprinted
by permission of Prentice-
Hall, Inc., Upper Saddle
River, NJ.

high academic and ethical standards. Although promoting students' academic progress has always been their primary responsibility, teachers are also expected to further students' social, emotional, and moral development and to safeguard students' health and well-being. Increasingly, the public calls on teachers and schools to address social problems and risk factors that affect student success.

The Public Trust

Teaching is subject to a high degree of public scrutiny and control. The level of trust that the public extends to teachers as professionals varies greatly. The public appears to have great confidence in the work that teachers do. Because of its faith in the teaching profession, the public invests teachers with considerable power over its children. For the most part, parents willingly allow their children to be influenced by teachers and expect their children to obey and respect teachers. However, the public trust increases and decreases in response to social and political changes that lead to waves of educational reform.

Teacher Competency and Effectiveness

Society believes that competent, effective teachers are important keys to a strong system of education. Accordingly, teachers are expected to be proficient in the use of instructional strategies, curriculum materials, advanced educational technologies, and classroom management techniques. They are also expected to have a thorough understanding of the developmental levels of their students and a solid grasp of the content they teach. To maintain and extend this high level of skill, teachers are expected to be informed of exemplary practices and to demonstrate a desire for professional development.

Teacher competency and effectiveness includes the responsibility to help all learners succeed. Though today's students come from a diverse array of backgrounds, society expects teachers to hold strong beliefs about the potential for all children. Regardless of their students' ethnicity, language, gender, socioeconomic status, family backgrounds and living conditions, abilities, or disabilities, teachers have a responsibility to ensure that all students develop to their fullest potential. To accomplish this, teachers are expected to have a repertoire of instructional strategies and resources to create meaningful learning experiences that promote students' growth and development.

Teacher Accountability

Teachers must "be mindful of the social ethic—their public duties and obligations—embodied in the practice of teaching ..." (Hansen 1995, 143). Society agrees that teachers are primarily responsible for promoting students' learning, though it is not always in agreement about what students should learn. In any case, society expects teachers to understand how factors such as student backgrounds, attitudes, and learning styles can affect achievement; and it expects that teachers will create safe and effective learning environments. Society also believes that teachers and schools should be accountable for equalizing educational opportunity and maintaining high professional standards.

Teacher accountability also means meeting high standards of conduct. Teachers are no longer required to sign statements such as the following, taken from a 1927 contract: "I promise to sleep at least eight hours a night, to eat carefully, and to take every precaution to keep in the best of health and spirits, in order that I may be better able to render efficient service to my pupils" (Waller 1932, 43). Nevertheless, society does expect teachers to hold high standards of professional ethics and personal morality and to model behaviours that match those standards.

How Do Good Teachers View Their Work?

Most Canadian teachers across the country feel good about their jobs. Of 11 000 teachers surveyed (Kuehn n.d.) overall sources of satisfaction from their work included student respect for them as a teacher (92 percent), financial rewards (51 percent), and being well-respected in their community (49 percent). Eighty-seven percent of teachers agreed that "teaching is a worthwhile job," 89 percent said they are "proud to be a teacher," and 77 percent said that they "look forward to coming to work each day" (Larry Kuehn n.d.).

Good teachers derive greatest satisfaction when they are effective in promoting students' learning—when they "make a difference" in students' lives. When you recall your most effective teachers, you probably think of particular individuals, not idealizations of the teacher's many roles. What good teachers do can be described in terms of five **modes of teaching**, which are more general and significant than a discussion of roles.

You may recognize these modes in your observations of teachers and in the writings of gifted teachers when they reflect on their work. You may even acknowledge these modes of teaching as deeper reasons for becoming a teacher.

A Way of Being

In becoming a teacher, you take on the role and let it become a part of you. Increasingly, the learning of facts can be achieved easily with good books, good TV, CD-ROMs, and access to the Internet. What cannot be done in these ways is teaching styles of life, teaching what it means to be, to grow, to become actualized, to become complete. The only way a teacher can teach these qualities is to possess them. "They become living examples for their students, showing that what they say is important enough for them to apply to their own lives. They are attractive models who advertise, by their very being, that learning does produce wondrous results" (Zehm and Kottler 1993, 16).

A Creative Endeavour

Teaching is a creative endeavour in which teachers are continually shaping and reshaping lessons, events, and the experiences of their students. In *The Call to Teach*, David Hansen (1995, 13) describes the creative dimensions of teaching this way: "In metaphorical terms, teaching is ... more than carrying brick, mortar, and shovel. Rather, it implies being the architect of one's classroom world."

With careful attention to the details of classroom life, effective teachers artistically develop educative relationships with their students; they "read" the myriad events that emerge while teaching and respond appropriately. One high school teacher, identified as highly successful by her principal, reported: "I have to grab the kids that don't want to do math at all and somehow make them want to do this work. I'm not sure how I do it, but kids just want to do well in my class. For some mysterious reason, and I don't care why, they really want to do well."

A Live Performance

Teaching is a live performance with each class period, each day, containing the unpredictable. Further, teachers are engaged in live dialogues with their classes and individual students. The experience of teaching is thus an intense, attention-demanding endeavour—an interactive one that provides minute-to-minute challenges.

Some teachers embrace the live performance aspect of teaching more than others, believing that within it lies true learning. They recognize that teaching "... is full of surprises; classroom lessons that lead to unexpected questions and insights; lessons that fail despite elaborate planning; spur-of-the-moment activities that work beautifully and that may change the direction of a course; students who grow and learn; students who seem to regress or grow distant" (Hansen 1995, 12).

A Form of Empowerment

Power is the dimension of teaching most immediately evident to the new teacher. It is recognized in the first-grader's awed "Teacher, is this good?" on through the high school senior's "How much will this paper count?" Customarily, teachers get respect, at least initially; the deference derives from their power to enhance or diminish their students' academic status and welfare.

What are the modes of teaching that define the essence of good teaching and distinguish gifted teachers? Which mode of teaching might this photo represent?

Even in the most democratic classrooms, teachers have more influence than students because they are responsible for what happens when students are with them, establishing the goals, selecting the methods, setting the pace, evaluating the progress, and deciding whether students should pass or fail. How you use this power is critical. As you know, students at any level can be humiliated by teachers who misuse their power or convey negative expectations to students. A student teacher in a Grade 5 class comments on the impact negative expectations can have on students:

They [students] can sense how a teacher feels, especially how she feels about them personally. Students often find themselves locked into a role that they have played for so long they don't know how to get out of it. Students deserve the right to have an education. They should not have to worry about what negative comments their teachers are saying about them (Rand and Shelton-Colangelo 1999, 107).

An Opportunity to Serve

To become a teacher is to serve others professionally—students, the school, the community, and the country, depending on how broad the perspective is. Most who come to teaching do so for altruistic reasons. The altruistic dimension of teaching is at the heart of the motivation to teach. The paycheque, the public regard, and the vacations have little holding power compared to the opportunity to serve. As the authors of *On Being a Teacher* observe:

Very few people go into education in the first place to become rich or famous. On some level, every teacher gets a special thrill out of helping others.... [The] teachers who flourish, those who are loved by their students and revered by their colleagues, are those who feel tremendous dedication and concern for others—not just because they are paid to do so, but because it is their nature and their ethical responsibility (Zehm and Kottler 1993, 8–9).

Prime Minister's Award for Teaching Excellence Recipients: George Findlay, Renee Boyce, and Lindsay Johnston.

Taking students outside the traditional classroom walls expands their horizons and allows them to experience learning in non-traditional ways. The three teachers profiled in this Teaching for Excellence feature show their students a world of opportunities to prepare them for lifelong learning beyond the classroom.

George Findlay

Princess Elizabeth Public School, Windsor, Ontario

Subjects Taught: Grades 6, 7, and 8

At the very time of their lives when they need to be learning about the range of possibilities that life offers them and about the incredible potential they have within them, children are trapped in a routine round of fact processing, explains George Findlay, who teaches students in the transition years (Grades 6, 7, and 8) at Princess Elizabeth Public School. Findlay tries to counter the feeling he sees in too many kids, that they will stay in a routine school-bound existence until they are 17 or 18 and then leave to take a routine-bound job for the rest of their lives.

For Findlay, hope and opportunities lie around every corner—even at the local campground. "It may seem a simple—even a corny—thing to take a class on a three-day camping trip," he says, "but the benefits are huge." Children learn valuable lessons far beyond the curriculum, about working and about reaching outside their immediate experiences, he explains. "For children in my school, going to a campground or a large building downtown, paying for their own meal, and figuring out how to tip in a restaurant can be very educational experiences."

Lindsay Johnston

Calgary Science Centre School, Calgary, Alberta

Subjects Taught: Science

In elementary school, Lindsay Johnston says, the most important thing a child can learn about science is that it is accessible. In the controlled environment that is all too common inside the classroom, students often learn that science is something closed. "Can you imagine a 10-year-old child believing that they can't do science?" asks Johnston incredulously. Unfortunately, she has, and it is her desire to counter that impression that drives her work at the Science Centre School—a very un-classroom-like setting.

Johnston and her students adopted a natural area a kilometre from the school for a year. They studied the wildlife and plants, and they hiked, bicycled and picnicked, getting to know every corner of the green space. When there was a local dispute about making the area more commercial, the students immersed themselves in the related social issues, such as land use in urban areas. Even at a young age, the students began to see how their learning is connected to the real world.

Renee Boyce

Bishops College, St. John's, Newfoundland

Subjects Taught: Physics

At the high school level, Renee Boyce worried about opening doors for her high school students who feared physics courses. This teacher countered widespread fear by printing a pamphlet telling students exactly what they needed to "do physics." An enthusiastic advocate for the subject, Boyce says that the "mystique that surrounds physics—Newton, Einstein, and Hawking struggling with the basic stuff of the universe—is exactly what captivates kids and fills them with wonder, giving them the drive to master the concepts and the math." This includes getting them out of the classroom, and into the real world that led scientists to start asking questions in the first place. For example, her students learn about navigation on the deck of an oceanographic vessel while they are learning about the ocean floor and currents.

Source: Reproduced with the permission of the Minister of Public Works and Government Services, 2003. Prime Minister's awards for teaching excellence: Exemplary practices. *Beyond the Classroom Walls*. Retrieved 22 January 2003, from pma-ppm.ic.gc.ca/exemplary/1999/Beyond.html

Whatever forms the altruistic rewards of teaching take, they ennoble the profession and remind teachers of the human significance of their work.

Teaching for Excellence

Many of our country's most talented youth and dedicated veterans in the teaching field retain the desire to teach. In part, the desire endures because teachers have been positively influenced by one or more teachers of their own, who enriched, redirected, or significantly changed their lives. The desire also endures because teachers recognize the many joys and rewards the profession offers.

Reflecting on dedicated teachers and their contributions to our lives, we are guided to teaching for the benefit it brings to others. Every year, the Prime Minister's Awards for Teaching Excellence recognizes the efforts of outstanding teachers in all disciplines who provide students with "the tools to become good citizens, to grow and prosper as individuals, and to contribute to Canada's growth, prosperity and well-being" (Industry Canada 1998, iv). Specifically, nominees are recognized for excelling in "some or all of the following areas: exemplary teaching practices; student interest and participation; student achievement/performance; student skills development; and teacher commitment and leadership" (Industry Canada). This textbook acknowledges recipients of the Prime Minister's Awards for Teaching Excellence in selected chapters in a special feature called *Teaching for Excellence*.

SUMMARY

Why Do You Want to Teach?

- An important reason for becoming a teacher is a desire to work with children and young people.

- Other reasons include a passion for teaching based on a love of subject, the teaching life, or the teaching–learning process; the influence of teachers in one's past; and a desire to serve others and society.

- Practical benefits of teaching include on-the-job hours at school, vacations, increasing salaries and benefits, job security, and a feeling of respect in society.

- In contrast to the diversity of student enrollments, the backgrounds of today's teachers are less diverse; thus teachers from diverse racial and ethnic backgrounds and teachers with disabilities will experience exceptional job opportunities for the foreseeable future.

What Are the Challenges of Teaching?

- Working conditions for teachers can be difficult and stressful; however, for most teachers satisfactions outweigh dissatisfactions.

- Though problems in schools vary according to size of community, location, and other factors, teachers in most schools face five challenges: classroom management, social problems that impact students, need for family and community support, long working hours and job stress, and need for professional empowerment.

- Maintaining discipline and avoiding school-based violence are major concerns among preservice teachers.
- Social problems that impact the lives of many children and youth include substance abuse, teen pregnancies, homelessness, poverty, family distress, child abuse, violence and crime, suicide, and health problems such as HIV/AIDS and fetal alcohol syndrome.
- Though job-related factors cause some teachers to experience high levels of stress, stress-reduction activities can help teachers cope and avoid burnout.

What Is Teaching Really Like?

- The outcomes of teaching, even in the best of circumstances, are neither predictable nor consistent.
- It is difficult to assess what students learn as a result of being taught.
- The teacher's ability to influence student behaviour is actually quite limited.
- With the role of teacher also comes the power to influence others by example.
- Interactive teaching is characterized by events that are rapid-changing, multidimensional, and irregular.
- Teaching involves a unique mode of being between teacher and student—a mode of being that can be experienced but not fully defined or described.

What Does Society Expect of Teachers?

- Society has high expectations of the teachers to whom it entrusts its children and youth.
- Society expects teachers to be competent and effective, and it holds teachers accountable for student achievement, for helping all learners succeed, and for maintaining high standards of conduct.

How Do Good Teachers View Their Work?

- Helping students learn and making a difference in students' lives provide teachers with their greatest satisfaction.
- The essence of good teaching can be described in terms of modes of teaching illustrating what good teachers do.
- Five modes of teaching are teaching as a way of being, a creative endeavour, a live performance, a form of empowerment, and an opportunity to serve.

KEY TERMS AND CONCEPTS

burnout
fringe benefits
interactive
    teaching
modes of teaching
preactive teaching

professional
    empowerment
professional portfolio
realities of teaching
student diversity
student-mobility rates

student variability
teacher accountability
teacher–student ratios
teachers' thought
    processes

APPLICATIONS AND ACTIVITIES

Teacher's Journal

1. Consider your reasons for deciding to become a teacher. How do they compare with those described in this chapter?

2. Describe a former teacher who has had a positive influence on your decision to teach. In what ways would you like to become like that teacher?

3. What is your impression of the public's image of teachers in your province, territory, or community today? What factors might be contributing to the kind of attention or lack of attention teachers are receiving?

4. Think about a time when a teacher truly motivated you to learn. What did that teacher do to motivate you? Do you believe other students in the class had the same reaction to this teacher? Why or why not?

5. Recall and describe specific experiences you had with teachers in elementary school, middle school or junior high school, or high school. Were you ever made uncomfortable because of a teacher's power over you? Were you ever ridiculed or diminished by a teacher? Or have you experienced the opposite—being elevated by a teacher's regard for you?

Teacher's Database

1. Make a list of recent portrayals of teachers in the movies, television, and other media. Analyze the portrayals in terms of the type of teacher image they present—positive, neutral, or negative.

2. Clip articles in a major newspaper that relate to one of the focus questions in this chapter. Analyze the clippings as sources of information and examples you can use to develop an answer to that question.

3. While you are on the web, use your favourite search engine and search for information by key words or topics such as: teacher burnout, cost of living, moonlighting, accountability, teacher–student ratios, and tenure.

Observations and Interviews

1. As a collaborative project with classmates, visit a local school and interview teachers to learn about their perceptions of the rewards and challenges of teaching. Share your findings with other groups in your class.

2. Arrange to observe a teacher's class. During your observation, note evidence of the five modes of teaching discussed in this chapter.

3. Ask your instructor to arrange group interviews between students in your class and students at the local elementary, middle, junior, and senior high schools. At each interview session, ask the students what characterizes good and not so good teachers. Also, ask the students what advice they would give to beginning teachers.

4. During an observation of a teacher's class, note evidence of the six realities of teaching discussed in this chapter. How many realities are evident during your observation? Which reality is most prevalent? Least prevalent?

5. Visit a first-year teacher (possibly a graduate from your institution) and ask about his or her first impressions of becoming a teacher. What aspects of teaching were difficult? Which easy? What surprises did this first-year teacher encounter? How would this person have prepared differently?

Professional Portfolio

To help you in your journey toward becoming a teacher, each chapter in this textbook includes suggestions for developing your **professional portfolio**, a collection of evidence documenting your growth and development while learning to become a teacher. At the end of this course you will be well on your way toward a portfolio that documents your knowledge, skills, and attitudes for teaching and contains valuable resources for your first teaching position.

For your first portfolio entry, expand on Teacher's Journal entry #1, which asks you to consider your reasons for becoming a teacher. In your entry (or videotaped version), identify the rewards of teaching for you. Identify the satisfactions. Also, describe the aspects of teaching that you will find challenging.

3

Learning to Teach

The mediocre teacher tells.
The good teacher explains.
The superior teacher demonstrates.
The great teacher inspires.
—William A. Ward

Taken from *Becoming a Teacher,* Second Canadian Edition, by Forrest W. Parkay, Beverly Hardcastle Stanford, John P. Vaillancourt, and Heather C. Stephens.

1. What essential knowledge do you need to teach?
2. What are five ways of viewing the teacher knowledge base?
3. How are Canadian teachers educated and certified?
4. What can you learn from observing in classrooms?
5. How can you gain practical experience for becoming a teacher?
6. How can you develop your teaching portfolio?
7. How can you benefit from mentoring relationships?
8. What opportunities for continuing professional development will you have?

The room was filled with the chatter of writing workshop. Nat puzzled over two crayons in his hand, one of them blue: "Mrs. Hankins, ain't you had you a blue bicycle when you was a little-girl-teacher?" Nat had a way of naming me for what I was: always a teacher—or was it always a little girl? I answered Nat's present question, remembering my past blue bicycle and a childhood story about it that I had shared with the children recently.

Perhaps it was one of those "tell-me-about-when-you-were-little" moments that brought writing memoirs to the forefront of my teaching journal. Perhaps it was the need to make some sense of the cacophonous days with my three special students, Nat, Loretta, and Rodney, who had all been damaged in utero by drugs or alcohol. The original impetus for these writings is lost to me now, but, as Lucy Calkins (1991, 169) says, writing memoirs "has everything to do with rendering the ordinariness of our lives so that it becomes significant." The past seemed to wrap itself around my present-day questions, and as the number of memoirs grew, my journal became a place for uncovering the significant....

I wrote up a study of Nat, Loretta, and Rodney's journey through Kindergarten and presented parts of the study at a conference. After the presentation, I wrote the following reflection in my journal:

So, I keep this journal. It was easier when no one else knew or cared that I wrote. It's a teaching journal. It's a personal journal. It's a research journal. It's both a personal and teaching journal because John Dewey first and Lucy Calkins later taught me to reflect on my day and my life in the same breath. It's both a teaching and research journal because I no longer believe that teaching can be separated from research. (Perhaps it CAN be but it shouldn't be.) The question is ... I guess ... Can it be both personal and research journal? That's what people really want me to defend. But how can I tell people what my heart and head do together in my classroom? (journal entry, April)

I wrote at nap time, while waiting for faculty meetings to begin, during the last ten minutes before turning out the light each night, and on the backs of church bulletins or napkins in restaurants. I had never heard of field notes at the time. I read recently a definition of ethnographic field notes as "the systematic ways of writing what one observes and learns while participating in the daily rounds of the lives of others" (Emerson, Fretz, and Shaw 1995, 18). As the year progressed, I fell into a system of sorts as I recorded the "lives of others." My journal served, then, as the field notes of a teacher. Mine were records of what Emerson et al. (1995) call "headnotes"—mental notes—"hard notes"—direct observations—and "heartnotes"—my feelings and reflections....

When I began seriously listening to my life, my teaching life, I also began to listen to my students' lives at a different level.... I became more tolerant of those who were different from me. When I began to stop and examine the flashes of memory that jolted me, I became a more patient teacher. I more often saw the students and their parents as people; people walking in and out of pain, in and out of joy, in and out of socially constructed prisons (Hankins 1998, 81, 83, 93).*

In the preceding excerpt from Karen Hale Hankin's article "Cacophony to Symphony: Memoirs in Teacher Research," Hale describes how reflective journal writing enabled her to see significant connections between her personal history and her present experiences in the classroom. By purposely examining her "mental notes," "direct observations," and "feelings and reflections," Hankins learned how to "reach and teach" the students with whom she once felt she had little in common. Her ability to reflect upon her experiences in the classroom and her appreciation for the interconnectedness of teaching and research are the hallmarks of a professional teacher. Furthermore, her reflections are reminders that teaching is a complex act—one that requires thoughtfulness, insight into the motivations of others, and good judgment.

What Essential Knowledge Do You Need to Teach?

Students preparing to become teachers must have three kinds of knowledge before they can manage effectively the complexities of teaching: knowledge of self and students, knowledge of subject, and knowledge of educational theory and research. It is to this essential knowledge that we now turn.

Self-Knowledge

Effective teachers are aware of themselves and sensitive to the needs of their students. Although it is evident that teachers should understand their students as fully and deeply as possible, it is less evident that this understanding depends on their level of self-knowledge. If teachers are knowledgeable about their needs (and, most important, able to take care of those needs), they are better able to help their students. As Arthur Jersild (1955, 3), one of the first educators to focus attention on the connection between the teacher's personal insight and professional effectiveness, pointed out, a teacher's self-understanding and self-acceptance are prerequisites for helping students to know and accept themselves.

Teachers' self-evaluations often are influenced by emotions that teachers may experience when they teach, such as anxiety or loneliness. Promoting anxiety are the realities of teaching outlined in Chapter 1. For example, three conditions that cloud teachers' efforts are (1) the interminable nature of teaching (i.e., their work is never completed), (2) the intangible and often unpredictable characteristics of teaching results, and (3) the inability to attribute learning results to specific teachers' instruction. Unlike architects, lawyers, and doctors, teachers can never stand back and admire their work. If a student does well, that success rightfully belongs to the student.

Teachers thus need to develop the ability to tolerate ambiguities and to reduce their anxieties about being observably effective. Without this ability, a teacher "can feel that one is 'wrong,' 'missing something,' a 'bad fit' with students and with teaching itself. One can feel that one's circumstances are unfair, that one is giving but not receiving. One can feel helpless, not knowing what to do, not even knowing how to get the frustration out of mind let alone how to resolve it in practice" (Hansen 1995, 60).

Teachers can also experience loneliness or psychological isolation, since most of their time is spent interacting with children and youth, not adults. Though increased opportunities for professional collaboration and networking are reducing teacher isolation, teachers are behind classroom doors most of the day, immersed in the complexities of teaching and trying to meet the diverse needs of their students. Most teachers would welcome more interaction with their colleagues, especially time to observe one another. Without opportunities to receive feedback from one's peers, teachers are deprived of an important catalyst for professional growth. As Elliot Eisner puts it: "The result of professional isolation is the difficulty that teachers encounter in learning what they themselves do in their own classrooms when they teach. [How] can a teacher learn that he or she is talking too much, not providing sufficient time for student reflection, raising low-order questions, or is simply boring students? Teachers unaware of such features of their own performance are in no position to change them" (1998, 160–61). Additionally, by observing how a colleague responds to the challenges of teaching, the observer has an opportunity to reflect on his or her approaches to meeting those same challenges. For example, a Grade 4 teacher came to the following insight as a result of observing his teaching partner: "Being a teacher is so much more than an extensive repertoire of strategies and techniques. [To] be a teacher is to find a way to live within an environment filled with dilemmas" (Hole 1998, 419).

Knowledge of Students

Knowledge of students is also important. Student characteristics such as their aptitudes, talents, learning styles, stage of development, and their readiness to learn new material are a part of the essential knowledge teachers must have. The importance of this knowledge is evident in comments made by an intern at a middle school: "To teach a kid well you have to know a kid well.... teaching middle school takes a special breed of teachers who understand the unique abilities and inabilities ... [of] those undergoing their own metamorphosis into teenagers" (Henry et al. 1995, 124–25). Teachers gain this kind of knowledge through study, observation, and constant interaction. Without considerable understanding of children and youth, teachers' efforts to help students learn and grow can be inappropriate and, in some cases, counterproductive. Teachers' expectations of students directly affect student achievement. The following Professional Reflection activity is designed to guide you in reflecting on opportunities you have already had to acquire knowledge about learners.

Professional Reflection   **Inventorying your knowledge of children and youth**

To be accepted into a teacher preparation program, you may be required by your college or university to have prior experiences working with children and youth. For instance, to be admitted to any of Nova Scotia's four teacher education programs, all applicants must have a significant amount of supervised work (paid or volunteer) in a "teaching" capacity with children or adolescents. The knowledge of children and youth acquired through such experiences provides an excellent foundation upon which to begin your preparation for becoming a teacher.

Use the following outline to inventory your experiences working with children and youth. Your experiences might include working with service clubs such as Scouts, 4-H, and youth groups; volunteering at a child care center; coaching a sport as part of a parks and recreation program; or tutoring young children in reading or mathematics.

After completing your inventory, reflect on your experiences. During which experiences were you functioning, at least partially, in the role of "teacher"? For example, did you have to demonstrate the skills involved in a particular sport? As a member of a club in high school, did you explain club activities to new members or to parents? While holding a leadership position in a group, were you expected to function as a "role model" to other members of the group?

Setting	Activity	Participants' Age and Sex	Your Role	Date
Example:				
Summer sports program	Taught swimming	Coed, ages 6–8	Camp counsellor	Summer 2000
1.				
2.				
3.				

Knowledge of Subject

With the title of *teacher* comes an assumption of knowledge. Those outside the field of education expect a teacher to be a ready reference for all sorts of information. Clearly, teachers who have extensive knowledge of their subjects are better equipped to help their students learn. However, knowledge of subject matter does not translate into an understanding of *how* to share that knowledge with students—a point illustrated in a case study that focused on "Mary," an undergraduate literature major enrolled in a teacher education program at a major university. By any standards, Mary was a subject-matter expert—she was valedictorian of a large, urban high school; had straight A's in the literature courses she had taken; and had a sophisticated understanding of literature, especially poetry. The case study revealed that Mary had little understanding of classroom activities that would show her students *how* to read with sophistication and concluded that "some prospective teachers may come to teacher education unaware of how they have learned the processes they use and that render them expert. Unaided by their disciplines in locating the underpinnings of their expertise, these skilled, talented, and desirable recruits may easily become, ironically, those who can *do* but who cannot *teach*" (Holt-Reynolds 1999, 43).

Extensive knowledge of subject matter is, by itself, insufficient. Effective, successful teachers possess what is sometimes called **pedagogical content knowledge**. They have an understanding of how students can efficiently learn facts, concepts, generalization and skills. They also have learned how to use various teaching techniques—such as simulations, demonstrations, and illustrations—to maximize student learning.

Knowledge of Methods for Applying Educational Theory and Research

Theories about learners and learning guide the decision making of professional teachers. Not only do such teachers know that a certain strategy works, but they also know *why* it works. Because they recognize the importance of theories, they have at their disposal a greater range of options for problem solving than teachers who have not developed their repertoire of theories. Your ultimate goal as a professional is to apply theoretical knowledge to the practical problems of teaching.

To illustrate the usefulness of research on students' learning, we present six teaching strategies that Barak Rosenshine (1995, 267) recommends, based on his and others' research on cognitive processing, studies of teachers whose students have higher achievement gains than students of other teachers, and research on cognitive strategies.

1. Present new material in small steps so that the working memory does not become overloaded.
2. Help students develop an organization for the new material.
3. Guide student practice by (a) supporting students during initial practice and (b) providing for extensive student processing.
4. When teaching higher level tasks, support students by providing them with cognitive strategies.
5. Help students to use cognitive strategies by providing them with procedural prompts (e.g., questions students ask themselves while learning new material— "who," "what," "why," "when," etc.) and modelling the use of procedural prompts.
6. Provide for extensive student practice.

Which type of knowledge do teachers need more— subject-matter knowledge or professional knowledge?

If you know your subject well, can you teach it well? If you know how to teach well, can you teach anything? Which of the two forms of knowledge is more important for teachers—subject-matter knowledge or professional knowledge?

Individuals preparing to become teachers usually specialize in either elementary or secondary education—although some provinces have a middle school stream for those who wish to teach at the Grade 6 to 8 level. In general, students enrolled in elementary programs are given a broad range of methodological courses in how to teach language arts, social studies, mathematics, and science. On the other hand, students enrolled in secondary programs, where depth of subject knowledge is more critical, are usually given subject-specific methodological courses in only one or two areas. Some educators believe that schools of education should place emphasis on pedagogy, stressing the importance of teaching skills and knowledge about learning, brain research, and communication. Others are still emphatic that it is more important that teachers be well-educated individuals who have an in-depth knowledge of the subjects that they teach. Where do you stand on this issue?

Subject-matter knowledge is most needed.

In addition to the argument that teachers need to be prepared with subject-matter knowledge in order to meet students' curricular needs is the recognition that teachers model to their students what an educated person is. For all teachers, but especially those at the elementary school level, what they teach most is themselves: who they are. Day in and day out, they show students their values, beliefs, and knowledge, even as they teach the subject matter they are required to teach. The illustrations they offer, the language they use, and the perspectives they take draw on their personal knowledge base.

Marva Collins, a teacher who stretched the minds of children with the writings of Aristotle and Shakespeare, was successful in her teaching in large measure because of who she was and what she knew. Her knowledge of history, economics, and literature, especially poetry, enriched the learning of her elementary school children. Similarly, Jaime Escalante attracted attention and became the subject of a popular film, *Stand and Deliver,* because of his success teaching his economically stressed students to perform impressively well on the Scholastic Achievement Test in calculus. Most who followed his story would agree that his effectiveness was more attributable to his personal spirit, his in-depth knowledge of mathematics, and his understanding of history and culture, than to his knowledge of pedagogy per se.

Subject-matter expertise is thus more important for teachers because they must offer students much more than limited, superficial information about increasingly complex topics, and because they should model to students what an educated person is.

Professional knowledge is most needed.

Today, some educational scholars support returning to a greater emphasis on professional knowledge. They base their position on research results such as the following:

- Many studies have found positive relationships between education coursework and teacher performance in the classrooms. These relationships are stronger and more consistent than those between subject matter knowledge and teacher performance (Darling-Hammond, Wise, and Klein 1995, 24).
- The premise is that subject-matter knowledge alone is not enough. To paraphrase author Walker Percy's observation, "Some people get all A's and flunk life," in education, some people get all A's and flunk teaching. Academic knowledge does not translate automatically to teaching effectiveness.

Proponents of greater professional knowledge for teachers observe that teaching has become an increasingly complex and challenging endeavour. Students in today's classrooms are more diverse than ever in their cultural backgrounds, educational needs, and communication and learning styles. As Linda Darling-Hammond (1999, 222–223) observes:

In a typical classroom of 25 students, today's teacher will have at least four or five students with specific educational needs that require professional expertise previously reserved to a few specialists... [and] will need considerable knowledge to develop curriculum and teaching strategies that address the wide range of learning approaches, experiences, and prior levels of knowledge the other students bring with them, and an understanding of how to work within a wide range of family and community contexts.

Professional knowledge is thus more important for teachers because simply knowing a subject well does not guarantee being able to transmit it well, especially in light of the diverse and complex needs of students in today's classrooms.

Where do you stand on this issue?

1. What arguments can you give to defend your position?

2. What compromise position would be feasible and effective?

3. How can students best learn each type of knowledge?

4. What other questions are raised within each position—for instance, how specific should subject matter knowledge be? Should one know all of "science" or only "biology"?

5. Which type of professional knowledge is most needed for new teachers and which would be more useful later in a teacher's career?

Recommended Sources

Darling-Hammond, L., Wise, A. E., and Klein, S. P. (1995). *A license to teach: Building a profession for 21st-century schools.* Boulder:Westview Press.

Darling-Hammond, L. (1999). Educating teachers for the next century: Rethinking practice and policy. In *The education of teachers: Ninety-eighth yearbook of the National Society for the Study of Education,* Part 1. Chicago: University of Chicago Press.

What kinds of basic knowledge and skills do teachers need to do their jobs well? How will you acquire and develop knowledge and skills in these areas?

Research on students' learning is not intended to set forth, in cookbook fashion, exactly what teachers should do to increase students' learning. Instead, it may be helpful to think of educational research as providing teachers with rules of thumb to guide their practice. For example, Rosenshine, Meister, and Chapman (1996, 198) point out that, in spite of extensive research on the effectiveness of procedural prompts, "at the present time, developing procedural prompts appears to be an art. [It] is difficult to derive any prescriptions on how to develop effective procedural prompts for cognitive strategies in reading, writing, and subject matter domains." Finally, noted educational psychologist Lee Cronbach (quoted in Eisner, 1998, 112) may have put it best when he said "[educational research] is to help practitioners use their heads."

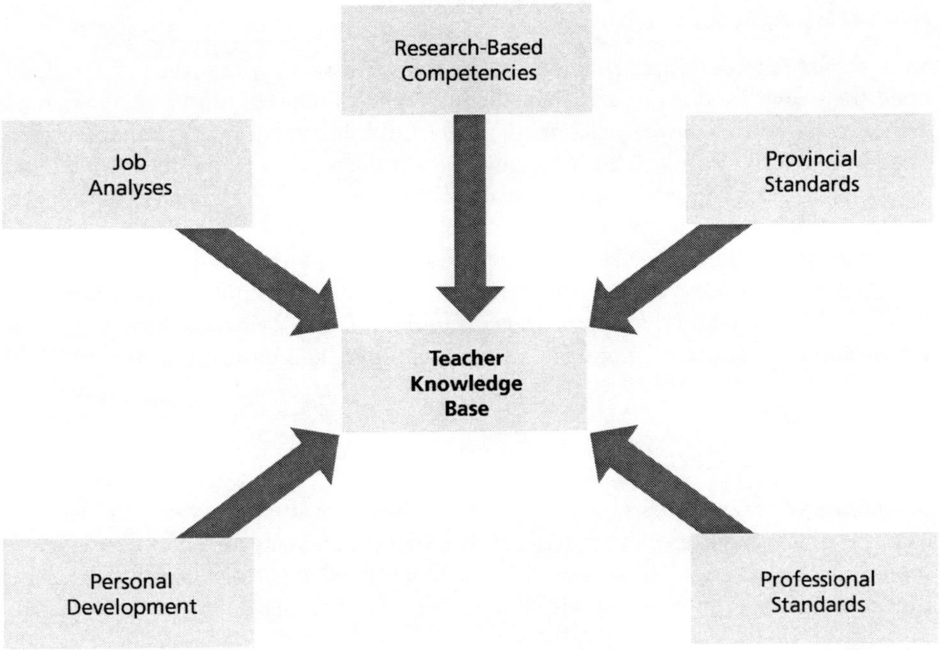

Figure 3.1

Five views of the
teacher knowledge base

What Are Five Ways of Viewing the Teacher Knowledge Base?

Just as people hold different expectations for schools and teachers, there are different views on the knowledge and abilities teachers need to teach well. The complexities of teaching make it difficult to describe in exact detail the **knowledge base** on which teaching as a profession rests. This difficulty results, in part, because there is no universally accepted definition of what good teaching is. Educational researchers are still learning *what* good teachers know and *how* they use that knowledge. Five widespread views of teachers' knowledge and abilities are portrayed in Figure 3.1.

A Personal Development View

One view of what teachers need to know and be able to do places primary emphasis on who the teacher is as a person. According to this view, teachers should be concerned with developing themselves as persons so that they may learn to use themselves more effectively. The importance of personal development is described as follows by the authors of *On Being a Teacher:* "... teachers who appear in charge of their own lives, who radiate power, tranquility, and grace in their actions, are going to command attention and respect. People will follow them anywhere.... What we are saying is that you have not only the option, but also the imperative, to develop the personal dimensions of your functioning, as well as your professional skills" (Zehm and Kottler 1993, 15).

What this approach requires, then, is that teachers continually develop their powers of observation and reflection so that they can most effectively respond to the needs of students. Teaching becomes an authentic, growth-oriented encounter between teacher and students. An important dimension of this **personal development view** is the teacher's need for self-knowledge, particularly in regard to oneself as a learner.

Research-Based Competencies

Since the late 1980s, most provinces, or the school districts within them, have developed their own lists of **research-based competencies** that beginning teachers must demonstrate. These competencies are derived from educational research that has identified what effective teachers do. Typically, many provinces have developed *behavioural indicators* for each competency, which trained observers use to determine to what extent teachers actually exhibit the target behaviours in the classroom. Teachers are required to demonstrate effective pedagogical behaviours in a number of domains: planning and preparation, effective classroom management, control of student conduct, instructional organization and development, presentation of subject matter, verbal and non-verbal communication, and testing (student preparation, administration, and feedback).

Provincial Standards

In addition to sets of research-based competencies for evaluating practicing teachers, some provinces have developed performance-based standards for what new teachers should know and be able to do. Known as **outcome-based** or **performance-based teacher education**, the new approach is based on several assumptions:

- Outcomes are demonstrations of learning rather than a list of teaching specializations, college courses completed, or concepts studied.
- Outcomes are performances that reflect the richness and complexity of the teacher's role in today's classrooms—not discrete, single behaviours.
- Demonstrations of learning must occur in authentic settings—that is, settings similar to those within which the teacher will teach.
- Outcomes are culminating demonstrations of what beginning teachers do in real classrooms.

Typically, outcome-based standards are developed with input from teachers, teacher educators, provincial department of education personnel, and various professional associations. However, outcome-based standards are not without their critics. Sharp criticism of the Atlantic Provinces Education Foundation (APEF) outcomes-based curriculum (see Appendix 3.1) is articulated by Dr David MacKinnon, author of *A Wolf in Sheep's Clothing: The Erosion of Democracy* in Education (Portelli and Solomon 2001, 136).

> [A]n outcomes-based approach to education provides an inadequate foundation for public education. Behavioral outcomes, by definition, are confined to that which is observable and measurable … [P]rojects like the APEF initiative are necessarily incomplete and, perhaps, unwittingly misguided … [T]he APEF initiative is a reductionist and anti-democratic exercise at increasing system accountability.

A Job-Analysis Approach

Another view of what teachers need to know and be able to do is based on the job analyses that some school districts conduct. Typically, a **job analysis** begins with a review of existing job descriptions and then proceeds to interviews with those currently assigned to the job and their supervisors regarding the activities and responsibilities associated with the job. These data are then analyzed to identify the dimensions of the job. Finally, interview questions based on the dimensions are developed and used by district personnel responsible for hiring.

The following excerpt from a study by the Urban Network to Improve Teacher Education (UNITE), an organization comprised of both Canadian and American universities, illustrates the knowledge, skills, and attitudes needed by successful urban teachers.

Twenty-two teachers and five administrators were involved in focus group interviews conducted during the study. Over half of the 27 participants have been working in the field of education for less than five years, although four have been teaching in their present school for over 15 years. On average, the participants graduated from a faculty of education 11 years ago. The teachers interviewed represented all grade levels, from Kindergarten to senior secondary, and represented a variety of subject areas and roles within a school community (eg., physical education, visual arts, resource teacher, special education teacher). All but one of the participants received their preservice education in the province of Ontario.

Characteristics of a Successful Urban Teacher

Eight characteristics were identified in all focus group interviews as being important for teachers to possess in order to be successful in an urban school. These eight characteristics are discussed in order of the degree of emphasis placed on them by the focus group participants.

Empathy—Because most teachers never experience many of the traumas and issues that their students deal with on a daily basis, they strongly believed that teachers in urban schools need to be empathetic. They mentioned the importance of "not placing your morals, judgments and values on the students and parents," and "making greater attempts at trying to understand the different cultures and religions."

Respect for the students—Teachers need to respect students and to operate on the belief that all students have the right to learn, and to achieve success. Participants stated that teachers in urban schools should not compromise expectations and that they should "believe that all students have a future."

Flexibility—Teachers in urban schools need to be flexible. Teachers reported that this flexibility was necessary when dealing with such things as curriculum guidelines, programming, evaluation, classroom disruptions, and student behaviour. One teacher stated, "You set up a wonderful day, and then it isn't working, and you have to step back and reassess. It's constant."

Self-care—In order to be a successful teacher in an urban school, participants stressed the need for caring for their personal needs. Since urban schools "really challenge you, you have to make sure you take care of the whole you, emotionally, physically, personally, and manage your stress. You have to find the balance."

Patience—Teachers in urban schools need to be patient. Dealing with the diverse population of students, and all of the other challenges previously mentioned, the need for 'infinite patience' was believed to be necessary in order to be successful as a teacher in an urban school.

Sense of humour—Participants in the focus group interviews strongly believed that in order to be a successful teacher in an urban school one must possess a sense of humour. One teacher described this need in connection with self-care, stating, "If you don't have the ability to laugh, you run the risk of becoming emotionally drained."

Collegiality—Another important characteristic for teachers in urban schools is collegiality and peer support. Participants described the need, in urban schools, for staff to work together, to "share their ups and downs," to share their resources, and to be there to support one another.

technology

highlights

What technology-related knowledge and skills do teachers need?

Today, thousands of teachers and students routinely use desktop and laptop computers with built-in modems, faxes, and CD-ROM players; camcorders; optical scanners; speech and music synthesizers; laser printers; digital cameras; and data projectors. In addition, they use sophisticated software for email, word processing, desktop publishing, presentation graphics, spreadsheets, databases, and multimedia applications.

To prepare teachers to use these new technologies, many teacher education programs and provincial departments of education have developed information technology competency guidelines for classroom teachers. For example, many teachers are now expected to have technology skills in three areas: basic computer/technology operations and concepts, personal and professional use of technology, and integration of technology into a standards-based curriculum. The following competencies are among the most common. How many of these competencies do you possess, and what steps can you take to acquire those you do not have?

1. Media Communications and Integration

   - Set up and operate video media [eg., videocassette recorders (VCRs) and digital video disks (DVDs)]
   - Connect video output devices and other presentation systems to computers and video sources for large-screen display
   - Use painting, drawing, and authoring tools
   - Plan, create, and use linear and non-linear multimedia presentations
   - Use imaging devices such as scanners, digital cameras, and/or video cameras with computer systems and software

2. Telecommunications

   - Connect to the internet or an online service
   - Use internet search engines
   - Use a web browser to access and use resources on the internet
   - Download and print resources from the internet
   - Use URL management tools (eg., bookmarks or favourites)
   - Telnet to a remote computer on the internet
   - Connect to and use resources from university libraries
   - Use email (compose, send, retrieve, read, reply to sender, reply to all, and forward)
   - Attach files to email messages
   - Retrieve and use attachments (eg., view, read, save and print)
   - Configure and use email distribution lists relevant to professional information needs
   - Create and use group addresses for email
   - Collaborate with peers through available tools (eg., email, websites, threaded and other online discussions)

Source: Adapted from Colorado Technology Competency Guidelines for Classroom Teachers and School Media Specialists, Education Telecommunications Unit, Colorado, Department of Education, January, 1999.

High energy level—In order to deal with the plethora of daily challenges facing urban school teachers, interview participants stated that these teachers need to have high energy levels. A number of participants extended this characteristic to include a willingness "to make the commitment of time, energy and effort it takes to work in a school like this."

Source: UNITE article reprinted with permission from Patricia J. Rawson Wheeler. Retrieved November 1, 2003 from www.umanitoba.ca/publications/cjeap/issue1/issue6.htm

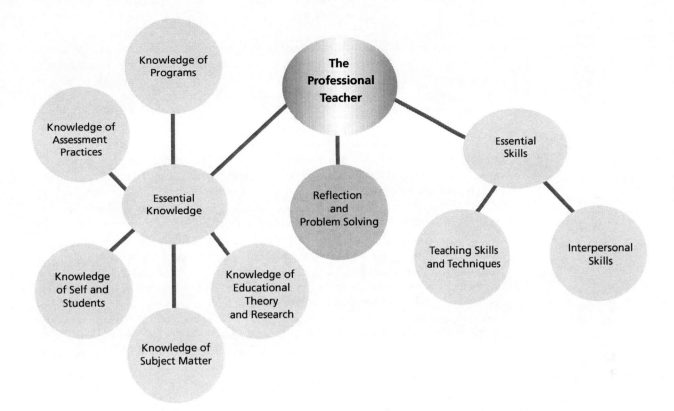

Figure 3.2

Essential knowledge and skills for the professional teacher.

Professional Views

While there are differing opinions regarding what teachers should be able to do, it seems evident that becoming a teacher is complex and demanding. For example, as part of its supervision policy, Manitoba's St. Boniface School Division No. 4 (now Louis Riel School Division) lists the following skills as essential to good practice (St. Boniface 1995).

- Classroom Learning Environment: The teacher provides appropriate learning resources, ... makes effective use of space ... [and] provides stimulating and creative experiences.
- Classroom Management: The teacher establishes a positive classroom environment ... promotes self-esteem ... [and] plans and organizes for success.
- Contribution to the Total School Environment: The teacher contributes to students ... parents/guardians and community partnerships ... the school ... colleagues ... [and] the St. Boniface System.
- Instructional Process: The teacher implements Manitoba Education, school and Board expectations and policies for curriculum and program planning ... understands the learner ... [and] employs a repertoire of instructional strategies.
- Interpersonal Relations: The teacher interacts positively with students ... with colleagues ... [and] with parents and community.
- Student Evaluation: The teacher understands the purpose of assessment and evaluation ... [and] implements a variety of assessment and evaluation strategies.

How Are Canadian Teachers Educated and Certified?

Because education is a provincial rather than a federal responsibility, each province has been free to elect its preferred method for educating those intent on pursuing careers as professional teachers. The result has been a patchwork quilt of Bachelor of Education programs, each with its own specific admission requirements, and each with its own particular curriculum.

Additionally, while the academic body bestows the Bachelor of Education degree on its graduates, each province and territory has a teacher certification body that establishes the requirements, which must be met before a teaching license will be awarded. In some provinces, such as Newfoundland and Nova Scotia, the certifying agency is each province's department of education. However, in other jurisdictions, such as BC and Ontario, independent agencies such as the British Columbia College of Teachers and the Ontario College of Teachers are responsible for teacher certification.

Most provinces and territories issue teaching certificates based upon the qualifications of the applicant. In general, the higher the level of certification, the higher the remuneration. (See Appendix 3.2, "Saskatchewan: Teacher Salary Classification"). Most provinces also give teachers annual raises for each of their first ten years of teaching experience. Saskatchewan has five levels of teacher certification and, as Table 3.1 indicates, has ten steps for years of experience.

In 2003 the Ontario Ministry of Education introduced the Ontario Teacher Qualifying Test (OTQT) as part of its teacher certification process (See Appendix 3.3).

Table 3.1

Salaries effective September 1, 2003, in dollars

Step	Class C	Class I-III	Class IV	Class V	Class VI
1	32 273	32 273	38 700	40 895	43 570
2		33 697	40 911	43 191	45 973
3		35 122	43 121	45 487	48 376
4		36 546	45 331	47 783	50 779
5		37 971	47 542	50 079	53 182
6		39 395	49 752	52 374	55 585
7		40 820	51 962	54 670	57 988
8		42 244	54 173	56 966	60 391
9		43 669	56 383	59 262	62 794
10		45 093	59 500	62 464	66 103

Source: Saskatchewan Teachers' Federation.

This is the first time any Canadian educational jurisdiction has administered what is effectively a teacher competency test to those whom it grants teaching certificates. The *Quality in the Classroom Act*, 2001, which provides the legislative requirements for the OTQT, also sets performance appraisal standards and processes for Ontario school districts to use in evaluating their teachers. The stated purposes of the new performance appraisal system (Ontario Ministry of Education 2002, 3) are as follows:

- To ensure that students receive the benefit of an education system staffed by teachers who are performing their duties satisfactorily
- To provide fair, effective and consistent teacher evaluation in every school
- To promote professional growth

For more information, see the sample "Rubric to Describe the Levels of Performance" for the "Domain Teaching Practice," Appendix 3.4, at the end of this chapter.

In Manitoba, Alberta, and Ontario, teacher associations negotiate their contracts at the regional or local level. In all other provinces and territories the negotiations are conducted between the teachers' associations and department of education personnel. Salary scales are quite variable. In some provinces a teacher with an approved undergraduate degree, with an additional eight-month Bachelor of Education degree, can earn an annual salary of $30 000 to $50 000; in other jurisdictions the same level of certification would result in annual pay of $40 000 to $70 000. The highest rates of teacher pay are offered by the Yukon, Nunavut, and the Northwest Territories, where starting salaries are $55 000 to $60 000.

Canadian Schools of Education: A Variety of Models

Concurrent Program

Students enrol in a Bachelor degree and take both regular academic courses and education courses at the same time. Most such programs are of four years' duration and provide their graduates with the least expensive route to a teaching degree. However, the majority of students in concurrent programs must decide at a very early stage in their lives that teaching is their chosen profession.

Eight-Month Post-Degree Program

This is by far the most common model. Applicants for admission to a school of education first obtain a three- or four-year undergraduate degree which contains the appropriate academic prerequisites as established by the university or department of education. Successful applicants then take a specified number of courses specifically designed to assist them with their teaching practice. As part of their program they also spend a specified amount of time—usually five to eight weeks—working with associate teachers in the field. Critics of eight-month programs argue that they do not provide sufficient time for student teachers to learn all of the things necessary for them to be truly effective educators. In addition, provinces with more comprehensive Bachelor of Education programs will sometimes decline to grant teaching licenses to those who have graduated from such programs.

Twelve-Month Post-Degree Programs

There are relatively few twelve-month Bachelor of Education programs available within Canada. Twelve-month programs have more coursework for students to complete and provide more time for fieldwork in classrooms. They are also more expensive for students but, as they are completed within an extended academic year, graduates of such programs can be employed as teachers in September of the year in which they graduate.

Two-Year Post-Degree Programs

At present, only Nova Scotia and Prince Edward Island have two-year post-degree Bachelor of Education programs. Applicants to these programs first obtain a three-year or four-year undergraduate degree, and then complete two academic years of educational studies in combination with 20 or more weeks of field experience. Some colleges and universities also offer two or more of the models described above. Hyperlinks to all of Canada's teacher education programs can be found at the following URL: www.oise.utoronto.ca/~mpress/eduweb/faculties.html

What Can You Learn from Observing in Classrooms?

Classroom observations are a vital element of many **field experiences**. Students report that these experiences aid them greatly in making a final decision about entering the teaching field. Most become more enthusiastic about teaching and more motivated to learn the needed skills, although a few decide that teaching is not for them. Recognizing the value of observations, many teacher education programs are increasing the amount of field experiences and placing such fieldwork earlier in students' programs.

Focused Observations

Observations are more meaningful when they are focused and conducted with clear purposes. Observers may focus on the students, the teacher, the interactions between the two, the structure of the lesson, or the setting. More specifically, for example, observers may note differences between the ways boys and girls or members of different ethnic groups communicate and behave in the classroom. They may note student interests and ability levels, study student responses to a particular teaching strategy, or analyze the question and response patterns in a class discussion.

Observations may also be guided by sets of questions related to specific areas. For instance, since beginning teachers are frequently frustrated by their lack of success in interesting their students in learning, asking questions specifically related to motivation can make an observation more meaningful and instructive. Figure 3.3 on page 61 presents a helpful set of focused questions on motivation. Similar questions can be generated for other focus areas such as classroom management, student involvement, questioning skills, evaluation, and teacher–student rapport.

Observation Instruments

A wide range of methods can be used to conduct classroom observations, ranging from informal, qualitative descriptions to formal, quantitative checklists. With reform efforts to improve education in Canada has come the development of instruments to facilitate the evaluation of teacher performance, a task now widely required of school administrators. Students preparing to teach can benefit by using these evaluative instruments in their observations.

Directions: As you observe, note the ways that students are motivated intrinsically (from within) and extrinsically (from factors outside themselves).

Intrinsic Motivation	Extrinsic Motivation
What things seem to interest students at this age?	How do teachers show their approval to students?
Which activities and assignments seem to give them a sense of pride?	What phrases do teachers use in their praise?
When do they seem to be confused? bored? frustrated?	What types of rewards do teachers give (eg., grades, points, tangible rewards)?
What topics do they talk about with enthusiasm?	What reward programs do you notice (eg., points accumulated toward free time)?
In class discussions, when are they most alert and participating most actively?	What warnings do teachers give?
What seems to please, amuse, entertain, or excite them?	What punishments are given to students?
What do they joke about? What do they find humorous?	How do teachers arouse concern in their students?
	How do students motivate other students?
What do they report as being their favourite subjects? favorite assignments?	What forms of peer pressure do you observe?
What do they report as being their least favourite subjects and assignments?	How do teachers promote enthusiasm for an assignment?
How do they respond to personalized lessons (e.g., using their names in exercises)?	How do teachers promote class spirit?
How do they respond to activity-oriented lessons (eg.,fieldwork, project periods)?	How do teachers catch their students' interest in the first few minutes of a lesson?
How do they respond to assignments calling for presentations to groups outside the classroom (eg., parents, another class, the chamber of commerce)?	Which type of question draws more answers—recall or open-ended?
	How do teachers involve quiet students in class discussions?
	How do teachers involve inactive students in their work?
How do they respond to being given a choice in assignments?	In what ways do teachers give recognition to srudents' accomplishments?

Figure 3.3

Guiding questions for observing motivation

How Can You Gain Practical Experience for Becoming a Teacher?

A primary aim of teacher education programs is to give students opportunities to experience, to the extent possible, the real world of the teacher. Through field experiences and carefully structured experiential activities, preservice teachers are given limited exposure to various aspects of teaching. Observing, tutoring, instructing small groups, analyzing video cases, operating instructional media, performing student teaching, and completing various non-instructional tasks are among the most common experiential activities.

Ruth's Dilemma

This case recounts a dilemma typical for many who decide to enter the teaching field. Ruth, who worked in the same department as one of the authors, faced this decision at the time this textbook was being written.

Ruth knew it was time to begin the process to become a teacher. She wondered what had influenced her decision most—her love of English literature, her youngest son's graduation from high school, or the fact that she was surrounded daily by people teaching or taking education classes. As secretary to the School of Education's associate dean, she oversaw the details of class schedules, textbook orders, room assignments, program evaluations, faculty teaching loads, and students' petitions, all to help smooth the way for others to become teachers. Now she had decided to enter the field herself.

She had applied to the program, outlined a plan, and sought her dean's permission to proceed. The former school superintendent was sincere in his encouragement. Certainly she could leave the office early on Tuesdays to attend classes. And what level did she plan to teach? High school or elementary? Ruth wasn't sure.

The question remained even after she had made several elementary and high school classroom observations in her Introduction to Teaching class. The answer wasn't as clear for Ruth as it seemed to be for many of her classmates. Like many of them, she had wanted to be a teacher for as long as she could remember, but unlike them, she had given up the idea because she was unable to gain the needed financial support until she learned that staff could participate in the university's degree completion program. Also, like a number of her classmates, a teacher had inspired her—her high school English teacher had made the subject come alive for her.

By the end of this course, she would have to choose between preparing to teach at the secondary or elementary school level, and her dilemma remained. She loved English literature. Whenever she talked about the books she had read, she felt that words were inadequate for capturing the experience. With other students in class, she thought

Classroom Experiences

Because of the need to provide opportunities to put theory into practice before student teaching, many teacher education programs enable students to participate in microteaching, teaching simulations, analyses of video cases, field-based practica and clinical experiences, and classroom aide programs.

Microteaching

Introduced in the 1960s, **microteaching** was received enthusiastically and remains a popular practice. The process calls for students to teach brief, single-concept lessons to a small group (five to ten students) while concurrently practicing a specific teaching skill, such as positive reinforcement. Often the microteaching is videotaped for later study.

As originally developed, microteaching includes the following six steps:

out loud about the problem: "In high school you have so many students. How could you possibly get to know 120, 150, or more students? It's just not possible. Just think about it. Over a hundred! You couldn't get to know all of them and not many very well. How much of an impact could I have on their lives?"

"In elementary school, it's different," she continued. "You really can get to know the children well. You would be with them every day, all day, all school year. And there wouldn't be that many, maybe 25 or 30. Even less in some places—only 18 or 21 in a class. You'd even know their families. And you certainly could have an impact on their lives. But then the curriculum isn't that interesting. I would miss teaching literature."

Ruth knew that at the end of her first education course she would have to decide between the two. The classes in the remainder of her program were focused on either elementary or secondary teaching, and she could not do both.

Questions

1. Should Ruth become a high school English teacher or teach children at the elementary level? On what basis should she make her decision?

2. Is teaching a generic skill or art that can be applied to any level, or does it require distinctive skills geared to the students' ages and educational needs?

3. What factors other than teaching skills need to be considered when making this decision? Do the two levels draw upon different personality strengths? Is there a greater demand for teachers at one level than at the other? How do salaries and benefits compare for the two levels?

4. How do motivations to teach vary with the stage of life in which the decision to become a teacher is made?

5. What research activities might help someone decide whether to teach at the elementary or the secondary level?

1. Identify a specific teaching skill to learn about and practice.
2. Read about the skill in one of several pamphlets.
3. Observe a master teacher demonstrate the skill in a short movie or on videotape.
4. Prepare a three- to five-minute lesson to demonstrate the skill.
5. Teach the lesson, which is videotaped, to a small group of peers.
6. Critique, along with the instructor and student peers, the videotaped lesson.

Simulations

As an element of teacher training, **teaching simulations** provide opportunities for vicarious practice of a wide range of teaching skills. In simulations, students analyze teaching situations that are presented in writing, on audiotape, in short films, or on videotape. Typically, students are given background information about a hypothetical school or classroom and the pupils they must prepare to teach. After this orientation, students role-play the student teacher or the teacher who is confronted with the problem situation. Following the simulation, participants discuss the appropriateness of solutions and work to increase their problem-solving skills and their understanding of the teacher's multifaceted role as a decision maker.

With recent advances in computer technology, some teacher education programs now use computer-based simulations that enable students to hone their classroom planning and decision-making skills. Students at Acadia University in Nova Scotia, for example, learn to deal with classroom management problems within an interactive virtual learning environment. In addition, continuing progress in the development of virtual reality technology suggests that preservice teachers will soon be able to practice their skills with computer-simulated "students" who learn by interacting with humans (VanLehn et al. 1994; Sigalit and VanLehn 1995).

Video Cases

Teacher education students who view, analyze, and then write about video cases have an additional opportunity to appreciate the ambiguities and complexities of real-life classrooms, to learn that "there are no clear-cut, simple answers to the complex issues teachers face" (Wasserman 1994, 606). Viewing authentic video cases enables students to see how "teaching tradeoffs and dilemmas emerge in the video 'text' as do the strategies teachers use, the frustrations they experience, the brilliant and less-brilliant decisions they make" (Grant, Richard, and Parkay 1996, 5).

Practica

A **practicum** is a short-term field-based experience (usually about two weeks long) that allows teacher education students to spend time observing and assisting in classrooms. Though practica vary in length and purpose, students are often able to begin instructional work with individuals or small groups. For example, a cooperating teacher may allow a practicum student to tutor a small group of students, read a story to the whole class, conduct a spelling lesson, monitor recess, help students with their homework, or teach students a song or game.

Classroom Assistants

Serving as a teacher assistant is another popular means of providing field experience before student teaching. A teacher assistant's role depends primarily on the unique needs of the school and its students. Generally, assistants work under the supervision of a certified teacher and perform duties that support the teacher's instruction. Assisting teachers in classrooms familiarizes teacher education students with class schedules, record-keeping procedures, and students' performance levels, and provides ample opportunity for observations. In exchange, the classroom teacher receives much needed assistance.

Student Teaching

The most extensive and memorable field experience in teacher preparation programs is the period of student teaching. As *The Student Teacher's Handbook* points out, student teaching "is the only time in a teaching career that one is an apprentice under the close guidance of an experienced mentor" (Schwebel et al. 1996, 4). Depending on the province, Bachelor of Education students may be required to have as few as five weeks of student teaching or, as in Nova Scotia, as many as fifteen weeks before being certified as teachers. The nature of student teaching varies considerably among teacher education programs. Typically, a student is assigned to a cooperating (or master) teacher in the school, and a university supervisor makes periodic visits to observe the student teacher. Some programs even pay student teachers during the student teaching experience.

Student teaching is a time of responsibility. As one student teacher put it, "I don't want to mess up [my students'] education!" It is also an opportunity for growth, a chance to master critical skills. Time is devoted to observing, participating in classroom activities, and actively teaching. The amount of time one actually spends teaching, however, is not as important as one's willingness to reflect carefully on the student teaching experience. Two excellent ways to promote reflection during student teaching are journal writing and maintaining a reflective teaching log.

Student Teacher Journal Writing

Many supervisors require student teachers to keep a journal of their classroom experiences so that they can engage in reflective teaching and begin the process of criticizing and guiding themselves. The following two entries—the first written by a student teacher in a Grade 4 classroom, the second by a student teacher in a high school English class—illustrate how journal writing can help student teachers develop strategies for dealing with the realities of teaching.

What strategies can you use to make your student teaching experience truly valuable? In what sense will you remain a student teacher throughout your career?

> Today I taught a geography lesson and the kids seemed so bored. I called on individuals to read the social studies text, and then I explained it. Some of them really struggled with the text. Mr. H. said I was spoon-feeding them too much. So tomorrow I am going to put them into groups and let them answer questions together rather than give them the answers. This ought to involve the students in the learning a bit more and enable some of the better readers to help out those who have difficulty, without the whole class watching. I feel bad when I see those glazed looks on their faces. I need to learn how to be more interesting (Pitton 1998, 120).

> I had good feedback on small groups in their responses to questions on *Of Mice and Men*. They were to find a paragraph that might indicate theme and find two examples of foreshadowing. We found five!

> The short story unit was awful during fourth hour. The kids just didn't respond. I quickly revamped my approach for the next hour. Fifth hour did seem to go better. (Mostly though, I think it was just that I was more prepared, having had one class to try things out.) I can see how experience really helps. Now that I've tried the story "The Tiger or the Lady," I would use the same material, but I would know HOW to use it more effectively! (Pitton 1998, 143).

Relatively unstructured, open-ended journals, such as the ones from which these entries were selected, provide student teachers with a medium for subjectively exploring the student teaching experience.

Reflective Teaching Logs

To promote the practice of reflecting more analytically, some supervisors ask their student teachers to use a more directed and structured form of journal keeping, the reflective teaching log. In this form a student lists and briefly describes the daily sequence of activities, selects a single episode to expand on, analyzes the reason for selecting it and what was learned from it, and considers the possible future application of that knowledge.

To illustrate the reflective teaching approach to keeping a log, we share here a partial entry for one episode that was recounted and critiqued by a college student tutoring a student in French. The entry is of particular interest because it provides us with a glimpse of a college student's first experience with a pupil's difficulty in understanding subject matter.

Log #1: February 14, 1991 (10:00–10:30am)

Sequence of Events: Worked with Richy on his French.

Episode: Because I wasn't sure of Richy's level, I asked him a few questions to see what he knew. His homework exercises involved work like reflexives, irregular verbs, and vocabulary. But when he and I started reviewing, he didn't remember the very basics of conjugation. He said, "I know this stuff, I just need review." We reviewed the conjugation of regular verbs. I set up a chart of *er* and *ir* endings and had him fill in the correct forms. He kept saying, "I just don't remember," or "Oh yeah, I knew that." His facial expressions reflected concentration and perhaps frustration. At times, he would just stare at the page until I gave him a hint. His forehead was scrunched up and he fidgeted a bit with his hands and legs. After working on the regular endings, he wanted to get a drink. I told him to go ahead....

Analysis: I guess that I was just shocked at how little Richy knew. What we went over was the most simple form of French grammar and in a way he was acting as if he had no idea what we were doing. I was surprised, like I said, but only on the inside. I just helped him along, showing him why the concepts made sense. I had no idea how we were going to do his homework assignments since they were considerably more difficult ... (Posner 1993, 116–117).

Though student teaching will be the capstone experience of your teacher education program, the experience should be regarded as an *initial* rather than a terminal learning opportunity—your first chance to engage in reflection and self-evaluation for a prolonged period.

Gaining Experience in Multicultural Settings

Canadian schools will enrol increasing numbers of students from diverse cultural backgrounds during the twenty-first century. As this trend continues, it is vitally important that those entering the teaching profession achieve an understanding of children's differing backgrounds. As a result, many teacher education programs now have courses that deal with equity issues. Such courses help prepare student teachers for the diversity that exists in almost every classroom.

As a teacher you can be assured that you will teach students from backgrounds that differ from your own—including students from the more than 100 racial and ethnic groups in Canada, and students who are poor, gifted, or have disabilities. You will have the challenge of reaching out to all students and teaching them that they are persons of worth and that they can learn. You will also be confronted with the difficult challenge of being sensitive to differences among students, while at the same time treating all equally and fairly. To prepare for these realities of teaching, you should make every effort to gain experiences in multicultural settings.

Supply Teaching

On completion of a teacher education program and prior to securing a full-time teaching assignment, many students choose to gain additional practical experience in classrooms by **supply teaching** or **substitute teaching**. Others, unable to locate full-time positions, decide to supply, knowing that many districts prefer to hire from their pool of supply teachers when full-time positions become available. Supply teachers replace regular teachers who are absent due to illness, family responsibilities, personal reasons, or professional workshops and conferences.

Each day, thousands of supply teachers are employed in schools across Canada. For example, during one school year at the fifteen high schools in a large urban district, the total number of absences for 1200 regular teachers equalled 14 229 days. Multiplying this figure by five (the number of classes per day for most high school teachers) yields 71 145 class periods taught by supply teachers that year (St. Michel 1995).

Qualifications for supply teachers vary from province to province. An area with a critical need for supply teachers will often relax its requirements to provide classroom coverage. In many districts, it is possible to supply without regular certification *if no fully certified teacher can be located.* Some districts have less stringent qualifications for short-term, day-to-day supply teachers and more stringent ones for long-term, full-time assignments. In many districts, the application process for supply teachers is the same as that for full-time applicants; in others, the process may be somewhat briefer. Often, supply teachers are not limited to working in their area of certification; however, schools try to avoid making out-of-field assignments. If you decide to supply, contact the schools in your area to learn about the qualifications and procedures for hiring supply teachers.

In spite of the significant role supply teachers play in the day-to-day operation of schools, "... research tells us that they receive very little support, no specialized training, and are rarely evaluated.... In short, the substitute will be expected to show up to each class on time, maintain order, take roll, carry out the lesson, and leave a note for the regular teacher about the classes and events of the day without support, encouragement, or acknowledgement" (St. Michel 1995, 6–7). While working conditions such as these are certainly challenging, supplying can be a rewarding, professionally fulfilling experience. Figure 3.4 presents several advantages and disadvantages of supplying.

How Can You Develop Your Teaching Portfolio?

Now that you have begun your journey toward becoming a teacher, you should acquire the habit of assessing your growth in knowledge, skills, and attitudes. Toward this end, you may wish to collect the results of your reflections and self-assessment in a **professional portfolio**. A professional portfolio is a collection

Figure 3.4

Advantages and disadvantages of supplying

Source: John F. Snyder, "The Alternative of Substitute Teaching." In *1999 Job Search Handbook for Educators.* Evanston, IL: American Association for Employment in Education, p. 38.

Advantages and Disadvantages of Substitute Teaching

Advantages
- Gain experience without all the nightly work and preparation
- Compare and contrast different schools and their environments
- Be better prepared for interviews by meeting administrators and teachers
- Teach and learn a variety of material
- Get to know people—network
- See job postings and hear about possible vacancies
- Gain confidence in your abilities to teach
- Practice classroom management techniques
- Learn about school and district politics—get the "inside scoop"
- Choose which days to work—flexible schedule

Disadvantages
- Pay is not as good as full-time teaching
- No benefits such as medical coverage, retirement plans or sick days
- Lack of organized representation to improve wages or working conditions
- May receive a cool reception in some schools
- Must adapt quickly to different school philosophies
- Lack of continuity—may be teaching whole language one day; phonetics the next

of work that documents an individual's accomplishments in an area of professional practice. An artist's portfolio, for example, might consist of a résumé, sketches, paintings, slides and photographs of exhibits, critiques of the artist's work, awards, and other documentation of achievement. Recently, new approaches to teacher evaluation have included the professional portfolio. Teacher education programs at several universities now use portfolios as one means of assessing the competencies of candidates for teacher certification.

Portfolio Contents

What will your portfolio contain? Written materials might include the following: lesson plans and curriculum materials, reflections on your development as a teacher, journal entries, writing assignments made by your instructor, sample tests you have prepared, critiques of textbooks, evaluations of students' work at the level for which you are preparing to teach, sample letters to parents, and a résumé. Non-print materials might include video- and audiotapes featuring you in simulated teaching and role-playing activities, audiovisual materials (transparencies, charts, or other teaching aids), photographs of bulletin boards, charts depicting room arrangements for cooperative learning or other instructional strategies, sample grade book, certificates of membership in professional organizations, and awards.

Your portfolio should represent your *best work* and give you an opportunity to become an advocate of *who you are* as a teacher. Because a primary purpose of the professional portfolio is to stimulate reflection and dialogue, you may wish to discuss what entries to make in your portfolio with your instructor or other teacher education students. In addition, the following questions from *How to Develop a Professional Portfolio: A Manual for Teachers* (Campbell et al. 1996) can help you select appropriate portfolio contents:

What questions might you ask a mentor teacher about developing your professional portfolio?

Would I be proud to have my future employer and peer group see this? Is this an example of what my future professional work might look like? Does this represent what I stand for as a professional educator? If not, what can I revise or rearrange so that it represents my best efforts? (p. 5).

Using a Portfolio

In addition to providing teacher education programs with a way to assess their effectiveness, portfolios can be used by students for a variety of purposes. Campbell et al. (1996, 7–8) suggest that a portfolio may be used as

1. A way to establish a record of quantitative and qualitative performance and growth over time.
2. A tool for reflection and goal setting as well as a way to present evidence of your ability to solve problems and achieve goals.
3. A way to synthesize many separate experiences; in other words, a way to get the "big picture."
4. A vehicle for you to collaborate with professors and advisors in individualizing instruction.
5. A vehicle for demonstrating knowledge and skills gained through out-of-class experiences, such as volunteer experiences.
6. A way to share control and responsibility for your own learning.
7. An alternative assessment measure within the professional education program.
8. A potential preparation for national, regional, and state accreditation.
9. An interview tool in the professional hiring process.
10. An expanded résumé to be used as an introduction during the student teaching experience.

How Can You Benefit from Mentoring Relationships?

When asked "What would have been most helpful in preparing you to be a teacher?" one first-year suburban high school teacher responded with: "I wish I had one [a mentor] here.... There are days that go by and I don't think I learn anything about my teaching, and that's too bad. I wish I had someone" (Dollase 1992, 138). In reflecting on how a mentor contributed to his professional growth, Forrest Parkay defined **mentoring** as

> ... an intensive, one-to-one form of teaching in which the wise and experienced mentor inducts the aspiring protégé [one who is mentored] into a particular, usually professional, way of life.... [T]he protégé learns from the mentor not only the objective, manifest content of professional knowledge and skills but also a subjective, non-discursive appreciation for *how* and *when* to employ these learnings in the arena of professional practice. In short, the mentor helps the protégé to "learn the ropes," to become socialized into the profession (Parkay 1988, 196).

An urban middle school intern's description of how his mentor helped him develop effective classroom management techniques exemplifies "learning the ropes": "'You've got to develop your own sense of personal power,' [my mentor] kept saying. 'It's not something I can teach you. I can show you what to do. I can model it. But I don't know, it's just something that's got to come from within you'" (Henry et al. 1995, 114).

Table 3.2

Problem-solving approaches used by a mentor

Prescription giving	Remedy given by the mentor with a rationale, examples, alternatives, parameters of use, or rules
Personal storytelling	The mentor gives an example of his or her own classroom experiences to set a context for the prescription
Rehearsal	Verbal practice or rehearsal by the mentor and novice teacher of a strategy to be implemented in the classroom the next day, together with problem anticipation and troubleshooting
Role-playing	Playing and reversal of roles by the mentor and novice teacher reflecting problem situations or concerns of the novice teacher; both teacher and student roles are played
Modelling	Verbalization by the mentor of a teaching strategy or interaction technique with demonstration
Oral blueprinting	Oral planning by the novice teacher with critique and refinement by the mentor
Replay	Reconstruction of the day's events by the novice teacher with probing and clarifying questions and feedback from the mentor

Source: J. A. Ponticel and S. J. Zepeda. "Making Sense of Teaching and Learning: A Case Study of Mentor and Beginning Teacher Problem Solving," in D. J. McIntyre and D. M. Byrd, eds., *Preparing Tomorrow's Teachers: The Field Experience: Teacher Education Yearbook IV.* Thousand Oaks, CA: Corwin Press, p.127. Copyright © 1996 by Corwin Press. Reprinted by permission of Corwin Press, Inc.

Those who have become highly accomplished teachers frequently point out the importance of mentors in their preparation for teaching. A **mentor** can provide moral support, guidance, and feedback to students at various stages of professional preparation. In addition, a mentor can model for the protegé an analytical approach to solving problems in the classroom. Table 3.2 shows several problem-solving approaches a mentor can demonstrate to a novice teacher.

What Opportunities for Continuing Professional Development Will You Have?

Professional development is a lifelong process; any teacher, at any stage of development, has room for improvement. Many school systems and universities have programs in place for the continuing professional development of teachers. Indeed, teachers are members of a profession that provides them with a "... continuous opportunity to grow, learn, and become more expert in their work" (Lieberman 1990, viii).

Self-Assessment for Professional Growth

Self-assessment, or **reflection**, is a necessary first step in pursuing opportunities for professional growth. The simplest level of reflection occurs when, after a particular lesson has been taught, a teacher asks such questions as: How did that lesson go?

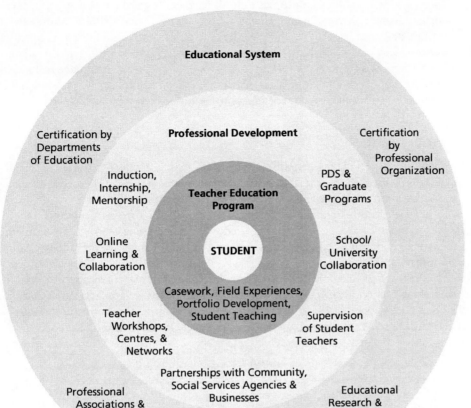

Educational System

Professional Development

Certification by
Departments
of Education

Certification
by
Professional
Organization

Induction,
Internship,
Mentorship

PDS &
Graduate
Programs

**Teacher Education
Program**

Online
Learning &
Collaboration

STUDENT

School/
University
Collaboration

Casework, Field Experiences,
Portfolio Development,
Student Teaching

Teacher
Workshops,
Centres, &
Networks

Supervision
of Student
Teachers

Partnerships with Community,
Social Services Agencies &
Businesses

Professional
Associations &
Other Stakeholders

Educational
Research &
Educational Reform

What might have been done to improve it? What were the good lesson elements which should be retained when I next teach it again? A deeper level of reflection might include such questions as: How has that lesson contributed to my students' overall educational growth? Is society as a whole in any way better off as a consequence of what my students just learned?

Several questions can help you make appropriate choices as a teacher: In which areas am I already competent? In which areas do I need further development? How will I acquire the knowledge and skills I need? How will I apply new knowledge and practice new skills? Answers to such questions will lead you to a variety of sources for professional growth: teacher workshops, teacher centres, professional development schools, the opportunity to supervise and mentor student teachers, and graduate programs. Figure 3.5 illustrates the relationship of these professional development experiences to your teacher education program.

Teacher Workshops

The quality of **in-service workshops** is uneven, varying with the size of school district budgets and the imagination and knowledge of the administrators and teachers who arrange them. It is significant that the most effective in-service programs tend to be the ones that teachers request—and often design and conduct.

Some workshops focus on topics that all teachers (regardless of subject or level) can benefit from: classroom management, writing across the curriculum, multicultural education, and strategies for teaching students with learning disabilities in the general education classroom, for example. Other workshops have a sharper focus and are intended for teachers of a subject at a certain level—for example, whole language techniques for middle school students, discovery learning for high school science students, and student-centred approaches to teaching literature in the high school classroom.

Teacher Centres

Teacher centres provide opportunities for teachers "to take the lead in the decision making and implementation of staff development programs based on the needs of teachers. Within limits they provide opportunities for teachers to have a level of control over their own professional development. In contrast to in-service programs, the initiatives undertaken are more clearly directed by teachers. Some centres cooperate with a local or neighbouring college of education and include members of the faculty on their planning committees.

Many teachers find teacher centres stimulating because they offer opportunities for collegial interaction in a quiet, professionally oriented setting. Teachers often find that The busy, hectic pace of life in many schools provides little time for professional dialogue with peers. Furthermore, in the teacher centre, teachers are often more willing to discuss openly areas of weakness in their performance. As one teacher put it:

> At the teacher centre I can ask for help. I won't be judged. The teachers who have helped me the most have had the same problems. I respect them, and I'm willing to learn from them. They have credibility with me.

Supervision and Mentoring of Student Teachers

After several years in the classroom, teachers may be ready to stretch themselves further by supervising student teachers. Some of the less obvious benefits of doing so are that teachers must rethink what they are doing so that they can explain and sometimes justify their behaviours to someone else, learning about themselves in the process. Furthermore, because they become a model for their student teachers, they continually strive to offer the best example. In exchange, they gain an assistant in the classroom—another pair of eyes, an aid with record keeping—and more than occasionally, fresh ideas and a spirit of enthusiasm.

Graduate Study

A more traditional form of professional development is to do graduate study. With the recent reforms, many provinces now require teachers to take some graduate courses to keep their certifications and knowledge up to date. Some teachers take only courses that are of immediate use to them; others use their graduate study to prepare for new teaching or administrative positions; and still others pursue doctoral work in order to teach prospective teachers or others in their discipline at the college level.

Study on the Internet

If you have access to the **internet**, you can locate many possibilities for continuing professional development. Teachers use the internet to exchange ideas and experiences and to acquire additional expertise in teaching or to share their expertise with others.

See the Appendix "Professional Development Opportunities on the Internet," on this book's website. Also at the website is a periodically updated list of professional development opportunities available online for teachers. If you decide to visit any of these sites, remember that web addresses change frequently or are taken off the internet. The web addresses given throughout this book were active at the time of printing. It is estimated that 10 000 websites are added to the internet every day, so you should regularly do internet searches using keywords related to education to gather the latest information and resources.

SUMMARY

What Essential Knowledge Do You Need to Teach?

- Professional teachers reflect upon their classroom experiences.
- Teachers need three kinds of knowledge: knowledge of self and students, knowledge of subject, and knowledge of educational theory and research.
- Teachers' self-knowledge influences their ability to understand students.
- The ambiguities of teaching can cause teachers to experience anxiety.
- Teachers can experience loneliness because they are isolated from adults.
- Teachers must know their students' aptitudes, talents, learning styles, stage of development, and readiness to learn new material.
- Teachers must understand their subjects deeply so that they can modify instructional strategies based on students' perception of content.
- Knowledge of educational theory enables professional teachers to know why certain strategies work.
- Educational research provides teachers with rules of thumb for practice.

What Are Five Ways of Viewing the Teacher Knowledge Base?

- There is no universally accepted definition of "good" teaching.
- The teacher knowledge base (essential knowledge and abilities) can place primary emphasis on personal development, research-based competencies, provincial or territorial standards, job analyses, or the views of professional organizations.
- Many provinces have developed standards for outcome-based or performance-based teacher education. Outcomes are based on what beginning teachers do in real classrooms.
- The job-analysis view of teaching is based on identifying job dimensions—the knowledge, skills, and attitudes teachers need.
- Effective teachers are guided by reflection and a problem-solving orientation.

How Are Canadian Teachers Educated and Certified?

- Provincial departments of education and independent professional organizations both set criteria for the certification of teachers.

What Can You Learn from Observing in Classrooms?

- The opportunity to observe in classrooms helps some students make a final decision about becoming a teacher.

- Many teacher education programs are providing students with more and earlier opportunities to observe in classrooms.

- Distance-learning classrooms, using compressed video, link teacher education programs to schools off campus.

- Observations can focus on a particular aspect of classroom life or be guided by a set of questions related to a specific area, such as how the teacher motivates students.

- Observation instruments range from informal, qualitative descriptions to formal, quantitative checklists.

How Can You Gain Practical Experience for Becoming a Teacher?

- Teacher education students can gain practical experience through focused classroom observations, microteaching, teaching simulations, analyses of video cases, field-based practica and clinical experiences, and classroom assistant programs.

- Distance-learning classrooms, using compressed video, link teacher education programs to schools off-campus.

- In microteaching, students practice specific skills by teaching brief lessons that are later analyzed.

- Computer simulations and virtual reality—as well as written, videotaped, and audiotaped cases—are being used for teaching simulations.

- Journal writing and reflective teaching logs increase the benefits of the student teaching experience.

- To prepare to teach students from diverse backgrounds, teacher education students should actively seek field experiences in multicultural settings.

- Supply teaching provides additional practical experience after completing a teacher education program.

How Can You Develop Your Teaching Portfolio?

- A portfolio documents professional growth and development over time.
- A portfolio can be organized around specific outcomes or standards.
- Portfolio contents should represent one's best work.
- Professional portfolios can be used in teacher evaluation, self-evaluation, and hiring.

How Can You Benefit from Mentoring Relationships?

- Ask for advice from teachers you admire.
- Mentoring can be a source of professional growth for experienced teachers.
- Mentoring enables the protegé to "learn the ropes."

What Opportunities for Continuing Professional Development Will You Have?

■ Self-assessment is necessary to select appropriate professional development experiences.

■ Opportunities for professional development include teacher workshops, teacher centres, professional development schools, supervision and mentoring of student teachers, graduate study, and the internet.

KEY TERMS AND CONCEPTS

field experiences
in-service
  workshops
internet
job analysis
knowledge base
mentor
mentoring
microteaching
observations

outcome-based teacher
  education
pedagogical content
  knowledge
performance-based teacher
  education
personal development
  view
practicum
professional portfolio

reflection
reflective teaching
  log
research-based
  competencies
self-assessment
substitute teaching
supply teaching
teacher centres
teaching simulations

APPLICATIONS AND ACTIVITIES

Teacher's Journal

1. What does self-knowledge mean to you? Why is self-knowledge important in teaching? What steps can you take to achieve greater self-knowledge?

2. As a teacher, you will encounter challenges related to student variability (differences in developmental needs, interests, abilities, and disabilities) and student diversity (differences in gender, race, ethnicity, culture, and socioeconomic status). To begin thinking about how you will acquire and use knowledge about your students, write a brief profile of yourself as a student in elementary school, in middle school or junior high school, and in high school.

3. Reflect on your education as a teacher. What are your primary concerns about the preparation you are receiving? What experiences do you think will be most helpful to you as you move toward becoming a teacher? What qualities would you look for in a mentor?

4. On the basis of your field experiences to date and the information in Chapters 1 and 2, ask yourself these questions and respond in your journal: Do I have the aptitude to become a good teacher? Am I willing to acquire the essential knowledge and skills teachers need? Do I really want to become a teacher?

Teacher's Database

1. Find out more about the use of technology to enhance teaching and learning. Join one of the internet teacher discussion groups that deal with the educational use of information technology.

2. Instead of using "outside experts" to deliver professional development workshops to teachers, some school districts and teacher associations have implemented teacher networks in which teachers address problems of mutual concern. For example, the Nova Scotia Teachers Union organizes an annual conference specifically designed to assist new teachers with the problems they encounter. You can visit the Nova Scotia Teachers Union website at www.nstu.ca/ for more information.

Observations and Interviews

1. Think about areas for focused observations of teaching, such as classroom management, student involvement, questioning techniques, evaluation, or teacher–student rapport. For one or more areas, brainstorm and order in logical sequence a set of questions you could use to guide your next observations. Include a list of questions to ask the teacher whom you will observe.

2. As a collaborative project with classmates, interview students who have completed student teaching at your university. What tips do they have for developing a positive relationship with a cooperating teacher? For establishing rapport with students? For developing confidence in presenting lessons?

3. Arrange to interview a school administrator about the knowledge, skills, and aptitude he or she thinks teachers must have. Which of the knowledge and skills discussed in this chapter does the administrator mention? Does he or she mention knowledge and skills not discussed in this chapter?

4. Observe a teacher in the classroom for the purpose of identifying examples that help to answer the following questions. How does the teacher demonstrate or use knowledge of self and students? Knowledge of subject matter? Knowledge of educational theory and research?

5. Observe a classroom in which there is likely to be some teacher–student interaction (for example, questions and answers, discussion, or oral review and feedback). On the basis of the data you collect, what conclusions can you draw about life in this classroom?

Professional Portfolio

1. Create a plan for developing your portfolio. What specific outcomes or standards will you use to organize your portfolio entries? What artifacts will you use to demonstrate your professional growth and development?

2. Evaluate the products of your studies in education so far in your preparation for becoming a teacher. Identify a few examples of your best work to include in your portfolio. Also, evaluate your Teacher's Journal, Teacher's Database, and Observations and Interviews for possible inclusions in your portfolio.

Appendix 3.1

Atlantic Canada Education Foundation: English Language Arts Outcome Statement

Broad focus	General curriculum outcomes
Speaking and listening	1. Students will speak and listen to, explore, extend, and reflect on their thoughts, ideas, feelings and experiences. 2. Students will be able to communicate information and ideas effectively and clearly, and to respond personally and critically. 3. Students will be able to interact with sensitivity and respect, considering the situation, audience, and purpose.
Reading and viewing	1. Students will be able to select, read, and view with understanding a range of literature, information, media, and visual texts. 2. Students will be able to interpret, select, and combine information using a variety of stategies, resources, and technologies. 3. Students will be able to respond personally to a range of texts. 4. Students will be able to respond critically to a range of texts, applying their understanding of language, form, and genre.
Writing and other ways of representing	1. Students will be able to use writing and other ways of representing to explore, clarify, and reflect on their thoughts, feelings, experiences, and learning; and to use their imagination. 2. Students will be able to create texts collaboratively and independently, using a variety of forms for a range of audiences and purposes. 3. Students will be able to use a range of strategies to develop effective writing and other ways of representing, and to enhance their clarity, precision, and effectiveness.

Source: Based on *Nova Scotia Education and Culture*, n.d., pp. 16–35.

Appendix 3.2

Teacher Salary Classification in Saskatchewan

Teachers in Saskatchewan schools, which are regulated by *The Education Act, 1995*, are classified for salary purposes based on their post-secondary education and the type of teaching certificate they hold. Section 200, *The Education Act* 1995, gives authority to the Board of Education for initial classification. The salary paid in each class is determined by the provincial collective agreement.

Classifications

Class C: Teachers will be placed in this class if they hold a probationary certificate but lack the two years of approved post-secondary education required for Class I.

Class I Requirements: A teacher in Class I is required to hold a valid Probationary Certificate and to have completed two years of recognized post-secondary education.

Class II Requirements: A teacher in Class II is required to hold: (i) a valid: (a) Standard "A" Certificate; or (b) Standard "B" Certificate (Endorsed); and to have completed a minimum of two years of recognized post-secondary education; or (ii) a valid Probationary Certificate, and to have completed a minimum of three years of recognized post-secondary education.

Class III Requirements: A teacher in Class III is required to hold: (i) a valid: (a) Standard "A" Certificate; or (b) Standard "B" Certificate (Endorsed) or (c) Vocational Teacher's Certificate (Endorsed); or (d) Technical Teacher's Certificate (Endorsed); and to have completed a minimum of three years of recognized post-secondary education; or (ii) a valid Probationary Certificate, and to have completed a minimum of four years of recognized post-secondary education including a bachelor's degree.

Class IV Requirements: A teacher in Class IV is required to have completed a minimum of four years of recognized post-secondary education and hold: (i) a valid: (a) Professional "A" Certificate; or (ii) Professional "B" Certificate (Endorsed) or (iii) a valid (a) Vocational Teacher's Certificate (Endorsed); or (b) Technical Teacher's Certificate (Endorsed); and to have completed sufficient additional training that only one year of university education is required to complete a four-year degree.

Class V Requirements: A teacher in Class V is required to have completed a minimum of five years of recognized post-secondary education and hold: (i) a valid: (a) Professional "A" Certificate, a Bachelor of Education (B.Ed.) degree, or a degree recognized as equivalent to a B.Ed. degree, and a second bachelor's degree; or (ii) a valid Professional "A" Certificate, an approved bachelor's degree, and one year of graduate study; or (iii) a valid Professional "A" Certificate and an approved four-year bachelor's degree other than a B.Ed. degree; or (iv) a valid Professional "B" Certificate and an approved four-year bachelor's degree other than a B.Ed. degree; or (v) a valid: (a) Vocational Teacher's Certificate (Endorsed); or (b) Technical Teacher's Certificate (Endorsed); and a B.Ed. or equivalent degree.

Class VI Requirements: A teacher in Class VI is required to have completed a minimum of six years of recognized post-secondary education and hold: (i) a valid Professional "A" Certificate, a B.Ed. degree, a second bachelor's degree and one year of graduate study; or (ii) a valid Professional "A" Certificate, a B.Ed. degree, and two years of graduate study; or (iii) a valid Professional "A" Certificate, an Honours degree and a B.Ed. degree; or (iv) a valid Professional "A" Certificate, an approved bachelor's degree and a Masters of Education degree (v) a valid (a) Vocational Teacher's Certificate (Endorsed); or (b) Technical Teacher's Certificate (Endorsed); and a B.Ed. degree and one year of graduate study.

Source: "Teacher Salary Classification in Saskatchewan," Reprinted by permission of the Saskatchewan Teachers' Federation, p. 2. Retrieved October 3, 2003 from www.stf.sk.ca/prof_growth/pdf/teacher_classification.pdf

Appendix 3.3

Q. What does the OTQT assess?

A. ■ The knowledge and skills judged to be important to carry out essential occupational responsibilities competently

■ Whether individuals possess occupation-relevant knowledge and skills at the time of entry into their occupation or profession

Q. What is included in the OTQT?

A. ■ The test has 36 multiple-choice questions that focus specifically on a particular theory, strategy, technique, term, concept, act, or regulation related to classroom instruction in Ontario.

■ The test also has four case studies, each with short-answer question (a total of 14).

■ Two case studies are seen by all test candidates, who are asked to write answers to the six questions associated with these case studies.

■ The other two case studies and the eight questions associated with them are matched to the candidate's certification level—Primary/Junior, Junior/ Intermediate, or Intermediate/Senior. In other words, each candidate will respond to a total of four case studies—two general ones and two for the candidate's specific certification level.

■ The test covers content areas such as the Ontario Curriculum, Planning Instruction, Human Development, Classroom Management, The Use of Technology, Acts and Regulations, Instructional Skills, Motivation and Communication, Diversity and Students with Special Needs, Assessment, Reflections on Teaching, and Parents, Colleagues, and Resources.

Q. What is a case study?

A. A case study consists of a teaching scenario of 800 to 1000 words. Typically a case study focuses on a teacher's experience with a class or on the learning experiences of a student or group of students. Each case study is followed by three or four open-ended questions that encourage synthesizing of knowledge, much as new teachers have to do in the day-to-day work of teaching. A sample of a case study is included later in this booklet. Answers to the case study questions included here are actual responses of student-participants from a pilot test.

Q. How are the case studies used on the test?

A. Each case study describes a classroom situation and is followed by a set of questions. You will be asked to provide a brief written answer for each question. For example, you may be asked to:

■ Analyze a student's behaviour

■ Suggest next steps in a classroom management situation

■ Discuss the merits and disadvantages of certain types of assessments

■ Describe ways of communicating with parents

■ Suggest teaching strategies to meet expectations based on the Ontario curriculum

■ Your answer should be brief and relevant to the question being asked. The quality and relevance of your response are the keys to a high score.

Source: © Queen's Printer of Ontario. (2002). *Ontario Teacher Qualifying Test Information Booklet*, Ontario Ministry of Education, 2002–2003, p.4. Reprinted with permission.

Appendix 3.4

Rubric to Describe the Levels of Performance

Domain: Teaching Practice

Competencies	Levels of Performance			
	Exemplary	**Good**	**Satisfactory**	**Unsatisfactory**
Teachers use their professional knowledge and understanding of the curriculum, legislation, teaching practices and classroom management strategies to promote the learning and achievement of their pupils.	The teacher always demonstrates use of professional knowledge and understanding of students, curriculum, legislation, teaching practices and classroom management strategies to promote the learning and achievement of his or her students.	The teacher consistently demonstrates use of professional knowledge and understanding of students, curriculum, legislation, teaching practices and classroom management strategies to promote the learning and achievement of his or her students.	The teacher generally demonstrates use of professional knowledge and understanding of students, curriculum, legislation, teaching practices and classroom management strategies to promote the learning and achievement of his or her students.	The teacher infrequently demonstrates use of professional knowledge and understanding of students, curriculum, legislation, teaching practices and classroom management strategies to promote the learning and achievement of his or her students.
Teachers communicate effectively with pupils, parents and colleagues.	The teacher is always effective in communicating with pupils, parents, and colleagues.	The teacher is consistently effective in communicating with pupils, parents, and colleagues.	The teacher is generally effective in communicating with pupils, parents, and colleagues.	The teacher is infrequently effective in communicating with pupils, parents, and colleagues.
Teachers adapt and refine their teaching practices through continuous learning and reflection, using a variety of sources and resources.	The teacher always adapts and refines teaching practice through continuous learning and reflection, using a variety of sources and resources.	The teacher consistently adapts and refines teaching practice through continuous learning and reflection, using a variety of sources and resources.	The teacher generally adapts and refines teaching practice through continuous learning and reflection, using a variety of sources and resources.	The teacher infrequently adapts and refines teaching practice through continuous learning and reflection, using a variety of sources and resources.
Teachers consistently use appropriate technology in their teaching practices and related professional responsibilities.	The teacher always uses appropriate technology in teaching practice and related professional responsibilities.	The teacher consistently uses appropriate technology in teaching practice and related professional responsibilities.	The teacher generally uses appropriate technology in teaching practice and related professional responsibilities.	The teacher infrequently uses appropriate technology in teaching practice and related professional responsibilities.

Source: Queen's Printer of Ontario. (2002). *Teacher performance appraisal manual and approved forms and guidelines*. Toronto: Ontario Ministry of Education, p. 75. Reprinted with permission.

Philosophical and Ethical Foundations

4

Educational philosophy is a way not only of looking at ideas, but also of learning how to use ideas in better ways.

—Howard A. Ozmon and Samuel M. Craver
Philosophical Foundations of Education, 6th ed., 1999

Ideas and Events That Have Shaped Education in Canada

Taken from *Becoming a Teacher,* Second Canadian Edition, by Forrest W. Parkay, Beverly Hardcastle Stanford, John P. Vaillancourt, and Heather C. Stephens.

Y ou are having an animated conversation in the teacher's lounge with four colleagues, Manjit, Yuliya, Kim, and Claude about educational reform and the changes sweeping across our nation's schools. The discussion was sparked by a television special everyone watched last night about new approaches to teaching and assessing students' learning.

"I was really glad to see teachers portrayed in a professional light," you say. "The message seemed to be 'Let's get behind teachers and give them the support and resources they need to implement new ideas and technologies. Effective schools are important to our nation's well-being.'"

"I think it's just a case of schools trying to jump on the bandwagon," Claude says. "All this talk about restructuring schools, developing partnerships with the community, and using technology—they're supposed to be the silver bullets that transform education. These ideas just take time away from what we should be doing, and that's teaching kids how to read, write, and compute. If we don't get back to what really matters, our country is going to fall apart ... that's my educational philosophy."

"But times have changed; the world is a different place," Manjit says. "Look at how the internet has changed things in just a few years. We can't return to the 'good old days.' Students need to learn how to learn; they need to learn how to solve problems that we can't even imagine today."

"Just a minute," Yuliya interjects. "I don't think the 'good old days' ever were. That's a nostalgia trap. What kids need is to see how education is the key to understanding themselves and others. If we can't get along as human beings on this planet, we're in trouble. Look at the ethnic cleansing in Kosovo, the killing in Rwanda, Angola, Northern Ireland.... Sure, we've got the internet and all this technology, but as a species we haven't evolved at all."

"Of course we can't return to the past," Kim says, "but we can learn a lot from it. That's one of the main purposes of education ... to see how the great ideas can help us improve things. Like I tell my students, there isn't one problem today that Shakespeare didn't have tremendous insights into 400 years ago—racism, poverty, war."

"Well, all I know is that when I started teaching 30 years ago, we taught the basics," Claude says. "It was as simple as that. We were there to teach, and the kids, believe it or not, were there to learn. Nowadays, we have to solve all of society's problems—eliminate poverty, racism, crime, or whatever."

Claude pauses a moment and then turns his attention to you. "What do you think ... what's your educational philosophy?"

What do you say?

Manjit is correct when she says we cannot return to the past, to the "good old days." On the other hand, Kim is also correct when she says we should learn from the past. We cannot understand schools today without a look at what they were yesterday. The current system of public and private education in Canada is an ongoing reflection of its philosophical and historical foundations and of the aspirations and values brought to this country by its founders and generations of settlers. Developing an appreciation for the ideas and events that have shaped education in Canada is an important part of your education as a professional.

Still, you may wonder, what is the value of knowing about the philosophy and history of Canadian education? Will that knowledge help you to be a better teacher? First, knowledge of the ideas and events that have influenced our schools will help you evaluate current proposals for change more effectively. You will be in a better position to evaluate changes if you understand how schools have developed and how current proposals might relate to previous change efforts. Second, awareness of ideas and events that have influenced teaching is a hallmark of professionalism in education.

The first half of this chapter presents several basic philosophical concepts that will help you answer five important questions that teachers must consider as they develop an educational philosophy:

1. What should the purposes of education be?
2. What is the nature of knowledge?
3. What values should students adopt?
4. What knowledge is of most worth?
5. How should learning be evaluated?

The second half presents brief overviews of how education developed in Canada's major geographical regions. This chapter will discuss the philosophical concepts, social forces, and events that, in our judgment, have had the greatest impact on education in our country.

What Determines Your Educational Philosophy?

In simplest terms, **educational philosophy** consists of what you believe about education—the set of principles that guides your professional action. Every teacher, whether he or she recognizes it, has a philosophy of education—a set of beliefs about how human beings learn and grow and what one should learn in order to live the good life. Teachers differ, of course, in regard to the amount of effort they devote to the development of their personal philosophy or educational platform. Some feel that philosophical reflections have nothing to contribute to the actual act of teaching. (This stance, of course, is itself a philosophy of education.) Other teachers recognize that teaching, because it is concerned with *what ought to be*, is basically a philosophical enterprise.

Your behaviour as a teacher is strongly connected to your personal beliefs and your beliefs about teaching and learning, students, knowledge, and what is worth knowing (see Figure 4.1). Regardless of where you stand in regard to these five dimensions of teaching, you should be aware of the need to reflect continually on *what* you believe and *why* you believe it.

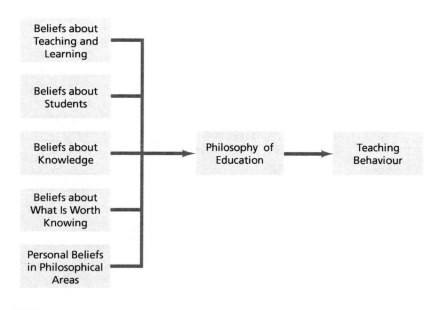

Figure 4.1

The influence of the teacher's educational beliefs on teaching behaviour

Beliefs about Teaching and Learning

One of the most important components of your educational philosophy is how you view teaching and learning. In other words, what is the teacher's primary role? Is the teacher a subject matter expert who can efficiently and effectively impart knowledge to students? Is the teacher a helpful adult who establishes caring relationships with students and nurtures their growth in needed areas? Or is the teacher a skilled technician who can manage the learning of many students at once?

Some teachers emphasize the individual student's experiences and cognitions. Others stress the

How can the web enhance your study of and interest in the philosophy and history of education?

The web has dramatically increased the amount of information that is easily available to anyone with a computer. The web, in a manner perhaps more dramatic than the invention of the printing press in the middle of the fifteenth century, has brought limitless information and expertise to people around the globe.

However, you might wonder, is there any connection between the web and the philosophy and history of education? Can the web enhance your study of and interest in these two areas? Prior to the availability of the web, it may have been more difficult for a student to develop an interest in the philosophy and history of education and to see their relevance to becoming a teacher. Only the most diligent students had the time, energy, and interest to do library research in these areas. Moreover, the outcomes of their research were limited to the size of the library collections they were using.

Today, however, the web makes available to you in a digitized form a huge amount of human culture. This means that you can easily access *more* information that is *more relevant* to your interests, experiences, and professional goals. The web makes available to you not only vast information on the philosophy and history of education, but also an extensive collection of original primary sources. Some internet sites you might visit are:

http://education.guardian.co.uk/netclass/schools/history/0,5607,80402,00.html

http://fcis.oise.utoronto.ca/~daniel_schugurensky/assignment1/1907montessori.html

http://gsnlists.org/pipermail/k12opps/2000-November/000280.html

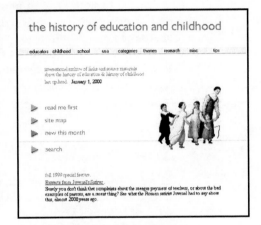

Source: Used with permission, from www.socsci.kun.nl/ped/whp/histeduc

---

student's behaviour. Learning, according to the first viewpoint, is seen as the changes in thoughts or actions that result from personal experience; that is, learning is largely the result of internal forces within the individual. In contrast, the other view defines learning as the associations between various stimuli and responses. Here, learning results from forces that are external to the individual.

Beliefs about Students

Your beliefs about students will have a great influence on how you teach. Every teacher formulates an image in her or his mind of what students are like—their dispositions, skills, motivation levels, and expectations. What you believe students are like is based on your unique life experiences, particularly your observations of young people and your knowledge of human growth and development.

Negative views of students may promote teacher–student relationships based on fear and coercion rather than on trust and helpfulness. Extremely positive views may risk not providing students with sufficient structure and direction and not communicating sufficiently high expectations. In the final analysis, the truly professional teacher—the one who has a carefully thought-out educational philosophy—recognizes that, although children differ in their predispositions to learn and grow, they all *can* learn.

Beliefs about Knowledge

How a teacher views knowledge is directly related to how she or he goes about teaching. If teachers view knowledge as the sum total of small bits of subject matter or discrete facts, their students will most likely spend a great deal of time learning that information in a straightforward, rote manner.

Other teachers view knowledge more conceptually, that is, as consisting of the big ideas that enable us to understand and influence our environment. Such teachers would want students to be able to explain how legislative decisions are made in the provincial capital, how an understanding of the eight parts of speech can empower the writer and vitalize one's writing, and how chemical elements are grouped according to their atomic numbers.

Finally, teachers differ in their beliefs as to whether students' increased understanding of their own experiences is a legitimate form of knowledge. Knowledge of self and one's experiences in the world is not the same as knowledge about a particular subject, yet personal knowledge is essential for a full, satisfying life.

Beliefs about What Is Worth Knowing

As we saw in this chapter's opening scenario, teachers have different ideas about what should be taught. Claude believes it is most important that students learn the basic skills of reading, writing, and computation. These are the skills they will need to be successful in their chosen occupations, and it is the school's responsibility to prepare students for the world of work. Kim believes that the most worthwhile content is to be found in the classics or the Great Books. Through mastering the great ideas from sciences, mathematics, literature, and history, students will be well prepared to deal with the world of the future. Duncan is most concerned with students learning how to reason, communicate effectively, and solve problems. Students who master these cognitive processes will have learned how to learn—and this is the most realistic preparation for an unknown future. Last, Manjit is concerned with developing the whole child and teaching students to become self-actualizing. Thus, the curriculum should be meaningful and contribute to the student's efforts to become a mature, well-integrated person.

What Are the Branches of Philosophy?

To provide you with further tools to formulate and clarify your educational philosophy, this section presents brief overviews of six areas of philosophy that are of central concern to teachers: metaphysics, epistemology, axiology, ethics, aesthetics, and logic. Each area focuses on one of the questions that have concerned the world's greatest philosophers for centuries: What is the nature of reality? What is the nature of knowledge and is truth ever attainable? According to what values should one live? What is good and what is evil? What is the nature of beauty and excellence? What processes of reasoning will yield consistently valid results?

Metaphysics

Metaphysics is concerned with explaining, as rationally and as comprehensively as possible, the nature of reality (in contrast to how reality *appears*). What is reality? What is the world made of? These are metaphysical questions. Metaphysics also is concerned with the nature of being and explores questions such as, What does it mean to exist? What is humankind's place in the scheme of things? Metaphysical questions such as these are at the very heart of educational philosophy. As two educational philosophers put it: "Our ultimate preoccupation in educational theory is with the most primary of all philosophic problems: metaphysics, the study of ultimate reality" (Morris and Pai 1994, 28).

Metaphysics has important implications for education because the school curriculum is based on what we know about reality. And what we know about reality is driven by the kinds of questions we ask about the world. In fact, any position regarding what schools should teach has behind it a particular view of reality, a particular set of responses to metaphysical questions.

Epistemology

The next major set of philosophical questions that concerns teachers is called **epistemology**. These questions focus on knowledge: What knowledge is true? How does knowing take place? How do we know that we know? How do we decide between opposing views of knowledge? Is truth constant, or does it change from situation to situation? What knowledge is of most worth? How you answer the epistemological questions that confront all teachers will have significant implications for your teaching. First, you will need to determine what is true about the content you will teach; then you must decide on the most appropriate means of conveying this content to students. Even a casual consideration of epistemological questions reveals that there are many ways of knowing about the world, at least five of which are of interest to teachers:

1. *Knowing Based on Authority*—for example, knowledge from the sage, the poet, the expert, the ruler, the textbook, or the teacher.
2. *Knowing Based on Divine Revelation*—for example, knowledge in the form of supernatural revelations from the sun god of early peoples, the many gods of the ancient Greeks, or the Judeo-Christian god.
3. *Knowing Based on Empiricism (Experience)*—for example, knowledge acquired through the senses, the informally-gathered empirical data that direct most of our daily behaviour.
4. *Knowing Based on Reason and Logical Analysis*—for example, knowledge inferred from the process of thinking logically.
5. *Knowing Based on Intuition*—for example, knowledge arrived at without the use of rational thought.

Axiology

The next set of philosophical problems concerns values. Teachers are concerned with values because "school is not a neutral activity. The very idea of schooling expresses a set of values. [We] educate and we are educated for some purpose we consider good. We teach what we think is a valuable set of ideas. How else could we construct education?" (Nelson, Carlson and Palonsky 2000, 304).

Among the axiological questions teachers must answer for themselves are: What values should teachers encourage students to adopt? What values raise humanity to our highest expressions of humaneness? What values does a truly educated person hold?

Axiology highlights the fact that the teacher has an interest not only in the *quantity* of knowledge that students acquire but also in the *quality* of life that becomes possible because of that knowledge. Extensive knowledge may not benefit the individual if he or she is unable to put that knowledge to good use. This point raises additional questions: How do we define quality of life? What curricular experiences contribute most to that quality of life? All teachers must deal with the issues raised by these questions.

Ethics

While axiology addresses the question "What is valuable?" **ethics** focuses on "What is good and evil, right and wrong, just and unjust?"

A knowledge of ethics can help the teacher solve many of the dilemmas that arise in the classroom. Frequently, teachers must take action in situations where they are unable to gather all of the relevant facts and where no single course of action is totally right or wrong. For example, a student whose previous work was above average plagiarizes a term paper: Should the teacher fail the student for the course if the example of swift, decisive punishment will likely prevent other students from plagiarizing? Or should the teacher, following her hunches about what would be in the student's long-term interest, have the student redo the term paper, and risk the possibility that other students might get the mistaken notion that plagiarism has no negative consequences? Another ethical dilemma: Is an elementary mathematics teacher justified in trying to increase achievement for the whole class by separating two disruptive girls and placing one in a mathematics group beneath her level of ability?

What might this teacher want her students to learn about aesthetics? How were aesthetic values reflected in the K–12 curricula you experienced?

Aesthetics

The branch of axiology known as **aesthetics** is concerned with values related to beauty and art. Although we expect that teachers of music, art, drama, literature, and writing regularly have students make judgments about the quality of works of art, we can easily overlook the role that aesthetics ought to play in *all* areas of the curriculum.

Aesthetics can also help the teacher increase his or her effectiveness. Teaching, because it may be viewed as a form of artistic expression, can be judged according to artistic standards of beauty and quality. In this regard, the teacher is an artist whose medium of expression is the spontaneous, unrehearsed, and creative encounter between teacher and student.

Logic

Logic is the area of philosophy that deals with the process of reasoning and identifies rules that will enable the thinker to reach valid conclusions. The two kinds of logical thinking processes that teachers most frequently have students master are *deductive* and *inductive* thinking. The deductive approach requires the thinker to move from a general principle or proposition to a specific conclusion that is valid. By contrast, inductive reasoning moves from the specific to the general. Here, the student begins by examining particular examples that eventually lead to the acceptance of a general proposition. Inductive teaching is often referred to as discovery teaching—by which students discover, or create, their own knowledge of a topic.

Perhaps the best-known teacher to use the inductive approach to teaching was the Greek philosopher Socrates (ca. 470–399 BC). His method of teaching, known today as the Socratic method, consisted of holding philosophical conversations (dialectics) with his pupils. The legacy of Socrates lives in all teachers who use his questioning strategies to encourage students to think for themselves. Figure 4.2 presents guidelines for using **Socratic questioning** techniques in the classroom.

The Spirit and Principles of Socratic Questioning

- Treat all thoughts as in need of development.
- Respond to all answers with a further question (that calls on the respondent to develop his or her thinking in a fuller and deeper way).
- Treat all assertions as a connecting point to further thoughts.
- Recognize that any thought can only exist fully in a network of connected thoughts. Stimulate students—by your questions—to pursue those connections.
- Seek to understand—where possible—the ultimate foundations for what is said or believed.
- Recognize that all questions presuppose prior questions and all thinking presupposes prior thinking. When raising questions, be open to the questions they presuppose.

Figure 4.2

The spirit and principles of Socratic questioning

Source: Richard Paul and Linda Eider, "The Art of Socratic questioning," *Critical Thinking*, Fall 1995, 16.

What Are Five Modern Philosophical Orientations to Teaching?

Five major philosophical orientations to teaching have been developed in response to the branches of philosophy we have just examined. These orientations, or schools of thought, are perennialism, essentialism, progressivism, existentialism, and social reconstructionism. The following sections present a brief description of each of these orientations, moving from those that are teacher-centred to those that are student-centred (see Figure 4.3).

Perennialism

Perennialism, as the term implies, views truth as constant, or perennial. The aim of education, according to perennialist thinking, is to ensure that students acquire knowledge of unchanging principles or great ideas. Like Karen, whom you met briefly in this chapter's opening scenario, perennialists believe that the great ideas continue to have the most potential for solving the problems of any era.

Socrates
(ca. 470–399 BC)

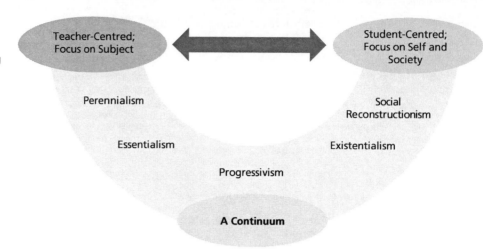

Figure 4.3

Five philosophical orientations to teaching

Teacher-Centred; Focus on Subject

Student-Centred; Focus on Self and Society

Perennialism

Social Reconstructionism

Essentialism

Existentialism

Progressivism

A Continuum

The curriculum, according to perennialists, should stress students' intellectual growth in the arts and sciences. To become "culturally literate," students should encounter in these areas the best, most significant works that humans have created. Thus, a high school English teacher would require students to read Melville's *Moby Dick* or any of Shakespeare's plays rather than a novel on the current best-seller list.

Similarly, science students would learn about the three laws of motion or the three laws of thermodynamics rather than build a model of the space shuttle.

Robert Maynard Hutchins (1899–1977)

Perennialist Educational Philosophers

Two of the best known advocates of the perennialist philosophy have been Robert Maynard Hutchins (1899–1977) and, more recently, Mortimer Adler, who together developed an undergraduate curriculum based on the study of the Great Books and discussions of these classics in small seminars. Noted educational philosopher Mortimer Adler, along with Hutchins, was instrumental in organizing the Great Books of the Western World curriculum. Through focusing study on over 100 enduring classics, from Plato to Einstein, the Great Books approach aims at the major perennialist goal of teaching students to become independent and critical thinkers. It is a demanding curriculum, and it focuses on the enduring disciplines of knowledge rather than on current events or student interests.

William C. Bagley (1874–1946)

Essentialism

Essentialism, which has some similarities to perennialism, is a conservative philosophy of education. It was originally formulated by William C. Bagley (1874–1946), an American professor of education, as a criticism of progressive trends in schools. Essentialists, like Claude, whom you met in this chapter's opening scenario, believe that human culture has a core of common knowledge that schools are obligated to transmit to students in a systematic, disciplined way. Unlike perennialists, who emphasize a set of external truths, essentialists stress what they believe to be the essential knowledge and skills (often termed "the basics") that productive members of our society need to know.

According to essentialist philosophy, schooling should be practical and provide children with sound instruction that prepares them to live life; schools should not try to influence or set social policies. Critics of essentialism, however, charge that such a tradition-bound orientation to schooling will indoctrinate students and rule out the possibility of change. Essentialists respond that, without an essentialist approach, students will be indoctrinated in humanistic and/or behavioural curricula that run counter to society's accepted standards and need for order.

Progressivism

Progressivism is based on the belief that education should be child-centred rather than focused on the teacher or the content area. The writing of John Dewey (1859–1952) in the 1920s and 1930s contributed a great deal to the spread of progressive ideas. Briefly, Deweyan progressivism is based on three central assumptions:

1. The content of the curriculum ought to be derived from students' interests rather than from the academic disciplines.
2. Effective teaching takes into account the whole child and his or her interests and needs in relation to cognitive, affective, and psychomotor areas.
3. Learning is essentially active rather than passive.

Progressive Strategies

The progressive philosophy also contends that knowledge that is true in the present may not be true in the future. Hence, the best way to prepare students for an unknown future is to equip them with problem-solving strategies that will enable them to discover meaningful knowledge at various stages of their lives.

John Dewey (1859–1952)

Educators with a progressive orientation give students a considerable amount of freedom in determining their school experiences. Contrary to the perceptions of many, though, progressive education does not mean that teachers do not provide structure or that students are free to do whatever they wish. Progressive teachers begin where students are and, through the daily give-and-take of the classroom, lead students to see that the subject to be learned can enhance their lives.

In a progressively oriented classroom, the teacher serves as a guide or resource person whose primary responsibility is to facilitate student learning. The teacher helps students learn what is important to them rather than passing on a set of so-called

How might you explain what is happening in this classroom from the perspective of progressivism? From the perspective of perennialism? From the perspective of essentialism?

enduring truths. Students have many opportunities to work cooperatively in groups, often solving problems that the group, not the teacher, has identified as important.

Existentialism

Existential philosophy is unique in that it focuses on the experiences of the individual. Other philosophies are concerned with developing systems of thought for identifying and understanding what is common to *all* reality, human existence, and values. **Existentialism**, on the other hand, offers the individual a way of thinking about *my* life, what has meaning for *me*, what is true for *me*. In general, existentialism emphasizes creative choice, the subjectivity of human experiences, and concrete acts of human existence over any rational scheme for human nature or reality.

The writings of Jean-Paul Sartre (1905–1980), well-known French philosopher, novelist, and playwright, have been most responsible for the widespread dissemination of existential ideas. According to Sartre (1972), every individual first exists and then he or she must decide what that existence is to mean. The task of assigning meaning to that existence is the individual's alone; no preformed philosophical belief system can tell one who one is. It is up to each of us to decide who we are.

**Jean-Paul Sartre
(1905–1980)**

Life, according to existential thought, has no meaning, and the universe is indifferent to the situation humankind finds itself in. Moreover, "existententialists [believe] that too many people wrongly emphasize the optimistic, the good, and the beautiful—all of which create a false impression of existence" (Ozmon and Craver 1999, 253). With the freedom that we have, however, each of us must commit him- or herself to assign meaning to his or her *own* life. As Maxine Greene, an eminent philosopher of education whose work is based on existentialism, states: "We have to know about our lives, clarify our situations if we are to understand the world from our shared standpoints ..." (1995, 21). The human enterprise that can be most helpful in promoting this personal quest for meaning is the educative process. Teachers, therefore, must allow students freedom of choice and provide them with experiences that will help them find the meaning of their lives. This approach, contrary to the belief of many, does not mean that students may do whatever they please; logic indicates that freedom has rules, and respect for the freedom of others is essential.

Existentialists judge the curriculum according to whether or not it contributes to the individual's quest for meaning and results in a level of personal awareness that Greene (1995) terms "wide-awakeness." The ideal curriculum is one that provides students with extensive individual freedom and requires them to ask their own questions, conduct their own inquiries, and draw their own conclusions.

**Maxine Greene
(b. 1917)**

Social Reconstructionism

As the name implies, **social reconstructionism** holds that schools should take the lead in changing or reconstructing society. Theodore Brameld (1904–1987), acknowledged as the founder of social reconstructionism, based his philosophy on two fundamental premises about the post–World War II era: (1) We live in a period of great crisis, most evident in the fact that humans now have the capability of destroying civilization overnight, and (2) humankind also has the intellectual, technological, and moral potential to create a world civilization of "abundance, health, and humane capacity" (Brameld 1959, 19). In this time of great need, then, social reconstructionists like Yuliya, whom we met in this chapter's opening scenario, believe that schools should become the primary agent for planning and directing social change. Schools should not only *transmit* knowledge about the existing social order; they should seek to *reconstruct* it as well.

Social Reconstructionism and Progressivism

Social reconstructionism has clear ties to progressive educational philosophy. Both provide opportunities for extensive interactions between teacher and students and among students themselves. Furthermore, both place a premium on bringing the community, if not the entire world, into the classroom. Student experiences often include field trips, community-based projects of various sorts, and opportunities to interact with people beyond the four walls of the classroom.

According to Brameld and social reconstructionists such as George Counts, who wrote *Dare the School Build a New Social Order?* (1932), the educative process should provide students with methods for dealing with the significant crises that confront the world: war, economic depression, international terrorism, hunger, inflation, and ever-accelerating technological advances. The logical outcome of such education would be the eventual realization of a worldwide democracy (Brameld 1956). Unless we actively seek to create this kind of world through the intelligent application of present knowledge, we run the risk that the destructive forces of the world will determine the conditions under which humans will live in the future.

George Counts
(1889–1974)

What Psychological Orientations Have Influenced Teaching Philosophies?

In addition to the five philosophical orientations to teaching described in previous sections of this chapter, several schools of psychological thought have formed the basis for teaching philosophies. These psychological theories are comprehensive world views that serve as the basis for the way many teachers approach teaching practice. Psychological orientations to teaching are concerned primarily with understanding the conditions that are associated with effective learning. In other words, what motivates students to learn? What environments are most conducive to learning? Chief among the psychological orientations that have influenced teaching philosophies are humanistic psychology, behaviourism, and constructivism.

Humanistic Psychology

Humanistic psychology emphasizes personal freedom, choice, awareness, and personal responsibility. As the term implies, it also focuses on the achievements, motivation, feelings, actions, and needs of human beings. The goal of education, according to this orientation, is individual self-actualization.

Humanistic psychology is derived from the philosophy of **humanism**, which developed during the European Renaissance and Protestant Reformation and is based on the belief that individuals control their own destinies through the application of their intelligence and learning. People "make themselves." The term "secular humanism" refers to the closely related belief that the conditions of human existence relate to human nature and human actions rather than to predestination or divine intervention.

In the 1950s and 1960s, humanistic psychology became the basis of educational reforms that sought to enhance students' achievement of their full potential through self-actualization (Maslow 1954, 1962; Rogers 1961). According to this psychological orientation, teachers should not force students to learn; instead, they should create a climate of trust and respect that allows students to decide what and how they learn, to question authority, and to take initiative in "making themselves." Teachers should be what noted psychologist Carl Rogers calls "facilitators," and the classroom should be a place "in which curiosity and the natural desire to learn can be nourished and enhanced" (1982, 31). Through their non-judgmental understanding of students, humanistic teachers encourage students to learn and grow.

Behaviourism

Behaviourism is based on the principle that desirable human behaviour can be the product of design rather than accident. According to behaviourists, it is an illusion to say that humans have a free will. Although we may act as if we are free, our behaviour is really *determined* by forces in the environment that shape our behaviour. "We are what we are and we do what we do, not because of any mysterious power of human volition, but because outside forces over which we lack any semblance of control have us caught in an inflexible web. Whatever else we may be, we are not the captains of our fate or the masters of our soul" (Power 1982, 168).

Founders of Behaviouristic Psychology

B. F. Skinner
(1904–1990)

John B. Watson (1878–1958) was the principal originator of behaviouristic psychology and B. F. Skinner (1904–1990) its best-known promoter. Watson first claimed that human behaviour consisted of specific stimuli that resulted in certain responses. In part, he based this new conception of learning on the classic experiment conducted by Russian psychologist Ivan Pavlov (1849–1936). Pavlov had noticed that a dog he was working with would salivate when it was about to be given food. By introducing the sound of a bell when food was offered and repeating this several times, Pavlov discovered that the sound of the bell alone (a conditioned stimulus) would make the dog salivate (a conditioned response). Watson came to believe that all learning conformed to this basic stimulus-response model (now termed classical or type S conditioning).

Skinner went beyond Watson's basic stimulus-response model and developed a more comprehensive view of conditioning known as operant (or type R) conditioning. Operant conditioning is based on the idea that satisfying responses are conditioned, unsatisfying ones are not. In other words, "The things we call pleasant have an energizing or strengthening effect on our behaviour" (Skinner 1972, 74). Thus the teacher can create learners who exhibit desired behaviours by following four steps:

1. Identify desired behaviours in concrete (observable and measurable) terms.
2. Establish a procedure for recording specific behaviours and counting their frequencies.
3. For each behaviour, identify an appropriate reinforcer.
4. Ensure that students receive the reinforcer as soon as possible after displaying a desired behaviour.

Constructivism

In contrast to behaviourism, **constructivism** focuses on processes of learning rather than on learning behaviour. According to constructivism, students use cognitive processes to *construct* understanding of the material to be learned—in contrast to the view that they *receive* information transmitted by the teacher. Constructivist approaches support student-centred rather than teacher-centred curriculum and instruction. The student is the key to learning.

Unlike behaviourists who concentrate on directly observable behaviour, constructivists focus on the mental processes and strategies that students use to learn. Our understanding of learning has been extended as a result of advances in **cognitive science**—the study of the mental processes students use in thinking and remembering. By drawing from research in linguistics, psychology, anthropology, neurophysiology, and computer science, cognitive scientists are developing new models for how people think and learn.

Teachers who base classroom activities on constructivism know that learning is an active, meaning-making process, that learners are not passive recipients of information. In fact, students are continually involved in making sense out of activities around them. Thus the teacher must *understand students' understanding* and realize that students' learning is influenced by prior knowledge, experience, attitudes, and social interactions.

How Can You Develop Your Educational Philosophy?

As you read the preceding brief descriptions of five educational philosophies and three psychological orientations to teaching, perhaps you felt that no single philosophy fit perfectly with your image of the kind of teacher you want to become. Or, there may have been some element of each approach that seemed compatible with your own emerging philosophy of education. In either case, don't feel that you need to identify a single educational philosophy around which you will build your teaching career. In reality, few teachers follow only one educational philosophy, and, as Figure 4.4 shows, educational philosophy is only one determinant of the professional goals a teacher sets.

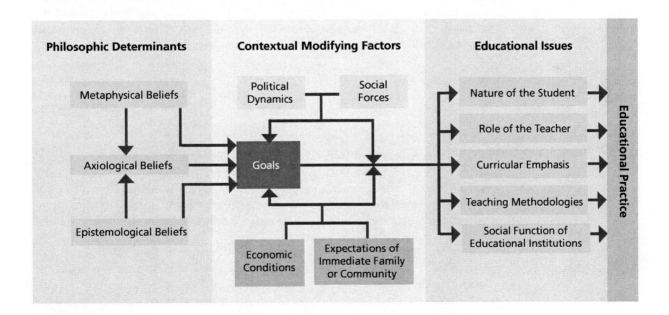

Figure 4.4

The relationship of philosophy to educational practice

Source: George R. Knight, *Issues & Alternatives in Educational Philosophy, 3rd ed.* Berrien Springs, MI: Andrews University Press, p. 34.

These children are active learners in a real or relevant context, and they are constructing their own meanings through direct experience. How might this lesson be seen as an eclectic blend of progressive, existential, and constructivist ideals?

Most teachers develop an *eclectic* philosophy of education, which means they develop their own unique blending of two or more philosophies. The self-knowledge you glean from the philosophical constructs presented in the first half of this chapter will provide a useful framework for studying the six periods in the historical development of schools that follow. For example, you will be able to see how philosophical orientations to education waxed and waned during each period—whether it was the perennialism and essentialism that characterized colonial schools, the progressivism of the 1920s and 1930s, the essentialism of the 1950s and 1980s, the humanism and social reconstructionism of the 1960s, or the constructivism of the 1990s.

What Cultural Traditions Have Led to the Development of the Canadian Educational Landscape?

The Canadian educational landscape has roots which can be traced to four cultural traditions. The earliest schools of New France were, for example, quite naturally modelled after the educational practices common in France. Later, after the fall of Quebec and the rise to governmental supremacy of the British, practices common to English schools were introduced. Later still, after the American Revolution of 1776 and the resultant emigration of the Loyalists to Canada, educational practices based upon the American model were given support. And finally, during the 1760–1840 period, thousands of Scots immigrated to Canada, bringing with them their strong regard for schools based upon democracy and merit. In areas of the country where only one cultural tradition was common, as in New Brunswick, where the Loyalists initially had the field to themselves, development of a coherent educational system was accomplished with a comparative degree of ease. However, in Nova Scotia, where the Scottish, English, and American traditions were all represented, several systems vied for supremacy with the consequence that factionalism, tumult and discord enriched the level of educational discourse.

The French Tradition

During the period 1650–1700, most adult citizens of New France—an area which extended from Cape Breton to the Great Lakes—had received their education in France. In the **French tradition**, the dominant educational philosophy was based upon the traditions of the Roman Catholic Church. Elementary **parochial schools**, known as **petites écoles**, were relatively common in most areas of France. While there was a general belief among the upper classes that the children of the lower classes should be educated, their education was to deal with only the most rudimentary of facts. Girls and boys attended separate schools, with the boys' education tending to be of a better quality. Instruction in the curriculum (catechism, singing, arithmetic, reading, writing, and grammar) was delivered by the parish priests or their assistants.

Funding for the support of the *petites écoles* was provided by the church and those parents who could afford to make contributions. Teacher colleges, also known as **normal schools**, were starting to appear, and several religious orders, most notably the Jesuits priests and the Ursuline nuns, were becoming involved in the educational process. Secondary schools, while not common, did exist and were almost exclusively the responsibility of specific religious orders.

The English Tradition

During the period 1760–1840, the English school system emerged. The **English tradition** reflected the beliefs and attitudes of the upper classes and had two salient characteristics. First, education was primarily a responsibility of the church rather than the state; second, education a was a function of class rather than merit. Education for the lower classes was primarily provided by the Church of England, although other organizations did have some modest involvement. While charitable groups sometimes provided schooling for the poor, some children attended **dame-schools** run by widows and housewives, who taught within their own homes and collected small fees from their students' parents. At the other end of the educational spectrum were the "public" schools reserved for the privileged and the wealthy.

There were various religious groups who wanted to improve the quality of education given to the lower classes, most notably, the Puritans, who eventually decamped to the American colonies. The group with the most outstanding success, however, was the Society for the Propagation of the Gospel in Foreign Parts (SPG). While its main goal was the teaching of the Bible for the benefit of overseas British settlers, the SPG soon involved itself with the development of schools in Canada and other parts of the British Empire.

The American Tradition

The United States' educational system, the **American tradition**, had its primary roots in English culture. The settlers initially tried to develop a system of schooling that paralleled the British two-track system. If students from the lower classes attended school at all it was at the elementary level for the purpose of studying an essentialist curriculum of reading, writing, and computation and receiving religious instruction. Students from the upper classes had the opportunity to attend Latin grammar schools, where they were given a college-preparatory education that focused on subjects such as Latin and Greek classics. Above all, the American colonial curriculum stressed religious objectives.

Generally, no distinction was made between secular and religious life in the colonies. The religious motives that impelled the Puritans to endure the hardships of settling in a new land were reflected in the schools' curricula. The primary objective of elementary schooling was to learn to read so that one might read the Bible and religious catechisms and thereby achieve salvation.

In the period immediately following the American Revolution of 1776, thousands of Loyalists fled to Canada. However, because they had a strong distrust of all things republican, and because they were staunchly loyal to Britain, the Loyalists tended to reinforce the provincial elites who were predominantly Anglicans in control of government counsels. In reality, the American influence upon early Canadian education was essentially a modified, somewhat more practical, version of the English influence. During the many nineteenth-century battles fought for control of Canadian schools, the Loyalists usually supported the entrenched "family compacts" who favoured the English educational tradition. It was a struggle they were destined to lose.

The Scottish Tradition

At the time of the great Scottish migration (1760–1840), the **Scottish tradition** of education, based upon a combination of parish and burgh (town) schools, had several characteristics which led to its easy transference to the New World. The first of these characteristics is of primary importance, for it resulted in the Scots having an educational impact which far outweighed their actual numbers as a percentage of the Canadian population. In Scotland almost every child attended a school, which frequently had students from *all ranks of society*. The class-based system of education found in England was absent. In addition, both male and female students often attended the same school, and had done so for hundreds of years. The practice of having separate schools for boys and girls, a dominant characteristic of the French educational tradition, was absent. Additionally, many Scottish schools provided education at both the elementary and secondary levels. There was no great divide between the two. Rather than placing a strong emphasis upon the classics as the foundation of the curriculum, subjects such as science and art were also taught. In combination with its strong democratic tradition, the characteristics of the Scottish educational system would flourish in Canada's frontier environment.

What Were Teaching and Schools Like in Canada Prior to 1875?

Canada can be roughly divided into five geographical regions: Atlantic Canada, Quebec, Ontario, the west, and the north. As each region was settled at a different time by immigrants from a variety of cultural, linguistic, and religious backgrounds, it is not surprising that the school systems which evolved had their own individual characteristics. In the early years almost all schooling was controlled by religious authorities. However, as Canada's population increased in size, and as economic development became more important to the life of the citizenry, the state began to take a greater interest in educational matters. This increased interest led to the two great educational questions of the eighteenth and nineteenth centuries: Who would control the schools? Who would pay for their maintenance and operation? These questions were largely answered by 1875—but how they were answered differed from one geographical region to another.

Quebec

1608–1760

The earliest Quebec schools were modelled exactly after the *petites écoles* of the mother country. There were separate schools for girls and boys with instruction usually provided by members of religious orders. However, lay teachers who met the moral and competency requirements of the clergy were present in small numbers. Student attendance (by those who had access to a school) varied and most students left soon after learning the rudiments of reading, writing, and arithmetic. Financial support for the *petites écoles* was provided by the church, the students' parents, and in some cases by the King of France. If an educational issue required resolution, an appeal was made to the bishop of Quebec. Indeed, it was not until after 1760 that any civil laws concerning the schools came into existence.

The *petites écoles* provided a very basic education. As early as 1635, however, when the population of New France numbered less than a thousand, the Jesuits established the Collège de Québec. For the next 150 years it remained the only secondary school in French North America. Its curriculum followed the French model, with courses in philosophy, grammar, rhetoric, mathematics, and the humanities.

An interesting development during the latter part of the 1600s was the establishment of craft and trade schools for those young men who were not suited by inclination, education, or personal circumstances, to a career in religion or one of the other professions. These schools, which offered courses in such varied subjects as carpentry, masonry, and shoemaking, provided a valuable service to a developing colony with a need for a skilled workforce. While the craft and trade schools had the support of both the secular and religious authorities, it was the latter who were responsible for their administration and support.

From 1700 until 1760, the pattern of education in New France underwent little change. The various religious societies continued to provide a modest degree of schooling to those children who lived in or near urban communities; children in rural areas had very limited access to schools and many received no education of any kind. However, the ecclesiastical school system established by the religious orders formed the basis for the system which would evolve after the start of British rule.

1760–1875

During the first 30 years of British rule, Protestant settlers from England, Scotland, Ireland, and other British colonies settled in the urban areas of Quebec. During this period, a few Anglo-Protestant schools were established through the initiative of interested clergy and lay persons. Nothing resembling a coherent school system for either the English-speaking or French-speaking citizens was evident. Education was still an essentially private or church-sponsored enterprise.

The first tentative steps towards the establishment of a centralized school system took place in the last ten years of the eighteenth century, when citizens of all religious groups recognized that economic and social development required a sound educational system. But there were some immediate problems. Should the schools be English or French; Protestant or Roman Catholic? Should the state or the church control the schools? And, most importantly, who should pay for the maintenance and operation of the educational system which would be established? It would take an additional 75 years of acrimonious political and social debate before these questions could be answered.

By 1875, all the elements of a systematic school system were in place. In actuality there were two distinct and totally separate school systems: one for Protestants, and one

Jean-Baptiste Meilleur, first superintendent of education in Lower Canada (1842–1855).

for Roman Catholics. While religious groups would continue to operate their schools, it would be the state, via a centralized bureaucracy, which would establish teaching standards, set curriculum and, through taxation based upon local assessment, pay for school maintenance and teacher salaries. The state would also provide grants for the establishment of normal schools for the training of teachers. And, by the late 1850s, three such schools had been successfully established. While this separate system of schools was a political solution acceptable to both religious groups, it created a divide between them which lasted well into the twentieth century.

Atlantic Canada

Despite their geographical proximity, the school systems which developed in the four Atlantic Provinces were the result of significantly different influences. During the formative years of its educational system, Nova Scotia had a population which was predominantly Scottish in origin, whereas New Brunswick was composed primarily of Loyalists. Both Prince Edward Island and Newfoundland had populations which were much more varied. The degree of difficulty each province would experience in its drive to establish a comprehensive school system became a function of the cultural traditions within each, and of how these cultural traditions interacted.

Nova Scotia

In 1710 the British conquered the French Garrison at Port Royal, and in 1713 the Treaty of Utrecht gave all of Nova Scotia to England. Later, after the British founded Halifax in 1749, they initiated the infamous expulsion of the Acadians in 1755. Shortly after the expulsion, 8000 New England citizens (traditionally referred to as the Planters) accepted the Governor of Nova Scotia's invitation that they move to Nova Scotia and take over the now vacant farm lands of the departed Acadians. These new settlers brought with them their tradition of self-government in church and state matters.

Prior to the arrival of the Planters, most of the schools which did exist were administered by the Church of England's Society for the Propagation of the Bible (SPG). While the quality of education provided by these schools was very limited, the SPG had strong connections with government officials. Therefore, in an effort to keep the Planters from establishing their own schools, during 1766 the SPG had the House of Assembly pass *An Act Concerning Schools and Schoolmasters*. This act, designed to protect the Church of England's monopoly over education, ironically marks the first official recognition that education was actually the responsibility of the state.

In the ten years following the 1776 American War of Independence, the Loyalists formed a second, larger wave of American immigrants to Nova Scotia. At approximately the same time, an even larger group of Scottish settlers started their migration to the province. The Scots arrived in such numbers that they quickly became the largest, and eventually most influential, faction within the colony.

Sir John William Dawson, first superintendent of education in Nova Scotia (1850–1853) and later president of McGill University (1855–1893).

By 1800, there was recognition that an effective school system was needed for an ever-expanding population. However, the questions which needed to be answered were somewhat simpler in nature. Should the state or the Church of England control the schools? Who should pay for the maintenance and operation of the educational system that would be established? The numerical strength of the Scots provided the answers to these questions. By 1875, after the usual series of acrimonious debates in the legislature, there was agreement that the state would be responsible for the governance and maintenance of schools, and that financial support for schools would be through taxation based upon local assessment. It was also agreed that a coeducational normal school should be established at Truro. The Planters and the Loyalists had a strong affinity for democratically operated schools, while the Scots had a high regard for the benefits of a school education for everyone. Working in tandem, these two traditions completely overwhelmed the influence of the British, who wanted control of schools to be a function of the Church of England.

New Brunswick

Prior to 1783, New Brunswick was sparsely settled. There were pockets of Acadians who had fled there as a result of their expulsion from Nova Scotia, and a few New England Planters were also present in small numbers. Therefore, when large numbers of Loyalists arrived in the 1775–1785 period, they quickly became the dominant group within the colony. The school system envisaged by the Loyalists, most of whom were Anglicans, was one in which church and state would work together in support of the aristocratic English tradition. Initially, this is what took place. The Society for the Propagation of the Bible (SPG) had the full support of the Executive Council of the legislature, and such grammar schools and other institutions of higher learning had their enrolments limited to members of the Anglican Church.

Unfortunately for the Loyalists, settlers from other areas of the world started arriving in large numbers during the period 1815–1825. In particular, there was a great influx of immigrants from Ireland. Scots, business people from other parts of the British Empire, and settlers from non-Anglican denominations were also becoming increasingly common, with up to one-third of the citizenry composed of Roman Catholics. Additionally, the children of the first Loyalists tended to have educational and social ideas which differed from those of their parents. All groups saw the need for tax assessment in support of free schools, an educational bureaucracy to govern the schools, and a normal school to provide qualified and effective teachers. After years of confused and rancorous debate, the situation began to improve. A normal school was established in 1847, as was a Board of Education. However, it was not until 1871 that the *Common School Act* made provision for free, non-sectarian schools supported by taxation based upon local assessment. Roman Catholics, who had diligently lobbied for separate schools supported by public funds, were deeply offended by the *Act*'s failure to grant their request.

Prince Edward Island

The early history of education in Prince Edward Island (PEI) is one of unrelenting sectarian strife. Acadians missed by the expulsion formed a small part of the population, but there were also Loyalists, Irish, Roman Catholic and Protestant Scots, and English immigrants. In the early part of the 1800s a small number of private schools were in existence. In general, they were operated by itinerant schoolmasters who made their services available to the residents of PEI's ethnic communities.

In 1800 there were fewer than 5000 people in the colony, a number which grew to 70 000 by 1855. Roman Catholics comprised approximately 40 percent of the population, while various Protestant denominations formed the remainder. It was this approximate balance between the two religious groups that lay at the heart of the sectarian warfare and dominated discussion in the provincial legislature. The fundamental issue upon which the two groups could not agree concerned authorization of the Bible for use in PEI public schools. Both groups recognized the needs for establishing a comprehensive system of schools, but the "Bible Question" hindered progress. Coincident with the Bible debate was the question of whether Prince Edward Island should join Confederation. The Roman Catholics tied the two issues together by saying that

Teaching for Excellence

Prime Minister's Award for Teaching Excellence Recipients: Blake Seward and Carmie MacLean.

Blake Seward
Smith Falls District Collegiate, Smith Falls, Ontario
Subjects Taught: Grade 9 to OAC History

Teaching Philosophy

Take students to the site; make history come to life

Outstanding Achievements

Blake Seward brought the relevance of history to life with an inspiring, unusual project—*Lest We Forget*. Grade 10 students were each given the name of a fallen soldier listed on the World War I section of the local cenotaph [monument] and given three weeks to find as much information as possible about the person. Students initially accessed regimental information from government websites, and quickly discovered that many names were misspelled and missing. Students searched relatives' attics, old newspapers and finally the National Archives of Canada for primary research material. The final result is a permanent written record of an almost—but not quite (thanks to Seward and his students)—forgotten band of men and period of history. Students received an award from the Minister of Veteran Affairs for their research and an Ontario Heritage award.

Seward is now working with the National Archives of Canada to expand the project. So far, several schools have signed up, with the formal launch taking place in September of 2003.

The history department has grown under Seward's leadership to be the largest in the school. He has redesigned and reintroduced the American History course, overseen the development of the World Issues and World Religions courses, written curriculum for several history courses, and is planning to launch a senior-level philosophy course.

Rave Reviews

"Students are like bloodhounds: they can sniff out a fake from the very first lesson of the year. But there is no fear that such a thing could occur in Blake's class."

—Colleague

"I believe that this project [*Lest We Forget*] is very important because not only does it inspire learning on several different levels, but it also invokes a deep respect for those who fought for our freedom, something that is not often felt by my generation."

—Student

Carmie MacLean
Tusarvik School, Repulse Bay, Nunavut
Subjects Taught: Grade 6, All Subjects

Teaching Philosophy

- Share the joy and excitement of lifelong learning with a community—children and their extended families—that, not that many years ago, was nomadic, focused mainly on day-to-day survival.
- Make every effort to ensure students think about learning—even after school hours and outside school walls.
- Balance understanding of many cultural differences with clear high expectations for students.

Outstanding Achievements

Created numerous incentives to improve English skills of Inuktitut-speaking students:
- An email account for all students with required literacy skills.
- Personal letters each week to students in response to their journal entries
- A daily letter to the class outlining new topics, discussing moral or behaviour issues, commenting on performance on tests, or introducing new vocabulary, which ensures students start each school day with reading that is personal, applicable, and pertinent.

Students who use English mainly at school and often have little opportunity to practice their skills at home improve their reading by at least one grade by the end of the year.

MacLean adjusts teaching strategies as necessary to address the learning styles and culture of the North while improving the academic skills of students. For example,

(continued on next page)

MacLean launched a campaign making homework completion a normal expectation of daily school life. The campaign includes lunchtime reminder notes to parents for missing homework, special draws for prizes, a daily visual record maintained by the students, and school-wide homework challenges with PA announcements and coloured bar graphs displayed in the office area.

MacLean also spearheaded an initiative to improve chronic low attendance. One month's perfect attendance earns Saturday morning blueberry muffin baking at MacLean's home, and photos of students displayed in the school foyer, a true incentive in a place where personal photos are rare. These efforts resulted in the outstanding accomplishment of three students having perfect attendance for one whole year.

Rave Reviews

"She is as solid as the rock we walk on in our barren-ground community."
—*Fellow teacher*

"My students, who are presently in Grade 9, still cannot read or write as well as Carmie's but neither did they have the benefit of Carmie's teaching for the last three years."
—*Colleague*

Source: Reproduced with the permission of the Minister of Public Works and Services. Prime Minister's Awards for Teaching Excellence. Retrieved October 4, 2003 from pma-ppm.ic.gc.ca/bio02-e.asp?prov=on and pma-ppm.ic.gc.ca/bio00-e.asp?prov=nu

the union should be opposed unless they were given a constitutional right to **separate schools**. Such a guarantee was not given, and in 1873 Prince Edward Island joined the Confederation of Canada. Shortly thereafter, the Public School Act was passed. This act established the office of Superintendent of Education, decreed that taxation based upon local assessment would support free, non-denomination schools, and created an improved Board of Education for administration of the new system of schooling.

Newfoundland and Labrador

While Prince Edward Island experienced a great deal of sectarian strife during its journey towards a system of publicly funded, non-sectarian schools, the situation in Newfoundland was more protracted and bitter, by several orders of magnitude. The roots of Newfoundland's educational system are similar to the roots of other systems in Canada. The first schools were established and operated by the Society for the Propagation of the Bible, and other groups soon began to provide schooling for the island's children. Roman Catholics, Methodists, and other Protestant groups established schools in various communities, and private schools also sprang up. However, for reasons deeply locked in Newfoundland's cultural history, the state's battle for free, non-denominational schools was lost. In 1874 the legislature gave its formal approval to funding all of the parochial schools which had been founded. Separate schools for everyone became part of the established educational order. Of all the British North American colonies, Newfoundland was the only one to develop such a unique educational model. It would be late in the twentieth century before this parochial system of schools was discontinued.

Labrador, with its harsh climate and very scattered and nomadic Inuit population, also had a church-based system of schooling. In the second half of the 1700s, the Church of the United Brethren (also known as the Moravian Church) took an interest in converting and educating the indigenous Inuit population. The Moravians carried

The Little Red School House

During the early days of Canadian education, any available room in a church, tavern, or public meeting house was pressed into service as a school. If a community did go to the trouble and expense of building a school, the structure was usually made of five-metre long, rough-cut logs. In very few instances was it ever painted red. The ceiling was relatively low and a simple fireplace was the only source of heat. Students were required to supply the firewood. During the winter months those who sat furthest from the fireplace were often uncomfortably cold.

The older students sat on simple benches arranged around three of the walls. In some cases these benches were accompanied by crude desks. Arranged around the centre of the room were more deskless, backless benches for the younger children. Other than a desk for the teacher, the room was almost completely empty. There were no blackboards, no maps, no reference books, and no teaching aids. However, quill pens were common and the students would practice their writing skills for as long as two hours each day. In cases where paper was scarce, birch bark was used. Writing slates, which the students would often "erase" by spitting and wiping them, became relatively common after 1825.

Textbooks were in very short supply and the modern concept of a "class set" was unknown. Students would bring to school any textbook which they might have been able to buy or borrow. Those who could not supply a textbook shared with students who did. The few textbooks which were available were often of American origin, a feature of much annoyance to the Loyalist faction.

The teaching strategies were simple. In many cases students were required to memorize and then recite material assigned to them by the teacher. Instruction of groups within the school was rare. In most cases the teacher dealt with individual students.

The strap was freely used to maintain discipline, and, depending on the seriousness of the offence, a specific number of lashes was administered to the offender. Arriving at school with dirty hands might result in two lashes, fighting might result in five, but swearing or playing cards at school would engender even more.

The teacher was usually an unmarried young woman who, if she did marry and became pregnant, would be expected to resign her position. The administration of the school was usually in the hands of three male trustees—some of whom might be illiterate.

out their work with skill and energy and helped to make their Inuit students literate in their own language. Unlike Newfoundland, where numerous religious groups vied for the souls and minds of the citizens, the Moravians carried out their work without competition from any other church.

Ontario

Prior to the arrival of approximately 6000 Loyalists in 1884–1886, Upper Canada (Ontario) had very few settlers. While most of the new Loyalist settlers were farmers, among them were small numbers of well-educated individuals with a high regard for good schooling. These Loyalists wanted their children to have access to American grammar (secondary) schools in addition to the locally supported non-denominational schools. Their educational concerns received support from a second wave of American settlers who, enticed by offers of free land grants, arrived in large numbers during the 20 years preceding the War of 1812. However, while these two groups of American settlers constituted a majority of the population, the government was primarily in the hands of British officials, who believed that the state should control education while leaving its administration to Church of England officials. As most of the population had religious affiliations which were non-Anglican, it is not surprising that a struggle between the English and American traditions developed.

In 1816 the passage of the *Common School Act* suggested that the free schools might come into existence with a minimum of difficulty. This act, which per-mitted any community with suf-

The District School in Cornwall, Ontario, ca. 1810.

ficient resources to establish a public school towards which the government would make an annual grant for a teacher's salary, was undermined by the 1820 *Common School Act*, which reduced the government grant. It effectively neutralized the Act of 1816 and established a pattern which would last for another 25 years. where acts regarding schools would be passed, and later rescinded or rendered irrelevant by later acts. While Upper Canada would not be spared the legislative struggles which had dogged the other Canadian provinces, it did continue to make incremental steps towards a comprehensive educational system. By the early 1840s, progress towards a centralized bureaucracy had been made, and provisions for a normal school had been put in place. Local assessment in support of schools was effectively introduced in 1846 and, the *School Act* having been passed in 1843, members of religious groups were permitted to operate their own schools. Interestingly, the impetus for separate schools came not from Roman Catholics, but from adherents of the Church of England and other protestant groups. By the early 1870s the major features common to Ontario's present system of schooling had been established.

The West of Canada

The Prairies

Until 1869, western Canada was under the control of the Hudson Bay Company, which had the fur trade as its exclusive interest. Prior to 1810, most of those living in what would eventually become Manitoba, Saskatchewan, and Alberta were either First Nations peoples or French-speaking Catholic Metis. However, in 1811, Thomas Douglas, the fifth Earl of Selkirk, made the first concerted effort to colonize this area. He wanted to provide relief to distressed Scottish farmers while also providing the Hudson Bay Company with a source of food and labour. To this end he established the agriculturally-based Red River Settlement near present-day Winnipeg. Early attempts to provide the settlers with a school were unsuccessful and it would be almost 40 years before a Presbyterian

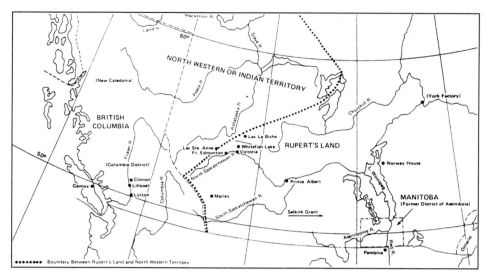

Figure 4.5

Centres where Western schools were established prior to 1873.

Source: Reprinted with permission from the University of Toronto Press.

school was established for them. In the interim, such schools as did exist for the French-speaking population were run by Roman Catholic priests or their French-Canadian lay recruits. By 1820 Roman Catholics had access to three schools, while Protestants had access to none.

Between 1820 and 1870, the population of the prairies experienced a slow but steady growth and a concurrent increase in the number of schools. In general, the schools which were established during this period were of a sectarian nature. By 1840 the Roman Catholics and Methodists were active in what is presently northern Alberta. By the late 1860s Saskatchewan also had a small number of Protestant schools. Despite the parochial nature of these prairie schools, 20 years after Manitoba joined Confederation in 1870, the province decreed that all schools should be non-denominational. Alberta and Saskatchewan, on the other hand, would eventually recognize separate schools based upon religious affiliation.

British Columbia

Like the prairies, British Columbia was initially under the control of the Hudson Bay Company. Prior to 1858 the non-indigenous population was less than a thousand. As a result, the first British Columbia school was not established until 1849. Nine years later, the gold rush of 1858 brought about dramatic changes. Thousands of gold seekers from all parts of the world descended on the territory and brought an end to the influence of the Hudson Bay Company. The new arrivals, who were of numerous cultural and ethnic backgrounds, immediately began to agitate for schools which were both non-denominational and free. Unlike other areas of Canada, where protracted battles for control of the schools had been waged by primarily sectarian interests, the conflict in BC was remarkably brief. The *Common School Act* of 1865, supplemented by the common *School Ordinance* of 1869, decreed that BC schools would be both free and non-sectarian. The state was now firmly in control of the educational system.

Confederation and the British North America Act of 1867

As Canada's colonial period came to an end, political figures from all parts of England's remaining North American provinces discussed a confederation that would bind them together as one nation. The **British North America Act (BNA Act)** of 1867 was the legal instrument used to set out the federal and provincial responsibilities of those provinces that wished to become part of this new country. Under Article 93 of this agreement, education was to be a provincial responsibility (see Figure 4.6). Careful reading of

Figure 4.6

The British North
America Act 1867

Education

93. In and for each Province the Legislature may exclusively make Laws in relation to Education, subject and according to the following Provisions:

(1) Nothing in any such Law shall prejudicially affect any Right or Privilege with respect to Denominational Schools which any Class of Persons have by Law in the Province at the Union;

(2) All the Powers, Privileges, and Duties at the Union, by Law conferred and imposed in Upper Canada on the Separate Schools and School Trustees of the Queen's Roman Catholic Subjects shall be and the same are hereby extended to the Dissentient Schools of the Queens's Protestant and Roman Catholic Subjects in Quebec:

Where in any Province a System of Separate or Dissentient Schools Exists by Law at the Union or is hereafter established by the Legislature of the Province, an appeal shall lie to the Governor General in Council from any Act or Decision of any Provincial Authority affecting a Right or Privilege of the Protestant or Roman Catholic Minority of the Queen's Subjects in relation to Education:

In case any such Provincial Law as from Time to Time seems to the Governor General in Council requisite for the due Execution of the Provisions of this Section is not made, or in case any Decision of the Governor General in Council on any Appeal under this Section is not duly executed by the proper Provincial Authority in that Behalf, then and in every such Case, and as far only as the Circumstances of each Case require, the Parliament of Canada may make remedial Laws for the due Execution of the Provisions of this Section and of any Decision of the Governor General in Council Under this section. (43)

Article 93 clearly indicates that the diverse school systems established in the various geographical areas of the country would not be threatened by the newly established federal government. Indeed, any separate school rights acquired by a miniority group prior to 1867 were constitutionally guaranteed by the BNA. The Act also placed Canada in a unique category. Today, Canada is one of the few developed countries in which there is no national system of education.

What Patterns Did Canadian Education Develop from 1875 to 1918?

In 1875 Canada's population was primarily rural. Most schools were relatively small with most of them accurately representing the concept of the little red school house. The curriculum was simple and concentrated on the 3 Rs. However, as Canada approached the twentieth century the number of immigrants increased significantly while industrialization and urbanization also began to place additional strains on every province's education system. The basic education provided by existing schools was becoming inadequate for the needs of a society, which was slowly but certainly changing from a rural focus to an urban one. A result of this evolving demographic was a philosophical debate over the basic goals of education. Is the purpose of schools to help individuals to read the Bible, do simple mathematical calculations and write simple communications, or is the purpose to provide skilled workers who can meet the demands of commerce and industry?

While the roots of science and technical education can be traced back to the work of educators such as Sir John William Dawson, President of McGill University from 1855–1896, by the early twentieth century, science had become a significant component of provincial curricula. Technical education had also made significant inroads, and by 1918 it was available in most urban centres. However, while urban-area schools were successfully making the transition to a more scientifically and technologically based curriculum, rural areas were experiencing serious educational distress. The Federal Census of 1871 indicated that almost 88 percent of Canada's population resided in rural areas; however, the Federal Census of 1911 indicated that those living in rural areas constituted only 54 percent of the population. Additionally, urban areas paid teachers salaries that were often twice as high as those available in rural communities. This led to most of the best qualified teachers moving to, and remaining in, urban centres. Rural groups, composed mainly of farmers, began to make demands for a more relevant curriculum, better teachers, and better educational opportunities for their children.

By the early 1900s, the demand for teachers had grown dramatically. An increasing number of women entered the teaching field at this time, beginning a trend often referred to as the "feminization of teaching." Female teachers were given less respect from the community than their male predecessors, though they were still more highly regarded than women who worked in factories or in the domestic sphere. In addition, they were expected to be of high moral character. They were subjected to a level of public scrutiny hard to imagine today, as illustrated by the following Professional Reflection.

Professional Reflection   Reflecting on changes in the image of teachers

The following is a public school contract that teachers were required to sign in 1927. Analyze the contract and then write a one-paragraph description of the image of teachers and teaching reflected in the contract. How does this image differ from the current image of teachers and teaching?

Teacher Contract

I promise to take vital interest in all phases of Sunday-school work, donating of my time, service, and money without stint for the uplift and benefit of the community.

I promise to abstain from all dancing, immodest dressing, and any other conduct unbecoming a teacher and a lady.

I promise not to go out with any young men except in so far as it may be necessary to stimulate Sunday-school work.

I promise not to fall in love, to become engaged or secretly married.

I promise not to encourage or tolerate the least familiarity on the part of any of my boy pupils.

I promise to sleep at least eight hours a night, to eat carefully, and to take every precaution to keep in the best of health and spirits, in order that I may be better able to render efficient service to my pupils.

I promise to remember that I owe a duty to the townspeople who are paying me my wages, that I owe respect to the school board and the superintendent that hired me, and that I shall consider myself at all times the willing servant of the school board and the townspeople.

Source: Willard Waller, *The Sociology of Teaching,* N.Y.: John Wiley, 1932, p. 43. Copyright 1932 by John Wiley.

Attempts by educational officials to meet the demands of their rural citizens encountered varying degrees of success. Perhaps the most successful of these efforts was the consolidation of small rural school districts into larger ones, a process which, to some degree, is still taking place as Canada's rural population continues to shrink. Because of their larger student bodies, consolidated schools could provide greater opportunities for curriculum diversity. However, rural education still faced many challenges. The prairie provinces, for example, had been subject to a large influx of settlers from eastern and central Europe. Some of these settlers wanted their children to be at home working the land rather than at school. Others wanted their children educated in their native tongue but, as there were few teachers with the linguistic knowledge to provide such a service, English became the language of instruction.

At the conclusion of World War I in 1918, the Canadian educational system was taking on the basic elements of its present form. All provinces had developed centralized educational bureaucracies. Curricular issues around the preparation of students for an industrially, urban-focused life were being discussed and implemented, secondary schools were becoming more prevalent, normal schools for the preparation of teachers were becoming more common and, while some provinces had separate schools, these schools were publicly funded.

What Is the History of Schooling for First Nations Peoples?

From the beginning, settlers' efforts to indoctrinate First Nations children with European values through education was a shameful exercise, undertaken only to try to exterminate First Nations peoples by assimilation. The settlers and the clerics—first Roman Catholic, and later also Protestant—shared a common belief that the Native way of life was inferior in every way to their own.

However, as Barman, Hebert, and McCaskill point out in *Indian Education in Canada, Volume 1: The Legacy* (1986, 2–4) there was much that was admirable about the education provided by First Nations for their children. They taught their children about the unity of all life, honourable conduct, family responsibilities, individual responsibility, the importance of sharing, self-reliance, and survival skills. Their history was transmitted through stories, myths, and legends.

Unfortunately for First Nations peoples, the colonial clerical and other designated educators were primarily interested in "civilizing" Native peoples by converting them to Christianity. Because Native languages, culture, and political structures were different and non-Christian, they were deemed barbaric, and thus worthy of eradication. This belief in Native inferiority was institutionalized in the Treaty of Utrecht (which transferred Acadia from France to Britain) and was incorporated into the British North America act in 1867.

When Canada was created in 1867, by the British Parliament enacting the British North America Act, Section 91:24 placed the responsibility for "Indians and Indian Lands" firmly in the hands of the federal government. The later *Indian Act* of 1876 was enacted by Canada's Parliament to manage that responsibility, with the goal being—following exactly the British example—the complete assimilation of Native Peoples.

The Indian Act of 1876 included paternalistic provisions for how the government would manage band membership, education, Indian estates, and practically every social service. Native governments were also made subservient to the federal government.

Residential schools for Native children were first established in the 1840s. Like Indian day schools, residential schools were created to assimilate Native peoples. Children were forcibly taken from their families, locked up, forbidden to speak their own tongues, and often subjected to harsh, or even criminal acts. The stories of mental, physical, and sexual abuse to which they were subjected are deeply disturbing. Fortunately, the National Indian Brotherhood's (NIB) 1972 call for greater Native control of education was eventually heeded.

While the funding for First Nations schools is provided by the federal government, some control of education, primarily through federal–provincial agreements, is now in the hands of various bands. There are still difficulties, however. High dropout rates are an ongoing problem and they perpetuate the shortage of First Nation teachers and other professionals. School funding and equipment shortages also continue to exist.

On the positive side, educational challenges faced by First Nations children are now well-recognized, and First Nation leaders are working toward the creation of a fairer and more effective system of schools. Thus, the wrongs of the past are unlikely to be repeated. The rest of Canadian society watches with supportive hope as Canada's First Nations attempt the recreation of a first class educational system that was taken from them over the last 350 years.

"What is the History of Schooling for First Nations Peoples?" was collaboratively written by one of the authors and Mr. Daniel Paul, a First Nations author and former District Chief for the Shubenacadie Mi'kmaq Bands.

See Table 4.1 for Aboriginal populations of First Nations peoples by province and territory.

Table 4.1

Aboriginal populations

Name	Total population	Aboriginal population[1]	North American Indian	Metis	Inuit	Non-Aboriginal populalion
Canada	29 639 030	976 305	608 850	292 305	45 070	28 662 725
Newfoundland and Labrador	508 080	18 775	7040	5480	4560	489 300
Prince Edward Island	133 385	1345	1035	220	20	132 040
Nova Scotia	897 565	17 010	12 920	3135	350	880 560
New Brunswick	719 710	16 990	11 495	4290	155	702 725
Quebec	7 125 580	79 400	51 125	15 855	9530	7 046 180
Ontario	11 285 545	188 315	131 560	48 340	1375	11 097 235
Manitoba	1 103 700	150 045	90 340	56 800	340	953 655
Saskatchewan	963 155	130 185	83 745	43 695	235	832 960
Alberta	2 941 150	156 225	84 995	66 060	1090	2 784 925
British Columbia	3 868 875	170 025	118 295	44 265	800	3 698 850
Yukon Territory	28 520	6540	5600	535	140	21 975
Northwest Territories	37 100	18 730	10 615	3580	3910	18 370
Nunavut	26 665	22 720	95	55	22 560	3945

[1] Includes the Aboriginal groups (North American Indian, Métis and Inuit), multiple Aboriginal responses and Aboriginal responses not included elsewhere.

The Aboriginal identity population comprises those persons who reported identifying with at least one Aboriginal group, that is, North American Indian, Metis or Inuit, and/or who reported being a Treaty Indian or a Registered Indian, as defined by the *Indian Act* of Canada, and/or who reported being a member of an Indian Band or First Nation.

Source: Reproduced with permission from the Minister of Public Works and Government Services.

Recommended Resources

Paul, Daniel N. (1993). *We were not the savages.* Halifax, NS: Nimbus.
www.danielnpaul.com/Images.html
www.shannonthunderbird.com/indian_act.htm
www.siouxme.com/rainface.html
www.aboriginalconnections.com/

What Educational Advancements Took Place between the Great Wars (1918–1939)?

World War I made government officials recognize the need for technical and industrial education. War was becoming more automated and scientific. Soldiers with technical experience were becoming a necessity of modern warfare. As a consequence, through the *Technical Education Act of 1919* the federal government made funds for the development of technical/vocational schools and programs available to the provinces. While all areas of the country participated to greater or lesser degree in the establishment of vocationally-based programs, the exact nature of the programs they developed varied. Some added programs to existing schools, some established schools devoted exclusively to technical and vocational training, while others set up correspondence courses or summer schools.

The problems associated with the decline of rural populations continued throughout this period. Studies of these problems were conducted in provinces such as Ontario, New Brunswick, and Alberta. However, other than through the continued amalgamation of rural school districts into ever larger consolidated ones, little could be done to alleviate the rural school issue.

The period between the wars also saw a dramatic increase in the number of students who went on to a post-elementary education. A partial explanation for this may lie with the great depression, which started in 1929. Students who might have wanted to enter the labour force could not do so as there were no jobs for them. However, other factors were likely involved. Schools were becoming more appealing places, and there was a growing recognition that a good education was often the prerequisite for a good job. An additional factor almost certainly relates to the school-leaving age requirements that were starting to be introduced. For example, in 1922, Ontario had a law that every child must attend school, and it also required children to attend until they were sixteen years of age.

Curriculum and student discipline were subjects of great concern and much discussion during this period. What exactly should be taught? Should the emphasis be placed upon traditional academic courses, such as English and mathematics? Should there be technical and vocational courses? Should some courses be required for all students to take, while other could be electives? Should junior high schools be established, thus changing the model of eight years of elementary education followed by three or four years of secondary school? What types of disciplinary procedures should be established? Opinions on these and related topics varied from province to province. However, there was little agreement, and definitive answers would not be determined until after 1945.

Other, newer ideas and issues also made their appearance during this period. The theories of psychologists such as Edward Lee Thorndike started to receive attention, as did the concepts of progressive education espoused by John Dewey, one of the most noteworthy American philosophers of the twentieth century. Universities started to take an interest in teacher education and, as early as 1923, the University of British Columbia established a school of education for university graduates. Other universities followed this lead and, within the next 50 years, most of the traditional normal schools would cease to exist.

The period from 1918 to 1939 did not result in a great number of truly significant changes to the Canadian educational system. However, the ideas and forces which were to give our present-day system its final characteristics were now in place. The extended period of peace and prosperity which followed World War II would provide the ideal environment for the final evolution of Canada's present system of education.

What Are the Major Characteristics of Today's Canadian System of Education?

At the end of World War II Canadian education continued its evolution into the system as we know it today. The trend evident by 1945 would, for the most part, become well established by the end of the twentieth century. While each of the ten provinces and four territories has its own distinctive features, there are many commonalities.

Elementary

Education is compulsory for all children between the ages of six and sixteen although most provinces and territories have a Kindergarten (called Primary in some jurisdictions) for students who are five years of age. The length of the elementary program varies from five years in Saskatchewan to eight years in Ontario and Manitoba. Depending on the length of their elementary program, students next proceed to a middle school (normally Grades 6 to 8), a junior high (Grades 7 to 9), or a secondary school (in many areas Grades 9 to 12).

Secondary

Secondary schools (high schools) offer a variety of courses which are both academic and vocational in nature. High school students have compulsory courses in areas such as mathematics, languages, social studies, and the sciences. Elective courses, such as music, drama, and geology also form part of the high school curriculum. Most schools have programs which prepare students for admission to university or to a community college. In Quebec, the model is somewhat different. At the end of Grade 11, students can attend a *collège d'enseignement général et professional* (**CEGEP**) for either two years of preparatory study towards admission to a university, or three years of study in a technical/vocational program.

School Year

The lengths of both the **school year** and the school day are set by each province or territory's department of education. The Canadian average is 188 student days, with seven additional professional development days for teachers. However, Alberta, Saskatchewan, and Quebec have set the school year at 200 days. An additional factor in determining what constitutes a school year is the length of the school day. On average, this is 300 min of teacher-student contact time per day, but there are variations.

All Alberta students receive 950 h of instruction per year, while secondary students in Ontario receive 925 h, and elementary students only 850. By way of comparison with other countries, Canada's school year is in the middle. China has 251 days in its school year, Taiwan has 222 days, and the United Sates has 178 days. At 172 days, the school years of Portugal and Ireland are the shortest.

Separate Schools

Canada's publicly funded separate schools reflect the country's religious and linguistic diversity. Alberta, Saskatchewan, Ontario, Quebec, New Brunswick, and Newfoundland all have separate school systems based upon religious affiliation or language. While Nova Scotia does not have a separate school system, it does have schools whose students are almost exclusively French Acadians.

How Are Canadian Schools Funded?

It costs approximately $40 billion a year to finance Canada's 5.4 million elementary and secondary students, who attend one of the country's 15 500 public and separate schools. Teacher salaries consume an estimated 80 percent of the school budget, while the remainder goes for maintenance, student transportation, school supplies, and new construction. On average, it costs $6500 to $7000 to educate one student for one year.

As Figure 4.7 indicates, Canada's per student level of educational spending is one of the highest in the world. The actual money required for the operation of schools is raised through taxation at the territorial/provincial and municipal levels. One of the most recent pressures in education has been created by governments which want to balance their budgets through the reduction of their school-operation expenses.

Figure 4.7

International comparison of direct public spending on education.

Source: Organization for Economic Cooperation and Development, *Education at a glance: OECD indicators, 2000.*

School Funding Formulas

School funding formulas are used to determine how much money is allocated to the operation of schools within a particular school district. While these formulas vary from one jurisdiction to another, the following constitutes a representative example.

Operating Formula for the Basic Costs of School Operation

- For every student in a school district the government gives the board a specified amount of money.
- A student is defined as someone who is under 21 years of age and listed on a class register as of September 30.

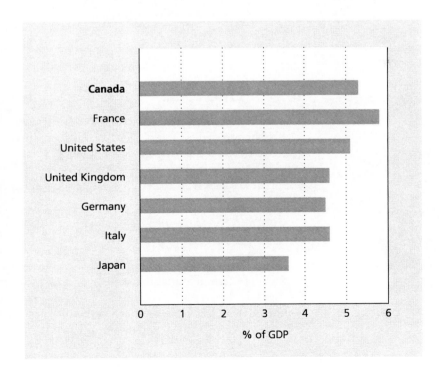

% of GDP

(Some provinces give schools half their funding for students enrolled on September 30, and the remainder for students enrolled as of May 30.)

■ Rural school districts receive a special allocation to cover the costs of student transportation.

■ Some students are more expensive than others to education. For example, a student who is deaf or blind might cost as much to educate as 2.2 students without such needs.

Maintenance Formula for the Upkeep and Repair of a School

■ Very similar to operating formulas but pertaining to buildings and equipment.

■ Boards are given a grant for each instruction area (classroom = 1.0) with adjustments made for laboratories (2.1) and gymnasium (4.5).

■ Telephone costs, paper costs, janitorial services, and other similar expenses are covered by this formula.

Capital Funding for Major Repairs or New Construction

■ A school board submits to its department of education a proposal for construction of a new school or major repairs to an existing school.

■ Department of education officials then review the proposal, compare it to other similar requests, and make a decision to accept or reject each on a case-by-case basis.

Local Funding

■ A municipality must pay a specified percentage of its board's operating expenses. Typically, this percentage can range from a low of 1 percent to as much as 20 percent. The municipality can, however, elect to allocate funds above the required percentage should it wish to do so.

■ Municipalities raise their required funding through the taxation of local property.

What Are Some Current Trends in Canadian Education?

While the tendency of territorial and provincial governments to reduce funding for the support of their schools is a concern, there are several other educational trends which have developed during the last ten years. Some of these have a very positive impact and reflect the vibrant nature of our collective public and separate school systems. Many of these topics will receive greater attention in later chapters.

Evaluation and Assessment

Most Canadians have a great interest in educational matters and are quick to express their concerns about curriculum issues and issues related to the quality of instruction their children receive. As a direct consequence of the criticism levelled at schools in these areas, there has been an increased emphasis placed upon the evaluation and assessment of the curriculum and the teachers who deliver it. The Council of Ministers of Education, Canada (CMEC) which meets regularly for the discussion of issues of common

Should school attendance beyond the elementary level become voluntary?

Should every child in Canada over twelve years old be required to attend high school? Should only those students who choose to be in school be permitted to attend? Should school attendance beyond the elementary level become voluntary?

Compulsory school attendance started to become a common feature of education in the early 20th century. By 1930 all provinces and territories had passed laws regarding this topic.

Over the years, individuals and groups dissatisfied with the schooling system in Canada have argued in favour of voluntary school attendance for a variety of reasons. Some believed that schools forced students to be too conforming and obedient. Others believed that compulsory attendance was simply a means of keeping disruptive adolescents off the streets. Today, many who home-school their children believe schools are unsafe, unhealthy, and poor settings for learning. On the other hand, opponents of voluntary school attendance say that the nation will be lost if citizens abdicate responsibility for the education of children over thirteen and release them to society with no further guidance. We would be giving up on them and limiting their futures, they say. Where do you stand on this issue? Should school attendance beyond the elementary level become voluntary?

In addition, many who oppose the idea of voluntary attendance believe strongly that the core of Canadian society is weakening, and lacking in such values of the past as honesty, perseverance, integrity, generosity, compassion, and service. Drugs, violence, sexual promiscuity, and the loss of ethics and morals have all taken their toll, they say, resulting in a society that is self-indulgent, irresponsible, and impatient for immediate gratification. Too many parents are unwilling to place demands on their children. In such a weakened society, is it wise to make school attendance after the age of twelve voluntary? Will parents choose the easy way out and let their children drop out of school when they are thirteen?

Furthermore, which children would remain in school if attendance were voluntary, the sons and daughters of the wealthy, or of the poor? Will the children who leave school when they are thirteen be short-changed in their career options? Will they be able to keep up with the expansion of technology and access to information? Will they acquire the knowledge and thinking skills necessary to make the important, complex decisions in their lives? Will they be able to negotiate as well in our increasingly complex society? Opponents to voluntary attendance after elementary school think not. They fear that the costs for those who leave, and for society as a whole, would be extensive and irreparable.

No, school attendance beyond elementary school should not become voluntary.

Opponents of voluntary school attendance believe that the original reason for requiring students to continue their schooling past the age of twelve remains valid today. Citizens need to be informed and able to think critically if democracy is to prevail. This necessity is especially important today because of the increasing complexity and diversity in society. As extensive immigration to Canada continues, new citizens and their children need to learn about the history, government, and values of their new land. In addition, the growing influence and sophistication of the news media requires an educated citizenry that can resist intellectual manipulation. Thus compulsory school attendance should be continued for the common good of the country.

Yes, school attendance beyond the elementary level should become voluntary.

"Education is wasted on the young!" say many people who return to college after being in the work world. they are more motivated to learn, bring more life experiences to their studies, use their time more efficiently, and earn higher grades after being out in the world for a while. Wouldn't adolescents discover the same thing if they weren't required to move on to middle or junior high school after elementary school? Instead of forcing thirteen-year-olds to stay in school, shouldn't we encourage them to travel, engage in meaningful service, or experience the work world before continuing their education? Their readiness to learn and their appreciation of the educational opportunities they were given would be greatly enhanced if that were the case, say those who favour voluntary school attendance.

The proponents also ask, "Do all adolescents benefit from having a secondary education?" Some students know exactly what they want to learn, but they are not able to find the instruction they desire in their high schools. Most secondary schools do not offer classes in such areas as paramedics, auto design, marketing, investments, computer graphics, song writing, art design, architecture, guitar playing, fashion design, script writing, film animation, flight training, river boat piloting, auto racing, skiing, broadcasting, scuba diving, parachuting, abnormal psychology, child development, and parenting. A resurgence of the apprenticeships of our colonial past may be the answer for some groups of today's young people.

Proponents of voluntary attendance argue that public schools would be more effective if they didn't have to deal with uncooperative students who wanted to leave but couldn't. These resistant students take teachers' and principals' time from the students who are there to learn. How much more productive schools would be if they were filled only with students motivated to learn! Educators, too, would find their work more rewarding, and teaching would become a more inviting profession. In addition, parent involvement in school would increase, because parents had chosen to have their children continue in school.

The tax money saved from having fewer students in school could enrich school offerings and extend students'

educational experiences. The extra money could even be spent on creative education and training alternatives that would appeal to and benefit those who chose to leave. Making school attendance voluntary after the age of twelve could result in a revitalized education system.

Where do you stand on this issue?

1. With which position do you agree and why?

2. What would you add to the list of subjects desired by students but not currently taught in secondary schools?

3. What do you think of the compromise position of giving people in Canada the option of having ten years of free education that they could take whenever they choose?

4. What other solutions can you suggest for helping students who don't want a traditional secondary education?

Recommended Sources

McGhan, B. (1997, Winter). Compulsory school attendance: an idea past its prime? *The Educational Forum.*

Noll, J. W. (Ed.). (1999). *Taking sides: clashing views on controversial educational issues,* 10th ed. Guilford, CT: McGraw-Hill.

interest, has advanced its School Achievement Indicators Program (SAIP) as one method for determining the effectiveness of provincial and territorial educational programs. Additionally, many school districts have created their own evaluation instruments to determine how well their schools are performing. While the CMEC, national teacher conferences, and other groups with an interest in education now share their practices regarding evaluation and assessment, they also deal with other topics as well. This mutual sharing of ideas has become one of the most valuable trends within Canadian education.

Students with Special Needs

The inclusive school movement has made significant gains in making schools more responsive to the needs of children with learning difficulties or physical disabilities. (Chapter 8 will deal with the complexities related to this topic.) The needs of groups such as the children of recent immigrants, members of our Aboriginal communities, and African-Canadian students are also being addressed. Indeed, many school districts now have departments or officials designated with the responsibility of meeting the needs of these minorities.

Ancillary Services

Canadian schools are responding to requests for additional services. Daycare facilities, for example, are now available in some secondary schools, as are programs in anger-management, peer mediation, peer drug-education, and respect-for differences. Schools are increasingly having their educational role intermixed with that of the family.

Technology

The advent of the internet and the need to prepare students for the world of information technology have led to increased funding for computers, data projectors, printers, scanners and other related pieces of hardware and software. Teachers now require increased professional development to deal with new teaching and learning methodologies which rely upon the new technology which confronts them. Persuading them to give up some of their more traditional teaching strategies is one of the many challenges facing the leaders of today's technology-enriched schools.

Curriculum Development

All departments of education now provide teachers with curriculum guides that contain lists of specific learning outcomes. There is an increased emphasis placed upon language development and use, mathematical skills and concepts, thinking skills, and the sciences. Teachers no longer have to develop a curriculum based upon some general guidelines for a particular subject at a specific grade level. The trend is now to give them a very specific curriculum to deliver along with concrete suggestions as to how they might deliver it effectively. On the one hand, this constitutes a reduction in teacher autonomy; on the other, it is a response to the criticisms of those who believe that teachers require more guidance to carry out their classroom responsibilities effectively.

Second Language Acquisition

Canada is a leader in the area of second language instruction. French as a second language is taught in most Canadian school districts and French Immersion (FI) programs are common in many areas. However, the shortage of qualified French Immersion teachers is generating concerns. While most FI programs start at some point in the lower elementary grades, the true difficulties arise at the secondary level where subjects such as physics, mathematics, and chemistry need to be taught in French. Finding a qualified English-speaking teacher for these subjects is already very difficult. Finding someone who can teach them in French is more difficult still.

There can be no doubt that Canadian schools are still in an evolutionary process. However, the independence of each province or territory, a characteristic which makes our educational system quite different from those of other countries, provides

Canadians with a great advantage. The provinces and territories are uniquely free to experiment with new educational practices without having to seek permission from a centralized federal bureaucracy. If a new practice is successful, the high degree of collaboration among the various Canadian units ensures that it may be instituted in other areas of the country. The cultural divisiveness and sectarian wrangling which characterized so much of Canada's educational history has actually been an exceptionally valuable gift. Rather than having a single, centralized bureaucracy within which a single bureaucrat might have the authority to stifle a good idea, Canada has fourteen independent departments of education. As a consequence, the possibilities for a novel educational practice to receive a valid field test are much higher here than in many other countries.

What Are Some Other Types of Canadian Schools?

While the large majority of Canadian students attend government-funded public or separate schools, there are several other options available to those parents who are unhappy with the education provided by these schools. While it is not possible to list all of these options, the following five examples provide a representative sample.

Independent Schools

Independent schools have existed from the earliest days of Canadian education. Often referred to as private schools (a term these schools dislike, because of its elitist connotation), these schools charge a tuition which can range from a low of $2000 per year to a high of over $25 000 per year. Most are religious in nature, or at least in origin, and often have a boarding school component. Parents who elect to send their children to independent schools do so for a variety of reasons. Some want the religious and/or social values of the home reinforced by the school, some believe the quality of the education delivered is better than in the public schools, while others believe that the characteristically small class sizes provide an environment in which their children are more likely to thrive.

In some provinces, such as Quebec and the western provinces, limited public funding is available under certain conditions. In all other areas the independent schools must provide their own funding. Overall, perhaps five to six percent of Canadian students attend independent schools.

Montessori Schools

Maria Montessori (1870–1952), an Italian physician who was influenced by Rousseau, believed that children's mental, physical, and spiritual development could be enhanced by providing them with developmentally-appropriate educational activities.

At Montessori's school for poor preschool-age children in Rome, teachers created learning environments based on students' levels of development and readiness to learn new material. According to the **Montessori method**, prescribed sets of materials and physical exercises are used to develop students' knowledge and skills, and students are allowed to use or not use the materials as they see fit. The materials arouse students' interest, and the interest motivates them to learn. Through highly individualized

Maria Montessori
(1870–1952)

instruction, students develop self-discipline and self-confidence. Montessori's ideas spread throughout the world. While most Canadian Montessori schools are located in Ontario and British Columbia, there are a few in other provinces. (Webb, Metha, and Jordan 1999). Today, Montessorian materials and activities are a standard part of the early childhood and elementary curricula in public schools throughout the nation.

Hutterite Schools

The Hutterites are a unique group within Canadian society. For over 400 years, they have maintained unchanged their rural, communal way of life. Located primarily, but not exclusively, in western Canada, they are deeply religious and avoid excessive contact with the outside world. Most Hutterites now speak English as a first language, and **Hutterite schools** teach German as a second language.

A day in the life of a Hutterite student begins with a communal breakfast at 6:30 AM, followed immediately by instruction in German until 8:30 AM. English school begins at 8:50 AM and, after a school day of nine hours, the students are home for the daily 6:00 PM evening church service which is then followed by supper. Unlike other Canadian students, Hutterite children go to school six days per week.

Home-Schooling

While there are laws requiring that all children be educated, there is no legal requirement that parents send their children to a publicly or privately funded institution. It is perfectly valid for children to be educated at home. Fifteen years ago there were fewer than 2000 Canadian children who were being home-schooled. However, the situation has changed and there are now over 30 000 children being taught at home by one or both of their parents. The **home-schooling** movement is growing at such a rate that provincial and territorial departments of education are developing new rules, regulations, and procedures for those who wish to take advantage of the home-schooling practice. While there is little formal research which compares the later academic success of home-schooled children with that of children who had a more traditional educational experience, the initial indications suggest that home-schooled children do as well on standardized achievement tests as those who attend publicly or privately funded schools. When one home-schooled child was asked what she did not like about the practice, her only complaint was: "We don't get storm days off like the other kids."

Virtual Schools

New **virtual schools** are becoming popular in Canada, especially in British Colombia and Alberta. Virtual schools vary in significant ways from traditional schools. First, the courses are taken electronically via the internet rather than in-person within a regular classroom; and second, while some courses are scheduled for a particular time, others may be taken at the convenience of the student. In the model which has specifically scheduled class times, all students taking a particular class are expected to be online at the same time. They can take part in discussions, listen to a lecture, and send or receive information. In the model where a specific time is not scheduled, the student takes the course at such times as she or he decides. There is no "real-time" discussion as in the other model and communication with the instructor is via email or a dedicated listserv.

What Determines Your Educational Philosophy?

- An educational philosophy is a set of beliefs about education—a set of principles to guide professional action.
- A teacher's educational philosophy is made up of personal beliefs about teaching and learning, students, knowledge, and what is worth knowing.

What Are the Branches of Philosophy?

- The branches of philosophy and the questions they address are (1) metaphysics (What is the nature of reality?), (2) epistemology (What is the nature of knowledge and is truth attainable?), (3) axiology (What values should one live by?), (4) ethics (What is good and evil, right and wrong?), (5) aesthetics (What is beautiful?), and (6) logic (What reasoning processes yield valid conclusions?).

What Are Five Modern Philosophical Orientations to Teaching?

- *Progressivism*—The aim of education should be based on the needs and interests of students.
- *Perennialism*—Students should acquire knowledge of enduring great ideas.
- *Essentialism*—Schools should teach students a core of "essential" knowledge and skills in a disciplined and systematic way.
- *Social reconstructionism*—In response to the significant social problems of the day, schools should take the lead in creating a new social order.
- *Existentialism*—In the face of an indifferent universe, students should acquire an education that will enable them to assign meaning to their lives.

What Psychological Orientations Have Influenced Teaching Philosophies?

- *Humanism*—Children are innately good, and education should focus on individual needs, personal freedom, and self-actualization.
- *Behaviourism*—By careful control of the educational environment and with appropriate reinforcement techniques, teachers can cause students to exhibit desired behaviours.
- *Constructivism*—Teachers should "understand students' understanding" and view learning as an active process in which learners construct meaning.

How Can You Develop Your Educational Philosophy?

- Instead of basing their teaching on only one educational philosophy, most teachers develop an eclectic educational philosophy.
- Professional teachers continually strive for a clearer, more comprehensive answer to basic philosophical questions.

What Cultural Traditions Have Led to the Development of the Canadian Education Landscape?

- Early Canadian education was founded upon the cultural traditions of France, England, Scotland, and the United States. The primary purpose of each tradition was the promotion of religion.

- The French tradition, in schools known as *petites écoles*, provided a rudimentary education. Instruction was provided by parish priests or their assistants. Boys and girls attended separate schools.

- The English tradition was primarily controlled by the Church of England with the quality of the education delivered being a function of class rather than merit. There were "public" schools for the wealthy and various other schools for the poor.

- The American tradition was originally modelled after the British tradition but the practicalities of frontier life led to its becoming increasing more practical.

- The Scottish tradition provided elementary and secondary education to students of both genders regardless of their social rank. Unlike the other traditions, the curriculum of Scottish schools also included subjects such as science and art.

What Were Teaching and Schools Like in Canada Prior to 1875?

- During this formative period of Canada's educational history, the school systems that evolved were a reflection of the cultural traditions that existed within Quebec, Atlantic Canada, Ontario, and the Northwest. In all areas, the struggle for state supported schools was the cause of much rancorous debate.

- In Quebec, during the period between its founding and fall (1608–1760), the school system was modelled after that of France. Later, with the arrival of English, Scottish, and Irish settlers tentative steps towards a more coherent school system took place. By 1875 Quebec had two schools systems: one for the English and one for the French. The government of Quebec paid for the support of the schools via taxation based upon local assessment.

- In Nova Scotia, Prince Edward Island, and New Brunswick, waves of settlers arrived from England, Scotland, and the United States. The school systems that evolved were state supported and operated. However, in Newfoundland and Labrador the schools eventually came to be supported by the state but operated by various religious denominations.

- In Ontario, where most of the settlers were either Loyalists or Americans who emigrated to that province, state supported and operated schools were firmly established by 1850.

- The Northwest was a thinly populated area during this period. However, by 1870 both Manitoba and British Columbia had state supported and operated schools. Alberta and Saskatchewan would later establish a system of state supported and operated separate schools based on religious lines.

- The British North America Act of 1867 established that education was to be a purely provincial responsibility.

What Patterns Did Canadian Education Develop from 1875 to 1918?

- In 1875 Canada's population was primarily rural; by 1918 it had become increasingly urban.
- All areas of the country developed centralized educational bureaucracies.
- Secondary schools became common and normal schools for the training of teachers became prevalent.

What Is the History of Schooling for First Nations Peoples?

- First Nations peoples used myths and legends to teach their children about the unity of all life, honourable conduct, individual and family responsibilities, and survival skills.
- Colonial clerical educators initially attempted to assimilate First Nations peoples by converting them to Christianity.
- Residential schools, established in the 1840s, were created to assimilate First Nations peoples into European culture. Children at these schools were forbidden to speak their native language and were often abused.
- Since the 1970s, control of education has been in the hands of various First Nations bands.

What Educational Advancements Took Place between the Great Wars (1918–1939)?

- Vocationally based education became common.
- Larger numbers of students went on to post-elementary education.
- Discussions about curricular and student discipline issues became common.
- The writings of educational psychologists and philosophers started to have an impact upon Canadian schools.

What Are the Major Characteristics of Today's Canadian System of Education?

- Education is compulsory for all children.
- Most provinces have an elementary component (Grades 1 to 6), a junior high component (Grades 7 to 9), and a high school program (Grades 10 to 12).
- The average school year in most provinces and territories is 188 days.
- Some jurisdictions have separate schools based upon either religion or language; others do not.

How Are Canadian Schools Funded?

- The costs of operating all of Canada's schools for one year is approximately $40 billion.

- Schools boards receive their operating, maintenance, and capital funding needs according to funding formulas, which differ from one province or territory to the next.

What Are Some Current Trends in Canadian Education?

- Evaluation and assessment are receiving increased attention.
- The inclusive school movement has led to students with special needs receiving increased attention and funding.
- Many Canadian schools now provide a variety of ancillary services such as day care and respect-for-differences programs.
- Information technology is now widely available in most schools.
- Curriculum guides with specific recommendations for teachers to follow are available in all school districts.
- French Immersion (FI) programs are available in all provinces and territories.

What Are Some Other Types of Canadian Schools?

- Independent schools, also known as private schools, charge tuition for the educational services they provide. Many of these schools have a religious affiliation. Some provide boarding facilities; other do not.
- Montessori schools, which base their curriculum upon the Montessori method, are most commonly found in Ontario and British Columbia.
- Some religious groups, such as the Hutterites of western Canada, operate their own schools.
- The home-schooling movement is becoming more popular. Departments of education are now developing regulations and procedures for those parents who wish to teach their children at home.
- Virtual schools are becoming more prevalent. Students "attend" class electronically via the internet.

KEY TERMS AND CONCEPTS

aesthetics
American tradition
axiology
behaviourism
British North America Act
   (BNA Act)
CEGEP
cognitive science
constructivism
dame-schools
educational philosophy
English tradition

epistemology
essentialism
ethics
existentialism
French tradition
home-schooling
humanism
humanistic psychology
Hutterite schools
independent schools
logic
metaphysics

Montessori method
normal schools
parochial schools
perennialism
petites écoles
progressivism
school year
Scottish tradition
separate schools
social reconstructionism
Socratic questioning
virtual schools

APPLICATIONS AND ACTIVITIES

Teacher's Journal

1. Imagine that you are a colleague of Claude, who was profiled in this chapter's opening scenario. Write a memo to him in which you react to his philosophical orientation to teaching.

2. Recall one of your favourite teachers in grades K–12. Which of the educational philosophies or psychological orientations to teaching described in this chapter best captures that teacher's approach to teaching? Write a descriptive sketch of that teacher in action.

3. Based on what you have read in this chapter, identify several broad or long-term trends in the development of Canadian education that continue even today. How are those trends reflected in educational policies and practices through the decade? How is this trend evident at different points in the past and now? How might this trend be manifested in the future?

4. Write a personal history of your experience as a student, focusing on the age or grade level of the students you plan to teach. Conclude with an analysis of how you expect your experience as a student will influence you as a teacher.

5. What does the history of textbooks tell us about education in Canada? What values and priorities do textbooks today seem to reflect in comparison to textbooks of the seventeenth, eighteenth, and nineteenth centuries?

6. Develop a proposal for researching the impact of the past on teaching today and record it in your teacher's journal. For suggestions on choosing a specific topic, locating information, and conducting the research, ask your instructor for Handout M 3.1, "Researching Impacts of the Past on Teaching Today."

Teacher's Database

1. Use your favourite internet search engine to go to the home page of Philosophy in Cyberspace, The History of Education Site, or another professional organization devoted to educational philosophy or history, and compile a list of online publications, associations, and reference materials that you could use in developing your educational philosophy further.

2. Explore encyclopedias, bibliographies, periodicals, news sources, and online reference works to research in greater detail the contributions of a pioneer in education or a historical development described in Chapter 4.

Observations and Interviews

1. Interview a teacher for the purpose of understanding his or her educational philosophy. Formulate your interview questions in light of the philosophical concepts discussed in this chapter. Discuss your findings with classmates.

2. Administer a philosophical inventory to a group of teachers at a local school. Analyze the results and compare your findings with classmates.

3. Observe the class of a teacher at the level in which you plan to teach. Which of the five philosophies or three psychological orientations to teaching discussed in this chapter most characterizes this teacher?

4. Visit a school and interview the principal about the school's educational philosophy. Ask him or her to comment on what is expected of teachers in regard to achieving the goals contained in the statement of philosophy.

5. Interview veteran teachers and administrators at a local school and ask them to comment on the changes in education that they have observed and experienced during their careers. What events do respondents identify as having had the greatest impact on their teaching? Tape record, videotape, or transcribe respondents' stories to share with classmates.

6. As a collaborative project with classmates, conduct on-site interviews and observations for the purpose of researching the history of a particular school and its culture or way of life. You might also collaborate with teachers and students of history or social studies at the school to help you in your investigation.

Professional Portfolio

1. Prepare a written (or videotaped) statement in which you describe a key element of your educational philosophy. To organize your thoughts, focus on *one* of the following dimensions of educational philosophy:

   - Beliefs about teaching and learning
   - Beliefs about students
   - Beliefs about knowledge
   - Beliefs about what is worth knowing
   - Personal beliefs about the six branches of philosophy

   Develop your statement of philosophy throughout the course, covering all dimensions. On completion of your teacher-education program, review your portfolio entry and make any appropriate revisions. Being able to articulate your philosophy of education and your teaching philosophy will be an important part of finding your first job as a teacher.

2. Prepare a video or audiotaped oral history of the school experiences of older members of the community. Focus on a topic or issue of special interest to you and prepare some questions and probes in advance. For instance, you might be interested in an aspect of curriculum or student relations. Analyze the oral histories in relation to the development of education in Canada and videotape or tape record your analysis.

5

Social and Cultural
Realities Confronting
Today's Schools

The educational system is part of the common life and cannot escape suffering the consequences that flow from the conditions prevailing outside the school building.

—John Dewey "Introduction,"
The Use of Resources in Education

Taken from *Becoming a Teacher*, Second Canadian Edition, by Forrest W. Parkay, Beverly Hardcastle Stanford, John P. Vaillancourt, and Heather C. Stephens.

focus questions

1. What are the aims of education today?

2. How can schools be described?

3. What are schools like as social institutions?

4. How is cultural diversity represented in Canadian schools?

5. What is multicultural education?

6. How is gender a dimension of multicultural education?

7. What characteristics distinguish successful schools?

8. What social problems affect schools and place students at risk?

9. What are schools doing to address societal problems?

J eff Banks, a history teacher at Lakeside High School, enters the faculty lunchroom and sees his friends, Sue Anderson, Nancy Watkins, and Bret Thomas, at their usual table in the corner. Lakeside is located in a medium-size city in Central Canada. The school, in the centre of a low- to middle-income area, has an enrolment of almost 1400 students. About 70 percent of these self-identify as Anglo-European Canadians, with the remaining 30 percent comprised of students from various ethnic and cultural groups. After English, the most common languages are Italian and East Indian. Lakeside has a reputation for being a "good" school—for the most part, students are respectful of their teachers. Parents, many of whom work in the several small businesses and industries found in the community generally support the school and are involved in school activities in spite of their heavy work schedules. The consensus among teachers is that most parents recognize that education is the key if their children are to "better themselves."

As soon as Jeff is within earshot of his friends, he knows they are talking about a tragic shooting at a Canadian high school. An unhappy student had brought a gun to school and shot a fellow student.

"It's so scary," Sue says, "Who knows, something like that could happen right here at Lakeside. We have no idea what kids have to deal with today."

"Yeah, we have no idea who might snap," says Bret. "With a lot of these school shootings lately, it seems to be a kid that no one would have expected. Quiet, polite, good student—you just never know."

"In some cases, that's true," Jeff says, placing his lunch tray on the table and then sitting down between Sue and Bret. "But a lot of times there are signs. A lot of these kids are loners and outcasts; they're into violent video games, cults, drugs, guns, you name it."

"What I want to know," says Sue, "is how we can prevent something like that from happening here? Since the Colorado shootings, there have been bomb scares, threats, guns confiscated at dozens of schools around the country."

"Well, I don't think metal detectors, more police in schools, and stiffer penalties for kids who bring guns to school are necessarily the answers," says Bret. "The question is, why are kids doing this?"

"Right, how can we prevent things like this?" says Jeff.

"If we're going to change things," says Sue, "we've got to figure out ways to identify and help kids who feel so desperate that they turn to violence."

"Well, that's all well and good," says Nancy with a sigh. "But I don't see where all of this is going to lead. Our responsibility as teachers is to educate our kids. We're not psychiatrists or social workers. We can't change society. Besides, we've got youth agencies, centres for families in crisis, and all kinds of social service agencies."

What is the role of schools at the start of the 21st century? Should teachers play a role in addressing social problems such as violence in our society? What would you say to a teacher who expresses views such as Nancy's?

The discussion among Jeff and his fellow teachers highlights the expectation of much of the public that schools (and teachers) have a responsibility to address problems that confront modern society. Those who agree with Nancy's point of view tend to believe that schools should teach only content to students. Others, however, believe that teachers have an obligation to address domestic social problems. Underlying both positions are conflicting views on the aims of education.

What Are the Aims of Education Today?

In Canada, people agree that the purpose of schools is to educate. Unlike other institutions in society, schools have been developed exclusively to carry out that very important purpose. That we are not always in agreement about what the **aims of education** should be, however, is illustrated by the fact that we disagree about what it means to be an educated person. Is a person with a college degree educated? Is the person who has overcome, with dignity and grace, extreme hardships in life educated?

Debate about the aims of education is not new. Fourth century BC philosopher Aristotle, for example, expressed the dilemma this way: "The existing practice [of education] is perplexing; no one knows on what principle we should proceed—should the useful in life, or should virtue, or should the higher knowledge, be the aim of our training; all three opinions have been entertained" (1941, 1306). Definitive answers to Aristotle's questions have not been achieved; instead, each generation has developed its own response to what the aims of education should be.

Education for Prosocial Values

Although there is widespread debate about what academic content the schools should teach, the public agrees that schools should teach **prosocial values** such as honesty, fairness, civility, and respect for the law. The well-being of any society requires support of such values; they enable people from diverse backgrounds to live together peacefully. Others we would add to this list include respect for others, industry or hard work, persistence or the ability to follow through, fairness in dealing with others, compassion for others, and civility and politeness (Elam, Rose, and Gallup 1994). The strong support for these prosocial values reflects the public's belief that the schools should play a key role in promoting the democratic ideal of equality for all.

Education for Socialization

Schools are places where the young become socialized—where they learn to participate intelligently and constructively in the Canadian society. Table 5.1 shows the percentage of the public in 1998 who believed that the practice of good citizenship was a "very important" measure of school effectiveness, even more important than going on to postsecondary education, getting a job, or scoring well on standardized tests.

Additionally, it is in our schools, more than any other institution within our society, that persons from various ethnic, racial, religious, and cultural backgrounds learn about Canadian values and customs. It is also through the schools that persons from such diverse backgrounds learn English or French, the nature of the Canadian parliamentary system, and the basic workings of our economic institutions.

Of the various aims that the schools have, achievement is the most universally agreed on. For most people, the primary purpose of schools is to impart to students the academic knowledge and skills that will prepare them either for additional schooling or for the world of work. Regardless of political ideology, religious beliefs, and cultural values, people want their schools to teach academic content.

Education for Personal Growth and Societal Improvement

Society places great value on the dignity and worth of the individual. Accordingly, one aim of schools is to enable the young to become all that they are capable of becoming. Unlike socialization or achievement, the emphasis on personal growth puts the individual first, society second. According to this view, the desired outcomes of education go beyond achievement to include the development of a positive self-concept and interpersonal skills, or what psychologist Daniel Goleman has termed "**emotional intelligence.**" According to Goleman (1997, 1998), schools should emphasize five

Table 5.1

What are the most important criteria for measuring school effectiveness?

	Very Important %	Somewhat Important %	Not Very Important %	Not at All Important %	Don't Know %
Percentage of students who graduate from high school	82	14	2	1	1
Percentage of high school graduates who practice good citizenship	79	15	3	1	2
Percentage of high school graduates who go on to college or junior college	71	24	3	1	1
Percentage who graduate from college or junior college	69	25	3	1	2
Percentage of graduates who get jobs after completing high school	63	28	5	2	2
Scores that students receive on standardized tests	50	34	9	3	4

Source: L. C. Rose and A. M. Gallup, "The 30th Annual Phi Delta Kappa/Gallup Poll of the Public's Attitudes toward the Public Schools," *Phi Delta Kappan,* September 1998, p. 48.

dimensions of emotional intelligence: self-awareness, handling emotions, motivation, empathy, and social skills. Emotional intelligence is essential for achievement in school, job success, marital happiness, and physical health; it enables students to live independently and to seek out the "good" life according to their own values, needs, and wants. The knowledge and skills students acquire at schools are seen as enabling them to achieve personal growth and self-actualization.

Schools also provide students with the knowledge and skills to improve society and the quality of life and to adapt to rapid social change. Naturally, there exists a wide range of opinions about how society might be improved. Some teachers, like Jeff, Sue, and Bret in this chapter's opening scenario, believe that one purpose of schooling is to address social problems such as violence in society; while other teachers, such as their friend, Nancy, believe schools should teach academic content and not try to change society. However, as James Banks (1999, 4) suggests, "Education within a pluralistic society should affirm and help students understand their home and community cultures. [To] create and maintain a civic community that works for the common good, education in a democratic society should help students acquire the knowledge, attitudes, and skills needed to participate in civic action to make society more equitable and just."

How Can Schools Be Described?

Given the wide variation in schools and their cultures, many models have been proposed for describing the distinguishing characteristics of schools. Schools can be categorized according to the focus of their curricula; for example, high schools might be college preparatory, vocational, or general. Another way to view schools is according to their organizational structure; for example, elementary (K–5), middle school (6–8), or high school (9–12).

Other models view schools metaphorically; that is, what is a school like? Some schools, for example, have been compared to factories; students enter the school as raw material, move through the curriculum in a systematic way, and exit the school as finished products. Terrence Deal and Kent Peterson (1999, 21) have suggested that exemplary schools "become like tribes or clans, with deep ties among people and with values and traditions that give meaning to everyday life." Others have suggested that schools are like banks, gardens, prisons, mental hospitals, homes, churches, families, and teams.

In the school-as-family metaphor, for example, the effective school is a caring community of adults who attend to the academic, emotional, social, and physical needs of the children and youth entrusted to their care.

Schools and Social Class

In spite of a general consensus that schools should promote social improvement and equal opportunity, some individuals believe that schools "reproduce" the existing society by presenting different curricula and educational experiences to students from different socio-economic classes. Students at a school in an affluent suburb, for example, may study chemistry in a well-equipped lab and take a field trip to a high-tech industry to see the latest application of chemical research, while students attending a school in another school district may learn chemistry from out-of-date texts, have no adequate lab in which to conduct experiments, and have limited opportunities for field trips because the school district has more limited funding. Schools, in effect, preserve the stratification within society and maintain the differences between the "haves" and the "have-nots." As Joel Spring puts it: "the affluent members of ... society can protect the educational advantages and, consequently, economic advantages, of their children by living in affluent school districts or by using private [independent] schools. Their children will attend the elite institutions of higher education, and their privileged educational background will make it easy for them to follow in the footsteps of their parents' financial success" (Spring 1999, 290–91).

What Are Schools Like As Social Institutions?

Schools are social institutions. An **institution** is an organization established by society to maintain and improve its way of life. Schools are the institutions our society has established for the purpose of educating the young. During the last 200 years, Canadian schools have developed complex structures, policies, and curricula to accomplish this mission. "The Institutional Structure of Education in Canada" is shown in Figure 5.1.

The School As a Reflection of Society

As you might expect, schools mirror the national, provincial/territorial culture and surrounding local culture and other special interests. Independent and parochial schools,

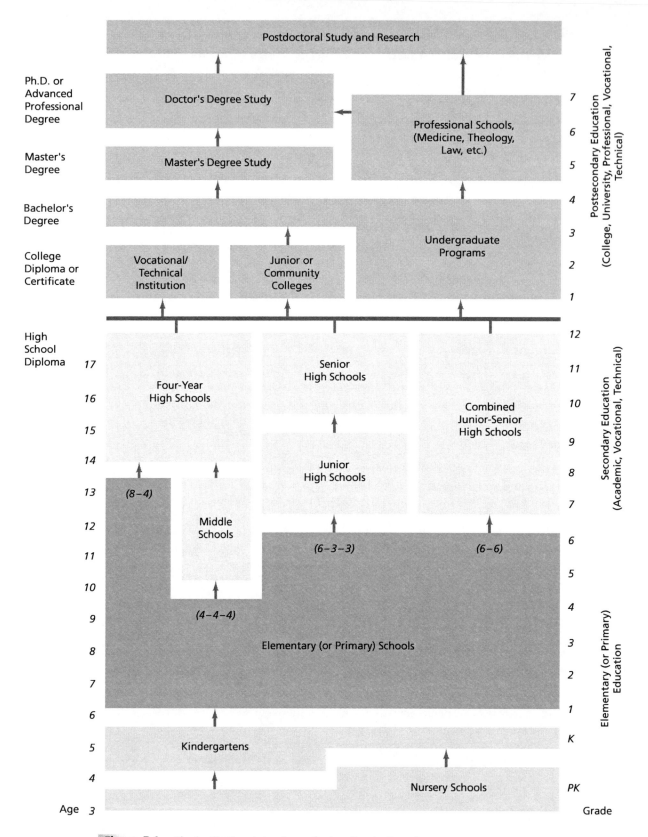

Figure 5.1 The institutional structure of education in Canada

for example, are often maintained by groups that see the school as a means of perpetuating their preferred way of life. Nevertheless, as Mary Henry (1993, 29) points out, "Schools are ... not simply puppets of the dominant mainstream society. They have their own unique concerns and their own 'poetry' of people and events. Whether public or private, all schools are not the same."

Rural, Suburban, and Urban Schools

Schools also reflect their location. Schools in rural, urban, and suburban settings often have significantly different cultures. Rural schools are often the focal point for community life and reflect values and beliefs that tend to be more conservative than those associated with urban and suburban schools. While the small size of a rural school may contribute to the development of a family-like culture, its small size may also make it difficult to provide students with an array of curricular experiences equal to that found at larger schools in more populated areas. In contrast, large suburban or urban schools may provide students with more varied learning experiences, but these schools may lack the cohesiveness and community focus of rural schools.

Schools and Community Environments

The differences among the environments that surround schools can be enormous. Urban schools, especially if located in less affluent districts, may reflect the social problems of the surrounding area. Middle-class families who can afford to, move away from such urban areas or place their children in independent schools. As a result, students in some urban school districts are increasingly from low-income backgrounds.

Though some communities may impact their schools in undesirable ways, many teachers at such schools find their work professionally stimulating and growth-enhancing. As one teacher said:

I taught in two different environments — middle school in an inner city and high school in a more rural area. I think that combination was the experience that made me become a teacher. When I did my student teaching, I enjoyed it so much, and I realized I had a knack for it. When recruiters looked at my résumé, they were impressed that I had two different experiences I could draw from and elaborate on. I know that's how I got my job (Sallie Mae Corporation 1995, 8).

In what ways do schools reflect their communities and the wider Canadian society? What difference might the community make for this school? for the students who attend it? for the teachers who work there?

The Culture of the School

Although schools are very much alike, each school is unique. Each has a culture of its own—a network of beliefs, values and traditions, and ways of thinking and behaving that distinguishes it from other schools.

Much like a community, a school has a distinctive culture—a collective way of life. Terms that have been used to describe **school culture** include *climate, ethos, atmosphere,* and *character.* Some schools may be characterized as community-like places where there is a shared sense of purpose and commitment to providing the best education possible for all students. Other schools lack a unified sense of purpose or direction and drift, rudderless, from year to year. Still others are characterized by internal conflict and divisiveness and may even reflect what Deal and Peterson (1999) term a "toxic" school culture; students, teachers, administrators, and parents may feel that the school is not sufficiently meeting their needs.

The Physical Environment

The physical environment of the school both reflects and helps to create the school's overall culture. Displays of student art, trophy cabinets, bulletin boards with a sections for "Student of the Week" and newspaper clippings highlighting school activities or accomplishments all play in the creation of a school's culture. "Whether school buildings are squeezed between other buildings or located on sprawling campuses, their fenced-in area or other physical separation distinguishes them from the community-at-large" (Ballantine 1997, 210). Some schools are dreary places or, at best, aesthetically bland. The tile floors, concrete block walls, long, straight corridors, and rows of fluorescent lights often found in these schools contribute little to their inhabitants' sense of beauty, concern for others, or personal comfort.

Other schools are much more attractive. They are clean, pleasant, and inviting; and teachers and students take pride in their building. Overall, the physical environment has a positive impact on those who spend time in the school; it encourages learning and a spirit of cohesiveness.

Formal Practices of Schools

The formal practices of schools are well known to anyone who has been educated in Canadian schools. With some exceptions, students attend school from five or six years of age through sixteen at least, and usually to eighteen, Monday through Friday, September through June, for twelve or thirteen years. For the most part, students are assigned to a grade level on the basis of age rather than ability or interest. Assignment to individual classes or teachers at a given grade level, however, may be made on the basis of ability or interest.

Teachers and students are grouped in several ways in the elementary school and in one dominant pattern in junior and senior high school. At the elementary school level, the **self-contained classroom** is the most traditional and prevalent arrangement. In this type of classroom, one teacher teaches all or nearly all subjects to a group of about 25 children, with the teacher and students remaining in the same classroom for the entire day. Often art, music, physical education, and computer skills are taught in other parts of the school, so students may leave the classroom for scheduled periods. Individual students may also attend special classes for remedial or advanced instruction, speech therapy, or instrumental music and band lessons.

In **open-space schools,** students are free to move among various activities and learning centres. Instead of self-contained classrooms, open-space schools have large instructional areas with movable walls and furniture that can be rearranged easily. Grouping for instruction is much more fluid and varied. Students do much of their work independently, with a number of teachers providing individual guidance as needed.

In middle schools and junior and senior high schools, students frequently study four or five academic subjects taught by teachers who specialize in them. In this organizational arrangement, called **departmentalization,** students move from classroom to classroom for their lessons. High school teachers often share their classrooms with other teachers and use their rooms only during scheduled class periods.

School Traditions

School traditions are those elements of a school's culture that are handed down from year to year. The traditions of a school reflect what students, teachers, administrators, parents, and the surrounding community believe is important and valuable about the school. One school, for example, may have developed a tradition of excellence in academic programs; another school's traditions may emphasize the performing arts; and yet another may focus on athletic programs. Whatever a school's traditions, they are usually a source of pride for members of the school community.

Ideally, traditions are the glue that holds together the diverse elements of a school's culture. They combine to create a sense of community, identity, and trust among people affiliated with a school. Traditions are maintained through stories that are handed down, rituals and ceremonial activities, student productions, and trophies and artifacts that have been collected over the years.

The Culture of the Classroom

Just as schools develop their unique cultures, each classroom develops its own culture or way of life. The culture of a classroom is determined in large measure by the manner in which teacher and students participate in common activities. An additional factor is the variety of cultural, ethnic, and linguistic groups represented within some classrooms. In Canada's larger urban areas it is not uncommon for an individual school to have students from as many as 50 different cultural, ethnic, or linguistic groups. In addition, "the environment of the classroom and the inhabitants of that environment—students and teachers—are constantly interacting. Each aspect of the classroom affects all others. (Woolfolk, 1998, 440) Indeed, as any teacher can attest, the addition, or removal, of as few as one or two students from a class's roll can positively or negatively affect the classroom's culture.

The quality of teacher–student interactions is influenced by the physical characteristics of the setting (classroom, use of space, materials, resources, etc.) and the social dimensions of the group (norms, rules, expectations, cohesiveness, distribution of power and influence). These elements interact to shape **classroom culture.** Teachers who appreciate the importance of these salient elements of classroom culture are more likely to create environments that they and their students find satisfying and growth-promoting. For example, during the second month of student teaching in Grade 2, "Miss Martin" reflects on her efforts to create classroom culture characterized by positive teacher–student interactions:

I started off with a big mistake. I tried to be their friend. I tried joining with them in all the jokes and laughter that cut into instruction time. When this didn't work, I overcompensated by yelling at them when I needed them to quiet down and get to work. I wasn't comfortable with this situation. I did not think it was like me to raise my voice at a child. I knew I needed to consider how they felt. I realized that if I were them, I'd hate me, I really would. In desperation, I turned to my education textbooks for advice.

This was a huge help to me, but a book can only guide you. It can't establish a personality for you or even manage your classroom for you. You have to do that yourself and as lovingly and effectively as possible. But I had so much trouble finding a middle ground: love them, guide them, talk to them, manage them, but don't control them (Rand and Shelton-Colangelo 1999, 8–9).

Similarly, a beginning teacher at an experimental school describes the classroom culture she wants to create: "What I'm trying to get to in my classroom is that they have power. I'm trying to allow students to have power—to know what their knowledge is and to learn to create their own ideas as opposed to my being the one who is the only holder of ideas in the universe. I want to transfer the authority back to them" (Dollase 1992, 101). The efforts of this teacher to create an empowering classroom culture were supported by the culture of the school itself: "Because her comments reflect the prevailing view of this small, neo-progressive public school, she is able to implement her philosophy in her upper-level middle school classroom. [T]he structure of the school and the organization of the school day, which permits more personalization and more time with each class, are school variables that allow her a chance to succeed in redefining the authority relationships in her class" (Dollase 1992, 101).

How Is Cultural Diversity Represented in Canadian Schools?

The percentage of ethnic minorities in Canadian schools has been growing steadily since the end of World War II. According to Statistics Canada's report on the census of 2001, 18.4 percent of Canada's population was born in other countries, the highest percentage of any country except for Australia. Statistics Canada also reports that 94 percent of these new citizens settled in large urban areas, with Montreal, Toronto, and Vancouver accounting for 73 percent of the total (Statistics Canada 2001b). (Table 5.2 provides a list of the most common ethnic origins.)

Clearly, the increasing **diversity** of Canadian society has extensive implications for schools. There is, for example, an increased demand for English as a Second Language (ESL) programs and teachers. All but a few school districts face a critical shortage of minority teachers. As well, there is a need to develop curricula and strategies that address the needs and backgrounds of all students—regardless of their social class, gender, sexual orientation, or ethnic, racial, or cultural identity.

The Meaning of Culture

Culture is *the way of life* common to a group of people. It consists of the values, attitudes, and beliefs that influence their traditions and behaviour. It is also a way of interacting with and looking at the world. Though at one time it was believed that Canada was a "melting pot" in which ethnic cultures would melt into one, ethnic and cultural differences have remained very much a part of life in Canada. A "salad-bowl"

Table 5.2

Population by selected ethnic origins, Canada

Definitions and notes	2001		
	Total responses	Single responses	Multiple responses
	Number	Number	Number
Total population	29 639 035	18 307 545	11 331 490
Ethnic origin			
Canadian	11 682 680	6 748 135	4 934 545
English	5 978 875	1 479 525	4 499 355
French	4 668 410	1 060 760	3 607 655
Scottish	4 157 210	607 235	3 549 975
Irish	3 822 660	496 865	3 325 795
German	2 742 765	705 600	2 037 170
Italian	1 270 370	726 275	544 090
Chinese	1 094 700	936 210	158 490
Ukrainian	1 071 060	326 195	744 860
North American Indian	1 000 890	455 805	545 085
Dutch (Netherlands)	923 310	316 220	607 090
Polish	817 085	260 415	556 665
East Indian	713 330	581 665	131 665
Norwegian	363 760	47 230	316 530
Portuguese	357 690	252 835	104 855
Welsh	350 365	28 445	321 920
Jewish	348 605	186 475	162 130
Russian	337 960	70 895	267 070
Filipino	327 550	266 140	61 405
Metis	307 845	72 210	235 635
Swedish	282 760	30 440	252 325
Hungarian (Magyar)	267 255	91 800	175 455
American (USA)	250 005	25 205	224 805
Greek	215 105	143 785	71 325
Spanish	213 105	66 545	146 555
Jamaican	211 720	138 180	73 545
Danish	170 780	33 795	136 985
Vietnamese	151 410	119 120	32 290

Source: Statistics Canada: Census 2001. Retrieved April 10, 2003 from www.statcan.ca/english/Pgdb/demo28a.htm. Reproduced with the permission of the Minister of Public Works and Services.

analogy more accurately captures the multicultural diversity of Canadian society. That is, the distinguishing characteristics of cultures tend be preserved and valued rather than blended into a single monoculture. An **ethnic group** is made up of individuals within a larger culture who share a self-defined racial or cultural identity and a set of beliefs, attitudes, and values. Members of an ethnic group distinguish themselves from others in the society by physical and social attributes. In addition, you should be aware that the composition of ethnic groups can change over time and there is often as much variability within groups as between them. The biological concept of **race** suggests that there are natural, physical variations among humans that are hereditary, reflected in body shape and/or skin coloration, and identifiable by terms such as Negroid, Caucasoid, and Mongoloid. While most individuals have a personal concept of what constitutes race, this issue is a complicated one that goes far beyond the scope of this text.

Dimensions of Culture

Within Canada, we find cultural groups that differ according to other distinguishing factors, such as religion, politics, economics, and geographic region. The regional culture of Newfoundland, for example, is quite different from that of Alberta. Similarly, British Columbians are culturally different from *les québécois*. However, everyone in Canada does share some common dimensions of culture. James Banks, an authority on multicultural education, has termed this shared culture the "national macro-culture" (Banks 1999). In addition to being members of the national macro-culture, people in Canada are often members of specific ethnic groups.

Cultural Identity

Students in today's classrooms have diverse cultural identities. As a teacher, what steps will you take to integrate *all* students into the classroom?

In addition to membership in the Canadian macro-culture, each individual participates in an array of subcultures, each with its customs and beliefs. Collectively, these subcultures determine an individual's **cultural identity**, an overall sense of who one is. Other possible elements that might shape a person's cultural identity include age, racial identity, exceptionalities, language, gender, sexual orientation, income level,

and beliefs and values. These elements have different significances for different people. For example, the cultural identity of some people is most strongly determined by their occupations; for others by their ethnicity; and for others by their religious beliefs.

Remember that your future students will have their own complex cultural identities, which are no less valid for being different. For some of them, these identities may make them feel "disconnected" from the attitudes, expectations, and values conveyed by the school. For example:

Students who come from homes where languages other than English are the medium of communication, who share customs and beliefs unique to their cultural community and/or home countries, or who face the range of challenges posed by economic insecurity will not often find much of their family, community, or national existence reflected in the school setting. Often these students feel that school is itself foreign, alienating, and unrelated to their beliefs and concerns (Rice and Walsh 1996, 9).

As a teacher, you will be challenged to understand the subtle differences in cultural identities among your students and to create a learning environment that enables all students to feel comfortable in school and "connected to" their school experiences.

Language and Culture

Culture is embedded in language, a fact that has sometimes resulted in historical conflicts between the English and French-speaking groups in our society. While Canadians generally support the preservation of ethnic cultures, most believe that new immigrants should learn one of the two official languages, English and French, if they are to function effectively within Canadian society. While the types of English as a Second Language (ESL) programs vary from one jurisdiction to another, Figure 5.2 contains most of the variants. Interestingly, Statistics Canada reports in its 2001 article, "Census: Ethnocultural portrait: Canada," that its Longitudinal Survey of Children and Youth indicates that, over time, children with immigrant parents "caught up to, and sometimes surpassed, the academic performance of their classmates with Canadian-born parents."

Advice for Monolingual Teachers

Teachers must continue to meet the needs of language-minority students. These needs are best met by teachers who speak their native language as well as English. However, this is often not possible, and monolingual teachers, particularly those in large urban areas, will find increasing numbers of such students in their classrooms.

Four Types of Bilingual Education Programs

Figure 5.2

Four types of bilingual education programs

Immersion programs: Students learn English and other subjects in classrooms where only English is spoken. Aides who speak the first language of students are sometimes available, or students may also listen to equivalent audiotaped lessons in their first language.

Transition programs: Students receive reading lessons in their first language and lessons in English as a Second Language (ESL). Once they sufficiently master English, students are placed in classrooms where English is spoken and their first language is discontinued.

Pull-out programs: On a regular basis, students are separated from English-speaking students so that they may receive lessons in English or reading lessons in their first language. These are sometimes called sheltered English programs.

Maintenance programs: To maintain the student's native language and culture, instruction in English and instruction in the native language are provided from Kindergarten through Grade 12. Students become literate.

The Concept of Multiculturalism

Multiculturalism is a set of beliefs based on the importance of seeing the world from different cultural frames of reference and on recognizing and valuing the rich array of cultures within a nation and within the global community. For teachers, multiculturalism affirms the need to create schools where differences related to race, ethnicity, gender, disability, and social class are acknowledged and all students are viewed as valuable members and as human resources for enriching the teaching–learning process. Furthermore, a central purpose of teaching, according to the multiculturalist view, is to prepare students to live in a culturally pluralistic world—a world that "contrasts sharply with cultural assimilation, or 'melting pot' images, where ethnic minorities are expected to give up their traditions and blend in or be absorbed by the mainstream society or predominant culture" (Bennett 1999, 11).

Stereotyping and Racism

Although teachers should expand their knowledge of and appreciation for the diverse cultural backgrounds of their students, they should also guard against forming stereotypes or overgeneralizations about those cultures. **Stereotyping** is the process of attributing behavioural characteristics to all members of a group. In some cases, stereotypes are formed on the basis of limited experiences with and information about the group being stereotyped, and the validity of these stereotypes is not questioned.

Within any cultural group that shares a broad cultural heritage, however, considerable diversity exists. For example, two Asian-Canadian children who live in the same community and attend the same school may appear alike to their teachers when, in reality, they are very different. One may come from a home where Mandarin is spoken and Chinese holidays are observed; the other may be Vietnamese, speak no language but English, and observe only Canada's official holidays.

To help immigrant students adjust to Canadian culture, Qiu Liang offers teachers the following advice based on his school experiences as a Chinese immigrant:

> They [teachers] should be more patient [with an immigrant child] because it is very difficult for a person to be in a new country and learn a new language. Have patience.

> If the teacher feels there is no hope in an immigrant child, then the child will think, "Well, if the teacher who's helping me thinks that I can't go anywhere, then I might as well give up myself" (Igoa 1995, 99–100).

Similarly, Dung Yoong offers these recommendations based on her educational experiences as a Vietnamese immigrant:

> Try to get them to talk to you. Not just everyday conversation, but what they feel inside. Try to get them to get that out, because it's hard for kids. They don't trust—I had a hard time trusting and I was really insecure because of that.

> [P]utting an immigrant child who doesn't speak English into a classroom, a regular classroom with Canadian students, is not very good. It scares [them] because it is so different. [Teachers] should start [them] slowly and have special classes where the child could adapt and learn a little bit about Canadian society and customs (Igoa 1995, 103).

In addition to being alert for stereotypes they and others may hold, teachers should learn to recognize **individual racism**, the prejudicial belief that one's ethnic or racial group is superior to others, and **institutional racism**, "established laws, customs, and practices which systematically reflect and produce racial inequalities in Canadian society ... whether or not the individuals maintaining those practices have racist intentions" (Jones 1981, 118).

As a teacher, you will not be able to eliminate stereotypic thinking or racism in society. However, you have an obligation to all your students to see that your curriculum and instruction are free of any forms of stereotyping or racism. To provide equal educational opportunity to all students means that teachers and schools promote the full development of students as individuals, without regard for race, ethnicity, gender, sexual orientation, socio-economic status, abilities, or disabilities. More specifically, educators fulfill this important mission by continually evaluating the appropriateness of the curricular and instructional experiences they provide to each student. The following Professional Reflection will help you examine, and possibly reassess, your cultural attitudes and values and determine whether you have stereotypes about other cultural groups.

Professional Reflection   **Reflecting on your cultural identity**

In a Teacher's Journal entry, describe your cultural identity. Who are you? What beliefs, customs, and attitudes are part of your culture? Which of these are most important to your cultural identity?

Next, think of the ethnic and cultural groups in Canada with which you are unfamiliar. When you become a teacher, some of your students may be from these groups. What are some stereotypes about these groups that you tend to believe? How might these stereotypes influence your teaching and teaching effectiveness? How will you test or change your beliefs as part of the process of becoming a teacher?

What Is Multicultural Education?

Multicultural education is committed to the goal of providing all students—regardless of socioeconomic status, gender, sexual orientation or ethnic, racial, or cultural backgrounds—with equal opportunities to learn in school. Multicultural education is also based on the fact that students do not learn in a vacuum—their culture predisposes them to learn in certain ways. And finally, multicultural education recognizes that current school practices have provided, and continue to provide, some students with greater opportunities for learning than students who belong to other groups.

Dimensions of Multicultural Education

According to James A. Banks, "Multicultural education is a complex and multidimensional concept" (Banks 1999, 13). More specifically, Banks suggests that multicultural education may be conceptualized as consisting of five dimensions: (1) content integration, (2) knowledge construction, (3) prejudice reduction, (4) an equity pedagogy, and

(5) an empowering school culture (see Figure 5.3). As you progress through your teacher education program and eventually begin to prepare curriculum materials and instructional strategies for your multicultural classroom, remember that integrating content from a variety of cultural groups is just one dimension of multicultural education. Multicultural education is not "something that is done at a certain time slot in the school day where children eat with chopsticks or listen to Peruvian music ... [it is] something that is infused throughout the school culture and practiced daily" (Henry 1996, 108).

Multicultural education promotes students' positive self-identity and pride in their heritage, acceptance of people from diverse backgrounds, and critical self-assessment. In addition, multicultural education can prompt students, perhaps with guidance from their teachers, to take action against prejudice and discrimination within their school. Indeed, as Joel Spring says, "multicultural education should create a spirit of tolerance and activism in students. An understanding of other cultures and of differing cultural frames of reference will ... spark students to actively work for social justice" (Spring 1998, 163). For example, students might reduce the marginalization of minority-group students in their school by inviting them to participate in extracurricular and after-school activities.

Figure 5.3

Banks' dimensions of multicultural education

Source: From James A. Banks, and Cherry A. McGee Banks. *Multicultural Education: Issues and Perspectives,* 3rd ed. Copyright © 1997 by Allyn & Bacon. Reprinted by permission, p. 24.

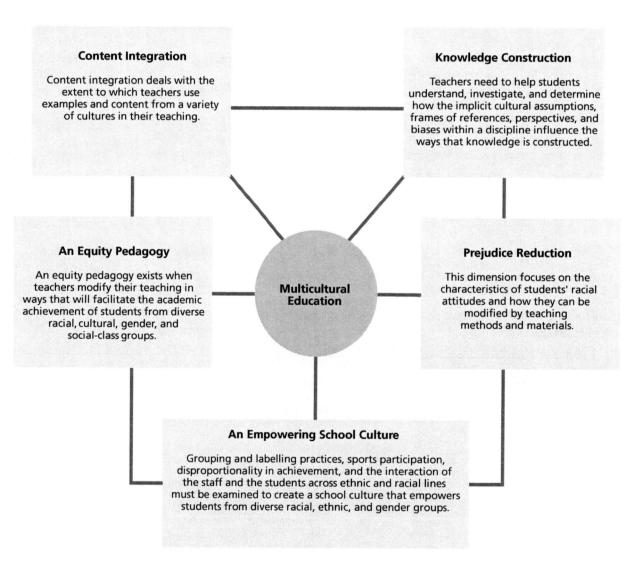

Prime Minister's Award for Teaching Excellence Recipients: Marie Louise Mastromonaco and Sharon Davis

Marie Louise Mastromonaco
Bishop Grandin High School, Calgary, Alberta
Subjects taught: Grades 10 to 12,
English as a Second Language (ESL)

Mrs. Mastromonaco created partnership programs that allow ESL students to work together and with community organizations to enhance their learning and discover opportunities for their future lives. More than 55 percent of ESL students now take part in these programs.

She developed adjunct classes tailored to help ESL students in mainstream English and social studies courses. Beginning with six students in 1999–2000, the program has already more than doubled in size, and participants have shown a marked improvement in their grades.

The Volunteer Host and Tutor program has had the same enthusiastic response. In the first semester of 2001–2002, 24 ESL students were paired with 28 tutors.

Mrs. Mastromonaco created special teaching units to help ESL students understand Canadian history and culture, including *Immigrants All*, *Spirit of the West* (in which she took part in a five-day cattle drive) and *Along the River's Edge* (an interactive unit on Calgary's early history).

> I have never met a teacher with such passion for teaching and caring for students until I met you.
> —*Former student*

> A lifelong commitment to improving each child's destiny is a major accomplishment by any measure. Mrs. Mastromonaco's outstanding contributions live on in her students who now call Canada home.
> —*Department head*

Sharon Davis
Jack Hulland Elementary School, Whitehorse, Yukon
Subjects taught: Counsellor, Kindergarten to Grade 7

Because Mrs. Davis has worked so long in the community, she has built a legacy of trust that enables her to bridge relations, particularly in the First Nations community, and provide a valuable historical perspective on conflicts in the school. She has done the following:

- Developed class meetings in which students raise problems and concerns. Students learn appropriate communications, conflict resolution and problem-solving skills, among others.
- Introduced Family Group Conferencing, a restorative justice program used as an alternative to suspension if parents wish, and as a vehicle for solving interpersonal conflict and dealing with bullying.
- Interaction problems needing to be referred to the office have declined during her tenure, and fights and incidents of bullying are almost non-existent.
- Students solve their own problems. Recently, a group of students asked Mrs. Davis to help them sort out a conflict. As they sat down in her office, one said, "You know what Mrs. Davis? I think we can solve this on our own."

> "What distinguishes Sharon from others "just doing their job" is her tireless dedication to her school community and that she genuinely cares."
> —*School Council member*

> "Mrs. Davis is the nicest person I have ever met. She makes us feel better and helps us all at work. She is there when we are sad and she helps us separate fights."
> —*Student*

Source: Government of Canada (2001). Prime Minister's awards for teaching excellence: Exemplary practices. Retrieved October 3, 2003 from http://pma-ppm.ic.gc.ca/bio01-e.asp?prov=al

Multicultural Curricula

As a teacher you will teach students who historically have not received full educational opportunity—students from the many racial and ethnic minority groups in Canada, students from low-income families or communities, students with exceptional abilities or disabilities, students who are gay or lesbian, and students who are male or female.

You will face the challenge of reaching out to all students and teaching them that they are persons of worth who can learn.

In your diverse classroom your aim is not to develop a different curriculum for each group of students—that would be impossible and would place undue emphasis on differences among students. Rather, your curriculum should help increase students' awareness and appreciation of the rich diversity in Canadian culture. A **multicultural curriculum** addresses the needs and backgrounds of all students regardless of their cultural identity. As Banks suggests, the multicultural curriculum "enable[s] students to derive valid generalizations and theories about the characteristics of ethnic groups and to learn how they are alike and different, in both their past and present experiences.... [It] focus[es] on a range of groups that *differ* in their racial characteristics, cultural experiences, languages, histories, values, and current problems" (Banks 1997, 15). Teachers who provide multicultural education recognize the importance of asking questions such as those posed by Valerie Ooka Pang: "Why is a child's home language important to keep? What strengths does culture give children? What impact does culture have on learning? What does racism, sexism, or classism look like in schools?" (Pang 1994, 292).

In developing a multicultural curriculum, you should be sensitive to how your instructional materials and strategies can be made more inclusive so that they reflect cultural perspectives, or "voices," that previously have been silent or marginalized in discussions about what should be taught in schools and how it should be taught. "Nondominant groups representing diversity in the school whose voices traditionally have not been heard include those defined by race, language, gender, sexual orientation, alternative family structures, social class, disability, bilingualism, and those with alien or refugee status" (Henry 1996, 108). Effective teachers attend to these previously unheard voices not as an act of tokenism but with a genuine desire to make the curriculum more inclusive and to "create space for alternative voices, not just on the periphery but in the center" (Singer 1994, 286).

Multicultural Instructional Materials and Strategies

To create classrooms that are truly multicultural, teachers must select instructional materials that are sensitive, accurately portray the contributions of ethnic groups, and reflect diverse points of view. Teachers must also recognize that "[s]ome of the books and other materials on ethnic groups published each year are insensitive, inaccurate, and written from mainstream and insensitive perspectives and points of view" (Banks 1997, 124). Some guidelines for selecting multicultural instructional materials follow.

- Books and other materials should accurately portray the perspectives, attitudes, and feelings of ethnic groups.
- Fictional works should have strong ethnic characters.
- Books should describe settings and experiences with which all students can identify and yet should accurately reflect ethnic cultures and lifestyles.
- The protagonists in books with ethnic themes should have ethnic characteristics but should face conflicts and problems universal to all cultures and groups.
- The illustrations in books should be accurate, ethnically sensitive, and technically well done.
- Ethnic materials should not contain racist concepts, clichés, phrases, or words.
- Factual materials should be historically accurate.

- Multiethnic resources and basal textbooks should discuss major events and documents related to ethnic history (Banks 1997, 125–26).

Yvonne Wilson, an elementary teacher from our aboriginal community, points out that a teacher's willingness to learn about other cultures is very important to students and their parents:

> People in the community know if you are trying to understand their culture. Students also see it. Becoming involved—going to a powwow or participating in other cultural events—shows people that here is a teacher who is trying to learn about our culture.

Participating wholeheartedly in cross-cultural experiences will help you to grow in the eight areas outlined in Figure 5.4 as essential for successful teaching in a diverse society.

Figure 5.4

Essential knowledge and skills for successful teaching in a diverse society

Source: Adapted from Forrest W. Parkay and Henry T. Fillmer, "Improving Teachers' Attitudes toward Minority-Group Students: An Experiential Approach to Multicultural Inservice," *New Horizons Journal of Education* (November 1984), pp. 178–79.

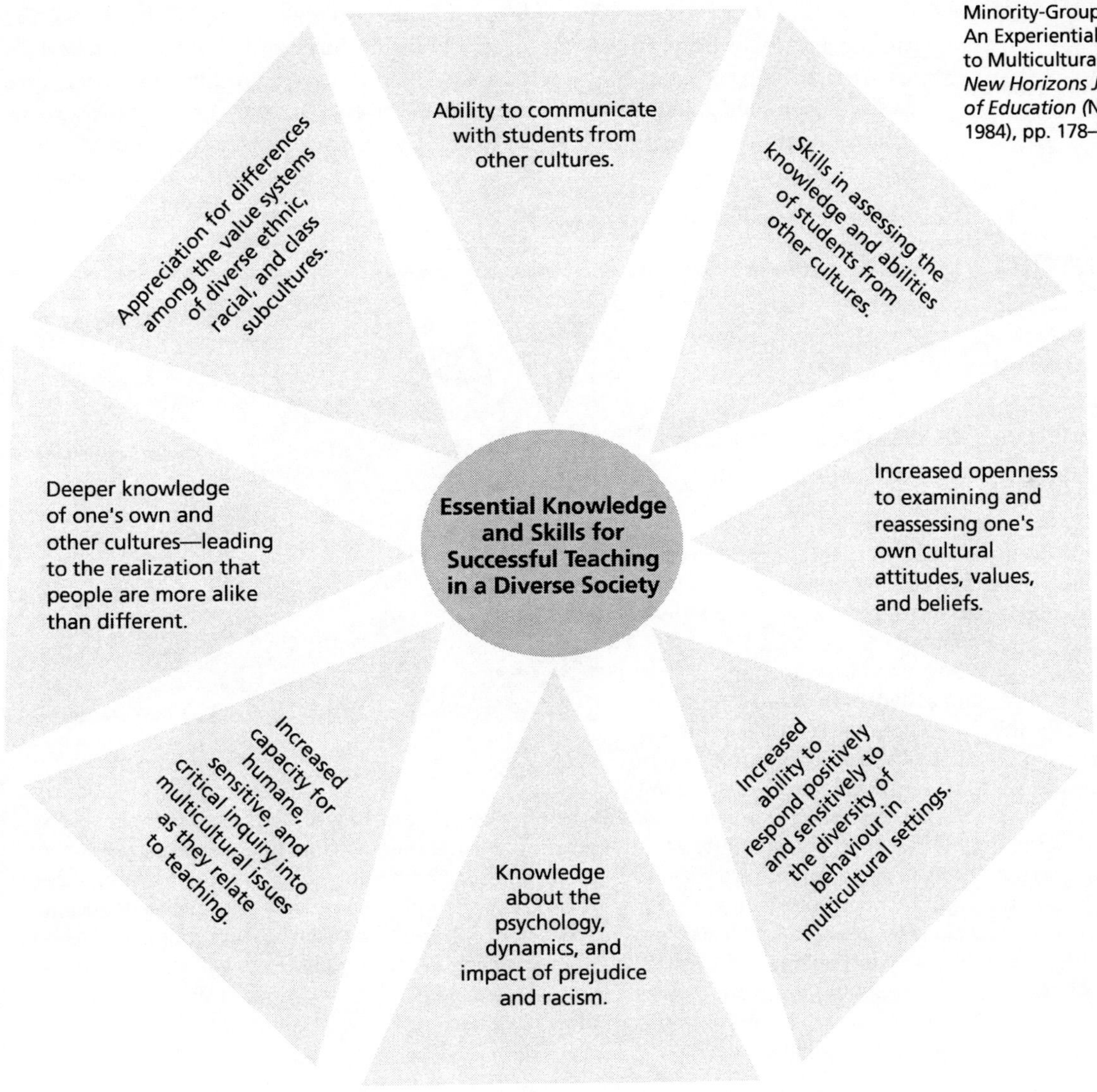

Essential Knowledge and Skills for Successful Teaching in a Diverse Society

- Ability to communicate with students from other cultures.
- Skills in assessing the knowledge and abilities of students from other cultures.
- Increased openness to examining and reassessing one's own cultural attitudes, values, and beliefs.
- Increased ability to respond positively and sensitively to the diversity of behaviour in multicultural settings.
- Knowledge about the psychology, dynamics, and impact of prejudice and racism.
- Increased capacity for humane, sensitive, and critical inquiry into multicultural issues as they relate to teaching.
- Deeper knowledge of one's own and other cultures—leading to the realization that people are more alike than different.
- Appreciation for differences among the value systems of diverse ethnic, racial, and class subcultures.

How Is Gender a Dimension of Multicultural Education?

Though it may be evident that gender affects students' learning in many ways, it may not be evident that gender is an important dimension of multicultural education. However, as Tozer, Violas, and Senese point out:

> Traditional definitions of culture have centered around the formal expression of a people's common existence—language, art, music, and so forth. If culture is more broadly defined to include such things as ways of knowing, ways of relating to others, ways of negotiating rights and privileges, and modes of conduct, thought, and expression, then the term "culture" applies not only to ethnic groups but to people grouped on the basis of gender. [G]ender entails cultural as well as physiological dimensions (Tozer, Violas, and Senese 1993, 310).

Gender Differences

Cultural differences between males and females are partially shaped by society's traditional expectations of them. Through **sex role stereotyping**, families, the media, the schools, and other powerful social forces condition boys and girls to act in certain ways regardless of abilities or interests. As we mentioned previously, one of the aims of schools is to socialize students to participate in society. One dimension of the **sex role socialization** process sometimes conveys to students certain expectations about the way boys and girls are "supposed" to act. We used to suggest that girls are supposed to

---

technology

highlights

Does gender equity exist in the use of educational technology?

Considerable evidence indicates that boys tend to have more experience with and positive attitudes toward computer technology than girls (Bitter and Pierson 1999; Comber et al 1997; Hammett 1997; Valenza 1997; Whitley 1997). In addition, boys participate in more elective technology courses and activities than girls. A partial explanation for this difference may stem from the fact that "Software generally tends to emphasize male-dominated activities. Games often include violence and competition as motivation. These software characteristics tend to attract males" (Bitter and Pierson 1999, 240). Also, some computer software and online advertisements promote gender stereotypes (Knupfer 1998). In addition, Cornelia Brunner and Dorothy Bennett (1997) suggest that the attitude of girls toward technology might reflect a tendency in schools to celebrate the speed and power of the machine (the "masculine view") rather than the social function of technology (the "feminine view").

In any case, as the use of technologies continues to become more widespread in society and schools, teachers must make a special effort to ensure that girls have equal access to technology and that their technology-related experiences are positive and growth-enhancing. What steps will you take to ensure that your use of technology reflects gender equity? How will you encourage your students, regardless of gender, to acquire additional knowledge and skills with computers?

play with dolls, boys with trucks. It was also believed that girls are supposed to be passive, boys active. Girls are supposed to express their feelings and emotions when in pain, boys to repress their feelings and deny pain.

Students may be socialized into particular gender-specific roles as a result of the curriculum materials they use at school. By portraying males in more dominant, assertive ways and portraying females in ways that suggest that they are passive and helpless, textbooks can subtly reinforce expectations about the way girls and boys "should" behave. Within the last few decades, though, publishers of curriculum materials have become more vigilant about avoiding these stereotypes.

In the mid-1990s, however, some gender equity studies had more mixed findings. In their analysis of data on achievement and engagement of 9000 Grade 8 boys and girls, researchers Valerie Lee, Xianglei Chen, and Becky A. Smerdon concluded that "the pattern of gender differences is inconsistent. In some cases, females are favored; in others males are favored" (Lee, Chen, and Smerdon 1996). Similarly, Larry Hedges and Amy Nowell found in their study of 32 years of mental tests given to boys and girls that, while boys do better than girls in science and mathematics, they were "at a rather profound disadvantage" in writing and scored below girls in reading comprehension (Hedges 1996, 3).

Why and in what ways does gender bias persist in many Canadian classrooms and schools?

Additional research and closer analyses of earlier reports on gender bias in education were beginning to suggest that boys, not girls, were most "shortchanged" by the schools (Sommers, 1996). Numerous articles as well as a 1999 PBS series that began with a program titled "The War on Boys" challenged the conclusions of the earlier AAUW report, *How Schools Shortchange Girls*. Other commentary discounted gender bias in the schools as a fabrication of radical feminism; among the first to put forth this view was Christina Hoff Sommers' (1994) controversial book, *Who Stole Feminism? How Women Have Betrayed Women*; and, more recently, Judith Kleinfeld's (1998) *The Myth That Schools Shortchange Girls: Social Science in the Service of Deception* and Cathy Young's (1999) *Ceasefire!*

To examine gender issues in the public schools, and to shed light on gender differences in academic achievement, Warren Willingham and Nancy Cole (1997) conducted a seminal study of the scores of 15 million United States students in the fourth, eighth, and twelfth grades on hundreds of standardized exams used by schools and college placement exams such as the SAT. Contrary to long-standing assumptions that there are pronounced differences between the performance of males and females on standardized tests, their study found that "There is not a dominant picture of one gender excelling over the other and, in fact, the average performance difference across all subjects is essentially zero." Boys and girls, Willingham and Cole found, were fairly evenly matched in verbal and abstract reasoning, math computation, and the social sciences. The superiority of boys in math and science was found to be surprisingly slight and "significantly smaller than 30 years ago." Boys were found to have a clear advantage in mechanical and electronic ability and knowledge of economics and history, while girls had a clear advantage in language skills, especially writing, and a "moderate edge" in short-term memory and perceptual speed. Furthermore, the authors concluded that gender differences in test scores are not the result of bias in the exams; instead, the differences are genuine and would be reflected also in more carefully designed tests.

However, in 2002 the Council of Ministers of Education, Canada (CMEC), as part of its School Achievement Indicators Program (SAIP), released the following data regarding the writing skills of Canadian 13- and 16-year-old students. These results indicate that a gender gap in the relative writing skills of boys and girls appears to be developing. The assessment was administered to approximately 24 000 students in all provinces and territories except Nunavut. Performance is reported on a five-point scale, with one being the lowest and five the highest.

Some major findings of the SAIP test:

1. More than 80 percent of 13-year-olds reached level 2 and above. According to the test designers, level 2 is the level that most 13-year-olds should reach. Over 40 percent reached level 3 and above.
2. Over 60 percent of 16-year-olds reached level 3 or above. Level 3 is the level most 16-year-olds should reach, according to test designers.
3. Significantly more girls in both age groups performed at higher levels than boys. This gender gap is consistent with current trends in Language Arts assessment as confirmed in the Programme for International Student Assessment (PISA) 2000 reading assessment.
4. Among francophones, students in Quebec outperformed francophone students in minority-language settings for both age groups.

Gender-Fair Classrooms and Curricula

Although research and debate about the bias boys and girls encounter in school will no doubt continue, it is clear that teachers must encourage girls and boys to develop to the full extent of their capabilities and provide them an education that is free from **gender bias**—subtle favouritism or discrimination on the basis of gender. In her article "The Quality Teacher" (1993, 6) Kimberley Burstall reports the results of a survey she administered to a gender-balanced group of 300 Nova Scotia students from Grades 5, 8, and 11. The survey asked the students to select, from an extensive list of options, the three characteristics they considered most important for a "good teacher." In first place, with a score of 200, was "Treats boys and girls equally." As it is through language that gender fairness is most easily observed, it is important for teachers to be very careful in the selection of words they use when interacting with students. To check your own sensitivity to gender-fair language, we suggest you complete the Gender-Neutral Questionnaire located in Appendix 5.1.

Following is a list of basic guidelines for creating a **gender-fair classroom**. Adherence to these guidelines will help teachers "address the inequities institutionalized in the organizational structure of schools, the curriculum selected to be taught, the learning strategies employed, and their ongoing instructional and informal interactions with students" (Stanford 1992, 88).

- Become aware of differences in interactions with girls and boys.
- Promote boys' achievement in reading and writing and girls' achievement in mathematics and science.
- Reduce young children's self-imposed sexism.
- Teach about sexism and sex role stereotyping.
- Foster an atmosphere of collaboration between girls and boys.

Sexual Orientation

In addition to gender bias, some students experience discrimination on the basis of their sexual orientation. To help all students realize their full potential, teachers should acknowledge the special needs of gay, lesbian, and bisexual students for "there is an invisible gay and lesbian minority in every school, and the needs of these students [a]re often unknown and unmet" (Besner and Spungin 1995, xi). One study of 120 gay and lesbian students ages 14 to 21 found that only one-fourth said they were able to discuss their sexual orientation with school counsellors, and less than one in five said they could identify someone who had been supportive of them (Tellijohann and Price 1993). Moreover, a similar study of lesbian and gay youth reported that 80 percent of participants believed their teachers had negative attitudes about homosexuality (Sears 1991).

Based on estimates that as much as 10 percent of society may be homosexual, a high school with an enrolment of 1500 might have as many as 150 gay, lesbian, and bisexual students (Besner and Spungin 1995; Stover 1992). Several professional organizations have passed resolutions urging members and school districts to acknowledge the special needs of these students.

Homosexual students can experience school-related problems and safety risks. The hostility which gay, lesbian, and bisexual youth can encounter may cause them to feel confused, isolated, and self-destructive (Alexander 1998; Jordan, Vaughan, and Woodworth 1997; Edwards 1997; Anderson, 1997). Teachers and other school personnel can provide much-needed support. Informed, sensitive, and caring teachers can play an important role in helping all students develop to their full potential. Such teachers realize the importance of recognizing diverse perspectives, and they create inclusive classroom environments that encourage students to respect differences among themselves and others and to see the contributions that persons from all groups have made to society.

What Characteristics Distinguish Successful Schools?

At this point in your professional education you may, because of the very diverse nature of today's school populations, be uncertain of your ability to develop a positive classroom climate within your classroom. However, a great many schools in all settings and with all kinds of students are highly successful, including inner city and isolated rural schools and schools that serve pupils of all socio-economic, racial, and ethnic backgrounds. What are the characteristics of these schools? Do they have commonalities that account for their success?

Measures of Success

First, we must define what we mean by a **successful school**. One measure of success, naturally, is that students at these schools achieve at a high level and complete requirements for graduation. Whether reflected in scores on standardized tests or other documentation of academic learning gains, students at these schools are learning. They are achieving literacy in reading, writing, computation, and computer skills. They are learning to solve problems, think creatively and analytically, and, most importantly, they are learning to learn.

Another valid measure of success for a school is that it achieves results that surpass those expected from comparable schools in comparable settings. The achievement of students goes beyond what one would expect. In spite of surrounding social, economic, and political forces that impede the educative process at other schools, these schools are achieving results.

Finally, successful schools are those that are improving, rather than getting worse. School improvement is a slow process, and schools that are improving—moving in the right direction rather than declining—are also successful.

Research on School Effectiveness

During the 1980s and early 1990s, much research was conducted to identify the characteristics of successful (or effective) schools. The characteristics of successful schools were described in different ways in several research projects. The following list is a synthesis of these findings.

- *Strong leadership*—Successful schools have strong leaders—individuals who value education and see themselves as educational leaders, not just as managers or bureaucrats. They monitor the performance of everyone at the school—teachers, staff, students, and themselves. These leaders have a vision of the school as a more effective learning environment, and they take decisive steps to bring that about.
- *High expectations*—Teachers at successful schools have high expectations of students. These teachers believe that all students, rich or poor, can learn, and they communicate this to students through realistic, yet high, expectations.
- *Emphasis on basic skills*—Teachers at successful schools emphasize student achievement in the basic skills of reading, writing, and mathematical computation.
- *Orderly school environment*—The environments of successful schools are orderly, safe, and conducive to learning. Discipline problems are at a minimum, and teachers are able to devote greater amounts of time to teaching.
- *Frequent, systematic evaluation of student learning*—The learning of students in successful schools is monitored closely. When difficulties are noticed, appropriate remediation is provided quickly.
- *Sense of purpose*—Those who teach and those who learn at successful schools have a strong sense of purpose. From the principal to the students, everyone at the school is guided by a vision of excellence.
- *Collegiality and a sense of community*—Teachers, administrators, and staff at successful schools work well together. They are dedicated to creating an environment that promotes not only student learning but also their own professional growth and development.
- *Strategies for effective schools*—Research has also focused on strategies for making schools more effective. A synthesis of research (Newmann and Wehlage 1995) conducted between 1990 and 1995 on school improvement identified four characteristics of successful schools:
- *Focus on student learning*—Planning, implementation, and evaluation focus on enhancing the intellectual quality of student learning. All students are expected to achieve academic excellence.
- *Emphasis on authentic pedagogy*—Students are required to think, to develop in-depth understanding, and to apply academic learning to important, realistic problems. Students might, for example, conduct a survey on an issue of local concern, analyze the results, and then present their findings at a town council meeting.
- *Greater school organizational capacity*—The ability of the school to strive for continuous improvement through professional collaboration is enhanced. For example, teachers exchange ideas to improve their teaching; they seek feedback from students, parents, and community members; and they attend conferences and workshops to acquire new materials and strategies.
- *Greater external support*—The school receives critical financial, technical, and political support from outside sources.

In short, the cultures of effective schools encourage teachers to grow and develop in the practice of their profession. As the Secondary Schools in Canada: The National Report of the Exemplary Schools Project, (Gaskell 1995, 278) states: "School success is a complex and constantly evolving concept; different communities place emphasis on different elements. Success is a fragile quality that always involves a balance among different demands and pressures. It needs to be constantly reevaluated as conditions change. Successful schools are consciously trying to improve themselves by continuing inquiry and deliberative change."

What Social Problems Affect Schools and Place Students at Risk?

A complex and varied array of social issues impact schools. These problems often detract from the ability of schools to educate students according to the seven aims discussed at the beginning of this chapter: educational goals, prosocial values, socialization, achievement, personal growth, social change, and equal opportunity. Furthermore, schools are often charged with the difficult (if not impossible) task of providing a front-line defense against such problems.

One of the most vocal advocates of the role of schools in solving social problems was George S. Counts, who said in his 1932 book, *Dare the School Build a New Social Order?* that "If schools are to be really effective, they must become centers for the building, and not merely the contemplation, of our civilization" (p. 12). Many people, however, believe that schools should not try to build a new social order. They should be concerned only with the academic and social development of students—not with solving society's problems. Nevertheless, the debate over the role of schools in regard to social problems will continue to be vigorous. For some time, schools have served in the battle against social problems by offering an array of health, education, and social service programs. Schools provide breakfasts, nutritional counselling, diagnostic services related to health and family planning, after-school child care, job placement, and sex and drug education, to name a few. In the following sections we examine several societal problems that directly influence schools, teachers, and students.

Identifying Students at Risk

An increasing number of young people live under conditions characterized by extreme stress, chronic poverty, crime, and lack of adult guidance. As James Garbarino (1999, 12) points out: "In almost every community ... growing numbers of kids live in a socially toxic environment." Frustrated, lonely, and feeling powerless, many youths escape into music with violence-oriented and/or obscene lyrics, violent video games, cults, movies, and television programs that celebrate gratuitous violence and sex, and cruising shopping malls or "hanging out" on the street. Others turn also to crime, gang violence, promiscuous sex, or substance abuse. Not surprisingly, these activities place many young people at risk of dropping out of school. **Students at risk** of dropping out tend to get low grades, perform below grade level academically, are older than the average student at their grade level because of previous retention, and have behaviour problems at school. It is estimated that the following percentages of 14-year-olds are likely to exhibit one or more at-risk behaviours (substance abuse, sexual behaviour, violence, depression, or school failure) and to experience serious negative outcomes as a result: 10 percent at very high risk, 25 percent at high risk, 25 percent at moderate risk, 20 percent at low risk, and 20 percent at no risk (Dryfoos 1998).

Many Canadian children live in families that help them grow up healthy, confident, and skilled, but many do not. Instead, their life settings are characterized by problems of alcoholism or other substance abuse, family violence, unemployment, poverty, poor nutrition, teenage parenthood, and a history of school failure. Such children live in communities and families that have many problems and frequently become dysfunctional, unable to provide their children with the support and guidance they need. Children who experience the negative effects of poverty are from families of all ethnic and racial groups.

The life experiences of students who are at risk of dropping out can be difficult for teachers to imagine; and, as the following comments by a student teacher in a Grade 3 classroom illustrate, encountering the realities of poverty for the first time can be upsetting.

> [Some] students came in wearing the same clothes for a week. Others would come in without socks on. No pencils, crayons, scissors, or glue. Some without breakfast, lunch, or a snack. My heart bled every day. I found myself becoming upset about their lives. I even found myself thinking about them at night and over the weekend. [I] noticed that they were extremely bright students, but their home life and economic status hindered them from working to their potential. Some of my students couldn't even complete their homework because they had no glue, scissors, or crayons at home (Molino 1999, 55).

Although Canada is one of the richest countries in the world, it has by no means achieved an enviable record in regard to poverty among children. According to Statistics Canada, 20 percent of children under eighteen years of age live in families below the poverty line.

Family Stress

The stress placed on families in a complex society is extensive and not easily handled. For some families, such stress can be overwhelming. The structure of families who are experiencing the effects of financial problems, substance abuse, or violence, for example, can easily begin to crumble. Health challenges where a family member has developed cancer or other serious disease can also lead to significantly increased levels of stress.

Stress within the family can have a significant negative effect on students and their ability to focus on learning while at school. Such stress is often associated with health and emotional problems, failure to achieve, behavioural problems at school, and dropping out of school.

With the high rise in divorce and women's entry into the workforce, family constellations have changed dramatically. No longer is a working father, a mother who stays at home, and two or three children the only kind of family in Canada. The number of single-parent families, stepparent families, blended families, and extended families has increased dramatically during the last decade. In 1996, Statistics Canada released Growing Up In Canada: The National Longitudinal Survey of [22 000] Canadian Children and Youth. This report indicated that:

■ 14.6 percent of children under age 12 lived in a lone-parent family headed by a woman. One in six (17 percent) of these children had some form of conduct disorder; one in nine (11 percent) had repeated a grade at school.

- 41 percent of children in female single-parent families had at least one kind of problem as compared with 26 percent of children in all families.
- A child with a single-parent mother was almost twice as likely to face academic or behavioural problems as were children in a two-parent family.

Just as there is diversity in the composition of today's families, so, too, there is diversity in the styles with which children are raised in families. Because of the number of working women and single-parent homes, an alarming number of **latchkey children** are unsupervised during much of the day. To meet the needs of these children, some schools offer before- and after-school programs.

In addition, many middle-class couples are waiting longer to have children. Although children of such couples may have more material advantages, they may be somewhat "impoverished" in regard to the reduced time they spend with their parents. To maintain their lifestyle, these parents are often driven to spend more time developing their careers. As a result, the care and guidance their children receive is inadequate, and "Sustained bad care eventually leads to a deep-seated inner sense of insecurity and inadequacy, emotional pain, and a troublesome sense of self" (Comer 1997, 83). To fill the parenting void that characterizes the lives of an increasing number of children from all economic classes, schools and teachers are being called on to play an increased role in the socialization of young people.

Substance Abuse

One of the most pressing social problems confronting today's schools is the abuse of illegal drugs, tobacco, and alcohol. The use of drugs among young people varies from community to community and from year to year, but overall it is disturbingly high. Mind-altering substances used by young people include the easily acquired glue, white correction fluid, and felt marker, as well as marijuana, amphetamines, and cocaine. The abuse of drugs not only poses the risks of addiction and overdosing, but is also related to problems such as HIV/AIDS, teenage pregnancy, depression, suicide, automobile accidents, criminal activity, and dropping out of school. For an alarming number of young people, drugs are seen as a way of coping with life's problems.

Violence and Crime

While Canada experienced a decline in serious violent crimes during the 1990s, crime rates among adolescents has remained relatively constant. Statistics Canada reports in *Crime Statistics 2001* the following:

- The youth crime rate, as measured by the rate of youths aged 12 to 17 formally charged by police, rose a slight 1 percent for the second straight year, after decreasing from 1991 to 1999.
- The violent crime rate for youths increased 2 percent, its second consecutive gain, but the youth property crime rate continued to drop, falling 3 percent. Police-reported data show that 16 is the peak age of offending among all youths and adults for both violent and property crimes.
- There were 30 youths accused of homicide in 2001—the lowest level in over 30 years and 18 fewer than the average of 48 over the past decade.
- The rate of youths charged with robbery climbed 10 percent in 2001, and youths charged with motor vehicle theft rose 7 percent. The rate of young people charged with breaking and entering fell 6 percent, the tenth consecutive decline.

Figure 5.5

Security measures

Source: Indicators of School Crime and Safety, 1998. Washington, DC: National Center for Education Statistics.

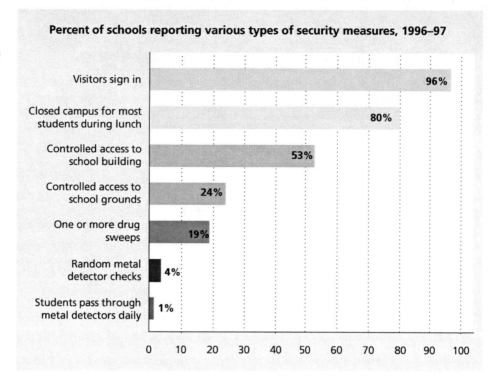

Percent of schools reporting various types of security measures, 1996–97

Canadian concern about school crime and safety heightened as a result of a string of American and Canadian school shootings between 1996 and 1999. Among the communities that had to cope with such tragic incidents were Moses Lake, Washington (1996); Pearl, Mississippi (1997); West Paducah, Kentucky (1997); Jonesboro, Arkansas (1998); Springfield, Oregon (1998); Littleton, Colorado (1999), and Taber, Alberta (1999). As a consequence, Canadian school officials have become much more concerned student safety and have started to initiate safety measures similar to those already common in many United States' schools. (See Figure 5.5.)

The American Psychological Association reviewed research studies and concluded that television violence *alone* is responsible for up to 15 percent of all aggressive behaviour by children and youth (Garbarino 1999). Lastly, David Grossman, a military psychologist, and his colleague pointed out that violent point-and-shoot video games are similar to those used to "desensitize" soldiers to shoot at human figures (Grossman and Siddle 1999).

As a result of the school shootings listed earlier and the public's concern with school crime and violence, many schools developed crisis management plans to cope with violent incidents on campus. Schools also reviewed their ability to provide students, faculty, and staff with a safe environment for learning. The following "School Safety Checklist" excerpted from the National Education Association's *School Safety Check Book* presents a starting point for evaluating school safety.

School Safety Checklist

Give your school a thorough crime prevention inspection now. Use this checklist as a guideline to determine your school's strengths and weaknesses.

1. Is there a policy for dealing with violence and vandalism in your school? (The reporting policy must be realistic and strictly adhered to.)
2. Is there an incident reporting system?
3. Is the incident reporting system available to all staff?
4. Is there statistical information available as to the scope of the problems at your school and in the community?
5. Have the school, school board and administrators taken steps or anticipated any problems through dialogue?
6. Does security fit into the organization of the school? (Security must be designed to fit the needs of the administration and made part of the site.)
7. Are the teachers and administrators aware of laws that pertain to them? To their rights? To students' rights? Of their responsibility as to enforcement of and respect for rules, regulations, policies, and the law?
8. Is there a working relationship with your local law enforcement agency?
9. Are students and parents aware of expectations and school discipline codes?
10. Are there any actual or contingency action plans developed to deal with student disruptions and vandalism?
11. Is there a policy as to restitution or prosecution of perpetrators of violence and vandalism?
12. Is there any in-service training available for teachers and staff in the areas of violence and vandalism and other required reporting procedures?
13. Is there a policy for consistent monitoring and evaluation of incident reports?
14. Is the staff trained in standard crime prevention behaviour?

Source: Excerpted from *The School Safety Check Book* by the National School Safety Center, 141 Duesenberg Dr., Suite 16, Westlake Village, CA, 91362, www.nssc1.org.

Now that you have completed the School Safety Checklist, consider the following excerpt that describes a program called "Peaceful Schools International." As explained below by V. Lois Ross, principal of Meadows School in Manitoba, the mandate of this program is to foster safe and peaceful school environments.

Peaceful Schools International

Imagine a school of about 350 students from Kindergarten to Grade 6 which is nestled on the outskirts of a mid sized city. Many of the educators and the principal have long standing experience at this school. Historically, this student body has been described as a rural and urban mixture from relatively stable, white, middle class families.

Now, imagine this same school which, over a period of three years, has been transformed to include nearly 500 students from Kindergarten to Grade 8. A number of educators have transferred into this school to teach at the new levels and a new principal has been assigned. Due to the opening of a large pork processing facility in the city, several families have moved into a high-density apartment residence located in the area, and as a result the student body now reflects much more diversity and transience. The school is now operating over capacity and space has become an issue.

Although the situation described above reflects challenges, it also poses opportunities for the staff, students and parent body to collaborate and implement a number of positive initiatives to foster the development of a healthy K to 8 learning community; one that attempts to negate the traumas of misbehaviour including bullying and other social concerns. One such initiative included the application for, and adoption of, Peaceful Schools International.

The appeal of this program comes from its mandate to support schools in their quest to establish and maintain a peaceful, caring and safe atmosphere. Acceptance into this organization is based on an application process which includes, for example, documentation of collaborative decision-making, multi-disciplinary approaches and overall commitment from all stakeholders at the school. Participants are challenged to generate creative, grassroots ideas, so instead of a "canned program," each school develops approaches which are uniquely tailored to its own setting.

Poetry, songs, drama, class challenges, community service and art are all being utilized, to date, to energize our focus of a safe, respectful, caring, peaceful K-8 learning community. Both staff and students are now strongly engaged in this focus. Just imagine the possibilities now!

Source: Reprinted by permission of V. Lois Ross.

Teen Pregnancy

Each year thousands of Canadian teenage women (one in every 20) between the ages of 15 and 19 will become pregnant, and about 85 percent of these pregnancies are unintended. Indeed, most teachers of adolescents today may expect to have at least some students who are, or have been, pregnant.

Since peaking in 1990, the teenage pregnancy, birth, and abortion rates have declined. About 20 percent of this decrease has been the result of decreased sexual activity and 80 percent the result of more effective contraceptive practices among sexually active teenagers (Alan Guttmacher Institute 1999). Nevertheless, teen pregnancies remain a serious problem in society. Because the physical development of girls in adolescence may not be complete, complications can occur during pregnancy and in the birthing process. Also, adolescents are less likely to receive prenatal care in the crucial first trimester; they tend not to eat well-balanced diets; and are not free of harmful substances such as alcohol, tobacco, and drugs, which are known to be detrimental to a baby's development. These young mothers "are at risk for chronic educational, occupational, and financial difficulties, and their offspring are also at risk for medical, educational, and behavioural problems" (Durlak 1995, 66). Because many teen mothers drop out of school, forfeiting their high school diplomas and limiting their access to decent, higher-paying job opportunities, they and their children tend to remain at the bottom of the economic ladder.

Suicide among Children and Youths

The increase in individual and multiple suicides is alarming for, in any given year, approximately 500 Canadian youths and adolescents will take their own lives. Among teenagers it is the third leading cause of death. Additionally, it is estimated that there are 8 to 25 attempted suicides for one completion. According to the Centers for Disease Control and Prevention (1998b), about 21 percent of high school students seriously considered committing suicide in 1997; about 16 percent made a specific suicide plan; about 8 percent actually attempted suicide; and about 3 percent required medical attention as a result of their suicide attempt.

Although female students are almost two times more likely than male students to have seriously considered attempting suicide during the preceding twelve months, about six times as many male students as females actually commit suicide. Also, lesbian and gay youth are two to three times more likely to attempt suicide than their heterosexual peers, and they account for up to 30 percent of all completed suicides among youth (Besner and Spungin 1995).

Should metal detectors be installed in schools?

Violence by or against students occurs in schools in many developed countries. Canada and the United states have had their own unfortunate occurrences—but so have others. In Dunblane, Scotland, a madman burst into a school and killed a teacher and 16 Kindergarten students. In Japan a middle school student was recently convicted of beheading another student, and other nations have experienced other horrific events. The question then becomes: How should schools react to this increased rate of violence?

In Canada, one popular response has been the Alberta Teachers' Association's Safe and Caring Schools program (SACS) (www.teachers.ab.ca/safe/Recognition.htm), which has, as its primary focus, the provision of advice and assistance required to communities wanting to develop the skills and knowledge essential for the provision of safe and caring schools. Supporters of the SACS program can now be found in British Columbia, Alberta, Saskatchewan, Ontario, and the Maritimes. The Ottawa–Carlton Board of Education has, for example, adapted the SACS curriculum outcomes to reflect the Ontario curriculum. In addition to the SACS program, the Lions Quest and the Peaceful Schools International are dedicated to the same objective of making schools safe for students. Unfortunately, it takes time to make all schools safe and caring places and some feel that other approaches should be taken.

In the United States, within ten days of the Columbine High School 1999 shooting spree, an event that that took the lives of fourteen students and a teacher while wounding over 20 others, the U.S. Secretary of Education, Richard Riley, sought to make sense of the tragedy. Speaking at Walt Whitman High School in Bethesda, Maryland, he told his audience, "We have always had schoolyard fights, but now there is a new level of fear because of these weapons of deadly violence." Crime statistics at the time indicated an actual decline in the juvenile violence rate, but lethality had increased, mainly due to guns.

"Guns and youth are a particularly deadly combination," observed a report by the Center for the Study and Prevention of Violence at the University of Colorado at Boulder. "Guns give youth the feeling of power, and during adolescence, abstract reasoning about the consequences of gun use and the capacity to read social cues are incomplete." The need to separate the two is obvious. But the way to do that is a challenge. Should metal detectors be installed in schools? Are there less ominous ways to handle the problem? Can schools be kept safe without becoming fortresses?

Metal detectors should be installed in schools.

A shooting in a school is like an earthquake in a city: It shakes the very foundation of what was thought to be solid, secure, and safe. Children and youth need to feel confident that their school is a safe and secure place. The thought of requiring students to spend their days in environments that make them vulnerable to violence is abhorrent. Expecting students to tackle their studies and find learning engaging when they are fearful for their lives is ludicrous. And yet that is exactly what we are doing if we fail to install metal detectors in schools.

After bombings occurred in air travel, metal detectors were installed in airports in order to protect passengers. Few complained, realizing that the personal inconvenience assured them of greater protection and peace of mind. They accepted the need to lose a liberty for the good of all. If adults are granted such protection from the violence in our society, should we not provide the same for our children and youth?

Metal detectors and similar devices are technological advances that help reduce crime in a variety of settings. In addition to the security they provide in airports, they prevent people from taking library books they haven't checked out and protect stores from shoplifters. Just as we have learned to accept metal detectors in libraries, airports, and stores, so their presence in schools would soon be hardly noticed.

Model programs that have decreased student weapon violations by 70 to 86 percent include weapon scanning with metal detectors along with random searches conducted by police. Other features of such model programs include eliminating building areas that cannot be viewed by surveillance cameras and training school security officers by local police forces. These model programs also call for teachers and students to be trained in how to handle dangerous situations and ways to avoid them. The installation of metal detectors is clearly where protection from school violence must begin.

Metal detectors should not be installed in schools.

Using metal detectors to prevent school violence is like putting an adhesive bandage on an infected wound. Not only will it not remedy the problem, but it could also make it even worse. Students who have not considered bringing a weapon to school might decide to do so simply to challenge the system. Like gang members who write graffiti on dangerous highway overpasses, similar minds will be motivated to find ways to bypass the metal detector. Metal detectors also present a foreboding welcome to a school campus and convey to students the messages "We have problems here" and "We don't trust you."

Instead, the way to prevent school violence is to get to the heart of students' problems. What causes the anger and alienation that eventually explodes in destructive, and sometimes deadly, acts? Teaching students how to solve their problems, handle disappointments, and seek help when it's needed are ways in which some schools have tried to reduce violence. Conflict management, peace building, using literature to teach empathy, forbidding teasing, and anti-bullying programs are other approaches.

In his speech at Walt Whitman High, Secretary Riley urged community members, parents, and students themselves to play active roles in reversing the trend toward greater violence. "I ask all Americans to believe as I do in this generation of young people…. We must send … a powerful message of hope and security. We will do everything we can to protect you, to listen to you, and to reach out to you so that you feel connected…. This is why I ask parents again and again to slow down your lives." He told students to speak to adults when they believe something violent is about to happen. He never mentioned metal detectors, and rightly so. Finding ways to reduce alienation and create community in our schools is a better approach to promoting school safety.

Where do you stand on this issue?

1. With which position do you agree? Why?
2. What are "zero tolerance" policies and should they be used?
3. How can teachers help prevent violence in schools?
4. How do schools and airports compare in their needs for metal detectors?
5. What compromise position can you suggest?

Recommended Sources

Center for the Study and Prevention of Violence, University of Colorado at Boulder (1991, April 21). Response to the Columbine school incident.

Department of Education (1999, April 30). Safe schools, healthy schools: remarks as prepared for delivery by U.S. Secretary of Education Richard W. Riley

Walters, L. S. (1999, January/February). What makes a good school violence prevention program? *Harvard Education Letter.*

Alberta Teachers' Association. Safe and Caring Schools program www.teachers.ab.ca/safe/Recognition.htm

What Are Schools Doing to Address Societal Problems?

Responding to the needs of at-risk students will be a crucial challenge for schools, families, and communities during the twenty-first century. Since most children attend school, it is logical that this pre-existing system be used for reaching large numbers of at-risk children (and through them, their families). During the last decade, many school districts have taken innovative steps to address societal problems that impact students' lives.

Though programs that address social problems are costly, the public believes that schools should be used for the delivery of health and social services to students and their families. However, there is some disagreement about the extent to which school facilities should be used for anything but meeting students' educational needs. For example, in a publication titled *Putting Learning First,* the Committee for Economic

Development (1994, 1) stated, "Schools are not social service institutions; they should not be asked to solve all our nation's social ills and cultural conflicts." In isolated instances, community groups and school boards have resisted school-based services such as family planning clinics and mental health services.

Intervention Programs

Under pressure to find solutions to increasing social problems among children and adolescents, educators have developed an array of intervention programs. In general, the aim of these programs is to address the behavioural, social, and academic adjustment of at-risk children and adolescents so they can receive maximum benefit from their school experiences.

In the following sections, we briefly review several comprehensive strategies that have proven effective in addressing academic, social, and behavioural problems among children and adolescents; these approaches to intervention are peer counselling, and school-based interprofessional case management. Chapter 5 presents additional information about recent, innovative steps schools are taking for the *prevention* of the effects of social problems on students. Also see Appendix 5.2 for "Selected Resources for Meeting Needs of Students Placed at Risk"—a list of publications, organizations, and online locations that are good sources of information on the problems children and youth may encounter.

Peer Counselling

To address the social problems that affect students, some schools have initiated student-to-student **peer counselling** programs—usually monitored by a school counsellor or other specially trained adult. In peer counselling programs, students can address problems and issues such as low academic achievement, interpersonal problems at home and at school, substance abuse, and career planning. Evidence indicates that both peer counsellors and students experience increased self-esteem and greater ability to deal with problems.

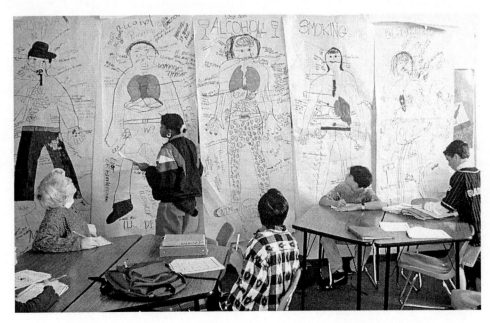

What approach to the education of students at risk does the scene in this photograph represent? What other risk factors affect children and youths? What are some other effective approaches for helping students at risk to succeed in school?

When peer counselling is combined with cross-age tutoring, younger students can learn about drugs, alcohol, premarital pregnancy, delinquency, dropping out, HIV/AIDS, suicide, and other relevant issues. Here the groups are often college-age students meeting with those in high school, or high school students meeting with those in junior high school or middle school. In these preventative programs, older students sometimes perform dramatic episodes that portray students confronting problems and model strategies for handling the situations presented.

School-Based Interprofessional Case Management

In responding to the needs of at-risk students, it has been suggested that schools "will need to reconceptualize the networks of community organizations and public services that might assist, and they will need to draw on those community resources" (Edwards and Young 1992, 78). One such approach to forming new home/school/community partnerships is known as **school-based interprofessional case management.** The approach uses professionally trained case managers who work directly with teachers, the community, and the family to coordinate and deliver appropriate services to at-risk students and their families. The case management approach is based on a comprehensive service delivery network of teachers, social agencies, and health service agencies.

Alternative Schools and Curricula

To meet the needs of students whom social problems place at risk, many school districts have developed alternative schools and curricula. Usually, an **alternative school** is a small, highly individualized school separate from the regular school; in other cases, the alternative school is organized as a **school-within-a-school.** Alternative school programs usually provide remedial instruction, some vocational training, and individualized counselling. Since they usually have much smaller class sizes, alternative school teachers can monitor students' progress more closely and, when problems do arise, respond more quickly and with greater understanding of student needs.

To reach students who are not successful at regular schools, alternative schools offer a program of individualized instruction, small class sizes, and various enrichment programs delivered in what school staff describe as a "supportive, non-coercive, nontraditional setting." Most students are expected to return to their regular schools after a minimum of four weeks.

While they don't work in alternative school settings, many highly effective regular teachers have developed alternative curricula to meet the unique learning needs of students at risk. Many teachers, for example, link students' learning to the business, civic, cultural, and political segments of their communities. The rationale is that connecting at-risk students to the world beyond their schools will enable them to see the relevance of education.

SUMMARY

What Are the Aims of Education Today?

- Though debate about the aims of education continues, the public believes that schools have a responsibility to address problems confronting Canadian society.

- Agreement exists regarding six additional broad educational aims—education for prosocial values, socialization, achievement, personal growth, social change, and equal opportunity.

How Can Schools Be Described?

- Schools can be categorized according to the focus of their curricula and according to their organizational structures.

- Metaphors for schools have suggested that schools are like families, tribes or clans, banks, gardens, prisons, and so on, with the school-as-family metaphor often describing schools that are successful.

- Some people believe that schools reproduce the existing social class structure, that they maintain the differences between the "haves" and "have-nots."

What Are Schools Like As Social Institutions?

- As social institutions that contribute to the maintenance and improvement of society, schools mirror Canadian culture and the surrounding local culture.

- Schools develop their own unique cultures, and the community environment that surrounds a school can impact it positively or negatively.

- Elements of a school's physical environment such as self-contained classrooms, open-space arrangements, and departmentalization contribute to a school's character and culture. Similarly, each classroom develops its own culture, which is influenced by the physical setting and the social dimensions of the group.

How Is Cultural Diversity Represented in Canadian Schools?

- The percentage of ethnic **minorities** in Canadian schools has been growing steadily since the end of World War II. According to Statistics Canada's report on the census of 2001, 18.4 percent of Canada's population was born in other countries, the highest percentage of any country except for Australia. Statistics Canada also reports that 94 percent of these new citizens settled in large urban areas with Montreal, Toronto, and Vancouver accounting for 73 percent of the total.

- Culture is defined as the way of life common to a group of people, including beliefs, attitudes, habits, values, and practices.

- Dimensions of cultural identity include beliefs, attitudes, and values; racial identity; exceptionalities; language; gender; ethnicity; income level; and occupation.

- **Ethnicity** refers to a commonly shared racial or cultural identity and a set of beliefs, values, and attitudes. The concept of race is used to distinguish among people on the basis of biological traits and characteristics. A minority group is a group of people who share certain characteristics and are fewer in number than the majority of a population.

- Stereotyping is the process of attributing certain behavioural characteristics to all members of a group, often on the basis of limited experiences with and information about the group being stereotyped. Individual racism is the prejudicial belief that one's own ethnic or racial group is superior to others, and institutional racism refers to laws, customs, and practices that lead to racial inequalities.

What Is Multicultural Education?

■ Five dimensions of multicultural education have been suggested: content integration, knowledge construction, prejudice reduction, an equity pedagogy, and an empowering school culture.

■ A multicultural curriculum addresses the needs and backgrounds of all students—regardless of their cultural identity—and expands students' appreciation for diversity. Effective multicultural materials and instructional strategies include the contributions of ethnic groups and reflect diverse points of view or "voices" that previously may have been silenced or marginalized in society.

How Is Gender a Dimension of Multicultural Education?

■ Gender includes ways of knowing and "modes of conduct, thought, and expression;" these are dimensions of culture.

■ Both boys and girls experience inequities in the classroom; teachers, however, can provide both sexes with an education free of *gender bias* by creating gender-fair classrooms and curricula.

■ Teachers should acknowledge the special needs of students who are gay, lesbian, or bisexual, and provide them with safe, supportive learning environments.

What Characteristics Distinguish Successful Schools?

■ Three aspects of successful schools have been suggested: (1) their students manifest a high level of learning; (2) their results surpass those for comparable schools; and (3) they are improving rather than getting worse.

■ Research has identified seven characteristics of effective schools: strong leadership, high expectations, emphasis on basic skills, orderly school environment, frequent and systematic evaluation of student learning, sense of purpose, and collegiality and a sense of community.

■ Research indicates that successfully restructured schools emphasize student learning, authentic pedagogy, building organizational capacity, and external support.

What Social Problems Affect Schools and Place Students at Risk?

■ Among the many social problems that impact the school's ability to educate students are poverty, family stress, substance abuse, violence and crime, teen pregnancy, HIV/AIDS, and suicide.

■ Children at risk, who represent all ethnic and racial groups and all socio-economic levels, tend to get low grades, underachieve, be older than other students at the same grade level, and have behaviour problems at school.

What Are Schools Doing to Address Societal Problems?

■ Schools have developed intervention and prevention programs to address social problems. Three effective intervention programs are peer counselling, and school-based interprofessional case management.

■ Many school districts have developed alternative schools or schools-within-a-school that provide highly individualized instructional and support services for students who have not been successful in regular schools. Also, highly effective teachers modify their techniques and develop alternative curricula to meet the needs of students at risk.

KEY TERMS AND CONCEPTS

aims of education
alternative school
classroom culture
cultural identity
culture
departmentalization
diversity
emotional intelligence
ethnic group
ethnicity
gender bias
gender-fair classroom
individual racism

institution
institutional racism
latchkey children
minorities
multicultural
   curriculum
multicultural
   education
multiculturalism
open-space schools
peer counselling
prosocial values
race

school-based
   interprofessional case
   management
school culture
school traditions
school-within-a-school
self-contained classroom
sex role socialization
sex role stereotyping
stereotyping
students at risk
successful school

APPLICATIONS AND ACTIVITIES

Teacher's Journal

1. Collect and summarize several newspaper and magazine articles that contain references to the public's expectations of education and the schools. To what extent do the articles address the four aims discussed in this chapter? To what extent do they identify social problems that schools are expected to address?

2. Identify and then defend your choice of school improvements that you consider most important for improving the quality of education in Canada. What aims of education do your choices reflect?

3. Reflect on your experiences with the impact of social problems on teaching and learning at the elementary, middle, or high school levels. Select one of the social issues or problems discussed in this chapter and describe its influences on you or your peers.

4. Reflecting on your experiences in schools and the five dimensions of multicultural education (see Figure 5.5 on page 190), describe the steps your teachers took to create an empowering school culture and social climate.

5. During your school years, did you ever experience discrimination as a member of a "different" group? Write about one outstanding incident that you feel affected your performance as a student.

6. As a teacher, what activities and materials might you use in a specific learning context to reduce the prejudices of students toward groups different from theirs?

7. Describe an example of sex-role stereotyping or gender bias that you experienced or observed in a school setting and how you felt about it.

1. Join or start an interactive online discussion on one or more of the following topics discussed in this chapter. You might join a newsgroup already in progress or request discussion partners via an email mailing list or via any one of the message board opportunities that are offered at many of the sites you have already explored. You might also establish a communication link among your classmates or with students in other schools who are taking a similar course.

teen pregnancies	effective schools
at-risk students	family stress
gender equity	English as a Second Language (ESL)
cultural diversity	multicultural education
substance abuse	latchkey children
crime and violence in schools	youth suicide
school improvement	school-based clinics
children in poverty	alternative schools

2. Formulate a research question concerning demographic aspects of students and their families, and go online to gather current national and provincial statistics on topics related to your question. For example, your question might relate to one or more of the above topics.

3. Develop a collaborative project with classmates to investigate and report on issues in drug abuse prevention, at-risk intervention, or violence prevention. Begin by exploring web sites such as Children, Youth and Families Education and Research Network (CYFERNet); and Children, Youth, and Families at Risk (CYFAR). Both sites have extensive resources, databases, and services for at-risk children, youth, and their families.

1. Visit a school in your community recognized as successful or effective. What evidence do you find of the characteristics of successful schools (or successfully restructured schools) discussed in this chapter? Are there other characteristics you would add to the list based on your observations?

2. Reflect on your experiences relating to social problems at the elementary, middle, or high school levels. Then gather statistics and information about how a local school or local school district is responding to the social problems discussed in this chapter.

3. Obtain at least one statement of philosophy, or mission statement, from a school with which you are familiar. Analyze the statement(s), identifying and highlighting portions that refer to the major aims of education discussed in this chapter (educational goals, prosocial values, socialization, achievement, cultural and ethnic groups, personal growth, social change, and equal educational opportunity).

4. If possible, visit a school that has an enrolment of students whose cultural or socioeconomic backgrounds differ from your own. What feelings and questions about these students emerge as a result of your observations? How might your feelings affect your teaching and teaching effectiveness? How might you go about finding answers to your questions?

5. Interview a teacher at the school identified in the above activity. What special satisfactions does he or she experience from teaching at the school? What significant problems relating to diversity does he or she encounter, and how are they dealt with?

Professional Portfolio

1. Analyze a school as a social institution. How is the school organized in terms of roles and statuses? How does the school's organization and functioning reflect the wider society as well as the community in which it is located? What characteristics of the school and its people relate to the urban, rural, or suburban nature of the school environment?

2. Develop a case study of a school's culture. Visit a local school or base your study on a school you have attended. Organize your case in terms of the following categories of information:

   - *Environment*—How would you describe the school facility or physical plant and its material and human resources? How is space organized? What is the climate of the school?
   - *Formal Practices*—What grades are included at the school? How is the school year organized? How is time structured? How are students and teachers grouped for instruction?
   - *Traditions*—What events and activities and products seem important to students, teachers, and administrators? What symbols, slogans, and ceremonies identify membership in the school? How do community members view and relate to the school?

   Draw conclusions from your case study: What aspects of the school culture seem to support learning and academic achievement? On the basis of your case study, draft a position statement on the kind of culture you would like to create or promote in your classroom.

3. Prepare an annotated directory of local resources for teaching students about diversity, implementing multicultural curricula, and promoting harmony or equity among diverse groups. For each entry, include an annotation—that is, a brief description of the resource materials and their availability.

   - Resources for your personalized directory should be available through local sources such as your university library, public library, community agencies, and so on. Among the types of resources you might include are the following:
   - Films, videos, audio tapes, books, and journal articles
   - Simulation games designed to improve participants' attitudes toward diversity
   - Motivational guest speakers from the community
   - Ethnic museums and cultural centres
   - Community groups and agencies dedicated to promoting understanding among diverse groups
   - Training and workshops in the area of diversity

Appendix 5.1

Gender-Neutral Language Test

The following questions are designed to determine how gender-neutral you are with respect to your normal speech patterns. When you respond to these questions, please answer honestly. Do not respond with what you consider to be the "correct" answer; rather, respond with an answer which truly reflects how you speak in the situations described.

	Yes	No
1. Would you refer to the boy who delivers your daily newspaper as the "paperboy"?		
2. Would you refer to a member of your local fire department as a "fireman"?		
3. Would you refer to a woman who works for your police department as a "policewoman"?		
4. Would you refer to the man who delivers your mail as the "mailman"?		
5. Do you almost invariably say "his and hers" as opposed to "hers and his"?		
6. Do you, or would you, use phrases such as the following: "Don't rag me" or "She ragged him out"?		
7. Do you comment on the dress or physical appearance of women far more often than you do of men?		
8. In your normal speech do you ever use the term "mankind" or "man" when referring to the human race?		
9. When referring to native peoples and early European settlers would you ever use the term "the white man"?		
10. When referring to people who fish do you call them "fishermen"?		
11. When referring to a clerk who has waited on you, would you ever use such a phrase as "the lady who works at the clothing store"?		
12. When talking of the woman who cleans your house or apartment would you refer to her as the "cleaning lady"?		
13. When speaking of artificial or synthetic products do you ever use the term "manmade" to describe such products?		
14. Would you use the word "guys" when speaking to, or about, a group comprised of females and males?		
15. If you were writing a formal paper and used the following quotation: "Every bank manager must watch his staff with care," would you fail to make an editorial insertion so the quotation read: "Every bank manager must watch his [or her] staff with care"?		
16. Would you ever refer to a medical doctor who treated you as a "woman doctor" or, in the case of a man who is a nurse, as a "male nurse"?		
17. Would you ever refer to a woman who was bothering you in some way as "a bitch"?		
18. Do you often use the pronouns "he" or "his" when referring to someone whose sex is unknown to you? eg., "I would like to speak to the manager if he's in"?		
19. Do you ever refer to the person who attends you on an airplane as the "stewardess"?		
20. To the best of your knowledge has anyone—within the last month—ever corrected you for what she or he considered to be your use of sexist language?		
Totals:		

Appendix 5.1 *(continued)*

Rating scale is based upon the number of "Yes" responses. If you do not know why a specific "Yes" response is considered inappropriate, you might visit one of the numerous "gender-neutral language" web sites.

16–20   *Watch your tongue or it may hurt you.*
Many of those involved in hiring teachers are language sensitive, will notice your speech patterns, and select someone else.

11–15   *Fair.*
You're trying, but you've still have a long way to go.

6–10   *Good.*
This probably puts you in the top 10 percent of the population with respect to gender-neutral language.

0–5   *Very impressive.*

Explanations as to why "Yes" answers are inappropriate can be found on the pages which follow.

Appendix 5.1 *(continued)*

Gender-Neutral Language Test: Responses

Languages tend to reflect the prejudices of the society from which they have evolved. English, which developed within a male-centred, patriarchal society, traditionally assigned the masculine gender to terms or individuals which might have been neutral or feminine in nature. A book title such as *The History of Western Man* provides a perfect example of this practice.

As our language continues to evolve it is appropriate for everyone, and educators in particular, to assist our language's progress towards a more inclusive model. Language which is exclusionary can alienate our readers or listeners who may feel personally diminished or—and this is the critical point for teachers—reject our message because they perceive us as sexist or insensitive to their existence.

A common reaction among those who take this test and score poorly on it is to say: "There is no need for me to become politically correct." This response suggests an insensitivity to the realities of today's society. The issue is not one of political correctness; rather, it is one of fairness and clarity. To speak of the "guys" when referring to a group that contains both male and female students is definitely misleading. Similarly, to speak about the "firemen" hosing down your burning house, several of whom are women, is both unfair and confusing.

The "Yes" answers within the *Gender-Neutral Language Test* are regarded as inappropriate. The explanations, and suggested gender-neutral alternative uses, follow.

1. Paperboy: Genderist. Some girls also deliver newspapers—as do many adult men and women. Newspaper publishers refer to all such individuals as "paper carriers."
2. Fireman: Genderist. Both men and women work for fire departments and all refer to themselves with the accurate and gender-neutral term of "firefighter."
3. Policewoman: Genderist. Both men and women work for police departments. All of them refer to themselves as "police officers."
4. Mailman: Genderist. Both men and women deliver mail to homes; both refer to themselves as "postal carriers."
5. His/Hers; Hers/His. To always place the masculine "his" first is regarded by many as insensitive. The recommendation is to alternate the use of his/hers with hers/his.

6. Don't rag me: Sexist and insulting. It is a reference to premenstrual syndrome (PMS) and women's use of sanitary napkins during menstruation.
7. Women's dress/appearance. If you comment equally about the dress and/or appearance of both men and women, there is little problem. However, if you single out women for special comment you are being sexist, whether you are a man or a woman.
8. Man/Mankind: Sexist. These usages, when referring to both men and women, are exclusionary. Use "humans," "humanity," "people," or another word or phrase that does not involve a particular gender.
9. White Man: Genderist. This suggests that all early settlers were white males. This is certainly erroneous on a number of levels. Use "Europeans" or, simply, "early settlers."
10. Fishermen: Genderist. There are many women who fish. If speaking about inshore people who fish, use the term "anglers" or "fishers;" if speaking about offshore people who fish, use "fishers."
11. Lady: Stereotypical. It is perfectly acceptable to say "Ladies and gentlemen" for this is a parallel use of masculine and feminine terms. However, to use lady as a generic synonym for a woman is inappropriate. A lady is a woman who acts and behaves in a socially prescribed manner. Using lady as the reference to a woman about whom you know little tends to suggest that (a) she is not necessarily viewed as a mature and responsible individual and (b) that she should act in a manner that befits a lady.
12. Cleaning lady: Genderist. (See #11 above). Men also clean houses. Use "cleaner."
13. Manmade: Genderist. Women also make things. Use "artificial," synthetic," or "manufactured."
14. Guys: Genderist. Guys are males. Using this word as a collective noun for a group of males and females is inappropriate; using it as a reference to a group comprised exclusively of females is even more inappropriate.
15. Editorial insertions: These are usually placed within material directly cited from another writer. To indicate to your readers that you are sensitive to language gender issues you should make such editorial insertions whenever the need arises.

16. Woman Doctor: Genderist. Expressions such as "woman doctor" or "male nurse" imply that the occupation in question normally "belongs" to a man or to a woman. Make women part of the rule, not the exception.
17. Bitch: Sexist and insulting. A bitch is a female dog with a perceived bad temper. To refer to a woman as a bitch is highly inappropriate.
18. He: Genderist. If a person's gender is unknown to you, do not automatically refer to that person with a masculine pronoun. Use any gender-neutral term such as: owner, manager, superior, etc.
19. Stewardess: Genderist. It has been 25 years since any flight attendant, male or female, used such a term. Although the term actress lives on, most words with the feminine *-ess* ending are being dropped from use.
20. Your use of sexist language. If someone has corrected you for such use, or if you scored poorly on the *Gender-Neutral Language Test*, perhaps you should visit one of the websites listed above.

Gender-Neutral Language Websites

www.ucc.ie/ucc/equalcom/language.html#Page4
www.otago.ac.nz/personnelservices/Policies/NonSexistLang Guide.html
http://langue.lc.chubu.ac.jp/jalt/pub/tlt/98/may/beebe.html
http://coral.wcupa.edu/stupaper/01gems.htm

Appendix 5.2

Selected Books for Meeting Needs of Students Placed at Risk

101 Ways to Develop Student Self-Esteem and Responsibility. Jack Canfield and Frank Siccone. Boston: Allyn and Bacon, 1994.

Against The Odds: How "At-risk" Children Exceed Expectations. Janie Bempechat. San Francisco: Jossey-Bass, 1998.

Assessment and Instruction of Culturally and Linguistically Diverse Students with or At-risk of Learning Problems: From Research to Practice. Virginia Gonzalez, Rita Brusca-Vega, and Thomas Yawkey. Boston: Allyn and Bacon, 1997.

At-risk Students: Tools for Teaching in Problem Settings. Susan L. Peterson. San Francisco: International Scholars Publications, 1998.

Beyond Discipline: From Compliance to Community. Alfie Kohn. Alexandria, VA: Association for Supervision and Curriculum Development, 1996.

Get to School Safely! Washington, DC: National Institute on the Education of At-Risk Students.

Hope at Last for At-Risk Youth. R.D. Barr and W.H. Parrett. Boston: Allyn and Bacon, 1995.

Last Chance High: How Girls and Boys Drop In and Out of Alternative Schools. Deirdre Kelly. New Haven, CT: Yale University Press, 1993.

Mentoring Students at Risk: An Underutilized Alternative Education Strategy for K-12 Teachers. Gary Reglen. Springfield, IL: Charles C. Thomas Publishers, 1998.

The New Circles of Learning: Cooperation in the Classroom and School. David W. Johnson, Roger T. Johnson, and Edythe J. Holubec. Alexandria, VA: Association for Supervision and Curriculum Development, 1994.

Open Lives, Safe Schools. Donovan R. Walling (Ed.). Bloomington, IN: Phi Delta Kappa Educational Foundation, 1996.

Reducing School Violence through Conflict Resolution. David W. Johnson and Roger T. Johnson. Alexandria, VA: Association for Supervision and Curriculum Development, 1995.

Resiliency in Schools: Making It Happen for Students and Educators. Nan Henderson and Mike M. Milstein. Thousand Oaks, CA: Corwin Press, 1996.

Safe Passage: Making It Through Adolescence in a Risky Society. Joy G. Dryfoos. New York: Oxford University Press, 1998.

A School for Healing: Alternative Strategies for Teaching At-risk Students. Rosa L. Kennedy and Jerome H. Morton. New York: P. Lang, 1999.

The School Safety Handbook: Taking Action for Student and Staff Protection. Kenneth Lane, Michael D. Richardson, and Dennis W. Van Berkum (Eds.). Lancaster, PA: Technomic Publishing Company, 1996.

Students at Risk. H. Lee Manning and Leroy G. Baruth. Boston: Allyn and Bacon, 1995.

Talk It Out: Conflict Resolution in the Elementary Classroom. Barbara Porro. Alexandria, VA: Association for Supervision and Curriculum Development, 1996.

Teaching Mainstreamed, Diverse, and At-risk Students in the General Education Classroom. Sharon Vaughn, Candace S. Bos, and Jeanne S. Schumm. Boston: Allyn and Bacon, 1997.

Teaching Social Competence: A Practical Approach for Improving Social Skills in Students At-risk. Dennis R. Knapczyk and Paul Rodes. Pacific Grove, CA: Brooks/Cole, Pub. Co., 1996.

Toward Resiliency: At-risk Students Who Make It to College. Laura J. Horn, Xianglei Chen, and Clifford Adelman. Washington, DC: U.S. Department of Education.

Treating Adolescent Substance Abuse: Understanding the Fundamental Elements. George R. Ross. Boston: Allyn and Bacon, 1994.

Using Educational Technology with At-risk Students: A Guide for Library Media Specialists and Teachers. Roxanne B. Mendrinos. Westport, CT: Greenwood Press, 1997.

Waiting for a Miracle: Why Schools Can't Solve Our Problems—And How We Can. James P. Comer. New York: Dutton, 1997.

6

Philosophical Approaches
to Classroom Management

Focus on the Principles of Classroom Management

1. How are theoretical approaches to classroom management useful to teachers as they manage their own and their students' behaviour?
2. What are the power bases that teachers can access in order to influence student behaviour?
3. Why is it important that the techniques a teacher employs to manage student behaviour be consistent with the teacher's beliefs about how students learn and develop?

Introduction

Teaching can be a threatening and frustrating experience, and all of us at some time entertain doubts about our ability to maintain effective classroom learning environments. For many teachers, however, these normal self-doubts, which are especially common early in a teaching career (Housego, 1992), lead to a frantic search for gimmicks, techniques, or tricks that they hope will allow them to survive in the real classroom world (Fast, Elliott, Hunter, and Bellamy, 2002). This is indeed unfortunate, as case 6.1 illustrates. When classroom management problems are approached with a frenetically sought-after bag of tricks instead of a carefully developed systematic plan for decision-making, teachers are likely to find themselves behaving in ways they later regret. The teachers who are most successful at creating a positive classroom atmosphere that enhances student learning are those who employ a carefully developed plan for

Taken from *Principles of Classroom Management: A Professional Decision-Making Model*, Canadian Edition, by James Levin, James F. Nolan, James W. Kerr, and Anne E. Elliott.

The Tricks-of-the-Trade Approach

Ms. Judy Knepp is a first-year teacher at Armstrong School. Although most of her classes are going well, she is having a great deal of difficulty with her grade six developmental reading class. Many of the students seem disinterested, lazy, immature, and rebellious. As a result of the class's continuous widespread chattering, Ms. Knepp spends the vast majority of her time yelling and reprimanding individual students. She has considered using detention to control students, but there are so many disruptive students that she doesn't know whom to give detention to first. The class has become such a battlefield that she finds herself hating to go to school in the morning.

After struggling on her own for a couple of long weeks, Ms. Knepp decides that she had better ask somebody for help. She is reluctant to go to any of the administrators because she thinks that revealing the problem will result in a low official evaluation for her first semester's work. Finally, she decides to go to Ms. Hoffman, a veteran teacher of 14 years with a reputation for striking fear into the hearts of her grade six students.

After she tells Ms. Hoffman all about her horrendous class, Ms. Knepp waits anxiously for some words of wisdom that will help her to get the class under control. Ms. Hoffman's advice is short and to the point: "I'd just keep the whole class in for detention. Keep them until about 4:30 just one day, and I guarantee you won't have any more trouble with them. These kids think they're tough, but when they see that you're just as mean and tough as they are, they'll melt pretty quickly."

Ms. Knepp is dismayed. She immediately thinks, "That's just not fair. What about those four or five kids who don't misbehave? Why should they have to stay in too?" She does not voice her objections to Ms. Hoffman, fearing Ms. Hoffman will see her as rude and ungrateful. She does ask, "What about parents who object to such punishment?" However, Ms. Hoffman assures her that she has never had any trouble from parents and that the principal, Dr. Kropa, will support the disciplinary action even if any parents do object.

Ms. Knepp feels trapped. She knows that Ms. Hoffman expects her to follow through, and she fears that Ms. Hoffman will tell the other veteran teachers if she doesn't take the advice. Like most newcomers, Ms. Knepp longs to be accepted.

Despite her misgivings, then, Ms. Knepp decides to follow the advice and to do so quickly before she loses her nerve. The next day, she announces that one more disrup-

classroom management. Clearly, any such plan must be congruent with their basic beliefs about the nature of the teaching and learning process. When teachers use this type of plan, they avoid the dilemma that Ms. Knepp encountered.

There are multiple models or systems of classroom management and hundreds of techniques for promoting positive student behaviour within these models. Most of these techniques are effective in some situations but not others, for some students but not others, and for some teachers but not others. "What most of the experts fail to mention is that the efficacy of a technique is contextually dependent. Who the teacher teaches

tion—no matter who is the culprit—will bring detention for the entire class. For five minutes silence reigns, and the class actually accomplishes some work. Ms. Knepp has begun to breathe a long sigh of relief when suddenly she hears a loud "you pig" from the back right-hand corner of the room. She is positive that all the students have heard the epithet and knows that she cannot ignore it. She also fears that an unenforced threat will mean disaster.

"That does it. Everyone in this class has detention tomorrow after school." Immediately the air is filled with "That ain't fair," and "I didn't do nothing," and "You wish," and "Don't hold your breath." Naturally, most of these complaints come from the biggest troublemakers. However, several students who never cause trouble also complain bitterly that the punishment is unfair. Deep down, Ms. Knepp agrees with them, but she feels compelled to dismiss their complaints with a fainthearted, "Well, life just isn't always fair, and you might as well learn that now." She stonewalls it through the rest of the class and is deeply relieved when the class is over.

When Ms. Knepp arrives at school the next morning, there is a note from Dr. Kropa in her box stating that Mr. and Mrs. Pennsi are coming in during her free period to talk about the detention of their son, Fred. Fred is one of the few students who rarely cause trouble. Ms. Knepp feels unable to defend her action. It contradicts her beliefs about fairness and how students should be treated. The conference is a disaster. Ms. Knepp begins by trying to convince the Pennsies that she is right but ends by admitting that she too feels that she has been unfair to Fred. After the conference, she discusses the punishment with Dr. Kropa, who suggests that it is best to call it off. Ms. Knepp drags herself, half in tears, to her class. She is going to back down and rescind the punishment. She believes that the kids will see this as a sign of weakness, and she is afraid of the consequences.

Questions to Consider

1. What might Ms. Knepp have done to avoid her dilemma with regards to following Ms. Hoffman's advice?

2. Why did the detention fail?

3. Should she rescind the punishment? What should she say to the class?

4. Most important, what can Ms. Knepp learn from the experience?

and who the teacher is dictate which technique will have the greatest potential for addressing the complex management problems evidenced in classrooms (Lasley, 1989). Because every technique is based implicitly or explicitly on some belief system concerning how human beings behave and why, classroom teachers must find prototypes of classroom management that are consistent with their beliefs and use them under appropriate circumstances.

How can teachers ensure that their behaviour in dealing with classroom management and classroom discipline problems will be effective and will match their beliefs about students, teachers, and learning? First, they can understand their own basic beliefs about classroom management. Second, they can develop, based on their beliefs, a systematic plan for promoting positive student behaviour and dealing with inappropriate behaviour. Numerous options exist which allow teachers to develop a personal plan for encouraging appropriate student behaviour and for dealing with unacceptable behaviour in a manner congruent with their own basic beliefs about management. Because there are numerous options, teachers can prioritize their options in a hierarchical format.

To help teachers and future teachers lay the philosophical foundation for their own classroom management plan, this chapter offers an overview of a variety of philosophical approaches to classroom management. So that they may be considered in a more systematic and orderly fashion, the approaches are grouped under two major headings: teacher power bases and theories of classroom management. The first section discusses the various types of power or influence that are available to teachers to promote appropriate student behaviour. The second section explains three theories of classroom management and their underlying beliefs and includes models and techniques for each of the theoretical approaches.

It is important to be aware of the inherent connection between the three theories and the four power bases. Each of the three theories relies on the dominant use of one or two power bases. Teachers can examine the foundations on which their own classroom management plans rest by comparing their beliefs with those inherent in each of the various teacher power bases and theories of classroom management.

Teacher Power Bases

Although the work has been expanded to include other elements (Erchul, Raven, and Whichard, 2001), the foundational work of French and Raven remains relevant for teachers (1960). They have identified four different types of power that teachers, as social agents, may use to influence student behaviour. The effective teacher is aware of the type of power he wants to use to influence student behaviour and is also aware of the type of power that is implicit in each of the techniques available. It cannot be emphasized enough that when teachers' beliefs and behaviours are consistent, they are more likely to be successful than they are when they are not consistent. When beliefs and behaviours are congruent, usually teachers follow through and are consistent in dealing with student behaviour. Students usually perceive such teachers as genuine; they practise what they preach. As you read the explanation of the four types of power, ask yourself which type or types fit your beliefs and which ones you could use comfortably. Although every teacher probably uses each of the four types of power at some time, teachers tend to have a dominant power base that they use most often.

The four teacher power bases are presented in a hierarchical format, beginning with those more likely to engender student control over their own behaviour and proceeding to those that foster increasing teacher control. If teachers believe, as we do, that one of the important long-range goals of schooling is to foster student self-direction, using those power bases at the top of the hierarchy as often as possible will be consistent with this belief. If teachers do not share this belief, the hierarchical arrangement of power bases is not as important for them. Whatever teachers believe about the long-range goals of education, they must understand the four teacher power bases because no single one is effective for all students, all classrooms, or all teachers. Thus, effective classroom management requires the use of a variety of power bases.

The Involved Teacher

Mr. Emig was envied by administrators and teachers alike at Spring Grove School. Even though he taught grade eight English to all types of students, he never sent students to the office, rarely gave detentions, and never needed parent conferences to discuss student behaviour. In fact, it seemed as if he never had any discipline problems with students.

Mr. Karr, the principal, decided that other teachers might be able to learn some techniques from Mr. Emig and so asked some of Mr. Emig's students why his classes were so well behaved. Students said that they liked Mr. Emig because he was always involved in activities with them. He sponsored the school newspaper, went on ski club trips, went to athletic events, coached track, chaperoned dances, and advised the student council. Because of his heavy involvement with them, students got a chance to see him as a person, not just as a teacher, and they felt that he was a really good person who cared a lot about kids. As a result, nobody hassled him in class.

Questions to Consider

1. How important is it to be liked by your students?

2. Describe the responsibilities and roles of teachers in student activities beyond the classroom.

Referent Power

Consider case 6.2. The type of power Mr. Emig uses to influence student behaviour has been termed *referent power* by French and Raven (1960). When a teacher has **referent power,** students behave as the teacher wishes because they like the teacher as a person. Students view the teacher as a good person who is concerned about them, cares about their learning, and demands a certain type of behaviour because it is in their best interests.

There are two requirements for the effective use of referent power: (1) teachers must perceive that the students like them, and (2) teachers must communicate that they care about and like the students. They do this through positive nonverbal gestures; positive oral and written comments; extra time and attention; and displays of sincere interest in students' ideas, activities, and especially, learning. Teachers with referent power are able to appeal directly to students to act a certain way. Examples of such direct appeals are, "I'm really not feeling well today. Please keep the noise level at a minimum," and "It really makes me angry when you hand assignments in late. Please have your assignments ready on time." These teachers might handle Ms. Knepp's problem with a statement such as, "You disappoint me and make me very angry when you misbehave and disrupt class time. I spend a great deal of time planning activities

Her Reputation Precedes Her

Ms. Sanchez is a chemistry teacher at Lakefront High School. Each year, Ms. Sanchez teaches an academic chemistry course to university-bound students. For the past five years, none of her students has failed the exam. As a result, each student has received an excellent foundation for a university credit in chemistry. Students in Ms. Sanchez's class recognize that she is very knowledgeable about chemistry and knows how to teach. If an observer walks into Ms. Sanchez's class, even during April and May, he will find the students heavily involved in class activities, with very little off-task behaviour.

Questions to Consider

1. What motivates Ms. Sanchez's students so highly?

2. What did Ms. Sanchez likely do over the past five years to build such a positive reputation?

that you will enjoy and that will help you to learn, but I must spend so much time on discipline that we don't get to them. I would really appreciate it if you would stop the misbehaviour."

Referent power must not be confused with attempts to be the students' friend. Teachers who want to be friends with students usually are dependent on students to fulfill their personal needs. This dependency creates an environment in which students are able to manipulate teachers. Over time, teacher and students become equals, and the teacher loses the ability to influence students to behave appropriately. In contrast, teachers who use referent power are authority figures and do make demands on students. Students carry out the teacher's wishes because they like the teacher as a teacher, not as a friend.

It is neither possible nor wise to use referent power all the time with all students. In any classroom, it may be difficult to establish referent power with some students. In these cases a different technique must be selected because the foundation for using referent power cannot be built. However, when students make it clear, through their general reactions before, during, and after class, that they like the teacher, and when the teacher has communicated caring and concern to students, the use of referent power can make classroom management easy.

Expert Power

Ms. Sanchez in case 6.3 is a teacher who uses **expert power** to influence student behaviour. When a teacher enjoys expert power, students behave as the teacher wishes because they view that teacher as someone who is good and knowledgeable and who can help them to learn. This is the power of professional competence. To use expert power effectively, two important conditions must be fulfilled: (1) the students must believe the teacher has both special knowledge and the teaching skills to help them acquire that knowledge, and (2) the students must value learning what the teacher is teaching. Students may value what they are learning for any number of reasons: the subject matter is inherently interesting, they can use that knowledge in the real world, they want good grades, or they want to reach some personal goal such as college or a job.

Teachers who use expert power successfully communicate their competence through mastery of content material, the use of motivating teaching techniques, clear explanations, and thorough class preparation. In other words, such teachers use their professional knowledge to help students learn. When expert power is employed successfully, students make comments similar to these: "I behave because he is a really good teacher," and "She makes biology interesting," and "He makes you really want to learn." A teacher with an expert power base might say to Ms. Knepp's disruptive class: "I'm sure you realize how important reading is. If you can't read, you will have a rough time being successful this year. You know that I can help you learn to read and to read well, but I can't do that if you won't behave as I've asked you to behave."

As is the case with referent power, a teacher may be able to use expert power with some classes and some students but not with others. A math teacher may be able to use expert power with an academic calculus group but not with a remedial math group; an auto mechanics teacher may be able to use expert power with the vocational-technical students but not with students who take auto mechanics to fill up their schedules.

One final caveat concerning this type of power: whereas most primary teachers are perceived as experts by their students, expert power does not seem to be effective in motivating these students to behave appropriately. Thus, unlike the other three power bases, which can be employed at all levels, the appropriate use of expert power seems to be confined to students beyond the primary grades.

Legitimate Power

The third type of power identified by French and Raven and used by Mr. Davis in case 6.4 is **legitimate power**. The teacher who seeks to influence students through legitimate power expects students to behave appropriately because the teacher has the legal and formal authority for maintaining appropriate behaviour in the classroom. In other words, students behave because the teacher is the teacher, and inherent in that role are a certain authority and power.

Teachers who wish to use a legitimate power base must demonstrate through their behaviour that they accept the responsibilities, as well as the power, inherent in the role of teacher. They must be viewed by students as fitting the stereotypical image of teacher (e.g., in dress, speech, and mannerisms). Students must believe that teachers and school administrators are working together. School administrators help teachers gain legitimate power by making clear, through words and actions, that students are expected to treat teachers as legitimate authority figures. Teachers help themselves gain legitimate power by following and enforcing school rules and by supporting school policies and administrators.

Students who behave because of legitimate power make statements such as, "I behave because the teacher asked us to. You're supposed to do what the teacher says." A teacher who employs legitimate power might use a statement in Ms. Knepp's class such as, "I do not like the way you people are treating me. I am your teacher. I will not put up with disrespectful behaviour. I am responsible for making sure that you learn, and I'm going to do that. If that means using the principal and other school authorities to help me do my job, I'll do just that."

"School Is Your Job"

Mr. Davis looked at the grade four students in front of him, many of whom were talking or staring into space instead of doing the seatwork assignment. He said, "You are really disappointing me. You're sitting there wasting precious time. School is not a place for wasting time. School is your job, just like your parents have jobs, and it is my job to see that you work hard and learn during school. Your parents pay taxes so that you'll have the chance to come to school and learn. You and I both have the responsibility to do what we're supposed to do. Now, cut out the talking and the daydreaming, and do your math."

Questions to Consider

1. Explain the effectiveness of Mr. Davis's strategy.

2. What might Mr. Davis have said that would have been more effective but yet contained the same message?

Because of societal changes, most teachers rightly believe that today's students are less likely to be influenced by legitimate power than students of 30 or 40 years ago were. However, it is still possible to use legitimate power with some classes and some students.

Reward/Coercive Power

Notice how the teacher in case 6.5 is using **reward and coercive power** to influence student behaviour. Although they may be considered two separate types of teacher authority, reward and coercive power are really two sides of the same coin. They are both based on behavioural notions of learning, they both foster teacher control over student behaviour, and they are both governed by the same principles of application.

There are several requirements for the effective use of this power base: (1) the teacher must be consistent in assigning and withholding rewards and punishments; (2) the teacher must ensure that students see the connection between their behaviour and the reward or punishment; (3) the rewards or punishments actually must be perceived as rewards or punishments by the student (many students view a three-day, out-of-school suspension as a vacation, not as a punishment).

Teachers using this base rely on a variety of rewards, such as oral or written praise, gold stars, free time, "good news" notes to parents, and release from required assignments, as well as a variety of punishments, including verbal reprimands, loss of recess or free time, detention, in-school suspension, and out-of-school suspension.

Students who behave appropriately because of reward/coercive power are apt to say, "I behave because if I don't, I have to write out a stupid saying 50 times and get it signed by my parents." A teacher using reward/coercive power to solve Ms. Knepp's problem might say, "I've decided that for every five minutes without a disruption this class will earn one point. At the end of each week, for every ten points it has accumu-

Going to Recess

"O.K., grade twos, it's time to put your spelling books away and get ready for recess. Now, we all remember that we get ready by putting all books and supplies neatly and quietly in our desks and then by folding our hands on top of the desk and by looking at me quietly. Let's see which row can get ready first. I see that Tammy's row is ready. O.K., Tammy's row, you can walk quietly out to the playground. Oh, no, wait a minute. Where are you going, Joe? You're not allowed to go out to recess this week because of your misbehaviour on the bus. You can go to Mr. Li's room and do your math assignment. I'll check it when I get back."

Questions to Consider

1. Name three strategies being used by this teacher.

2. Explain why you agree or disagree with Joe's punishment and the reminder to him in this context.

---

lated, the class may buy one night without homework during the following week. Remember, if there are any disturbances at all, you will not receive a point for the five-minute period." This point system is an example of a behaviour modification technique. More information on the use of behaviour modification in the classroom may be obtained from many sources (e.g., Alberto and Troutman, 1999; Kerr and Nelson, 1998; Axelrod, 1983; Winter, 1983).

As is true for the other three power bases, reward/coercive power cannot be used all the time. As students become older, they often resent obvious attempts to manipulate their behaviour through rewards and punishments. It is also difficult with older students to find rewards and punishments under the classroom teacher's control that are powerful enough to motivate them. (Still, some teachers have found their control of student time during school has allowed them to use reward/coercive power successfully with some students and some classes at all levels of schooling.) It should be noted that there are some inherent dangers in the use of reward/coercive power. Research has indicated that when students are rewarded for engaging in an activity, they are likely to perceive the activity as less inherently interesting in the future and are less likely to engage in that activity without external rewards (Lepper and Green, 1978). Also, overuse of punishment is likely to engender in students negative attitudes toward school and learning.

It is important for a teacher to recognize what power base he uses to influence students in a given situation and to recognize why that base is appropriate or inappropriate. It is also important for the teacher to recognize the power base he uses most frequently as well as the power base he is comfortable with and would like to use. For some teachers, the two things may be quite different. Examining your beliefs about teacher power bases is one important step toward ensuring that your beliefs about classroom management and your actions are congruent. Table 6.1 offers a brief comparison of the four power bases on several significant dimensions.

Of course, most teachers use a combination of power bases in the classroom. They use one for one type of class and student and another for another type of class and student. They may even use a variety of power bases with the same students. This approach may, indeed, be the most practical and effective one, although combining certain power bases—for example, coercive and referent—may be difficult to do.

Theories of Classroom Management

In this section, we will describe three theories of classroom management. In order to make the differences clear between the three theories, we will describe each theory as if it were completely independent of the others. In reality, however, the three theories are more like three points on a continuum, moving from student-directed toward teacher-directed practices. On such a continuum, collaborative models represent a combination of the two end points. Of course, the classroom behaviour of most teachers represents some blending of the three theories. According to Martin and Sugarman, "There inevitably is a big gap between theory and practice. Even when theory (principles) is supported by research ..., it still does not tell teachers exactly what to do in any classroom situation" (1993, p.12). As Bob Strachota has noted, "Theories about

Table 6.1

Teacher Power Bases

	Referent	Expert	Legitimate	Reward/Coercive
Motivation to behave	Student likes teacher as a person	Teacher has special knowledge	Teacher has legal authority	Teacher can reward and punish
Need for teacher management of student behaviour	Very low	Very low	Moderate	High
Requirements for use	Students must like the teacher as a person	Teacher expertise must be perceived and valued	Students must respect legal authority	Rewards and punishments must be effective
Key teacher behaviours	Communicates caring for students	Demonstrates mastery of content and teaching skills	Acts as a teacher is expected to act	Has and uses knowledge of student likes and dislikes
Age limitations	Useful for all levels	Less useful at primary level	Useful at all levels	Useful at all levels but less useful at senior high level
Caveats	Teacher is not the student's friend	Heavily dependent on student values	Societal changes have lessened the usefulness of this power base	Emphasizes extrinsic over intrinsic motivation

Punishment and rewards are often used by teachers; however, they may not be the most effective means to manage student behaviour.

how to best help children learn and change have to be broad enough to encompass the vitality and ambiguity that come with life in a classroom. If relied on too exclusively, behaviourism or constructivism end up living awkwardly in school" (1996, p. 133). Still, if a teacher's behaviour is examined over time, it is usually possible to classify the teacher's general approach to working with students and goals for classroom management into one of the theories on a fairly consistent basis.

Before reading the specific theories, determine your answers to the following nine basic questions about classroom management. Inherent in each theory are answers, either implicit or explicit, to these questions. If you are aware of your own beliefs about classroom management before you begin, you will be able to identify the theory that is aligned most closely with those beliefs.

1. Who has primary responsibility for managing student behaviour?
2. What is the goal of classroom management?
3. How do you view time spent on management issues and problems?
4. How would you like students to relate to each other within your management system?
5. How much choice will you give students within your management system?
6. What is your primary goal in handling misbehaviour?
7. What interventions will you use to deal with misbehaviour?
8. How important to you are individual differences among students?
9. Which teacher power bases are most compatible with your beliefs?

Readers of other versions of this text will recognize that the labels of the three theories have changed from *non-interventionist* to *student-directed*, from *interventionist* to *teacher-directed*, and from *interactionalist* to *collaborative*. We believe the new labels describe the theories more clearly than the former labels, which were taken from Wolfgang and Glickman (1995). Because the student-directed approach is used less frequently in schools than the other two approaches and may be unfamiliar, more specific details are provided for it than for the other two.

Student-Directed Management

Advocates of the **student-directed classroom management** theory believe that the primary goal of schooling is to prepare students for life in a democracy, which requires citizens—who are able to—to control their behaviour, to care for others, and to make wise decisions. Previously, student-directed models of classroom management were drawn primarily from counselling models. Gordon's teacher effectiveness training (1989), Berne's and Harris's transactional analysis (1964 and1969, respectively), and Ginott's communication model (1972) relied almost exclusively on one-to-one conferencing between teacher and student to deal with behaviour issues. Such models were difficult to implement in the reality of a classroom filled with 25 to 30 students, each with a variety of talents, needs, interests, and problems. As a result, **teacher-directed management** models dominated most classrooms. During the past five years, however, there has been considerable progress in developing student-directed management models that can be employed effectively within classrooms. Alfie Kohn (1996), Bob Strachota (1996), Ruth Charney (1992), Martin and Sugarman (1993), Putnam and Burke (1992) and Schwartz and Pollishuke (2002) have provided a variety of practical strategies that classroom teachers can use effectively.

The student-directed theory of classroom management, which Ms. Koskowski in case 6.6 uses to handle David's behaviour, rests on two key beliefs: (1) students must have the primary responsibility for controlling their behaviour; and (2) students are capable of controlling their behaviour if given the opportunity to do so. Given these beliefs, student-directed models of management advocate the establishment of classroom learning communities, which are designed to help students become more self-directed, more responsible for their own behaviour, more independent in making appropriate choices, and more caring toward fellow students and teachers. The well-managed classroom is one in which students care for and collaborate successfully with each other, make good choices, and continuously strive to do high quality work that is interesting and important to them.

When viewed from a student-directed perspective, time spent on management is seen as time well spent on equipping students with skills that will be important to them as adult citizens in a democracy (Novak, 2002). "Learning to behave in manners consistent with the goal of accepting individual responsibilities within a democratic social context is a functional strategy for individual development" (Martin and Sugarman, 1993, p.33). In attempting to develop a student-directed learning environment in which students develop self-regulation skills, collaborative social skills, and decision-making skills, the teacher relies heavily on several major concepts: student ownership, student choice, community, and conflict resolution and problem solving.

Student ownership is established in several ways. Although the teacher takes responsibility for the arrangement of the classroom and for the safety of the environment, students are often responsible for deciding how the room should be decorated, for creating the posters, pictures, and other works that decorate the walls, and for maintaining the room. In fact, sharing the responsibility of establishing a positive learning environment can empower students to take control of their own learning (Schwartz and Pollishuke, 2002). Throughout the year, students rotate through committees (the art supplies committee, the plants and animals committee, the cleanup committee, and so forth) that are responsible for various aspects of the class's work. Often these committees are structured so that students gain experience in planning, delegating, and evaluating their own work in a fair and equitable manner.

Students are also given a great deal of responsibility for determining classroom rules. Typically a class meeting is held during which the teacher and students discuss how they want their classroom to be. Students are asked to think about the ways they are treated by others that make them feel good or bad. These experiences are then used as a springboard for a discussion about how the students want to treat each other in the classroom. The students' words become the guidelines for classroom behaviour.

Choice plays a key role in student-directed learning environments because it is believed that a student can learn to make good choices only if he has the opportunity to make choices. In addition to making choices about the physical environment of the room and the expectations for behaviour, students are given choices about classroom routines and procedures, topics and questions to be studied in curriculum units, learning activities, and the assessment of their learning, including assessment options and criteria. Creating rubrics together, prior to a learning task, is a good example of providing students with meaningful choices about their own learning. Classroom meetings, which are viewed as important vehicles for establishing and maintaining a caring classroom community, provide more opportunities for choices. Agendas for the meetings, which may be planning and decision-making meetings, check-in meetings, or problem-solving and issues-oriented meetings, are often suggested by the students.

Through the physical arrangement of the room, class meetings, and planned learning activities, the teacher attempts to build a community of learners who know and care for each other and work together productively. A great deal of time is spent at the beginning of the year helping students to get to know each other through get-acquainted activities, meetings, and small group activities. Throughout the year, the teacher uses cooperative learning activities stressing individual accountability, positive interdependence, face-to-face interaction, social skill development, and group processing. These types of activities are emphasized because student-directed theorists believe that students learn more in collaborative activities and that when they know and care for those in their classroom community, they are more likely to choose to behave in ways that are in everyone's best interest.

Student-directed teachers see interpersonal conflict as a teachable moment. They realize that conflict is inevitable when individuals are asked to work closely together. In fact, the absence of conflict is probably a good indication that individuals are not working together very closely. Thus, these teachers believe that helping students to deal with interpersonal conflict productively is an important goal of classroom management. Conflict resolution, peer mediation, and interpersonal problem-solving skills are taught just as academic content is taught. Students are encouraged to use these skills when conflicts arise. Issues that concern the class as a whole—conflicts concerning the sharing of equipment, class cliques, and relationship problems—become opportunities for using group problem-solving skills during class meetings. Some teachers even use class meetings to involve the entire class in helping to improve the behaviour of a particular student. It is important to note that encouraging caring relationships and teaching ways to deal with conflict productively go hand-in-hand and demand ongoing efforts and consistency on the part of the teacher. If students do not know or care about each other, conflict is hard to resolve. Conversely, if students do not acquire the ability to resolve conflict productively, they are unlikely to build caring relationships with each other.

Student misbehaviour is seen not as an affront to the teacher's authority but rather as the student's attempt to meet needs that are not being met. In response to misbehaviour, the teacher tries to determine what motivates the child and to find ways to meet those unmet needs. A student-directed teacher would view the behaviour problems in Ms. Knepp's class, in case 6.1, as a clear indication that the learning activities and curriculum were not meeting the student needs. The teacher probably would hold a class meeting to address the problem behaviours in the classroom. He would articulate his feelings and reactions to the class and would elicit student feelings about the class as well. Through a discussion of their mutual needs and interests, the teacher and the

Handling Disruptive David

M Ms. Koskowski, Ms. Sweely, and Mr. Green teach grade four at Longmeadow School. Although they work well together and like each other, they have very different approaches to classroom discipline. To illustrate their differing approaches, let's examine their behaviour as each one deals with the same situation.

In the classroom there are three students at the reading centre in the far right-hand corner and two students working quietly on insects at the science interest centre near the chalkboard located in the front of the room. Five students are correcting math problems individually, and 10 students are working with the teacher in a reading group. David, one of the students working alone, begins to mutter out loud, "I hate this math. It's too hard to do. I never get them right. Why do we have to learn about fractions anyway?" As his monologue continues, David's voice begins to get louder and clearly becomes a disruption for the other students.

Ms. Koskowski

Ms. Koskowski recognizes that David, who is not strong in math, is really frustrated by the problems on fractions. She walks over to him and quietly says, "You know, David, the other night I was trying to learn to play tennis, and I was getting really frustrated. It helped me to take a break and get away from it for a minute, just to clear my head. How about if you do that, now? Go, get a drink of water, and when you come back, you can get a fresh start." When David returns to his seat and begins to work, Ms. Koskowski helps him to think through the first problem and then watches and listens as he does the second one on his own.

class would develop a solution to the problem that would probably include some redesign of the tasks that students were asked to perform.

Kohn suggests that the first questions the teacher should ask when a child is off task are (1) What is the task? and (2) Is it really a task worth doing (1996)? Many teachers try to identify with the child. Strachota calls this " getting on their side" (1996). This strategy seems especially appropriate when coping with students who seem out of control and unable to behave appropriately. If a teacher can identify experiences in which he has felt out of control, he is usually more empathetic and helpful. In case 6.6 Ms. Koskowski employs this strategy with David.

Student-directed teachers also believe in allowing students to experience the consequences of their behaviour. Natural consequences (consequences that do not require teacher intervention) are the most helpful because they allow the student to experience the results of his behaviour directly. However, sometimes the teacher must use logical consequences. The teacher's role in using consequences is neither to augment nor to alleviate the consequences but rather to support the child or the class as the consequences are experienced. This can be a difficult role for teachers and parents to play. Even when a teacher can predict that a given choice is going to lead to negative conse-

Ms. Sweely

As soon as she sees that David is beginning to interrupt the other students, Ms. Sweely gives the reading group a question to think about and walks toward David's desk. She quietly approaches David until she is right beside him, but the muttering continues. She says, "David, you are disrupting others; please stop talking and get back to math." David stops for about five seconds but then begins complaining loudly again. "David, since you can't work with the group without disrupting other people, you will have to go back to the castle [a desk and rocking chair partitioned off from the rest of the class] and finish your math there. Tomorrow, if you believe that you can handle it, you may rejoin your math group."

Mr. Green

As soon as David's muttering becomes audible, Mr. Green says, "David, that behaviour is against our class rules. Stop talking and concentrate on your math." David stops talking momentarily but begins again. Mr. Green walks calmly to David's desk and removes a small, round, blue chip. As he does, he says, "Well, David, you've lost them all now. That means no more recess for the rest of the week and no good-news note to your mom and dad."

Questions to Consider

1. Whose approach would likely receive the best learning response from David? Why?

2. What would the other students be learning by observing each of the teachers interact with David?

quences, student-directed theorists argue, the student should experience the consequence unless it will bring great harm to the child. Students learn to make wise choices, according to student-directed theorists, by recognizing that their behaviour inevitably has consequences for themselves and others.

Some student-directed theorists also believe that restitution is an important part of dealing with misbehaviour when a behaviour has hurt other students. In order to emphasize that the classroom is a caring community and that individual behaviour has consequences for others, a student whose behaviour has hurt others is required to make amends to those harmed. One strategy used by some teachers is called "an apology of action" (Forton, 1998). In this strategy, the student who has been hurt is allowed to decide what the offending student must do to make restitution. The strategy not only helps students to recognize that inappropriate behaviour hurts others but also can be a powerful way to mend broken relationships.

Referent and expert teacher power bases seem most compatible with student-directed management theory. Each power base emphasizes students' control over their own behaviour. At the same time, the student-directed perspective adds a new dimension to the notion of expert power. Students must recognize the teacher's specialized

Cooperative learning activities can help students realize that they have responsibilities to both themselves and the class.

knowledge and his ability to build a caring classroom community in which students are given the opportunity to make choices and take responsibility for directing their own behaviour. Putting this philosophy into practice demands highly competent and committed teachers who truly believe that enabling students to become better decision-makers who are able to control their own behaviour is an important goal of schooling. These teachers must be committed to establishing more democratic classrooms that are true caring communities (Novak, 2002). A teacher who is not committed to these beliefs will be unwilling to invest the time and effort needed to establish a student-directed learning environment. Long-term commitment is one key to success.

It is important to note that student-directed classrooms are not laissez-faire situations or classrooms without standards. In fact, the standards for student behaviour in most of these classrooms are exceptionally high. When student efforts fall short of meeting agreed-upon standards for behaviour and work, the teacher plays the role of encourager, helping students to identify ways to improve. The teacher's role is not to punish the student with behaviour or academic problems but rather to find ways to help the student overcome the problems.

Student-directed strategies are effective in all teaching situations and are especially well suited for self-contained early childhood and elementary settings—for several reasons. First, students and teachers in these settings typically spend a large portion of the day together, which gives them the opportunity to build close relationships with each other. Second, because the classes are self-contained, it is possible to build a community in which students really know and care about each other. Finally, teachers in these settings have greater control over the allocation of time during the day than most secondary teachers. Because they are not "bell bound," they are free to spend more time dealing with classroom management issues with individual students or the class as a whole. The current practice of teacher looping, in which teachers stay with one group of students for two or three years (for example, from grades one through three), provides an outstanding opportunity to create a student-directed environment because teachers and students work together for an extended period of time. Secondary schools would seem to be well served by adopting similar structures to personalize the environment and make it more student-directed—i.e., by using an integrated curriculum (Drake, 1998). At present, in many secondary schools students and teachers spend about

80 minutes together per day, and an individual teacher may teach 120 students or more per day. In such environments, although it may be more difficult, it is still possible to get to know each other personally, to understand each other's needs, and to establish a caring community.

Collaborative Management

The collaborative theory of classroom management is based on the belief that the control of student behaviour is the joint responsibility of the student and the teacher. Although those who adopt the collaborative approach to management often believe in many of the tenets of the student-directed theory, they also believe that the number of students in a class and the size of most schools make it impractical to put a student-directed philosophy into practice. With the current provincial trend toward standardized testing and prescriptive and extensive curriculum, the time required to work collaboratively with students under this model is becoming more difficult for teachers to attain (Elliott and Woloshyn, 1996). In fact, many secondary teachers, in particular, feel that the size of their classes and the limited time they have with students make it imperative for them to place the needs of the group above the needs of any individual student. Under the collaborative theory, then, students must be given some opportunity to control their own behaviour because a long-range goal of schooling is to enable students to become mature adults who can control their own behaviour; but the teacher, as a professional, retains primary responsibility for managing student behaviour because the classroom is a group learning situation.

In case 6.6 Ms. Sweely represents the **collaborative management** theory in action. Note that she tries to protect the reading group activity and, at the same time, deal with David. While the group is occupied, she uses proximity interference to signal David that he should control his behaviour. When he cannot, she emphasizes the effect of his behaviour on others and separates him from the rest of the group to help him recognize the logical consequences of being disruptive in a group situation. Thus, the teacher oriented toward the collaborative theory promotes individual control over behaviour but sometimes subordinates this goal to the right of all students to learn. From the collaborative perspective, the goal of classroom management is to develop a well-organized classroom in which students are (1) engaged in learning activities; (2) usually successful; (3) respectful of the teacher and fellow students; and (4) cooperative in following classroom guidelines because they understand the rationale for the guidelines and see them as appropriate for the learning situation. From the collaborative point of view, then, students become capable of controlling their own behaviour not by simply following rules but, rather, by understanding why rules exist and then choosing to follow them because they make sense. Neither blind obedience to rules nor complete freedom in deciding what rules should exist is seen as the best route toward self-regulated behaviour.

In collaborative classrooms the teacher and students develop rules and procedures jointly. Some teachers begin with a minimum list of rules, those that are most essential, and allow students to develop additional ones. Other teachers give students the opportunity to suggest rules but retain the right to add rules or veto suggested rules. Both of these techniques are intended to help the teacher maintain the ability to use his professional judgment to protect the rights of the group as a whole.

Teachers who adopt a collaborative approach to classroom management often give students choices in other matters as well. Typically, the choices are not as open-ended as those provided by student-directed advocates. For example, instead of allowing students to develop the criteria for judging the quality of their work, a collaborative teacher might present a list of 10 potential criteria and allow students to choose the five criteria that will be used. Thus, the students are provided with choices, but the choices are confined to some degree by the teacher's professional judgment. This same system of providing choice within a given set of options may be followed in arranging and decorating the classroom or selecting topics to be pursued during academic units.

Advocates of a collaborative approach see time spent on classroom management issues as potentially productive for the individual but not for the class as a whole unless there is a major problem interfering with the learning of a large number of students. Thus, collaborative teachers, whenever possible, do not take time away from group learning to focus on the behaviour of an individual or a few students. Interpersonal conflicts are treated in a similar way. They are not dismissed, but collaborative teachers usually do not use classroom time to deal with them unless they involve many students. When an interpersonal conflict arises, the teacher deals with the individuals involved when there is a window of time to do so. Class meetings are used to deal with management issues or conflicts involving large numbers of students. Collaborative teachers tend to view a class meeting as a means for solving problems as a way to maintain the classroom community.

While collaborative management advocates believe that outward behaviour must be managed to protect the rights of the group, they also believe the individual's thoughts and feelings must be explored to get at the heart of the behaviour. Therefore, collaborative teachers often use coping skills to manage student behaviour in a group situation and then follow up with a conference with the student. Because collaborative theorists believe that relating behaviour to its natural or logical consequences helps students learn to anticipate the consequences of their behaviour and thus become more self-regulating, they advocate consequences linked as closely as possible to the misbehaviour itself. A student who comes to school five minutes late, for example, might be required to remain five minutes after school to make up work.

The teacher power bases most compatible with collaborative management theories are the expert and legitimate bases. Each of these power bases rests on the belief that the primary purpose of schools is to help students learn important processes and information. Therefore, the teacher must protect the rights of the group while still nurturing the learning of individual students. A collaborative teacher in Ms. Knepp's class might decide to hold a class meeting to review the classroom expectations and the rationale for them, to answer any questions or concerns regarding those expectations, and to remind students that the expectations will be enforced through the use of logical consequences. The teacher might also allow the class to make some choices concerning upcoming activities and events from a presented list of options. Three well-known collaborative management models come from the work of Dreikurs, Grundwald, and Pepper (1998), Glasser (1992), and Curwin and Mendler (1988).

Teacher-Directed Management

Advocates of the teacher-directed management theory believe that students become good decision-makers by internalizing the rules and guidelines for behaviour that are given to them by responsible and caring adults. The teacher's task, then, is to develop a set of guidelines and rules that will create a productive learning environment, to be sure that the students understand the rules, and to develop a consistent system of rewards and punishments that make it likely that students will follow the guidelines and rules. The goal of the teacher-directed theory is to create a learning environment, in which management issues and concerns play a minimal role, to discourage misbehaviour and to deal with it as swiftly as possible when it does occur. In this theory, the teacher assumes primary responsibility for managing student behaviour. Time spent on management issues is not seen as productive time because it reduces time for teaching and learning. The well-managed classroom is seen as one in which the management system operates efficiently and students are cooperative and consistently engaged in learning activities. The primary emphasis in teacher-directed classrooms is on academic content and processes. Current Canadian trends are prompting more teachers to adhere to this model of management in light of increased curriculum expectations and standardized testing. Pressure from the public—exerted through the media—as well as from provincial ministries of education for increased teacher accountability, is also contributing significantly to this trend (e.g., *Alberta Department of Education*, 2003; *Newfoundland and Labrador Department of Education*, 2003; *Ontario Ministry of Education*, 2003).

In teacher-directed environments, the teacher makes almost all of the major decisions, including room arrangement, seating assignments, classroom decorations, academic content, assessment devices and criteria, and decisions concerning the day-to-day operation of the classroom. Students may be given a role to play in implementing teacher decisions—for example, they may be asked to create a poster—but they are usually restricted to implementing the teacher's decisions. Advocates of teacher-directed models view the teacher as a trained professional who understands students, teaching, and the learning process and therefore is in the best position to make such choices.

Usually the teacher presents rules and a system of consequences or punishments for breaking those rules to students on the first or second day of school. Often students are asked to sign a commitment to obeying the rules, and frequently their parents are asked to sign a statement declaring that they are aware of the rules. Often punishments for misbehaviour are not directly related to the misbehaviour itself but rather are universal consequences that can be applied to a variety of transgressions. For example, the student's name may be written on the board, a check mark may be made in the grade book, or a call may be made to the student's parents. Teachers may also establish a set of rewards that are provided to the class as a whole if everyone follows the rules consistently. Punishments and rewards are applied consistently to ensure that the management system and rules are internalized by all.

Although teachers who follow teacher-directed approaches do use cooperative learning strategies, their management techniques usually are not focused on the creation of a caring classroom community in which caring is a primary motivator for choosing to behave appropriately. In a teacher-directed classroom, the primary relationship is usually the relationship between the teacher and individual students. Students tend to be seen as a collection of individuals who should not interfere with each other's right to learn or with the teacher's right to teach. Self-control is often viewed as a matter of will. If students want to control their own behaviour, they can.

Given this, conflict is seen as threatening, nonproductive, and disruptive of the learning process. The teacher deals swiftly with any outward manifestations of a conflict but usually not with the thoughts and feelings that have led to the conflict. Students have a right to feel upset, it is argued, but not to act in inappropriate ways. Using the predetermined list of punishments or consequences, the teacher redirects the misbehaving student to appropriate behaviour by applying the appropriate consequence. For the most part, punishments are sequenced so that second or third offences bring more stringent consequences than first offences. While individual differences may play an important part in the academic aspects of classroom work, they do not play a major role in the management system. Consider the actions of Mr. Green in case 6.6. As an advocate of teacher-directed management, he moves quickly to stop the misbehaviour, emphasizes classroom rules, employs blue chips as rewards, and uses punishments in the form of loss of recess privileges and good-news notes.

Clearly, reward and coercive power is the teacher power base that is most compatible with the teacher-directed theory. Advocates use clear, direct, explicit communication, behaviour contracting, behaviour modification, token economy systems, consistent reinforcement of appropriate behaviour, and group rewards and punishments. A teacher following this theory might handle Ms. Knepp's dilemma by setting up a group management plan in which the group earns points for appropriate behaviour. The points could then be exchanged for meaningful rewards. At the same time the teacher uses a predetermined set of punishments to punish any students who misbehave.

The teacher who wants to use a teacher-directed approach should be aware of some important considerations. A thorough understanding of the principles of behavioural psychology is necessary in order to apply behaviour modification appropriately. Individual student differences do play a role in the management system because they must be considered in developing rewards and punishments. After all, a reward to some individuals may be a punishment to others. Thus, most teacher-directed theorists are concerned with students' thoughts and emotions; however, the primary goal in dealing with misbehaviour is management of the student's outward behaviour, not inner feelings. Therefore, individual differences do not play a role in determining which behaviours are acceptable. Some well-known authors of classroom management systems derived from the teacher-directed perspective are Axelrod (1983), Canter and Canter (1992), Cangelosi (1997), and Valentine (1987).

Table 6.2

Theories of Classroom Management

Question	Student-Directed	Collaborative	Teacher-Directed
Primary responsibility for management	Student	Joint	Teacher
Goal of management	Caring community focus and self-direction	Respectful relationships, academic focus	Well-organized, efficient, academic focus
Time spent on management	Valuable and productive	Valuable for individual but not for group	Wasted time
Relationships within management system	Caring, personal relationships	Respct for each other	Noninterference with each other's rights
Provision of student choice	Wide latitude and freedom	Choices within teacher-defined options	Very limited
Primary goal in handling misbehaviour	Unmet need to be explored	Minimize in group; pursue individually	Minimize disruption; redirect
Interventions used	Individual conference, group problem solving, restitution, natural consequences	Coping skills, natural and logical consequences, anecdotal record keeping	Clear communication, rewards and punishments, behaviour contracting
Individual differences	Extremely important	Somewhat important	Minor importance
Teacher power bases	Referent, expert	Expert, legitimate	Reward/coercive
Theorists	Charney, Faber and Mazlish, Gordon, Kohn, Strachota, Putnam and Burke	Curwin and Mendler, Dreikurs, Glasser	Axelrod, Cangelosi, Canter and Canter, Valentine

Table 6.2 provides a summary of the three theories of management in terms of their answers to the nine basic questions about classroom management introduced at the beginning of this section.

SUMMARY

The first section of the chapter provides an explanation of the four teacher power bases: referent, expert, legitimate, and reward/coercive. Each base is presented in terms of the underlying assumptions about student motivation to behave, the assumed need for teacher control over student behaviour, the requirements for employing the base effectively, the key teacher behaviours in using the base, and limitations and caveats concerning its use.

The second section discusses nine basic questions that are useful for articulating beliefs about classroom management:

1. Who has primary responsibility for managing student behaviour?
2. What is the goal of classroom management?
3. How do you view time spent on management issues and problems?
4. How would you like students to relate to each other within your management system?
5. How much choice will you give students within your management system?
6. What is your primary goal in handling misbehaviour ?
7. What interventions will you use to deal with misbehaviour?
8. How important to you are individual differences among students?
9. Which teacher power bases are most compatible with your beliefs?

Articulating one's beliefs is the initial step toward developing a systematic plan for managing student behaviour. These nine basic questions are used to analyze three theories of classroom management: student-directed, collaborative, and teacher-directed.

Teachers may use the information and questions provided in this chapter to develop a plan for preventing classroom management problems and for dealing with disruptive student behaviour that is congruent with their basic beliefs about teaching and learning.

KEY TERMS

Collaborative management: the belief that the control of student behaviour is the joint responsibility of the student and the teacher.

Expert power: where students view the teacher as a good, knowledgeable teacher who can help them to learn; the power of professional competence.

Legitimate power: where students behave because the teacher is the teacher; inherent in that role are a certain authority and power.

Referent power: where students behave as the teacher wishes because they like the teacher as a person and they feel the teacher cares about them.

Reward/coercive power: where students behave to avoid some form of punishment or to gain a predetermined reward.

Student-directed management: where the primary goal of schooling is to prepare for life in a democracy.

Teacher-directed management: the belief that students become good decision-makers by internalizing rules and guidelines for behaviour that are provided by a responsible and caring teacher.

REFERENCES

Alberta Department of Education. (2003). *Curriculum by subject.* Retrieved July 16, 2003, from **ednet.edc.gov.ab.ca/k_12/curriculum/bySubject/**

Alberto P. A., and Troutman A. C. (1999). *Applied Behavior Analysis for Teachers* (5th ed.). Upper Saddle River, NJ: Merrill.

Axelrod, S. (1983). *Behaviour Modification for the Classroom Teacher.* New York: McGraw Hill.

Berne, E. (1964). *Games People Play: The Psychology of Human Relations.* New York: Avon.

Cangelosi, J. S. (1997). *Classroom Management Strategies: Gaining and Maintaining Students' Cooperation.* New York: Longman.

Canter, L., and Canter, M. (1992). *Assertive Discipline: Positive Behaviour Management for Today's Classrooms.* (rev. ed.). Santa Monica, CA: Canter Associates.

Charney, R. (1992). *Teaching Children To Care: Management in the Responsive Classroom.* Greenfield, MA: Northeast Foundation for Children.

Alberta Department of Education. (2003). *Curriculum by subject.* Retrieved July 16, 2003, from **ednet.edc.gov.ab.ca/k_12/curriculum/bySubject/**

Curwin, R. L., and Mendler, A. (1988). *Discipline with Dignity.* Alexandria, VA: Association for Supervision and Curriculum Development.

Drake, S. M. (1998). *Creating Integrated Curriculum.* Thousand Oaks, CA: Corwin Press Inc.

Dreikurs, R., Grundwald, B., and Pepper, F. (1998). *Maintaining Sanity in the Classroom: Classroom Management Techniques.* (2nd ed.). Washington, DC: Taylor and Francis.

Elliott, A. and Woloshyn, V. (1996). Adopting collaborative strategies in the classroom. *The Canadian School Executive 15(9),* 3–9.

Erchul, W. P., Raven, B. H., and Whichard, S. M. (2001). School psychologist and teacher perceptions of social power in consultation. *Journal of School Psychology 39(6),* 483–97.

Faber, A., and Mazlish, E. (1995). *How To Talk So Kids Will Learn at Home and in School.* New York: Simon & Schuster.

Fast, L., Elliott, A., Hunter, R., and Bellamy, J. (2002). Perspectives from the other side of the (new teacher's) desk. *Brock Education 12(12),* 1–16.

Forton, M. B. (1998). Apology of action. *Responsive Classroom, 10,* 1, 6–7.

French, J. R. P., and Raven, B. (1960). The bases of social power. In D. Cartwright and A. Zander (Eds.), *Group Dynamics: Research and Theory.* Evaston, IL: Row-Peterson.

Ginott, H. (1972). *Between Teacher and Child.* New York: Wyden.

Glasser, W. (1992). *The Quality School: Managing Students without Coercion.* New York: HarperCollins.

Gordon, T. (1989). *Teaching Children Self-Discipline at Home and in School.* New York: Random House.

Harris, T. (1969). *I'm O.K., You're O.K.: A Practical Guide to Transactional Analysis.* New York: Harper & Row.

Housego, B. E. J. (1992). Monitoring student teachers' feelings of preparedness to teach: personal teaching efficacy and teaching efficacy in a new secondary teacher education program. *The Alberta Journal of Educational Research XXXVIII (1),* 49–64.

Kerr, M. M., and Nelson, C. M. (1998). *Strategies for Managing Behavior Problems in the Classroom* (3rd ed.). Toronto, ON: Prentice-Hall.

Kohn, A. (1996). *Beyond Discipline: From Compliance to Community*. Alexandria, VA: Association for Supervision and Curriculum Development.

Lasley. T. J. (1989). A teacher development model for classroom management. *Phi Delta Kappan, 71*, 1, 36–38.

Lepper, M., and Green, D. (1978). *The Hidden Costs of Reward: New Perspectives on Human Motivation*. Hillsdale, NJ: Erlbaum.

Martin, J., and Sugarman, J. (1993). *Models of Classroom Management* (2nd ed.). Calgary, AB: Detselig Enterprises Ltd.

Newfoundland and Labrador Department of Education. (2003). *Curriculum and related documents*. Retrieved July 16, 2003, from **www.gov.nf.ca/edu/sp/main.htm**

Novak, J. M. (2002). *Inviting Educational Leadership*. Toronto, ON: Pearson Education.

Ontario Ministry of Education. (2003). *Curriculum and policy*. Retrieved July 16, 2003, from **www.edu.gov.on.ca/eng/document/curricul/curricul.html**

Putnam, J., and Burke, J. (1992). *Organizing and Managing Classroom Learning Communities*. New York: McGraw Hill.

Schwartz, S., and Pollishuke, M. (2002). *Creating the Dynamic Classroom*. Toronto, ON: Irwin.

Strachota, R. (1996). *On Their Side: Helping Children Take Charge of Their Learning*. Greenfield, MA: Northeast Foundation for Children.

Valentine, M. (1987). *How to Deal with Discipline Problems in the Schools: A Practical Guide for Educators*. Dubuque, IA: Kendall-Hunt.

Wolfgang, C., and Glickman, C. (1995). *Solving Discipline Problems: Methods and Models for Today's Teachers* (2nd ed.). Boston: Allyn and Bacon.

Winter, S. (1983). Rewarding work output of a child with poor attention: you get what you reward. *Behavioural Approaches with Children, 7(4)*, 12–16.

Exercises

1. If one of the long-term goals of classroom management and discipline is for students to gain control over their own behaviour, what are some advantages and disadvantages of using each of the four teacher power bases to help students achieve that goal?

2. Given your knowledge of cognitive and moral development, what factors facilitate or limit the use of each of the four teacher power bases at (a) the primary elementary grades, (b) the intermediate elementary grades, (c) the junior high level, and (d) the senior high level?

3. Do you think there is any relationship between teacher job satisfaction and the power base the teacher uses most frequently to influence student behaviour?

4. Which specific teacher behaviours would indicate to you that a teacher was trying to use (a) referent power and (b) expert power?

5. Using referent authority successfully requires the teacher to communicate caring to students. (a) How can a teacher communicate caring without initiating personal friendships? (b) As you see it, is there a danger in initiating personal friendships with students?

6. How would teachers operating at each of the four authority bases respond to the following situations?

Behaviour	Referent	Expert	Reward/ Legitimate	Coercive
a. A student throws a paper airplane across the room.				
b. A student publicly shows disrespect for the teacher.				
c. A student makes funny noises while another student is giving an oral report.				

7. If one of the long-range goals of classroom management is to help students gain control over their own behaviour, what are the advantages and disadvantages of each of the three theories of classroom management in helping students meet that goal?

8. Given your knowledge of cognitive and moral development, what factors facilitate or limit the use of each of the three theories of classroom management at (a) the primary elementary level, (b) the intermediate elementary level, (c) the junior high level, and (d) the senior high level?

9. How would each of the theories of classroom management respond to the following situations?

Behaviour	Student-Directed	Collaborative	Teacher-Directed
a. A student uses power equipment in a dangerous way.			
b. A student chews gum loudly and blows bubbles.			
c. A student draws moustaches and beards on all the pictures in a textbook.			

10. Is there any danger in using techniques to manage student behaviour that are not consistent with your basic beliefs about student learning and behaviour?

11. Think of the best teacher that you have ever had. Which authority base and classroom management theory was this teacher using the majority of the time?

12. Think of the worst teacher you have ever had. Which authority base and classroom management theory was this teacher using the majority of the time?

Web Sites

The Master Teacher
www.disciplinehelp.com/default.htm)
Includes topics like behaviour management overview and foundations, solutions for handling 117 misbehaviours, behaviour of the day, etc.

The Really Best List of Classroom Management Resources
drwilliampmartin.tripod.com/reallybest.htm
A site that has links to many resources that may help teachers with classroom management challenges.

University of New Orleans College of Education, Classroom Management Links
ss.uno.edu/ss/homepages/cmanage.html
A site that provides links to various resources for classroom management.

7

The Ethics of Teaching

Kenneth A. Strike

Mrs. Porter and Mr. Kennedy have divided their third-grade classes into reading groups. In her class, Mrs. Porter tends to spend the most time with students in the slowest reading group because they need the most help. Mr. Kennedy claims that such behavior is unethical. He maintains that each reading group should receive equal time.

Miss Andrews has had several thefts of lunch money in her class. She has been unable to catch the thief, although she is certain that some students in the class know who the culprit is. She decides to keep the entire class inside for recess, until someone tells her who stole the money. Is it unethical to punish the entire class for the acts of a few?

Ms. Phillips grades her fifth-grade students largely on the basis of effort. As a result, less-able students who try hard often get better grades than students who are abler but less industrious. Several parents have accused Ms. Phillips of unethical behavior, claiming that their children are not getting what they deserve. These parents also fear that teachers in the middle school won't understand Ms. Phillips' grading practices and will place their children in inappropriate tracks.

The Nature of Ethical Issues

The cases described above are typical of the ethical issues that teachers face. What makes these issues ethical?

First, ethical issues concern questions of right and wrong—our duties and obligations, our rights and responsibilities. Ethical discourse is characterized by a unique vocabulary that commonly includes such words as *ought* and *should, fair* and *unfair.*

Kenneth A. Strike is professor of philosophy of education at Cornell University, Ithaca, N.Y. Strike, Kenneth A., "The Ethics of Teaching," *Phi Delta Kappan,* October 1988. Copyright © 1988 by Phi Delta Kappa. Reprinted by permission of author and publisher.

Second, ethical questions cannot be settled by an appeal to facts alone. In each of the preceding cases, knowing the consequences of our actions is not sufficient for determining the right thing to do. Perhaps, because Mrs. Porter spends more time with the slow reading group, the reading scores in her class will be more evenly distributed than the scores in Mr. Kennedy's class. But even knowing this does not tell us if it is fair to spend a disproportionate amount of time with the slow readers. Likewise, if Miss Andrews punishes her entire class, she may catch the thief, but this does not tell us whether punishing the entire group was the right thing to do. In ethical reasoning, facts are relevant in deciding what to do. But by themselves they are not enough. We also require ethical principles by which to judge the facts.

Third, ethical questions should be distinguished from values. Our values concern what we like or what we believe to be good. If one enjoys Bach or likes skiing, that says something about one's values. Often there is nothing right or wrong about values, and our values are a matter of our free choice. For example, it would be difficult to argue that someone who preferred canoeing to skiing had done something wrong or had made a mistake. Even if we believe that Bach is better than rock, that is not a reason to make people who prefer rock listen to Bach. Generally, questions of values turn on our choices: what we like, what we deem worth liking. But there is nothing obligatory about values.

On the other hand, because ethics concern what we ought to do, our ethical obligations are often independent of what we want or choose. The fact that we want something that belongs to someone else does not entitle us to take it. Nor does a choice to steal make stealing right or even "right for us." Our ethical obligations continue to be obligations, regardless of what we want or choose.

Ethical Reasoning

The cases sketched above involve ethical dilemmas: situations in which it seems possible to give a reasonable argument for more than one course of action. We must think about our choices, and we must engage in moral reasoning. Teaching is full of such dilemmas. Thus teachers need to know something about ethical reasoning.

Ethical reasoning involves two stages: applying principles to cases and judging the adequacy or applicability of the principles. In the first stage, we are usually called upon to determine the relevant ethical principle or principles that apply to a case, to ascertain the relevant facts of the case, and to judge the facts by the principles.

Consider, for example, the case of Miss Andrews and the stolen lunch money. Some ethical principles concerning punishment seem to apply directly to the case. Generally, we believe that we should punish the guilty, not the innocent; that people should be presumed innocent until proven guilty; and that the punishment should fit the crime. If Miss Andrews punishes her entire class for the behavior of an unknown few, she will violate these common ethical principles about punishment.

Ethical principles are also involved in the other two cases. The first case involves principles of equity and fairness. We need to know what counts as fair or equal treatment for students of different abilities. The third case requires some principles of due process. We need to know what are fair procedures for assigning grades to students.

However, merely identifying applicable principles isn't enough. Since the cases described above involve ethical dilemmas, it should be possible to argue plausibly for more than one course of action.

For example, suppose Miss Andrews decides to punish the entire class. It could be argued that she had behaved unethically because she has punished innocent people.

She might defend herself, however, by holding that she had reasons for violating ethical principles that we normally apply to punishment. She might argue that it was important to catch the thief or that it was even more important to impress on her entire class that stealing is wrong. She could not make these points by ignoring the matter. By keeping the entire class inside for recess, Miss Andrews could maintain, she was able to catch the thief and to teach her class a lesson about the importance of honesty. Even if she had to punish some innocent people, everyone was better off as a result. Can't she justify her action by the fact that everyone benefits?

Two General Principles

When we confront genuine ethical dilemmas such as this, we need some general ethical concepts in order to think our way through them. I suggest two: the principle of benefit maximization and the principle of equal respect for persons.

The principle of benefit maximization holds, that we should take that course of actions which will maximize the benefit sought. More generally, it requires us to do that which will make everyone, on the average, as well off as possible. One of the traditional formulations of this principle is the social philosophy known as utilitarianism, which holds that our most general moral obligation is to act in a manner that produces the greatest happiness for the greatest number.

We might use the principle of benefit maximization to think about each of these cases. The principle requires that in each case we ask which of the possible courses of action makes people generally better off. Miss Andrews has appealed to the principle of benefit maximization in justifying her punishment of the entire class. Ms. Phillips might likewise appeal to it in justifying her grading system. Perhaps by using grades to reward effort rather than successful performance, the overall achievement of the class will be enhanced. Is that not what is important?

It is particularly interesting to see how the principle of benefit maximization might be applied to the question of apportioning teacher time between groups with different levels of ability. Assuming for the moment that we wish to maximize the overall achievement of the class, the principle of benefit maximization dictates that we allocate time in a manner that will produce the greatest overall learning.

Suppose, however, we discover that the way to produce the greatest overall learning in a given class is for a teacher to spend the most time with the *brightest* children. These are the children who provide the greatest return on our investment of time. Even though the least-able children learn less than they would with an equal division of time, the overall learning that takes place in the class is maximized when we concentrate on the ablest.

Here the principle of benefit maximization seems to lead to an undesirable result. Perhaps we should consider other principles as well.

The principle of equal respect requires that our actions respect the equal worth of moral agents. We must regard human beings as intrinsically worthwhile and treat them accordingly. The essence of this idea is perhaps best expressed in the Golden Rule. We have a duty to accord others the same kind of treatment that we expect them to accord us.

The principle of equal respect can be seen as involving three subsidiary ideas. First, it requires us to treat people as ends in themselves, rather than as means to further our own goals. We must respect their goals as well.

Second, when we are considering what it means to treat people as ends rather than as means, we must regard as central the fact that people are free and rational moral agents. This means that, above all, we must respect their freedom of choice. And we must respect the choices that people make even when we do not agree.

Third, no matter how people differ, they are of equal value as moral agents. This does not mean that we must see people as equal in abilities or capacities. Nor does it mean that we cannot take relevant differences between people into account when deciding how to treat them. It is not, for example, a violation of equal respect to give one student a higher grade than another because that student works harder and does better.

That people are of equal value as moral agents does mean, however, that they are entitled to the same basic rights and that their interests are of equal value. Everyone, regardless of native ability, is entitled to equal opportunity. No one is entitled to act as though his or her happiness counted for more than the happiness of others. As persons, everyone has equal worth.

Notice three things about these two moral principles. First, both principles (in some form) are part of the moral concepts of almost everyone who is reading this article. These are the sorts of moral principles that everyone cites in making moral arguments. Even if my formulation is new, the ideas themselves should be familiar. They are part of our common ethical understandings.

Second, both principles seem necessary for moral reflection. Neither is sufficient by itself. For example, the principle of equal respect requires us to value the well-being. But to value the welfare of ourselves *and* others is to be concerned with maximizing benefits; we want all people to be as well-off as possible.

Conversely, the principle of benefit maximization seems to presuppose the principle of equal respect. Why, after all, must we value the welfare of others? Why not insist that only our own happiness counts or that our happiness is more important than the happiness of others? Answering these questions will quickly lead us to affirm that people are of equal worth and that, as a consequence, everyone's happiness is to be valued equally. Thus our two principles are intertwined.

Third, the principles may nevertheless conflict with one another. One difference between the principle of benefit maximization and the principle of equal respect is their regard for consequences. For the principle of benefit maximization, only consequences matter. The sole relevant factor in choosing between courses of action is which action has the best overall results. But consequences are not decisive in the principle of equal respect; our actions must respect the dignity and worth of the individuals involved, even if we choose a course of action that produces less benefit than some other possible action.

The crucial question that characterizes a conflict between the principle of benefit maximization and the principle of equal respect is this:

When is it permissible to violate a person's rights in order to produce a better outcome? For example, this seems the best way to describe the issue that arises when a teacher decides to punish an entire class for the acts of a few. Students' rights are violated when they are punished for something they haven't done, but the overall consequence of the teacher's action may be desirable. Is it morally permissible, then, to punish everyone?

We can think about the issue of fair allocation of teacher time in the same way. Spending more time with the brightest students may enhance the average learning of the class. But we have, in effect, traded the welfare of the least-able students for the welfare of the ablest. Is that not failing to respect the equal worth of the least-able students? Is that not treating them as though they were means, not ends?

The principle of equal respect suggests that we should give the least-able students at least an equal share of time, even if the average achievement of the class declines.

Indeed, we might use the principle of equal respect to argue that we should allocate our time in a manner that produces more equal results—or a more equal share of the benefits of education.

I cannot take the discussion of these issues any further in this short space. But I do want to suggest some conclusions about ethics and teaching.

First, teaching is full of ethical issues. It is the responsibility of teachers, individually and collectively, to consider these issues and to have informed and intelligent opinions about them.

Second, despite the fact that ethical issues are sometimes thorny, they can be thought about. Ethical reflection can help us to understand what is at stake in our choices, to make more responsible choices, and sometimes to make the right choices.

Finally, to a surprising extent, many ethical dilemmas, including those that are common to teaching, can be illuminated by the principles of benefit maximization and equal respect for persons. Understanding these general ethical principles and their implications is crucial for thinking about ethical issues.

POST NOTE

Ethics seems to be making a comeback. We may not be behaving better, but we are talking about it more. Street crime and white-collar crime, drugs and violence, our inability to keep promises in our personal and professional lives—all these suggest a renewed need for ethics.

Kenneth Strike points out that teaching is full of ethical issues, and it is true that teachers make promises to perform certain duties and that they have real power over the lives of children. This article, however, speaks to only one end of the spectrum of ethical issues faced by the teacher: what we call "hard case" ethics, complex problems, often dilemmas. Certainly these are important, but there are also everyday teaching ethics—the issues that fill a teacher's day. Should I correct this stack of papers or watch *The Simpsons?* Should I "hear" that vulgar comment or stroll right by? Should I read this story again this year before I teach it tomorrow or spend some time with my colleagues in the teachers' lounge? Should I bend down and pick up yet another piece of paper in the hall or figure I've done my share for the day?

Like hard-case ethical issues, these questions, in essence, ask, What's the right thing to do? Our answers to these everyday questions often become our habits, good and bad. These, in turn, define much of our ethical behavior as teachers.

8

Teaching Themes of Care

Nel Noddings

Some educators today—and I include myself among them—would like to see a complete reorganization of the school curriculum. We would like to give a central place to the questions and issues that lie at the core of human existence. One possibility would be to organize the curriculum around themes of care—caring for self, for intimate others, for strangers and global others, for the natural world and its non-human creatures, for the human-made world, and for ideas.[1]

A realistic assessment of schooling in the present political climate makes it clear that such a plan is not likely to be implemented. However, we can use the rich vocabulary of care in educational planning and introduce themes of care into regular subject-matter classes. In this article, I will first give a brief rationale for teaching themes of care; second, I will suggest ways of choosing and organizing such themes; and, finally, I'll say a bit about the structures required to support such teaching.

Why Teach Caring?

In an age when violence among schoolchildren is at an unprecedented level, when children are bearing children with little knowledge of how to care for them, when the society and even the Schools often concentrate on materialistic messages, it may be unnecessary to argue that we should care more genuinely for our children and teach them to care. However, many otherwise reasonable people seem to believe that our educational problems consist largely of low scores on achievement tests. My contention is, first, that we should want more from our educational efforts than adequate academic achievement and, second, that we will not achieve even that meager success unless our children believe that they themselves are cared for and learn to care for others.

There is much to be gained, both academically and humanly, by including themes of care in our curriculum. First, such inclusion may well expand our students' cultural literacy. For example, as we discuss in math classes the attempts of great mathematicians to prove the existence of God or to reconcile a God who is all good with the reality of evil in the world, students will hear names, ideas, and words that are not part of the standard curriculum. Although such incidental learning cannot replace the systematic and sequential learning required by those who plan careers in mathematically oriented fields, it can be powerful in expanding students' cultural horizons and in inspiring further study.

Second, themes of care help us to connect the standard subjects. The use of literature in mathematics classes, of history in science classes, and of art and music in all classes can give students a feeling of the wholeness in their education. After all, why should they seriously study five different subjects if their teachers, who are educated people, only seem to know and appreciate one?

Third, themes of care connect our students and our subjects to great existential questions. What is the meaning of life? Are there gods? How should I live?

Fourth, sharing such themes can connect us person-to-person. When teachers discuss themes of care, they may become real persons to their students and so enable them to construct new knowledge. Martin Buber put it this way:

> Trust, trust in the world, because this human being exists—that is the most inward achievement of the relation in education. Because this human being exists, meaninglessness, however hard pressed you are by it, cannot be the real truth. Because this human being exists, in the darkness the light lies hidden, in fear salvation, and in the callousness of one's fellow-man the great love.[2]

Finally, I should emphasize that caring is not just a warm, fuzzy feeling that makes people kind and likable. Caring implies a continuous search for competence. When we care, we want to do our very best for the objects of our care. To have as our educational goal the production of caring, competent, loving, and lovable people is not anti-intellectual. Rather, it demonstrates respect for the full range of human talents. Not all human beings are good at or interested in mathematics, science, or British literature. But all humans can be helped to lead lives of deep concern for others, for the natural world and its creatures, and for the preservation of the human-made world. They can be led to develop the skills and knowledge necessary to make positive contributions, regardless of the occupation they may choose.

Choosing and Organizing Themes of Care

Care is conveyed in many ways. At the institutional level, schools can be organized to provide continuity and support for relationships of care and trust.[3] At the individual level, parents and teachers show their caring through characteristic forms of attention: by cooperating in children's activities, by sharing their own dreams and doubts, and by providing carefully for the steady growth to the children in their charge. Personal manifestations of care are probably more important in children's lives than any particular curriculum or pattern of pedagogy.

However, curriculum can be selected with caring in mind. That is, educators can manifest their care in the choice of curriculum, and appropriately chosen curriculum can contribute to the growth of children as carers. Within each large domain of care, many topics are suitable for thematic units: in the domain of "caring for self," for example, we might consider life stages, spiritual growth, and what it means to develop an admirable character; in exploring the topic of caring for intimate others, we might include units on love, friendship, and parenting; under the theme of caring for strangers and global others, we might study war, poverty, and tolerance; in addressing the idea of caring for the human-made world, we might encourage competence with the machines that surround us and a real appreciation for the marvels of technology. Many other examples exist. Furthermore, there are at least two different ways to approach the development of such themes: units can be constructed by interdisciplinary teams, or themes can be identified by individual teachers and addressed periodically throughout a year's or semester's work.

The interdisciplinary approach is familiar in core programs, and such programs are becoming more and more popular at the middle school level. One key to a successful interdisciplinary unit is the degree of genuinely enthusiastic support it receives from the teachers involved. Too often, arbitrary or artificial groupings are formed, and teacher are forced to make contributions that they themselves do not value highly. For example, math and science teachers are sometimes automatically lumped together, and rich humanistic possibilities may be lost. If I, as a math teacher, want to include historical, biographical, and literary topics in my math lessons, I might prefer to work with English and social studies teachers. Thus it is important to involve teachers in the initial selection of broad areas for themes, as well as in their implementation.

Such interdisciplinary arrangements also work well at the college level. I recently received a copy of the syllabus for a college course titled "The Search for Meaning," which was co-taught by an economist, a university chaplain, and a psychiatrist.[4] The course is interdisciplinary, intellectually rich, and aimed squarely at the central questions of life.

At the high school level, where students desperately need to engage in the study and practice of caring, it is harder to form interdisciplinary teams. A conflict arises as teachers acknowledge the intensity of the subject-matter preparation their students need for further education. Good teachers often wish there were time in the day to co-teach unconventional topics of great importance, and they even admit that their students are not getting what they need for full personal development. But they feel constrained by the requirements of a highly competitive world and the structures of schooling established by that world.

Is there a way out of this conflict? Imaginative, like-minded teachers might agree to emphasize a particular theme in their separate classes. Such themes as war, poverty, crime, racism, or sexism can be addressed in almost every subject area. The teachers should agree on some core ideas related to caring that will be discussed in all classes, but beyond the central commitment to address themes of care, the topics can be handled in whatever way seems suitable in a given subject.

Consider, for example, what a mathematics class might contribute to a unit on crime. Statistical information might be gathered on the location and number of crimes, on rates for various kinds of crime, on the ages of offenders, and on the cost to society; graphs and charts could be constructed. Data on changes in crime rates could be assembled. Intriguing questions could be asked: Were property crime rates lower when penalties were more severe—when, for example, even children were hanged as thieves? What does an average criminal case cost by way of lawyers' fees, police investigation, and court processing? Does it cost more to house a youth in a detention center or in an elite private school?

None of this would have to occupy a full period every day. The regular sequential work of the math class could go on at a slightly reduced rate (e.g., fewer textbook exercises as home-work), and the work on crime could proceed in the form of interdisciplinary projects over a considerable period of time. Most important would be the continual reminder in all classes that the topic is part of a larger theme of caring for strangers and fellow citizens. It takes only a few minutes to talk about what it means to live in safety, to trust one's neighbors, to feel secure in greeting strangers. Students should be told that metal detectors and security guards were not part of their parents' school lives, and they should be encouraged to hope for a safer and more open future. Notice the words I've used in this paragraph: caring, trust, safety, strangers, hope. Each could be used as an organizing theme for another unit of study.

English and social studies teachers would obviously have much to contribute to a unit on crime. For example, students might read *Oliver Twist,* and they might also study and discuss the social conditions that seemed to promote crime in 19th-century England. Do similar conditions exist in our country today? The selection of materials could include both classic works and modern stories and films. Students might even be introduced to some of the mystery stories that adults read so avidly on airplanes and beaches, and teachers should be engaged in lively discussion about the comparative value of the various stories.

Science teachers might find that a unit on crime would enrich their teaching of evolution. They could bring up the topic of social Darwinism, which played such a strong role in social policy during the late 19th and early 20th centuries. To what degree are criminal tendencies inherited? Should children be tested for the genetic defects that are suspected of predisposing some people to crime? Are females less competent than males in moral reasoning? (Why did some scientists and philosophers think this was true?) Why do males commit so many more violent acts than females?

Teachers of the arts can also be involved. A unit on crime might provide a wonderful opportunity to critique "gangsta rap" and other currently popular forms of music. Students might profitably learn how the control of art contributed to national criminality during the Nazi era. These are ideas that pop into my mind. Far more various and far richer ideas will come from teachers who specialize in these subjects.

There are risks, of course, in undertaking any unit of study that focuses on matters of controversy or deep existential concern, and teachers should anticipate these risks. What if students want to compare the incomes of teachers and cocaine dealers? What if they point to contemporary personalities from politics, entertainment, business, or sports who seem to escape the law and profit from what seems to be criminal behavior? My own inclination would be to allow free discussion of these cases and to be prepared to counteract them with powerful stories of honesty, compassion, moderation, and charity.

An even more difficult problem may arise. Suppose a student discloses his or her own criminal activities? Fear of this sort of occurrence may send teachers scurrying for safer topics. But, in fact, any instructional method that uses narrative forms or encourages personal expression runs this risk. For example, students of English as a second language who write proudly about their own hard lives and new hopes may disclose that their parents are illegal immigrants. A girl may write passages that lead her teacher to suspect sexual abuse. A boy may brag about objects that he has "ripped off." Clearly, as we use these powerful methods that encourage students to initiate discussion and share their experiences, we must reflect on the ethical issues involved, consider appropriate responses to such issues, and prepare teachers to handle them responsibly.

Caring teachers must help students make wise decisions about what information they will share about themselves. On the one hand, teachers want their students to express themselves, and they want their students to trust in and consult them. On the other hand, teachers have an obligation to protect immature students from making disclosures that they might later regret. There is a deep ethical problem here. Too often educators assume that only religious fundamentalists and right-wing extremists object to the discussion of emotionally and morally charged issues. In reality, there is a real danger of intrusiveness and lack of respect in methods that fail to recognize the vulnerability of students. Therefore, as teachers plan units and lessons on moral issues, they should anticipate the tough problems that may arise. I am arguing here that it is morally irresponsible to simply ignore existential questions and themes of care; we must attend to them. But it is equally irresponsible to approach these deep concerns without caution and careful preparation.

So far I have discussed two ways of organizing interdisciplinary units on themes of care. In one, teachers actually teach together in teams; in the other, teachers agree on a theme and a central focus on care, but they do what they can, when they can, in their own classrooms. A variation on this second way—which is also open to teachers who have to work alone—is to choose several themes and weave them into regular course material over an entire semester or year. The particular themes will depend on the interests and preparation of each teacher.

For example, if I were teaching high school mathematics today, I would use religious/existential questions as a pervasive theme because the biographies of mathematicians are filled with accounts of their speculations on matters of God, other dimensions, and the infinite—and because these topics fascinate me. There are so many wonderful stories to be told: Descarte's proof of the existence of God, Pascal's famous wager, Plato's world of forms, Newton's attempt to verify Biblical chronology, Leibnitz' detailed theodicy, current attempts to describe a divine domain in terms of metasystems, and mystical speculations on the infinite.[5] Some of these stories can be told as rich "asides" in five minutes or less. Others might occupy the better part of several class periods.

Other mathematics teachers might use an interest in architecture and design, art, music, or machinery as continuing themes in the domain of "caring for the human-made world." Still others might introduce the mathematics of living things. The possibilities are endless. In choosing and pursuing these themes, teachers should be aware that they are both helping their students learn to care and demonstrating their own caring by sharing interests that go well beyond the demands of textbook pedagogy.

Still another way to introduce themes of care into regular classrooms is to be prepared to respond spontaneously to events that occur in the school or in the neighborhood. Older teachers have one advantage in this area: they probably have a greater store of experience and stories on which to draw. However, younger teachers have the advantage of being closer to their students' lives and experiences; they are more likely to be familiar with the music, films, and sports figures that interest their students.

All teachers should be prepared to respond to the needs of students who are suffering from the death of friends, conflicts between groups of students, pressure to use drugs or to engage in sex, and other troubles so rampant in the lives of today's children. Too often schools rely on experts— "grief counselors" and the like—when what children really need is the continuing compassion and presence of adults who represent constancy and care in their lives. Artificially separating the emotional, academic, and moral care of children into tasks for specially designated experts contributes to the fragmentation of life in schools.

Of course, I do not mean to imply that experts are unnecessary, nor do I mean to suggest that some matters should not be reserved for parents or psychologists. But our society has gone too far in compartmentalizing the care of its children. When we ask whose job it is to teach children how to care, an appropriate initial response is "Everyone's." Having accepted universal responsibility, we can then ask about the special contributions and limitations of various individuals and groups.

Supporting Structures

What kind of schools and teacher preparation are required, if themes of care are to be taught effectively? First, and most important, care must be taken seriously as a major purpose of our schools; that is, educators must recognize that caring for students is fundamental in teaching and that developing people with a strong capacity for care is a major objective of responsible education. Schools properly pursue many other objectives—developing artistic talent, promoting multicultural understanding, diversifying curriculum to meet the academic and vocational needs of all students, forging connections with community agencies and parents, and so on. Schools cannot be single-purpose institutions. Indeed, many of us would argue that it is logically and practically impossible to achieve that single academic purpose if other purposes are not recognized and accepted. This contention is confirmed in the success stories of several innercity schools.[6]

Once it is recognized that school is a place in which students are cared for and learn to care, that recognition should be powerful in guiding policy. In the late 1950s, schools in the U.S., under the guidance of James Conant and others, placed the curriculum at the top of the educational priority list. Because the nation's leaders wanted schools to provide high-powered courses in mathematics and science, it was recommended that small high schools be replaced by efficient larger structures complete with sophisticated laboratories and specialist teachers. Economies of scale were anticipated, but the main argument for consolidation and regionalization centered on the curriculum. All over the country, small schools were closed, and students were herded into larger facilities with "more offerings." We did not think carefully about schools as communities and about what might be lost as we pursued a curriculum-driven ideal.

Today many educators are calling for smaller schools and more family-like groupings. These are good proposals, but teachers, parents, and students should be engaged in continuing discussion about what they are trying to achieve through the new arrangements. For example, if test scores do not immediately rise, participants should be courageous in explaining that test scores were not the main object of the changes. Most of us who argue for caring in schools are intuitively quite sure that children in such settings will in fact become more competent learners. But, if they cannot prove their academic competence in a prescribed period of time, should we give up on caring and on teaching them to care? That would be foolish. There is more to life and learning than the academic proficiency demonstrated by test scores.

In addition to steadfastness of purpose, schools must consider continuity of people and place. If we are concerned with caring and community, then we must make it possible for students and teachers to stay together for several years so that mutual trust can develop and students can feel a sense of belonging in their "school-home."[7]

More than one scheme of organization can satisfy the need for continuity. Elementary school children can stay with the same teacher for several years, or they can work with a stable team of specialist teachers for several years. In the latter arrangement, there may be program advantages; that is, children taught by subject-matter experts who get to know them well over an extended period of time may learn more about the particular subjects. At the high school level, the same specialist teaching might work with students throughout their years in high school. Or, as Theodore Sizer has suggested, one teacher might teach two subjects to a group of 30 students rather than one subject to 60 students, thereby reducing the number of different adults with whom students interact each day.[8] In all the suggested arrangements, placements should be made by mutual consent whenever possible. Teachers and students who hate or distrust one another should not be forced to stay together.

A policy of keeping students and teachers together for several years supports caring in two essential ways: it provides time for the development of caring relations, and it makes teaching themes of care more feasible. When trust has been established, teachers and students can discuss matters that would be hard for a group of strangers to approach, and classmates learn to support one another in sensitive situations.

The structural changes suggested here are not expensive. If a high school teacher must teach five classes a day, it costs no more for three of these classes to be composed of continuing students than for all five classes to comprise new students—i.e., strangers. The recommended changes come directly out of a clear-headed assessment of our major aims and purposes. We failed to suggest them earlier because we had other, too limited, goals in mind.

I have made one set of structural changes sound easy, and I do believe that they are easily made. But the curricular and pedagogical changes that are required may be more difficult. High school textbooks rarely contain the kinds of supplementary material I have described, and teachers are not formally prepared to incorporate such material. Too often, even the people we regard as strongly prepared in a liberal arts major are unprepared to discuss the history of their subject, its relation to other subjects, the biographies of its great figures, its connections to the great existential questions, and the ethical responsibilities of those who work in that discipline. To teach themes of care in an academically effective way, teachers will have to engage in projects of self-education.

At present, neither liberal arts departments nor schools of education pay much attention to connecting academic subjects with themes of care. For example, biology students may learn something of the anatomy and physiology of mammals but nothing at all about the care of living animals; they may never be asked to consider the moral issues involved in the annual euthanasia of millions of pets. Mathematics students may learn to solve quadratic equations but never study what it means to live in a mathematicized world. In enlightened history class students may learn something about the problems of racism and colonialism but never hear anything about the evolution of childhood, the contributions of women in both domestic and public caregiving, or the connection between the feminization of caregiving and public policy. A liberal education that neglects matters that are central to a fully human life hardly warrants the name,[9] and a professional education that confines itself to technique does nothing to close the gaps in liberal education.

The greatest structural obstacle, however, may simply be legitimizing the inclusion of themes of care in the curriculum. Teachers in the early grades have long included such themes as a regular part of their work, and middle school educators are becoming more sensitive to developmental needs involving care. But secondary schools—where violence, apathy, and alienation are most evident—do little to develop the capacity to care. Today, even elementary teachers complain that the pressure to produce high test scores inhibits the work they regard as central to their mission:

the development of caring and competent people. Therefore, it would seem that the most fundamental change required is one of attitude. Teachers can be very special people in the lives of children, and it should be legitimate for them to spend time developing relations of trust, talking with students about problems that are central to their lives, and guiding them toward greater sensitivity and competence across all the domains of care.

NOTES

1. For the theoretical argument, see Nel Noddings, *The Challenge to Care in Schools* (New York: Teachers College Press, 1992); for a practical example and rich documentation, see Sharon Quint, *Schooling Homeless Children* (New York: Teachers College Press, 1994).

2. Martin Buber, *Between Man and Man* (New York: Macmillan, 1965), p. 98.

3. Noddings, chap. 12.

4. See Thomas H. Naylor, William H. Willimon, and Magdalena R. Naylor, *The Search for Meaning* (Nashville, Tenn.: Abingdon Press, 1994).

5. For many more examples, see Nel Noddings, *Educating for Intelligent Belief and Unbelief* (New York: Teachers College Press, 1993).

6. See Deborah Meier, "How Our Schools Could Be," *Phi Delta Kappan,* January 1995, pp. 369–73; and Quint, op. cit.

7. See Jane Roland Martin, *The Schoolhome: Rethinking Schools for Changing Families* (Cambridge, Mass.: Harvard University Press, 1992).

8. Theodore Sizer, *Horace's Compromise: The Dilemma of the American High School* (Boston: Houghton Mifflin, 1984).

9. See Bruce Wilshire, *The Moral Collapse of the University* (Albany: State University of New York Press, 1990).

POST NOTE

Getting over selfishness and self-preoccupation is a major task of one's young years. Schools have a responsibility to help children develop the habit of caring for others, as Nel Noddings demonstrates in this article. She makes a strong case for giving this task a more prominent place in our educational planning.

As children get older, however, they need to develop some sterner virtues to complement caring. They need to acquire self-discipline and self-control. They need to acquire the habit of persistence at hard tasks. They need, too, to learn how to strive for individual excellence and to compete against others without hostility. We could argue that both a strong individual and a strong nation need a balance of strengths. To pursue one strength, such as caring, without developing the full spectrum of human virtues, leaves both the individual and the nation vulnerable.

Section 3

Classroom Engagement

9

Creating a Community of Learners

Teacher-oriented, passive-student approaches to instruction are outdated ... we cannot effectively conduct our classes as if students were sponges who sit passively and absorb attentively.

—A middle school mathematics teacher, quoted in Burden and Byrd (1999, 103)

Taken from Becoming a Teacher, Second Canadian Edition, by Forrest W. Parkay, Beverly Hardcastle Stanford, John P. Vaillancourt, and Heather C. Stephens.

September 26

I set up a classroom library. We don't use the reading textbook. What for? Grown-ups don't read textbooks unless they're forced. I told them we could read real books so long as they don't steal any. I make a big show of counting the books at the end of the day. The kids sigh audibly when they're all there. They look beautiful, like a bookstore, facing out in a big wooden display my uncle made for me. Plus, it covers the bullet-riddled window that never was repaired.

We don't call the subjects the old-fashioned names in Room 211. Math is "Puzzling," science is "Mad Scientist Time," social studies is "T.T.W.E." which stands for "Time Travel and World Exploring," language arts is "Art of Language," and reading is "Free Reading Time." I did this because I figured kids at this age come to me with preconceived notions of what they are good at. This way, a kid who thinks she's no good in math might turn out to be good at Puzzling, and so on.

In the morning, three things happen religiously. I say good morning, real chipper, to every single child and make sure they say good morning back. Then I collect "troubles" in a "Trouble Basket," a big green basket into which the children pantomime unburdening their home worries so they can concentrate on school. Sometimes a kid has no troubles. Sometimes a kid piles it in, and I in turn pantomime bearing the burden. This way, too, I can see what disposition the child is in when he or she enters. Finally, before they can come in, they must give me a word, which I print on a piece of tagboard and they keep in an envelope. It can be any word, but preferably one that they heard and don't really know or one that is personally meaningful. A lot of times the kids ask for *Mississippi,* just to make me spell it. We go over the words when we do our private reading conferences. I learned this from reading *Teacher* by Sylvia Ashton-Warner, who taught underprivileged Maori children in New Zealand. She says language should be an organic experience. I love her approach.

It takes a long time to get in the door this way, but by the time we are in, I know every kid has had and given a kind greeting, has had an opportunity to learn something, and has tried to leave his or her worries on the doorstep. Some kids from other classrooms sneak into our line to use the Trouble Basket or to get a word card.

Then the national anthem blares over the intercom. The kids sing with more gusto now that we shout "Play ball!" at the end. We do Puzzling until 10:30, then we alternate Mad Sciencing with T.T.W.E., lunch, reading aloud, Free Reading and journaling, and Art of Language.

At the end of the day, as the kids exit, they fill in the blanks as I call out, "See you in the [morning!]." "Watch out for the [cars!]." "Don't say [shut up!]." "I love [you!]." This is a game I played with my father at bedtime growing up. It gives the day a nice closure (Codell 1999, 29–31).

The opening scenario for this chapter, taken from *Educating Esmé: Diary of a Teacher's First Year,* by Esmé Raji Codell, a Grade 5 teacher, illustrates how one teacher organized her classroom to create a positive learning environment. Sensitivity to the elements that combine to give a day in the classroom a "nice closure" is the hallmark of a professional, reflective teacher. For teacher education students such as you, making the transition between the study of teaching and actual teaching can be a challenge. The more you understand how "the classroom learning environment develops gradually, in response to the teacher's communication of expectations, modelling of behaviour, and approach to classroom management" (Good and Brophy 1997, 129), the better prepared you will be to make the transition smoothly.

What Determines the Culture of the Classroom?

As you learned in Chapter 5, one definition of *culture* is the way of life common to a group of people. In much the same way, each classroom develops its own culture. The culture of a classroom is determined by the manner in which teachers and students participate in common activities.

The activities that teachers and students engage in are influenced by several factors. As a teacher, you will make countless decisions that will shape the physical and social milieus of your classroom. From seating arrangement, to classroom rules and procedures, to the content and relevance of the curriculum, you will have a strong influence on the culture that emerges in your classroom. You will have many methodological choices to make—when to shift from one activity to another, when to use discussion rather than lecture, or whether to make one requirement rather than another.

Classroom Climate

Part of the environment of the classroom is **classroom climate**—the atmosphere or quality of life in a classroom. The climate of your classroom will be determined by how you interact with your students and "by the manner and degree to which you exercise authority, show warmth and support, encourage competitiveness or cooperation, and allow for independent judgment and choice" (Borich 1996, 470).

Classroom climates are complex and multidimensional; their character is determined by a wide array of variables, many of which are beyond the teacher's control. Nevertheless, our observations of high-performing teachers have confirmed that they take specific steps to create classroom climates with the following eight characteristics:

- A productive, task-oriented focus
- Group cohesiveness
- Open, warm relationships between teacher and students
- Cooperative, respectful interactions among students
- Low levels of tension, anxiety, and conflict
- Humour
- High expectations
- Frequent opportunities for student input regarding classroom activities

These dimensions of classroom climates are within teachers' spheres of influence and are promoted, consciously or unconsciously, by their styles of communicating and treating students. As the following reflections by a student teacher indicate, creating a classroom climate characterized by these eight dimensions is not easy; teachers must make moment-to-moment judgments about what actions will enhance students' motivation to learn.

> The next day, as I was going over the instructions for a science experiment I noticed Sheila and Devon leaning over and whispering. I immediately stopped my presentation and said, "Sheila and Devon, you need to turn around in your seats and stop whispering while I am talking." Both girls rolled their eyes and slowly turned their bodies around in their seats. Neither of them made eye contact with me as I continued the lesson. Although the class was now quiet, I felt uncomfortable myself. As the students gathered the science materials they needed to carry out the experiment in their cooperative learning groups, I noticed that Theresa was passing a note to Sheila. Trying to hide my anger and frustration, I said, "Theresa, you need to get rid of that note now. You can come up and put it in the wastebasket. It is time to be working on science, not note passing." Although singling out the girls worked in the short term, to tell the truth I did not feel comfortable dealing with the situation as I did.
>
> I didn't want to feel as if I was spending half the time handling misbehaviour, but that's just what I was doing. I had learned in school to reach for student strengths, so I am trying to practice the strategy of giving the students a better attitude

about themselves through praise. I explained to them that by correcting their behaviour I was just trying to create a climate in which they could learn. I am trying to be a supportive teacher who still corrects misbehaviour—always with the goal of redirecting students toward meaningful classroom work.

That same afternoon, I began to gather the students together for literature circles. I had four groups reading different novels. Today I was planning to have the students discuss their reactions to the first chapter and make predictions about the rest of the book. For the first five minutes or so, the groups were very productive, and I felt a surge of hope that all would go well. Just then, I noticed Devon lean back in her chair to pass a note to Theresa, who was in a different group. I wanted to shout across the room at them, but I kept my calm and tried to figure out what I should do now (Rand and Shelton-Colangelo 1999, 10–11).

How would you describe this classroom climate using the eight dimensions listed earlier? What changes in the student teacher's behaviour could transform the overall climate?

Although teachers influence the classroom climate by the way they regard and treat students, they also shape it by their instructional decisions. David Johnson and Roger Johnson, two researchers in the area of classroom communication and dynamics, delineate three types of interactions promoted by instructional decisions: cooperative or positive interdependence, competitive or negative interdependence, and individualistic or no interdependence (Johnson and Johnson 1999). To illustrate the three types, Johnson and Johnson suggest that a group project to measure classroom furniture would promote cooperative interdependence; a race to be the first student to measure the furniture would call for competitive interdependence; and having a student measure the furniture independently would be an example of no interdependence. Johnson and Johnson believe that teachers should use strategies that foster all three forms of interactions, depending on their instructional goals, but that, ideally, the emphasis should be on furthering cooperative interdependence.

What words would you use to describe the apparent climate of this classroom? In what ways does this classroom appear to be an effective learning environment? What would you look for to determine if this is a caring classroom?

Classroom Dynamics

Interactions between teachers and students are the very core of teaching. The quality of these interactions reveals to students how the teacher feels about them. Teachers who empathize with students, genuinely respect them, and expect them to learn are more likely to develop a classroom climate free of management problems. In classrooms with positive group dynamics, teachers and students work toward a common goal—learning. In classrooms with negative interactions, the energy of teachers and students may be channeled into conflict rather than into learning.

There is no precise formula to guarantee success in the classroom; however, educational psychologist Anita Woolfolk (1998, 427) suggests four "necessary conditions" to increase student learning through positive interactions:

1. The classroom must be relatively organized and free from constant interruptions and disruptions.
2. The teacher must be a patient, supportive person who never embarrasses students for mistakes.
3. The work must be challenging but reasonable.
4. The learning tasks must be authentic.

Teacher Communication

Successful teachers possess effective communication skills. They express themselves verbally and nonverbally (and in writing) in a manner that is clear, concise, and interesting. They "are able to communicate clearly and directly to their students without wandering, speaking above students' levels of comprehension, or using speech patterns that impair the clarity of what is being presented" (Borich 1996, 11). In addition, they are good listeners. Their students feel that not only are they heard, they are understood.

Effective teachers relish the live, thinking-on-your-feet dimensions of classroom communication. Their communication skills enable them to respond appropriately to events that could sabotage the plans of less effective teachers: a student's clowning, announcements on the public address system, interruptions by other teachers or parents, students' private arguments or romances, or simply the mood of the class at that particular time.

Student Interaction

In addition to engaging in positive, success-oriented interactions with their students, effective teachers foster positive, cooperative interactions among students. As a result, students feel supported by their peers and free to devote their attention to learning. Richard Schmuck and Patricia Schmuck (1997) describe the climate of such classrooms as "mature" and "self-renewing." Their research on classroom group processes has led them to identify the four sequential stages of group development portrayed in Figure 9.1.

Figure 9.1

Characteristics of groups at four stages of development

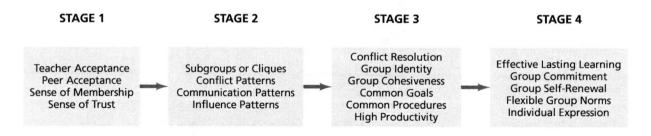

STAGE 1	STAGE 2	STAGE 3	STAGE 4
Teacher Acceptance Peer Acceptance Sense of Membership Sense of Trust	Subgroups or Cliques Conflict Patterns Communication Patterns Influence Patterns	Conflict Resolution Group Identity Group Cohesiveness Common Goals Common Procedures High Productivity	Effective Lasting Learning Group Commitment Group Self-Renewal Flexible Group Norms Individual Expression

During Stage 1 of a class's group development, students are on their best behaviour. Teachers who are aware of this "honeymoon period" use it to their advantage; they discuss and teach classroom rules and procedures, outline their goals, and deliberately set the classroom tone and standards they want. During Stage 2, teachers seeking to promote group development are advised to encourage student participation and communication and to discourage the formation of cliques.

Groups that have met the requirements of the preceding stages move into Stage 3, which lasts for the majority of the expected life of the group (in other words, the semester or the school year). This stage is characterized by the group's willingness to set clear goals, share tasks, and agree on deadlines. At Stage 4, the final stage, group members fully accept responsibility for the group's quality of life, and they continuously strive to improve it.

In addition, teachers who effectively orchestrate group processes in their classrooms recognize that, for good or ill, students as well as teachers exert leadership in classrooms. Wise teachers quickly identify student leaders and develop ways to focus their leadership abilities on the attainment of goals that benefit the entire class. Teachers should also encourage their students to develop leadership skills.

How Can You Create a Positive Learning Environment?

A positive classroom climate and positive classroom dynamics are prerequisites for a good learning environment. Creating and then maintaining a positive learning environment is a multidimensional challenge. While no single set of strategies will ensure success in all situations, educational researchers have identified teacher behaviours that tend to be associated with high levels of student learning. Effective teachers also know how to use these behaviours and *for what purposes* they are best suited. The following sections address three important dimensions of positive learning environments: the caring classroom, the physical classroom environment, and classroom organization, including procedures for grouping students for instruction and managing time.

The Caring Classroom

At this point in your preparation to become a teacher, you may feel uncertain of your ability to create a positive classroom climate and to orchestrate the complex dynamics of the classroom so that you and your students become a cohesive, productive, and mutually supportive group. In your quest to achieve these aims, it will help to remember that an authentic spirit of caring is at the heart of an effective learning environment. "[C]aring interactions between teachers, students, and parents often make the difference between positive school experiences and frustration or alienation" (Chaskin and Rauner 1995, 667–68).

How do teachers establish a **caring classroom?** First, teachers demonstrate caring through their efforts to help all students learn to their fullest potential. "Teachers display genuine caring for students when they find out about students' abilities and motivations. They continue this pervasive caring by providing all their students with the appropriate amount of support, structure, and expectations they need in order to be self-directed, responsible learners" (Zehm and Kottler 1993, 54). In addition, teachers realize that how they speak and listen to students determines the extent to which students believe their teachers care about them. In a synthesis of research on classroom environments that enhance students' learning, Herbert Walberg and Rebecca Greenberg (1997, 46) found that "students learn more when their classes are satisfying, challenging, and friendly and they have a voice in decision making. [When] classes are unfriendly, cliquish, and fragmented, they leave students feeling rejected and therefore impede learning." Table 9.1, based on Walberg and Greenberg's work, presents fifteen dimensions of classroom life and how each influences students' learning at the junior and senior high levels.

While students learn best in caring classrooms, Nel Noddings has suggested that students also must learn to care for others. Toward this end, she recommends reorganizing the school curriculum around "themes of care" and points out that "educators must recognize that caring for students is fundamental in teaching and that developing people with a strong capacity for care is a major objective of responsible education" (Noddings 1995, 678).

Table 9.1

Fifteen dimensions of classroom environment

Dimension	Percent Positive Influence on Learning		Description
Satisfaction	100	(17)	Students enjoy classroom work and find it satisfying.
Challenge	87	(16)	Students find the work difficult and challenging.
Cohesiveness	86	(17)	Students know one another well and are helpful and friendly toward one another.
Physical Environment	85	(15)	Adequate books, equipment, space, and lighting are available.
Democracy	85	(14)	Students share equally in making decisions that affect the entire class.
Goal Direction	73	(15)	Learning goals are clear.
Competition	67	(9)	Competition among students is minimized.
Formality	65	(17)	Class is informal, with few formal rules to guide behaviour.
Speed	54	(14)	Students have sufficient time to finish their work.
Diversity	31	(14)	Students' interests differ and are provided for.
Apathy	14	(15)	Students don't care about what the class does.
Favouritism	10	(13)	All students do not enjoy the same privileges; the teacher has favourites.
Cliquishness	8	(13)	Certain students work only with close friends and refuse to interact with others.
Disorganization	6	(17)	Activities are disorganized and confusing, rather than well organized and efficient.
Friction	0	(17)	Tension and quarreling among students characterize the classroom.

Note: Percent indicates the percentage of research studies that reported a positive influence on learning for that dimension; number in parenthesis indicates number of research studies that investigated that dimension.

Source: Adapted from Herbert J. Walberg and Rebecca C. Greenberg, "Using the Learning Environment Inventory," *Educational Leadership,* May 1997, p. 47.

The Classroom As a Physical Environment

When you become a teacher, the physical environment you work in will probably be similar to that of schools you attended. However, we encourage you, with the help of your students, to make your surroundings as safe, pleasant, and convenient as possible. Fresh air; plants; clean, painted walls; displays of students' work; a comfortable reading or resource area; and a few prints or posters can enhance the quality of teacher–student relationships. Seating arrangements and the placement of other classroom furniture also do much to shape the classroom environment. Although seating by rows may be very appropriate for whole-group instruction or examinations, other arrangements may be more beneficial for other activities. For example, you can enhance small-group activities by moving desks into small clusters in different parts of the room. Figure 9.2 shows the arrangement of a classroom at an exemplary elementary school. The room is designed to encourage students to learn through discovery at learning centres located around the room.

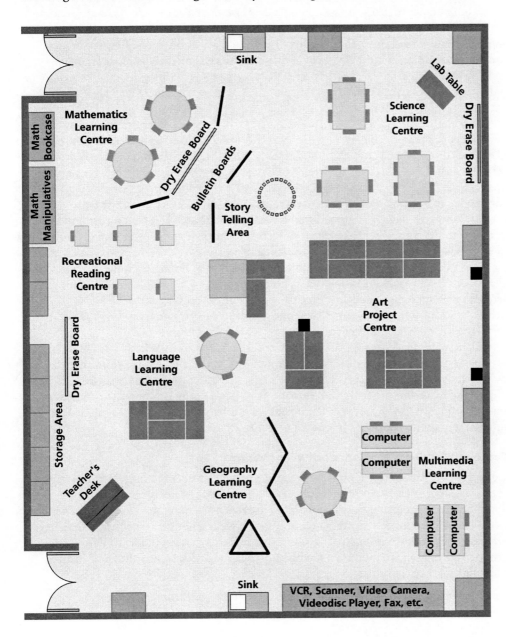

Figure 9.2

Learning centres in an elementary classroom

However you design your classroom, take care to ensure that seating arrangements do not reduce the opportunity of some students to learn. For example, students in some classrooms receive more attention if they are seated in the "action zone," the middle front-row seats and seats on the middle aisle. Teachers often stand near this area and unknowingly give students seated there more opportunities to speak.

Classroom Organization

A factor in positive learning environments is **classroom organization**—the way teachers and students are grouped for instruction, the way learning tasks are structured, and other resources used. The following sections focus on these aspects of classroom organization.

Grouping Students by Ability

Two common approaches for grouping students on the basis of shared characteristics are between-class ability grouping, often called tracking, and within-class ability grouping. Students who attend schools where **between-class ability grouping** is practiced are assigned to classes on the basis of ability or achievement. This practice is not common in Canadian schools. Another form of between-class ability grouping, especially at the high school level, is based on students' goals after graduation. Many high schools, for example, offer honours classes or French Immersion programs.

Research suggests that, for the most part, between-class ability grouping does not contribute to greater achievement (Good and Brophy 2000). Supporters nevertheless claim that teachers are better able to meet the needs of students in homogeneous groupings. Among the alternatives to between-class ability grouping are heterogeneous (or mixed-ability) grouping, regrouping by subject area, the Joplin Plan (regrouping students for reading instruction by ability across grade levels), and cooperative learning.

Within-class ability grouping often is used for instruction in reading and mathematics within a class, where a teacher instructs students in homogeneous, small groups. Within-class grouping is used widely in elementary classrooms. Perhaps you can recall learning to read in a small group with a name such as the Sparrows, the Robins, or the Bluejays. Like tracking, within-class ability grouping can heighten preexisting differences in achievement between groups of students, especially if teachers give high-achieving groups more attention. Also, once students are grouped, they tend not to be regrouped, even when differences in achievement are reduced.

At best, evidence to support student groupings is mixed. Whether students are grouped on the basis of ability, curricular interests, or disabling condition, there is a danger that some group labels can evoke negative expectations, causing teachers to "underteach" certain students, and their peers to isolate or reject them. The most serious consequence, of course, is that students so labelled are taught to feel inadequate, inferior, and limited in their options for growth.

Grouping Students for Cooperative Learning

Cooperative learning is an approach to teaching in which students work in small groups, or teams, sharing the work and helping one another complete assignments. Student-Team-Learning, for example, is a cooperative approach teachers use to increase the basic skills achievement of at-risk students. In cooperative learning arrangements, students are motivated to learn in small groups through rewards that are made available to the group as a whole and to individual members of the group. Cooperative learning includes the following key elements:

- Small groups (four to six students) work together on learning activities.
- Assignments require that students help one another while working on a group project.

Prime Minister's Award for Teaching Excellence Recipient: Sharon Davis

Jack Hulland
Elementary School, Whitehorse, Yukon

Teachers are in the best position to listen to fears and worries that parents express and tie these to educational objectives. Sharon Davis, the school counsellor at Jack Hulland Elementary School in Whitehorse, Yukon cites an interesting example. Parents came to her because they were concerned about the number of fights on the playground. Because of her training as a teacher-counsellor, Davis recognized that the fights were occurring because children did not know how to play.

> "Today's children spend so much time in structured activities that they are unable to play without a referee or coach overseeing them. Anytime something goes wrong, and there is no authority to refer to, a fight breaks out. A group of parents got together and started a group called POPs (Peace on the Playground). The parents trained some Grade 7 students who then showed the younger children ways to resolve problems when playing games."

This effective program was born when parents and a teacher, Davis, had a chance to actually talk with and listen to one another. These exchanges have become a regular part of school life at Jack Hulland Elementary. Groups meet regularly so that parents can share their concerns.

It is important to recognize parents who make the effort and take time out of their busy days to volunteer at school. Every year, Jack Hulland Elementary has a volunteer tea to show appreciation to those individuals, and each volunteer gets a certificate. Davis points out that when children see themselves as part of a community that includes both their teachers and their parents, it changes the way they make decisions that have lifelong consequences.

Source: Reproduced with the permission of the Minister of Public Works and Government Services, 2003. Prime Minister's awards for teaching excellence: Exemplary practices. *Beyond the Classroom Walls*. Retrieved 22 January 2003, from pma-ppm.ic.gc.ca/exemplary/1999/Beyond.html

- In competitive arrangements, groups may compete against one another.
- Group members contribute to group goals according to their talents, interests, and abilities.

In addition, cooperative learning is an instructional method that can strengthen students' interpersonal skills. When students from different racial, ethnic, and cultural backgrounds and mainstreamed special-needs students all contribute to a common group goal, friendships increase and group members tend to view one another as more equal in status and worth.

Cooperative learning also enables students to learn a variety of roles and responsibilities, as the following comments by a Grade 5 science teacher indicate:

> I have the class divided into groups of five students and each group works as a team. The job duties are as follows: principal investigator (PI), materials manager (MM), reader, recorder, and reporter. The PI is the leader of the group and helps mediate when problems occur. The PI is the only student who can come to me with questions during the actual procedure. This rule enables me to monitor the groups and also teaches the group to work independently.

> Students change job duties within their group [for] each activity and every six weeks students change groups. This plan gives each student the experience of working with different classmates as well as learning the responsibility of group participation through performing the different job duties.

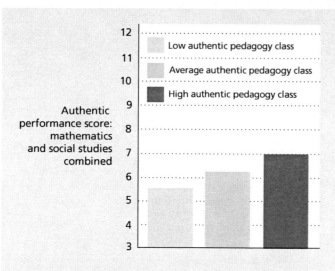

Figure 9.3

Level of authentic student performance for students who experience low, average, and high authentic pedagogy in restructuring elementary, middle, and high schools.

Source: Fred M. Newmann and Gary G. Wehlage, *Successful School Restructuring: A Report to the Public and Educators by the Center on Organization and Restructuring of Schools.* University of Wisconsin-Madison: Center on Organization and Restructuring of Schools, 1995, pp. 21, 55.

Note: The analysis included 2,100 students in 125 classrooms in 23 schools. Most students had either a mathematics or social studies score, and the two subjects were scored on the same 12-point scale. There were no major differences in the effect of authentic pedagogy on achievement between the two subjects.

Delivering Instruction

The delivery of instruction is a key element in creating positive learning environments. What the teacher does and what students do have powerful influences on learning and on the quality of classroom life. A common activity format in elementary schools consists of students doing seatwork on their own or listening to their teachers and participating in whole-class recitations. In addition, students participate in reading groups, games, and discussions; take tests; check work; view films; give reports; help clean up the classroom; and go on field trips.

A teacher must answer the question, "What activity will enable me to accomplish my instructional goals?" Teachers also must realize that learning activities should meet *students'* goals; that is, the activities must be meaningful and authentic for students. **Authentic learning tasks** enable students to see the connections between classroom learning and the world beyond the classroom—both now and in the future. To understand how authentic learning tasks can motivate students to learn, reflect upon your own school experiences. Do you recall memorizing facts only because they would appear on a test? Did you ever wonder why a teacher asked you to complete a learning task? Did you ever feel that a teacher asked you to do "busywork"? What kinds of learning tasks motivated you the most?

Herbert A. Thelen (1981, 86) contends that authenticity is "the first criterion all educational activity must meet." According to Thelen, an activity is authentic for a person if he or she "feels emotionally 'involved' and mentally stimulated ... is aware of choices and enjoys the challenge of making decisions," and feels he or she "has something to bring to the activity and that its outcome will be important" (Thelen 1981, 86). A comprehensive nationwide study of successfully restructured schools reported that "authentic pedagogy" helps students to (1) "construct knowledge" through the use of higher-order thinking, (2) acquire "deep knowledge" (relatively complex understandings of subject matter), (3) engage in "substantive conversations" with teachers and peers, and (4) make connections between substantive knowledge and the world beyond the classroom (Newmann and Wehlage 1995; Newmann et al. 1996). In addition, as Figure 9.3 shows, high authentic pedagogy classes boost achievement for students at all grade levels. The following Professional Reflection illustrates the differences between high and low authentic pedagogy.

Professional Reflection How do low and high authentic pedagogy differ?

Read the following descriptions of low and high authentic pedagogy classes in social studies. What differences do you notice between the two classes? What do you think Mrs. Allen's students thought about the learning tasks they were asked to complete? Ms States' students? When you were a Grade 5 or 6 student, which teacher would you have preferred? Why?

Low Authentic Pedagogy

The task for a class of Grade 5s required them to copy a set of questions about famous explorers from a worksheet and to add the correct short-answer responses in the appropriate spots. The class spent thirty minutes on this exercise, which was part of a larger unit on exploration and which the teacher, Mrs. Allen, described as very consistent with the typical assessment.

During the four times that [researchers] observed Allen's hour-long classes, students read aloud from the textbook, a routine occasionally punctuated with Allen's asking them factual recall questions. During one class, students copied a chart from the board organizing the facts from the reading into categories. After finding more facts to fill up the chart, the students then completed a worksheet crossword puzzle built from the vocabulary words of the lesson (Marks, Newmann, and Gamoran 1996, 59–60).

High Authentic Pedagogy

As an assessment of their learning, Ms States had her class of 5s and 6s research and write a paper on ecology, an assignment that occupied forty hours of class time during the twelve-week grading period. Each student produced several drafts of the paper and met individually with the teacher several times to discuss the drafts. Before they began the project, students received eleven pages of written directions on how to research, organize, and write the paper, including a step-by-step checklist for completing the assignment, a sample outline, and sample bibliography entries. The paper counted for 75 percent of the student's grade for the twelve-week period (Marks, Newmann, and Gamoran, 1996, 60).

Structuring the Use of Time

How teachers use time affects student learning. **Allocated time** is the time teachers allocate for instruction in various areas of the curriculum. Teachers vary widely in their instructional use of time. Educational researchers Tom Good and Jere Brophy report, for example, that "some students [may receive] as much as four times more instructional time in a given subject than other students in the same grade" (Good and Brophy 1997, 29–30).

Researchers have shown that **time on task**—the amount of time students are actively engaged in learning activities—is directly related to learning. As anyone who has ever daydreamed while appearing to pay attention can confirm, time on task is difficult to measure. In response to this difficulty, researchers have introduced the concept of **academic learning time**—the amount of time a student spends working on academic tasks with a high level of success (80 percent or higher) Not surprisingly, learning time, like allocated time, varies greatly from classroom to classroom.

An additional concept that is proving useful in understanding teachers' use of time in the classroom is known as **opportunity to learn** (OTL). OTL is based on the premise that teachers should use time to provide all students with challenging content through appropriate instruction.

In some Canadian provinces, the Departments of Education are making specific minimum daily guidelines regarding how time should be used in classrooms. For example, in 2002, the Nova Scotia Education Department specified how much time elementary students should spend learning the basics. The minimum daily guidelines are:

Grades Primary to 2—Language arts, 90 min; math, 45 min
Grade 3—Language arts, 1 h, 55 min; math, 60 min

Grades 4 to 6—Language arts, 90 min; math, 60 min

Similar time standards are expected to be introduced in junior high schools in 2003. (*Halifax Herald* 2003).

To increase the time available for active learning, many high schools have implemented block scheduling arrangements. **Block scheduling** uses longer blocks of time each class period, with fewer periods each day. Longer blocks of time allow more in-depth coverage of subject matter and lead to deeper understanding and higher-level applications. Block scheduling also gives teachers more time to present complex concepts and students more time to practice applying those concepts to authentic problems.

What Are the Keys to Successful Classroom Management?

For most new teachers, classroom management is a primary concern. How can you prevent discipline problems from arising and keep students productively engaged in learning activities? While effective **classroom management** cannot be reduced to a cookbook recipe, there are definite steps you can take to create an effective learning environment in your classroom. First, it is important to understand that classroom management refers to how teachers structure their learning environments to prevent, or minimize, behaviour problems; *discipline* refers to the methods teachers use *after* students misbehave. *Classroom management* is prevention-oriented, while *discipline* is control-oriented. Second, it is important to recognize that "the key to good management is use of techniques that elicit student cooperation and involvement in activities and thus *prevent* problems from emerging in the first place" (Good and Brophy 1997, 129). In addition, sound classroom management techniques are based on the guidelines for creating an effective learning environment presented previously in this chapter—in other words, (1) creating a caring classroom, (2) organizing the physical classroom environment, (3) grouping students for instruction, (4) providing authentic learning tasks, and (5) structuring the use of time to maximize students' learning. Positive leadership and preventive planning thus are central to effective classroom management.

The Democratic Classroom

Research findings suggest that teachers who allow students to participate in making decisions about the physical classroom environment, classroom rules and procedures, modifications to the curriculum, and options for learning activities also have fewer discipline problems. Students in **democratic classrooms** have both more power and more responsibility than students in conventional classrooms. On the premise that if students are to live in a democracy, they must learn to manage freedom responsibly, teachers model democracy by giving their students some choices and some control over classroom activities. William Glasser, well-known psychiatrist and author of *Quality School* (1998a), *The Quality School Teacher* (1998b), *Choice Theory* (1998c), and (with Karen Dotson) *Choice Theory in the Classroom* (1998), recommends that teachers develop "quality" classrooms based on democratic principles. According to Glasser, many teachers struggle with classroom management because their actions are guided by stimulus–response theory; that is, they try to coerce students through rewards or punishment, or what many teachers term "logical consequences." Instead, Glasser maintains that teachers should establish "quality" environments in the classroom by following **choice theory**—that is, recognizing that human beings make choices that enable them to create "quality worlds" that satisfy four needs: the need to belong, the need for power, the need for freedom, and the need for fun. From a *choice theory* perspective, misbehaviour in the classroom arises when students' learning experiences do not enable them to create quality worlds for themselves. Therefore, teachers "must give up bossing and turn to 'leading'" (Glasser 1997, 600). We follow leaders, Glasser says, because we believe they are concerned about our welfare. To persuade students to do quality schoolwork, teachers must establish warm, noncoercive relationships with students; teach students meaningful skills rather than ask them to memorize information; enable them to experience satisfaction and excitement by working in small teams; and move from teacher evaluation to student self-evaluation.

Preventive Planning

In what other ways can teachers prevent discipline problems from occurring? The key to prevention is excellent planning and an understanding of life in classrooms. In addition, teachers who have mastered the essential teaching skills have fewer discipline problems because students recognize that such teachers are prepared, well organized, and have a sense of purpose. They are confident of their ability to teach all students, and their task-oriented manner tends to discourage misbehaviour.

In a seminal study of how teachers prevent discipline problems, Jacob Kounin looked at two sets of teachers: those who managed their classrooms smoothly and productively with few disruptions and those who seemed to be plagued with discipline problems and chaotic working conditions. He found that the teachers who managed their classrooms successfully had certain teaching behaviours in common: (1) they displayed the proverbial eyes-in-the-back-of-the-head, a quality of alertness Kounin referred to as *withitness,* (2) they used individual students and incidences as models to communicate to the rest of the class their expectations for student conduct—Kounin's *ripple effect,* (3) they supervised several situations at once effectively, and (4) they were adept at handling transitions smoothly (Kounin 1970). In addition to the principles of effective classroom management that emerge from Kounin's study, two key elements of preventive planning are establishing rules and procedures and organizing and planning for instruction.

Establishing Rules and Procedures

Educational researchers have found that effective classroom managers have carefully planned rules and procedures, which they teach early in the year using clear explanations, examples, and practice (Evertson et al. 1997; Good and Brophy 1997). Your classroom rules should be clear, concise, reasonable, and few in number. For example, five general rules for elementary-age students might include: (1) be polite and helpful; (2) respect other people's property; (3) listen quietly while others are speaking; (4) do not hit, shove, or hurt others; and (5) obey all school rules. Rules for the secondary level might stipulate the following: (1) bring all needed materials to class; (2) be in your seat and ready to work when the bell rings; (3) respect and be polite to everyone; (4) respect other people's property; (5) listen and stay seated while someone else is speaking; and (6) obey all school rules (Evertson et al. 1997).

It is important to enforce classroom rules consistently and fairly. "Consistency is a key reason why some rules are effective while others are not. Rules that are not enforced or that are not applied evenly and consistently over time result in a loss of prestige and respect for the person who has created the rules and has the responsibility for carrying them out" (Borich 1996, 364).

Procedures—the routines your students will follow as they participate in learning activities—also are essential for smooth classroom functioning and minimizing opportunities for misbehaviour. How will homework be collected? How will supplies be distributed? How will housekeeping chores be completed? How will attendance be taken? How do students obtain permission to leave the classroom? Part of developing classroom rules and procedures is to decide what to do when students do not follow them. Students must be made aware of the consequences for failing to follow rules or procedures. For example, consequences for rule infractions can range from an expression of teacher disapproval to penalties such as loss of privileges, detention after school, disciplinary conference with a parent or guardian, or temporary separation from the group.

Organizing and Planning for Instruction

The ability to organize instructional time, materials, and activities so that classes run smoothly are skills that will enable you to keep your students engaged in learning, thereby reducing the need for discipline. Time spent planning authentic learning activities that are appropriate to students' needs, interests, and abilities will enable you to enjoy the professional satisfaction that comes from having a well-managed classroom.

In the following, a remedial algebra teacher in an urban school tells how organization and planning helped her effectively teach a class of 27 students, Grades 9 through 12, who enrolled in the class "for a myriad of reasons, [including] absenteeism, learning disabilities, course failure, unwillingness to do required course work, personal problems, nonconformity, and a need for credits":

> I am consistently rewarded by the creative thinking and quickness of these students when they are asked to do something other than listen to my thinking, take notes, and copy examples from the board. I have learned that planning meaningful activities, choosing engaging tasks, organizing small groups and pair problem-solving experiences, valuing thinking, and carefully assessing understanding promote an improved classroom atmosphere where learning is the objective for everyone (Schifter 1996, 75–76).

Effective Responses to Student Behaviour

When student misbehaviour does occur, effective teachers draw from a repertoire of problem-solving strategies. These strategies are based on their experience and common sense, their knowledge of students and the teaching-learning process, and their knowledge of human psychology. There are many structured approaches to classroom management; some are based on psychological theories of human motivation and behaviour, while others reflect various philosophical views regarding the purposes of education. None of these approaches, however, is appropriate for all situations or for all teachers or for all students, and the usefulness of a given method depends, in part, on the teacher's individual personality and leadership style and ability to analyze the complex dynamics of classroom life. In addition, what works should not be the only criterion for evaluating structured or "packaged" approaches to discipline; what they teach students about their self-worth, acting responsibly, and solving problems is also important (Curwin and Mendler 1988, 1989).

Severity of Misbehaviour

Your response to student misbehaviour will depend, in part, on whether an infraction is mild, moderate, or severe and whether it is occurring for the first time or is part of a pattern of chronic misbehaviours. For example, a student who throws a wad of paper at another student might receive a warning for the first infraction, while another student who repeatedly throws objects at other students might receive an after-school detention. Definitions of the severity of misbehaviour vary from school to school and from province to province. Table 9.2 presents one classification of examples of mild, moderate, and severe misbehaviours and several alternative responses.

Table 9.2

Mild, moderate, and severe misbehaviours and some alternative responses

Misbehaviours	Alternative Responses
Mild misbehaviours	**Mild responses**
Minor defacing of school property or property of others	Warning
Acting out (horseplaying or scuffling)	Feedback to student
Talking back	Time out
Talking without raising hand	Change of seat assignment
Getting out of seat	Withdrawal of privileges
Disrupting others	After-school detention
Sleeping in class	Telephone/note to parents
Tardiness	
Throwing objects	
Exhibiting inappropriate familiarity (kissing, hugging)	
Gambling	
Eating in class	
Moderate misbehaviours	**Moderate responses**
Unauthorized leaving of class	Detention
Abusive conduct toward others	Behaviour contract
Noncompliant	Withdrawal of privileges
Smoking or using tobacco in class	Telephone/note to parents
Cutting class	Parent conference
Cheating, plagiarizing, or lying	In-school suspension
Using profanity, vulgar language, or obscene gestures	Restitution of damages
Fighting	Alternative school service (eg., clean up, tutoring)
Severe misbehaviours	**Severe responses**
Defacing or damaging school property or property of others	Detention
Theft, possession, or sale of another's property	Telephone/note to parents
Truancy	Parent conference
Being under the influence of alcohol or narcotics	In-school suspension
Selling, giving, or delivering to another person alcohol, narcotics, or weapons	Removal from school or alternative school placement
Teacher assault or verbal abuse	
Incorrigible conduct, noncompliance	

Source: Gary Bovich, *Effective Teaching Methods,* 3rd ed. Englewood Cliffs, NJ: Merrill, 1996, p. 527. © 1996.
Reprinted by permission of Prentice-Hall, Inc., Upper Saddle River, NJ.

Constructive Assertiveness

The effectiveness of your responses to students' misbehaviour will depend, in part, on your ability to use "constructive assertiveness" (Evertson et al. 1997). Constructive assertiveness "lies on a continuum of social response between aggressive, overbearing pushiness and timid, ineffectual, or submissive responses that allow some students to trample on the teacher's and other students' rights. Assertiveness skills allow you to communicate to students that you are serious about teaching and about maintaining a classroom in which everyone's rights are respected" (Evertson et al, 1997 139). Communication based on constructive assertiveness is neither hostile, sarcastic, defensive, nor vindictive; it is clear, firm, and concise.

Evertson and colleagues (1997) suggest that constructive assertiveness has three basic elements:

- A clear statement of the problem or concern
- Body language that is unambiguous (eg., eye contact with student, erect posture, facial expressions that match the content and tone of corrective statements)
- Firm, unwavering insistence on appropriate behaviour

Lee Cantor developed an approach to discipline based on teacher assertiveness. The approach calls on teachers to establish firm, clear guidelines for student behaviour and to follow through with consequences for misbehaviour. Cantor (1989, 58) comments on how he arrived at the ideas behind assertive discipline: "I found that, above all, the master teachers were assertive; that is, they *taught* students how to behave. They established clear rules for the classroom, they communicated those rules to the students, and they taught students how to follow them." **Assertive discipline** requires teachers to do the following:

1. Make clear that they will not tolerate anyone preventing them from teaching, stopping learning, or doing anything else that is not in the best interest of the class, the individual, or the teacher.
2. Instruct students clearly and in specific terms about what behaviours are desired and what behaviours are not tolerated.
3. Plan positive and negative consequences for predetermined acceptable or unacceptable behaviours.
4. Plan positive reinforcement for compliance. Reinforcement includes verbal acknowledgment, notes, free time for talking, and, of course, tokens that can be exchanged for appropriate rewards.
5. Plan a sequence of steps to punish noncompliance. These range from writing a youngster's name on the board to sending the student to the principal's office (MacNaughton and Johns 1991, 53).

Teacher Problem Solving

When a teacher's efforts to get a student to stop misbehaving are unsuccessful, a problem-solving conference with the student is warranted. A problem-solving conference may give the teacher additional understanding of the situation, thus paving the way for a solution. A conference also helps teacher and student understand the other's perceptions better and begin to build a more positive relationship.

The goal of a problem-solving conference is for the student to accept responsibility for his or her behaviour and make a commitment to change it. While there is no "right way" to conduct a problem-solving conference, Glasser's choice theory lends itself to a conferencing procedure that is flexible and appropriate for most situations.

Students will usually make good choices (ie., behave in an acceptable manner) if they experience success and know that teachers care about them. The following steps are designed to help misbehaving students see that the choices they make may not lead to the results they want.

1. Have the misbehaving student evaluate and take responsibility for his or her behaviour. Often, a good first step is for the teacher to ask, "What are you doing?" and then, "Is it helping you?"
2. Have the student make a plan for a more acceptable way of behaving. If necessary, the student and the teacher brainstorm solutions. Agreement is reached on how the student will behave in the future and the consequences for failure to follow through.
3. Require the student to make a commitment to follow the plan.
4. Don't accept excuses for failure to follow the plan.
5. Don't use punishment or react to a misbehaving student in a punitive manner. Instead, point out to the student that there are logical consequences for failure to follow the plan.
6. Don't give up on the student. If necessary, remind the student of his or her commitment to desirable behaviour. Periodically ask, "How are things going?"

Developing Your Own Approach to Classroom Management

No approach to classroom management is effective with all students at all times. How you respond to misbehaviour in your classroom will depend on your personality, value system, and beliefs about children and will range along a continuum from the "minimum power" of giving students nonverbal cues to the "maximum power" of physical intervention.

Classroom management expert Charles Wolfgang points out that teachers usually present one of three "faces" (or attitudes) to students who misbehave:

1. The *relationship-listening* "face" involves the use of minimum power. This reflects a view that the student has the capabilities to change his or her own behaviour, and that if the student is misbehaving, it is because of inner emotional turmoil, flooded behaviour, or feelings of inner inadequacy.
2. The *confronting-contracting* "face" is one of "I am the adult. I know misbehaviour when I see it and will confront the student to stop this behaviour. I will grant the student the power to decide how he or she will change, and encourage and contract with the student to live up a mutual agreement for behavioural change."
3. The *rules and consequences* "face" is one that communicates an attitude of "This is the rule and behaviour that I want and I will set out assertively to get this action" (Wolfgang 1999, 5–6).

In your journey toward becoming a professional teacher, you will develop a repertoire of strategies for classroom management; then, when you encounter a discipline problem in the classroom, you can analyze the situation and respond with an effective strategy. The ability to do so will give you confidence, like the following beginning teacher:

> I went into the classroom with some confidence and left with lots of confidence. I felt good about what was going on. I established a comfortable rapport with the kids and was more relaxed. Each week I grew more confident. When you first go in you are not sure how you'll do. When you know you are doing OK, your confidence improves.

What Teaching Methods Do Effective Teachers Use?

As we pointed out in our discussion of educational philosophy in Chapter 3, beliefs about teaching and learning, students, knowledge, and what is worth knowing influence the instructional methods a teacher uses. In addition, instruction is influenced by variables such as the teacher's style, learners' characteristics, the culture of the school and surrounding community, and the resources available. All of these components contribute to the "model" of teaching the teacher uses in the classroom. A model of teaching provides the teacher with rules of thumb to follow to create a particular kind of learning environment, or, as Bruce Joyce, Marsha Weil, and Emily Calhoun point out in *Models of Teaching* (2000, 13), a model of teaching is "a description of a learning environment." Table 9.3 presents brief descriptions of four widely used models of teaching.

Table 9.3

Four instructional models

	Goals and Rationale	Methods
Cooperative Learning	Students can be motivated to learn by working cooperatively in small groups if rewards are made available to the group as a whole and to individual members of the group.	■ Small groups (four to six students) work together on learning activities. ■ Assignments require that students help one another while working on a group project. ■ In competitive arrangements, groups may compete against one another. ■ Group members contribute to group goals according to their talents, interests, and abilities.
Theory into Practice	Teachers make decisions in three primary areas: content to be taught, how students will learn, and the behaviours the teacher will use in the classroom. The effectiveness of teaching is related to the quality of decisions the teacher makes in these areas.	The teacher follows seven steps in the classroom: 1. Orients students to material to be learned 2. Tells students what they will learn and why it is important 3. Presents new material that consists of knowledge, skills, or processes students are to learn 4. Models what students are expected to do 5. Checks for student understanding 6. Gives students opportunity for practice under the teacher's guidance 7. Makes assignments that give students opportunity to practice what they have learned on their own
Behaviour Modification	Teachers can shape student learning by using various forms of enforcement. Human behaviour is learned, and behaviours that are positively reinforced (rewarded) tend to increase and those that are not reinforced tend to decrease.	■ Teacher begins by presenting stimulus in the form of new material. ■ The behaviour of students is observed by the teacher. ■ Appropriate behaviours are reinforced by the teacher as quickly as possible.
Nondirective Teaching	Learning can be facilitated if teachers focus on personal development of students and create opportunities for students to increase their self-understanding and self-concepts. The key to effective teaching is the teacher's ability to understand students and to involve them in a teaching–learning partnership.	■ Teacher acts as a facilitator of learning. ■ Teacher creates learning environments that support personal growth and development. ■ Teacher acts in the role of a counsellor who helps students to understand themselves, clarify their goals, and accept responsibility for their behaviour.

Effective teachers use a repertoire of teaching models and assessment strategies, depending upon their situations and the goals and objectives they wish to attain. Your teaching strategies in the classroom will most likely be eclectic, that is, a combination of several models and assessment techniques. Also, as you gain classroom experience and acquire new skills and understanding, your personal model of teaching will evolve, enabling you to respond appropriately to a wider range of teaching situations.

Methods Based on Learning New Behaviours

Many teachers use instructional methods that have emerged from our greater understanding of how people acquire or change their behaviours. **Direct instruction,** for example, is a systematic instructional method that focuses on the transmission of knowledge and skills from the teacher (and the curriculum) to the student. Direct instruction is organized on the basis of observable learning behaviours and the actual products of learning. Generally, direct instruction is most appropriate for step-by-step knowledge acquisition and basic skill development but not appropriate for teaching less structured, higher-order skills such as writing, the analysis of social issues, and problem solving.

Extensive research was conducted in the 1970s and 1980s on the effectiveness of direct instruction (Gagné, 1974, 1977; Good and Grouws, 1979; Rosenshine, 1988; Rosenshine and Stevens, 1986). The following eight steps are a synthesis of research on direct instruction and may be used with students ranging in age from elementary to senior high school.

1. Orient students to the lesson by telling them what they will learn.
2. Review previously learned skills and concepts related to the new material.
3. Present new material, using examples and demonstrations.
4. Assess students' understanding by asking questions; correct misunderstandings.
5. Allow students to practice new skills or apply new information.
6. Provide feedback and corrections as students practice.
7. Include newly learned material in homework.
8. Review material periodically.

A direct instruction method called **mastery learning** is based on two assumptions about learning: (1) virtually all students can learn material if given enough time and taught appropriately and (2) students learn best when they participate in a structured, systematic program of learning that enables them to progress in small, sequenced steps (Carroll 1963; Bloom 1981):

1. Set objectives and standards for mastery.
2. Teach content directly to students.
3. Provide corrective feedback to students on their learning.
4. Provide additional time and help in correcting errors.
5. Follow a cycle of teaching, testing, reteaching, and retesting.

In mastery learning, students take diagnostic tests and then are guided to do corrective exercises or activities to improve their learning. These may take the form of programmed instruction, workbooks, computer drill and practice, or educational games. After the corrective lessons, students are given another test and are more likely to achieve mastery.

Methods Based on Child Development

As you learned in Chapter 6, children move through stages of cognitive, psychosocial, and moral development. Effective instruction includes methods that are developmentally appropriate, meet students' diverse learning needs, and recognize the importance of learning that occurs in social contexts. For example, one way that students reach higher levels of development is to observe and then imitate their parents, teachers, and peers, who act as models. As Woolfolk (1998, 229) points out:

> Modeling has long been used, of course, to teach dance, sports, and crafts, as well as skills in subjects such as home economics, chemistry, and shop. Modeling can also be applied deliberately in the classroom to teach mental skills and to broaden horizons—to teach new ways of thinking. Teachers serve as models for a vast range of behaviors, from pronouncing vocabulary words, to reacting to the seizure of an epileptic student, to being enthusiastic about learning.

Effective teachers also use **modelling** by "thinking out loud" and following three basic steps of "mental modelling" (Duffy and Roehler 1989):

1. Showing students the reasoning involved
2. Making students conscious of the reasoning involved
3. Focusing students on applying the reasoning

In this way, teachers can help students become aware of their learning processes and enhance their ability to learn.

Since the mid-1980s, several educational researchers have examined how learners *construct* understanding of new material. "Constructivist views of learning, therefore, focus on how learners make sense of new information—how they construct meaning based on what they already know" (Parkay and Hass 2000, 168). Teachers with this constructivist view of learning focus on students' thinking about the material being learned and, through carefully orchestrated cues, prompts, and questions, help students arrive at a deeper understanding of the material. The common elements of **constructivist teaching** include the following:

- The teacher elicits students' prior knowledge of the material and uses this as the starting point for instruction.
- The teacher not only presents material to students, but he or she also responds to students' efforts to learn the material. While teaching, the teacher must *learn about students' learning.*
- Students not only absorb information, but they also actively use that information to construct meaning.
- The teacher creates a social milieu within the classroom, a community of learners, that allows students to reflect and talk with one another as they construct meaning and solve problems.

Constructivist teachers provide students with support, or "scaffolding," as they learn new material. By observing the child and listening carefully to what he or she says, the teacher provides **scaffolding** in the form of clues, encouragement, suggestions, or other assistance to guide students' learning efforts. The teacher varies the amount of support given on the basis of the student's understanding—if the student understands little, the teacher gives more support; conversely, the teacher gives progressively less support as the student's understanding becomes more evident. Overall, the teacher provides just enough scaffolding to enable the student to "discover" the material on his or her own.

The concept of scaffolding is based on the work of L. S. Vygotsky, a well-known Soviet psychologist. Vygotsky (1978, 1980) coined the term *zone of proximal development* to refer to the point at which students need assistance in order to continue learning. The effective teacher is sensitive to the student's zone of development and ensures that instruction neither exceeds the student's current level of understanding nor underestimates the student's ability.

Methods Based on the Thinking Process

Some instructional methods are derived from the mental processes involved in learning, thinking, remembering, problem solving, and creativity. **Information processing,** for example, is a branch of cognitive science concerned with how people use their long- and short-term memory to access information and solve problems. The computer is often used as an analogy for information processing views of learning:

> Like the computer, the human mind takes in information, performs operations on it to change its form and content, stores the information, retrieves it when needed, and generates responses to it. Thus, processing involves gathering and representing information, or *encoding;* holding information, or *storage;* and getting at the information when needed, or *retrieval.* The whole system is guided by *control processes* that determine how and when information will flow through the system (Woolfolk 1998, 249-50).

Although several systematic approaches to instruction are based on information processing—teaching students how to memorize, think inductively or deductively, acquire concepts, or use the scientific method, for example—they all focus on how people acquire and use information. Table 9.4 presents general teaching guidelines based on ideas from information processing.

In **inquiry learning** and **discovery learning** students are given opportunities to inquire into subjects so that they "discover" knowledge for themselves. When teachers ask students to go beyond information in a text to make inferences, draw conclusions, or form generalizations; and when teachers do not answer students' questions, preferring instead to have students develop their own answers, they are using methods based on inquiry and discovery learning. These methods are best suited for teaching

---

Table 9.4

Using information processing ideas in the classroom

- Make sure you have the students' attention. For example, begin a lesson by asking a question that stimulates interest in the topic.
- Help students separate essential from nonessential details and focus on the most important information as it relates to instructional objectives.
- Help students make connections between new information and what they already know.
- Provide for repetition and review of information and the practice of skills.
- Present material in a clear, organized, concrete way. For example, give students a brief outline to follow and summarize lessons.
- Focus on meaning, not memorization.

Source: Adapted from Anita E. Woolfolk, *Educational Psychology,* 7th ed. Boston: Allyn and Bacon, 1998, p. 265–68.

concepts, relationships, and theoretical abstractions, and for having students formulate and test hypotheses. The following example shows how inquiry and discovery learning in a Grade 1 classroom fostered a high level of student involvement and thinking.

> The children are gathered around a table on which a candle and jar have been placed. The teacher, Jackie Wiseman, lights the candle and, after it has burned brightly for a minute or two, covers it carefully with the jar. The candle grows dim, flickers, and goes out. Then she produces another candle and a larger jar, and the exercise is repeated. The candle goes out, but more slowly. Jackie produces two more candles and jars of different sizes, and the children light the candles, place the jars over them, and the flames slowly go out. "Now we're going to develop some ideas about what has just happened," she says. "I want you to ask me questions about those candles and jars and what you just observed" (Joyce, Weil, and Calhoun 2000, 3).

Methods Based on Peer-Mediated Instruction

Student peer groups can be a deterrent to academic performance (Steinberg et al. 1996), but they can also motivate students to excel. Because school learning occurs in a social setting, **peer-mediated instruction** provides teachers with options for increasing students' learning. Cooperative learning, described earlier in this chapter, is an example of peer-mediated instruction. Another example is **group investigation**, in which the teacher's role is to create an environment that allows students to determine what they will study and how. Students are presented with a situation to which they "react and discover basic conflicts among their attitudes, ideas, and modes of perception. On the basis of this information, they identify the problem to be investigated, analyze the roles required to solve it, organize themselves to take these roles, act, report, and evaluate these results" (Thelen 1960, 82).

The teacher's role in group investigation is multifaceted; he or she is an organizer, guide, resource person, counsellor, and evaluator. The method is very effective in increasing student achievement (Sharan and Sharan 1989/90, 17–21), positive attitudes toward learning, and the cohesiveness of the classroom group. The model also allows students to inquire into problems that interest them and enables each student to make a meaningful, authentic contribution to the group's effort based on his or her experiences, interests, knowledge, and skills.

Other common forms of peer-mediated instruction include peer tutoring and cross-age tutoring. In **peer-tutoring** arrangements, students are tutored by other pupils in the same class or the same grade. **Cross-age tutoring** involves, for example, Grade 6 students tutoring Grade 2 students in reading. Research clearly shows that with proper orientation and training, cross-age tutoring can greatly benefit both "teacher" and learner (Henriques 1997; Schneider and Barone 1997; Utay and Utay 1997; Zukowski 1997). Pilot programs pairing students at risk of dropping out of school with younger children and with special-needs students have proved especially successful.

What Are Some Characteristics of Effective Teaching?

The *outcomes* of effective teaching are relatively easy to enumerate: (1) students acquire an understanding of the subject at hand; (2) they can apply what they have learned to new situations; and (3) they have a desire to continue learning. However, if we wish to identify the *characteristics* of effective teaching, we find ourselves confronted with a more difficult task.

Domain 1: Planning and Preparation

- Demonstrating knowledge of content and pedagogy
- Demonstrating knowledge of students
- Selecting instructional goals
- Demonstrating knowledge of resources
- Designing coherent instruction
- Assessing student learning

Domain 3: Instruction

- Communicating clearly and accurately
- Using questioning and discussion techniques
- Engaging students in learning
- Providing feedback to students
- Demonstrating flexibility and responsiveness

Domain 2: The Classroom Environment

- Creating an environment of respect and rapport
- Establishing a culture for learning
- Managing classroom procedures
- Managing student behaviour
- Organizing physical space

Domain 4: Professional Responsibilities

- Reflecting on teaching
- Maintaining accurate records
- Communicating with families
- Contributing to the school and district
- Growing and developing professionally
- Showing professionalism

What do effective teachers do when they are teaching? How do they communicate with students? How do they manage classroom activities? What models of teaching do they use? As the previous discussions of classroom cultures, learning environments, classroom management, and teaching methods suggest, answers to questions such as these are not easy to formulate. However, one broad helpful view of the characteristics that underlie all effective teaching is the "Framework for Teaching," developed as part of the Praxis Series: Professional Assessments for Beginning Teachers. According to the Praxis framework, teachers must be proficient in four domains: planning and preparation, structuring classroom environment, instruction, and professional responsibilities. Teachers must be effective within these domains while taking into account individual, developmental, and cultural differences among students and differences among subjects. Figure 9.4 shows the tasks teachers should be able to perform within the four domains.

Figure 9.4

The Praxis framework for teaching

Source: Charlotte Danielson, *Enhancing Professional Practice: A Framework for Teaching.* Alexandria, VA: Association for Supervision and Curriculum Development, 1996.

Establishing Goals

One characteristic of successful teachers is that they focus on the outcomes—the results or consequences of their teaching. Regardless of the instructional method used, with clear goals to provide guidance, teachers can make good decisions about classroom activities to select or develop.

Goals are general statements of purpose that guide schools and teachers as they develop instructional programs. **Instructional goals** can be derived from the curriculum or

From this photo, what can you tell about this teacher's proficiency in planning and preparation, structuring classroom environment, instruction, and professional responsibilities?

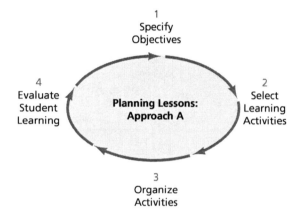

1
Specify
Objectives

4
Evaluate
Student
Learning

**Planning Lessons:
Approach A**

2
Select
Learning
Activities

3
Organize
Activities

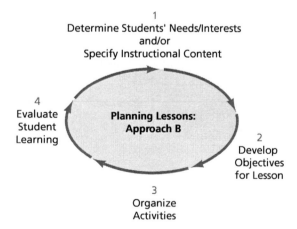

1
Determine Students' Needs/Interests
and/or
Specify Instructional Content

4
Evaluate
Student
Learning

**Planning Lessons:
Approach B**

2
Develop
Objectives
for Lesson

3
Organize
Activities

Figure 9.5

Two approaches to planning lessons

content being taught; or, as you saw in Chapter 4, they can be derived from various educational philosophies. Goals range from very broad statements of purpose that apply to a large number of students to those that apply to students in a particular classroom. In addition, teachers evaluate their teaching by how well students master certain objectives. **Learning objectives** are specific, measurable outcomes of learning that students are to demonstrate. For example, "Students will identify the structural elements of cells and explain their functions" might be a specific objective toward a larger goal of "understanding biological concepts and principles."

Successful teachers also realize that the quality of their teaching depends on what students can *do*, not only on what they *know*. To evaluate their effectiveness in this area, teachers assess students' mastery of performance tasks in which they apply their learning to a new problem. Figure 9.5 illustrates two different approaches to lesson planning that take into account targeted goals, objectives, and performance tasks.

Appendix 9.1 provides guidelines for teachers in providing students with Study Skills information, which can be incorporated into lessons for effective instruction.

Linking Assessment with Instruction

In assessing students' learning, teachers make judgments about the performance of students and about their own performance as teachers. Successful teachers use **assessment** to evaluate the effectiveness of their teaching because they recognize that how well students learn depends on how well they teach.

Should the use of standardized testing be increased?

Assessment of student learning is essential: students, teachers, school administrators, parents, and the public need to know how schools and students are doing. Not knowing is like shooting arrows at a target out of your line of vision and never being told how close you are to the bull's-eye. Simply to be told "Shoot another one, shoot another one" will not help you get closer to the target. Madeline Hunter, UCLA teacher educator and author of *Enhancing Teaching* (1994), used that illustration to emphasize the importance of feedback. Although most educators agree with Hunter in general principle, they disagree as to which type of assessment is best and how extensive it should be.

Canada is beginning to take the lead of the United States, Great Britain, and New Zealand in instituting standardized testing. Testing has been an integral part of Canadian schools since their inception and all provinces engage in some form of large-scale assessment. Under the Constitution, individual Canadian provinces are responsible for education. Provincially, testing varies with some provinces assessing Grades 3, 6, and 9, or 4, 7, 10 and Grade 12. A number of Canadian provinces also participate in international assessment programs such as the Third International Math and Science Study (TIMSS).

The Canadian Council of Ministers of Education (CMEC) developed the school Achievement Indicators Program (SAIP) in 1993 to provide information to the Canadian public on how well their education systems were meeting the needs of students and society. The SAIP is a cyclical program of pan-Canadian assessment of student achievement in math, reading and writing, and science (Council of Ministers of Education, Canada).

Opponents of increasing the use of standardized testing note that alternative forms of assessment—teacher-constructed tests, student portfolios, evaluations of student performances, and teacher judgments—are better ways to determine how well students are learning. They fear that mandating more standardized testing will discriminate against schools with greater populations of language-minority students and students from lower socio-economic groups. They also warn that curricula will be narrowed by teaching to the test and express concern that the consequences of poor test results can negatively affect the lives of students and teachers.

Where do you stand on this issue? Should the use of standardized testing be increased?

Yes, the use of standardized testing should be increased.

Educators must be held accountable for student learning. Parents entrust their children to schools to educate them well. The community invests in school buildings, teachers' salaries, and curricular resources, and thus people have a right to know how well the schools are doing. For schools to expect to proceed without any accountability is unreasonable and irresponsible.

Educators themselves also need to know how they are doing. As in Madeline Hunter's archery illustration, if educators do not know whether they are on target, they are unable to improve their performance. Teachers should be continually evaluating their strategies and education programs in terms of the programs' effectiveness in promoting students' learning. If teachers do not do this, students, who are the centre of the education enterprise, are the losers. The portion of their lives that students spend in school can be a waste rather than a life-changing boon. For teachers not to take care in assessing their own effectiveness is to risk short-changing children and youth.

Canada spends proportionally more money on education than most other industrialized countries. Tests such as the Canadian SAIP can provide Canada-wide data on the achievement levels of 13 and 16 year old students; the results are used to assess whether students know more or less than expected and to assist provincial departments of education with future curriculum decisions (Osborne 1999). A recent study commissioned for the Advancement of Excellence in Education, Student Assessment in Canada, calls for a broad level of testing in all provinces in order to measure and improve school and student performance (Smythe 2001).

No, the use of standardized testing should not be increased.

The arguments against using more standardized testing are summarized succinctly and dramatically by George

Madaus, Boston College Professor of Education and Director of the Center for the Study of Testing:

The tests can become the ferocious master of the educational process, not the compliant servant they should be. Measurement-driven instruction invariably leads to cramming; narrows the curriculum; concentrates attention on those skills most amenable to testing (and today this means skills amenable to the multiple-choice format); constrains creativity and spontaneity of teachers and students; and, finally, demeans the professional judgment of teachers. (Madaus 1999)

Other opponents are especially concerned about the misuse of the resulting scores. W. James Popham, author of *Testing! Testing! What Every Parent Should Know about School Tests* (1999), points out that "even the standardized test items that actually measure knowledge and skills that might be taught in school will often fail to coincide with the content stressed in a specific school." When that is the case, the school rates poorly in comparison to other schools even though it may have been doing a superior job teaching the content it deems important.

Some districts evaluate teachers in terms of how well their students score on standardized tests, ignoring the fact that the tests are more reflective of "what children bring to school, not what they learn there," Popham argues. He urges teachers to "become thoroughly familiar with the innards of any standardized test being used in their setting. These tests are not sacrosanct instruments." Teachers should investigate a test's history, development, current use, norming population, fit with the school's curriculum and goals, and the number of questions in each skill area. Such knowledge is essential for interpreting the results to children, parents, principals, district administrators—and the news media. The last group can unfairly damage a school's reputation, a realistic fear that drives some administrators to overstress test scores, promoting teaching to the test and narrowing curriculum in the process.

Most important is the impact the scores of questionable standardized tests can have on the education and lives of children and young people. An overreliance on standardized test scores can lead to inappropriate assignments to remediation programs, unjustified retentions of students, increases in dropout rates, and reduced career opportunities for students. Adriana Steinberg, in a 1999 *Harvard Education Letter,* provides one illustration of the human dimension of the problem:

Standardized test scores do not differentiate between a newly mainstreamed bilingual student who rewrites each paper four or five times and meets twice a week after school with a math tutor, but who does not yet know enough academic English to decipher arcane test items, and a student whose disengage-

ment from school and low estimation of his own academic abilities cause him to give up midway through the first section of the test and leave much of the rest blank.

The Canadian Teachers Federation has written extensively against the rising tide of standardized testing. In their *Standardized Testing: Undermining Equity in Education*, they argue that standardized tests are inadequate in assessing complex student learning and development. The publication examines the effects of standardized testing on educational equity with particular emphasis on the impact of testing bias and the misuse of test data (Froese-Germain 1999).

Teachers know better than developers of tests how *their* students are doing, why they are doing well or poorly, and how to assist them individually. Their opinions matter much more than scores on standardized tests taken in an artificial setting on one or two days of the entire school year. Their judgments deserve the public's trust. Standardized testing should not be increased, because teachers need all the time they can get to do their most important work—teaching.

Where do you stand on this issue?

1. What is your position on increasing standardized testing? Why do you hold this position?

2. Which form of assessment has been most helpful to you as a student? How can you tell?

3. Propose a compromise position regarding standardized testing.

4. How would you interpret children's standardized test scores for their parents?

5. Find two examples of standardized tests and evaluate the aspects of tests that Popham cites.

Recommended Sources

Alberta Teachers Association. (2001). The Learning Team, "Teachers and Parents Need to Fight Standardized Testing," Volume 3, April 3, 2001. Retrieved October 24, 2003 from: www.teachers.ab.ca/resources/ata.learningteam/index.cfm?p_ID=1809&Volume=4&Issue=3

British Columbia Teachers' Federation. (1997). *Opportunities to learn: Accountability in education in British Columbia.* A Brief to the Minister of Education, Skills, and Training for the British Columbia Teachers' Federation. Retrieved October 24, 2003 from www.bctf.ca/publications/briefs/ocg/

Canadian Teachers Federation. (2000). *Assessment and eval-uation: National Testing.* Retrieved October 24, 2003 from: www.ctf-fce.ca/en/default.htm

Earl, L.M. (1999). Assessment and accountability in educa-tion: improvement or surveillance" Education Canada. 39 (3). 4-6.

Madaus, G. F. (1999). *The influence of testing on the curricu-lum.* In Margaret J. Early and Kenneth J. Rehage (Eds.). *Issues in curriculum: A selection of chapters from past NSSE yearbooks: Ninety-eighth yearbook of the national society for the study of education, Part II.* Chicago: Uni-versity of Chicago Press.

Osborne, K. (1999). *Education: A guide to the Canadian school debate—or, who want what and why?* Montreal: Penguin/McGill Institute.

Popham, W. J. (1999, May 12). Commentary: assessment apa-thy. *Education Week.*

Rose, L. C. and Gallup, A. M. (1998, September). The 30th annual Phi Delta Kappa/Gallup poll of the public's atti-tudes toward the public schools. *Phi Delta Kappan.*

Steinberg, A. (1999, March/April). The human cost of over-reliance on tests. *Harvard Education Letter.*

To assess students' learning, teachers use measurement and evaluation techniques. **Measurement** is the gathering of quantitative data related to the knowledge and skills students have acquired. Measurement yields scores, rankings, or ratings that teachers can use to compare students. **Evaluation** involves making judgments about or assign-ing a value to those measurements. **Formative evaluation** occurs when the teacher measures students' learning for instruction. **Summative evaluation** is used by teachers to determine grades at the end of a unit, semester, or year and to decide whether stu-dents are ready to proceed to the next phase of their education.

Authentic assessments (sometimes called *alternative assessments*) require students to use higher-level thinking skills to perform, create, or solve real-life problems—not just choose one of several designated responses as on a multiple-choice test. The authen-tic assessments a teacher might use include evaluating the quality of individual and small-group projects, videotaped demonstrations of skills, or participation in com-munity-based activities. In science, for example, students might design and conduct an experiment; in mathematics, they might explain in writing how they solved a problem. Authentic assessments require students to solve problems or to work on tasks that approximate as much as possible those they will encounter beyond the classroom. **Portfolio assessment** is based on a collection of student work that "tell[s] a story of a learner's growth in proficiency, long-term achievement, and significant accomplish-ments in a given academic area" (Tombari and Borich 1999, 164). For students, an important part of portfolio assessment is clarifying the criteria used to select work to be included in the portfolio. **Performance assessment** is used to determine what stu-dents can do as well as what they know. In some cases, the teacher observes and then evaluates an actual performance or application of a skill; in others, the teacher eval-uates a product created by the student.

Examples of Effective Teachers

This chapter concludes with comments by several effective teachers in which they describe strategies that help them create communities of learners. As you read the teach-ers' comments, identify how each has put into practice many of the concepts dis-cussed in this chapter. In addition, reflect on the degree to which that teacher's approach would "fit" your personality and value system.

How do effective teachers use technology to enhance their instruction?

Effective teachers recognize that educational technologies should be used to enhance students' inquiry, reflection, and problem solving rather than merely "grafted" onto existing practices. They also recognize that "schools need not be technology rich to be 'information age.' Rather, the phrase 'information age' signals that the schools focus on developing students' critical habits of mind with regard to ideas and evidence—the ability to use their minds well" (Brunner and Tally 1999, 32).

In the following excerpt, a teacher from Newfoundland describes in her own words how she effectively integrated technology into her Grade 9 curriculum.

Anna Gosse,
Middle School Science Teacher, Newfoundland

The challenge for teachers is to actively involve students in curriculum that is enhanced by the use of technology and that illustrates how the technological skills that they possess can be used for practical purposes.

This is my fourth year teaching and the internet was really just coming onto the scene in educational terms when I was in university. The integration of technology into the classroom has been my most recent personal objective.

Technology can and should be used in more meaningful ways other than typing up assignments and finding information. I have created several lessons and assignments around the use of technology. Being a science teacher, the use of technology extends beyond the regular computer image to include graphical analysis, electronic probes, and monitoring devices of unlimited sources. One of my favourite lessons in the Grade 9 science curriculum is on dichotomous keys. The students research five organisms from the same family and create a dichotomous key web page to properly identify the organisms by scientific names. Each project requires about 10 web pages with limited information contained on each page, so that means lots of links. For example, each question leads to a link, which takes you either to the correct identification of an organism or the next question until you have identified the organism. The students really enjoy it. I have only one student who did not complete the assignment this year and that was due to absenteeism. Generally, the submissions of high quality assignments of a non-technology nature are much lower. A sample can be viewed at the following website. www.k12.nf.ca/lms/keyweb/. I recommend the Penguin or Whale page.

This was my first time giving this assignment which was prepared with Composer. Since then, upon evaluation, changes have been made and this year we are now using FrontPage to create some awesome projects soon to be online.

James Turner, Teacher in an Alternative High School, Southwest Regional School Board, Nova Scotia

Teaching in an alternate school, everything we do is somehow "altered" to give personal meaning to the students within the context of their lives. Their lives in so far as school is concerned, have not been positive experiences to date. Often this negative experience stretches into nearly all aspects of their lives.

Each day we begin with a meeting called a "round up." Information is exchanged, the day is defined or redefined as needed, issues from the previous days are addressed, students may address things they want to talk about concerning school, their classes, their classmates, etc. The day ends the same way and this meeting is often quite long as we address whatever has happened that may be a "teachable moment."

We also concern ourselves with the students' lives outside of school. In the end what we change the most is the fact that they are not just one of the herd; they are one of the family and we care what they do and what happens to them. Daily!

Marie Church, Grade 1 Teacher, Inner City School, Rothesay, New Brunswick

Four years ago, I was teaching in an inner city school with 99 percent minority enrollment. From the beginning, I was convinced that all these children could learn. My goal each day was to provide material and present in such a way that ensured every student would experience some degree of success. I will never forget one particular series of lessons.

As part of the primary language arts curriculum children spend a great deal of time building a reading vocabulary. Our newest program includes wonderful stories, poems, and songs as well as important emphasis on phonemic awareness. To provide personal meaning for each child, regardless of social background or culture, we also write experience stories (one of their favourite activities) where each child composes sentences about himself/herself in relation to the current theme. They write about personal preferences, experiences, family, friends, or pets and later share them with their families at home, as well as their classmates. As young children read and write about themselves and others within their immediate social world, it gives true meaning and relevancy to curriculum, while sparking interest and motivation.

Rona Howald, Grade 4 Teacher, Quispamsis, New Brunswick

Saint John's Cherry Brook Zoo is used by our students as a learning resource and features many endangered species and models of extinct animals. The city has eliminated its funding to the zoo and in order to remain in the area, it has undertaken an appeal for funds from the local community. In the past, we have had a day at the zoo for our entire school population of 450 students but in winter this is impractical and the zoo is only open on the weekends.

Instead of holding our usual Valentine's Day activities in February, we decided to put our "Hearts into the Zoo"! We asked that funds normally devoted to cards and treats be made available to students to help support the animals. We did not just ask for donations, we provided activities in return for their support. We had Frances Helyar, a local storyteller and song writer, entertain us with animal stories. Other features of the week before Valentine's Day were face painting, photos with school mascots (the "pride of Lakefield lions"), guessing games, raffles, a heart tree, and class cheers. Students were encouraged to bring their favourite stuffed animal to school for a parade. We integrated our language arts, math, art, and music to include our theme. The students and staff had an enjoyable week and we raised over $2400 for the zoo.

This showed everyone that curriculum can be integrated and expanded beyond the classroom walls and that students can learn valuable lessons about caring for the world around them while still having fun.

Source: Contributions in this section are reproduced with permission from the teachers themselves.

SUMMARY

What Determines the Culture of the Classroom?

- From seating arrangements, to classroom rules and procedures, to the content and relevance of the curriculum, teachers make many decisions that influence the culture of the classroom.

- Classroom climate refers to the atmosphere or quality of life in a classroom. The climates established by high-performing teachers are characterized by a productive, task-oriented focus; group cohesiveness; open, warm relationships between teacher and students; cooperative, respectful interactions among students; low levels of tension, anxiety, and conflict; humour; high expectations; and frequent opportunities for student input regarding classroom activities.

How Can You Create a Positive Learning Environment?

- An important element of a positive learning environment is a caring classroom climate. Teachers show care for students by providing support, structure, and appropriate expectations.

- The physical environment of a classroom—seating arrangements and the placement of other classroom furniture, for example—can make a positive contribution to students' learning.

- Classroom organization, how students are grouped for instruction and how time is used, is an important element of the effective learning environment. Among the patterns for organizing classrooms are grouping students by ability, grouping students for cooperative learning, using activity formats based on authentic learning tasks, and using time to maximize students' learning.

What Are the Keys to Successful Classroom Management?

- The key to successful classroom management is preventing problems before they occur. Teachers who prevent problems foster effective, harmonious interpersonal interactions; understand how their leadership style influences students; and facilitate the development of the classroom group so that it becomes more cohesive and supportive.

- Teachers who establish a democratic classroom climate that allows students to participate in making decisions about the classroom environment, rules and procedures, curriculum materials, and learning activities have fewer discipline problems.

- When management problems occur, effective teachers use a repertoire of problem-solving skills based on experience, common sense, and understanding of the teaching–learning process. Regardless of the management strategy used, effective teachers base their response to problems on three elements of "constructive assertiveness": a clear statement of the problem or concern; unambiguous body language; and a firm, unwavering insistence on appropriate behaviour.

What Teaching Methods Do Effective Teachers Use?

- Although it is difficult to identify all the skills teachers need, research indicates that effective teachers use a repertoire of models of teaching based on students' learning behaviours, child development, the thinking process, and peer mediation.

- Direct instruction and mastery learning are based on the view that learning is the acquisition of new behaviours.

- Modelling, constructivism, and scaffolding are based primarily on an understanding of how students construct meaning as they learn new material.

- Information processing, inquiry learning, and discovery learning are based on our understanding of the cognitive processes involved in learning.

- Peer-mediated instruction, which views learning as taking place in social situations, includes cooperative learning, group investigation, and peer- and cross-age tutoring.

What Are Some Characteristics of Effective Teaching?

- Effective teaching focuses on outcomes—the results or consequences of teaching. Outcomes include clear goals, objectives, and performance tasks that students are to master.

- Successful teachers modify their instruction based on assessments of students' understanding.

- Measurement refers to gathering data related to students' knowledge and skills, while evaluation involves making judgments about or assigning value to those judgments. In addition to traditional tests, teachers can use authentic assessments, portfolio assessments, and performance assessments to measure and evaluate students' learning.

KEY TERMS AND CONCEPTS

academic learning time
allocated time
assertive discipline
assessment
authentic assessments
authentic learning tasks
between-class ability
    grouping
block scheduling
caring classroom
choice theory
classroom climate
classroom management
classroom organization

constructivist teaching
cooperative learning
cross-age tutoring
democratic classrooms
direct instruction
discovery learning
evaluation
formative evaluation
group investigation
information processing
inquiry learning
instructional goals
learning objectives
mastery learning

measurement
modelling
opportunity to learn (OTL)
peer-mediated instruction
peer-tutoring
performance assessment
portfolio assessment
scaffolding
summative evaluation
time on task
within-class ability
    grouping

APPLICATIONS AND ACTIVITIES

Teacher's Journal

1. Recall the teachers and classmates you had during your school career. Select one class and analyze its group processes in terms of the stages of group development discussed in this chapter. At what stage of development was the group near the end of the school year? What conditions facilitated or impeded the development of this group?

2. Describe the "ideal" physical classroom environment for you. How would the seating arrangement facilitate the attainment of your instructional goals and objectives? How would you involve students in arranging the classroom?

3. Describe your leadership style as it relates to classroom management. In which aspects of leadership and classroom management do you feel most and least confident? What might you do, or what skills might you acquire, to strengthen your effectiveness in areas you feel you lack confidence? Develop your ideas into a statement of professional goals.

Teacher's Database

1. Visit the home pages of three or more of the following research publications on the web. These journals focus on educational research, learning theories, student and teacher attitudes and behaviours, and the effectiveness of teaching methods. Some journals especially emphasize the implications of educational psychology theory and research for educational policy and applications to teaching practice. Note the kinds of studies and research topics each selected journal reports. How might articles in these journals help you as an education major? as a classroom teacher? as a teaching professional?

   Cognition and Instruction
   Contemporary Educational Psychology
   Educational Psychologist
   Educational Psychology Review
   Educational Researcher
   Journal of Educational Psychology
   Review of Research in Education
   Journal of Teaching and Teacher Education
   Social Psychology of Education
   Review of Educational Research

2. What resources are available on the internet for developments in educational assessment? Begin in the ERIC Clearinghouse on Assessment and Evaluation. This clearinghouse contains the Test Locator service, searchable testing databases, tips on how to best evaluate a test, and information on fair testing practices.

Observations and Interviews

1. Observe several teachers at the level for which you are preparing to teach and try to identify the teaching methods they are using as part of their instructional repertoires.

2. Interview a classroom teacher about the assessment of students' learning. How do the assessment methods used by this teacher relate to his or her goals and objectives? To what extent does the teacher use authentic assessments?

Professional Portfolio

1. Prepare a poster depicting a classroom arrangement appropriate for the subject area and grade level for which you are preparing to teach. The poster should indicate the seating arrangement and location of other classroom furniture. In addition, make a list of classroom rules that will be posted in the room. You may wish to organize the rules according to the following categories.

- Rules related to academic work
- Rules related to classroom conduct
- Rules that must be communicated on your first teaching day
- Rules that can be communicated later

2. Last, prepare a flow chart depicting routine activities for a typical day. This chart could include procedures for the following:

- Handling attendance, tardy slips, and excuses
- Distributing materials
- Turning in homework
- Doing seatwork or various in-class assignments
- Forming small groups for cooperative learning activities
- Returning materials and supplies at the end of class

Appendix 9.1

Study Skills

While what follows are technically study skills, an effective teacher can take advantage of the principles and incorporate them into her/his instructional lessons.

A. The more senses involved in learning a fact, concept, generalization or skill, the greater the likelihood that it will be remembered.

1. Assume you are learning the steps required for proper use of a word processor. Here is the probability of your recalling all of the instructions you received 24 h later under various learning conditions.

	Percent probability of recall
– hear instructions only	15
– hear/read instructions	30
– hear/read/say aloud	45
– hear/read/say/write	60
– hear/read/say/write/do	75
– add one rehearsal	90

(Obviously, these percentages are only approximate and will vary widely from one individual to another.)

2. In general, students should be taught to use the following practices for use when studying.
   – write down key words or phrases
   – use a highlighter to mark key words or phrases
   – underline key words or phrases (not as good as highlighting)
   – say important things aloud
   – make mental pictures of things to be remembered

B. The importance of scheduled review: Retaining studied material

1. Student reviews classroom material that evening .... 5 min
2. Student reviews same material the next day .... 4 "
3. Student reviews same material one week later .... 3 "
4. Student reviews same material one month later .... 3 "

5. Six months later the student has probably still remembered the material. A further three-minute review at the six-month point would likely result in retention of the learned material for life.

C. The importance of interrupted study

Because it is necessary for the mind to rest, and because there is a greater tendency for items to be transferred from short-term to long-term memory with repeated exposures, the following two study habits should be adopted by students. If studying for a two-hour period, breaks should be taken at increasingly shorter periods. Perhaps the first might be taken after 30 to 40 min and the final break after only 20 min or so. The length of the break should be 10 min; anything less hurts study effectiveness and anything longer has been demonstrated to be unnecessary. Two hours of study with breaks will lead to a greater degree of learning than two hours of non-stop study.

D. If faced with a choice between going over test material once during a two-hour study session, or going over it two times (but somewhat less thoroughly) the second of these methods will usually lead to a higher mark.

When students study and immediately go to sleep, there is an approximate 5 percent loss of learned material. Since the loss when awake is roughly the same rate per hour, the most effective time to study for a test is just before bedtime—especially if the material is being learned for the first time.

E. Music can increase or decrease the effectiveness of the study process. Certain types of music, such as classical Baroque, have the same rhythm as the brain's delta waves. Since we learn best when our delta waves are operating smoothly, and since some music can encourage their appearance (delta waves disappear when we are upset or listening to discordant music) selective use of some softly-played background music may help the study process.

F. Visualization can be a powerful tool for learning new material. Not only does it make learning easier for most people, it greatly encourages the retention of the learned material. Teachers who can bring a strong visualization component to their teaching will increase the learning that their students experience.

G. Mnemonic devices can be useful devices for learning certain specialized types of information, eg., HOMES, which stands for the Great Lakes: Huron, Ontario, Michigan, Erie, Superior.

H. Reductionism can also be helpful. For example, reduce an entire course to a point outline format with all important topics/phrases/concepts listed.

I. Writing tests or examinations:
   (a) Read the test or exam over before starting to write. This allows the subconscious to bring forth information which may have already been forgotten. It also allows the student to write down a few notes on topics which he/she may forget before the test ends.
   (b) After completing the writing of a test, read the question sheet over to be certain all questions have been answered.

Source: Based on information from *Accelerated Learning* by Colin Rose (1987). Dell Publishing: New York.

10

Planning and
Conducting Instruction

Taken from *Classroom Management for Elementary Teachers*, Seventh Edition, by Carolyn M. Evertson, Edmund T. Emmer, and Murray E. Worsham.

How do you think students learn? How do you know when someone is learning? What is your own preferred style of learning? How will these beliefs affect your choice of teaching strategies? As you read this chapter, consider how each suggestion supports or fails to support the kinds of learning you believe to be most important.

Let's assume that the steps you have taken so far to ensure that your classroom will run smoothly have worked. Your classroom is organized, you have thought about the climate to be established and the expectations you want to communicate, you've developed and taught your rules and procedures, and you have systems in place to manage student learning. Now that your students are attentive and ready to participate, what do you do? Remember, your purpose is not just to have a smoothly running classroom; your purpose is to help students learn, and to help them ultimately take responsibility for their learning.

It is at this point that management and instruction meet. Well-planned lessons with a variety of developmentally appropriate activities support the positive learning environment that your careful management decisions intend to create. Dry lessons with limited opportunities for students to participate are boring and erode students' motivation; this is when management problems begin. Interesting, relevant, well-planned lessons are the key to holding student attention.

As you may have noticed, not all people learn in the same way. These different modes have been called learning styles or learning preferences. These preferences generally consist of four styles: (1) Sensory/Logical, using a step-by-step approach to gather, rehearse, and explain information; (2) Sensory/ Emotional, using interpersonal relationships to help review and master information; (3) Intuitive/Logical, using natural curiosity to solve problems and understand big ideas; (4) Intuitive/Emotional, using opportunities for creative projects to deepen understanding. Because children learn in different ways, by varying the activities and the formats for learning, you will have a better chance of meeting the different learning preferences in your class. You should not think, however, that you have to determine each child's preferred learning style and accommodate that style in every subject. It is just as important for students to understand that they can be successful in instructional formats that may not seem easiest to them (Brophy, 2004).

This chapter describes how to plan and conduct instruction in ways that support the kinds of learning you want for your students regardless of content area. Combining this information with knowledge from your content area will help you teach each subject more effectively. The chapter is divided into three sections. The first part discusses the planning decisions you must make. The second section discusses how to implement those plans as you conduct instruction. The final section discusses common problems such as transitions between activities and clarity of instruction.

Planning Instructional Activities

When you choose instructional activities for your classes, consider primarily whether an activity will lead to learning and what kind of learning you want to encourage. Activities that lead to better memorization are different from those that enhance reflective thinking or problem solving. Next, consider whether the activity will maintain student involvement. Also consider the sequence of activities for and the amounts of time spent on the various subjects in the curriculum. Such considerations lead many elementary teachers to plan reading and at least some language arts activities for the first two hours or so of the morning. These activities usually require sustained effort and often involve a combination of small-group, whole-group, and individual work formats. Involvement in these activities is more difficult to maintain later in the day when students are less alert and more fatigued.

Establishing a daily schedule with specific times for various subjects will help you remain conscious of time so that you do not shortchange subjects taught later in the day. Furthermore, students will be better able to pace their own work if they know the schedule. When you plan your schedule, try to arrange change-of-pace activities to follow periods of sustained effort or intense concentration. For example, you might arrange reading or language arts activities so that they come before recess or physical education. If you cannot schedule such activities conveniently, at least give students a brief break and lead them in exercises or a song or two, or give them time to stand and stretch if they have not had the opportunity to move around.

When you plan your daily schedule, you may find that your school district has established guidelines for the amount of time to be allotted to each subject. Also, special teachers may be assigned to teach a particular subject for certain days and times of the week. Thus, you may find that your class will be taught physical education on Tuesdays and Thursdays from 1:30 to 2:00 and will have music on Mondays and Wednesdays from 10:30 to 11:00. Obviously, your schedule will have to be set accordingly.

At the beginning of the school year, good planning requires extra effort. Overplanning (preparing more activities than can be accomplished in a particular time) and underplanning (preparing too little for the amount of time available) can occur, particularly with inexperienced teachers. It is better to overplan, then be flexible in implementing the plan. Activities not completed one day can serve as starters for second and third days.

Types of Planning

You will engage in several levels of planning, both long range (i.e., by the year and by the term) and short range (i.e., by the unit, the week, or the day). These levels of planning should be coordinated. Accomplishing the longer plan requires dividing the work into terms, the terms into units, and the units into weeks and days.

The lesson outcomes you envision will determine your planning goals and objectives, and your plans should reflect these intended outcomes. Many of these outcomes are determined by state or local curriculum guidelines or by mandated testing, but you should keep in mind that you are also teaching for understanding, appreciation, and application. Thus, your plans, provide road maps that help transform the available curriculum into activities, assignments, and learning experiences that are meaningful. In developing your plans, keep two important considerations in mind: first, which skills and concepts students must learn; and second, through which activities can they become interested partners in the learning enterprise.

Types of Instructional Activities

For each subject you teach, you will design activities to help students construct new knowledge, acquire and practice skills, consolidate and extend knowledge, and receive feedback about their learning. The basic steps in teaching are (1) content development, (2) discussion, (3) recitation or reinforcement, and (4) feedback. These steps may be followed by using a variety of instructional formats (see Table 10.1). Chapter 6 is devoted to Cooperative Learning. In the following sections, the most common types of instructional activities are described. These are whole-group instruction, grouped basic skill instruction, individual work, and feedback.

Content Development (or Whole-Group Instruction)

Although teachers sometimes present content to students individually or in small groups, whole-class presentation is often the major vehicle for introducing and teaching content activities. During content development, you may present new information, elaborate on or extend a concept or principle, conduct a demonstration, show how to perform a skill, or describe how to solve a problem. Whole-group content development activities are appropriate for learning goals such as exposure and familiarity and for the efficient presentation of new material.

During content development, the teacher takes an active role focused on helping students think about the new content, relate it to what they know, and apply it. One chief management concern is making sure that students are active, not passive. Therefore, you will have to find ways to involve students in the development of the lesson.

Table 10.1

Formats for Instruction

Format	How Formed	Purpose	Advantages	Disadvantages
Whole Group	Whole group	To deliver information on new content or skill(s) to all at one time	▦ Cover much information in little time ▦ Everyone hears the same information	▦ Does not meet needs of many students when used as the only method of instruction
Small Teacher-Led Group	Teacher formed T homogeneous groups using set criteria	To provide activities to meet specific needs, either remedial or enrichment	▦ Able to check more accurately for student understanding	▦ Some students may be engaged in long periods of seatwork without being actively monitored
Small Cooperative Group	Teacher formed equivalent heterogeneous groups based on performance, gender, race, and so forth	To reinforce previously taught content and foster social skills (Note: Individual grades are a must to achieve these purposes.)	▦ More opportunity for students to "interact" with material being presented	▦ Sometimes only two or three of the four to five students benefit from doing the work
Small Noncompetitive Group	Random selection with teacher guidance as needed to form hetero-geneous groups	To experience a process or produce a product with no individual or group academic grading involved	▦ Social skills fostered	▦ Difficult to check for individual student's understanding during activity
Student Pairs	Teacher or student selected based on reciprocal learning needs	To enhance collaborative learning through collaborative/reciprocal processes	▦ Can involve both students ▦ Fosters social skills ▦ Facilitates reciprocal learning	▦ One student may do all the work/thinking
Individualized Instruction	One student	To meet individual student needs, (IEPs, absentee makeup work, enrichment, remediation of content or skills)	▦ Teacher-student ratio a plus ▦ Remedial/enrichment help easily given	▦ May be time consuming ▦ Some students may not be actively monitored
Centers and Stations	Teacher created with equitable student access designated in a variety of ways	To enrich, extend, practice, apply new learning, and/or remediate content and/or skills	▦ Enriches student understanding ▦ Students can practice skills ▦ Students can apply new learning	▦ Difficult to manage time at center and problematic for nonreaders ▦ Requires preparation time ▦ Difficult to monitor

Adapted from Evertson & Harris (2003). © Vanderbilt University, reprinted with permission.

Teacher questions are also used for this purpose, allowing the teacher to check student understanding, to encourage students to contribute to steps in problem solving, to apply concepts or principles, and to analyze ideas.

In addition to presentations and questions, content development should include sample problems or other demonstrations of understanding of the new content. These not only help students learn the new content but also provide you with information about how well the class is understanding the lesson. Activities and questions should be thoughtfully designed to expose student thinking and understanding. For example, when a student gives a correct answer, you can probe with further questions: "What led you to that answer?" "What do you mean by . . . ?" "What would come next?" "How else could you do that?"

Another way to develop content is to help students engage in research and problem solving, individually and in groups.

Grouped Basic Skill Instruction

In this format, you work with small groups of students, one group at a time, while the rest of the class works independently. This mode of instruction is most commonly used for reading and frequently for mathematics. Its purpose is to accommodate a wide range of achievement levels in basic skill subjects. Because small-group instruction is used so extensively for basic skills, we will describe its features in detail.

A critical aspect of small-group instruction is that at least two different activities occur simultaneously. The teacher leads one group while students outside the group participate in a variety of independent activities. Because the teacher is actively involved with the small group, it is more difficult to monitor the behavior of other students and give them assistance. And because students may work independently for a long period, careful planning and extra effort are required to keep them involved in their work.

The first step in setting up effective small-group instruction is to plan the stage for the out-of-group activities. Give directions to the whole class at once: instructions for each assignment, a description of needed materials, and a suggested time for completing each activity. This list of assignments should also be posted or written on the board. Check whether students understand the directions by asking students in each group to review them before beginning.

Before calling the first group, monitor the beginning of independent work for a short time. After you are certain that students have started, signal the first group. During your work with the small group, monitor out-of-group students by scanning the room frequently. If you observe inappropriate behavior that is interfering with work, try to stop it with eye contact or some nonverbal signal, by calling the student's name once, or by reminding the student of what he or she should be doing. A "time-out" desk near you can also be used for a student who persists in misbehavior: You can signal such a student to go to the desk for a while, without your having to leave the group.

Another consideration is how students needing help on an independent task can obtain it without interrupting you. Some teachers tell students to skip work they cannot do and go on to another activity until the teacher is available. Others allow students to help each other, or they assign a few students (perhaps one for each table or group) the role of helper. This works best if students are seated in mixed-ability groups. Finally, students can sign up on the board or on a clipboard sheet to indicate the need for assistance when it is available. If you must leave the small group to help a student or to deal with a problem, be sure to give students in the group something to do. One student in the group may be able to lead the activity for a short time.

When work with one small group has been completed, the next group should not be called immediately. Instead, take the opportunity to check the progress of the students who will be continuing individual assignments and help them with any problems they may have. Briefly inspect all students' work to determine whether they have requested assistance. Students who were off-task while you were teaching the small group can be given delayed feedback at this time. Be sure to encourage and give positive feedback to students who are participating appropriately. The students who have left the small group and are moving to other activities should also be monitored to be sure they begin their activity promptly. Then signal the next group to come for instruction.

Individual Work

In this activity, students engage in assignments that build on presented material. In the upper elementary grades, the portion of the assignment not completed in class often becomes a homework assignment unless the materials or resources needed are available only in the classroom.

Good management of individual activities has several components. First, adequate content development must precede the independent student activity so that students can work productively on their own. Second, you must communicate clearly the requirements and objectives of the students' work and arrange for access to needed materials or resources. A good strategy is to begin the independent work assignment as a whole-class activity (for example, by working several of the exercises, problems, or questions together) before the independent work phase. This gets students started, gives them an opportunity to ask questions, and enables you to observe and correct common problems in a whole-class format rather than having to deal with the same problem with multiple individuals. Third, actively monitor the students' work so that problems are detected early and corrective feedback is provided.

Independent activities are best used for consolidating or extending prior learning rather than for acquiring new content. Therefore, be careful not to overuse independent activities; a rule of thumb is to devote at least as much time to content development as to independent work. Moreover, student engagement is more difficult to maintain in lengthy individual work activities. If you do find yourself assigning long periods of time to individual assignments, try breaking the activity into smaller segments and having a discussion or review between segments. The change in lesson format will help refocus attention, and it will give you an opportunity to check comprehension and clear up problems.

Feedback

Feedback may be provided during discussion, recitation, or checking, and each of these may occur before, during, or after content development. For example, in presenting new material you may build on prior knowledge, and you might want to begin with a group discussion that leads to a new idea or problem to be solved. Also check individual work to be sure that students' levels of understanding allows for the introduction of new content or skill development. Wherever these feedback activities occur in the instructional sequence, planning and management skills can make them more productive.

Discussion

Discussions are helpful in encouraging students to evaluate events, topics, or results; to clarify the basis for their opinions; to help them become aware of other points of view; or to help them improve their oral expression skills. Sometimes discussions start with a recitation activity (described next) in which the facts of the content to be discussed are reviewed. Compared to a recitation, however, discussion questions are more likely to elicit the students' judgments, impressions, ideas, and opinions; also, teachers are less likely to evaluate the responses directly. Instead, students are encouraged to express themselves, to examine their opinions and beliefs, and to understand other perspectives. Students may respond to each other rather than only to the teacher. The teacher's role becomes one of encouraging, clarifying, and using student ideas rather than evaluating their correctness.

Management of a discussion calls for a number of skills, including warmth or friendliness (to promote security), conflict resolution, and encouraging expression of divergent points of view (to foster acceptance and openness). Although it is more common for some students to contribute to a discussion, avoid allowing a few students to monopolize the discourse; less verbal students should be included skillfully. Inviting reticent members to speak from time to time by asking for their opinions or views of what has previously been discussed is a good way to do so. Giving students opportunities to paraphrase, clarify, and elaborate on their own or other students' remarks helps keep a discussion moving and on target; also, transferring some of the responsibility for maintaining the discussion to students can keep the conversation moving. Getting students to listen to each other rather than treating the discussion as a dialogue with the teacher is sometimes difficult. Therefore, it is important to emphasize that students should respond to each other as well as to the teacher's comments or questions.

If you choose to use a whole-group discussion format, you must plan questions in advance. This can keep the discussion focused and productive. However, many teachers encourage students to formulate their own discussion questions, especially if these follow from group or individual research projects. Whether discussions are student-led or teacher-led, ground rules for participation must be clear (e.g., raise hands, listen carefully, respect others' right to speak).

Recitation

Recitation is a question-and-answer sequence in which the teacher asks questions, usually of a factual nature, and accepts, guides, or corrects student responses. The sequence of question/answer/evaluation is repeated frequently, with many students being asked to respond until a body of content has been covered. In effect, a recitation is a form of checking that is done orally. It can be used as a skill drill or to review student understanding of a previous lesson or assigned reading. It can also be used to check spelling, knowledge of vocabulary words, or other factual recall.

When recitation is used to check understanding, it is important to distribute questions to all students, not just to those who are eager to answer. Calling on only those who volunteer can give you an inaccurate impression of what students know. Develop a way to check systematically on which students get a turn to answer. This can be done by using a checklist or a shuffled stack of name cards. Some teachers place a strip of construction paper on each student's desk as a marker. As a student contributes, her or his marker is removed. It is helpful to ask the question, allow time for students to think, and then call on individual students. Limit the time you call on only students who volunteer. Sometimes you can use choral or whole-group responses as a way of keeping everyone alert and active. These kinds of responses are usually helpful only at the beginning of concept development as new material is being introduced and practiced. Sometimes teachers do not allow students enough time to respond, thus reducing opportunities for those who are slow to answer. Some experts recommend a "wait time" of several seconds before giving a prompt or calling on another student.

Checking

In this activity, students check their own classwork or homework. The checking activity is appropriate only when the judgment of correctness can be made easily. Checking provides quick feedback, and it allows the teacher to identify and discuss common errors on assignments. Careful monitoring during checking is important to be sure that students are doing it correctly. Students must be taught to check papers accurately, so it is important to explain the procedures as well as model them and allow students opportunities to practice. When student checking is used, you should collect the papers and examine them to remain aware of progress and problems.

Arranging Activities within a Lesson

In any given subject, lessons usually consist of a series of activities. A common activity sequence in basic skill areas is this:

1. Checking or recitation
2. Content development
3. Classwork
4. Independent work, group work, or discussion

The first activity allows the previous day's assignment or homework to be corrected. If there was no homework, the teacher leads a review of prior content important for the day's lesson. During content development, new content or skills are taught. Following this, a short classwork activity is used to review the new content and to preview the new assignment. Then practice is provided through independent work, group work, or discussion.

The problem with this sequence is that it requires that the presentation of lesson content and the practice period each be handled in two, usually lengthy, segments. A variation of the sequence that accommodates more complex content and that does not demand as much sustained attention is this:

1. Checking or recitation
2. Content development
3. Classwork or independent work, usually brief, with checking
4. Content development
5. Classwork, usually brief
6. Independent work, group work, or discussion

This sequence allows you to divide the lesson content into two parts, with practice and feedback following the first content development activity. Teaching new content in two parts with an intervening practice period helps students consolidate learning from the first part before they are asked to address new learning required in the second part. The sequence also allows you to check student understanding and to provide prompt feedback before moving on to more complex content. Furthermore, when individual activities are divided into shorter segments, student attention is usually easier to maintain. A problem with this sequence is that it produces more transition points and thus greater potential for student disengagement. Usually these transitions can be managed without difficulty, however, because student movement, new materials, or drastically changed lesson focus are not required in the content development-classwork-independent work cycle. Thus, the various activities blend together, usually without conspicuous transitions.

Of course, not all lessons fit either of the activity patterns just described. For instance, a science or social studies lesson may consist of a relatively long period of active student exploration or problem solving in small groups, followed by a whole-class content development discussion. Ongoing projects may entail long segments of individual seatwork or small-group work interspersed with short segments of whole-class or small-group instruction. Nevertheless, the two common patterns described here provide useful frameworks for building most teacher-directed lessons.

Planning for Clear Instruction

When you have an idea of the range and sequence of activities available to you, examine the content, concepts, and goals of the lessons and units that you will be teaching. One way to start is to review the unit and lesson in the teacher's edition of your textbook(s). Pay careful attention to suggestions for lesson development and activities. Study the exercises, questions, problems, and other activities in the textbook and decide which items provide appropriate review of lesson objectives. Note examples, demonstrations, and key questions and activities to use in the development of the main concepts. Put yourself in the lesson. Try to anticipate problems students may encounter in the lesson or assignments. Check for new terms and be ready to define them and present examples.

The textbook suggestions should not be limiting. Remember, you want your students to understand the content, not just retain it. Many educators talk about the importance of constructing knowledge, having students actively involved in making new information relevant to what they already know. This may be as simple as introducing a problem and exploring possible solutions or reframing a lesson through a thoughtful discussion of how it relates to individual experiences. You are targeting understanding, appreciation, and application.

Consider the interest the lesson is likely to have for students. Will you be enthusiastic about teaching this material to your class in this way? Your enthusiasm about the lesson is contagious and signals to students how you feel about its importance. If you find it interesting and exciting and you communicate this excitement to your class, students will probably respond with interest. However, if you find yourself unenthusiastic about a lesson or topic, chances are your students will share your feelings. Consider approaching the lesson in a different way. For example, rather than giving a lecture presentation of material, perhaps you can find ways for students to contribute through large- or small-group discussions that address the same issues.

Finally, organize your lesson parts into a coherent sequence. Write down or outline the main components. Then you will be well prepared for a clear lesson presentation.

Presenting New Content

If students understand where a lesson is going, they are more likely to be with you at the end. Tell students what the lesson objectives are, either at the beginning of the activity or during it. If the lesson is complex, give them an outline to help them follow its organization. An outline helps organize the content for the students and provides a road map to keep them on course.

If students are to understand content from silent reading or from viewing a video, provide a content outline with a few items filled in and spaces for students to supply the rest. This task focuses attention and helps motivate them to read or watch carefully. Go over these items with the class after the film, especially if the students use the outline for further work or study. Alternatively, use the video as an opportunity to teach note-taking skills. Guide students in determining the questions they need answered by the film, and then help them identify important information as the video progresses.

As you present a lesson, stay with the planned sequence unless an obvious change is needed. Avoid needless digressions, interruptions, or tangential information. Inserting irrelevant information into a lesson only confuses students about what they are expected to learn. Displaying key concepts, new terms, major points, and other critical information on the overhead transparency screen or the board underscores their importance.

Presentations should be as focused and concrete as possible. Use examples, illustrations, demonstrations, props, charts, and any other means of providing substance and dimension to abstractions in the lesson. Avoid the vague expressions and verbal time fillers that, at best, communicate little information and make presentations difficult to follow. Then allow students time and opportunity to process the information you're presenting.

Checking for Understanding

Find out whether students understand a presentation during the lesson; do not wait until the next day. As content development activities unfold, ask students questions to verify their comprehension of main points. You can also ask students to provide a written response to key questions and then check some or all of their answers either orally or by examining the written work. Asking students to demonstrate comprehension at several points during a presentation not only allows you to verify their progress but also keeps students more involved in the lesson.

You can also check student understanding and emphasize main points by conducting an oral recitation after a presentation. Do this by asking a series of questions that recapitulate the lesson sequence and its major concepts. Be sure to involve many students in answering these questions so that you can identify the overall level of understanding in the class and reteach what has not been satisfactorily learned.

Other methods of checking for understanding include having students respond to your questions in these ways:

- Displaying the correct one of two or more possible answers by holding up prepared color-coded cards

- Using designated body movement (e.g., thumbs up or thumbs down, arms crossed or arms uncrossed)
- Folding a piece of notebook paper into fourths, using each of the eight sections to write responses, and holding them up for you to see
- Writing in their own words explanations of the concept studied and turning these in for your inspection
- Pairing with a designated neighbor and quietly explaining a concept or process to the other while you circulate and listen
- Keeping a journal or a learning log that includes entries on each lesson in a particular unit

Technology in the Classroom

Using computers, whether for content development, research, or practice, requires awareness and planning. Few classrooms have as many computers as teachers would like, but almost all have at least one. Develop strategies to make technology a productive tool in helping students reach their academic goals. Unless your school has a computer classroom, you probably will have to devise activities to be carried out at a computer station. As noted in Chapter 4, this requires that procedures for the use of the station be taught and rehearsed. In addition, you may want to appoint one or more student "computer experts" who can assist quietly while you continue with whole- or small-group instruction.

Making the best possible use of shared technology is a challenge. Useful strategies include using CD-ROMs or the Internet for research or setting up specific content software to reinforce skills. E-mail and word processing software may enable students to improve their organizational and writing skills. You may set up your own base of notes, games, and puzzles to engage your students.

Internet access in the classroom makes it possible for students to find information more easily than ever before. Unfortunately, not all of the information available to them is appropriate, and many schools now use Internet filters. Certain precautions must be taken when including Internet use in your lessons. Some school systems require that parents give written permission before their child is allowed on the Internet. The teacher must find alternative ways for students without that permission to gather information. Children should be cautioned not to give their last names or any personal information over the Internet. All teachers should receive written permission before publishing a child's likeness on the Internet. Additionally, you should preview the sites you have assigned so you can easily recognize a screen that does not reflect the assigned task.

To make more efficient use of browsing time while students search for information, you may want to encourage them to print the resources they find. Teach them to skim headings for appropriate material and print it out rather than reading it on line. Even if the material turns out not to be relevant, it saves time, and other uses for the printed pages may be found.

Students should be monitored frequently as they access information on the Web. By giving them specific information to find and a limited time in which to find it, you can avoid many hazards. It is a good idea to set up guidelines for use at the beginning of the year. For example, have the students sign a contract that states, "I will use the Internet for school use only. If I knowingly search for inappropriate materials, I will lose the privilege of using the Internet for the remainder of the year." To eliminate the argument that a site was accidentally found, teach students to click the "back" button on the browser and get your attention immediately if they access an inappropriate site by mistake.

Kounin's Concepts for Managing Whole-Group Instruction

A central theme in managing teacher-led activities well is the idea of activity flow—the degree to which a lesson proceeds smoothly, without digressions, diversions, or interruptions. Lessons with good flow keep student attention and prevent deviation because most of the cues for behavior during the lesson are focused on behaviors appropriate for the lesson. When lesson flow is jerky, with frequent interruptions and side trips, there is more competition for attention from cues external to the focus of the lesson. Therefore, there will be a greater tendency for students to disengage.

A series of classroom research studies by Kounin and his colleagues (Kounin 1970; Kounin & Gump 1974) identified several concepts that contribute to effective management of interactive group activities, leading to smooth activity flow. According to Kounin, activity flow is maintained through three types of teacher practices, summarized in Table 10.2. Within each class of behavior there are two or three related concepts. Look at how each is defined and consider some examples.

Preventing Misbehavior

Classrooms are complex settings. Many events can occur at the same time. One cannot always predict with certainty what will occur when. New teachers run the risk of focusing too closely on single events or on select areas of the classroom and missing the big picture. Understanding two of Kounin's (1970).

Withitness is the degree to which the teacher corrects misbehavior before it intensifies or spreads to more students and also targets the correct student when doing so. A teacher who is not "with it" either will fail to stop the problem until it has escalated and may require a major intervention or else will fail to catch the perpetrator and instead target the wrong student. It is apparent that underlying aspects of withitness include good monitoring and prompt handling of inappropriate behavior.

Overlapping refers to how the teacher handles two or more simultaneous events. Here are some examples: a visitor comes to the door in the middle of a lesson, a child from out of the group comes up to the teacher during reading group time, or several students get into a squabble while the teacher is busy helping other children across the room. A teacher who has good overlapping skills will handle both events in some way instead of dropping one event to handle the other or else ignoring the second event. To handle an interruption, for example, a teacher might tell the class or group to continue working or to get out some work, and then deal with the interrupter. The squabble taking place away from the teacher might be handled by eye contact or a brief verbal desist while the teacher stays where he or she is.

Notice that a teacher who is with it and exhibits good overlapping skills is able to insulate lessons from the intrusions that student misbehavior or external interruptions might cause. Furthermore, by reacting promptly to problems (but not overreacting), the teacher is often able to use simple measures (eye contact, redirection, a quiet desist) that do not interfere with ongoing activities or distract students very much. If a teacher is not with it or does not overlap when needed, lessons may be interrupted by student misbehavior and by the teacher's subsequently more visible and tardy reactions.

Table 10.2

How Effective Managers Maintain Activity Flow Kounin (1970)

Issue	Skills	Definition	Example
Preventing misbehavior	Withitness	Communicating general awareness of the lassroom to students; cidentifying and correcting misbehavior promptly and correctly	The teacher makes eye contact with a student who is about to "shoot a basket" with a wad of paper. The student puts the paper away. A student behind him, who has seen the interaction, decides he's not likely to get away with shooting a basket either.
	Overlapping	Attending to two or more simultaneous events	The teacher is leading a class discussion when a student comes in late. The teacher nods to him, continuing the discussion. Later, when students have begun a seat-work assignment, she attends to him and signs his tardy slip.
Managing movement	Momentum	Keeping lessons moving briskly; planning carefully to avoid slowdowns	The teacher notices that the explanation of a relatively minor concept is taking too long and distracting attention from the primary focus of the lesson. The teacher makes a mental note to go more in-depth on this concept in a separate lesson the next day, and moves on.
	Smoothness	Staying on track with the lesson; avoiding digressions and divergences that can lead to confusion	While being responsive to student interests, the teacher avoids comments that tend to draw attention away from the key points of the lesson.
Maintaining group focus	Group alerting	Engage the attention of the whole class while individuals are responding	Each student has a number that was drawn from a hat on the way into class. The teacher draws numbers and uses them to call on students during a fast-paced review.
	Encouraging accountability	Communicating to students that their participation will be observed and evaluated	At the end of discussion and practice of a new skill, students are told to turn to a neighbor and explain the process to him or her.
	High-participation formats	Using lessons that define behavior of students when they are not directly answering a teacher's question	While some students work problems at the board, students at their desks are instructed to check them by working the problems on paper.

Managing Movement

Whereas withitness and overlapping are accomplished by handling external interruptions and student intrusions into the flow of the lesson, movement management is accomplished by avoiding teacher-caused intrusions or delays. Good movement management is achieved through momentum and smoothness.

Momentum refers to pacing and is indicated by lessons that move along briskly. Teachers can cause slowdowns in momentum by dwelling on individual parts of a lesson, direction, or skill and by unnecessarily breaking an activity into too many parts. For example, teachers should provide a standard heading for assignments that can be used routinely rather than altering its form and having to explain it over and over.

Smoothness, as opposed to jerkiness, is epitomized in lesson continuity. A smoothly flowing lesson keeps student attention. If a teacher leaves a topic or activity to do something else or to insert new material, students may be distracted and miss the point of the lesson.

Maintaining Group Focus

Classroom instruction involves teaching children in groups, often a whole class at a time. Doing so means that a teacher must be conscious of the group influence on the instruction. Like a conductor leading an orchestra, the teacher must elicit the performance of the individuals and still provide signals and direction to the whole class. Group focus can be maintained through several techniques.

Group alerting means taking action to engage the attention of the whole class while individuals are responding. It can take the form of creating suspense, telling students they might be called on next, calling on students randomly, asking students not reciting to listen carefully because they might be called on to add to the answer, or using some new visual aid, display, or attention-getting strategy. Engaging in a dialogue with one student or calling on students before asking questions are examples of poor group alerting.

Accountability occurs when the teacher lets students know that their performance will be observed and evaluated in some manner. It does not require a letter grade or a score (although it might); it simply communicates some degree of awareness of how students are performing. For example, the teacher might ask everyone who knows an answer to raise a hand and then call on one or more of those students. The teacher could have all students write answers and circulate to check them. The teacher might also have students keep notebooks and check them from time to time.

High-participation formats are lessons that program the behavior of students when they are not directly involved in answering a teacher's question. Such lessons have a higher built-in rate of participation than do lessons that merely assume that students will sit and watch when other students respond. Higher-participation formats occur when students are expected to write answers, solve problems, read along, manipulate materials, or perform some other concurrent task.

Some activities lend themselves more to one type of group focus than another. When planning instruction, it is helpful to consider which of the three aspects to use. For example, during a demonstration that involves expensive materials, it might be difficult to use a high-participation format, but group alerting might be easy to incorporate.

Kounin's concepts for managing group instruction not only help identify key aspects of effective teaching, but they can also be used to diagnose instructional problems and identify possible solutions. For example, if lessons seem to drag and student response is unenthusiastic, there may be a problem with group focus; a solution may be to work on alerting or accountability or to increase the degree of participation. Activities that take too long and that seem to get off track constantly may have a problem with movement management. Perhaps the teacher should check for slowdowns and jerkiness.

Common Problems in Conducting Instruction

Two areas give many teachers difficulty in conducting instruction: transitions and clarity. This section focuses on common problems in these areas and suggests possible solutions.

Transitions

The interval between any two activities is a transition. Several management problems can occur during transitions, including long delays before starting the next activity, which can contribute to high levels of inappropriate or disruptive behavior. Transition problems can be caused by a lack of readiness by the teacher or the students for the next activity, unclear student expectations about appropriate behavior during transitions, and faulty procedures for transitions. Here are some examples of transition problems, along with suggested ways of correcting them.

The preceding items summarize the major problems that occur in classrooms at and around transition times. If you feel that your class is wasting time or if you are having difficulty keeping control during transitions, the suggested solutions may prove helpful.

Transition Problem	Suggested Solution
Students talk loudly at the beginning of the day. The teacher is interrupted while checking attendance, and the start of content activities is delayed.	Establish a beginning-of-day routine, and clearly state your expectations for behavior at the beginning of the day.
Students talk too much during transitions, especially after an assignment has been given but before they have begun working on it. Many students do not start their work activity for several minutes.	Be sure students know what the assignment is. Post it where they can see it easily. Work as a whole class on the first several exercises so that all students begin the lesson successfully and at the same time. Watch what students do during the transition and urge them along when needed.

Transition Problem	Suggested Solution
Students who go for supplemental instruction stop work early and leave the room noisily while the rest of the class is working. When these students return to the room, they disturb others as they come in and take their seats. They interrupt others by asking for directions and assignments.	Have a designated signal that tells these students when they are to get ready to leave, such as a special time on the clock. Have them practice leaving and returning to the room quietly. Acknowledge appropriate behavior. Leave special instructions in a folder, on the board, or on a special sheet at their desks for what they are to do when they return. Or for younger students, establish a special place (e.g., the reading rug) for returning students to wait and an activity for them to engage in until you can give them personal attention.
During the last afternoon activity, students quit working well before the end; they begin playing around and leave the room in a mess.	Establish an end-of-day routine so that students continue their work until the teacher gives a signal to begin preparations to leave; then instruct students to help straighten the room.
Whenever the teacher attempts to move the students from one activity into another, a number of students don't make the transition but continue working on the preceding activity. This delays the start of the next activity or results in confusion.	Give students a few minutes' notice before an activity is scheduled to end. At the end of the activity, students should put all materials from it away and get out any needed materials for the next activity. Monitor the transition to make sure that all students complete it; do not start the next activity until students are ready.
The teacher delays the beginning of activities to look for materials, finish attendance reporting, pass back or collect papers, or chat with individual students while the rest of the class waits.	Have materials organized ahead of time, and when transitions begin, avoid doing anything that interferes with your ability to monitor and direct students.

Clarity

Communicating information and directions in a clear, comprehensible manner is an important teaching skill. Clear instruction helps students learn faster and more successfully; it also helps students understand your directions and expectations for behavior more readily. Although clarity is important in all classroom activities, it is crucial during content development, when nearly all new subject matter is introduced and taught.

Clear instruction results from several factors: organization of information into a coherent sequence, use of an adequate number of illustrations or examples, precision and concreteness of expression, keeping in touch with student comprehension, and providing enough practice to ensure mastery.

Clarity involves stating goals or major objectives and making sure that students know what they are accountable for knowing or doing; carefully outlining a lesson sequence, moving from simpler to more complex ideas; providing instructions both orally and in writing; checking understanding by asking specific questions or obtaining work samples; and providing for meaningful practice and feedback through classwork or homework assignments that review all lesson skills and content.

FURTHER READING

Alvermann, D. E., O'Brien, D. G., & Dillon, D. R. (1990). What teachers do when they say they're having discussions of content area reading assignments: A qualitative analysis. *Reading Research Quarterly, 25,* 296–322.

Although teachers often say they utilize discussion activities, this study found that the nature of discussion varies greatly from class to class. Maintaining control was very important to many of the teachers, and the more this dominated their perspective, the more their discussions resembled recitations rather than open forums for expressing views.

Brophy, J. E., & Alleman, J. (1991). Activities as instructional tools: A framework for analysis and evaluation. *Educational Researcher, 20*(4), 9–23.

The authors provide a detailed analysis of the design, selection, and evaluation of activities, with a central concern being how activities contribute to learning. Several major principles underlying activity design are proposed in this comprehensive analysis.

Casey, M. B., & Tucker, E. C. (1994). Problem-centered classrooms: Creating lifelong learners. *Phi Delta Kappan, Oct.,* 139–143.

The authors give guidelines for establishing a problem-centered instructional program. They address the teacher's role in posing open-ended questions, teaching the steps in thinking, and connecting lessons to children's interests. Their summary of strategies at the end of the article is especially useful.

Fuchs, D., Fuchs, L. S., Mathes, P. G., & Simmons, D. G. (1997). Peer-assisted learning strategies: Making classrooms more responsive to diversity. *American Educational Research Journal, 34*(1), 174–206.

Reporting a study on peer tutoring as a portion of planned reading instruction, the authors identify that students at low, average, and high levels of achievement all had achievement gains when involved in peer tutoring in comparison to students who were not part of planned reading instruction involving peer tutoring.

www.lessonplanspage.com

This website for educators, maintained by the University of Scranton, contains more than 2,500 sample lesson plans for all subjects (PreK–12).

www.teachervision.fen.com

This is the website for the Family Education Network; it has tips for teachers and a lesson planning center.

www.lburkhart.com

This website includes useful suggestions about technology integration in the classroom for elementary, middle, secondary, and special needs students.

SUGGESTED ACTIVITIES

1. Use Checklist 10 at the end of the chapter to plan one or more lessons.

2. Read Problems 10.1 through 10.3, which describe problems three teachers are experiencing with the management of instruction. After reading each paragraph,

review this chapter and decide what strategies they might use to help overcome their problems. You might use each problem as a basis for a group discussion and generate a list of many possible solutions or strategies. Then compare your list with the keys at the end of this chapter.

3. Read Problem 10.4. How many examples of Kounin's concepts noted on page 263 can you identify in this problem? Create a lesson outline that will improve the sequence of Mr. Case's instruction.

4. Case Study 10.1 illustrates problems that can arise in conducting instruction. Use the concepts in this and previous chapters to diagnose Ms. Lake's problems. Compare your list with the keys at the end of this chapter.

5. Teachers are sometimes caught between the need to cover a broad range of content quickly and the need to develop more specific content to deepen students' understanding. Interview several experienced teachers to get their ideas on how to meet this challenge.

6. Go to either www.lessonplanspage.com or www.teachervision.fen.com and select a few lesson plans. How well are they organized around powerful ideas, long-range goals, and supporting objectives and activities? If you were to teach from one of these plans, what changes would you make? Why?

Problem 10.1

Ms. Kendall is beginning her first year of teaching fourth graders. She is writing out her plans for the first few days of class. She has familiarized herself with the scope and sequence of the fourth-grade curriculum. One of the first decisions she will make is about her class schedule. She must decide how best to organize her students' day. What should she consider as she develops her daily schedule? What long-term plans should she make to ensure that students learn to manage their own academic work and develop good work skills?

Problem 10.2

During reading instruction, Mr. Hart generally works with a small group of students while the remaining students do assigned work. Lately, Mr. Hart has noticed that some students are not following seatwork directions and never finish their work, although he feels he allows appropriate amounts of time for work to be completed and gives thorough instructions before the reading groups start. A few students finish early, turn in their papers, and then wander around, interrupting other students and socializing excessively. Mr. Hart has to stop his work with the group to quiet the students. What can Mr. Hart do to get students to work more productively during seatwork?

Problem 10.3

Ms. Jackson is trying to include more science lessons in her curriculum. She wants to try a discovery approach with her third graders. For a lesson on how sound is made, Ms. Jackson passes out paper cups in two sizes. Her plan is to have the students hum into the cups and feel the different vibrations. However, as soon as students receive their cups, they begin to plop them noisily on the desks. Some students poke holes in the bottoms with pencils. Other students place them over their ears and show their neighbors, while another group tries to figure out how to make the cups stay on their heads as hats. Ms. Jackson cannot get their attention back to the lesson. How could advance planning have helped her to avoid these problems? Use Checklist 10 to help you analyze this lesson.

Problem 10.4

As he is about to begin class after lunch, Mr. Case makes eye contact with two students who are exchanging notes; the students quickly get out their class materials. "Let's begin by working some of the exercises at the end of the chapter; you will need a piece of paper with a heading." As students begin to get out their materials, Mr. Case calls out, "Oops! I forgot to tell you to bring money for tomorrow for the field trip. How many of you will be going?" After a brief discussion, students finish getting out their materials. Mr. Case says, "We'll go through these exercises orally, but I also want you to write the answers on your papers as part of today's classwork. I'll come around later and check your answers. Now, who can answer the first question? Hands please. Tyrone?"

Mr. Case conducts the lesson by calling on various students, some with hands up, others seemingly at random from the nonvolunteers. About halfway through the exercises, a student enters the room and says that he is new to the school and has been assigned to the class. Mr. Case goes to his desk, sits down, and says, "Okay, come here. I'll check out some of your books to you. I wish the school office wouldn't send children in the middle of the day. Where are you from, anyway? That's a nice shirt you are wearing."

After finishing with the student and sending him to a seat, Mr. Case leaves his desk and says to the class, "Now where were we? Oh, yes, question 7. Say, where did Kim and Lee go? I didn't give them permission to leave."

After several more minutes, Mr. Case calls a halt to the activity and says, "Now, I'd like us to discuss the test coming up this Thursday. Let's make sure that you are all clear on what will be on the exam and what you will need to get ready for it." After a pause, he adds, "I almost forgot. Get your questions from before and look at the next to the last one. We have to add an important point that was left out. . . ." After finishing the item, Mr. Case turns the topic back to the upcoming test: "Now, where were we? Oh, yes. I want to show you some items that will be similar to those on the test. Here's one." He writes it on the chalkboard, then pauses: "Well, I don't want to give away the test, do I?"

Without discussing the test further, he turns to another topic: "Just wait until you hear about the videotape we will be viewing tomorrow. I borrowed it from another teacher, and she said that her students thought it was one of the most interesting, exciting stories they had ever seen!"

A Science Lesson in a Sixth-Grade Class

M s. Lake has been having great difficulty obtaining acceptable or even completed work from many of her sixth-grade students. They never seem to be able to follow instructions or directions, even for assignments in the textbook. Only the most able four or five pupils are actually doing good-quality work. Ms. Lake likes to challenge the students with new ideas to stimulate their curiosity and promote independent thinking. Although much of the class appears to enjoy her presentations, the students don't seem to be able to transfer their enthusiasm to their assignments. For example, in a recent science assignment, students were supposed to draw pictures illustrating stages in the evolution of birds from reptiles; most students did not perform satisfactorily. The lesson preceding this assignment included a five-item test containing questions on birds, reptiles, and vertebrates, reviewing some content covered during the preceding week. Students checked their own answers to this test in class and then passed them in. Although it was not a difficult test, most students got three or fewer items correct. After the checking activity, the teacher began a twenty-minute presentation on the possible evolution of birds from reptiles. The following topics were discussed:

- The meaning of adaptation, with an example supplied by students.
- An example of environmental action in the local community. This topic was introduced by a student, and other students added comments.
- The possibility of life on other planets, including a discussion of the number of solar systems in our galaxy.
- A consideration of the question of why birds might evolve from reptiles, with a student's answer, "To get away from enemies, they would take to the air," as the only reason given.
- The classification system of living organisms: kingdom, phylum, class, order, family, genus, and species.

At this point in the presentation, students were instructed to copy the classification system from the board. Ms. Lake also provided an example of classification, using the lion in the animal kingdom, vertebrate phylum, mammal class, and so on. Two similar examples were also presented and listed on the board. The teacher asked whether students understood and whether they had any questions. No questions were forthcoming, so the teacher gave the assignment of illustrating the stages in the evolution of a reptile to a bird. Students were given twenty-five minutes and told, "Use some color in your picture, make it neat, and use three stages." As was the case with many of the assignments Ms. Lake gave, only a few students completed their work satisfactorily, although most seemed to make an effort to do some drawing, and many students checked frequently with Ms. Lake to see whether their pictures were acceptable.

What problems are evident, and what changes might Ms. Lake make to achieve more success in helping students complete assignments satisfactorily?

Checklist 10

Check When Complete	Before the Lesson Ask Yourself	Notes
☐	A. What are the most important concepts or skills to be learned?	
☐	B. What kind of learning is your goal (memorization, application, appreciation)? Have you communicated this to your students?	
☐	C. What learning style is targeted by this lesson? Are you varying learning modalities?	
☐	D. Are there difficult words or concepts that need extra explanation?	
☐	E. How will you help students make connections to previous learning?	
☐	F. What activities will you plan to create interest in the lesson?	
☐	G. How will you make transitions between activities?	
☐	H. What materials will be needed? Will students need to learn how to use them?	
☐	I. What procedures will students need to know to complete the activities?	
☐	J. How much time will you allocate for the lesson? For different parts of the lesson?	
☐	K. If activities require that students work together, how will groups be formed? How will you encourage productive work in groups?	
☐	L. What examples and questioning strategies will you use? Prepare a list of examples for explanations and list higher-order questions.	
☐	M. How will you know during and after the lesson what students understand?	
☐	N. What are some presentation alternatives if students have trouble with concepts (peer explanation, media, etc.)?	
☐	O. Are there extra- or special-help students?	
☐	P. How will you make sure that all students participate?	
☐	Q. How will you adjust the lesson if time is too short or too long?	
☐	R. What kind of product, if any, will you expect from students at the end of the lesson?	
☐	S. What will students do when they finish?	
☐	T. How will you evaluate students' work and give them feedback?	
☐	U. How will the concepts you present be used by students in future lessons?	

Chapter 10

Activity 2

Problem 10.1

In organizing her students' day, Ms. Kendall must plan to accommodate both "school givens" of time and space and "pupil givens" of numbers and abilities. Before developing her daily schedule, Ms. Kendall must check the school's master schedule to learn what times have been assigned to her class for lunch, recess, music, art, physical education, and so on. In planning around these time constraints, she must consider how many students will be in the class, the range of their ability levels, and the size of the classroom. She must take into consideration both student attention patterns throughout the day and attention spans within the day. Because students tend to be more alert in the morning and less alert after lunch, she will want to schedule academic subjects accordingly. Also, she will have to provide a variety of activities, with none lasting too long. Room size, however, will determine the number of centers and individual study areas available.

On the first day of school, Ms. Kendall's plans should include the following: greet the students; give a brief introduction of herself and her class; explain the areas of the room and procedures needed for the first week; begin a presentation and discussion of class rules, procedures, and consequences; direct a student get-acquainted activity; provide whole-class, uncomplicated academic activities; allow time to complete administrative tasks; and have constructive "time fillers" ready for use if needed.

Problem 10.2

The following suggestions for Mr. Hart could improve his students' performance during independent work.

- He should make sure that everyone understands instructions before starting groups. Explanation alone may not be sufficient; students should be questioned and should repeat key directions. Mr. Hart can also write the directions on the chalkboard. Students should be told what will be checked and when.
- If independent work includes silent reading, reading comprehension questions can be listed on the board so that students have a focus for their reading and know what they will be accountable for when they are called to the reading circle.
- Students may need help pacing themselves. The teacher can show them on the clock how much time the first assignment should take or set a timer to signal when they should be finished with a particular assignment.
- To have time to get the independent work group started, Mr. Hart can give the first reading group a getting-ready activity to complete before he joins them. This will enable him to monitor all out-of-group students at the beginning of the activity to be sure they have made a good start.
- After working with the reading group for a while, the teacher can give these students a short activity to do on their own while he checks on the progress of out-of-group students and answers their questions. When out-of-group students are wasting time and in danger of not completing other necessary activities, their papers can be marked to show each student's progress on the first assignment. They can then start on their next assignment, but they should be required to finish the first

assignment at home or later in class.

- Students should not be allowed to interrupt the teacher with questions during small-group instruction. They should be told to skip troublesome parts until the teacher can talk to them, or student monitors can be assigned the responsibility of giving assistance to children who need it.
- A visual signal, such as a sign or a flag, can be used to inform students when they may approach the teacher with questions and when they may not.
- A "help" list for the class may be established. Children can sign the list if they want to talk to the teacher when he is busy. The teacher must be conscientious about checking the list and going to the children as soon as possible (e.g., between reading groups).
- Students need to know what they may and may not do after their assignments have been completed. They should be given free-time enrichment activities or provided with a good set of interesting materials for free reading.

Problem 10.3

Apparently, this type of instruction is new for Ms. Jackson's class, so students will have to learn a new set of procedures. They may be accustomed to highly directed lessons, and they may not have had much science instruction. Ms. Jackson will have to explain the procedures for a discovery lesson, including how to work on your own and with a partner, and the purposes for this science lesson. She should make sure she has everyone's attention before beginning the explanation. She should start by introducing the lesson and its purposes and demonstrating appropriate uses of the cups. She must make clear at the beginning what uses of the cups she sees as inappropriate.

Ms. Jackson must consider how to create a balance between overdirecting students and leaving them too much on their own. She should work through questions like those in Checklist 10 to focus on her purposes for this lesson and which aspects of it are new to her students. For example, what kind of product does she expect from her students? Will they demonstrate their findings, write a lab report, apply their findings to another situation? If pairs or groups work independently, what will they do if they finish at different times?

Ms. Jackson has to develop a system for distributing and collecting materials to minimize the time the teacher is unavailable to circulate and provide assistance. For example, she might appoint one student from each group as "Materials Manager" and set up a central place for that student to pick up cups for the group.

Activity 3

Problem 10.4

See how many examples of Kounin's concepts noted on page 263 you can find in the following description.

As he is about to begin class after lunch, Mr. Case makes eye contact with two students who are exchanging notes; the students quickly get out their class materials. (**Withitness**) "Let's begin by working some of the exercises at the end of the chapter; you will need a piece of paper with a heading." As students begin to get out their materials, Mr. Case calls out, "Oops, I forgot to tell you to bring money for tomorrow for the field trip. How many of you will be going?" (**Lack of smoothness**) After a brief discussion, students finish getting out their materials. Mr. Case says, "We'll go through these exercises orally, but I also want you to write the answers on your papers as part of today's classwork. I'll come around later and check your answers. (**High-participation format and accountability**) Now, who can answer the first question? Hands please. Tyrone?" Mr. Case conducts the lesson by calling on various students, some with hands up, others seemingly at random from the nonvolunteers. (**Group alerting**) About halfway through the exercises, a student enters the room and says that he is new to the school and has been assigned to the class. Mr. Case goes to his desk, sits down, and says, "OK, come here. I'll check out some of your books to you. (**Lack of overlapping**) I wish the school office wouldn't send children in the middle of the period. Where are you from anyway? That's a nice shirt you are wearing." (**Lack of smoothness**) After finishing with the student and sending him to a seat, Mr. Case leaves his desk and says to the class, "Now where were we? Oh, yes, question 7. Say, where did Kim and Lee go? I didn't give them permission to leave." (**Lack of withitness**) After several more minutes, Mr. Case calls a halt to the activity and says, "Now, I'd like us to discuss the test coming up this Thursday. Let's make sure that you are all clear on what will be on the exam and what you will need to get ready for it." After a pause, he adds, "I almost forgot. Get your questions from before and look at the next to the last one. We have to add an important point that was left out. . . ." After finishing the item, Mr. Case turns the topic back to the upcoming test. (**Lack of momentum**) "Now, where were we. Oh, yes. I want to show you some items that will be similar to those on the test. Here's one." He writes it on the board, then pauses: "Well, I don't want to give away the test, do I?" Without discussing the test further, he turns to another topic. (**Lack of smoothness**) "Just wait until you hear about the videotape we will be viewing tomorrow. I borrowed it from another teacher, and she said that her students thought it was one of the most interesting, exciting stories they had ever seen!" (**Group alerting**)

Activity 4

Case Study 10.1

Diagnosis

Although Ms. Lake has planned interesting presentations, her students seem to be floundering during the follow-up activities. A large part of Ms. Lake's problem lies with poor instructional clarity, poor sequencing of activities, and unclear directions. Students' poor showing on the five-item test suggests that related content from the previous week had not been understood. The twenty-minute presentation contains several indicators of poor clarity, including presenting information out of sequence, backtracking, inserting extraneous information, and moving from one topic to another without warning. In addition, the assignment does not support the content development activity. The assignment is made without checking for understanding, and the directions are vague and indefinite.

Suggestions

Ms. Lake would achieve more success with her class if she concentrated on the following items:

■ Information should be presented systematically. Plan the lesson sequence and stick to it; state major goals and objectives; pace the lesson so that adequate time is available to cover major points; and avoid vagueness by being specific and using familiar words.

- Ms. Lake should review her procedures for keeping students responsible for work, especially in the areas of communicating work requirements and giving directions clearly. She should be sure that step-by-step directions are given for complex assignments, and she should ask students to repeat directions if there is a possibility that they do not understand them.
- During content development activities, frequent work samples should be obtained and other checks on comprehension used. With this information, available instruction can be adjusted as needed.
- The amount of information being presented in any one lesson should be considered carefully. It might be better to present less information and leave sufficient time to check classwork before assigning homework.
- Complex lessons should be broken down into smaller parts, and later concepts should not be presented until primary ones are mastered.
- If some students still do not seem to understand after a presentation and discussion, the teacher can meet with them in a small group to review the presentation and answer questions. If one or two students consistently have difficulty, they can be seated near the teacher's desk so that it is easier to work with them.
- During the independent work portion of lessons, the teacher should circulate to check student progress and to make sure that assignment directions are being followed.

11

Managing Problem Behaviors

Taken from *Classroom Management for Elementary Teachers*, Seventh Edition, by Carolyn M. Evertson, Edmund T. Emmer, and Murray E. Worsham.

Teachers' reactions to the problem behaviors described in this chapter are often affected by the adult models they observed and the type of discipline they received as children, both at home and at school. Recall your early experiences in this area and consider their implications. To what extent do these earlier models provide a positive guide for managing problems of varying severity? Would the strategies that were effective for you be equally appropriate or effective for the varied kinds of students you may teach? Are there current behaviors or environmental problems that you did not experience (e.g., drug culture, poverty, single parent/guardian homes, bullying)? Where should you add to or modify your approach?

In this chapter, we describe strategies for dealing with some problem behaviors you may encounter. Although previous chapters described preventive measures as well as tactics for managing inappropriate behavior, it is helpful to consider a full range of approaches. We hope that you will not encounter problems, especially serious ones, in large numbers. However, as you work with students, you will undoubtedly face difficult situations that must be resolved to preserve the climate for learning or to assist a student in developing behaviors more compatible with group life and learning. The aim of this chapter is to pull together and organize a wide array of possible strategies from which you can select. By having a broad array of approaches to draw on, you will be better able to choose one that fits your specific conditions. Having some alternatives in mind is very useful too, in case your first plan doesn't work.

We hope this chapter's concern with behavior problems will not be taken as a grim comment on the teacher's role. In particular, this extensive list of strategies should be considered within the context of the other chapters in this book. We have advocated generally for a positive, supportive climate with heavy reliance on preventive measures. Within that framework, however, you must be ready to deal with problems when they arise. With a variety of strategies at hand, you can tailor your approach to fit the situation, keep interruptions to the instructional program to a minimum, and promote positive behavior.

This chapter's focus is on problem behaviors rather than problem students. Only a small percentage of students exhibit maladaptive behaviors with such consistency and to such a degree that they warrant being labeled emotionally disturbed or behaviorally disordered. With a few students you may have to "teach" acceptable behavior. Most students do, however, behave inappropriately on occasion; we think it is much more constructive in the long run to help students learn how to behave rather than impute internal causes for their behavior and assume the students are restricted in the capacity to make good choices.

On occasion, problem behaviors result from stressors (e.g., abuse, a death in the family, parental unemployment, serious illness, or divorce) the student is experiencing at home or elsewhere. If a student's behavior changes, or if inappropriate behavior persists after reasonable attempts to deal with it have been made, a discussion of the situation with a parent, guardian, school counselor, or social worker is in order. Sometimes the student's previous teacher can provide additional information. When you talk with the student about what is happening, use listening skills to try to understand the situation. Be empathic, but help the child understand that acting out will not help the problem. By all means, follow up if you discover that a situation outside the classroom is affecting the child's behavior.

What Is Problem Behavior?

The concept of problem behavior is broad. Rather than enumerate all possible misbehaviors that might occur in classrooms, it is more manageable to think of categories.

Nonproblem

Brief inattention, some talk during a transition between activities, small periods of daydreaming, and a short pause while working on an assignment are examples of common behaviors that are not really problems for anyone because they are of brief duration and don't interfere with learning or instruction. Everyone is the better for their being ignored. To attempt to react to them would consume too much energy, interrupt lessons constantly, and detract from a positive classroom climate.

Minor Problem

This includes behaviors that run counter to class procedures or rules but that do not, when occurring infrequently, disrupt class activities or seriously interfere with learning. Examples are calling out or leaving seats without permission, reading or doing unrelated work during class time, passing notes, eating candy, scattering trash around, and talking excessively during independent work or group work. These behaviors are minor irritants as long as they are brief in duration and are limited to one or a few students. You would not give them much thought except for two reasons: Unattended, they might persist and spread; if the behaviors have an audience, not to respond might cause a perception of inconsistency and potentially undermine an important aspect of the overall management system. Also, if students engage in such behavior for an extended period of time, their learning is likely to be adversely affected.

Major Problem but Limited in Scope and Effects

This category includes behaviors that disrupt an activity or interfere with learning but whose occurrence is limited to a single student or perhaps to a few students not acting in concert. For example, a student may be chronically off-task. Another student may rarely complete assignments. A student may frequently fail to follow class rules for talk or movement around the room or may refuse to do any work. This category also includes a more serious but isolated violation of class or school rules, for example, an act of vandalism or hitting another student.

Escalating or Spreading Problem

This category includes any minor problem that has become commonplace and thus constitutes a threat to order and the learning environment. For example, when many students roam around the room at will and continually call out irrelevant comments, content development activities suffer; social talking that continues unabated even when the teacher repeatedly asks for quiet is distracting to others; and talking back and refusal to cooperate with the teacher are frustrating and may lead to a poor classroom climate. Frequent violations of behavioral guidelines cause the management and instructional system to break down and interfere with the momentum of class activities.

Goals for Managing Problem Behavior

In dealing with problem behavior, several types of goals must be considered. You have to judge the short- and long-term effects of any management strategy you choose. In the short term, the desired results are that the inappropriate behaviors cease and the students resume or begin appropriate behaviors. In the long run, it is important to prevent the problem from recurring. At the same time, you must be watchful for potential negative side effects and take steps to minimize them. Also, consider the effects on the individual student or students causing the problem as well as the effect on the whole class.

Joel is talking and showing off to a group of students during independent work. The teacher could squelch Joel by using a sarcastic put-down or a strong desist but chooses instead to redirect Joel's behavior and stand close by until he is working on the assignment. The put-down or strong desist might get faster results in the short run, but it may lead to resentment or even conflict if Joel tries a rejoinder. Redirection and proximity control take a little more effort but do not have negative side effects. In addition, they offer more support for appropriate behavior.

The ideal strategy is one that maintains or restores order in the class immediately without adversely affecting the positive learning environment; in addition, an ideal strategy prevents a repetition of the problem and results in subsequent appropriate behavior in similar situations. In practice, classrooms are busy places, and you rarely have sufficient time to mull over the various options and their effects whenever a problem arises, especially in the midst of a crisis. If only there were a "pause" button on classroom events! The need for prompt reaction should not, however, deter us from evaluating the results of our efforts and from seeking alternative approaches, especially when our initial efforts do not meet with success. It is, therefore, useful to have a repertoire of strategies to apply to various problem situations.

Management Strategies

This section includes useful strategies for dealing with a variety of classroom behavior problems. The first several strategies can be utilized without much difficulty, require little teacher time, and have the great virtue of being relatively unobtrusive. They have much to recommend them because they do not give undue attention to the misbehavior and do not interfere with the flow of instructional activity. As we move down the list, we encounter strategies that are more direct attempts to stop the behaviors and to do so quickly; however, the strategies have more negative features: they demand more of the teacher's time, they may have unintended consequences on students, or they interrupt class activities. A general principle helpful in selecting a strategy is to use an approach that is effective in stopping the inappropriate behavior promptly and that has the least negative impact. An implication is that minor problems should usually be dealt with by limited interventions. As problems become more serious, the limited interventions may be ineffective in quickly ending the disruptive behavior and thus a more time-consuming or intrusive intervention may be required. With every level of problem and strategy chosen, however, you must be consistent and fair with all students.

Most elementary schools have prescribed procedures for dealing with certain types of major problems and sometimes even minor ones. For example, teachers' responses to events such as fighting, obscene language, stealing, vandalism, and unexcused absence are likely to be directed by school (or district) policies. Therefore, a beginning teacher must learn what policies are in force and follow them. When no specific policy is established for particular problems or when teachers are given latitude in their responses, the alternatives listed later in the chapter can be helpful.

It is a given that preventive measures are more desirable than reactive ones. Thus, the earlier chapters have mainly been devoted to setting up the classroom environment to eliminate the need for frequent recourse to major interventions. Sometimes responsive strategies are still needed. However, when teachers find themselves frequently using major interventions to deal with minor problems, it is time to reevaluate expectations and the overall management and instructional plan and make needed modifications. To this end, reviewing suggestions for management presented in prior chapters and perhaps using the checklists to provide focus could result in changes that help reduce the problems. Teachers should also be aware that sometimes the source of the problem lies in frustration with content that the student does not grasp or with tasks that the student lacks skills to perform. When the problem is one of a poor fit between a student's capabilities and academic requirements, the source must also be addressed by developing more appropriate class activities and assignments or by giving the student more assistance.

If you have a special needs student whose behavior is causing a problem, you may find it helpful to discuss the situation with a special education teacher and ask for suggestions. In particular, find out whether the student has a special discipline program as part of an individualized education plan (IEP). Sometimes such a plan specifies particular ways to respond to the student or gives useful alternative strategies. Even if no specific discipline plan is included in the IEP, you may be able to obtain helpful ideas for working with the student.

In the pages that follow we describe classroom strategies that have a wide range of application, but the list is not exhaustive. Readers interested in additional ways of coping with behavior problems will find articles by Shukla-Mehta and Albin (2003) and Myles and Simpson (1994) helpful. Books that contain good descriptions of strategies for dealing with specific problems or with crisis management include Poland and McCormick (1999), Cohen and Fish (1993), and Stoner, Shinn, and Walker (1991). Many of the recommendations in these books are for school administrators or school psychologists, but there is much of value for teachers as well. Finally, the *Handbook of Classroom Management* (Evertson & Weinstein in press) has many excellent chapters that describe strategies for managing problems.

Minor Interventions

Use Nonverbal Cues

Make eye contact with the student and give a signal such as a finger to the lips, a head shake, or a hand signal to issue a desist. Sometimes lightly touching a student on the arm or shoulder helps signal your presence and has a calming effect. Never touch a student when you are angry, though, and avoid touching students when they are angry. Touching in these cases is likely to escalate the situation.

Get the Activity Moving

Often student behavior deteriorates during transition times between activities or during "dead" time when no apparent focus for attention is present. Students leave their seats, talk, shuffle restlessly, and amuse themselves and each other while waiting for something to do. The remedy is obvious: move through the transition more quickly and reduce or eliminate the dead time. This entails planning activities so that all materials are ready and adhering to a well-conceived lesson plan. Trying to catch and correct inappropriate behaviors during such times is usually futile and misdirected. Just get the next activity under way and direct students to the desired behaviors.

Use Proximity

Move closer to students. Combine proximity with nonverbal cues to stop inappropriate behavior without interrupting the instruction. Be sure to continue monitoring the students at least until they have begun an appropriate activity.

Use Group Focus

Use group alerting, accountability, or a higher-participation format (see Chapter 10) to draw students back into a lesson when attention has begun to wane or when students have been in a passive mode for too long and you observe off-task behavior spreading.

Redirect the Behavior

When students are off-task, remind them of appropriate behavior: "Everyone should be writing answers to the chapter questions," "Be sure your group is discussing your project plan," "Everyone should be seated and quiet unless you have been given permission to leave your seat or talk." If only one or two students are engaged in inappropriate behavior, a private redirection will be less likely to interrupt the activity or to direct attention toward the incorrect behavior. A redirection strategy that works well with younger children is the use of group and individual public praise for appropriate behavior. For example, if several students are talking and inattentive at the beginning of a new activity, the teacher should identify students who are behaving correctly: "I see many students who are sitting quietly, ready to begin. . . . I really appreciate the boys and girls who are ready for our next activity. John is listening, Donica is being very quiet. Oh, good, Demetrius, Richard, and Corby are ready. . . ." In most cases, off-task students quickly come around.

Provide Needed Instruction

Especially during individual work or group work, off-task behaviors may reflect poor comprehension of the task. Check the work or ask brief questions to assess understanding; give necessary assistance so students can work independently. If many students can't proceed, stop the activity and provide whole-class instruction. Next time, be sure to check comprehension before starting the independent work activity.

Issue a Brief Desist

Tell the students to stop the undesirable behavior. Make direct eye contact and be assertive (see Chapter 8). Keep your comments brief, and monitor the situation until the student complies. Combine this strategy with redirection to encourage desirable behavior.

Give the Student a Choice

Tell the student that he or she has a choice: either to behave appropriately or to continue the problem behavior and receive a consequence. Be sure to describe the desired behavior. Telling a student to "behave appropriately" does not communicate clearly what the desired behavior should be. For example, suppose a student has refused to clean up properly after completing a project: "You may choose to clean up now; if not, you are choosing to stay in during recess until your area is clean." To a student who continues to distract nearby students: "You may choose to work quietly on your assignment at your seat, or you will have to sit in the time-out area to do your work." The purpose of stating the consequence as a choice is to emphasize the student's responsibility for his or her behavior. Also, making the consequence clear increases the chance that the student will choose to self-regulate.

Moderate Interventions

These strategies are more confrontational than the limited interventions described previously and thus have greater potential for eliciting resistance. In cases in which the student's behavior is not especially disruptive, it is desirable to use a minor intervention or to issue a warning to the student before using these interventions. Doing so permits the student to exercise self-control and may save the teacher time and effort.

Withhold a Privilege or Desired Activity

Students who abuse a privilege (e.g., being allowed to work together on a project, sitting near friends, or having the freedom to move around the classroom without permission) can lose the privilege and be required to earn it back with appropriate behavior. Sometimes teachers allow quiet talking during independent activities and removing this privilege can be an effective way to limit unproductive social behavior. Other teachers allow a class to choose a favorite activity or a short period of free time on one or more days each week as incentives. Time lost from such activities can then be a strong deterrent to inappropriate behavior at other times. Although withholding a privilege is a form of punishment, it usually has fewer side effects than punishment that requires directly applying an aversive consequence.

Isolate or Remove Students

Students who disrupt an activity can be removed to another area of the room, away from other students. It is helpful to have a carrel with sides, or at least a desk at the back of the room facing away from other students, to discourage eye contact from the time-out area. If no suitable place is available, the student may have to have time-out in the hall outside the door, although not if your school has a policy prohibiting this because of the problem of adequately supervising the student.

Time-out is a variation on the preceding consequence in that it takes away the student's privilege of participating in the activity. It is a good idea to allow excluded students to return to the activity in a short time, as long as their behavior in time-out is acceptable. Some teachers prefer to let them retain some control over the return, using a direction such as, "You may come back in five minutes if you decide that you can follow our class rules." Other teachers prohibit the student from returning until the activity is completed or until they have a brief conference with the student.

A problem with time-out is that some students may find it rewarding. They receive attention when it is administered, and it allows them to avoid an activity they dislike. When this occurs, you should switch to another strategy. Another problem is that a student may refuse to go to the time-out area. Usually this is a temporary problem; if you are firm, ignoring the student's protests and continuing with the activity, the student will go eventually. One way to move a recalcitrant body is to offer a choice: "You can either take time-out or walk to the principal's office. It's your decision."

Time-out has another risk. Its use clearly identifies a student as someone who is excludable, and it may result in implicit labeling by the teacher, by other students, or by the excluded student. If used frequently with a particular student, it may cause resentment and anger. Therefore, be sure to provide opportunities for the student to resume full participation in the class and use other strategies to promote appropriate behavior at the same time.

Use a Penalty

Sometimes a small amount of repetitious work is required as payment for inappropriate behavior. For example, in physical education students may be required to run an extra lap or do push-ups. In math, students may work extra problems. The advantage of this type of consequence is that it can usually be administered quickly with a minimum of the teacher's time and effort. A disadvantage is that the task is being defined as punishing, and therefore the student's attitude toward the content may be negatively affected. Another problem with the use of penalties is that their ease of use can lead to overuse, detracting from the overall climate.

Assign Detention

Another penalty commonly used is to require that the student serve a detention, whether at lunch, during recess, or before or after school. Because of the logical relationship between the problem and the consequence, this penalty is often used for misbehaviors that involve time (e.g., extended goofing off and time wasting; behavior that interferes with instruction or work time). Other common uses of the penalty are for repeated rule violations and for frequent failure to complete assignments. You may have to supervise the detention in your room, or your school might have a detention hall with an assigned monitor. The time in detention need not be lengthy, especially for misbehaviors that are not severe or frequent; a ten- or fifteen-minute detention is often sufficient to make the point.

An advantage of detention as a penalty is that it is disliked by most students, and they want to avoid it; at the same time, it is administered away from other students in the class and thus does not give undue attention to the behavior. Also, it is a common punishment, so extensive explanations and unusual procedures aren't needed. Finally, the teacher can sometimes use a little of the detention time to hold a conference with the student and perhaps work out a plan for improving the situation.

A disadvantage of detention is that it does take the teacher's time, especially when he or she must supervise it. Even when the school has a D-Hall, the teacher must write a referral. Another disadvantage is that students might be able to avoid detention, at least in the short run, simply by not showing up. Thus, the teacher or the school must have a backup plan, such as doubling the time; moreover, records must be kept and often additional time is required to deal with such students.

Use a School-Based Consequence

If your school has a prescribed consequence for particular problem behaviors and you are allowed some latitude in its administration, you should consider utilizing it after you have not had desired results with other strategies. For example, some schools have a system of referral to the principal, who then deals with the student. Often a first referral consequence is limited to detention or to a warning, with subsequent referrals resulting in a parent conference. It is necessary to apprise the administrator of the basis for the referral and to discuss what outcome is desirable. An advantage of this approach is that it does not require much of the teacher's time. A disadvantage is that the usefulness of this strategy is dependent on others for its effectiveness; also, extensive and frequent external support for handling in-class problems is not a realistic option in most schools.

More Extensive Interventions

When students do not respond to minor or moderate interventions and their behavior continues to disrupt classroom activities and to interfere with their own and others' learning, one or more of the following strategies can be helpful.

Use Problem Solving

Problem solving was described extensively in Chapter 8, so it is not discussed in this chapter. However, the next three strategies, which share features with problem solving, are sufficiently difficult to warrant separate presentations.

Use a Five-Step Intervention Procedure

Jones and Jones (2001) recommend following five steps when dealing with disruptive student behavior.

STEP 1: Use a nonverbal signal to cue the student to stop.

STEP 2: If the behavior continues, ask the student to follow the desired rule.

STEP 3: If the disruption continues, give the student a choice of stopping the behavior or choosing to develop a plan.

STEP 4: If the student still does not stop, require that the student move to a designated area in the room to write a plan.

STEP 5: If the student refuses to comply with Step 4, send the student to another location (e.g., the school office) to complete the plan.

The five-step intervention process requires students to complete a form for the plan (Figure 11.1). When the approach is introduced to students, preferably at the beginning of the year, the teacher explains its purpose and how to fill out the form. Role playing the use of the five steps is recommended, both to teach the procedures and to provide a positive model of their application. It is helpful to laminate a couple of examples of appropriate plans so students have models.

Advantages of this approach include its emphasis on student responsibility and choice. Also, a graduated response to the problem allows the teacher to intervene nonpunitively at first and thus provides a means of settling the matter quickly, with a minimum of disturbance to the ongoing activity. The steps are simple and straightforward, which promotes consistency by the teacher; students, in turn, are aided by the structure and predictability of the approach.

A disadvantage of the system is that movement from Step 1 to Step 5 can occur very rapidly, and intermediate strategies may be necessary to avoid excessive reliance on sending students out of the classroom. In addition, some students, especially in early primary grades, have difficulty writing an acceptable plan by themselves. Finally, set-

---

Choose to Be Responsible

Figure 11.1

Problem-Solving Form

Name_____Date_____

Rules we agreed on:

1. Speak politely to others.
2. Treat each other kindly.
3. Follow teacher requests.
4. Be prepared for class.
5. Make a good effort at your work and request help if you need it.
6. Obey all school rules.

Please answer the following questions:

1. What rule did you violate? _____
   _____

2. What did you do that violated this rule? _____
   _____

3. What problem did this cause for you, your teacher, or classmates? _____
   _____

4. What plan can you develop that will help you be more responsible and follow this classroom rule? _____
   _____

5. How can the teacher or other students help you? _____
   _____

I, _____, will try my best to follow the plan I have written and to follow all other rules and procedures that we created to make the classroom a good place to learn.

_____

ting up the system and, later, meeting with students to discuss their plans and monitoring implementation require at least a moderate investment of time.

Use the "Think Time" Strategy

Designed to help students learn self-control and to prevent a reciprocally escalating sequence of student noncompliance–teacher warnings and reprimands, the Think Time strategy removes a noncompliant student to another teacher's classroom to provide time for the student to gain focus and reenter the classroom after making a commitment to change the behavior (Nelson & Carr 2000). Using the Think Time strategy requires the cooperation of another teacher whose classroom is in close proximity. The partner teacher reserves a location in the room that is not in a high-traffic area and that will minimize attention to the entering student. After arriving at the receiving classroom, the student waits quietly in the designated area and thinks about what happened. As soon as is practicable (e.g., three to five minutes), the receiving teacher makes contact with the student and gives him or her a debriefing form to fill out that asks "What was your behavior?" and "What behavior do you need to display when you go back to your classroom?" The student is asked if he or she can do it, or if a conference is needed with the teacher. If the student completes the form acceptably, the receiving teacher sends the student back to the original class.

If you use this strategy, you will need to partner with another teacher. After preparing a location in your rooms to receive think time students, you each need to teach your students about Think Time. Nelson recommends treating this task as you would any other complex procedure: explain the purpose of the strategy (e.g., to help students learn self-control and to minimize disruption to learning) and what behaviors might result in Think Time. You also need to describe the signal you will use to send someone to Think Time (e.g., hand them a pass card) and model how students will be expected to leave the room and enter the other teacher's room. The students should also be shown an example of the debriefing form with examples of appropriate responses. For high school applications, Nelson recommends having a back-up administrative sanction, such as an office referral, if a student becomes disruptive. Likewise, if a student is required to use Think Time more than once in a class period or after the third time in a semester, then an office referral or In School Suspension (ISS) assignment is used along with a parent contact.

Think Time gives the teacher a way to manage students who don't respond to simpler desist techniques, and at the same time it short circuits the reciprocal escalation of hostile interaction that can develop when a student resists a teacher's attempt to stop misbehavior. Another advantage is that Think Time provides a "ceasefire" opportunity in which students acknowledge their part in the problem and identify a solution. In this respect, it is similar to other problem-solving strategies. Limitations in the use of the strategy are that it takes the cooperation and commitment of another teacher, and it requires planning and systematic application to be successful. A training videotape is available through Sopris West (www.sopriswest.com).

Use the Reality Therapy Model

William Glasser's (1975, 1977) ideas about reality therapy have been widely applied in education. The essential features when working with an individual student include establishing a caring relationship with the student, focusing on present behaviors, getting the student to accept responsibility, developing a plan for change, obtaining a commitment to follow the plan, and following up. Glasser believes strongly that students choose behavior depending on their perceptions of its consequences. Most students choose appropriate behaviors when they believe these will lead to desirable outcomes, and they avoid behaviors they perceive will lead to undesirable consequences. Glasser's plan can be put into effect using the following steps.

STEP 1: Establish involvement with the students. If students believe the teacher cares for them and has their best interests in mind, they will be more likely to follow the teacher's guidance when evaluating and changing their behavior. Teachers can show commitment to and caring for students in numerous ways: commenting favorably to the students about their work; being friendly; and showing an interest in student activities, families, likes and dislikes, and hobbies. Teachers can also get involved by demonstrating school spirit, joking, being good listeners, and taking time to talk with students about their concerns. The best time to establish involvement is before a student becomes disruptive, but even if a student has begun to exhibit problem behavior, it is not too late to begin. When a teacher makes a special effort to have two or three friendly contacts a day with such a student, it can be helpful in creating a more positive climate for change.

STEP 2: Focus on behavior. When a problem has occurred, Glasser recommends that a brief conference be held with the student. The initial concern should be to determine what the problem is. To this end, the teacher should ask only questions about "what happened" or "what's going on" and avoid trying to fix blame. Even if the teacher knows exactly what the problem is, it is wise to obtain the student's perspective.

STEP 3: The student must accept responsibility for the behavior. This means the student acknowledges that he or she did engage in the behavior. No excuses are accepted. Admitting responsibility is difficult, especially when there are so many other handy things to blame, but in the end, it is a form of denial to try to assign responsibility elsewhere when it was the student who engaged in the behavior. Of course, it is possible that more than one individual is responsible for the problem, but that should not be an excuse for irresponsibility.

STEP 4: The student should evaluate the behavior. If students have difficulty perceiving their part or they minimize it, Glasser suggests asking, "Has the behavior helped or hurt you? Has it helped or hurt others?" The teacher may have to point out the negative consequences of continuing to misbehave. Unless the student sees that the behavior leads to negative consequences and that changing it will produce desirable consequences, there isn't much reason to expect a change.

STEP 5: Develop a plan. The teacher and student identify ways to prevent the problem from recurring and the new behaviors needed. The plan can be written as a contract.

STEP 6: The student must make a commitment to follow the plan. Progress will be limited at best if students do not seriously intend to make a change. It may help if the teacher makes clear the positive and negative consequences of following or not following the plan. The plan should be do-able in a reasonable time.

STEP 7: Follow up and follow through. If the plan doesn't work, it should be modified with the student; if a negative consequence was called for in the plan, it should be used. Glasser also proposes several additional steps beyond the classroom if a student continues to be a problem. For example, use of in-school suspension could be a consequence of continuing misbehavior; before the student is allowed to return to the classroom, an acceptable plan must be agreed on. Only after several failed attempts to obtain a change should the teacher refer the student to the principal.

The reality therapy approach to dealing with individual discipline problems has several positive aspects. It is a systematic way for teachers to deal with many kinds of individual problems, and it provides a simple, yet effective, process for getting right at the issues and avoiding being sidetracked by fault finding, conning, or excuse making. Research on the effects of this aspect of reality therapy is generally supportive for applications to individual students (Emmer & Aussiker 1990).

Confer with a Parent

Sometimes a telephone call or an e-mail to a parent can have a marked effect on a student's behavior, signaling to the child that accountability for behavior extends beyond the classroom. This assumes you have established with parents how they wish to be contacted. Parents react best if they don't feel they are being held responsible for their child's behavior in school (after all, they aren't there), so don't put the parent on the defensive. Describe the situation briefly and say that you would appreciate whatever support the parent can give in helping you understand and resolve the problem. Acknowledge the difficulty in rearing children as well as in teaching them. Be sure to use listening skills during the conversation, and be alert for information that might help you determine an appropriate strategy for dealing with the student. Have your grade book handy so you can give the parent specific information about the student's progress if the information is requested or needed.

Rather than a phone conference, you might have to schedule a face-to-face conference with a parent. Sometimes, but by no means always, when such conferences are arranged, it is because a problem has become severe, and other school personnel (e.g., a counselor or principal) may have to be present. If you have initiated the meeting, brief the others and plan your approach ahead of time; inform parents of other staff members who will be attending the meeting.

The secret to successful parent-teacher conferences is planning. If you have back-to-back conferences, provide a place for the next arrivals to sit and wait. Arrange chairs for all participants in a circle, a semicircle, or around a table. Decide which issues need to be addressed with the parent. Bring documentation and a collection of the child's work over time to support those issues. Have the child's grades written on a separate piece of paper; showing the entire gradebook may infringe on another child's right to privacy.

Begin the conference by describing some of the child's strengths. During the meeting, avoid "teacher talk," acronyms, or technical terms the parents may not understand. Encourage comments and questions. If possible, include the child in all or part of the conference. Keep a written record of suggestions, concerns, and plans of action. End the conference by reiterating any responsibilities that have been assumed. Thank the parents for supporting their child's education.

The chief drawback to parent conferences is the time and energy they require. The effort is frequently worth it. Although not every conference is successful, many times the student's behavior improves. Another potential problem is identifying beforehand the strategy that is best to follow with the parent. Occasionally parents overreact and punish children excessively. As the year progresses, you will get to know parents better and be able to gauge the probable effects of your call or conference.

Create an Individual Contract with the Student

When a student's inappropriate behavior has become chronic or a problem is severe and must stop immediately, try an individual contract. You should discuss the nature of the problem with the student, including the student's perspective on it. Then you and the student can identify appropriate solutions and agree on which course of action to take. Typically, the contract specifies changes the student will make, but it might also call for the teacher to alter some behavior or activity. You should make clear the consequences that will occur if the plan is not followed, and you can also identify an incentive to encourage the student to follow through with the contract. The plan and consequences are written down and signed by the student. Contracts can also be used with other strategies (see the Five-Step Plan and Reality Therapy sections).

Special Problems

Children sometimes behave in ways that require stronger measures than those described in the preceding sections. These behaviors include rudeness, chronic avoidance of work, fighting, bullying, and defiance or hostility toward the teacher. Although these behaviors are not pleasant to contemplate, they are an inevitable result of close contact with up to thirty students for long periods of time. Fortunately, few teachers encounter these behaviors in large numbers. Regardless of their frequency, it is wise to be aware of ways to cope with them if they occur.

Before discussing each type of problem, general guidelines applicable to aggressive behaviors will be considered. Consider coping with these behaviors in two phases: the immediate response and a long-range strategy. At the time the behavior occurs, your immediate concern is to bring it to a halt with the least disruption possible. Because these behaviors are annoying and can arouse your anxiety or anger, be careful not to exacerbate the problem. By staying calm and avoiding overreaction, rather than becoming overbearing or dictatorial, you are more likely to bring the situation to a successful conclusion. You may tell the student how you feel, but by avoiding an argument or an emotional confrontation you will be in a better position to deal with the student and the problem. Thinking about ways to handle disruptive behavior ahead of time and consulting with more experienced teachers will help you to act rather than react.

Long-range goals are to prevent a recurrence of the behavior and to help the student learn a more constructive means of dealing with others. Preventing a recurrence of the behavior is best accomplished by (1) finding out what triggered the incident and resolving the cause if possible, and (2) having a predictable classroom environment with reasonable and consistently used rules, procedures, and consequences. Aggressive behavior rarely occurs in such classrooms. Helping these students acquire better behavior may require much individual attention from you over a period of time. The extent to which this goal is feasible is, of course, limited by many factors, including your time constraints and the severity of the student's problem. In dealing with students who have chronic problems, you may need consultation and assistance from the student's parents, the school counselor, a special education resource teacher, or the principal. Suggestions for handling specific types of behavior follow.

Bullying

Bullying is a pervasive problem in many schools and communities. It is unacceptable behavior characterized by harassment or intimidation of one student through a pattern of threats, teasing, or physical abuse by one or more other students. Bullying is typically learned from peer groups, the home, or the media. Because of its damaging effects on students' self-esteem, some schools have a "zero tolerance" policy for bullying.

Bullying is certainly contrary to the climate of respect you want to develop early in the year, and it can lead to serious and long-term emotional difficulties both for the bully and for the victim. Make sure your students understand from the first day that bullying is not acceptable and should be reported. Bullying is sometimes hard to detect because victims are reluctant to report it for fear of reprisals, and victimizers often intimidate onlookers as well. Most bullying occurs on the playground, in the cafeteria, in hallways, or on school buses; be alert to the possibility of these types of abusive incidents.

The most effective programs aimed at decreasing bullying are schoolwide programs (see Olweus, *Bullying Prevention Program* at www.stopbullyingnow.com) that create a climate in which bullying is considered by everyone to be unacceptable behavior. In your classroom, emphasize social skills training (see *Bully Busters or Steps to Respect* at www.cfchildren.org). Students also need to learn deflective responses for potential victims and positive roles for bystanders. Loss of peer support is a major deterrent to bullying. In addition to group discussions on bullying and recognizing feelings generated in both the victim and the victimizer, provide lessons on friendship skills, assertive behavior, and respectful problem solving.

If you encounter bullying, evaluate the seriousness of the behavior. For instance, teasing because of racial differences, physical disfigurement, home issues, or other unique aspects should never be allowed. After meeting with the individual students involved, determine whether to contact school administrators, school counselors, and parents. Stopping pervasive bullying will need coordinated efforts. Your ultimate goal is to prevent bullying from being seen as acceptable. Changing individual and group perceptions of the behavior is critical to the mental and emotional health of your students.

Tattling

Although tattling is often not disruptive, it can nevertheless become a problem when it becomes a common practice. Most teachers in the early grades develop standard practices for dealing with tattling and apply them when it happens. To prevent tattling from occurring in the first place, let students know what kinds of information they should and should not report to you. For example, you need to be told about situations in which students are hurt or in danger. This includes bullying as previously described. You do not need to be told when students are whispering in class or not doing their work. If you move around the classroom and monitor well, you will see behavior occur, and students will not have to call your attention to it.

If it appears that several of your students are tattling frequently, plan a brief lesson with the class to clarify the difference between tattling and being socially responsible. Provide examples of tattling, such as (1) trying to get someone else in trouble, (2) trying to get someone else to solve a problem you could handle, or (3) trying to get help for someone else who is actually capable of solving the problem alone. One way to illustrate the differences between social responsibility and tattling is to draw a chart on the board with these two headings and help students think of examples to write under each one. For example, under the Tattling heading would be such things as "Someone called me a name," "Someone squirted some water from the water fountain outside." Under the Social Responsibility heading you would include such things as "Someone pushed me down and hurt me, and my elbow is bleeding," "Someone is in the restroom crying and won't come out."

In deciding how you will handle tattling if it should occur, keep in mind that students who tattle are usually seeking attention from the teacher. If tattlers are successful in getting you to intervene with the alleged misbehavior, other students are likely to follow suit. It is usually sufficient to remind tattlers of what they are supposed to be doing at that moment and have them return to it.

Do be sensitive to situations in which the student may really need your support. If you discuss other options for the student to try, encourage the student to tell you how the other strategy worked if the situation recurs. Another response to the tattler may be, "I'm glad you know not to behave that way. I'll deal with Jimmy (or whoever the other student is) if I see him do that." Do not pull the other student in for a "you did too/no I didn't" confrontation with the tattler. And do not apply consequences to another child based on one student's report. It is also probably prudent for you to follow up and check out the situation for yourself. If other students report similar problems with the same student, you will need to monitor that student more closely.

Other interventions that may be useful for persistent tattlers include pointing out the natural consequences of tattling (peers are likely to shun a tattler); coaching the student in strategies for handling situations without tattling (e.g., walking away); and teaching specific problem-solving techniques (identify the problem, decide on a goal, develop a strategy and plan for action, carry out the plan).

Rudeness toward the Teacher

Rudeness may take the form of back talk, arguing, crude remarks, or gesturing. Although this kind of behavior may trigger your anger, it is best to maintain a low-key, respectful, and professional manner in your response. In this way, you can model the kind of behavior you expect from students, and you will be more effective in interacting with the student in question. Determine if the student knows this is unacceptable. Frequently, the student is using such behavior as a means of getting attention from you or from peers, or to avoid an assignment that she or he does not feel able to complete successfully.

Avoid sarcasm, overreacting, arguing, or being trapped in a power struggle. To some extent, your response will depend on the degree of rudeness and on how public it was. In borderline cases, the student may not even realize that a comment was offensive, or the student may be impulsively reacting to frustration with an instruction or task that may be unclear or too difficult. A reasonable first reaction is to inform the student that the behavior is not acceptable, possibly referring to a general classroom rule such as "respect others" or "be polite," followed by an offer to work with the student individually as soon as you have finished giving instruction to the class. If the incident is repeated or if the original comment was intentionally rude, conferring with the student to find out the reasons for this behavior or penalizing the student may be necessary. Should disrespectful behavior disrupt the class or persist, the student may have to be isolated from other students or sent to the school office and not allowed to return until he or she agrees to behave appropriately. Most schools have a standard policy for dealing with extreme cases, and you will be able to rely on whatever procedures have been established.

Chronic Avoidance of Work

You may have students who frequently do not complete assigned work. Sometimes they do not complete assignments early in the school year; more often, a student begins to skip assignments occasionally and then with increasing regularity until he or she is habitually not completing them. This behavior can be minimized by a carefully planned accountability system. However, even in classrooms with a strong accountability system, some students may still avoid work.

It is much easier and better for the teacher to correct this problem before the student gets so far behind that failure is almost certain. To take early action, you must collect and check student work frequently and maintain good records. When a student has begun to miss assignments, talk with the student, seek information to help identify the problem, and then take corrective action. If the student is simply unable to do

" . . . and suddenly there were teachers all over the place!" © 1968 by Bill Knowlton. Reprinted from *Classroom Chuckles,* published by Scholastic Book Services, a Division of Scholastic, Inc., by permission of Bill Knowlton.

the assigned work, you should provide appropriate assistance or modify the assignments. If the student feels overwhelmed by the assignments, break them up into parts whenever possible. Have the student complete the first part of the assignment within a specific time (perhaps five or ten minutes); then check to see that it has been done. A bonus of a few minutes of free time at the end of the period can be offered for completion of the portion within the time limit or for working steadily without prodding. Sometimes you can provide a list of assignments for the student to check off. This can serve as a self-monitoring device and can provide a sense of accomplishment.

If ability is not the problem, the following procedures can be used in addition to talking with the student. Call the student's parents and discuss the situation with them. Often they can supply the extra support needed to help motivate the student. A simple penalty of requiring that the student remain after school until assignments have been completed can prove effective. If the student rides a bus, you won't be able to use the procedure, of course, without making special arrangements with the parents. Any time the child is likely to be detained for more than a few minutes, alert the parents ahead of time. Another procedure that can be used when the parents are cooperative is for the child to take home daily a list of incomplete assignments and all books or materials needed to complete the work. Be cautious about using this procedure lest the student waste time thinking all work may be done at home.

Be sure not to soften the negative consequences of repeated failure to complete work by giving students higher grades than they have earned. Doing so teaches them to avoid responsibility. Provide added incentives for good effort and completed work. Set up a reward system that encourages students to do their best.

Fighting

Fighting is less likely to occur in classrooms than on the playground, in the cafeteria, or in some other area of the school. In the elementary grades, you can often stop a fight without undue risk of injury. (If for some reason you cannot intervene directly, alert other teachers and administrators so that action can be taken.) When you do intervene, first give a loud verbal command to stop. This alone may stop the fight; it at least alerts the combatants that a referee has arrived. Instruct a student in the group of onlookers to go immediately for help; be specific about where the student should go. If you feel it is safe for you to do so, separate the fighters; as you keep them separate, instruct the other students to leave, to return to their play, or to go to their classes. Without an audience before which the fighters need to save face, you are more likely to be able to keep them apart until help arrives or until you can get them to a different location.

Your school will undoubtedly have a procedure for dealing with fighting; you should carry it out. Students may be questioned by the principal, who may call the student's home, arrange a conference, and determine the next step.

If school policy leaves the teacher with the responsibility and wide discretion for following up on such incidents, decide on your procedures. Unless the fighting was very mild or stopped immediately, you will have to talk with the children's parents before the children go home. In any case, it is generally best to arrange a cooling-off period. If you cannot find someone to supervise your class, let the fighters wait in separate areas of your classroom or in the school office. Older children can cool off by writing their versions of how the fight started. If you do not know what started the fight, try to find out from uninvolved students. As soon as you have an opportunity, meet with the offenders and get each one's point of view. The conference should focus on the inappropriateness of fighting and the need to resolve problems in ways other than physical aggression, accusations, or personal criticism. Help each student understand the other's point of view so they have a basis for better communication. Finally, stress the importance and your expectations of cooperativeness and friendliness toward one another, or at the least, the need to stay away from each other for the time being.

During the next day or two, watch for any indications of residual hostility. If the issue seems not to have been resolved, follow up by contacting the children's parents, discussing the matter with your principal, or talking with the students again.

Power Struggles

Dealing effectively with power struggles requires understanding what motivates this behavior and using techniques that deescalate the anger. What drives people to attack others generally arises from needs for power, belonging, and respect. For students who act out hostile and aggressive feelings, one or more of these needs is unmet in their lives. Allen Mendler (1997) (Power Struggles: Successful techniques for educators, Rochester, NY: Discipline Associates) has a number of suggested strategies for handling this problem.

Defiance or hostility is understandably threatening to teachers. They feel, and rightfully so, that if students are allowed to get away with it, the behavior may continue, and other students will be more likely to react in the same way. A student who has provoked a confrontation, usually publicly, feels that backing down would cause a loss of face in front of peers. The best way to deal with such an event is to try to defuse it by keeping it private and handling it individually with the student.

If an incident occurs during a lesson and is not extreme, deal with it by trying to depersonalize the event and avoid a power struggle: "This is taking time away from the lesson. I will discuss it with you in a few minutes when I have time." If the student does not accept the opportunity you have provided and presses the confrontation further, instruct the student to leave the room and wait in the hall. After the student has had time to cool off, give your class something to do and discuss the problem with the student.

When discussing the incident, remain objective. Remember—act, don't react. Listen to the student's point of view and respond to it, but do not engage in an argument. Separate the student's reason or excuse from the behavior itself, and point out that the behavior was not acceptable. State the consequence clearly, and implement it. If you are not sure how to respond, give yourself time by saying that you will think about it and discuss it later. However, you should still administer the penalty.

In an extreme (and rare) case, the student may be totally uncooperative and refuse to keep quiet or leave the room. If this happens, you can escort the student from the room yourself or, when dealing with a student who is older or larger, call or send another student to the office for assistance. In most cases, however, as long as you stay calm and refuse to get into a power struggle with the student, the student will accept the opportunity to cool down.

Although large-scale school violence is still extremely rare, heightened concern over isolated events in recent years has led many districts and schools to develop emergency plans similar to those for fires or natural disasters. Of course, you will need to familiarize yourself with these plans, which probably include steps such as remaining calm, moving students quickly to a safe area, and contacting administration and emergency personnel.

A Final Reminder: Think and Act Positively

In this chapter, many of the strategies for dealing with problem behaviors involve some form of punishment. This is especially the case for the strategies in the moderate and extensive categories. A drawback to punishment is that, by itself, it doesn't teach the student what behaviors should be practiced, so it may not help them change their behavior in the way you intend. Consequently, it is important for teachers using one of these approaches also to communicate clearly about the desired behaviors. That is, the focus should remain on teaching appropriate behaviors. Furthermore, a classroom in which the main consequences are negative does not have a good climate. Thus, teachers using strategies in the moderate and extensive categories more than occasionally should try to incorporate additional incentives or a reward system into their overall classroom management to help mitigate the effects of using punishment. After correcting student behavior, a teacher who supplies a generous helping of warmth and affection, offers ways to earn back points, and so on, reassures them that all is not lost and that they have been restored to good grace.

FURTHER READING

Cutona, C., & Guerin, D. (1994). Confronting conflict peacefully: Peer mediation in schools. *Educational Horizons, 72*(2), 95–104.

Problem behavior that pits student against student can escalate to threaten schoolwide climate and safety. These behaviors often frustrate teachers and are difficult to resolve through adult intervention alone. This article describes the use of peer mediation to resolve conflicts. Examples of such programs are also presented, along with an analysis of their benefits.

Davis, Stan. (2004). *Schools where everyone belongs: Practical strategies for reducing bullying.* Wayne, Maine: Stop Bullying Now.

This book outlines research on effective bullying prevention and interventions and presents specific practices and skills that help schools implement that research.

Evertson, C. M., and Weinstein, C. S. (Eds) (in press). *Handbook on classroom management: Research, practice and contemporary issues.* Hillsdale, N.J.: Erlbaum.

Johnson, D. W., & Johnson, R. T. (1994a). Constructive conflict in the schools. *Journal of Social Issues, 50*(1), 117–137.

Learning how to handle conflict constructively is a major accomplishment that eludes many adolescents and children (not to mention adults). This article describes the peer mediation approach to handling conflict, along with championing the use of cooperative strategies and structured controversy. Procedures involved in classroom-based and schoolwide peer mediation programs are carefully described, along with their rationale and supporting research.

Martin, H., & Hayes, S. (1998). Overcoming obstacles: Approaches to dealing with problem pupils. *British Journal of Special Education, 25*(3), 135–139.

This study highlights the fact that the context within which behavior difficulties occur plays a role in their occurrence. Students with behavior difficulties are more engaged and better behaved when they enjoy the lesson and when they are able to quickly experience some level of success with the lesson. However, appropriate behavior does not always indicate student on-task involvement with a lesson.

McCarney, S. B., & McCain, B. R. (1995). *The behavior dimensions intervention manual.* Columbia, Mo.: Hawthorne Educational Services, Inc.

This book presents clearly described interventions to address the most common and disruptive behavior problems reported in schools. Some interventions may be used as a general approach for groups of students; others are quite specific and are to be used for an individual student.

Mendler, Allen. (1997). *Power struggles: Successful techniques for educators.* Rochester, N.Y.: Discipline Associates.

This short, easy-to-read book outlines specific steps teachers and other school staff can take to deescalate the cycle of hostility that can occur when students are confrontational. It includes checklists and other aids to help identify causes of power struggles and other hostile behavior.

Myles, B. S., & Simpson, R. L. (1994). Prevention and management considerations for aggressive and violent children and youth. *Education and Treatment of Children,* 17, 370–384.

Aggression is typically preceded by warning signs and follows a sequence of stages. This article describes prevention and intervention strategies keyed to these stages. Many of the suggested strategies are also useful for nonaggressive inappropriate behaviors.

Shores, R. E., Gunter, P. L., & Jack, S. L. (1993). Classroom management strategies: Are they setting events for coercion? *Behavioral Disorders,* 18(2), 92–102.

In describing the difference between positive and coercive interactions between students, especially those with behavior difficulties, and teachers, the authors suggest that most often teachers have coercive interactions with their students. To counter this potential difficulty, the authors present the value of positive interactions and the likelihood that these types of interactions will increase student performance, enhance the classroom climate, and make classroom management more effective.

Sprick, R. (1995). *The teacher's encyclopedia of behavior management: 100 problems/500 plans.* Longmont, Colo.: Sopris West.

This book addresses individual and classwide problems common to schools. It includes model plans along with specific interventions.

www.state.ky.us/agencies/behave/homepage

Organized by the Kentucky Department of Education, it assists parents and teachers in gaining access to information and sharing effective practices regarding a full range of behavior problems.

www.cfchildren.org

Committee for Children is an international organization committed to social, emotional, and academic learning. Special topics include bullying, youth violence, and emergent literacy. "Steps to Respect" is an award-winning program to combat bullying.

www.stopbullyingnow.com

This site presents practical research-based strategies to reduce bullying in schools. The Power Point presentation summarizing the basics of bullying prevention is very informative.

SUGGESTED ACTIVITIES

1. Review the descriptions of problem types presented at the beginning of the chapter. Decide which interventions would be best suited for each type. Given several alternative interventions for any type of problem, how would you decide which to use?

2. Within each type of intervention—minor, moderate, or extensive—are there any strategies that you distinctly prefer? Do you reject any? Discuss your reasons for liking or disliking particular approaches.

3. In this list of problem behaviors, decide on a strategy for dealing with each and also an alternative response if your first approach does not produce good results. Indicate any assumptions you are making about the teaching context as you choose your strategy.

   - *Situation 1.* Ardyth and Melissa talk and pass notes as you conduct a class discussion. Several other students whisper or daydream.
   - *Situation 2.* Desi and Bryce talk constantly. They refuse to get to work, and they argue with you when you ask them to open their books.
   - *Situation 3.* Joe manages to get most of his work done, but in the process he is constantly disruptive. He teases the girls sitting around him, keeping them constantly laughing and competing for his attention. Joe makes wisecracks in response to almost anything you say. When confronted, he grins charmingly and responds with exaggerated courtesy, much to the delight of the rest of the class.
   - *Situation 4.* When someone bumped into Marc at the drinking fountain, he turned around and spit water at the other child. Later Marc ordered a boy who was standing near his desk to get away, and he then shoved the boy. On the way back from the cafeteria, Marc got into a name-calling contest with another boy.

4. Make a list of student behaviors including defiance, rudeness, aggression, and unresponsiveness that are the most likely to embarrass you or make you uncomfortable. Think in advance about how you might handle each one.

5. Find out if your school has a policy regarding bullying and how that policy is communicated to students and parents.

12

Maintaining
Appropriate
Student Behavior

Taken from *Classroom Management for Middle and High School Teachers*, Seventh Edition, by Edmund T. Emmer, Carolyn M. Evertson, and Murray E. Worsham.

As you have seen in the first six chapters, good classroom management depends on very careful planning of classroom organization, rules, procedures, and instruction. All the preparation will pay large dividends when the students arrive. Readiness alone, however, is not sufficient to sustain good behavior throughout the year. You will have to be actively involved in maintaining student cooperation and compliance with necessary classroom rules and procedures. You cannot assume that students will behave appropriately just because you once discussed what was expected of them.

In particular, do not be lulled into complacency by the good behavior of your students during the first few days of school. Most classes are cooperative initially even if the teacher does not pay careful attention to maintaining good behavior, but a class that seems to begin very well may ultimately become disruptive and difficult to control. Behavior problems can have a gradual onset, developing over several weeks or even months. It is usually possible to avoid these problems, but doing so depends on understanding why they occur and what to do to prevent them. Because problems develop gradually, the causes are not always apparent to the teacher or even to an observer unfamiliar with the history of the classroom.

Teachers who are able to maintain a high level of cooperative, appropriate student behavior often share a number of characteristics and skills. One of these is observant monitoring of students. Such teachers have greater awareness of classroom events and behaviors, which improves their ability to detect and treat problems and help students who are having difficulty. Another characteristic of good managers is consistency in the use of rules and procedures and in their dealings with students who do not follow them. A third attribute is prompt management of inappropriate behavior, before it escalates or spreads. Finally, good behavior is maintained by creating a positive classroom climate, with an emphasis on encouraging appropriate behavior. This chapter discusses ways in which these concepts can be implemented.

Monitoring Student Behavior

To be an effective monitor of classroom behavior, you must know what to look for. Two categories of behavior are especially important.

1. Student involvement in learning activities
2. Student compliance with classroom rules and procedures

Student involvement is indicated by many behaviors, including attention during presentations and discussions, and progress on seatwork and other assignments.

Students' compliance with classroom rules and procedures will be easy to monitor if you have a clear set of expectations for student behavior and have communicated them to the class.

Monitoring student behavior during presentations requires that you stand or sit so that you can see the faces of all of the students and that you scan the room frequently. Actively monitoring a class by walking among students tends to increase student attention (Fifer 1986). Some teachers are not very good monitors of student behavior during whole-class activities because they focus their attention on a limited number of students, especially those seated in the middle rows and at the front desks. Other teachers "talk to the chalkboard." In either case, the teacher does not have a very clear perception of overall student response to the presentation or of what may be occurring at the periphery of the class. During your presentations, therefore, try to move around and develop "active eyes." If you notice commotion involving several students and you have no idea what is going on, this is a sign that you have not been monitoring closely enough.

When students are working on individual assignments, monitoring should be done by circulating around the classroom to check each student's progress periodically and to provide individual feedback. You will, of course, help students who request assistance; however, you should not just "chase hands." If you do, you will not be aware of the progress of all students. It is very difficult to monitor student progress on assignments from your desk or from any other fixed location, so spend as little time as possible at one place. If you must work at your desk for a time, get up periodically and circulate around the room to check on students' progress and to make sure that directions are being followed correctly. If you must spend a long time (e.g., more than a minute or two) helping an individual student, avoid doing it at the student's desk unless you can monitor the rest of the class from that position. For instance, if the student's seat is in the middle of the room, half of the class will be behind you. In such a case, call the student to your desk, to the front of the room, or to some other location from which you can easily see all students. Finally, if for some reason you must work at your desk or at any other location, don't let students congregate around the area. They will obstruct your view of the class, and they may distract students seated nearby. Instead, call students to you one at a time.

A technique for monitoring at the beginning of seatwork that is effective in getting everyone started is to begin the work as a whole-group activity. Have students get out the necessary materials (be sure to look for these on the students' desks), head their papers, and then do the first exercise or answer the first question or two under your direction. Check and discuss this work with the class. This makes it easy for you to scan the room to be sure that everyone has begun and to determine whether students understand what to do.

A critical monitoring task is checking assignments. Collect them regularly and look them over even when students do the checking in class. Keep your grade book current so that you will be able to detect students who are doing poor work or who skip assignments. If you give a long-term assignment, be sure to check progress regularly. You may even wish to give a grade or assign points toward a grade at these progress checkpoints. To encourage self-monitoring, you may also have students keep their own checklists of assignments.

Consistency

The dictum "be consistent" has been repeated more frequently than the Pledge of Allegiance. It is still worth some discussion, however, because its meaning is not always clear. In the classroom, consistency means retaining the same expectations for behaviors that are appropriate or inappropriate in particular activities; it also means that these expectations apply to every student on all occasions. For example, if students are expected to work silently during seatwork activities on Monday, the same procedure is in effect for all students on Tuesday, Wednesday, and so on. Consistency also applies to the use of penalties. For example, if the penalty for tardy arrival to class is detention, the teacher makes sure that all tardy students receive the penalty and that this procedure is followed even on the days when it is inconvenient to administer it or in spite of the pleading of individual students that an exception be made. Obvious inconsistency in the use of procedures or in the application of penalties usually causes students to "test the limits" by not following the procedure or by repeating whatever behavior was to have evoked the penalty. These events can rapidly escalate and force the teacher either to abandon the procedure or to tolerate high levels of inappropriate behavior. Because neither outcome is desirable, it is best to avoid the problem by resolving to be consistent in the first place.

Of course, it is not possible to be totally consistent, as there will be occasions when the most reasonable course of action is to make an exception to a rule or procedure. For example, if a student's individualized education program stipulates a particular way to handle rule violations for a special student, the plan must be followed even if you might respond differently to other students who committed the same infraction. Or a deadline for an assignment may be extended when a student has a valid reason, or some procedures might be changed to accommodate a special event. Note that procedures used routinely for some activities but not for others are not inconsistent. For example, you may stipulate that students should remain in their seats during discussions or presentations but that during seatwork they may get materials, sharpen pencils, or turn in papers as needed without permission. As long as you have differentiated between the activities when you explain the procedures to the students, no problems should occur.

Undesirable inconsistency usually arises from three sources. First, the procedures or rules are not reasonable, workable, or appropriate. Second, the teacher fails to monitor students closely and does not detect inappropriate behavior. This gives the appearance of inconsistency when the teacher does detect misbehavior and tries to stop it. Finally, the teacher may not feel strongly enough about the procedure or rule to enforce it or to use the associated penalty. If you find yourself caught in an inconsistency that is becoming a problem, you have the following alternatives:

- Reteach the procedure. Take a few minutes to discuss the problem with the class and reiterate your desire that the rule or procedure be followed. Then enforce it.
- Modify the procedure and then reintroduce it.
- Abandon the procedure or consequence and possibly substitute another in its place.

The alternative you choose depends on the circumstances and on the importance of the component to your classroom management system.

Prompt Management of Inappropriate Behavior

Prompt handling of inappropriate behavior helps to prevent its escalation. Behaviors of concern include lack of involvement in learning activities, prolonged inattention or work avoidance, and obvious violations of classroom rules and procedures. Effective managers have a high degree of "withitness"; that is, they are so attuned to the class that they are able to detect off-task behavior and stop it before it escalates. It is not a good idea to ignore persistent off-task behavior because prolonged inattention makes it difficult for the students both to learn and to complete assignments. Violations of rules and failure to follow procedures create many problems we have already discussed. These behaviors should be dealt with directly but without overreaction. A calm, reasoned tone or approach is more productive and less likely to lead to confrontation. The following alternatives are recommended.

Four Simple Ways to Manage Inappropriate Behavior

We will assume that the classroom tasks are within the capabilities of the students. If not, then the first priority in addressing problem behaviors is to provide suitable instruction or to modify the tasks. If the suitability of the task is not at issue, the following simple strategies are often effective.

1. Make eye contact with or move closer to the student. Use a signal, such as a finger to the lips or a head shake, to prompt the appropriate behavior. Monitor until the student complies.
2. If the student is not following a procedure correctly, a simple reminder of the correct procedure may be effective. You can either state the correct procedure or note other students who are doing what is expected.
3. When the student is off-task—that is, not working on an assignment—redirect his or her attention to the task: "Robert, you should be writing now." Or "Becky, the assignment is to complete all of the problems on the page." Check the student's progress shortly thereafter to make sure that work is continuing.
4. Ask or tell the student to stop the inappropriate behavior. Then monitor until it stops and the student begins constructive activity.

Sometimes it is inconvenient or would interrupt an activity to use these procedures immediately. In such a case, make a mental note of the problem and continue the activity until a more appropriate time occurs. Then tell the student you saw what was occurring, and discuss what the appropriate behavior should have been. When possible, discussions with individual students about their inappropriate behaviors should be conducted as privately as feasible. Of course, privacy in a classroom is not likely to be complete unless you remove the student from the room, a strategy that you will usually not employ because of your responsibility for the entire class. Ways to achieve partial privacy include conferring with a student at your desk, whispering or speaking in a low tone, and using nonverbal signals to convey a message to a student. When you use such strategies, you also communicate to other students your intention that the conversation be considered private. This will reduce the amount of peer attention the student receives and is less likely to intrude into the ongoing activity.

The four procedures just listed are easy to use, cause little interruption of class activities, and enable students to correct their behavior. If a student persists in the behavior, however, some other alternatives must be used. If the rest of the class is working and does not need your immediate attention, a brief talk with the student and/or assessing an appropriate penalty may be sufficient. If that doesn't settle the matter or if an immediate conference isn't desirable or feasible, tell the student to wait after class to speak to you. If the student is being disruptive, send him or her either to a "time-out" desk in another part of the room or to the hall. Then talk with the student when you have time. Your goal in discussing the problem behavior with the student is to determine the reason for the problem, to make clear what the unacceptable behavior is and what the student should be doing, and then to obtain a commitment from the student for acceptable behavior. Some teachers like to have the student put the commitment in writing in a brief "contract" or "plan," specifying what he or she agrees to do, before being allowed to return to class.

Building a Positive Climate

This chapter has emphasized maintaining appropriate behavior by applying procedures and rules consistently, handling problems promptly, and using nonintrusive interventions when possible to maintain activity flow and student involvement in lessons. We now want to emphasize the importance of keeping a positive perspective and avoiding overdwelling on student misbehavior or inadequacies. Sometimes teachers get caught in the trap of seeing only faults and problems and overlooking the better features of students' behavior. Instead of rejoicing when twenty-nine students are involved in learning, we complain about the one student who is off-task.

> *Mr. Acerbic's ninth-grade physical education class could do no right. Although most of the students initially participated willingly in the class activities, students never seemed to perform quickly or well enough for their teacher. "Come on, you horseflies, quit buzzing and listen up," he would yell when he heard talking. "Laps" around the gym were given for even slight infractions such as inattention; there always seemed to be three or four students making the rounds at any given time. Instead of feedback about good performance, criticism was usually given for inadequacies. Although students took the constant carping in stride, they displayed little zest for the class.*

Although poor performance should not be ignored—students need specific, corrective feedback to know what to improve—it is important that the climate for learning be positive. This means that students should look forward to the class. They should expect to learn and to receive assistance when they encounter difficulty and should feel supported in their efforts. Such a climate can be fostered by communicating positive expectations to students, praising good performance, and at times, using additional rewards.

Teacher expectations can be communicated in a variety of ways, some obvious and others subtle. (For a thorough description of this aspect of teacher behavior, see Good & Brophy 2003, chap. 3.) Teachers can:

- Identify appropriate instructional goals and discuss them with students so that they are clear about what is expected.
- Insist that students complete work satisfactorily.
- Refuse to accept excuses for poor work.
- Communicate acceptance of imperfect initial performance when students struggle to achieve new learning.
- Convey confidence in the students' ability to do well.
- Display an encouraging, "can do" attitude that generates student excitement and self-confidence.
- Avoid comparative evaluations, especially of lower ability students, that might cause them to conclude that they cannot accomplish the objectives.

By communicating positive expectations, teachers lay the foundation for students to attempt new tasks and reach new goals. When students know that their teacher believes them to be capable, they are more likely to work harder.

A positive climate for learning is also created by appropriate teacher praise. When used well, teacher praise can be uplifting and provide great encouragement to a student. The most powerful type of teacher praise provides the student with information about what aspect of student performance is praiseworthy and also demonstrates that the teacher is impressed with the quality of the student's work. In other words, effective praise provides both informative feedback and genuine teacher approval. It can also accompany suggestions for improvement (constructive criticism) without loss of effect.

Public praise that focuses on student *accomplishment* works better than praise for student effort. When the teacher praises only for "working hard," students may assume that the teacher thinks they aren't very able. When you know that a student put forth considerable effort and you want to acknowledge it, be sure the praise also includes an emphasis on the student's achievement. "Gloria, all your hard work paid off because your project was beautifully done. The organization of ideas and the extra details in the descriptions were outstanding!" Likewise, praise should be deserved and it should not be too easily obtained. Public praise of a student for success on an easy task can suggest to the rest of the class (and the student who was praised) that the teacher believes he or she has little ability.

It is a good idea to look for private ways to provide praise. Written comments on papers, tests, and other assignments offer excellent opportunities for quality praise. Private conversations, conferences with parents, notes home, and informal contacts also offer opportunities for praising students. Private praise avoids some of the complications of public praise and permits the teacher to include a greater variety of performances and behaviors as its focus. Further discussion of the uses of teacher praise can be found in Emmer (1988) and Brophy (1998).

Improving Class Climate through Incentives or Rewards

Extra incentives or rewards can help build a positive climate. The improvement in class climate occurs because the incentives add interest or excitement to the class routine, while also directing attention toward appropriate behavior and away from inappropriate behavior. Moreover, when students are rewarded rather than punished, they are more likely to respond positively to the teacher, contributing to a mutually supportive pattern of interaction.

Before introducing an external incentive, you should consider several factors that might affect its appropriateness and effects. Check your school or district policies because sometimes the use of incentives is restricted. You would not want to promise a field trip or party only to find out that it was prohibited by school board policy.

Your rewards should target the behaviors you would like to encourage. Rewards too easily earned or too difficult to achieve lose their motivational effect. Also, you should be concerned about whether the use of a reward takes too much class time for recordkeeping or other administrative tasks. Avoid using complex systems that distract you and your students from a focus on learning. Start with simple procedures and add to them when reasonable.

Be careful not to set up incentives that only the most able students can achieve. Systems that encourage excessive competition for scarce rewards will discourage students who don't have much chance. The examples in this section and in the case at the end of the chapter include a variety of types. Combine these ideas with those of other teachers and your own experience to develop some alternatives for use at various

times of the year. Many different types of rewards, including symbols, recognition, activities, and materials, can be used with secondary students. Each of these types is described in the following sections with examples.

Grades and Other Symbols

The most prevalent form of incentive is the letter or numerical grade, although other symbols such as checks or stars are sometimes used with students in middle school classes. Good grades are a powerful incentive for most students when they are perceived to be a direct reflection of their achievement and competence. Therefore, it is important to tie as many facets of student work to grades as possible. In addition, you should make clear to students the basis for determining grades to help them know what they have to do to achieve good grades. Procedures for managing student work have already been discussed at length in earlier chapters, so we do not dwell on them here.

One caveat is worth noting. Occasionally, teachers react negatively to the grading system because they feel that too much emphasis is placed on grades and not enough on learning. This feeling may cause the teacher to project a casual attitude about grades and be vague about the grading criteria. This is a mistake; the teacher is still required to assign grades, and the students are left with less control over their fate. A more constructive reaction would be for the teacher to work hard to make the grading criteria reflect the course's learning objectives.

Recognition

These rewards involve some means of giving attention to the student. Examples are the display of student work; awarding a certificate for achievement, improvement, or good behavior; and verbally citing student accomplishments. Some adolescents are embarrassed by being singled out for attention, so giving public recognition to several students at the same time is a better strategy. At a school or grade level, recognition awards are often given at the end of the year or semester, with teachers nominating the recipients. If this is the case in your school, be sure to find out what awards are commonly given. Then tell your students what they are (e.g., awards for attendance, achievement, improvement, honor students, hard work, conduct, good citizens, etc.) early in the year. Early discussion of these awards may motivate your students to work toward them. A similar procedure is to establish and display an honor roll (e.g., an all-star list, honor society, gold record club) to reward students at the end of each grading term. Certificates, stickers with designs appealing to teenagers, or treats can be used in conjunction with the awards, especially for younger secondary students. It is a good idea to spread the honors around to include a good portion of your students. Thus, don't give awards only for outstanding achievement; have awards for improvement, excellent effort, good conduct, and so on.

For Reflection

Think back to your middle school and high school years and recall a class that had a very positive climate. List some of the characteristics of that class and what the teacher did to promote it. Compare notes with a friend. To what extent do you recognize concepts from this chapter in these recollections? How can you put these into practice in your own teaching?

Activities as Rewards

Granting privileges, such as working with a friend, free reading time, visits to the school library, or helping to decorate a bulletin board, are examples of activity rewards. A more elaborate activity reward would be a field trip or party. Because school policy may affect your use of the latter activities, check these out before announcing them to your classes. You should, of course, be certain to describe clearly what students need to do to receive such privileges.

Teachers who use activity rewards as incentives for the whole class can permit students to participate in their identification and selection. Thus, a list of possibly desirable (and acceptable) activities can be presented to a class or solicited from students during a discussion; either way, the class can vote on whichever one it wishes to seek. Some whole-class activities that might be used include watching a videotape, fifteen minutes of free time, playing games, listening to music, having a popcorn party, or no homework. A group activity reward should be made contingent on specific desirable behaviors; if the group cooperates, students will receive the incentive. If not, they will lose some or all of the time in the activity. Because the purpose of an activity reward is, at least in part, to promote positive climate building, it is important not to let one or two students spoil the fun for the rest of the class. A chronically uncooperative student or two can be invited to participate, but if they persist in noncompliance, the teacher may exclude them from the activity. Of course, they should be encouraged to participate and given the opportunity to make that choice.

Finding a supervised place for the excluded student during the activity is a drawback to using this incentive. Sometimes teachers solve the problem by arranging ahead of time for the student to go to another teacher's classroom. The student then works on assigned seatwork during that time.

Material Incentives

These rewards include awarding objects of value to students. Examples include food, discarded classroom materials, games, toys, or books. In addition to ascertaining school policy, you must consider your own financial circumstances before deciding to use such rewards. Because you will have a large number of students and limited resources, your use of material rewards will be restricted at best.

When you consider what types of rewards to use in your classes, several factors should be kept in mind. Your rewards should be related to the student behaviors that are most important to you. Obviously, one such set of student behaviors is satisfactory completion of assignments, participation in academic activities, and attainment of

learning objectives. For these student behaviors, grades are effective and relevant rewards. Another set of important student behaviors are those related to following rules and major procedures. For these behaviors, recognition and activity rewards can be used effectively. Some teachers hold competitions among their class sections, rewarding the class that has the best behavior record, punctuality, or homework completion rate for a grading period. With the cooperation of other teachers and administrators, good student behavior can be rewarded by a party or dance at the end of the semester for all students who have stayed off the detention list and maintained good attendance records. An incentive on such a grand scale requires much planning and effort as well as the cooperation of large numbers of people.

Caution in the Use of Rewards

Some researchers (e.g., Deci & Ryan 1985; Lepper & Greene 1978) have urged caution in the use of extrinsic rewards, pointing out that under some circumstances their use may reduce students' intrinsic motivation to engage in the rewarded activity. In studies conducted by motivational researchers, subjects are given a reward for engaging in an activity or for reaching some predetermined level of performance. Later, the reward is withdrawn and the subjects are observed when they are free to choose the activity and how long to engage in it. Compared to subjects who do not receive an external incentive, the previously rewarded subjects tend to choose other activities more or to engage in the rewarded activity for a shorter time. From such results, it is inferred that receiving a reward reduces motivation for an activity if subsequently the extrinsic reward is no longer available.

Explanations of this dampening effect on motivation usually focus on the thinking processes that occur when individuals are given rewards. "This is an unpleasant or boring task, so a reward is needed to maintain engagement" is the implicit message communicated by the use of external rewards. Consequently, the recipient tends to devalue the rewarded activity.

Before concluding that teachers should never use incentives, however, it should be noted that research in this area has a number of limitations with respect to its generalization to classroom practice. For one thing, much of the research has been conducted in laboratory settings in which the activity or task and its accompanying reward occur on only one occasion; in addition, the rewarded activity or task has usually been a highly interesting one, such as a game or puzzle. Thus, the research setting and the tasks are often not very representative of the nature of classroom work for which rewards might usually be used. Furthermore, some research has found that incentives can enhance interest rather than reduce it. After reviewing numerous studies, Cameron and Pierce (1994) concluded, "The present findings suggest that verbal praise and positive feedback enhance people's intrinsic interest. . . . Rewards can have a negative impact on intrinsic motivation when they are offered to people for engaging in a task without consideration of any standard of performance" (p. 397). Bandura (1986) argues that the conflicting findings mean that the effect of extrinsic rewards on intrinsic motivation is weak and that many other factors operate to mediate the effects of the use of incentives.

We believe that the most reasonable application of the research results for classroom use of rewards is to be thoughtful about their use. No purpose will be served by adding a reward to an activity that is already highly interesting to students, and the evidence suggests that to do so may cause reduced motivation. However, many classroom tasks are not highly interesting, especially during the extensive repetition that is needed to produce skilled performance and learning. When student motivation flags, external incentives help to maintain engagement. In fact, the use of incentives is much more desirable than lowering expectations and accepting poor performance or using punishment and threats to attempt to keep students working. Finally, when rewards are used, the teacher can counteract the potential for negative effects on intrinsic motivation by making the reward contingent on some desired level of performance (not only completion of the task), by pointing out the usefulness of the skill, by choosing materials and activities that have more potential for sustaining student interest, by describing long-term outcomes of value to the students, and by demonstrating personal interest in and enthusiasm for the task.

FURTHER READING

Freiberg, H. J. (1996). From tourists to citizens in the classroom. *Educational Leadership, 54,* 32–36.

An emphasis on creating a positive classroom climate characterizes this article. Based on research he has conducted, Freiberg recommends including increasing student participation in rule setting, allowing students to volunteer for classroom jobs, and making the school a more caring and personal place.

Hidi, S., & Harackiewicz, J. M. (2000). Motivating the academically unmotivated: A critical issue for the 21st century. *Review of Educational Research, 70,* 151–179.

The authors review research on how goals and interests influence motivation for school tasks. While acknowledging the benefits of intrinsic motivation, external reinforcement, situational interest, and performance goals are reviewed and suggested as helpful when working with unmotivated students.

Mueller, C. M., & Dweck, C. S. (1998). Praise for intelligence can undermine children's motivation for performance. *Journal of Personality and Social Psychology, 75,* 33–52.

In a series of six studies, the authors demonstrate that students who receive positive feedback based on their effort continue to exert effort in learning. These students associate struggles with a lack of effort. Students who receive positive feedback based on their intelligence seek to continue looking smart and may choose activities with less challenge. These students associate struggles with lack of ability and therefore may not make further attempts.

Positive school climate. (1998). *Educational Leadership, 56*(1), 1–85.

This issue of the journal has articles that describe a variety of approaches to positive climate setting. Included are such ideas as what makes a high school an inviting place

Examples of Incentives and Rewards

Some examples of incentives and rewards that we have observed in secondary school classrooms are described in the following pages. These examples are grouped according to type, although it should be noted that some incentives combine features of several types.

Awards and Other Recognition

An attractive award certificate was designed by a teacher and used for individual students at different times during the year. The certificates were especially impressive because each was signed by the principal as well as the teacher. Students were recognized for outstanding effort, along with improvement or accomplishment. To save time, the teacher made many copies of the blank certificates before school began and asked the principal to sign them all at once. She filled them in as needed with students' names and accomplishments. The certificates were awarded both publicly and privately, according to the student and the accomplishment. (Note: Blank achievement/appreciation certificates can also be purchased from school supply stores.)

Honor roll systems are common. Generally, these schoolwide systems have incentive value for better students and don't provide much motivation for the less academically successful. One teacher who taught several classes of low achievers in a school that used ability grouping developed an in-class honor roll that was more accessible to his students. At the end of each grading period, students who had improved their performance or who had participated well in class activities were named to a "Best in the West" honor roll. Their names were placed on a bulletin board honor roll, and they received attractive stickers to display on their notebooks or textbook covers.

Competitions

For some subjects, long-range incentives are available in the form of city, regional, or statewide competitions (e.g., spelling or composition contests, science and math fairs). Other competitions can be conducted within a school, with classes competing against one another, or they may even be limited to the classes taught by one teacher. The teacher can establish a reward for the first class completing a project or for the class in which all students complete the project first. Within-class rewards can also be offered. One teacher posted spelling grades by class on a bulletin board display. The class with the highest overall score at the end of each month received a special prize or treat.

Teachers who use some form of cooperative groups frequently use group competitions. Students in winning groups may receive a reward, such as extra time in desirable activities (e.g., free reading, computer use, library passes), recognition, certificates, appreciation notes sent home, or bonus points. Competitions can be based on average test scores of students in the group, performance criteria for projects or assignments, desirable group behavior, or improvement on some criterion. When using group competitions, it's best to have a fairly short time frame (e.g., group-of-the-week rather than group-of-the-semester awards).

Encouraging Improvement

One of the defining characteristics of the mastery learning approach is the opportunity to retake tests and redo assignments until a predetermined criterion, such as 80 or 90, is reached. Even if mastery learning is not adopted *in toto*, some teachers allow students to redo incorrectly done assignments to improve their grade. Students might be allowed to earn enough points to bring their grade up to a B level, for example.

Extra-Credit Assignments

Extra-credit activities are frequently popular with students, and the extra credit earned toward improving a grade is an important incentive for most students. One teacher kept an extra-credit logic problem on the side board, changing it every week or two depending on its difficulty. She also had extra-credit puzzles and worksheets on a front table. These puzzles covered material currently being studied by the class, and students were encouraged to work on them after they had finished their required work. They could also copy them and work on them at home. This teacher had students keep their completed extra-credit problems in a special section of their notebooks, where they were checked when the teacher graded the notebooks. Each correct problem was worth one point and was added to the notebook grade at the end of the grading period.

A science teacher kept a list of extra-credit projects for students to work on individually or in groups. Along with the list of projects was a description of the requirements for each project, its complexity, a deadline for completion, and the number of points earned toward a report card grade. English and social studies teachers frequently have book lists from which students may choose extra-credit reading. A form for students to use when reporting on the book should also be available.

Sometimes bulletin boards are used to display extra-credit work. One math teacher had a picture of a mountain, with math problems relevant to current lessons at each of several elevations. Beneath the mountain were lines for ten student names. The first ten students (from all classes) correctly completing the problems had their names posted under the mountain. When the tenth name was posted, the teacher taped a piece of gum or candy beside each name for the student to remove.

Special Activities and Privileges

Allowing students special privileges or permitting them to participate in desired activities is a commonly used reward, and it is often combined with another kind of reward such as recognition. For example, one teacher chose outstanding students each week, based on their attitude, grades, and attendance. The teacher would put students' names on a bulletin board display, and students would receive a special treat on Friday. The teacher also included in the special activity or treat all students who had not received demerits for misbehavior during that week. Another teacher recognized consistent performance by naming all students who had turned in all their work during the previous week as a "Student of the Week" and by placing their names on a special bulletin board display. After being named "Student of the Week" five times during a six-week grading period, the student was entitled to claim an A for one of the four major components of the report card grade. One teacher allowed fifteen or twenty minutes of free reading or game time on Friday when a class had been well behaved throughout the week. Another teacher made an "activity chain" from construction paper, adding a link when class behavior was good each day. When the chain reached a certain length, the class was permitted to have part of a period for a special activity such as free reading or a class competition.

Weekly Point System

Point systems are useful because in addition to giving students clearly specified incentives, they encourage them to take responsibility for keeping track of their own work. One teacher gave a handout to students at the beginning of each week with the week's assignments on it. The students recorded points they earned for each assignment, with up to 100 points awarded weekly. Some bonus points were also available for extra-credit assignments, and the teacher could add extra points for good behavior and class participation. These weekly records of points were then used along with test scores to determine report card grades. A common modification of this system is to allow the summary sheet to cover a longer period of time, such as two or three weeks, instead of one week. With older and more mature students, such as those in the upper grades in high school, teachers who apply this system often use a summary sheet for the grading period rather than for each week.

for students, preventing violence, modifying in-school suspension to make it more effective, helping students avoid risky behavior, and building a sense of community.

Raffini, J. P. (1996). *150 ways to increase intrinsic motivation in the classroom.* Boston: Allyn and Bacon.

Many useful strategies are presented in this compendium of classroom activities designed to enhance student motivation.

SUGGESTED ACTIVITIES

1. Find out about school policies that affect your use of rewards and penalties. Also, note any schoolwide policy that you will need to incorporate into your own classroom's procedures.

2. Read the descriptions of the various incentive systems and rewards in Case Study 12.1. What are some of the hoped-for consequences and what are some potential drawbacks of their use? Consider, for example, effects on student attitudes, motivation, and behavior in the short and long run, as well as teacher time and effort. Are there any incentives that especially appeal to you? Any that you would not use with middle school or high school students? Discuss the rationale for your preferences and dislikes. Are there circumstances that would make you more or less inclined to use any of these incentives?

3. Identify any individual or group rewards you intend to use with major conduct and work procedures. By planning ahead, you will be better able to explain these incentives and be consistent in their use.

13

Positive Discipline in the Classroom

Reflection Box

What I Believe About

The importance of discipline . . .
Culturally sensitive discipline . . .
Criteria for evaluating my discipline plan . . .
Preventive discipline . . .
Establishing classroom rules . . .
Underlying causes of misbehavior . . .
Asking for parent cooperation . . .
Positive discipline methods . . .

The word *discipline* strikes more fear into the hearts of teachers than it does into the hearts of misbehaving students. The overriding anxiety of beginning teachers is focused on control of the classroom. Even though you may have heard much of what is said here in other courses, you may need to refocus on the subject when you contemplate your first day in the classroom.

Even experienced teachers are concerned about discipline. Why? One explanation is that today's children come to school with different experiences in their book bags and go home to very different family configurations than they did years ago. Drugs, gangs, violent neighborhoods, homelessness, hunger, abuse, and neglect are just some of the social ills you will see reflected in the behavior of some of your students. Single-parent and dual-income families may have less time and energy for their children, and even

Taken from *Your First Year of Teaching and Beyond*, Fourth Edition, by Ellen L. Kronowitz.

wealthy families often relegate child rearing to someone else. Schools by default have taken on more of the responsibility for meeting children's needs in all developmental areas, including self-control and self-esteem. Charles and Senter (2002) suggest additional reasons for the persistence of discipline problems: Children have been raised more permissively; some parents increasingly take the child's side against the school; and some teachers and administrators have been worn down by the discipline struggle.

Discipline has never received as much attention as it has in the past few years. When I began teaching, there was only one golden rule: *Do not smile until Christmas*. All the rest was left up to the individual. Now books on discipline proliferate, as do workshops, seminars, and inservices. Along with the fitness craze, and the dressing-for-success seminars come the discipline disciples, each with a no-fail system for keeping kids in order. Teachers flock to these workshops, waiting for the definitive word. If the various exercise emporiums and health spas offered discipline classes along with life cycle and aerobics classes, memberships would soar and profits would triple.

Discipline is an aspect of human behavior, and as such, it derives from a complex interaction between the individual and the environment. It is the latter that must be established before the other facets of discipline can be explored. In this chapter the focus is on prevention of discipline problems through an organized plan for learning and a well-managed environment. Specific techniques for dealing with minor infractions will be discussed along with strategies for dealing with serious behavior problems in positive, reasonable, respectful, and dignified ways.

A Note from the Teacher

For the first two months as a middle school teacher, if you are going to smile, make it a scary smile.

—B. Dahnert

Why Discipline?

Developing a rationale for your discipline plan is the first step toward an effective system. It's simply not enough to adopt someone else's system, although this appears to be the easiest approach. The recipes abound, but they simply may not meet your tastes. No one system of discipline will suit you perfectly, and no one system will work for all students in your classroom. This is one aspect of classroom life that must be custom-fit, both to your needs and to the needs of your students. Take a few minutes to think about some reasons for discipline and then compare your answers to those that follow.

- *Safety.* Children need to feel physically safe and secure and free from threat and intimidation both in the classroom and outside. School may be the safest place in their lives. Children also need to feel emotionally safe and secure. When an atmosphere of mutual respect and consideration prevails in the classroom, children will more likely risk being open and honest and true to themselves. These safety needs are the most basic human concerns after the physiological needs of survival (Maslow, 1987), and a safe physical and emotional environment free from harm can be achieved only when discipline prevails.
- *Limits.* Children need to have limits and learn what is appropriate and inappropriate behavior. This is the other side of the safety issue. To ensure an environ-

ment that is safe for everyone, each one of us must limit our individual freedoms and must temper individual rights for the good and welfare of all. In a democratic society we all live by a code of law that is created by us through our representatives and that, ideally, is enforced equally and consistently.

- *Acceptance.* According to Maslow (1987), acceptance needs come after survival needs and safety needs are met. Kids need and desire the approval and love of others. When they are behaving in a socially acceptable manner, they will feel good about themselves and feel they are behaving in ways that bring them acceptance from others and a sense of belonging in the classroom.

- *Self-Esteem.* Self-esteem needs follow closely those of acceptance (Maslow, 1987). Children who can control their behavior will gain a sense of mastery and will feel competent and respected by their classroom community. Feeling competent in one area of life can help shore up poor self-esteem in other areas.

- *Learning.* Self-actualizing needs emerge after all others are met (Maslow, 1987). A classroom teacher who wants to encourage these needs in students must try to create an environment that helps children develop their gifts, talents, and abilities. Children have both the need to reach their potential and the right to an orderly classroom environment free from distractions, interruptions, and behavioral disruptions that interfere with their learning.

- *Responsibility.* Children need to learn that for every action there is a logical and sometimes equal reaction. Taking responsibility for one's actions is a cornerstone of democratic society. Any consequences should be related to the offense and must respect the dignity of the child. (A complete discussion of logical consequences follows later in the chapter.)

- *Democratic Training.* John Dewey (1980) advocated schools that would be mini-communities, training grounds for citizenship. In a workable discipline system, the foundations of democratic society should pertain: one person, one vote; the rule of law; self-responsibility; the rule of the majority, with respect for minority views; consequences for actions against the greater good; individual freedoms balanced against the common good; and respect for all, regardless of viewpoint.

Your Philosophy

Children, then, have some basic needs that are met through a discipline system, including physical and emotional safety needs, acceptance and belonging needs, and self-esteem and self-actualizing needs. Discipline also teaches students about the democratic processes and the tension that exists among individual rights, the rights of the majority, and respect for minority opinions. What your ultimate system will be depends very much on your own belief system about children and discipline. This chapter has been written with a philosophy in mind, which will become more apparent as you read further. I have sifted and winnowed through all the competing philosophies, the research studies, and the experiences of many teachers to formulate my own philosophy. You will be doing the same.

All of our actions are derived from our belief systems. If we believe that children are little gremlins who must be controlled, then control them we will, at all costs. If we believe that children must express themselves without constraint, then express themselves they will, by throwing paint or pencils, as we sit and marvel at their creativity. Take some time to complete Worksheet 13.1, Discipline Clarification Activity. Rank-order these positions vis-à-vis discipline from 1 to 8, with 1 being the position most like your own. This will help you conceptualize your own starting position regarding discipline. You may want to reach consensus with others if you are doing this activity in class.

These positions reflect a continuum of discipline strategies from the laissez-faire to the strict authoritarian. In between one finds the counseling approach, the democratic approach, the logical consequences approach, and the behavior modification approach. It was probably hard for you to rank these statements, as most people are eclectic in their beliefs and practice walking the thin line between laissez-faire and total authoritarianism. Do your best balancing act.

The emphasis on eclecticism and value-based discipline and real suggestions from real teachers makes this discussion of discipline different from others you may have read. The various discipline models or systems are elaborated in other books, and are just briefly mentioned in this chapter. You will find a list of suggested readings at the end of the chapter for more information. The purpose here is to help you articulate a humane, positive, reasonable, and respectful system of discipline based on what you can extract from the information provided by teachers who have been through all the discipline fads and models and have synthesized what is meaningful and achievable. Teachers combine elements of many approaches. What follows is a smorgasbord for you to sample; remember, however, to check and recheck the tidbits you choose against your beliefs about children, your value system, your rationale for discipline, and your own philosophy of discipline. As you read, you might also consider that, whatever plan you ultimately design, it should be checked against the criteria discussed below and listed on Worksheet 13.2, Discipline System Criteria.

Your overall discipline system should be, first and foremost, reasonable, respectful, dignified, and sensitive to cultural norms. If we accept Maslow's (1987) assertion that we all require a sense of significance, belonging, acceptance, security, and safety, then discipline plans cannot undermine children's intrinsic needs. Children new to this country, whose primary language is different, have even greater safety and security needs that must be considered. Any plan that is unfair or unreasonable, or that humiliates or demeans children in any way, will simply backfire. Put yourself in your students' place. Would you find the discipline system reasonable, respectful, and dignified? Dreikurs, Grunwald, and Pepper (1998) tell us that misbehavior is symptomatic, a message from a discouraged child who feels that he or she doesn't belong and is insignificant. Any system we choose should not add to the discouragement that the child already feels. It should, instead, encourage and satisfy the child's basic human needs.

Especially as a new teacher, you should develop a discipline plan that will ultimately be consistent with the overall school plan. This is especially important in middle and high school where, conceivably, there could be seven sets of rules in seven different periods. Find out first if there are schoolwide rules that your class is expected to follow. These are usually pretty general, and you will probably have an easy time living with them. If the school has adopted any one system of discipline that simply goes against your grain, it is imperative that you discuss the issue with the principal as soon as possible and see if there is any wiggle room for you. The best time to do this is at your interview, before you are hired. You will be very unhappy if you are expected to follow a plan that is counter to your own belief system about children and contrary to your general value system.

Your discipline system should also be appropriate for the age group and flexible enough to take individual differences into account. Although young children may respond to happy faces as rewards, middle school students would justifiably feel patronized. Watch out for whole systems of discipline that are so rigid that you have no flexibility in dealing with hyperactive children who are unable to sit still or be silent, or for systems that have stringent penalties that require, for example, that you call parents, when you know that certain parents are capable of overreaction or potential abuse. Make sure that your plan takes into account that culture influences children's reaction to being disciplined. In Latino cultures, for instance, lowered eyes are a sign of respect, and, therefore, the teacher who asks for direct eye contact is discounting individual differences and being culturally insensitive.

Your ultimate discipline plan should be time-efficient, easy to administer, and stress-free. You don't want to implement a plan that is ultimately more burdensome to you than the discipline problems themselves. Will you spend more time administering your plan than teaching children? Will your plan turn you into a police officer or a secretary keeping track of points or a candy machine dispensing food rewards? Will your system create in you positive feelings, or will it add anxiety to your already stressful life? Will your system make you feel like the professional educator you have been trained to be?

Can your plan be easily communicated to the students and their parents without a 10-page manual of directions? Is it easily translatable to a child's primary language for parents? Is it a system that a substitute can understand should the need arise? Can you articulate it simply and easily to your principal when asked? If it's too complicated to write down in one paragraph in a letter to parents, it's probably too complicated for you to manage without hiring an Assistant Teacher in Charge of Discipline, a Secretary in Charge of Tracking Points, and a Treasurer in Charge of Dispensing Rewards.

Preventing Discipline Problems

Much of what has preceded this chapter has set the stage for what follows. If you accept the premise that students respond and react to the situation at hand, then the more you control the variables of instruction, including the physical arrangement of the classroom, the less likely it is that you will have to control the class. I am not proposing that good teaching and organized, efficient classroom management will solve or prevent all discipline problems. I am suggesting that as long as these variables are under your control, it's best to start with a look at the context in which problems arise.

The Physical Environment

It is 105 degrees outside as I sit in an air-conditioned office that has been cleaned and organized to help me concentrate. Likewise, starting out in a comfortable classroom environment may increase the likelihood that children will attend to their learning tasks with minimum distraction and disruption. Pay attention to these parameters:

- a well-ventilated room
- glare-free lighting
- colorful and informative bulletin boards
- a clean and orderly room with clear organization
- private spaces for kids to get away from it all
- visibility from all areas of the room for you and the pupils
- compatible seatmates
- teaching style conducive to your furniture arrangement

Meeting Individual Differences

Some underlying causes of behavior disruptions are related to instruction and include the inability to do the work, sheer boredom, lack of challenging assignments, and expectations that are too high. These can be countered by your recognition that each student is an individual and deserves to have his or her learning needs met as much as is humanly possible. Unmet needs lead to trouble—that is, attention-getting behavior that undermines your classroom control.

Differentiated Assignments

Make sure each pupil can succeed at the tasks you assign. This may necessitate rewriting some assignments, tape-recording assignments, or providing more challenging work for the advanced learner. Plan for extension and enrichment activities as well.

Grouping

Individual needs can also be met by grouping, when appropriate, according to specific needs, abilities, and interests. Cooperative learning groups promote social skills as students engage in tasks that foster positive interdependence and problem solving. Other ad hoc groups can be formed on the basis of a specific skill need, a common interest (rock collecting or dinosaurs), common reading materials (kids who all are reading detective stories or biographies), a project (a class play or a newspaper).

Choices and Decisions

Students' individual differences may also be met by providing choices whenever possible: in creative writing topics, in art assignments, in P.E. games, and in seating. Choice empowers kids and thus may inhibit them from exercising power in unacceptable ways.

Realistic Expectations

One of the ways to determine if your expectations are too high or too low is to put yourself in your students' place. Try sitting in one spot yourself for five and one-half hours, totally still and quiet. I've tried, and it's quite difficult. Realize perhaps that giving 50 examples of a particular skill is tedious or that the literature selection is boring. Make revisions whenever you have the sense that you wouldn't be able to complete the assignment if you were in the students' shoes.

Capitalizing on Interests

Finding out what motivates each student and gearing instruction around common interests will accomplish two goals. First, you will capture attention more easily; and, second, you will convey the message that you care about individuals. Developing rapport with students is easy if you are honest, sincere, and genuine with them. Conduct an interest inventory. Using current fads as themes in your instruction may just be the spark to keep students involved and out of trouble. Expand your musical tastes, and pick up a few of the teen magazines your middle and high school students are reading.

Planning

Your planning, both long range and short term, if thorough and well formulated, will help you cut down on potential disruptions.

Plan for Success

If your planning allows for every student to succeed, you are maximizing your chances for effective discipline. It is far better to underestimate your class's abilities during the first few days than it is to go over their heads. Err on the side of easy before you have actual diagnostic data. The worst thing that can happen is that they will feel successful!

Worthwhile and Meaningful Activities

If kid's feel the work is worthwhile and meaningful, they are less likely to question your authority and rebel through negative behavior. Motivate individual lessons and let students know the purpose or objective of the lesson. Use a variety of media and technology in your instruction and vary your teaching strategies. Plan a balance among individual work, cooperative learning in groups, and teacher-directed instruction, to create variety and to maintain involvement and interest. Glasser (1998) sets forth six criteria for quality schoolwork. These are:

a warm, supportive classroom environment

useful work

students are asked to exert their best effort

students evaluate their own work and improve it

quality work feels good

and is never destructive

Orderly Procedures

The clarity of your directions and the availability of all teaching resources will allow the smoother operation of all activities within the classroom. Make sure you have gone through the lesson in your mind as well as written it on paper so you can anticipate any skipped steps or procedures that potentially might sandbag your lesson. Make sure materials are at the ready. If you have to go back to a closet to get the scissors, you will interrupt the flow and undermine your lesson.

A Note from the Teacher

It is much easier to have students do it "right" the first time than it is to undo the bad habits they may develop when you ignore the misbehaviors or overlook them out of sheer exhaustion.

—T. Beck

Sponges

Cutting down on lag time can be accomplished by overplanning and the use of "sponge" activities. You can always cut down on activities, but it's hard to think on your feet if you have an extra few minutes after you complete a lesson. If you don't have something to keep students actively involved, they may create their own diversions, ones you may not approve. Some ideas for sponges are listed below, but the sponges should relate to the curriculum:

Name a geometric shape.

Name a gem or mineral.

Name an organ in the body.

Name things with wheels.

List one country for each letter
of the alphabet.

Name things that fly.

Name things that run on electricity.

Name musical instruments.

Name something found in
King Tut's tomb.

Name things found in space.

Having a general list of things to do after students complete their work will also help. These activities must be rewarding in some way. Making more work the reward for early completion soon will lose its appeal, and students, wise to your scheme, will slow down and even avoid finishing in the allotted time. Keep a basket or box of books on each table grouping and rotate the book baskets as needed. This gives the students something to do at all times without leaving their seats.

Instruction

During instructional time, you can cut down on potential disruptions by adhering to principles of good teaching. Although good instruction cannot guarantee good discipline at all times, you can reduce potential problems by considering the possibility that a strong link exists between the two. Many of the following principles of good instruction, which correlate with effective classroom management, were first identified by Jacob Kounin (1977) in his seminal book, *Discipline and Group Management in Classrooms*. The terms in *italics* are his.

Focus Attention/Group Alerting

Before beginning any lesson, make sure the children are looking at you and you have everyone's undivided attention. If you begin while kids are talking or inattentive, the situation can only get worse. Clear desks will alleviate the probability that children will find something to play with during teacher-directed lessons. *Group alerting* is a key element in well-managed classrooms. Keeping the group alerted involves encouraging individual and unison responses and not calling on someone before you ask the questions; otherwise, the other students will tune out. It means keeping everyone on his or her toes. Calling on students randomly with name sticks or a deck of cards are two ways of keeping them on their toes.

Pacing

Make sure that lessons proceed at a steady clip. If you allow yourself to be distracted or slowed down, the delays will enable minor disruptions to erupt like mini-wildfires. Be careful of *overdwelling* and *fragmentation*. A teacher engaging in overdwelling is spending too much time on directions, on irrelevant details, or on the physical props of the lesson. A teacher engaged in fragmentation divides the lesson into too many unnecessary steps or procedures or has each student do something individually when a group or the entire class could do it more efficiently all at once.

Monitoring Attention

Kounin (1977) invented the term *withitness* to describe teachers who have eyes in the backs of their heads. They seem to know what's going to happen and who the culprit will be, and they move in quickly to nip the misbehavior in the bud. Observe and be alert during all presentations. Maintain eye contact with each student and move around the room. Pretend you are a bat hovering over the room with everyone under your wing. Students are less likely to act out when they feel they are in direct contact with you.

Stimulate Attention

Avoid boredom by showing enthusiasm yourself, by enabling the kids to feel they are making progress or getting somewhere as a result of all their effort, and by including variety. Vary the lesson formats, the group size, the media and materials; and to keep everyone involved, ask stimulating and sometimes unpredictable questions. Use "every pupil response" techniques whenever possible, as these allow everyone to be involved in responding at the same time. They enable you to diagnose on the spot who understands the lesson and who doesn't, saving you hours of grading written work. Some ways of engaging the whole group are:

Say it aloud.

Use a finger signal (thumbs up or down, for example).

Display responses on individual sets of flash cards.

Select students' names from a bundle of ice cream sticks or a deck of cards that have been individualized with their names and then randomized.

Display responses on individual chalkboards or laminated cardboards or white boards.

Overlappingness

Kounin's (1977) term *overlappingness* is a key to effective classroom management and simply refers to the ability to handle two or more things at the same time. An example would be walking over to a student who is tapping his or her pencil while still conducting the lesson, or checking a paper while working with a small math group and not missing a beat.

Smooth Transitions

Avoid *dangles*, *flip-flops*, *thrusts*, and *truncations*. While these sound like terms used in aerobic dancing, here are the definitions: *Dangles* and *flip-flops* occur when the teacher leaves one activity dangling or hanging, goes on to another, and returns once again to the initial activity. *Thrusts* occur when a teacher barrels into an activity without attention to pupil readiness. *Truncations* occur when a teacher aborts an activity and never returns to it.

Closure

Terminate lessons that have gone on too long. Know when students have reached their saturation point, and attempt to bring closure to the lesson before that time. Always leave students asking for more.

Checking for Understanding

Before dismissing a group after a teacher-directed activity, make sure your students know what to do next. This can be accomplished by asking one to summarize the lesson's content and directions for seat work or follow-up. Always ask if anyone has any questions about what to do next. This will prevent the sudden rash of questions that develop when you are happily engaged and settled in with the next group. When kids persist, just nonverbally motion to them to get to work. They are often testing to see if you mean it.

Organization

A well-organized classroom is not, to paraphrase a current slogan, the sign of a sick mind but rather a signal to students that all is safe and secure. Disruptions are less likely to occur in such a well-prepared environment.

Procedures and Routines

Everything you wanted to know (and probably more than you ever wanted to know) about routines and procedures has already been covered in the previous chapter. An efficiently run classroom will cut down on disruptions and delays, which are the precursors of some discipline problems. Most important are transitions, exits, and entrances. The smoothness with which these are orchestrated has a direct bearing on the behavior of pupils. The more adept you become as efficiency expert, classroom traffic controller, systems analyst, and employment agent for monitors, the less effort you will have to expend on discipline.

Signals

Most teachers use some sort of signal when they want the students' attention. This signal is explained on the first day of class, and its use is reinforced from that day forth. You might consider asking students to answer your signal with one of their own. For example, when your hand goes up, they need to raise their hands too. When you clap out a pattern, they respond with the same pattern. Some of the most common signals are lights off, a chord on the piano, a bell, a note on the xylophone, a red light up on the traffic signal, two fingers or a hand raised, a finger to the lips, a message on the chalkboard, and so on. In middle and high school, play some music students like to listen to; this will be their signal to quiet down.

Materials

A common cause of disturbance is the slow or unequal distribution of materials and supplies. Countless arguments occur over paste, scissors, and other items. Although sharing is a virtue to strive for, making sure you have enough supplies to go around is a preventive measure. Keep a basket of supplies on each table grouping.

Use Worksheet 13.3, Setting the Stage for Discipline Checklist, to help you determine whether your stage is set to prevent discipline problems. Any No column responses should start you thinking about how your variables of instruction can be restructured and reshaped to discourage behavioral disturbances.

A Note from the Teacher

Do yourself a favor, review classroom rules every morning or class period. No excuses!
—N. Rader

Off to a Good Start

The first day of school is not too early to discuss with students a rationale for discipline and to set down with children the rules and regulations they are to follow for the entire year.

In this section you will have the opportunity to reflect on how to introduce a needs-based and democratic discipline system to students. Some steps you may want to consider include discussing the importance of discipline, establishing classroom rules, establishing logical consequences for infractions, institutionalizing the class meeting as a problem-solving forum, and informing parents about the rules and consequences.

The Importance of Discipline

To bring home the importance of rules to my fourth through sixth graders, at least in my more radical days, I neither made rules nor extracted any from my class during the first week of school. I sat back as disruption became chaos and bit my tongue more than once during that week. On Friday afternoon I called a classroom meeting (not sure that the children would even come to the circle). When they did, we discussed the problems that had arisen during the previous week. These included noise, inconsiderate behavior, a messy room, assorted arguments, and general confusion. The children themselves suggested the need for some classroom rules and boiled all the suggestions down to two: *Respect each others' rights,* and *Clean up the room.*

While I would not suggest this approach to all but the most experienced and courageous among you, you can use the scenario as a guided fantasy to accomplish the same end. Questions such as the following will get you started:

1. Why do we have rules at all?
2. What would happen if we had no rules?
3. What makes a good rule?
4. What rules do you think are necessary for our room?

Students should ultimately come to understand the concepts of costs and benefits. While rules and laws help us remain safe and secure, we also have to give up something in return. This something is most often freedom to do what we want when we want to. Students should be helped to understand that classroom rules are a specific application of these basic concepts of law. Time spent in discussing the need for rules is time well spent. You are laying a foundation for life in a democratic society where rules, legislated by representatives for the good of all, may sometimes impinge on the total freedom of some, if not all, of the members of society to do whatever they please.

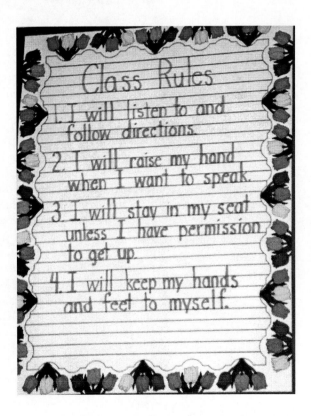

Establishing Classroom Rules

Experienced teachers report setting rules on the first day of school. Common practices include:

eliciting rules from the students

ranking the rules with the children and selecting a maximum of five

stating the rules positively

telling the children that as school progresses they can add or delete rules

having middle school students derive rules in groups

Good rules tend to be needed, fair, applied equally and consistently, enforceable, reasonable, and respectful.

Good rules are sensitive to cultural norms and understandable to nonnative speakers.

The most common rules in classrooms, both elementary and secondary, are listed below. If you find that your students do not come up with a rule for your pet peeve, simply cue them into thinking along those lines.

Elementary Rules	Secondary Rules
Respect rights and property of others.	Obey all school rules.
Follow directions.	Be in your seat when the bell rings.
Work quietly in the classroom.	Bring all needed materials, books, and homework to class.
Be a good listener.	Raise your hand to speak, and listen to others.
Raise hands to speak or leave seat.	Be responsible, respectful, and safeguard your reputation.
Be kind and courteous.	

These rules were mentioned time and time again by experienced teachers. In fact, the first rule in each column covers a lot of ground and was one of the two rules in my classroom. The other was to clean up after yourself. One teacher posts the following as the sole guiding principle: *When I am responsible, I will have a good day. When I am irresponsible, I will pay the consequences.* When children are given the opportunity to learn what makes a good rule, to discuss why rules are needed, to make up a limited set of good rules, and to monitor their enforcement, they are more likely to follow them.

Rules (and translations for nonnative speakers) should be posted in a prominent place in the room. Some teachers really go all out and call this list the Classroom Constitution. A good creative writing experience for older children is to write a fancy preamble. All students can then sign and date the rules to reinforce ownership of these self-imposed limits.

The Classroom Meeting

In a democratically run classroom, students can share not only in rule making but also in the process of monitoring and enforcing the rules. William Glasser (1975, 1998) believes that children can control themselves and will choose the appropriate behavior if those behaviors satisfy their basic needs for survival, love, power, fun, and freedom. It is the teacher's role to assist pupils to make positive choices by setting up a learning environment in which teaching strategies (e.g., cooperative learning) and noncoercive management strategies satisfy these basic needs. One vehicle Glasser proposes for this decision making is the classroom meeting.

Entire class or individual problems are appropriate for a class meeting, and they can be introduced by any student or by the teacher. During the meeting, everyone sits in a tight circle and the problem is exposed and solutions are discussed with everyone participating. The discussion is directed toward solutions, not punishment or faultfinding. The teacher facilitates the discussion, although it is the students' role (not the teacher's) to make the value judgments about the behavior. In simple terms, the children weigh the costs and benefits of continuing the behavior against the costs and benefits of desisting. Then they brainstorm and debate the effectiveness of various proposed ways of redressing the wrong or solving the problem. After a solution is agreed upon, the kids are expected to commit to it or sign a paper saying they are unwilling to commit to it. It is the very act of learning how to solve problems that is empowering, not any one particular solution. The class meeting has been simplified by Jane Nelsen (2000).

Consistency

Veteran teachers agree that once the rules are elicited, consolidated, voted on, and posted, they should be strictly enforced the first day and in the weeks that follow until they are set in the minds and hearts of your students. You should generally follow through on rule enforcement by:

encouraging students' efforts to follow the rules

demonstrating *withitness*

reminding, privately and immediately, those who forget

conveying your commitment to rule-bound behavior through your own actions, voice, and nonverbal behavior

bringing rule-enforcement issues to the class meeting

Communicating Rules to Parents

On the first day most teachers send a note home to parents (in translation, if needed) explaining the classroom rules, or they have the kids rewrite the rules for their parents to sign. While this might not be feasible on the first day given all you have planned, don't delay very long. Parents need to know the ground rules so they can help you. Should infractions occur, parents will have been forewarned about rules and will more likely accept the news that their child has broken one or two of them. A typical letter for elementary grades follows. In secondary schools, the letters are usually generic.

> Dear Parent or Guardian,
>
> Thank you for sharing your child with me this school year. I will do my best to help your child reach his or her full potential. In order to have a safe, secure, happy place to learn, we have written these classroom rules: (list your rules).
>
> I know the children will work hard to follow the rules they developed. At school, I will encourage them in their efforts at self-control. If I need your help at home, I will be in touch with you by phone or note.
>
> If you have any questions or wish to speak with me, I can be reached at the school (phone number) between 8:00 and 8:30 a.m. and during recesses (10:00–10:15 or 2:15–2:30). If these times are inconvenient for you, please leave a message and I'll return your call as soon as possible. I am looking forward to working with you and your child during the coming school year.
>
> Sincerely,
Mrs. Leticia Jones
Class 4B
Public School #94
>
> My child and I have read this letter and we will support the rules regarding behavior as best we can.
>
> Signature _____
>
> Child's signature _____
>
> Comments or Conference Request:

Should it become necessary, phone parents about any serious infractions. You can gauge their reaction on the phone and direct them to positive strategies for working the problem through with you and their child. Notes are far more impersonal, and you need to be careful about provoking an unreasonable overreaction.

Communication with parents regarding discipline should not be confined to instances where children are remiss. Rather, make liberal use of certificates of effort and achievement (translated if necessary) for self-control (Figure 13.1). These awards can go home weekly, and parents will appreciate the positive feedback. Catch a child trying to be on his or her best behavior, award a behavior certificate, and you'll get more mileage out of it from parents and students alike than you will from all the detention notices in the world.

A Note from the Teacher

To motivate them, lighten up, get off their backs, put away the stick, and dangle the carrots.

—C. Burns

Looking for Causes

The orientation of this chapter has been prevention of discipline problems through careful arrangement of the physical environment, attention to the variables of instruction, collaborative rule making, and classroom meetings.

Another way to prevent discipline problems is by looking for underlying causes and dealing with them before they break out in more serious, attention-seeking symptoms. As I noted earlier, Dreikurs and others (1998) tell us that all behavior is related to goals we are seeking. The primary goals we all seek are *to belong and to feel significant.* A misbehaving child is a discouraged child who, when thwarted from seeking these primary goals, substitutes four mistaken goals: attention, power, revenge, and assumed inadequacy.

The teacher, according to Dreikurs and colleagues, must be a detective and find the mistaken goal, so that children's behavior can be redirected—primarily through encouragement, mutual respect, and understanding—to return to the original goals. The teacher has three clues to go on. The first, the *recognition reflex,* is a child's smile that gives it away when you seek and get permission from the child to guess why he or she is behaving this way: "Could it be that . . . ?" The second clue is your visceral reaction to the misbehavior. The third clue is what the child does when told to cease and desist.

Figure 13.1

Behavior Certificate

Attention

An attention-seeking child irritates or annoys us, and when the child is told to stop, he or she ceases and then resumes or substitutes another attention-getting behavior. Remedies include spending special time with the child, redirecting the behavior, ignoring the behavior, imposing a consequence that is related, respectful, and reasonable, and presenting choices to the child (Nelsen, 2000). A now-retired kindergarten teacher was often heard to tell her block-throwing students, "Make a better choice," and they did. Other terminology is, "Make a different choice," or "Make a choice: either (expected behavior) _____ or (logical consequence) _____."

Power

A power-seeking child threatens us and, when told to stop, may passively resist or defy you. Remedies include withdrawing from the situation, cooling off first, problem solving with the child, redirecting the child's power needs, focusing on what you will do instead of what you will make the child do, and scheduling special time with the child (Nelsen, 2000).

Revenge

A revenge-seeking child makes us feel hurt and, when asked to stop, is destructive or hurtful. Remedies include allowing a cooling-off period, engaging in problem solving with the child, giving encouragement, and scheduling special time with the child (Nelsen, 2000).

Assumed Inadequacy

Not surprisingly, a child whose goal is assumed inadequacy makes us feel inadequate, and the child remains passive when confronted. Remedies include making success incremental, training the child in what to do, using encouragement, not giving up, and arranging for special time with the child (Nelsen, 2000).

Nelsen (2000) presents a very clear and concise discussion of the work of Dreikurs and of Glasser. You may want to read more about them either in Nelsen's interpreted version or in the original works listed in the references at the end of the chapter.

This is but one framework for understanding children's underlying motivation to misbehave. You need not accept it fully; in general, however, you will do well to try to see things from the child's point of view. Ask yourself, "Why is the student doing this?" Make some good guesses. Instead of just meting out punishment, which works only in the short haul and builds up long-term resentment in children, stop and think about probable causes or motives. Your hypotheses may be incorrect some of the time, but there is a possibility that some of your theories may be tested out and even proven. You gain much more by canceling out a negative with a positive solution than by doubling the negativity by assessing an immediate penalty.

Two Views of Changing Behavior

A prominent psychiatrist and expert on discipline remarked in a speech that if Pavlov had experimented with cats instead of dogs, his behavior reinforcement theories would have been long forgotten. But Pavlov didn't, and behavior modification techniques are much in vogue in schools today. Positive reinforcement and penalties are imposed by teachers to modify behavior extrinsically.

There is an alternative view of effecting change in children's behavior that capitalizes, instead, on children's intrinsic motivation to belong and to feel significant. This view relies on encouragement and logical consequences to effect change. The two viewpoints will be compared and contrasted in this section.

Rewards and Penalties

In most behavior modification systems, after the rules are handed down (or, in some instances, established with the children) and then practiced, an intricate system of rewards and penalties is initiated. Canter's work in *assertive discipline* (2002) is an example of a system based on rewards and penalties. Some of the positive rewards that teachers use for appropriate behavior are shown in the following lists:

Individual Elementary	Whole Class Elementary	Middle School/High School
certificates	popcorn parties	activities the students enjoy
special activities	field trip	recognition certificates
stickers, small gifts	extra P.E. time	fast-food coupons
food	ice cream party	homework passes
homework exemption	special cooking activity	gel pens, key chains
verbal praise	verbal praise	posters
Honor Roll	free time	computer time
		bonus "bucks" they can trade for any of the above

A Note from the Teacher

My emotionally disturbed children find it difficult to be positive toward others in the room (euphemism). I have a soup can decorated with a colorful sleeve for each of them. There are ten kids in the room and at the end of each day, each gets nine tokens to distribute in the cans of those students who have been nice to them or with whom they have gotten along during the day. We tally the tokens at the end of the week, and the Top five MVPs (most valued people) get to use the limited number of study carrels for the following week. Within weeks of starting this, they were able to see the glimmerings of quid pro quo and what goes around, comes around.

—D. Gillman

Rewards can be earned individually, in groups, or as a whole class. Designing a record-keeping system is fairly easy; maintaining it is difficult. Teachers make a chart of students' names and use stars or move pushpins or color in the spaces when children earn points. If the record keeping is done by groups at a table, the entire table is listed and points accrue when all the children at the table are doing the right thing. Some teachers run the system by total class and add marbles or popcorn kernels to a jar when everyone is behaving appropriately. A full jar means a popcorn party or special treat. Some teachers announce the number of points or marbles to be earned before each activity begins.

As you can see, this procedure takes time, and you must be consistent and fair in using the system if you choose it. Students will clamor for points and keep you on your toes if you forget. Beware of the management problems! Also, beware of making your students reward junkies who behave only because of the material rewards they will receive. *If discipline is ultimately self-control, you may be acting counterproductively by relying too much on extrinsic motivation. The management of these systems may cause more disruption in your class than the behaviors they were designed to correct in the first place.*

On the flip side of the rewards system are the various penalties that teachers assess for infractions of the rules. When this happens, depending on the system, children gather negative checks, on the board or on a teacher's clipboard, that translate into increasingly more negative consequences. These may include staying in for recess, staying after school, going to the principal, carrying a note home, or missing favorite activities. In middle and high school, punishments may include detention, isolation, fines, suspension, and contact with parents. I recently compiled a list of the more unusual penalties first-year teachers use, and some of the most medieval punishments follow anonymously:

A Note from the Teacher

I keep a cell phone on my desk and have the misbehaving kid call home on the spot.
I add or take away the letters that spell QUIET. If they are all erased, the class gets no free time.
I make the "bad kids" sit in the middle of the circle.
I make everyone put their heads down.

Although punishment may stop the behavior immediately, Nelsen (2000) cautions that over the long term, punishment results in the four Rs: *revenge, resentment, rebellion,* and *retreat.* You may win the battle but lose the war if you base your strategy on punishment. One teacher has changed the omnipresent pocket chart of increasingly negative color-coded tickets to a color progression that stands for positive consequences. She flips the card when the child or group is doing the "right thing." The first color stands for good, flips to great, then to terrific, and last to excellent. Special rewards are given to those who reach excellent. This turnaround of ever-increasing negatives to ever-increasing positives has had a profound effect on the climate of the classroom.

Encouragement and Logical Consequences

Encouragement is offered by Dreikurs and others (1998) as an alternative to praise. While praise is showered upon those who succeed, those who have not yet succeeded need encouragement. Encouraging the small steps on the way to success is as important as completion of the whole task. If a misbehaving child is a discouraged child, as Dreikurs and colleagues assert, then the teacher's goal is not to give false praise that the child knows is not deserved but rather to help each child achieve small victories by encouraging and praising in a positive direction. Teachers need to provide all children, and especially the discouraged ones, with opportunities to experience success. Ways of encouraging children suggested by Dreikurs and veteran teachers include recognizing effort, pointing out useful contributions, sharing with children the improvements you see, finding special jobs that the child can succeed in, having the child share a special interest or talent with the class, asking the child to assist others who need help, displaying the child's work, and showing the child in every way that you believe in him or her. Reimer (1967) offers a list of encouraging words, which include:

Keep trying. Don't give up.   You do a good job of. . . .

You have improved in. . . .   You can help me by. . . .

Let's try it together.   I'm sure you can straighten this out.

A Note from the Teacher

What students really yearn for is some extra attention from the teacher, either academic or personal. I make "private deals" with them, like the opportunity to be a monitor or to spend lunch with the teacher, to assist me with yard duty or be my special teaching assistant. These "disruptive" students often become my greatest success stories.

—T. Hong

Just as encouragement is an alternative to praise, logical consequences (Dreikurs, 1998) are an alternative to punishment. While punishment is applied by an outsider, in the logical consequences approach the child experiences the natural or logical consequences of his or her own behavior. What further distinguishes logical consequences from penalties or punishment, according to Nelsen (2000), are the three Rs. Logical consequences are always *related* to the offense, *reasonable*, and *respectful*. A student who writes on the desk cleans it up; a child who fights on the playground sits on the bench for a day or two; a child who spills the paint mops it up. Children are usually given the choice between stopping the misbehavior and accepting the logical consequence. Logical consequences are never humiliating, and they teach kids about responsibility and the relationship between actions and consequences. Remember to use the phrase "make a better choice" before you try anything else.

Counteracting Misdemeanors

Less is really more in dealing with minor infractions in the classroom. Although you may simply want to react at once, it's best to take a breath, examine any possible causes, and then intervene in the least obtrusive way possible. I caution "least obtrusive" because some reactions to infractions may be more disruptive to the learning process than the original sin. Be sure that students understand their choice of improper behavior, because language, cultural, and socioeconomic differences may create misunderstandings. What follows are some laid-back measures that experienced teachers use to nip minor infractions in the bud.

Overlooking Minor Incidents

If every single infraction received your attention, you would never get any teaching accomplished. Use your judgment, and don't make mountains out of mole hills. We all forget ourselves from time to time, and a margin of error should be allowed. Henkes

(1996) has the right idea when Lily the rodent brings an attention-getting purple purse to school in his book, *Lily's Purple Plastic Purse*. Yes, the teacher, Mr. Slinger, takes it away, but he returns it with a note: "Today was a difficult day. Tomorrow will be better." Emmer and his colleagues (2002) suggest that secondary teachers should think and act as if they expect complete compliance with the rules.

Nonverbal and Low-Key Interventions

If you want to continue the flow of classroom interaction, practice overlappingness and deal with minor infractions nonverbally, if possible, without missing a beat. Some of the more effective low-key techniques that teachers use follow.

The Look

Establishing eye contact with the offender and staring until the behavior diminishes works for some teachers. Jones (1992) advocates this practice, along with other nonverbal interventions. Remember that cultural norms may disallow the student from looking directly back at you.

Physical Proximity

Walking toward the offender will usually stop the behavior (Jones, 1992). You may need to move closer to the student and stand nearby. The increasing invasion of the child's space will usually cause him or her to desist. A hand on the desk as you pass is also effective, if moving to the edge of the desk hasn't achieved the desired outcome. You may want to learn more about nonverbal limit setting by reading the work of Jones (1992).

Signals

Signals can be established ahead of time with individuals. A finger to your cheek tells John you see what he is doing and want him to stop. This helps John save face, because the preestablished signal is private. Signals that work in general are a shake of the head, the raising of the eyebrows, a quick arc of the finger.

Enlisting Cooperation

When you notice someone starting to act out, you can check the misbehavior by enlisting the child's aid for some small task relevant to the lesson. You might ask the culprit to erase the board or to be an assistant in handing out materials. Whatever the job, both you and the offender will know why he or she has been chosen, and you still won't miss a beat in your instruction.

Questioning

Often, by posing a question to the student who has just started to act out, you can halt the behavior before it causes disruption by redirecting his or her attention to the task. Make sure it is a question that can be answered easily, as your goal is not to embarrass the child but to channel his or her attention in a productive way. If you feel the student cannot answer the question, have him or her select someone whose hand is raised to supply the answer.

The Encouraging Moment

If you catch the offender doing something right or trying to do the right thing among all the "wrong" things, you are better off waiting for that moment to take your chance to turn a child in the direction of success. Strike when the iron is hot and encourage the child. Having gotten your attention, the offender may cease and desist.

"See Me" Cards

You can duplicate cards that you can unobtrusively place on a child's desk that say something equivalent to "See me" (Figure 13.2). You may also have a place for students to write in why they think they received the card and what a better choice would have been. Have them sign and date it for your records.

Figure 13.2

"See Me" Card

Delayed Reaction

Rather than interrupt the flow of instruction, if the preceding techniques don't work for you, simply and firmly tell the child in question that you want to speak to him or her at the end of the lesson. This invitation to a private conference, only one sentence in length, may in fact cause the child to shape up, negating the need for a long conference. The delayed reaction also gives you a chance to cool off and consider an appropriate response. Nelsen (2000) suggests that this cooling off is most important when you are angry or frustrated and are likely to exacerbate the situation by responding in kind to the child's discouraged behavior. When the infraction involves two students, tell them to write their names on the class meeting agenda and let them cool off as well.

Dangerous and Disruptive Behaviors

These suggestions and techniques have no money-back guarantee that all misbehaviors can be handled without sacrificing instructional time. There will be times (it is hoped not too many) when the misbehavior steps over the line from misdemeanor to classroom felony. These behaviors include fighting, name calling, stealing, destruction of property, constant defiance, refusal to work, and profane language. These serious acts need to be treated differently from the rule-breaking behaviors or the manifestations of mistaken or misdirected goals.

There are no tried-and-true recipes for dealing with these behaviors either, but certain general principles obtain. Except when children are in danger, it is best to deal with serious infractions when you are calmer and better able to act in a rational manner. Keep detailed records (anecdotal) of the child's behavior, with dates, descriptions of behavior, and your response. This is a time to look for causes and seek assistance. Although the following list is far from inclusive, especially symptomatic behaviors to look for are:

anger	abusive language	suicidal ideation
withdrawal	threats to do violence	violent drawings
procrastination	threatening clothing and	any extreme changes in
lateness	insignia	behavior
bullying	absences	threats to other students

defiance	signs of physical or mental	weapons brought to
clowning around	abuse	school
moodiness	depression	manic behavior

Detailed anecdotal records will be helpful when discussing the problem and seeking solutions with school personnel or with parents. It's best to devise some long-range plans or strategies by enlisting the aid of your principal, school or district psychologist or counselor, student study team, special-education resource teacher, and the child's parents. Other, more experienced teachers can help as well, especially those who have encountered the child in earlier grades.

When you suspect that a child will persist in the inappropriate behavior, ask for help early on. By using resource persons available to you at the school or district level, you are demonstrating that you are resourceful, not incapable! After speaking with the principal and the school or district counselor, enlist the aid of the child's parents or guardians. Make your first contacts by phone, and, if you need to, initiate a conference. Use an interpreter on the phone as needed, and make sure one is available during the conference. The parent should already have a great deal of information from your prior contacts. During the conference:

■ Make the parent comfortable. Say something positive about the child.
■ Describe the inappropriate behavior, using anecdotal data. Watch for overreactions by the parents and head them off.
■ Stress to the parent that the child is capable of behaving and has many positive attributes despite his or her negative behavior.
■ Elicit data from parents about the child's attitude toward school, the child's behavior at home, how inappropriate behavior is dealt with at home, and what the parents see as possible causes of misbehavior at school.
■ Devise a plan together that is grounded in encouragement and logical consequences and does not run counter to cultural norms.
■ Follow up and inform parents about the child's progress.

Responses To Avoid

The hardest part of dealing with discipline problems of the more serious kind is repressing some of the very human responses that serious offenses provoke. If there is ever a time to put on your angel's wings and sit under a halo, it's when a serious offense occurs in your classroom. A calm, cool manner on the part of the teacher will not only disarm the offender but will also soothe the other students, who may be as upset as you are. What follows are various responses to avoid. They have been suggested by experienced teachers who know that it is impossible to avoid all of them. But they try!

■ *Holding a Grudge.* When the behavior has been dealt with, try to wipe the slate clean and forgive and forget. Begin each day anew. As one teacher phrased it, "Never let the sun go down on your anger."
■ *Taking It Personally.* Separate yourself from the situation and realize that the behavior is symptomatic of some disturbance within the child and doesn't necessarily reflect his or her attitude toward you. This may require that you schedule frequent pep talks with yourself.
■ *Everyone Suffers.* It simply isn't fair to apply consequences to the entire class, such as no recess or no art project, because a few of your charges are misbehaving.

One student continued to misbehave during a lesson so I sent him to the back of the room to stand for a timeout. Unfortunately, the fire extinguisher was at the back of the room and the student, seeking revenge, proceeded to spray the room. I immediately escorted the class out of the sand and dust cloud so we could breathe. Needless to say, that was the last time I ever used time out.

—D. Clark

Discriminate between the offenders and the nonoffenders and go on with business as usual.

- *Ejection from the Room/Time Out.* It is illegal in many districts to place children outside the room unsupervised. Were it not, it is still not a good solution. Kids will simply fool around in the halls or on the playground. You can be sure they won't stay where you put them. Avoid sending them to another classroom or to the principal except in rare instances. Not only does this burden the other teachers and the principal, but if you exercise this option too frequently, your actions may send a message to your class and to your administrator that you cannot deal with misbehavior. Try to tough it out and deal with problems in your own classroom.
- *Physical Contact.* Although you may be driven to distraction, never grab, pinch, or hit children. They will magnify some of the slightest restraining techniques, and you need to protect yourself. Also, you don't want to model a physical response to the rest of the class, as you are hoping to extinguish this kind of behavior in them.
- *Humiliation.* Included in this category of don'ts are using sarcasm, nagging, or imposing other public embarrassments. Kids need to save face, and if you can talk with the child privately, you are denying him or her an audience for further defiance or face-saving entrenchment of the negative behavior.
- *More Work.* Writing sentences 25 times or more or doing extra work may not change the behavior. Rather, it may negatively associate work, which should be intrinsically pleasurable, with punishment.
- *Threats You Can't/Won't Carry Out.* You will lose your credibility if you back down, so avoid this by thinking carefully about consequences before you announce them. Try withdrawing from the situation and establishing a cooling-off period. Find a way out for both of you to win if you are in a stand-off situation. Simply saying, "I am choosing to let that go this time, Sam, although I expect that you will not be fighting again" allows you both an easy out, and you are still in control of the situation by making the choice. Or have the kid choose between desisting and the logical consequence that pertains.

A Final Don't

Try to relax in regard to discipline and adopt the attitude, "I did the best that I knew how in that situation." If you make an error in judgment, you have the opportunity to recoup your losses the next day. Kids are very forgiving and flexible. If you've been too lax, then tighten the discipline the next day. If you've been too harsh, then lighten up. Remember that until a few years ago, teachers had few written guidelines for dealing with discipline problems.

Try not to become obsessed with classroom discipline matters, because it is not the only component of effective instruction. In fact, if you are too focused on discipline and too concerned about control, you may not risk some of the more active learning and inquiry activities that aren't easy to manage. If you play it safe and opt for a quiet classroom as your highest value, you may be tempted to go the worksheet or lecture route, and education will suffer as a result. This is the biggest *don't* of all.

Now it is your turn to synthesize all you have read and articulate your own comprehensive plan for discipline. On Worksheet 13.4, Discipline Letter to Parents, make a first attempt at conceptualizing your own system, based on your beliefs about children and your philosophy of discipline. Then use Worksheet 13.2 to apply the criteria for discipline systems to your own discipline plan. You will have time to refine your views over the years.

Trust yourself and your intuition. Your experience, the experiences of colleagues, and the kids themselves will help you figure out what works and doesn't work for you.

Reflection Box

In what ways, if any, has the chapter changed my beliefsabout discipline?
Questions I Still Have . . .

Reflection Box

What practices actually worked for me in my first year?

FURTHER READING

Charles, C. M. (2002). *Essentials of effective discipline*. Boston: Allyn & Bacon.

Charles, C. M., & Senter, G. (2002). *Elementary classroom management* (3rd ed.). Boston: Allyn & Bacon.

Evertson, C. M., Emmer, E. T., Clements, B. S., Sanford, J. P., & Worsham, M. E. (2003). *Classroom management for elementary teachers* (6th ed.). Boston: Allyn & Bacon.

Jones, F. (2000). *Tools for teaching*. Santa Cruz, CA: Fred Jones & Associates.

Nelsen, J., Lott, L., & Glen, H. S. (2000). *Positive discipline in the classroom*. (3rd rev. ed.). Roseville, CA: Prima Publishing.

Thorson, S. A. (2003). *Listening to students: Reflections on secondary classroom management*. Boston: Allyn & Bacon.

REFERENCES

Canter, L., & Canter, M. (2002). *Assertive discipline: Positive behavior management for today's classrooms* (3rd ed.). Santa Monica, CA: Lee Canter and Associates.

Charles, C. M. (2002). *Building classroom discipline: From models to practice* (7th ed.). Boston: Allyn & Bacon.

Dewey, J. (1980). *The school and society* (paperback ed.). Carbondale: Southern Illinois University Press.

Dreikurs, R., Grunwald, B., & Pepper, F. (1998). *Maintaining sanity in the classroom: Classroom management techniques* (2nd ed.). Levittown, PA: Taylor and Francis.

Emmer, E. T., Evertson, C. M., & Worsham, M. E. (2002). *Classroom management for secondary teachers,* 6th ed. Boston: Allyn & Bacon.

Glasser, W. (1998). *The quality school teacher.* New York: HarperCollins.

Glasser, W. (1975). Schools without failure (paperback ed.). New York: HarperCollins.

Henkes, K. (1996). *Lily's purple plastic purse.* New York: Greenwillow.

Jones, F. (1992). *Positive classroom discipline.* New York: McGraw-Hill.

Kounin, J. (1977). *Discipline and group management in classrooms.* New York: Krieger Publishing.

Maslow, A. (1987). *Motivation and personality* (3rd ed.). New York: HarperCollins.

Nelsen, J. (2000). *Positive discipline* (Rev. ed.). New York: Ballantine Books.

Reimer, C. (1967). Some words of encouragement. In V. Soltz, *Study group leader's manual* (pp. 67–69). Chicago: Alfred Adler Institute.

Worksheet 13.1

Discipline Clarification Activity

Rank from 1–8 alone and then in a group.

Me	Group	
_____	_____	Discipline is manipulation and isn't appropriate for kids.
_____	_____	I'll figure discipline out as I go along.
_____	_____	I believe in talking out discipline problems with individuals.
_____	_____	Students should participate in setting up classroom rules and working out classroom problems.
_____	_____	Discipline is helping kids make the right choices.
_____	_____	Kids should experience the logical consequences of their behavior.
_____	_____	Kids respond best to rewards and punishments.
_____	_____	A classroom is a dictatorship, and I make the rules.

Worksheet 13.2

My Discipline Plan Is:

	Yes	No
Reasonable	☐	☐
Respectful	☐	☐
Dignified	☐	☐
Consistent with school plan	☐	☐
Flexible	☐	☐
Time efficient	☐	☐
Easy to administer	☐	☐
Stress-free	☐	☐
Easy to communicate	☐	☐
Consistent with my philosophy and beliefs	☐	☐

Worksheet 13.3

	Yes	No
I. Physical Environment		
A. Room is properly ventilated.	☐	☐
B. Room is well lit.	☐	☐
C. Room is an attractive and stimulating environment.	☐	☐
D. Room is clean and uncluttered.	☐	☐
E. Private spaces are provided.	☐	☐
F. Students can see and be seen from all angles.	☐	☐
G. Seating arrangement promotes good management.	☐	☐
II. Meeting Individual Differences		
A. Assignments are differentiated for slower and faster learners.	☐	☐
B. Students are grouped according to needs, interests, abilities.	☐	☐
C. Students have some choices.	☐	☐
D. Teacher expectations are realistic.	☐	☐
E. Instruction is geared to pupil interests.	☐	☐
III. Planning		
A. Success is built in.	☐	☐
B. Activities are worthwhile and meaningful.	☐	☐
C. All materials are ready.	☐	☐
D. Procedures are clear.	☐	☐
E. Each day is overplanned, and "sponges" are ready for use when needed.	☐	☐
IV. Instruction		
A. Attention is focused prior to beginning instruction.	☐	☐
B. Lessons are well paced.	☐	☐
C. Attention is monitored.	☐	☐
D. Lessons are varied, and pupils are involved.	☐	☐
E. Overlapping is practiced.	☐	☐
F. Transitions are smooth.	☐	☐
G. Lessons are brought to closure.	☐	☐
H. Procedural questions are encouraged.	☐	☐
V. Organization		
A. Procedures and routines are set.	☐	☐
B. Signals for attention are consistently reinforced.	☐	☐
C. Materials are equally and efficiently distributed.	☐	☐

VI. Other _____

Worksheet 13.4

Discipline Letter to Parents

Dear Parent or Guardian:

14

Assessing
Student Learning

The typical teacher will spend one-quarter to one-third of his or her professional time involved in assessment-related activities. . . . without question, teachers need to know and understand the principles of sound assessment.

—Rick Stiggins, "New Assessment Beliefs for a New School Mission," *Phi Delta Kappan,* September 2004

Taken from *Curriculum and Instruction for Becoming a Teacher,* by Forrest W. Parkay.

Y ou are a first-year teacher at a school in a city of about 500,000 people. Your state has an induction program that provides support for teachers during their first year of teaching. As part of this induction program, new teachers are required to observe in classrooms of other teachers during the year. Throughout the year you have observed two fifth- and sixth-grade social studies teachers—Mrs. Allen and Ms. Rodriguez. The following are excerpts from the notes you took during two recent observations. The excerpts describe how Mrs. Allen and Ms. Rodriguez typically assess student learning.

Mrs. Allen's Classroom

The task for [Mrs. Allen's] fifth-graders required them to copy a set of questions about famous explorers from a work sheet and to add the correct short-answer responses in the appropriate spots. The class spent thirty minutes on this exercise, which was part of a larger unit on exploration and which the teacher, Mrs. Allen, described as very consistent with the typical assessment.

During the four times that [I] observed Allen's hour-long classes, students read aloud from the textbook, a routine occasionally punctuated with Allen's asking them factual recall questions. During one class, students copied a chart from the board organizing the facts from the reading into categories. After finding more facts to fill up the chart, the students then completed a work sheet crossword puzzle built from the vocabulary words of the lesson.

Ms. Rodriguez's Classroom

As an assessment of their learning, Ms. Rodriguez had her class of fifth- and sixth-graders research and write a paper on ecology, an assignment that occupied forty hours of class time during the twelve-week grading period. Each student produced several drafts of the paper and met individually with the teacher several times to discuss the drafts. Before they began the project, students received eleven pages of written directions on how to research, organize, and write the paper, including a step-by-step checklist for completing the assignment, a sample outline, and sample bibliography entries. The paper counted for 75 percent of the student's grade for the twelve-week period (Marks, Newmann, and Gamoran, 1996, 59–60).

Guiding Questions

1. What is the role of assessment in teaching?
2. What methods can you use to assess student learning?
3. What are emerging trends in classroom assessment?
4. How can you develop high-quality classroom assessments?

Newspaper headlines and special reports on television frequently remind us that the public is concerned about declining test scores, the performance of U.S. students on international comparisons of achievement, and our nation's standing in a competitive global economy. Pressure to get "back to the basics" and drives by parents, citizen groups, and politicians to hold teachers accountable have led to a nationwide push to develop more effective ways to assess student learning.

Despite the increased emphasis on assessing student learning, it is difficult to determine what students really know as a result of being taught. As a veteran teacher of twenty-seven years noted: "How do we truly know when our students have sufficient knowledge, understanding, and the skills required to be successful with the learning? In short, how do we know that our students know?" (Tileston 2004, 13).

Clearly, the purpose of teaching is to develop within students an understanding of the world around them. However, our knowledge of human nature tells us that it is hard to determine precisely what another person does or does not understand. Though the aims of teaching may be specified in carefully worded standards, one of the realities of teaching, as the following junior high school teacher points out, is that some of what students learn may be hard to measure:

> There is no clear end result. . . . That frustrates me. I want so badly for my joy [of teaching] to be neatly tied up so that I can look at it admiringly. . . . I want so badly to see my successes—I don't know, give me certificates or badges or jelly beans. Then I can stack them up, count them, and rate myself as a teacher (Henry et al. 1995, 68–69).

Currently, there is a nationwide emphasis on high-stakes testing. That is, the tests have "high-stakes" consequences for students, teachers, and administrators. For example, students' performance on a test may determine if teachers at a school receive a merit pay increase. High-stakes tests are one way to hold teachers accountable for student learning.

However, the conventional wisdom among teachers is that they are often uncertain about just what their students have learned. We have enormous amounts of assessment data, but often little understanding of what lies behind a student's written response and little understanding of what the assessment experience really means to a student. As one educational researcher concludes: "The inaccessibility of data is similar both in science and in learning. We cannot directly 'see' subatomic particles, nor can we 'see' the inner-workings of the mind and emotions of the child. Both are inferential: both are subject to human interpretation" (Costa 1984, 202).

On the one hand, then, when you become a teacher you must be realistic about the challenges of assessing student learning; on the other, you must continuously work to become aware of the latest approaches to assessing students' learning. Figure 14.1 presents a set of guiding principles for teachers to follow in developing a student-centered approach to classroom assessment.

As the opening scenario for this chapter illustrates, teachers can use very different methods for assessing student learning. For example, what differences did you notice between the assessment activities in Mrs. Allen's classroom and Ms. Rodriguez's classroom? What do you think Mrs. Allen's students thought about the learning tasks they were asked to complete? Ms. Rodriguez's students? When you were a fifth- or sixth-grade student, which teacher would you have preferred? Why?

Figure 14.1

The principles of sound assessment: A critical blend.

Source: Adapted from Richard J. Stiggins, *Student-Involved Classroom Assessment,* 3rd ed. Upper Saddle River, NJ: Merrill, 2000, p. 18.

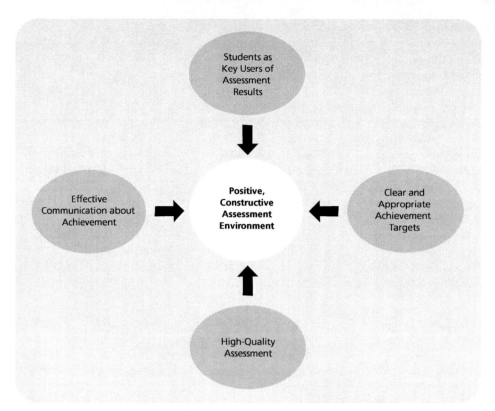

What Is the Role of Assessment in Teaching?

During the 1980s and early 1990s, numerous studies were conducted to identify the characteristics of successful (or effective) schools. A common finding in these studies was that successful schools place primary emphasis on assessing student learning. The environment, or culture, of these schools emphasizes the achievement of academic excellence *for all students.* Toward this end, successful schools have definite procedures in place for making frequent, systematic assessments of student learning. In short, the learning of students at these schools is monitored closely. When problems in student learning are noticed, appropriate remediation is pro-vided quickly.

The role of assessment in teaching is twofold: (1) assessment helps students learn more effectively, and (2) assessment helps teachers teach more effectively. Assessment of student learning is an important part of teaching. **Assessment** is the process of gathering data to determine students' knowledge, skills, and attitudes within a certain area of the school curriculum. As the final question in the Tyler rationale for curriculum development points out, teachers must ask "How can we determine whether [our] purposes have been attained." In other words, how can we assess students' learning? Similarly, the last element in the "Generic Lesson Plan for a Unit of Study" outline presented in Appendix 14.1 lists three assessment-related questions that all teachers must ask:

1. How will I measure and evaluate students' progress or achievement?
2. How will I know if I have achieved the objectives for the unit?
3. What assessments will I use to measure students' learning: quizzes, tests, observations of classroom behavior, portfolios, projects, performances, etc.?

Formal and Informal Assessments

Assessment of student learning may be formal or informal. **Formal assessments** are developed prior to having students complete the assessments. Formal assessments include final exams, tests, and quizzes on the subject matter studied; in-class seatwork and homework; and critiques of performances, for example, tryouts for a school play or athletic team.

Informal assessments occur during teaching, and they are made spontaneously. The teacher might, for example, note students' facial expressions to determine their level of understanding of the material taught, listen carefully to a student's explanation of how she solved a problem in mathematics; or ask questions to monitor students' level of understanding during a lecture. Teachers frequently make informal assessments of their students at the beginning of each school day or class session.

Informal assessments are less obvious to the classroom observer. In other words, during a classroom observation, an observer may not know just when a teacher is making informal assessments of student learning. Actually, professional teachers continuously assess students' responses to their teaching.

How Teachers Use Assessments

For most people, the term *classroom assessment* brings to mind a four-step process: (1) the teacher prepares a test (or selects a preexisting test) to cover material that has been taught, (2) students take the test, (3) the teacher corrects the test, and (4) the teacher assigns grades based on how well students performed on the test. Classroom assessment, however, involves more—it provides information teachers use (1) to determine how well students are learning the material being taught; (2) to identify the type of feedback that will enhance student learning; (3) to develop strategies for improving their effectiveness as teachers; and (4) to determine if students have reached certain levels of performance. For example, the Teachers' Voices feature on page 140 illustrates how two teachers used assessments of students' learning to evaluate their effectiveness as teachers.

What Methods Can You Use to Assess Student Learning?

The assessment of student learning will enable you to make judgments about the performance of students and about your performance as a teacher. You will use assessment to evaluate your effectiveness because you recognize that how well students learn depends on how well you teach. Furthermore, you will realize that "assessment is more than a collection of techniques. It is a systematic process that plays a significant role in effective teaching" (Linn and Gronlund 2000, xiii).

Assessment has been defined as "the full range of procedures used to gain information about student learning (observations, ratings of performances or projects, paper-and-pencil tests) and the formation of value judgments concerning learning progress" (Linn and Gronlund 2000, 31). As a professional teacher, you will strive to become aware of the latest approaches to assessing student learning. You will understand the critical role that assessment plays in teaching and the importance of "establishing credible performance standards, communicating these standards to students, and providing feedback to students on their progress" (McMillan 2001, xiii). In addition, the classroom assessments you develop will reflect four "guiding principles": "(1) Students

Eric Learns to Read: Learning Styles at Work

June Hodgin and Caaren Wooliscroft

We have seen dramatic changes in many students in our inclusive classroom since we have employed learning styles strategies. In our class of twenty-two students (ten Hispanic, twelve Anglo), four students were identified as learning disabled and qualified for special education and another three had attention deficit disorders. The students' IQs ranged from 74 to 126.

We introduce learning styles to our students at the beginning of each school year. We expose them to a variety of learning styles elements (for example, working with the lights off, while listening to classical music, or with everyone sitting on the floor) and discuss how the different elements help or hinder learning ability. After reading stories about learning styles and explaining the Learning Styles Model, we hold class discussions.

Our students' scores on the Texas Assessment of Academic Skills (TAAS) during the three-year period from 1993 to 1996 demonstrate the effectiveness of reading styles and inclusion practices. During 1993–94, the year before we implemented reading styles and inclusion, only 50 percent of the regular student population passed the test, and none of the special education children passed. We saw dramatic improvements during the next two years as we implemented the reading styles strategies and inclusion practices. All the regular education students passed the test both years, with 25 percent of special education students passing in 1994–95, and 20 percent in 1995–96. In addition, student mastery of all test objectives increased from 11 percent in 1994, to 67 percent in 1995, to 80 percent in 1996.

We saw another indicator of success in the classroom climate. Our students worked together in heterogeneous small and large groups. Because we did not separate students by ability level, our students were not aware of any labels. The self-esteem, motivation, and attitude of all students improved because they did not feel stress, learning was fun and pleasurable, and it was easy to succeed. We had created a real community of learners.

Questions

1. For Hodgin and Wooliscroft, their students' scores on the TAAS demonstrated the effectiveness of reading styles and inclusion practices. What other types of assessments might they have used to determine the effectiveness of reading styles and inclusion practices?

2. Hodgin and Wolliscroft used their students' scores on the TAAS to reflect on their effectiveness as teachers. How might teachers misuse students' scores on state-mandated tests like the TAAS?

3. Hodgin and Wooliscroft state that "We had created a real community of learners." What are the characteristics of a community of learners?

June Hodgin is a consultant for the Special Education Department in Abilene, Texas; *Caaren N. Wooliscroft* is a third-grade teacher at Alta Vista Elementary School in Abilene. The preceding is excerpted from their article in the March 1997 *Educational Leadership,* pp. 43–45.

are the key assessment users, (2) Clear and appropriate targets are essential, (3) Accurate assessment is a must, (4) Sound assessments must be accomplished by effective communication" (Stiggins 2001, 17–23).

Quantitative and Qualitative Assessments

To assess student learning, you can use both quantitative and qualitative ap-proaches. Quantitative approaches make use of measurement and evaluation techniques—such as teacher-made classroom tests composed of multiple-choice, true-false, matching, or essay items—or performance-based assessments. **Quantitative assessments** yield numerical scores that teachers use to evaluate student learning as well as the effectiveness of their teaching.

Qualitative approaches may include formal and informal observations of students' performance on various learning tasks, the manner with which they approach those learning tasks, or students' self-reports of their interests and attitudes. For example, teachers routinely assess students' work habits. *Work habits* is a term suggested by the Coalition of Essential Schools for various dispositions important for effective thinking and learning, including reading with curiosity; reflecting critically on one's own work; developing independence, clarity, and incisiveness of thought; willingness to work hard; an ability to manage time effectively; persistence; accuracy and precision; and working collaboratively. **Qualitative assessments** are more subjective than quantitative assessments. However, quantitative assessments are also subjective because teachers must interpret the meaning of the scores.

Classroom Assessment

To assess student learning, you will use measurement and evaluation techniques. **Measurement** is the gathering of quantitative data related to the knowledge and skills students have acquired. Measurement yields scores, rankings, or ratings that teachers can use to determine the degree to which students have attained specified standards. At some point in your teacher education program, you will be introduced to basic statistical methods for comparing the learning of students within a group and between groups of students.

Evaluation is a critical teaching skill. In your role as an evaluator, you will make judgments about the performance of students *and* about your own effectiveness as a teacher. **Evaluation** involves making judgments about or assigning a value to measurements the teacher makes of student learning. Successful teachers continually evaluate the effectiveness of their teaching because they recognize that how well students learn depends on how well they teach.

Formative Evaluation

When teachers measure students' attainment of knowledge and skills for the purpose of making decisions about their teaching, they are engaging in **formative evaluation.** Teachers use the results of formative evaluations to make decisions about what learning activities are appropriate for students. For example, as an aid to planning for a new unit of instruction, you may assess students' understanding of a subject by having them take a short diagnostic test or quiz, complete homework or seatwork assignments, or participate in a group project.

As a teacher, you will also conduct informal formative evaluations while you are teaching. For example, you will pay close attention to what students say; you will use probing questions to gauge students' understanding of the subject; and you will note students' facial expressions and behavior. During these informal formative evaluations, you will not only assess students' understanding; you will also assess students' attitudes toward learning the subject. For example, in the following, a teacher makes some candid comments about his informal formative evaluations while teaching:

I'd become dissatisfied with the closed Q & A style that my unthinking teaching had fallen into, and I would frequently be lazy in my acceptance of right answers and sometimes even tacit complicity with a class to make sure none of us had to work too hard. . . . They and I knew that if the Q & A wasn't going smoothly, I'd change the question, answer it myself, or only seek answers from the "brighter students." There must have been times (still are?) where an outside observer would see my lessons as a small discussion group surrounded by many sleepy onlookers (Black et al. 2004, 11).

Summative Evaluation

When teachers use measurements of student learning to determine grades at the end of a unit, semester, or year and to decide whether students are ready to proceed to the next phase of their education, they are engaging in **summative evaluation.** Summative evaluations usually provide the teacher with an overview of student learning across a broad range of knowledge and skills. In contrast, formative evaluations are usually more focused and cover a narrower range of knowledge and skills. Teachers also use summative evaluations to make changes in their teaching that might be beneficial with the next group of students. Figure 14.2 illustrates the essential elements of effective classroom assessment and the questions that guide teachers' decision making in this important area of teaching.

Standardized Assessments

Standardized assessments (or standardized tests) are pencil-and-paper tests that are taken by large groups of students and scored in a uniform manner. The test items, the conditions under which students take the test, how the tests are scored, and how the scores are interpreted are "standardized" for all who take the test. This standardization enables educators to compare scores for different groups of students in different schools around the country. **Standardized assessments** are administered at the district, state, and national levels.

The first standardized test in the United States was administered by Horace Mann, Secretary of the Massachusetts State Board of Education, in the mid-1800s. Mann, who eventually came to be known as "father of the common school," wanted to classify students by ability and gather evidence for the effectiveness of the state school system. He hoped to use the results of the state test to further his educational reform efforts. Prior to the use of this standardized test, teachers conducted their own assessments at the individual classroom level.

Figure 14.2

Effective classroom assessment.

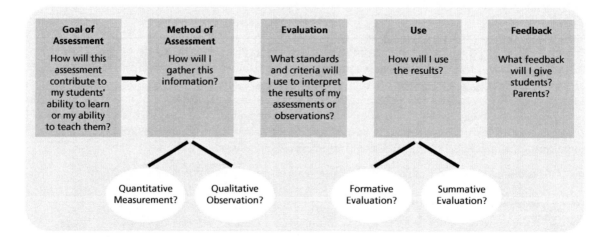

What might be some of the pressures felt by students and teachers as a result of the increased emphasis on testing?

Current examples of standardized tests are the Iowa Test of Basic Skills, the California Achievement Test, the Metropolitan Achievement Tests, the Stanford Achievement Test, the Scholastic Assessment Test (SAT), and the American College Test (ACT) Assessment. In addition, the federal government funds the National Assessment of Educational Progress (NAEP). The NAEP is periodically used to sample student achievement around the country. On a biannual basis, the performance of national samples of nine-, thirteen-, and seventeen-year-olds is assessed. Educational policy makers then use the results—reported by geographic region, gender, and ethnic background—to guide their decision making. First administered in 1969, the NAEP has assessed student learning in all areas of the curriculum.

International Assessments

In 1991, the first **International Assessment of Educational Progress** (IAEP) was conducted, and the achievement of U.S. students was compared to that of students in more than thirty nations. The results indicated that the achievement levels of U.S. students were often below those of students from other countries. Subsequent IAEP comparisons have shown some improvement in the rankings of American students in mathematics and science. Figure 14.3(a), for example, which is based on the **Third International Mathematics and Science Study** (TIMSS) sponsored by the International Association for the Evaluation of Educational Achievement (1997a, 1997b), shows how the mathematics and science achievement levels of fourth-grade U.S. students compare with those of students from several other countries. However, as Figure 14.3(b) shows, the relative standing of U.S. students in these subject areas was significantly lower by the final year of secondary school. Gains in literacy, however, have been more significant; for example, *A First Look—Findings from the National Assessment of Educational Progress* (National Center for Education Statistics 1995) reported that U.S. fourth-graders ranked second in 1995 on a thirty-two-nation survey of reading skills.

Since the publication of *A Nation at Risk* (National Commission on Excellence in Education 1983), there has been an unbroken trend for the media and some observers

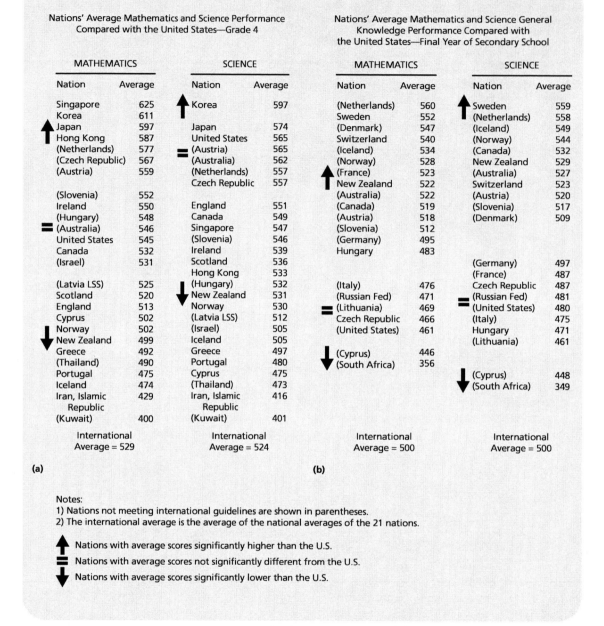

Nations' Average Mathematics and Science Performance Compared with the United States—Grade 4

MATHEMATICS			SCIENCE	
Nation	Average		Nation	Average
Singapore	625		Korea	597
Korea	611			
Japan	597		Japan	574
Hong Kong	587		United States	565
(Netherlands)	577		(Austria)	565
(Czech Republic)	567		(Australia)	562
(Austria)	559		(Netherlands)	557
			Czech Republic	557
(Slovenia)	552			
Ireland	550		England	551
(Hungary)	548		Canada	549
(Australia)	546		Singapore	547
United States	545		(Slovenia)	546
Canada	532		Ireland	539
(Israel)	531		Scotland	536
			Hong Kong	533
(Latvia LSS)	525		(Hungary)	532
Scotland	520		New Zealand	531
England	513		Norway	530
Cyprus	502		(Latvia LSS)	512
Norway	502		(Israel)	505
New Zealand	499		Iceland	505
Greece	492		Greece	497
(Thailand)	490		Portugal	480
Portugal	475		Cyprus	475
Iceland	474		(Thailand)	473
Iran, Islamic Republic	429		Iran, Islamic Republic	416
(Kuwait)	400		(Kuwait)	401

International Average = 529   International Average = 524

(a)

Nations' Average Mathematics and Science General Knowledge Performance Compared with the United States—Final Year of Secondary School

MATHEMATICS			SCIENCE	
Nation	Average		Nation	Average
(Netherlands)	560		Sweden	559
Sweden	552		(Netherlands)	558
(Denmark)	547		(Iceland)	549
Switzerland	540		(Norway)	544
(Iceland)	534		(Canada)	532
(Norway)	528		New Zealand	529
(France)	523		(Australia)	527
New Zealand	522		Switzerland	523
(Australia)	522		(Austria)	520
(Canada)	519		(Slovenia)	517
(Austria)	518		(Denmark)	509
(Slovenia)	512			
(Germany)	495			
Hungary	483		(Germany)	497
			(France)	487
(Italy)	476		Czech Republic	487
(Russian Fed)	471		(Russian Fed)	481
(Lithuania)	469		(United States)	480
Czech Republic	466		(Italy)	475
(United States)	461		Hungary	471
			(Lithuania)	461
(Cyprus)	446			
(South Africa)	356		(Cyprus)	448
			(South Africa)	349

International Average = 500   International Average = 500

(b)

Notes:
1) Nations not meeting international guidelines are shown in parentheses.
2) The international average is the average of the national averages of the 21 nations.

▲ Nations with average scores significantly higher than the U.S.

≡ Nations with average scores not significantly different from the U.S.

▼ Nations with average scores significantly lower than the U.S.

Figure 14.3

Nation's average mathematics and science performance compared with the United States.

Source: National Center for Education Statistics. *Pursuing Excellence: A Study of U.S. Fourth-Grade Mathematics and Science Achievement in International Context,* Figures 1 & 2. Washington, DC, NCES, 1997.

of U.S. education to decry the perceived poor performance of U.S. students on international comparisons of achievement. A closer examination of international comparisons, however, reveals the seldom-reported fact that the United States' position in country-by-country rankings is based on *aggregate* achievement scores—in other words, achievement scores of all students are used to make the comparisons. Not taken into account is the United States' commitment to educating all students (not just the academically able or those from home environments that encourage education), the widely varying quality of U.S. schools, and differences in students' *opportunity to learn* the content covered in achievement tests. That is, when only the top students of each country are compared, the rankings of U.S. students improve dramatically. As David Berliner and Bruce Biddle point out in *The Manufactured Crisis: Myths, Fraud, and the Attack on America's Public Schools* (1995, 52), "If one actually looks at and thinks about the comparative evidence, [o]ne discovers that it does not confirm the myth of American educational failure. Indeed, it suggests that in many ways American education stands head and shoulders above education in other countries."

To illustrate their point, Berliner and Biddle summarize Ian Westbury's (1992) analysis of data from the International Association for the Evaluation of Educational Achievements' (IEA) Second International Mathematics Study, which purported to show that U.S. eighth-graders were significantly behind their Japanese peers in mathematics achievement. Westbury noted that Japanese eighth-grade students were *required* to take courses that covered algebra, whereas U.S. students typically take such courses a year or two later. When Westbury compared the achievement of U.S. and Japanese students who had taken prealgebra and algebra, the achievement of U.S. students matched or exceeded that of Japanese students (see Figure 14.4).

Berliner and Biddle (1995, 63) go on to offer the following cautions about interpreting cross-national studies of educational achievement:

- Few of these studies have yet focused on the unique values and strengths of American education.
- Many of the studies' results have obviously been affected by sampling biases and inconsistent methods for gathering data.
- Many, perhaps most, of the studies' results were generated by differences in curricula—in opportunities to learn—in the countries studied.

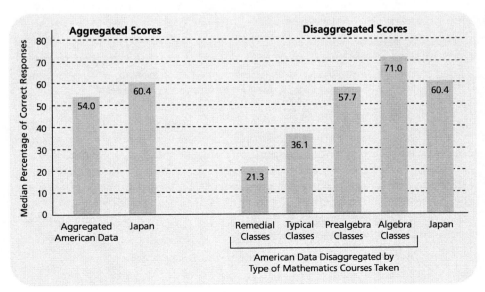

Figure 14.4

Japanese and American achievement scores for students age thirteen—from The Second International Mathematics Study of the IEA.

Source: Ian Westbury. "Comparing American and Japanese Achievement: Is the United States Really a Low-Achiever?" *Educational Researcher, 21*(5), 1992, pp. 18–24. Taken from David C. Berliner and Bruce J. Biddle, *The Manufactured Crisis: Myths, Fraud, and the Attack on America's Public Schools.* Reading, MA: Addison-Wesley Publishing Company, 1995, p. 57.

- Aggregate results for American schools are misleading because of the huge range of school quality in this country—ranging from marvelous to terrible.
- The press has managed to ignore most comparative studies in which the United States has done well.

Norm-Referenced Assessments

Some standardized assessments are norm-referenced—that is, students' scores are compared with scores of other students who are similar. The comparison group of students, called the *norm group,* is usually from the same age group and grade level. An individual student's score is then compared to the average, or mean, score for the total group. Norm-referenced tests are used to determine where a student is compared to the "typical" performance of other students at the same age and grade level. Thus, **norm-referenced assessments** enable teachers to rank students in terms of their achievement.

To understand the meaning of scores on a norm-referenced assessment, imagine that a student received a total of seventy-five points on a one hundred-point norm-referenced assessment. If the mean, or average, score for the comparison group of students was also seventy-five, the student would be at the fiftieth percentile. That is, 50 percent of the students in the comparison group scored higher, and 50 percent scored lower. However, if the mean score for the comparison group was ninety, the student might be in the thirtieth percentile. That is, 70 percent of students in the comparison group scored higher, and 30 percent scored lower.

The preceding example can also be used to illustrate why scores on norm-referenced tests should be interpreted carefully. Norm-referenced test scores can be misused. If the student scored in the thirtieth percentile, it would be a mistake to assume that score is evidence that the student is doing poorly. The student might not have done well on the material covered by the norm-referenced assessment; however, the student might be doing quite well in other areas not included in the test. Following are four examples of norm-referenced interpretations of students' performance:

1. Frank won the one-mile race.
2. On the test of basic skills, Susan's scores were near the average.
3. On the districtwide chemistry test, our school had the best scores.
4. On the test of physical fitness, Paul was in the ninetieth percentile.

Criterion-Referenced Assessments

Other standardized assessments are criterion referenced—that is, students' learning is compared with clearly defined criteria or standards, rather than with the performance of other students. **Criterion-referenced assessments** do not indicate what is "average" or "typical" for students from the same age group and grade level. Criterion-referenced assessments indicate what students know and can do within a specific subject area. Students' scores are not compared with the scores of other groups of students.

A teacher might use a criterion-referenced assessment to assess a student's ability to calculate the square root of a number, to write a well-organized paragraph, or to type sixty words per minute on a computer keyboard. In other words, the assessment is made with reference to an instructional objective, rather than the performance of other students on the assessment. Similarly, the student's score is interpreted without reference to how other students performed. Following are four examples of criterion-referenced interpretations of students' performance:

1. In the chemistry lab, Mary can correctly light a Bunsen burner.
2. Frank can identify each element on the periodic table.

3. Yiming can calculate the sine, cosine, and tangent of angles.
4. Using a map of the world, Karen can identify the countries that were involved in World War II.

What Are Emerging Trends in Classroom Assessment?

Declining test scores, international comparisons of student achievement, and calls to hold teachers more accountable for student learning have fueled a movement to assess student learning with an ever-increasing number of standardized tests. Test scores are frequently used to make "high-stakes" decisions about teacher accountability and the promotion of students to the next grade level.

The majority of the public supports testing in schools. According to the 2004 Phi Delta Kappa/Gallup Poll, 40 percent believe there is "about the right amount" of testing, whereas 22 percent believe there is "not enough" (Rose and Gallup 2004). However, the percentage believing that there is "too much" testing increased from 20 percent in 1997 to 32 percent in 2004. According to the 2004 poll, the public is almost evenly divided regarding the use of standardized test scores to judge the quality of teachers (49 percent favor, 47 percent oppose, and 4 percent "don't know") and to determine whether a student should receive a high school diploma (51 percent favor, 47 percent oppose, and 2 percent "don't know").

The drive for more testing has, in some cases, led to a lowering of standards. For example, some states have changed their assessment criteria to avoid the penalties that The No Child Left Behind Act of 2001 imposes on schools whose students score poorly on standardized tests. According to NCLB, states that fail to comply risk losing federal education money. Schools deemed failing several years in a row must offer tutoring to low-achieving students and, eventually, can be forced into complete reorganization. But the law leaves it up to the states to establish their own standards of success. The following states are among those that have modified their assessment criteria:

- Texas reduced the number of questions that students must answer correctly to pass the third-grade reading exam, from twenty-four out of thirty-six, to twenty.
- Michigan lowered the percentage of students who must pass statewide tests to certify a school as making adequate progress. For example, the percentage of high school students that must pass English tests has been reduced from 75 to 42 percent.
- Colorado changed the grading system used on its tests, combining students previously characterized on the basis of test scores as "partially proficient" with those called "proficient."

Although the push to assess student learning more frequently has led to some modifications in assessment criteria, new forms of assessment are being used more widely. Innovations in assessment are partly in response to criticisms of the fairness and objectivity of standardized tests, such as the Iowa Test of Basic Skills, the SAT, and the ACT. Educators and the public have criticized these tests not only for the class and gender bias in their content, but also for failing to measure accurately students' true knowledge, skills, and levels of achievement. For all of these reasons, educators are increasingly going beyond traditional pencil-and-paper tests, oral questioning, and formal and informal observations. In addition, they are using an array of new assessment tools—individual and small-group projects, portfolios of work, exhibitions, videotaped demonstrations of skills, and community-based activities, to name a few. The following

in Teaching

How can educational software be used to assess students' problem-solving skills?

Today's teachers can use an array of exciting educational software to assess students' problem-solving skills and higher-order thinking. For example, *the Astronomy Village: Investigating the Universe,* developed by the National Aeronautics and Space Administration (NASA) and available at a modest cost, promotes ninth- and tenth-grade students' learning within a virtual observatory community (see accompanying figure) that includes extensive multimedia resources and sophisticated exploration tools. The *Astronomy Village* requires that teams of three students select one of the following ten investigations, develop a plan, and carry it out.

- *Search for a Supernova*—Uses neutrino data to locate a supernova
- *Looking for a Stellar Nursery*—Views Omega nebula using different wavelengths
- *Variable Stars*—Identifying a Cepheid-variable star in another galaxy
- *Search for Nearby Stars*—Movement of stars' positions as Earth circles the Sun
- *Extragalactic Zoo*—Different galaxies and clusters
- *Wedges of the Universe*—Viewing depths of space in two wedges of sky
- *Search for a "Wobbler"*—Looking for stars that wobble in their motion
- *Search for Planetary Building Blocks*—Examines the Orion nebula for proplanetary disks
- *Search for Earth-Crossing Objects*—Looks for asteroids that cross Earth's path
- *Observatory Site Selection*—Selects a site for an observatory (Jonassen, Peck, and Wilson 1999, 94–95).

Included as part of the *Astronomy Village* are a star life-cycle simulator, an orbital simulator, and a three-dimensional star simulator. In addition, the student teams can use the program's digitized video clips, images from the Hubble space telescope and other instruments, audio clips of astronomers discussing their work, and book chapters, NASA publications, and articles from astronomy journals and magazines.

Technology in Teaching feature illustrates how teachers can use educational software to assess students' problem-solving skills and higher-order thinking.

Increasingly, teachers are using alternative assessments—that is, "forms of assessment that require the active construction of meaning rather than the passive regurgitation of isolated facts" (McMillan 2001, 14). The following sections examine several forms of **alternative assessments:** authentic assessments, portfolio assessments, peer assessments, self-assessments, performance-based assessments, alternate assessments, and project-based learning.

Authentic Assessment

Authentic assessment (sometimes called *alternative assessment*) requires students to use higher-level thinking skills to perform, create, or solve a real-life problem, not just choose one of several designated responses, as on a multiple-choice test item. A teacher might use **authentic assessment** to evaluate the quality of individual or small-group projects, videotaped demonstrations of skills, or participation in community-based activities. In science, for example, students might design and conduct an experiment to solve a problem and then explain in writing how they solved the problem.

Authentic assessments require students to solve problems or to work on tasks that approximate as much as possible those they will encounter beyond the classroom. For example, authentic assessment might allow students to select projects on which they will be evaluated, such as writing a brochure, making a map, creating a recipe, writing and directing a play, critiquing a performance, inventing something useful, producing a video, creating a model, writing a children's book, and so on. In addition, authentic assessment encourages students to develop their own responses to problem situations by allowing them to decide what information is relevant and how that information should be organized and used.

When teachers use authentic assessment to determine what students have learned—and the depth to which they have learned—student achievement and attitudes toward learning improve. For example, a study of eleven pairs of K–12 science and math teachers found that when teachers assess student learning in real-life problem-solving situations, learning and attitudes toward school improve (Appalachia Educational Laboratory 1993). Similarly, a synthesis of research on successfully restructured schools (Newmann and Wehlage 1995) revealed that teachers in those schools emphasized authentic assessment. Their assessments focused on students' ability to think, to develop in-depth understanding, and to apply academic learning to important, realistic problems.

Portfolio Assessment

Professionals in the fine arts, architecture, photography, and advertising routinely compile portfolios to document their best work. They show their portfolios to prospective clients or employers. Periodically, the professional will update the portfolio contents to reflect his or her latest, and best, accomplishments.

Similarly, **portfolio assessment** is based on a collection of student work that "tell[s] a story of a learner's growth in proficiency, long-term achievement, and significant accomplishments in a given academic area" (Tombari and Borich 1999, 164). In short, a portfolio provides examples of important work undertaken by a student, and it represents that student's *best* work. For example, a high school physics student might include in a portfolio (1) a written report of a physics lab experiment illustrating how vector principles and Newton's laws explain the motion of objects in two dimensions, (2) photographs of that experiment in progress, (3) a certificate of merit received at a local science fair, and (4) an annotated list of Internet sites related to vector principles and Newton's laws.

For students, an important part of portfolio assessment is clarifying the criteria used to select the work to be included in the portfolio and then selecting, organizing, and presenting that work for the teacher to assess. The following purposes have been suggested for student portfolios:

- Growth monitoring, in which portfolio content is used to document student progress toward goals or improvement in proficiency
- Skill certification, in which the portfolio is used to establish which instructional goals the student has adequately accomplished
- Evidence of best work, in which the portfolio contains a student's exemplary work and presents the highest level of proficiency the student has achieved with each goal

- External assessment, in which the portfolio is used to establish student proficiency by agencies outside the classroom, such as the school, school district, or a state agency
- Communication with parents, in which a portfolio is taken home or maintained at home to convey how the child is performing at school (Oosterhof 2003, 186)

As students prepare portfolios, four general guidelines should be followed to maximize the learning that results from their involvement in the process of portfolio development:

1. Have students individualize their portfolios—that is, portfolios should focus on the attainment of instructional goals that are important and meaningful for the students.
2. Portfolios should focus on students' accomplishments, their best work—not on their mistakes or limitations.
3. Portfolios should be collaboratively evaluated by teacher and students.
4. Use students' portfolios to discuss their progress with parents, counselors, and other teachers.

Peer Assessment

Peer assessment occurs when students assess one another's work. Typically, peer assessment is done informally during a class session. At times, a student may be more open to accepting critical feedback from a peer than from the teacher. Also, a peer may use a manner of speaking typical of his of her age level (word choice, for example), and it may be easier for another student to understand the feedback. Lastly, as the following teacher indicates, peer assessment frees the teacher to observe the **peer assessment** process and to provide input when necessary:

> We regularly do peer marking—I find this very helpful indeed. A lot of misconceptions come to the fore, and we then discuss these as we are going over the homework. I then go over the peer marking and talk to pupils individually as I go round the room (Black et al. 2004, 14).

Self-Assessment

Self-assessment occurs when students assess their own work and their thought processes while completing that work. It has been suggested that "[self-assessment] is the most underused form of classroom assessment but has the most flexibility and power as a combined assessment and learning tool" (Tileston 2004, 99). When students assess their own work, they become more aware of the factors that promote, or hinder, their learning. Students may, for example, ask assessment questions such as the following: What have I learned as a result of this activity? What problems did I encounter during my learning? How will I overcome these problems in the future?

As a teacher, you should help your students develop skills of **self-assessment**, particularly low achieving students. As the following teacher indicates, once students develop self assessment skills, their learning can improve dramatically:

> The kids are not skilled in what I am trying to get them to do. I think the process is more effective long term. If you invest time in it, it will pay off big dividends, this process of getting the students to be more independent in the way that they learn and to take the responsibility themselves (Black et al. 2004, 14).

Some teachers have taught students how to assess their work with reference to a common "traffic light." Students label their work green, yellow, or red based on whether they have good, partial, or little understanding. Teachers then have the "greens" and the "yellows" meet in small groups to help one another, while the teacher meets with the "reds" to address their learning problems.

Performance-Based Assessment

Put simply, **performance-based assessment** is based on observation and judgment (Stiggins 2001). Performance-based assessment focuses on assessing students' mastery of learning objectives or outcomes. We observe a student perform a task or review a student-produced product, and we judge its quality. We could observe a student's science experiment and judge the quality of the thinking involved, or we could read a student's research report in history and judge the quality of argumentation and writing. Performance-based assessment is used to determine what students can do as well as what they *know*. In some cases, the teacher observes and then evaluates an actual performance or application of a skill; in others, the teacher evaluates a product created by the student.

State-Level Performance-Based Assessments

Many states have developed statewide performance-based curriculum goals. Washington State, for example, developed the Essential Academic Learning Requirements (EALRs), which includes mandatory assessments of students' performance at the elementary, middle, and high school levels. The EALRs are based on the following four goals, each of which includes several outcomes and essential learning requirements:

Goal 1. READ with comprehension, WRITE with skill, and COMMUNICATE effectively and responsibly in a variety of ways and settings.

Goal 2. KNOW and APPLY the core concepts and principles of mathematics, social, physical and life sciences; civics; history and geography; arts; and health and fitness.

Goal 3. THINK analytically, logically, and creatively, and INTEGRATE experiences and knowledge to form reasoned judgments and solve problems.

What type of assessment is taking place in this classroom?

Goal 4. UNDERSTAND the importance of work and how performance, effort and decisions directly affect future career and educational opportunities (Commission on Student Learning 1993).

The EALRs are intended to improve student achievement and raise academic standards. Instruments for measuring student achievement were developed for the fourth-, seventh-, and tenth-grade levels. "Benchmarks"—points in time used to measure students' progress—were developed for the three grade levels, predicated on the assumption that students would have mastered certain skills and knowledge upon completion of those grades. Participation in the fourth-grade assessment became mandatory for all schools in Washington as of spring 1998. Assessments for seventh- and tenth-grade students were voluntary until spring 2001.

Washington's assessment system has four major components: state-level assessments, classroom-based assessments, professional staff development, and a "context indicator" system. The state-level assessments allow students to select and/or create responses to demonstrate their skills, knowledge, and understanding for each of the EALRs. Unlike traditional norm-referenced assessments, none of the state assessments are timed, so students feel little pressure to rush through their work.

The second component of the system is classroom-based assessment. These assessments address learning requirements not easily measured by the state assessment (e.g., oral presentations or group discussion); offer teachers opportunities to gather evidence of learning that best fit the needs of individual students; and assist teachers in gathering valid evidence of student learning (Ensign, 1998).

The third component of the new assessment system is professional development. Ongoing, comprehensive training and support for teachers and administrators improves their understanding of the EALRs, the elements of sound assessment, and effective instructional techniques that enable students to achieve the state standards. Learning and Assessment Centers have been established in several locations across the state to further facilitate use of the assessment system (Ensign, 1998).

The last component is the "context indicator" system. The context indicators provide insight into why some students do not achieve to the desired level and identify factors that both inhibit and support students' learning. Context indicators may include such information as faculty experience and training, instructional strategies employed, condition of facilities and equipment, availability of appropriate instructional materials and technology, relevant characteristics of the students and the community, and school dropout and graduation rates (Ensign, 1998).

Performance-based assessment focuses on students' ability to apply knowledge, skills, and work habits through the performance of tasks they find meaningful and engaging. While traditional testing helps teachers answer the question, "Do students *know* content?", performance-based assessment helps answer the question, "How well can students *use* what they know?"

Students should find that performance tasks are interesting and relevant to the knowledge, skills, and work habits emphasized in the curriculum. If appropriate, students can help teachers construct performance-based assessments. For example, the author observed elementary level and high school level students helping their teachers construct the following two performance-based assessments, each of which required students to create graphs.

Example 1—Elementary Level

At various times during the school day, students observe and count, at fifteen-minute intervals, the number of cars and trucks that crossed an unlit intersection near their school. Students also gather the same information for a lit intersection near the school.

Using data for both intersections, students construct graphs to illustrate the results. If the data suggest the need for a light at the unlit intersection, the graphs will be sent to the local police department.

As students work on various parts of this performance task, the teacher would observe students and make judgments about the quality of their work. Do the counts of cars and trucks appear to be accurate? Do the graphs illustrate the results clearly? Is the students' decision about the need for a traffic light supported by the data they have gathered?

Example 2—High School Level

Students go online to find data on traffic accidents in their state. Based on the data they locate, students prepare graphs that show, by driver's age, various types of accidents, fatalities, speed at the time of accident, and so on. Exemplary graphs will be displayed in the driver education classroom.

As with the elementary level example, the teacher would make judgments about the quality of the high school students' work. Naturally, these judgments would reflect the teacher's beliefs about the characteristics of exemplary student work at the high school level. Did students visit online sites that have extensive, accurate data on traffic accidents? Were students exhaustive in their online search? Do their graphs show a high degree of technical accuracy? Do the graphs "look professional"?

Alternate Assessments

Alternate assessments are designed to measure the performance of students who are unable to participate in traditional large-scale assessments used by districts and states. This approach to assessment emerged as a result of the reference to "alternate assessment" in the 1997 reauthorization of the Individuals with Disabilities Education Act (IDEA), which called for states to have alternate assessments in place by the year 2000. An alternate assessment is an alternative way of gathering data about what a student, regardless of the severity of his or her disability, knows and can do. Alternate strategies for collecting data might consist of observing the student during the school day, asking the student to perform a task and noting the level of performance, or interviewing parents or guardians about the student's activities outside of school.

The primary purpose for alternate assessments in state assessment systems is to provide information about how well a school, district, or state is doing in terms of enhancing the performance of *all* students. Gathering data through alternate assessments requires rethinking traditional assessment methods.

An alternate assessment is neither a traditional large-scale assessment nor an individualized diagnostic assessment. Alternate assessments can be administered to students who have a unique array of educational goals and experiences and who differ greatly in their ability to respond to stimuli, solve problems, and provide responses.

Most states are in the process of developing alternate assessments for students with severe disabilities. The National Center on Educational Outcomes at the University of Minnesota suggests six principles for developing inclusive assessment and accountability systems:

Principle 1. All students with disabilities are included in the assessment system.

Principle 2. Decisions about how students with disabilities participate in the assessment system are the result of clearly articulated participation, accommodation, and alternate assessment decision-making processes.

Principle 3. All students with disabilities are included when student scores are publicly reported, in the same frequency and format as all other students, whether they participate with or without accommodations, or in an alternate assessment.

Principle 4. The assessment performance of students with disabilities has the same impact on the final accountability index as the performance of other students, regardless of how the students participate in the assessment system (i.e., with or without accommodation, or in an alternate assessment).

Principle 5. There is improvement of both the assessment system and the accountability system over time, through the processes of formal monitoring, ongoing evaluation, and systematic training in the context of emerging research and best practice.

Principle 6. Every policy and practice reflects the belief that *all students* must be included in state and district assessment and accountability systems (Guenemoen, Thompson, Thurlow, and Lehr 2001).

The U.S. Department of Education decided in 2003 that the achievement of students with severe learning problems could be compared to the achievement of students without learning problems. The new ruling would enable more schools to demonstrate that they had made adequate yearly progress (AYP), a key requirement of The No Child Left Behind Act.

Prior to the Department of Education ruling, students who took alternate assessments could not be considered "proficient." In addition, many schools failed to make adequate yearly progress because their students with disabilities scored low on "regular" assessments or did not take the assessments. Thus, schools were "penalized" when they reported their yearly achievement scores for all students. Furthermore, schools that received federal aid for the poor but failed to make adequate yearly progress faced increasing sanctions from the government.

According to the new ruling, states can develop their own criteria to identify students with "significant cognitive disabilities." The federal government requires that standards for students with disabilities be tied to state academic standards, however. Identified students would be tested against standards appropriate for their intellectual development, and their scores counted as part of their school's overall academic performance.

Project-Based Learning (PBL)

A growing body of research supports the use of **project-based learning** (PBL) as a way to engage students, cut absenteeism, boost cooperative learning skills, and improve test scores. In project-based learning, students work in teams to explore real-world problems and create presentations to share what they have learned. Compared with learning solely from textbooks, this approach has many benefits for students, including deeper knowledge of subject matter, increased self-direction and motivation, and improved research and problem-solving skills. Furthermore, as George Lucas, founder of the George Lucas Educational Foundation and Director of *Star Wars,* points out, project-based learning has benefits that go beyond academic learning: "[Project-based learning] promotes emotional intelligence, which is actually much more important in the real world than a high degree of intellectual intelligence, because what you're really doing is working with other people" (George Lucas Educational Foundation 2001).

A three-year 1997 study of two British secondary schools—one that used open-ended projects and one that used more traditional, direct instruction—found striking differences between the two schools with regard to students' understanding of mathematics and standardized achievement data. Students at the project-based school did better than those at the more traditional school both on math problems requiring analytical or conceptual thought and on those requiring memory of a rule or formula. Three times as many students at the project-based school received the top grade achievable on the national examination in math (George Lucas Educational Foundation 2001).

Project-based learning, which transforms teaching from *teachers telling* to *students doing,* includes five key elements:

1. Engaging learning experiences that involve students in complex, real-world projects through which they develop and apply skills and knowledge.
2. Recognizing that significant learning taps students' inherent drive to learn, their capability to do important work, and need to be taken seriously.
3. Learning for which general curricular outcomes can be identified up front, while specific outcomes of the students' learning are neither predetermined nor fully predictable.
4. Learning that requires students to draw from many information sources and disciplines in order to solve problems.
5. Experiences through which students learn to manage and allocate resources such as time and materials (Oaks, Grantman, Pedras 2001, 443).

These five key elements are reflected in the following examples of project-based learning:

- At Mountlake Terrace High School in Mountlake Terrace, Washington, teams of students in a high school geometry class design a state-of-the-art high school for the year 2050. The students create a site plan, make simple architectural drawings of rooms and a physical model, draw up a budget, and write a narrative report. They present their work to real architects, who judge the projects and "award" the contract.
- At Newsome Park Elementary School in Newport News, Virginia, second-graders curious about the number of medicines a classmate takes and her frequent trips to the doctor investigate—with the classmate's permission—the causes of cystic fibrosis. They invite experts to tell them about the disease, write up their research, use graphs and Microsoft PowerPoint to tell the story, sell pledges to a cystic fibrosis walkathon, and participate in the walkathon.
- At the Mott Hall School in New York City's Harlem, a fifth-grade project on kites involves using creative writing skills in poems and stories with kite themes. While designing their own kites on the computer and then making them by hand, students learn about electromagnetism and the principles of ratios and proportions. A casual remark by one student leads to an in-depth study of the role of kites in various cultural celebrations.

How Can You Develop High-Quality Classroom Assessments?

To develop high-quality classroom assessments, you should focus on what *you* do to ensure that assessments fairly and accurately measure students' knowledge, skills, and levels of achievement. You should use various criteria to grade the assignments students complete and the tests they take. Among the criteria you may consider are effort, neatness, correctness, how well students did compared with other students or with their own past performance, and how long students had been studying the topic. These criteria, of course, focus on what *students* do to demonstrate their learning. To assess student learning, you should be skilled in the following:

Assessing Student Learning

As the following standards indicate, highly accomplished teachers use a variety of approaches for assessing student learning. These assessment strategies are linked to instructional objectives, and they are used to promote student learning rather than to determine what students do not understand.

- "Teacher candidates accurately assess and analyze student learning, make appropriate adjustments to instruction, monitor student learning, and have a positive effect on learning for all students." (National Council for Accreditation of Teacher Education [NCATE], 2002, 16. Standard 1: Candidate Knowledge, Skills, and Dispositions, "target" level of knowledge.)
- "Accomplished teachers can assess the progress of individual students as well as that of the class as a whole. They employ multiple methods for measuring student growth and understanding and can clearly explain student performance to parents." (National Board for Professional Teaching Standards [NBPTS], 2002, 4. "Supporting statements" for Proposition #3: Teachers are responsible for managing and monitoring student learning.")

- "The teacher appropriately uses a variety of formal and informal assessment techniques (e.g., observation, portfolios of student work, teacher-made tests, performance tasks, projects, student self-assessments, peer assessment, and standardized tests) to enhance her or his knowledge of learners, evaluate students' progress and performances, and modify teaching and learning strategies." (Interstate New Teacher Assessment and Support Consortium [INTASC], 1992, 29. "Performance" statement for Principle #8: "The teacher understands and uses formal and informal assessment strategies to evaluate and ensure the continuous intellectual, social and physical development of the learner".)
- "The [teacher's] approach to assessment is completely congruent with the instructional goals, both in content and process." (Praxis Series, "distinguished" level of performance for Domain 1: Planning and Preparation, Component 1f: Assessing Student Learning.) (Danielson 1996, 78)

- Choosing and/or developing assessment methods appropriate for attaining instructional goals and objectives
- Administering, scoring, and interpreting the results of both externally produced and teacher-produced assessment methods
- Using assessment results when making decisions about individual students, planning teaching, developing curriculum, and school improvement
- Developing valid grading procedures based on high-quality assessment of student learning
- Communicating assessment results to students, parents, other nonteaching audiences, and other educators
- Recognizing unethical, illegal, and otherwise inappropriate assessment methods and uses of assessment information

This chapter's Relevant Standards feature stresses the need for teachers to be proficient in using various approaches to assessing student learning.

Validity and Reliability

Two important qualities of classroom assessments—whether teacher made or commercially prepared—are validity and reliability. Because high-quality assessments are directly related to teaching effectiveness, assessments must be valid and reliable. **Validity** refers to the extent to which assessments measure what they are supposed to measure. If assessments fail to do this, they are useless. Valid assessments, however, ensure that what students are asked to do is a direct reflection of stated stan-dards, goals, expectations, and/or targeted learning outcomes. If assessments are valid, teachers can use that information to improve their teaching, and students can use that information to improve their learning.

Perhaps surprisingly, examples of assessments that lack sufficient validity can be found among state-mandated tests of student learning. For example, Beverly Falk observes that

> Numerous accountability systems use tests that have little relation to the standards they are supposed to evaluate. As recently as 1999, at least 25 states that claimed to be implementing new standards were still using old-style, norm-referenced tests to measure student progress. Although the rhetoric of new and lofty standards is used when discussing what the tests measure, their actual content includes few performance items, and their formats provide scant opportunities for students to demonstrate the higher-order thinking of the new standards (2002, 614).

Reliability refers to the degree to which an assessment provides results that are consistent over time. In other words, an entire test (or individual test item) is considered to be reliable if it yields similar results at different times and under different conditions. For example, imagine that Mr. Jones wants to assess his students' multiplication and division skills using whole numbers by giving them a forty-point quiz (twenty points for multiplication, twenty points for division). After scoring his students' quizzes, Mr. Jones is uncertain about whether he should begin teaching the more complex skills of multiplying and dividing using fractions. He decides to gather more information by giving another quiz three days later on the same multiplication and division skills. The following table presents the scores several students received on both quizzes.

	Multiplication		Division	
Student	*Quiz #1*	*Quiz #2*	*Quiz #1*	*Quiz #2*
Carlos	20	18	17	9
Kim	14	13	13	17
Shawn	11	11	12	17
Nong	16	17	16	12
Mary	20	19	15	14

The items that assessed students' multiplication skills, Mr. Jones notes, are quite consistent (or reliable). On quiz #1 and #2, all five students received comparable scores, with Carlos and Mary receiving the highest scores on both quizzes, and Shawn and Kim receiving the lowest scores. The items that assessed students' division skills are less consistent (or reliable). On quiz #1, Carlos and Nong received the highest scores on the division items; Kim and Shawn received the highest scores on the items for quiz #2.

At this point, Mr. Jones must make a judgment about the reliability of the information he has gathered. Because the results for the multiplication items are fairly consistent and those for the division items fairly inconsistent, he decides to spend one more class session instructing students on division using whole numbers before he proceeds to teach multiplication and division using fractions.

Scoring Rubrics

Teachers also frequently have students conduct a self-assessment by using *rubrics* (guides for evaluating the performance of a learning task) and/or benchmarks to assess their work. When students are involved in self-assessment, they are also engaged in self-evaluation—that is, interpreting information from the assessment of their own work.

Rubrics are an important element of quality classroom assessments. Sometimes called *scoring guides,* **scoring rubrics** are rating scales that consist of preestablished performance criteria. As a teacher, you can use rubrics to differentiate between levels of student performance on a rating scale, and your students can even use them to guide their learning. Rubrics can be used to specify performance criteria for a variety of learning activities—writing an essay, conducting a science experiment, or delivering an informative speech.

Because students can benefit from seeing examples of excellent work appropriate to their grade and ability levels, you should collect "models" of exemplary performances and products by your students. Besides using a scoring rubric to learn about the specific elements that will be used to assess the quality of their work, students must see what quality looks (sounds, feels, smells, or tastes) like. Over time, you should collect sets of excellent work such as graphs, nonfiction writing, solutions to open-ended math problems, and designs for science experiments from students. Less than exemplary work may also be used in the process of teaching students how to use the rubrics.

Rubrics are typically used as scoring instruments when teachers evaluate student performances or products resulting from a performance task. There are two types of rubrics: holistic and analytic.

Holistic Rubrics

A **holistic rubric** requires the teacher to score the overall process or product as a whole, without judging the component parts separately (Nitko 2001). Figure 14.5 presents a "generic" framework for developing a holistic scoring rubric based on a five-point scale.

Figure 14.5

Generic framework for a holistic scoring rubric.

Score	Description
5	Performance or product reflects complete understanding of the assessment task or problem. The performance or product reflects all requirements of the task or problem.
4	Performance or product reflects considerable understanding of the assessment task or problem. The performance or product reflects all requirements of the task or problem.
3	Performance or product reflects partial understanding of the assessment task or problem. The performance or product reflects nearly all requirements of the task or problem.
2	Performance or product reflects little understanding of the assessment task or problem. Many requirement of the task or problem are missing.
1	Performance or product reflects no understanding of the assessment task or problem.
0	Task or problem not undertaken.

As an illustration, a high school English teacher might use the framework presented in Figure 14.5 for a holistic assessment of students' ability to write a clear, well-organized essay. A score of 5 would mean the essay reflected characteristics such as clear organization, accurate and precise use of words, adequately developed ideas, insightful analysis of the topic, and effective transitions from paragraph to paragraph. An essay with a score of 3 might have grammatical errors, problems with logic, confusing sentences, and a lack of transitions from paragraph to paragraph. And an essay with a score of 1 might be very confusing and contain only a few sentences that are clear and understandable.

Analytic Rubrics

Unlike the holistic scoring rubric, an analytic rubric requires that the teacher score separate, individual parts of the product or performance according to prespecified criteria and then add the individual scores to obtain a total score (Moskal 2000; Nitko 2001). Figure 14.6 presents a "generic" framework for developing an analytic scoring rubric based on a five-point scale.

Continuing with the example that focuses on teaching essay writing at the high school level, a teacher might evaluate students' essays with reference to the following four criteria, each of which would be evaluated according to Figure 14.6's description of performances at the "beginning," "developing," "accomplished," and "highly accomplished" levels:

- *Criteria 1:* The essay is organized clearly—the introduction "sets the stage" for what follows and the conclusion summarizes key ideas.
- *Criteria 2:* The essay is free of grammatical errors.
- *Criteria 3:* The essay has a unifying idea that is clear and easy to follow.

Figure 14.6

Generic framework for an analytic rubric.

	Beginning	Developing	Accomplished	Highly Accomplished	Score
Criteria #1	Performance or product reflects beginning level of performance.	Performance or product reflects emerging performance at the mastery level.	Performance or product reflects performance at the mastery level.	Performance or product reflects performance at the highest level of mastery.	
Criteria #2	Performance or product reflects beginning level of performance.	Performance or product reflects emerging performance at the mastery level.	Performance or product reflects performance at the mastery level.	Performance or product reflects performance at the highest level of mastery.	
Criteria #3	Performance or product reflects beginning level of performance.	Performance or product reflects emerging performance at the mastery level.	Performance or product reflects performance at the mastery level.	Performance or product reflects performance at the highest level of mastery.	
Criteria #4	Performance or product reflects beginning level of performance.	Performance or product reflects emerging performance at the mastery level.	Performance or product reflects performance at the mastery level.	Performance or product reflects performance at the highest level of mastery.	

- *Criteria 4:* Effective paragraphing and transitions from one paragraph to the next provide an organizing structure and facilitate movement from one idea to the next.

To help you develop scoring rubrics for eventual use in your classroom, Figure 14.7 presents a step-by-step process for designing holistic and analytic scoring rubrics.

Figure 14.7

Designing scoring rubrics: a step-by-step procedure.

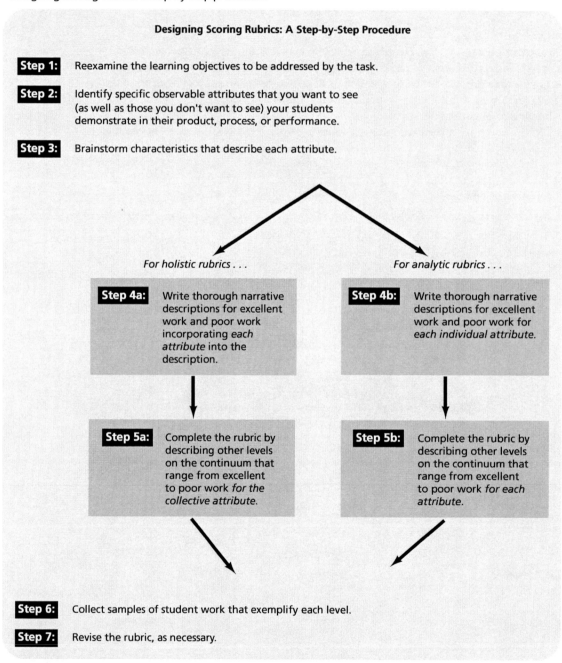

Source: Craig A. Mertler, "Designing Scoring Rubrics for Your Classroom," *Practical Assessment, Research & Evaluation,* 2001, 7(25). Used with permission.

Reflection

Using Different Methods to Assess Student Learning

The following transcription from an actual classroom session shows how a teacher skillfully uses different techniques to assess students' learning. First, the teacher focuses on the memorization of rules and vocabulary; then she turns to completion and fill-in exercises; and last, she has students practice their oral delivery.

MRS. LEFLUIR: Today we will study the gender of nouns. In Spanish, all nouns are either masculine or feminine. Nouns ending in *o* are generally masculine, and those ending in *a* are generally feminine. Tisha, can you identify the following nouns as either masculine or feminine? (writes on board) *libro pluma cuaderno gramatica*

TISHA: (Correctly identifies each.)

MRS. LEFLUIR: Now, let's see how you identified each of the words and what each word means.

TISHA: Well, I followed the rule that if it ends in an *o* it will be masculine but if it ends in an *a* it will be feminine. I think the words are *book, pen, notebook,* and *grammar.*

MRS. LEFLUIR: Good. Now for the next step, you've all used indefinite articles *a* or *an* many times in your speaking and writing. In Spanish, the word *un* is used for *a* or *an* before a masculine noun, and *una* is used for *a* or *an* before a feminine noun. In Spanish, the article is repeated before *each* noun. Now, using the vocabulary words on the board, let's place the correct form of the indefinite article in front of each word (shifting the task demand). Why don't you take the first one, Ted?

TED: It would be *un libro.*

MRS. LEFLUIR: Mary.

MARY: *Una pluma.*

MRS. LEFLUIR: Bob and Mike, take the next two.

BOB: *Un cuaderno.*

MIKE: *Una gramatica.*

MRS. LEFLUIR: OK. Now, we are ready to put our knowledge to work. I will give you a sentence in English and you translate it into Spanish, being sure to include the correct form of the indefinite article (shifting the task demand again). For this you will need to remember your vocabulary from last week. If you need to, look up the words you forgot. Mark, let's start with you. Come up to the board and write: Do you want a book?

MARK: (writes on board) *Desea usted un libro?*

MRS. LEFLUIR: Good. And how did you decide to use *un* instead of *una?*

MARK: The noun ended in *o.*

MRS. LEFLUIR: (continues with three other examples) (Borich 1996, 406–407).

Questions

1. How does Mrs. LeFluir promote her students' critical thinking?
2. When Mrs. LeFluir says "Now, we are ready to put our knowledge to work," how does this statement facilitate students' learning?
3. Within the short time covered by this transcription, why does Mrs. LeFluir change the "task demand" so frequently?

Multiple Measures of Student Learning

There is no single "right way" to assess student learning. Clearly, it will be important for you to provide your students with multiple opportunities to demonstrate what they know and are able to do. If your students know that they have different ways to demonstrate their success, they will develop more positive views of themselves as learners. They will find learning to be an enjoyable experience.

Students who previously might have disliked a subject because they associated assessments of learning in that area with failure can develop positive views about a subject if they know they have different ways to demonstrate their learning. They know that they have multiple opportunities to be successful. As assessment expert Rick Stiggins puts it, "We [now] understand how to use classroom assessment to keep students confident that the achievement target is within reach. . . . We must build classroom environments in which students use assessments to understand what success looks like and how to do better next time. . . . If teachers assess accurately and use the results effectively, then students prosper" (Stiggins 2004, 24–26).

SUMMARY

What Is the Role of Assessment in Teaching?

- Effective schools frequently and systematically assess student learning.
- Classroom assessments of student learning enable teachers to make judgments about the performance of students and about their own performance as teachers.
- Assessment is the process of gathering data to determine students' knowledge, skills, and attitudes within a certain area of the school curriculum.
- Formal assessments—such as final exams, tests, and critiques of performances—are developed prior to having students complete the assessments.
- Informal assessments occur during teaching, and they are made spontaneously.
- Teachers use classroom assessments for four purposes: (1) to determine how well students have learned, (2) to identify feedback that will enhance student learning, (3) to develop strategies to improve their teaching effectiveness, and (4) to determine if students have reached a certain level of performance.

What Methods Can You Use to Assess Student Learning?

- To assess student learning, teachers use quantitative and qualitative approaches, measurement and evaluation techniques, and formative and summative evaluation.
- Standardized assessments (or standardized tests) are pencil-and-paper tests taken by large groups of students and are scored in a uniform manner.
- Norm-referenced assessments compare students' scores with scores of other students who are similar.
- Criterion-referenced assessments compare students' learning with clearly defined criteria or standards.

What Are Emerging Trends in Classroom Assessment?

- Among the emerging trends in classroom assessment are authentic assessments, portfolio assessments, peer assessments, self-assessments, performance-based assessments, alternate assessments, and project-based learning.

How Can You Develop High-Quality Classroom Assessments?

- Validity and reliability are two qualities of high-quality classroom assessments.
- Scoring rubrics are rating scales that consist of preestablished performance criteria.

- Holistic rubrics are used to evaluate student perform-ances or products related to a performance task.
- Analytic rubrics are used to score separate, individual parts of a performance or product.
- There is no single "right way" to assess student learning, and students' views of themselves as learners improve if they know that they have different ways to demonstrate their learning.

KEY TERMS AND CONCEPTS

alternate assessments
alternative assessments
analytic rubric
assessment
authentic assessment
criterion-referenced assessments
evaluation
formal assessments
formative evaluation
holistic rubric
informal assessments

International Assessment of Educational Progress (IAEP)
measurement
norm-referenced assessments
peer assessment
performance-based assessment
portfolio assessment
project-based learning (PBL)

qualitative assessments
quantitative assessments
reliability
scoring rubrics
self-assessment
standardized assessments
summative evaluation
Third International Mathematics and Science Study (TIMSS)
validity

REFLECTIVE APPLICATION ACTIVITIES

Discussion Questions

1. How much emphasis do you think teachers should place on using alternative assessments in the classroom?
2. What are the advantages of peer assessment? Disadvantages? To what extent do you plan to use peer assessment in your classroom?

Professional Journal

1. Reflecting on the K–12 schools you attended, how often did you take norm-referenced assessments? How did you feel about taking those assessments of your learning?
2. Again, reflect on your K–12 school experiences. To what extent did you practice self-assessment of your own learning? What effect(s) did this have on your motivation to succeed?

Online Assignments

1. Using your favorite search engine, gather online information and resources about authentic assessments that you will use in your classroom.
2. With classmates, join in an online discussion on one or more of the following topics presented in this chapter:

criterion-referenced assessments
norm-referenced assessments
peer assessment
performance-based assessment
portfolio assessment
project-based learning (PBL)
scoring rubrics
standardized assessments

Observations and Interviews

1. Interview one or more teachers to find out how they assess students' learning. To what extent do they use the alternative forms of assessment discussed in this chapter?
2. Interview a group of students in the subject area and at the grade level you plan to teach to find out how they assess their own learning. What are the effects of self-assessment on their motivation to succeed?

Professional Portfolio

Using the "'Generic' Lesson Plan for a Unit of Study" presented in Appendix 14.1, prepare a lesson plan at the grade level and in the subject area for which you are preparing to teach. Include at least one authentic classroom assessment of students' learning in your plan.

Appendix 14.1

Teacher _____ Grade Level _____ Subject _____

Unit Topic_____ Length of Time _____

1. **Introduction:** What is the nature and scope of the unit? How will the unit benefit students? Briefly, what skills, concepts, issues, and activities will the unit address?

2. **Objectives:** (expected learning outcomes—i.e., what will students be expected to be able to do? Objectives can cover the cognitive, psychomotor, and affective domains).
   a. What do I expect students to be able to do?
   b. What changes in students' behavior do I wish to see?
   c. What should each be able to do to demonstrate that he/she has mastered each objective in the unit?

3. **Content of Unit:**
   a. What topics will I cover in my teaching? When will I teach those topics?
   b. Skills, topics, subtopics, concepts, issues, information, etc., covered in unit.
   c. List of activities and time for each (e.g., one week, two class sessions).

4. **Methods and Activities:**
   a. How am I going to teach the unit?
   b. What methods will I use: large group discussions, cooperative learning groups, discovery learning, mastery learning, etc.?
   c. In what activities will students participate: e.g., preparing oral and/or written reports, working in small committees, going on field trips, playing educational games, listening to guest speakers, etc.?

5. **Teaching Materials and/or Resources:**
   a. What materials and/or resources will you need to teach the unit?
   b. What materials will students need?
   c. What textbooks, software, or reference materials will be used?

6. **Assessment of Student Learning:**
   a. How will I measure and evaluate students' progress or achievement?
   b. How will I know if I have achieved the objectives for the unit?
   c. What assessments will I use to measure students' learning: quizzes, tests, observations of classroom behavior, portfolios, projects, performances, etc.?

Dealing with Issues of Conflict and Violence in Schools

15

Reacting to Conflict—An Overview

Reaction to conflict, while it may vary from individual to individual, falls into three basic categories:

> AVOIDANCE
> CONFRONTATION
> PROBLEM-SOLVING

Typical Behaviours Associated with Conflict Resolution Styles

Avoidance	Problem-Solving	Confrontation
Tendency to:	*Tendency to:*	*Tendency to:*
▩ Allow self to be interrupted, subordinated and stereotyped.	▩ State feelings, needs, and wants directly.	▩ Interrupt, subordinate, and stereotype others.
▩ Have poor eye contact.	▩ Have good eye contact.	▩ Have intense and glaring eye contact.
▩ Have poor posture and defeated air.	▩ Have straight posture and competent air.	▩ Have invading posture and arrogant air.
▩ Withhold information, opinions and feelings.	▩ Be able to disclose information, opinions and feelings.	▩ Conceal information, opinions, and feelings.
▩ Be an ineffective listener.	▩ Be an effective listener.	▩ Be an ineffective listener.
▩ Be indecisive.	▩ Initiate and take clear positions.	▩ Dominate.
▩ Apologize, avoid, and leave.	▩ Approach with skill.	▩ Be loud, abusive, blaming, and sarcastic.

Reprinted from *Managing Conflict* (1992), Ontario Secondary School Teacher's Federation.

It is important to keep in mind that each of these reactions is effective under some circumstances and conversely ineffective at other times. Understanding more about each of these approaches is essential for understanding our personal reaction to conflict. Developing a better understanding also creates the base from which we can begin to consider conflict resolution strategies or responses in the next chapter. Figure 15.1 presents an overview of these reactions to conflict.

It bears repeating that generally our culture does not like conflict and will typically avoid it. There is a tendency to view a good relationship as one where there is a minimum of interpersonal friction. Further, a relationship that is marked by considerable friction and perhaps open conflict may be identified as a "bad" one. It is not surprising that many of us learn at an early age to **avoid** conflict, sometimes at any cost. A variation on this theme is the tendency in some of us to deny conflict altogether.

Avoidance can be viewed two ways. On one hand there are indeed times when avoiding conflict makes much sense. Crises are a good example. In a crisis it is often best to go with one person's plan, any plan, so as to alleviate the crisis. This is not the time or place to call into question a particular approach to an extreme set of circumstances. Later there may be an appropriate time and space for this sort of analysis. On the other hand, continually avoiding conflict in many relationships can be very harmful. Often, while a conflict may be averted, residual feelings of anger or hurt remain to colour the future course of a relationship. Quite simply, avoiding conflict can in the end strangle a relationship.

Accommodation is another way of avoiding conflict. Sometimes if an issue is not important to a person, then adapting to others is an easy task. But often accommodation is based on it being easier to agree than to disagree, even if you don't like what is happening. This accommodation comes at a cost of course: unresolved resentment or some sense that one is "owed" and will need to be paid back in the future.

Confrontation is based on either the idea of confronting the problem and moving on to problem-solving or confronting the person. In the latter case confrontation is based on a notion of win-lose in a conflict situation. Those who tend to confront others usually believe that there is a "right" and "wrong" side and it is their duty to show, often at any cost, that they are on the side of "right". This approach will result in a person clinging to her/his "position" to the final moment or in more extreme, aggressive situations a person will abuse or threaten another person so as to get his/her own way.

Again, a direct approach to a conflict situation isn't always bad. As some would say at least you know where you stand and can get on with solving the problem. In general though, confrontation is likely to escalate a conflict situation. It can make mountains out of molehills. As well, an aggressive, confrontational reaction to conflict can make it even harder for individuals to talk easily in order to find a reasonable resolution or even to consider more creative responses or strategies to use on the problem.

When confrontation leads to the problem, a **problem-solving** approach results. In this approach a "win-win" philosophy prevails: any resolution to the difficulty will try to give each disputant something. Problem-solving takes two forms: compromise and collaboration. Compromise, when it is a true compromise, is a reasonable and often efficient way to resolve dispute. It is important though, to clearly indicate that a compromise is being reached, not just an accommodation of one person to another's needs. If someone goes for the quick and easy "compromise" because it is easier to agree than to disagree, then the situation, as before, can often lead to resentment and future unhappiness.

Collaboration, where the disputants pool their talents and abilities and where each person speaks honestly about his/her interests and needs, is an ideal way of reacting to conflict. At the outset of discussions it is rarely the case that both parties are working in a collaborative mode. But through persistence by one disputant, the other can

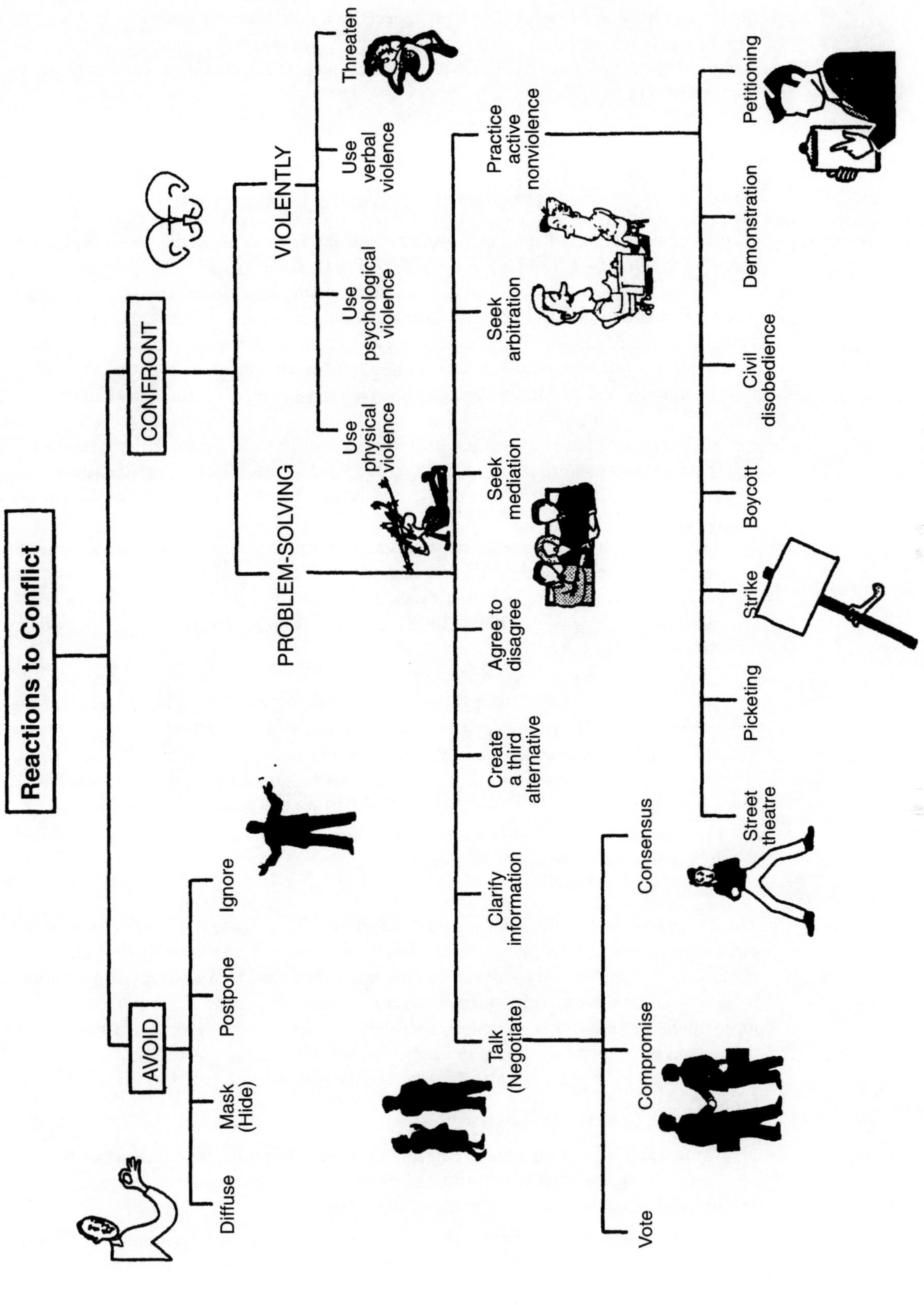

Reactions to Conflict

AVOID
- Diffuse
- Mask (Hide)
- Postpone
- Ignore

CONFRONT

VIOLENTLY
- Use physical violence
- Use psychological violence
- Use verbal violence
- Threaten

PROBLEM-SOLVING
- Talk (Negotiate)
  - Vote
  - Compromise
  - Consensus
- Clarify information
- Create a third alternative
- Agree to disagree
- Seek mediation
- Seek arbitration
- Practice active nonviolence
  - Street theatre
  - Picketing
  - Strike
  - Boycott
  - Civil disobedience
  - Demonstration
  - Petitioning

Figure 15.1

often be encouraged to work at the problem in a more collaborative frame of mind. A problem-solving approach to conflict, especially if collaborative, not only can lead to a more satisfying resolution to the present problem but also will contribute to the future ability of the disputants to deal with conflict in their relationship. This may be its greatest benefit of all.

The Thomas-Kilmann Conflict Mode Instrument

(*Copies of the **Thomas-Kilmann Conflict Mode Instrument** are available from: Xicom Inc., Woods Road – RR2, Tuxedo, NY. 10987. 1-800-759-4266.*)

One of the most popular instruments for assessing how an individual might react in a conflict situation is the **Thomas Kilmann Conflict Mode Inventory.** This is an individualized, forced-choice inventory that seeks to measure the degree to which an individual uses the following five reactions to conflict: Avoiding. Competing, Collaborating, Compromising, and Accommodating. The inventory operates on these principles:

- The user specifies the conflict situation so that there is a point of reference for the results. The authors are clear that we tend to use different modes for different situations and that the results could be quite different if a different situation is specified.
- The user must complete the entire inventory and must choose one of the paired statements even if he/she isn't comfortable with either statement. This allows the inventory to assess preferences or tendencies not absolutes. The authors are interested in preferences, not in labelling individuals as one type of person or another. As the authors state:

"Each of us is capable of using all five conflict-handing modes: none of us can be characterized as having a single, rigid style of dealing with conflict. However, any given individual uses some modes better than others and therefore, tends to rely upon those modes more heavily than others, whether because of temperament or practice.

The conflict behaviours that individuals use are therefore the result of both their personal predispositions and the requirements of the situation in which they find themselves." (p. 11)

The Thomas-Kilmann Inventory is particularly useful because it provides an accessible, graphic look at how people tend to deal with conflict. An individual's behaviour is analyzed in terms of two elements: **assertiveness,** the extent to which a person attempts to satisfy his/her needs, and **co-operativeness,** the extent to which a person tries to meet the needs of another person. Using these parameters, the five conflict-handling modes can be graphed as shown in Figure 15.2.

As indicated by the graph, the five conflict-handling modes are described as follows:

Competing is both an assertive and unco-operative mode. The individual tries to "win" by defending their "position" with whatever power seems necessary. The individual's concerns are pursued at the expense of the other person.

Accommodating is unassertive but co-operative. This could be based on altruism and a genuine concern for others or simply, a fear of causing offense and difficulty for the other person.

Thomas-Kilmann Conflict Mode Inventory

Figure 15.2

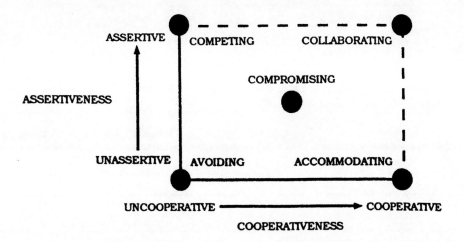

Avoiding is neither assertive nor co-operative. The individual can be side-stepping an issue for good reason or withdrawing because they are unable to cope with a conflict that threatens them.

Compromising is both assertive and co-operative although it differs from collaboration mainly in matter of degree. Often compromise offers itself as a "natural" and easy solution. In doing so, a quick compromise can preclude the kind of discussion that usually accompanies collaboration and thus not allow some more creative and often better resolutions to come forward. Compromise is often good but may not produce the best resolution of a difficulty.

Collaborating is both assertive and co-operative. The individuals work together to consider their mutual interests and needs while orienting their efforts towards consensus formation. This demands considerable interpersonal skill, commitment to the issue, and time for things to be fully discussed. In this respect not all conflicts are worth the effort, although the solution often empowers both parties and allows for a long lasting resolution to a problem.

The Thomas-Kilmann Inventory is an interesting exercise for groups of all ages and experience at the secondary level. Most people seem curious about their results and eager to compare and discuss their scores with others. One note of caution should you decide to use this inventory. It is essential to emphasize that the inventory only measures tendencies and does not label someone as one type of person or another. It is important, according to Thomas-Kilmann, to stress the situational nature of conflict resolution.

Activities

The following activities are designed to help an individual to examine her/his tendencies when reacting to conflict situations. For many of us this is the beginning of a better understanding of how we approach conflict and this understanding can in turn lead us to the development of the strategies discussed in the next chapter.

Exercise 1

Directions: After each of the following techniques, indicate whether you use it frequently, occasionally, or rarely, by placing a check mark in the appropriate column.

	Frequently	Occasionally	Rarely
1. Avoid the person.			
2. Change the subject.			
3. Try to understand the other person's point of view.			
4. Try to turn the conflict into a joke.			
5. Admit that you are wrong, even if you do not believe you are.			
6. Give in.			
7. Apologize.			
8. Try to narrow down the conflict by identifying specific areas of agreement and disagreement.			
9. Try to reach a compromise.			
10. Pretend to agree.			
11. Get another person to decide who is right.			
12. Threaten the other person.			
13. Fight it out physically.			
14. Whine or complain, until you get your way.			
15. Play the martyr; give in, but let the other person know how much you are suffering.			

Analyze your responses on the chart, and determine whether you handle conflict constructively, or seek negative responses too frequently. Explain.

Exercise 2

Most of us use different techniques for resolving conflicts with different people. Sometimes people in different situations require different techniques—you may not be able to talk to your boss the way that you talk to your best friends. But often we use a very limited number of techniques with certain people.

After each group of people listed below, indicate by number the techniques listed in Exercise 1 that you most frequently use to resolve conflict with them. (For example, if you frequently change the subject with parents, place a 2 in the first column after "Parents".) Disregard any groups of people that do not apply to you. Then, for each group, list any techniques you *might be able to use effectively that you do not now use.*

	Techniques now used	Techniques you might be able to use
Parents	_____	_____
Older people	_____	_____
Teenagers	_____	_____
Children	_____	_____
Brothers and sisters	_____	_____
Teachers	_____	_____
Employers	_____	_____
Members of other racial groups	_____	_____
Friends	_____	_____
People you do not know well	_____	_____

Exercise 3

When I disagree with someone, I sometimes (check all that apply):

_____ Put off dealing with the situation

_____ Try to meet the other person half way

_____ Cite authority to show I'm right

_____ Try to help the other person get what (s)he wants

_____ Explain my point of view and ask the other person to do the same

_____ Insist the other person do it my way

_____ Keep my ideas to myself

The person I find it easiest to resolve a disagreement with is _____, because

The person I find it hardest to resolve a disagreement with is _____, because

I'd like someone who disagrees with me to approach me this way:

When someone disagrees with me, I find it hardest to handle when the person approaches me this way:

Exercise 4

Are You Someone Who . . . ?

Objectives: To identify one's usual type of reactions to conflict

Group Size: Small groups of four to six people

Time Required: One hour

Materials Utilized: A copy for each person of the two worksheets accompanying this activity

Physical Setting: Small groups of tables and chairs

Content and Process:

1. Introduce the purpose of the activity.

2. Review with the participants how styles of behaving are developed. Review the ten types of reactions.

3. Ask participants to recall several different conflicts they experienced recently.

4. For each conflict listed, participants should determine which type of reaction they had, and put a check mark in the appropriate column(s) on the chart. Have them refer to the worksheet. *Are You Someone Who . . . ?* to help them determine their type by matching their behavior and words to those on the chart. They may find that they reacted with a variety of types.

5. In small groups, participants may discuss the following questions with one another.

   a. Which types of reaction do I generally use when I face conflict?

   b. Would others who know me agree with this perception?

   c. Which of my styles of reacting were most appropriate for the conflict situation I was facing at the time? Which were inappropriate?

   d. Which type would I like to increase the use of in the future?

Variations/Comments:

This activity assists awareness of one's conflict style when facing real experiences. It could be used in conjunction with other activities in this chapter, *e.g. sculpting.*

Type	Behaviours	Favourite Phrases
1. Defender	Justifies and defends position	"Let me explain." "Yes, but . . . ." "You don't understand."
2. Soldier	Fights back, threatens, punishes, seeks revenge, insults, or berates other person	"Oh, yeh?" "Says who?"
3. God	Dictates the resolution, uses power of established authority	"Of course I'm right." "Do it my way."
4. Diverter	Diverts discussion entirely or focuses on superficial issues, postpones conflict, complains to third party	"The real problem is . . . ." "Let's discuss this later."
5. Avoider	Avoids at all costs, ignores, doesn't become involved in situations that are conflict prone	"Let's forget it." "That doesn't bother me."
6. Harmonizer	Smooths over conflict; emphasizes harmony, peace, and warmth	"This isn't important enough to fight over. Both of us are right."
7. Apologizer	Expresses regret	"I'm sorry."
8. Abdicator	Agrees with other person, takes the blame, feels it is hopeless and gives up	"You're right. I did that wrong." "Oh well, it's hopeless to try."
9. Feeler	Expresses reaction by describing feelings	"When you . . . I feel . . ." "I'm feeling . . ..
10. Negotiator	Tries to find a compromise, bargains	"Let's talk this over so we can find a solution."

Charting My Reactions to Conflicts

Recent Conflicts	Defender	Soldier	God	Diverter	Avoider	Harmonizer	Apologizer	Abdicator	Feeler	Negotiator	Observations, Comments

16

Bullying

When push turns to shove, when meanness intrudes on play—when someone selects a target and inflicts pain and the payoff is someone else's humiliation—then it's outright bullying. (Marano, 1995, p. 68)

In every school, bullying is a problem for some children. It is pervasive, but often ignored by adults. Those who are bullied will avoid the washrooms, try to stay inside at recess, or feign illness to stay home. They rarely inform teachers or parents about the problem. It is estimated that in a school of 300 pupils, 60 likely attend in fear (based on numbers from Ziegler & Rosentstein-Manner, p. 18). Not a new problem, bullying seems to have been part of schooling since schools began.

The definition of bullying comprises several components. *"A person is being bullied when he or she is exposed, repeatedly and over time to negative actions on the part of one or more other persons."* (Olweus, 1993, p. 9) The pattern of activity that characterizes bullying is the imbalance of strength between the bully and the victim, the frequent and repeated attacks, and the intention to hurt. Bullies always pick on the most vulnerable youngsters, those who are defenseless; thus it is not a random activity.

Why Is Bullying A Problem In Our Schools?

Bullying is, not surprisingly, a problem in our schools since this is where the children of the community congregate. It affects as many as 35 percent of the children in the school, either as bullies or victims. (Ziegler & Rosenstein-Manner, p. 26) The pain

---

Reprinted from *Violence* (1998), Ontario Secondary School Teacher's Federation.

suffered by victims is immediate and affects their school work. At the same time, bullies acquire attitudes that hinder their development.

The other children are also affected by bullying. The vast majority, 90 percent, say that it is unpleasant to see someone bullied. (Ziegler & Rosenstein-Manner, p. 24) They find it threatening personally, but they feel conflicting emotions about whether or not to interfere and whether or not the victim carries at least some of the blame for what is happening. If this activity is not stopped, it may be increasingly accepted by the onlookers. Like a contagion it may spread through the school, accepted and supported as normal by the other children. During a bullying incident they are often aroused by the drama and the excitement. Seeing aggression rewarded, they may adopt it as a way to solve their problems, feeling less guilty and less inhibited when they are aggressive since others are doing it. When they join the bully in an act of aggression they may feel less responsible for what is happening. In this situation the bully may claim an enhanced reputation and greater respect; consequently the other children will likely turn to the bully for protection or for support. In contrast, the victim, labelled as someone who deserves the hurt, may be at greater risk. (Olweus, 1993; Pepler & Craig, 1994)

The behaviour of both bullies and victims is maladaptive and not helpful for their future lives. The bullies are more likely to become involved in criminal activity when they grow up. For example, in a longitudinal study, Olweus found that 60 percent of those who bullied had at least one criminal conviction by the age of 24, and 40 percent had three such convictions by this age. In a similar study conducted by Eron, in which he followed 518 children from the age of eight into their forties, he found *"that the kids who were named by their peers — at age eight — as most aggressive commit more crimes, and more serious crimes, as adults." (Marano, 1995, p. 69)* In a third longitudinal study, Huesmann discovered that aggression by younger boys and girls predicted aggressive personality scores and criminal acts. This should not surprise us since the bully's schoolyard behaviour is anti-social and often criminal.

Victims may also have personal difficulties in adulthood. Olweus found that they "were more likely to be depressed and had poorer self-esteem" although they might have grown past their earlier victimization. (1993, p. 33) The onlookers may grow up with the view that aggressive behaviour is after all natural and normal.

Incidence

A substantial body of research helps our understanding of the phenomenon of bullying. Olweus, who has studied bullying in Scandinavia, has established a base for this knowledge. He found that:

- 15 percent of the children in Norwegian schools were engaged in bullying problems now and then, or more frequently;
- 9 percent were involved as victims and 7 percent as bullies;

- "the percentage of students who are bullied decreases with higher grades. It is the younger and weaker students who reported being most exposed. . . . From the Bergen study it can also be reported that a considerable part of the bullying was carried out by older students." (1993, p. 15);
- the incidence of bullying is not affected by the socioeconomic condition of the family, housing, level of education, the size of class or school, the school's location in the country or city, or failing grades in school; *and*
- boys are more likely to be bullies and victims, but Olweus cautioned that his questionnaire may not uncover the more subtle forms of bullying displayed by girls.

In Toronto Ziegler and Rosenstein-Manner employed a similar data collection instrument to the one used by Olweus. They drew on 211 students in 14 classes from Grades 4 to 8. They found that:

- 35 percent of the children were engaged in bullying problems more than once or twice in the school term;
- 20 percent were victims and 15 percent bullies (This rate is twice as high as that reported by Olweus.);
- the common locations for bullying, in order, were playgrounds, hallways, classrooms, lunchrooms, and washrooms;
- most bullies are boys (75 percent);
- bullying peaks in the age group 11 to 12 years old;
- 38 percent of special education students compared to 18 percent of other students reported being bullied;
- 24 percent of students reported that race-related bullying occurred now and then or often; *and*
- 23 percent of the victims, and 71 percent of the teachers, reported that teachers intervened often or almost always. (Ziegler & Rosenstein-Manner, 1991)

Similar studies using Olweus' survey have been conducted in England, the United States and Australia. They yield comparable results regarding the decrease in bullying as children grow older and the low rate of teacher intervention. The latter may be a strong acknowledgement of the covert nature of bullying and the success of the bully in intimidating the victim.

Pepler, and her associates at York University, have studied bullying employing naturalistic observation rather than the self-reports used in other studies. She taped (video and audio) children in two Toronto schools, and then analyzed the results. Here are the numbers:

- 404 bullying episodes occurred during 52 hours of taping;
- one incident occurred every 7 minutes on average;
- a typical incident lasted 37 seconds, a remarkably short time;
- 79 percent of the episodes were direct bullying, 18 indirect, and 3 both;
- 90 percent of the incidents involved one bully and 92 percent one victim;
- 72 percent of the attacks were by boys and 28 percent by girls;
- in 4 percent of the episodes a weapon was visible;
- between 26 and 33 percent of the children in a school bullied between 18 and 22 percent of the other children;
- school staff were visible in 17 percent of the incidents; yet they intervened in 4 percent only;
- peers intervened in 11 percent of the episodes; *and*
- 2 percent of the incidents appeared to be motivated by race. (Craig & Pepler, 1995)

The Bullying Cycle

Bullying tends to start off in a tentative way, with some trial and error as the bully settles on a victim. *At first, the incidents may be playful* consisting of pranks, jokes and some rough and tumble. As victims succumb to this treatment and prove submissive, *the incidents become more hurtful*, escalating from criticizing the victim, to name-calling and taunting, then to personal attacks and public humiliation. In response to this increasingly hostile treatment, *the victims change and become more accepting and submissive. The rough and tumble play gives way to slapping, punching, kicking and beatings. The attacks become more systematized* as victims are scapegoated. (Floyd, 1985, p. 10)

A teacher told me of two twelve-year olds enmeshed in this typical escalation. At first, George would push Carl out of the way when they were waiting for the school bus. He would engage in "play fights" with Carl, daring the latter to challenge this description of what was happening. As time went on, George began to jump on Carl and knock him to the ground, or grab him by the arm and wrestle him to the ground. When Carl complained to George, George would ask aggressively: "Are you looking for a fight?" On one such occasion, he punched Carl in the face because "he was being mouthy." On another, he grabbed Carl's arm and swung him so violently that he tore his winter jacket.

Bullying is often sorted into direct and indirect forms. The direct style of bullying, as described in the above incident, is typically associated with boys. It involves a great deal of physical aggression. On the other hand, indirect bullying, associated more often with girls, is more subtle and more likely to be verbal. The following are typical examples of both forms of bullying:

Direct Bullying	**Indirect Bullying**
▪ shoving and poking	▪ name-calling
▪ throwing things	▪ taunting
▪ taking things	▪ rumour
▪ slapping and hitting	▪ gossiping
▪ choking	▪ arguing others into submission
▪ punching and kicking	▪ threats of withdrawing friendship
▪ beatings	▪ the silent treatment
▪ stabbings	▪ exclusion from the group

Typically, girls have been regarded as less physically aggressive than boys. They tend to express aggression through damaging or manipulating their relationships. (Marano, 1995; Pepler, 1996) However, recent indications reveal that this may be changing. In a series of self-reports summarized in the Ontario Child Health Study, the differences between boys and girls were not very large: 7 percent of adolescent girls and 12 percent of adolescent boys reported attacking others physically and 21 percent of girls and 30 percent of boys admitted being involved in many fights. (Pepler, 1996, p. 10) In her naturalistic observations Pepler concluded: **"Our observations of aggression and bullying on the school playground revealed no gender differences in the rates of verbal and physical aggression among children in Grades 1 to 6."** (1996, p. 8) In her discussion of these results, Pepler notes several possible explanations: a decline in gender differences, a corresponding change in norms and roles, and a change in socialization that encourages girls to be more competitive and achievement-oriented.

Why Do Young People Bully and Where Do Their Parents Fit In?

There are several reasons why children bully. As noted earlier, physical size and aggressive attitude combined with the human need for power and social influence may encourage bullying. Bullies satisfy these needs through dominating others and inflicting pain on them. They use power and their physical size inappropriately. They possess a positive view of violence as a way to settle problems. They process information in a way that supports their generally hostile view of the environment. When faced with an unclear situation, they are more likely than other children to read hostile intentions into the motivations of others. Interestingly, they tend to view themselves positively, suffering very little anxiety or insecurity about their behaviour and hostility.

At the same time, the use of physical force to meet their needs may be more normative among children than we have acknowledged in the past. In their discussion of their naturalistic observations, Pepler and Craig comment:

> *Bullying was surprisingly normative on the school playground: children identified by teachers as nonaggressive were just as likely to bully as those identified as aggressive. Given the wide range of children observed bullying, it appears that bullies do not simply represent the most deviant children in the school. This problem behaviour is widespread and is characteristic of both boys and girls and both older and younger children on the school playground. (1995, p. 17)*

The social density of the playground may add to the likelihood of bullying. In a crowded yard youngsters will bump into each other and will compete for space; thus, the rough and tumble of play may easily spill over into aggression. At the same time, bullying may simply have become normal school-yard behaviour.

"Several studies have shown parenting practices to be highly influential in controlling or encouraging aggressive behaviour." (Besag, 1989, p. 36) The experiences of childhood are powerful in developing values, attitudes, and behaviours. Children learn to become part of the family or community in which they undergo these early experiences. *Bullies who grow up in an environment that tends to encourage aggressiveness will develop many anti-social tendencies.*

Research indicates that their parents often:
- *exercise very little restraint on aggressive expression;*
- *give implicit or open permission to be aggressive;*
- *expect neither guilt nor remorse when their children are hurtful;*
- *often appreciate their children's public displays of strength;*
- *neither control nor supervise their offspring;* (Craig & Pepler, 1995)
- *rely on coercion and harsh physical discipline;*
- *abuse these children and expose them to a specific model of relationships where the strong exploit the weak;*
- *are cold and aloof, lacking warmth and empathy; and*
- *are permissive in regard to hostility, exercising no limits.*

The combination of aloofness and permissiveness leads to a situation in which parents provide too little love and too much freedom. (Olweus, 1993)

In the various surveys conducted on bullying, adults consistently underestimate its prevalence and severity. They appear not to take it very seriously. This attitude sends children a clear message that if they are victims they are on their own; if bullies, they have permission to continue. One teacher told me a typical story of being bullied himself in the junior grades. For several months in a new school he was bullied. At first, it was names and taunting, but then the bully got bolder. Raised not to fight, he submitted to the taunts and attacks for months, until one day, in desperation, he struck back. Along with the bully, he was sent to the office where he was scolded for fighting and told that he should have reported the bullying to teachers. Although he was no longer bullied, he was unaware of anything being done to curb the bully in the yard. He felt that the school should have been aware of the situation and should have acted to support him.

Finally, bullying pays off. Victims submit to the bully's demands. Adults are unaware of what is going on and do not intervene. As a consequence, the behaviour is rewarded.

Myths That Sustain Bullying

As noted above, adults tend to underestimate the prevalence of bullying and its consequences. They may view this activity as normal and be unable to distinguish between rough and tumble and genuine bullying. In discussions with parents and teachers about bullying, I have found them resorting to some form of the following myths to explain their thoughts on bullying:

- **"BOYS WILL BE BOYS"**
  This myth assumes that all boys are physically aggressive and cruel. It assumes that aggressive boys are necessarily aggressive. It equates rough and tumble play with bullying. It reveals a belief that bullying is simply a natural part of a boy's growing up.
- **"YOU SHOULD NEVER TATTLE"**
  We need to ask: "Who benefits from this rule?" This puts the victims at the mercy of the bully, unable to seek out help and support from those charged with protecting them. It treats bullying casually as part of the price of growing up. If we do not know what is happening in the schoolyard or hallways, we will never change things. A report by British educators stated: **"It is a damning indictment of the system in which we operate that victims of abuse of this nature feel they have to suffer in silence."** (Erling & Munthe, 1989, p. 11)
- **"SHE ASKED FOR IT"**
  This myth suggests that victims either enjoy being bullied or take a perverse delight in being hurt and humiliated. No one ever deserves humiliation and hurt. The message for the victim is that she deserves the bullying.
- **"IF ATTACKED, STAND UP FOR YOURSELF"**
  This appeal to self-reliance is most unhelpful and impractical. It challenges the most vulnerable children in the yard to look after themselves. It prevents peers from intervening, since many of them believe that the victims should fend for themselves. Worse, if the advice is followed and is effective, it teaches that aggression is the way to solve problems.
- **"HE WILL ALWAYS BE A VICTIM"**
  This myth suggests that victims are born that way and that they will continue as victims throughout their lives. This is a dangerous self-fulfilling prophecy that encourages us not to act. It denies that behaviour is learned, can be unlearned, and can be modified.
- **"BULLIES SUFFER FROM A LACK OF SELF-ESTEEM"**
  This myth serves to support programs that teach bullies social skills and self-esteem that, too often, they neither need nor pay attention to. Most bullies have a positive view of themselves; they are self-confident and may require very different programs or, at least, concrete applications of pro-social behaviour.

Strategies To Reduce Bullying

As part of a campaign to educate parents, teachers, and educational support staff about the concerns raised by bullying, *principals must make it clear that bullying is never acceptable*. They must make it clear that bullying is prevalent in the school and that they expect staff to deal with it. They must raise the myths and discuss them fully so that everyone has an opportunity to consider how such myths affect our attitudes to bullying and victimization.

Effective principals and teachers acknowledge the importance of dealing with bullying in a forthright way. They aim for a school climate that emphasizes caring for one another, respect for others, and protection of the younger and weaker students. They publicly state everyone's right to feel safe at school. They acknowledge that aggressive behaviour raises moral questions. They organize programs that explore pro-social skills and the consequences of hurting others. Most students understand this message and do not hurt others. Bullies, with these very pro-social skills, may apply them inconsistently and bully relentlessly. For example, a primary teacher told me about Teddy, a quiet and good pupil academically. On the surface, he is polite and cooperative to teacher and class-mates. Behind the teacher's back or in her absence, he bullies other boys smaller than he. He will write or scribble on their material. He pinches, shoves and pushes, and trips others. He grabs their toys out of their hands and runs off with them. All of this is done slyly, so, for a long time, the teacher was unaware of a problem. In fact, she became aware of this behaviour by accident and by good observation. She explained that he knows his behaviour is wrong. When caught, he shrugs or smiles in response to the message that he should not hurt someone, behaving as if he has no social conscience.

Building on the desire of all students to be in a safe environment and to see bullying stopped, *principals establish clear, easily-understood rules about bullying. Olweus suggests a simple statement such as:* **"We shall not bully other students; we shall try to help students who are being bullied."** (1995, p. 81) The rules send a signal to bullies that the school does not condone their aggressive behaviour. Moreover, calling on the other students to support the rules, and the victims, puts social pressure on bullies to conform.

More important than the rules is the determination to enforce them fairly and consistently. In all instances of aggression in the school, *the principal follows up to find out what happened and why. In the case of a bully who seems not to follow the rules, teachers may monitor his/her activity in the halls, washrooms and yard.* Extra vigilance may convince the bully that the school is aware of what is going on and intends to stop it.

When the bully continues to offend, the consequences are clear and applied. The consequences will range from admonition to suspension. Where it is possible, principals may transfer a bully to another class away from a victim, or make special arrangements for recess and lunch so that the bully is unable to get at a victim, while at the same time, counselling the bully.

Since social density may be a concomitant to bullying, principals may reduce the number of children in the yard and halls at any one time, by staggering recess and lunch time and by reorganizing a rotary schedule. *At the same time, they train teachers to patrol the yard, halls, and washrooms more vigilantly, with a greater awareness of what is happening.*

Teachers include lessons about bullying in the curriculum. They instruct students about bullying: what it is and why it occurs. In this way, *they dispel its mystique and encourage students to talk about their experiences with bullies. They draw on the reading program to increase understanding about bullying and victimization. They may have pupils role-play an incident from the school yard* to capture the issues and their resolution or have pupils create a drama on conflict and ways to reduce it. With both role-playing and drama, they encourage the pupils to suggest different endings to a story and then act out the new ending to test it. They may identify those students who require help with their language skills, and provide suitable assistance to them. In the aftermath of an incident, they may hold a circle meeting to have the students discuss their feelings, the issues of bullying, and solutions to yard problems.

Principals and teachers take time to listen to children, parents, and educational support staff when they complain about bullying. In this way, they ascertain its prevalence in the school. A frank discussion with the school council may also yield information about the state of bullying in the school and community. Principals and teachers ensure opportunities for victims to talk about their fears, and about incidents. They talk with bullies in an attempt to educate them about the effect of their bullying, to give notice that their behaviour is known and being watched, and to convince them that there will be follow-up on incidents. As part of this counselling, teachers and counsellors will attempt to help bullies with anger control and the development of empathy. They will also deal with the myths that support bullying: for example, insisting that no one deserves to be bullied.

In respect to girls, intervention has to be aimed at encouraging positive peer relations and optimum school performance. Teachers will help those in difficulty to increase their competence and self-concept, in the hope that if their need for self-worth is met, they will find aggression unnecessary. They will sensitize them to the hurt caused by gossip, exclusion, and manipulation. They will make it clear that these activities are also bullying and that they too are unacceptable.

17

Violence in Schools: School Treatable or Beyond School Control

Can schools deal effectively with violent or potentially violent students?

Position 1: Schools Can and Should Curb Violence

I believe that school is primarily a social institution. Education being a social process, the school is simply that form of community life in which all of those agencies are concentrated that will be most effective in bringing the child to share in the inherited resources of the race, and to use his own powers for social ends. . . . I believe that education, therefore, is a process of living and not a preparation for future living.

—Dewey, 1897, "My Pedagogic Creed," Reprinted in Dworkin, 1959, p. 22

John Dewey helped define the relationship between Americans and their public schools. Schools are extensions of the community in this country, he argued. Schools share in the burden of caring for the community's children and for equipping them with skills and habits necessary to survive and succeed. Schools take the community's highest ideals and translate them into academic and social programs for all children. As Dewey wrote, "What the best and wisest parent wants for his own child, that must the community want for all its children" (Dworkin, 1959, p. 54).

Dewey recognized social conditions constantly change and schools always have to adjust to new demands placed on communities. When social problems overwhelm community resources, schools are expected to lend strength and assistance. In a speech

Reprinted from *Critical Issues in Education: Dialogues and Dialectics,* Sixth Edition (2006), by permission of The McGraw-Hill Companies.

delivered in 1899, he said, "It is useless to bemoan the departure of the good old days of children's modesty, reverence, and implicit obedience, if we expect merely by bemoaning and by exhortation to bring them back. It is radical conditions which have changed, and only an equally radical change in education suffices" (Dworkin, 1959, p. 37).

In the late nineteenth century, the Industrial Revolution had upset the community's traditional structure and nature of work. Parents were working long hours, away from home, separated from their children. Many children also worked, at hard and often dangerous jobs. As a result, families had changed, and were not able to carry out the full range of their former functions. Schools were pressed to expand their role, to go beyond providing instruction in reading and arithmetic and help children adjust to the "radical conditions" of the day. Helping children adjust to the problems of a new industrial economy imposed a great burden on public education. Helping children understand and overcome the radical conditions of the twenty-first century may require even greater effort, but it is not a problem schools can shirk. The community's problems are always the school's problems. We are concerned with violence here, a social problem with a long history and many causes.

The Violent Community

Violence is among the most "radical conditions" now confronting the nation and its school-age children. Violence increasingly affects the daily lives of children, and violence-prevention and aggression-management programs have become part of the common curriculum in schools. Society has changed in the past decades, and students' lives are filled with problems never before the concern of schools. Testifying before Congress, the principal of a Miami high school notes:

> The primary differential between the high school environment we as adults recall and the present is the nature of the challenges the youth of today confront. Many of these issues, such as H.I.V., did not even exist when we were in school. Many students today face enormous pressures, isolation, and lack of support network mechanisms enjoyed by previous generations. . . . The primary concern of parents 20 years ago was academic progress; this has been replaced by a different concern—I want my child back in the same shape they left this morning. (School Crime Prevention Programs, 2001, p. 32)

In some ways school violence is a new American problem; in other ways, it is as old as the nation. American society is violent, and has been so for a long time. You may recall that Andrew Jackson shot and killed a man who made insulting comments about his wife,[1] and Aaron Burr killed political rival Alexander Hamilton in a New Jersey gun duel. The United States was born of revolution. It has made heroes of gunfighters and warriors. Americans have witnessed assassinations of national figures, racial lynchings, and riots by organized labor, farmers, and students. Until the 1930s it was not possible to quantify the rate of violence, but since that time, the FBI's *Uniform Crime Reports* document a dramatic increase in violent crime, including murder, forcible rape, robbery, and aggravated assault over time. The U.S. murder rate is the highest in the industrialized world, and we remain a leader in school violence.

---

[1]One scholar argues that retaliatory violence reflected in today's "street code" is simply a crude version of the "code of honor" that nineteenth-century gentlemen claimed as a right in protecting the reputation of their ladies (Spina, 2000, p. 12).

Violence and the Media

Violence currently presents unprecedented dangers to school-age children. U.S. films, music videos, and television are the most violent in the world. Messages about aggressive behavior enter the world of children no matter how hard families work to screen them out. These messages flow not only from children's direct experiences, but also from news reports, film, music, and advertising. War toys line store shelves; cartoon heroes destroy villains on television and in films; music videos play darkly on themes of anger and destruction; and computer games encourage interactive simulations of murder and mayhem. Many children suffer nightmares stemming from the violence in their lives (Jordan, 2002).

Television brings a steady volume of vicarious violence into living rooms. Over 97 percent of U.S. households have at least one television set, and young children watch about four hours of television daily. They likely watch passively—typically without adults present—acts of violence at unprecedented levels. The typical child in the United States views an estimated 8,000 murders and 100,000 acts of televised violence before the end of elementary school (Galezewski, 2005) and another 100,000 hours before the end of high school. Among other things, researchers have found that viewing portrayals of violence leads to aggressive behavior (Galezewski, 2005). Regular watching of media violence can desensitize viewers to real violence as well as make them excessively fearful of the potential for violence in their own lives.

Violence is an increasingly familiar aspect of students' lives, and bullying has become a common experience for school-age children. Some 90 percent of students report that they have been victims of bullying, beginning as early as preschool (Galezewski, 2005). Almost half of all middle and high school students report avoiding school bathrooms for fear of being assaulted or harassed (Smith-Heavenrich, 2005). It may be naive for us to think we are not vulnerable to violence. Although violence is more prevalent in urban areas and among the poor and minorities, no one in any neighborhood is immune. School violence affects the suburbs and rural areas as well as cities, white children as well as minority children.

> Violence is also increasing in suburban and rural schools, especially among white male students. Although not necessarily disadvantaged, white male students can be marginalized in other ways. Those who do not conform to accepted roles and expectations are often alienated from the dominant culture and at the bottom of the social hierarchy of schools (nerds, geeks, fags, etc.). These "minority" students are indoctrinated with almost the same message as inner-city students: pretty girls, strong boys, thin, rich, smart kids are the ones who matter.[2] (Spina, 2000, p. 13)

Recent reports of school crime contain both bad news and good news. The bad news is that in 2003, students between the ages of 12 and 18 were victims of 1.75 million crimes at school, and of that number 88,100 were victims of serious crimes—rape, sexual assault, and aggravated assault. The good news is that, as startling as these numbers are, they represent a decline in the nonfatal victimization rate, and students report a greater degree of safety in school in 2003 than in the previous decade (U.S. Department of Justice, 2004).

The bad news may not be getting worse, but it is disturbing nonetheless. From the standpoint of any victim of school violence or the parents whose children are victim-

---

[2]If you think of violence only as the use of physical force that causes bodily harm, this example of psychological violence may come as a surprise. Violence is not limited to acts that cause bodily harm; violence includes actions that deny others the ability to be effective actors in their world. Bullies trade in threats and intimidations as often as they deliver physical blows. The victims of bullying suffer more embarrassment, rejection, and anxiety than bruises, but their pain is real and lasting (MacNeil, 2002).

Figure 17.1

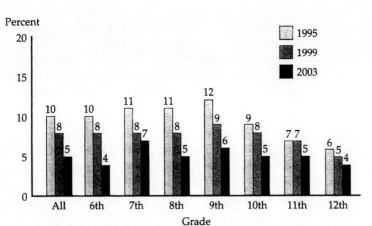

Note: This figure represents the prevalence of total victimization, which is a combination of violent victimization and theft. "At school" means in the school building, on school property, or on the way to and from school.

Source: National Center for Education Statistics, Indicators of School Crime and Safety. (2004). http://permanent.access.gpo.gov/lps9947/2004.

ized, there are no acceptable levels of violent behavior in schools (Astor et al., 2002). Reports of childhood aggression are especially troubling considering the research linking a child's inability to manage aggression with violent behavior in adulthood (Reiss and Roth, 1993; Caspi et al., 1994; Goldstein, Harootunian, and Conoley, 1994).

Violence-Prevention Curricula

The bad news is easy to tabulate. The statistics are alarming: Violence is common in schools; too many children feel unsafe in schools; many schools have to invest in metal detectors and guards instead of books and field trips. The good news is harder to quantify, but it should be reassuring: School programs can make a difference in preventing childhood aggressive behavior and future adult violence (*Recess from Violence,* 1993; Reiss and Roth, 1993; Bodine and Crawford, 1998; Astor et al., 2002; Bowen et al., 2002). While schools alone cannot overcome the problem of violence, they are central in the struggle to protect children from violence and teach them physical aggression is never the preferred solution to problems. The problem of violence is complex, and there are no simple solutions. It is not the sort of problem, however, likely to be solved by applying zero-tolerance policies and simple punitive measures. To solve the problem of school violence, children must learn how to understand and control their anger and practice using nonviolent problem-solving techniques. Schools can help students manage their aggression by teaching alternatives to violence through violence-prevention curricula. [3]

---

[3] Schools across the country now are experimenting with hundreds of new curricular interventions designed to reduce violence. You may want to examine some examples in your community or check national sources. Information from the National School Safety Center (NSSC) is available on the Internet at www.nssc1.org. NSSC is a nonprofit organization, established by presidential directive in 1984, and is charged with promoting violence-free and crime-free schools. NSSC provides information about programs that support safe schools worldwide. Its website also contains current statistics about school crime and school violence.

Consider a few violence-prevention strategies suggested by national organizations. We present them as illustrative examples rather than prescriptive remedies. Many schools now are using schooltime conflict-resolution approaches, teaching children to handle their own disputes and assume responsibility for helping other children find peaceful resolutions to their disagreements. These programs are disarmingly simple and effective. First, children are taught conflicts are inevitable, and in most disputes, both sides are apt to believe they and they alone are in the right. Conflict resolution approaches encourage students to listen to each other and take responsibility for ensuring they resolve conflicts by conversation and negotiation rather than by physical means. The process is similar for younger children and students in secondary schools. What varies is the nature and complexity of the problems. Consider this example for resolving a classroom conflict in elementary school: The teacher begins the activity by distributing an "activity card" to the class with a conflict that might be familiar to them.

> *Mariah is riding the bus to school. Kateesha, another girl on the bus, is having a bad day, and she calls Mariah a bad name. Mariah is very upset and mad at Kateesha. When they get off the bus, they start yelling at each other and shoving each other until a teacher breaks up the fight. Both children are taken to the office for fighting, and both children are still mad at each other. What is the solution to their problem? (Osier and Fox, 2001, p. 10)*

The teacher reads the card to the class and asks students to identify the problem. When the class agrees about the nature of the problem, the teacher asks students to recommend actions they could take to solve it. Younger children may draw a picture of the solution; older children write one. The teacher then asks the class to share their solutions and identifies those supported by students in the class. Students are asked to save the favored solutions and apply them when a new conflict arises in or outside of class.

Secondary school students are encouraged to use similar role-playing strategies to examine critical incidents in their lives. The goal is to have students see how simple, commonplace events can escalate into violence. In this example, taken from a videotape transcript written by eighth-grade students, one young woman taunts another:

"I heard that she was at the movies with your boyfriend last night. All over him."

"I wouldn't take it," adds another girl.

"She doesn't need your boyfriend. What was she doing with him anyhow?"

The young women simulate pushing and shoving. They break off from the simulation with self-conscious laughter, recognizing, perhaps, that in real life the angry words they scripted all too often escalate into real acts of violence. On the videotape, the classroom teacher applauds the students' effort, and the class examines what has taken place. A rumor was spread; it led to an exchange of words; verbal accusations threatened to become physical. In real life, it could easily have resulted in injury. The teacher asks, how could this have been avoided? What did others do to make the situation worse? What could they have done to help? (*Violence in the Schools*, 1993).

Many schools have adopted schoolwide prevention programs that teach students a series of consistent, reasonable approaches to contend with conflict. Students learn to view conflict situations as constructive rather than destructive experiences (Smith and Daunic, 2005). In these schools, when a playground dispute occurs, an older child, trained by the teachers, asks both parties to tell their sides of the story. Certain ground rules are agreed to beforehand: no yelling, no cursing, no interrupting, no put-downs of the other person. The older student, acting as a conflict manager, seeks to guide the disputants to solutions of their problems. If they cannot, the conflict manager tries to help. A teacher or administrator always is available. The goal is to provide a caring community in which all children feel safe, where they can resolve their problems, and where everyone is responsible for others' well-being. Caring communities teach children to handle problems without resorting to violence, and violence prevention is promoted by student vigilance and an increased sense of shared responsibility (Davies, 2004).

School programs can help students find alternatives to violence. Nonviolence can be an important curriculum strand running through social studies, language arts, and other subject areas. Violence is a learned response, and because it is learned, it can be unlearned (Noguera, 1995; Sautter, 1995). Schools, working with social service agencies and psychologists, can replace antisocial behaviors with prosocial behaviors and provide positive role models for children. Violence-prevention curricula are new and their successes have not been carefully evaluated or scientifically assessed (Devine and Lawson, 2003). The evidence collected thus far, however, supports the effectiveness of conflict resolution programs and other violence-prevention interventions (such as anger management and anger-coping programs) in teaching students to manage conflicts through nonviolent means (Bodine and Crawford, 1998; Bowen et al., 2002). Even more convincing is the observable difference these curricula bring to schools. As one school administrator notes, "It makes a difference in my school, and I have a reduction of 10 percent in some problems. These materials are OK by me, and I don't need researchers to say it works" (Lawton, 1994, p. 10).

College and university students can help through mentorship programs. The absence of appropriate parental supervision is a strong predictor of trouble complying with school discipline. Once thought of as a problem confined to the poor, lack of supervision and absence of positive role models now are recognized as much broader problems. Students from all social classes need sources of support other than the family. Many undergraduate programs now match volunteer mentors with at-risk students. The mentors act as role models, older brothers or sisters, and surrogate parents. They help with homework and teach study skills. They are models of problem solvers who do not resort to violence and examples of successful adults who have not succumbed to the temptations of crime. Above all, they offer at-risk children a caring, thoughtful person in their lives. Their presence cannot be underestimated. Children at risk for violence have had too few positive role models in their lives. Schools and teachers can help. Research indicates that "the involvement of just one caring adult can make all the difference in the life of an at-risk youth" (Sautter, 1995, p. K8).

Viewed simply, violence is irrational destruction, an explosion of spontaneous rage. But violence doesn't just happen. It is not an act without cause or one that defies understanding. To prevent violence, schools and society should examine how history, economics, and culture find an outlet in violent behavior. Violent acts cannot be prevented unless schools and communities attend to social and political forces producing them. Violent behavior is one of the most frequently studied social phenomena of our day. The social and behavioral sciences have learned a lot about violence, and we have every reason to assume schools can successfully stem the tide of violent behavior and protect children and society from the violent among us. We are ultimately very optimistic about schools and the ability of school personnel to make schools more just and more satisfying places for all students. Teachers and principals can extend the power of schooling into students' daily lives. Schools can help to reduce social conflicts and individual violence. The process likely will be slow and expensive, but if not begun in schools, future social and personal costs will be more costly. Potentially violent children and their problems will not go away by themselves. To paraphrase John Dewey, what the best and wisest parents in the community want for their children should be made available to all children through the agency of the schools.

Position 2: The Problem of School Violence is Beyond School Control

> *Social scientists and educators have developed school-based antibullying programs in an effort to combat the perceived problem of school violence. These programs are unnecessary because, contrary to public belief, school violence is decreasing rather than increasing. They are also ineffective because they do not impart useful tools for responding to bullying but simply teach children how to identify and express their feelings. Several rigorous studies have failed to prove such programs actually reduce bullying. Antibullying programs may do more harm than good by leaving children even less prepared for the interpersonal conflicts that have always been a normal, albeit unpleasant, part of school life.*
>
> —Labash, 2005, p. 13

U.S. schools began with modest academic goals: teach children to read and write. Over the years, schools enhanced their curricula to include academic instruction in content as well as skills, subject matter from art to social studies. The argument in this section is simple, direct, and straightforward: Schools should teach academic content in the most compelling and academically legitimate ways possible. This is the job schools are entrusted with, and is what teachers are trained to do. Without academic skills, students are at a disadvantage, will be unable to compete for places in the best colleges, earn scholarships, land good jobs, or launch satisfying careers. Schooling is primarily about teaching and learning academic subject matter and mastery of skills necessary for success in life. When society asks schools to engage in social engineering programs—such as preventing violence or solving the problems of crime and delinquency—it blurs the focus on cognitive learning, and spreads their efforts across too many areas (Finn, 1993). Schools must teach about our history and literature and instill in students a sense of civic responsibility, if we are to survive as a nation. School must equip students with intellectual skills necessary to understand science, math, the arts, and humanities, if they are to succeed individually. School focus should not be on social reform, but academic achievement. A school's success is measured by the rigor and quality of teaching, not by the extent to which it confronts social problems (Ravitch, 2001).

We will further argue that (1) violence in schools is an overstated problem; (2) violence-prevention curricula are of questionable value; and (3) schools should not try to do the job of welfare agencies, police, or social psychologists.

Decline of Family Values

To spend much energy arguing that these are not normal times is to belabor the obvious. Everyone knows that the family is in disarray, and family values are all but lost to many Americans. Thirty percent of all children are born to single mothers, and the problem is even greater in some minority populations. Too many youngsters have no one to teach them basic skills, socially appropriate behavior, and other family values. Too many children show up at the doors of the nation's schools with only a vague sense of right and wrong, no self-discipline, and a limited ability to get along with other children. Increasing numbers of today's youth claim that the counterculture or gang life offers the sense of belonging, worth, and purpose they fail to find within their families. Too many students refuse to accept responsibility for their actions, and teachers commonly report hearing excuses such as, "It's not my fault; other kids were doing it," and, "I wasn't late; the bell just rang before I got there" (Conrath, 2001, p. 586).

Children do not show up for the first day of kindergarten as blank slates: The experiences of their early lives have etched upon them many complex impressions, both good and bad. Most children are ready to begin school; their parents have invested tremendous amounts of time and energy in them. These children are self-controlled. They demonstrate mastery over their emotions, enthusiasm for learning, and respect for the teacher's authority. Others are not ready for school. Victims of poor parenting or no parenting at all, they come to school with insufficient preparation for the academic side of school and inadequate control over their own behavior to get along with classmates. Teachers spot these students quickly. They are overly impulsive, physically aggressive, and uncooperative. Psychologists have developed profiles of school bullies and other potentially violent youth. Among other things, they tend to be loners who lack empathy for others; frequently are victims of violence at home; have a great deal of pent-up anger, a low frustration tolerance, a record of involvement in substance abuse and other risky behavior, and a lack of moral conscience (MacNeil, 2002). They have been described as "youth with murdered souls" (Sandhu, Underwood, and Sandhu, 2000, p. 27). These troubled youth likely have average or above-average intelligence, but are not likely to do well in school, and threaten the educational quality and physical well-being of other children and themselves.

Only a small fraction of students, however, exhibit aggressive behaviors or other traits that predict violence. In fact, school violence is an overstated problem. Potentially violent students represent only 1 percent of children who enter school, and the rate of violence in school has not increased in twenty years. In 2005, the website of the National Center for Education Statistics (http://nces.ed.gov) reported data indicating a general decline in the victimization rate for violent crime between 1992 and 2002. According to self-reports, the rate of violent crimes committed against students declined 50 percent, from 48 to 24 crimes per 1,000 students. Students indicate that they feel more secure in school than students have in the past. Furthermore, the data suggest students are safer in school than out of school. (See Figure 17.2.) In 2002, 309,000 students ages 12 to 18 were victims of serious, violent crime while away from school, compared with about 88,000 of the same age group who were victims at school.

Despite widespread publicity depicting schools as dangerous places, rife with crime and violence, the conclusion drawn from student reports of violence seems to say school violence may be more of a media creation than a serious school problem. After reviewing the research literature on school crime, Lawrence (1998) argues that "It is difficult to conclude that schools are violent places, when data indicate that on average 99 percent of students are free from attack in a month's time" (p. 29). For the moment, at least, it seems fair to argue that schools are probably less dangerous for students than they have been in the past two decades. Every year since 1969, Phi Delta Kappa and the Gallup Organization conduct a poll of the public's attitude toward the public schools. For the first sixteen years of the poll, when asked to identify the biggest problem the schools in their communities faced, most of those polled put "discipline" at the top of the list. "The use of drugs" replaced discipline in the top spot until 1991, when it was tied with "lack of financial support." Since 2000, "lack of financial support" has been unchallenged in the public's view as the major problem facing the public schools. In 2004, "lack of discipline" was in third place among school problems, identified by only 10 percent of the public as the major problem faced by the schools in their communities (Rose and Gallup, 2005, pp. 4–5).

Teaching is among the nation's safest professions: According to statistics compiled by the Department of Justice, teaching remains one of the nation's safest occupations during the period studied, 1993 to 1999. By comparison, police officers hold the nation's riskiest job; 261 of every 1,000 officers were physically attacked or threatened during the period. The rate for junior high/middle school teachers was 54 per

Figure 17.2

Number of Nonfatal Crimes Against Student Ages 12–18 per 1,000 Students, by Type of Crime and Location: 1992–2002

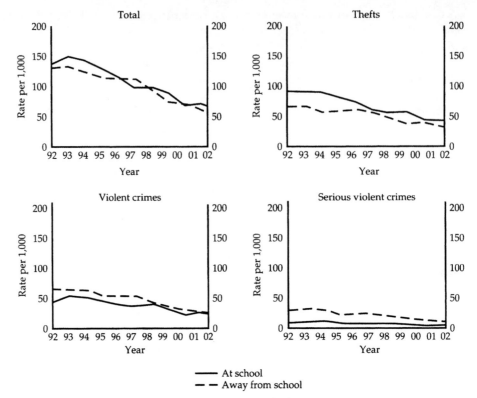

Note: Serious violent crimes include rape, sexual assault, robbery, and aggravated assault. Violent crimes include serious violent crimes and simple assault. Total crimes include violent crimes and theft. "At school" includes inside the school building, on school property, or on the way to or from school.

Source: National Center for Education Statistics. (2004).

1,000. Special education teachers were attacked or threatened with violence at a rate of 68.4 per 1,000, and preschool and elementary school teachers experienced these problems at a rate of 7.1 and 17 per 1,000, respectively, over the period (www.ojp.usdoj.gov/bjs/).

Schools are generally safe places, but disruptive students do exist. What responsibilities do schools have to teach the distracting handful of children who are unable to control their aggression? This is a difficult question. None of us wants to appear callous or indifferent to children, but schools are not social welfare agencies. Teachers are not social workers or psychiatrists. Educators are trained to teach children reading, math, social studies, and other important content and skills. We cannot reasonably expect schools and teachers to function as anger-management therapists or violence-control specialists. Violence-prevention curricula sound noble and high-minded, but they are a diversion from the schools' academic mission and are of doubtful benefit. After reviewing 70 federally funded programs with a total of $2.4 billion in funds aimed at reducing school violence and substance abuse, the General Accounting Office concluded these programs had not demonstrated their worth:

> *Insufficient information exists on the programs' performance. Although we identified some promising approaches for preventing substance abuse and violence, our work suggests that additional research is needed to further test these approaches' effectiveness and their applicability to different populations in varied settings. (U.S. General Accounting Office, 1997, p. 85)*

In other words, a great deal of money is being spent on a small minority of children with little to show for the expenditure. Today a small group of problem students is attracting a disproportionate share of curriculum attention as well as federal and state dollars. The education of the majority of cooperative students is being held ransom by an unruly minority.

Who Are the Potentially Violent?

We know who is likely to commit crimes, the early experiences that lead to violent behavior, and the personal and family traits that tend to protect children from becoming violent adults. We know behaviors that alert teachers and administrators to the potentially troublesome. (See Table 17.1.) Unfortunately, beyond identifying troubled students, research has not yet developed a strong knowledge base about the causes of violent behavior or the ways it can be prevented (Reiss and Roth, 1993). No one knows how to prevent potentially violent children from becoming violent adults. Schools now embracing one violence-management curriculum or another are

Table 17.1

Characteristics of Troubled Students*

1. Has a history of tantrums and uncontrollable angry outbursts.
2. Characteristically resorts to name calling, cursing, or abusive language.
3. Habitually makes violent threats when angry.
4. Has previously brought a weapon to school.
5. Has a background of serious disciplinary problems at school and in the community.
6. Has a background of drug, alcohol, or substance abuse or dependency.
7. Is on the fringe of his or her peer group with few or no close friends.
8. Is preoccupied with weapons, explosives, or other incendiary devices.
9. Has previously been truant, suspended, or expelled from school.
10. Displays cruelty to animals.
11. Has little or no supervision and support from parents or a caring adult.
12. Has witnessed or been a victim of abuse or neglect in the home.
13. Has been bullied and/or bullies or intimidates peers or younger children.
14. Tends to blame others for difficulties and problems she/he causes her/himself.
15. Consistently prefers TV shows, movies, or music expressing violent themes or acts.
16. Prefers reading material dealing with violent themes, rituals, and abuse.
17. Reflects anger, frustration, and the dark side of life in school essays or writing projects.
18. Is involved with a gang or an antisocial group on the fringe of peer acceptance.
19. Is often depressed and/or has significant mood swings.
20. Has threatened or attempted suicide.

*The National School Safety Center tracks school-associated violent deaths in the United States and has developed a checklist of behaviors to alert teachers and administrators to troubled students.

Source: www.nssc1.org/reporter/checklist.htm.

doing so without adequate evidence of its effectiveness. Many causes of violence are not within the schools' control (Weishew and Peng, 1993). Violent children become violent adults, and if children have not learned to control their aggression by the time they come to school, it may not be possible for them to disentangle the patterns of violence that took shape in their early years.

In a perfect world, all children would come to school with no violent inclinations. All children would be raised in loving, drug-free, nurturing homes. They would all bond with an adult who dispenses love freely and teaches them they belong to someone and someone belongs to them. Children's earliest experiences would have shown them that disagreements are part of life, but discord can be settled through calm discussions rather than rancor or violence. We would like all children to have high IQs, to have parents who are literate adults, free from alcohol and drug addiction, who study books about child rearing, read stories to their children, and place limits on television viewing. We would like all these things and more, but social policies cannot create them. Too many children are born to single mothers unprepared for the task or unable to give them what they need to be successful in life. Drug addiction, crime, and poverty are beyond school control. Schools cannot redistribute wealth or solve social problems. For better or worse, schools reflect society; they are not now nor have they ever been agents of social change. They have a mission to educate students and have little power and no authority to do anything else.

Although public schools must work with all students, they do not have to mix the disruptive and the potentially violent with the well behaved; nor do they have to encourage violent students to stay in school until graduation. Students who arrive at school ready to learn should be introduced to a rigorous, sound academic education. The academic side of school will matter to them in life. Children come to school to improve their academic skills and increase their store of intellectual capital—the knowledge needed for success in life. As Hirsch notes, "Sociologists have shown that intellectual capital (i.e., school knowledge) operates in almost every sphere of modern society to determine social class, success or failure in school, and even psychological and physical health" (1996, p. 19). Students are disadvantaged by too small a share of intellectual capital, and need to start early and move quickly in securing as much of it as they can. The vast majority of students do not need special curriculum treatments to teach them how to get along with others, settle disputes without violence, or manage aggression. They need academic content to succeed in life, and that's what schools should deliver.

Conflict-resolution curricula distract students from academic pursuits and send students an undesirable, if unintended, message: "We expect school to be violent, so let's talk about it" (Devine, 1996, p. 165). Violence is not a way of life for most children. Directing conflict-management programs to all students, rather than at the violent minority, sends a negative message that violence is a normal part of life and everyone must learn to manage it or otherwise cope with it.

Schools and Violence

Let's look at what we know about potentially violent children and what schools can reasonably do about them: Overly aggressive children should be identified in kindergarten and trained to work on anger management. Although a school cannot replace the family, it can provide some supports found in homes of self-controlled, high-achieving students. For example, school discipline policies should incorporate the reward-and-punishment systems successfully used by middle-class parents. Students should learn that appropriate behavior earns teacher praise and special privileges, while inappropriate behavior results in loss of praise and privilege. This would be reasonable, inexpensive, and not too intrusive on the privacy rights of students or their parents. Working individually with counselors—and not consuming instructional time—violent and potentially violent students should be the focus of appropriate intervention and prevention strategies (Bemak and Keys, 2000).

Schools alone cannot solve problems of violence (Burstyn, 2001; Casella, 2001; Bowen et al., 2002). Influences of early family experiences and the greater society are pervasive (Caspi et al., 1994). Research provides little encouragement that school interventions successfully prevent violence, and the research may simply be confirming public knowledge. Of course, schools should try to help all students, but not impede the progress of the well behaved. Schools should try every measure to help young children adapt to school and school discipline. But some children never will adjust to academic demands and self-discipline required for success. According to one analysis of U.S. Justice Department statistics, about 6 percent of adolescents are responsible for two-thirds of violent crimes committed by juveniles (Bodine and Crawford, 1998, p. 6). This tiny percentage of students should not be a major focus of school attention and a constant drain on school budgets. If these students have not learned to control themselves by early adolescence, schools should waste no more time or money on them.

Alternative Schools

A good but disaffected student who opts for the smaller, less formal environment [of an alternative school] may be told, "Only students who have messed up can go there," to which the student may reply, "How bad do I have to mess up?" (Gregory, 2001, p. 578)

Educators have long recognized that alternatives in public education are sometimes necessary to serve special populations of students—teenage mothers, for example, or the physically disabled. The one-size-fits-all model of the comprehensive public high school does not serve everyone equally well, and some students rebel against the competition, perceived conformity, and order of traditional education. Many educators now recognize the academic demands and social structure of traditional high schools may contribute to school violence. Students unaccustomed to impersonal rules governing school behavior and emphasis schools place on quiet compliance may lash out at teachers and other students (Epp and Watkinson, 1997; Lawrence, 1998). By the time they reach middle school, students learn the focus of schooling is on academic achievement, and unfortunately students who do not achieve well often develop indifferent or hostile attitudes. As one supporter of alternative schools notes, "Their behavior is not irrational. Just as it is rational to embrace the repetition of successful experiences, it is equally rational to avoid repetitions of unsuccessful experiences" (Conrath, 2001, p. 587).

Alternative schools can siphon off the troubled, disaffected, potentially violent, and others for whom traditional schooling is not a good fit. Alternative schools often are better able to serve nonacademic students while allowing traditional schools to focus on the majority's academic needs. Sometimes housed within the regular school building, and sometimes in separate facilities of their own, alternative schools are designed for students who, because of any number of problems—academic but more often behavioral or social—are not able to learn well in a traditional school environment. Today, 40 percent of all public school districts have some form of alternative school program, sometimes as part of the school, other times as separate buildings with their own faculty and administrators. Alternative schools and programs serve students who are at risk of dropping out of school for any number of reasons (National Center for Education Statistics, 2003).

Alternative schools are likely to be less formal than traditional schools, and typically offer a lower student-to-teacher ratio. The record indicates these schools can go a long way toward ameliorating the anonymity and isolation some students experience in traditional schools (Dunbar, 2001; McGee, 2001). Many formerly disruptive students behave better when they work in a small, supportive setting. They are able to find a niche that eluded them in traditional schools and teachers willing to focus on personal and social problems they bring with them to school (McPartland et al., 1997).

Alternative schools can be very effective, and should be viewed as appropriate educational options for disruptive students who have not responded to special curricular treatment and counseling in regular schools and classes. Unfortunately, although alternative schools try to accommodate students with a wide range of problems, they do not work for everyone. In fact, they may not work well for many of the most disruptive students (Lawrence, 1998). The same students that caused problems in traditional schools often continue to present problems when they transfer to alternative schools. For these students, more dramatic action is likely to be in order.

Schools should embrace all students equally when they first begin school. Special curriculum interventions—the so-called conflict-and dispute-resolution curricula—should be reserved exclusively for students who demonstrate behaviors associated with violence in adults (for example, physical aggression and lack of self-control). Schools should use every technique at their disposal to curb disruptive behavior and bring the unruly child back into the fold. However, by middle school, students who impede the learning process of their classmates or threaten the welfare of other children should be considered as candidates for alternative schools. Students who are not likely to succeed in one kind of school should be given another chance in a different kind of school. These alternative schools have amassed a sound, though not perfect, record for educating the disaffected. For the small handful of very disruptive students who are unable to cooperate in an alternative school, expulsion is a harsh but sensible last resort.

Will expelling problem students from the public school system be likely to increase their inclination toward further violence and criminality? Will these students inevitably wind up in the criminal justice system? It is hard to know. Research indicates future dropouts have high levels of criminal behavior while in school, but some evidence indicates that after these students drop out of school, they may have less trouble with the law (Herrnstein and Murray, 1994). Schools often add to the problems of young people. Many students who do not succeed academically feel frustrated. Others feel confined by school rules and the abrasiveness of school crowding (Noguera, 1995; Sautter, 1995; Lawrence, 1998). Some students may learn better in another environment, and schools should find places for such students. Schools are ultimately academic institutions designed to teach cognitive skills. Students who cannot learn to play by the rules of civilized behavior—to exercise self-discipline, order, and respect for others—ultimately have no place in school.

FOR DISCUSSION

1. Teenage boys are the most frequent perpetrators as well as the most common victims of school violence. One researcher argues that young males suffer from the

Boy Code: "Violence committed by and acted upon boys seems to be, more often than not, from what we teach (or do not teach) boys about the behavior we expect from them. It comes from society's set of rules about masculinity, the Boy Code that says, 'To become a man, you must hold your own if challenged by another male. You can show your rage, but you must not show any other emotions. You must protect your honor and fight off shame at all costs'" (Pollack, 2005, p. 64).

Is violence in boys an inevitable consequence of what our society expects of males and male behavior? Can schools discourage or modify the Boy Code without running afoul of established, social expectations?

2. Some social critics argue violence should be viewed as a legitimate protest against the injustices of a school system that include racial segregation, funding disparities among schools, a curriculum that avoids multicultural issues, and the wholesale discrimination against schools in African American and Hispanic neighborhoods (Casella, 2001, p. 11).

Do you consider these arguments to offer insights into school violence? Should perspectives of the potentially violent be taken into consideration in the design of school violence-prevention strategies? How?

3. In Scandinavian countries, corporal punishment is prohibited by law in schools and in homes. Minnesota is the only state in the United States to prohibit corporal punishment of any sort, even by parents (Smith, 2003). The 2006 Program Accreditation Criteria of the National Association for the Education of Young Children include the following statement about the interactions among teachers and children in preschools, kindergarten, and childcare centers: "Teachers [should] abstain from corporal punishment or humiliating or frightening discipline techniques."

Is this a reasonable standard? Should parents have the right to determine whether or not corporal punishment can be used as a form of discipline on their own children at home or in the public schools they attend?

REFERENCES

Astor, R. A., et al. (2002). "Public Concern and Focus on School Violence," in *Handbook of Violence,* ed. L. A. Rapp-Paglicci et al. New York: John Wiley & Sons.

Barbour, S. (2005). *How Can School Violence Be Prevented?* Detroit, MI: Greenhaven.

Bemak, F., and Keys, S. (2000). *Violent and Aggressive Youth: Intervention and Prevention Strategies for Changing Times.* Thousand Oaks, CA: Corwin Press.

Bodine, R. J., and Crawford, D. K. (1998). *The Handbook of Conflict Resolution Education: A Guide to Building Quality Programs in Schools.* San Francisco: Jossey-Bass.

Bowen, G. L., et al. (2002). "Reducing School Violence: A Social Capacity Framework," in *Handbook of Violence,* ed. L. A. Rapp-Paglicci et al. New York: John Wiley & Sons.

Burstyn, J. N., ed. (2001). *Preventing Violence in Schools: A Challenge to American Democracy.* Mahwah, NJ: Erlbaum.

Casella, R. (2001). *"Being Down": Challenging Violence in Urban Schools.* New York: Teachers College Press.

Caspi, A., et al. (1994). "Are Some People Crime Prone?" *Criminology* 32:163–196.

Conrath, J. (2001). "Changing the Odds for Young People: Next Steps for Alternative Education." *Kappan* 82:585–587.

Davies, L. (2004). *Education and Conflict; Complexity and Chaos.* New York: Routledge Falmer.

Devine, J. (1996). *Maximum Security.* Chicago: University of Chicago Press.

Devine, J., and Lawson, H. A. (2003). "The Complexity of School Violence: Commentary from the US," in *Violence in Schools: The Response in Europe,* ed. P. K. Smith. New York: Routlege Falmer

Dunbar, C. (2001). "Does Anyone Know We're Here?" *Alternative Schooling for African American Youth.* New York: Peter Lang.

Dworkin, M. S. (1959). *Dewey On Education.* New York: Teachers College Press.

Epp, J. R., and Watkinson, A. M. (1997). *Systemic Violence in Education: Broken Promise.* Albany: State University of New York.

Finn, C. E., Jr. (1993). "Whither Education Reform?" in *Making Schools Work,* ed. C. L. Fagnano and K. N. Hughes. Boulder, CO: Westview Press.

Galezewski, J. (2005). "Bullying and Aggression Among Youth," in *Violence in Schools: Issues, Consequences, and Expressions,* ed. K. Sexton-Radek. Westport: Praeger.

Goldstein, A. P., Harootunian, B., and Conoley, J. C. (1994). *Student Aggression: Prevention, Management, and Replacement Training.* New York: Guilford.

Gregory, T. (2001). "Fear of Success: Ten Ways Alternative Schools Pull Their Punches." *Kappan* 82:577–581.

Herrnstein, R. J., and Murray, C. (1994). *The Bell Curve: Intelligence and Class Structure in American Life.* New York: Free Press.

Hirsch, E. D., Jr. (1996). *The Schools We Need and Why We Don't Have Them.* New York: Doubleday.

Jordan, K. (2002). "School Violence Among Culturally Diverse Populations," in *Handbook of Violence,* ed. L. A. Rapp-Paglicci et al. New York: John Wiley & Sons.

Labash, M. (2005). "Antibullying Programs Are Ineffective and Unnecessary," in *How Can School Violence Be Prevented?* ed. S. Barbour. Detroit, MI: Greenhaven.

Lawrence, R. (1998). *School Crime and Juvenile Justice. New York: Oxford University Press.*

Lawton, M. (1994). "Violence-Prevention Curricula: What Works Best?" *Education Week* November 9: pp. 1, 10–11.

MacNeil, G. (2002). "School Bullying: An Overview," in *Handbook of Violence,* ed. L. A. Rapp-Paglicci et al. New York: John Wiley & Sons.

McGee, J. (2001). "Reflections of an Alternative School Administrator." *Kappan* 82:588–591.

McPartland, J., et al. (1997). "Finding Safety in Small Numbers." *Educational Leadership* 55:14–17.

National Association for the Education of Young Children. (2005). "Early Childhood Program Standards and Accreditation Criteria." www.naeyc.org/accreditation/criteria98.asp.

National Center for Education Statistics. (2003). "Public Alternative Schools For At-Risk Students." www.nces.ed.gov/programs/coe/2003.

Noguera, P. A. (1995). "Preventing and Producing Violence: A Critical Analysis of Responses to School Violence." *Harvard Educational Review* 65:189–212.

Osier, J., and Fox, H. (2001). *Settle Conflicts Right Now! A Step-by-Step Guide for K–6 Classrooms.* Thousand Oaks, CA: Corwin Press.

Pollack, W. S. (2005). "Changing Society's Expectations of Boys Can Prevent School Violence," in *How Can School Violence Be Prevented?* ed. S. Barbour. Detroit, MI: Greenhaven.

Potter, W. J. (1999). *On Media Violence.* Thousand Oaks, CA: Sage.

Ravitch, D. (2001). "Education and Democracy," in *Making Good Citizens: Education and Civil Society,* ed. D. Ravitch and J. P. Viteritti. New Haven, CT: Yale University Press.

Recess from Violence: Making Our Schools Safe. (1993). Hearings Before the Subcommittee on Education, Arts, and Humanities of the Committee on Labor and Human Resources. U.S. Senate, One Hundred Third Congress, First Session on S. 1125 (Sept. 23). Washington, DC: U.S. Government Printing Office.

Reiss, A. J., Jr., and Roth, J. A. (1993). *Understanding and Preventing Violence.* Washington, DC: National Academy Press.

Rose, L. C., and Gallup, A. M. (2005). The 37th Annual Phi Delta Kappa/Gallup Poll of the Public's Attitudes Toward the Public Schools. www.pdkintl.org/kappan/k0509pol.htm.

Sandhu, D. S., Underwood, J. R., and Sandhu, V. S. (2000). "Psychocultural Profiles of Violent Students: Prevention and Intervention Strategies," in *Violence in American Schools: A Practical Guide for Counselors,* ed. D. S. Sandhu and C. B. Aspy. Alexandria, VA: American Counseling Association.

Sautter, C. R. (1995). "Standing Up to Violence." *Kappan* 76:K1–K12.

School Crime Prevention Programs. (2001). Hearing of the Committee on the Judiciary, United States Senate, One Hundred Sixth Congress, Second Session (May 15). Washington, DC: U.S. Government Printing Office.

Smith, P. K., ed. (2003). *Violence in Schools: The Response in Europe.* New York: Routledge Falmer.

Smith, S. W., and Daunic, A. P. (2005). "Conflict Resolution and Peer Mediation," in *School Violence,* ed. K. Burns. Detroit, MI: Greenhaven.

Smith-Heavenrich, S. (2005). "Bullies in the Schoolyard," in *School Violence,* ed. K. Burns. Detroit, MI: Greenhaven.

Spina, S. U., ed. (2000). *Smoke and Mirrors: The Hidden Context of Violence in Schools and Society.* New York: Rowman & Littlefield.

U.S. Department of Justice. (2004). "National Crime Victimization Survey, 1995–2003." http://permanent.access.gpo.gov/lps9947/2004.

U.S. General Accounting Office. (1997). "Substance Abuse and Violence Prevention." Testimony before the Subcommittee on Oversight and Investigations, Committee on Education and the Workforce, House of Representatives. Washington, DC: Author.

Violence in the Schools. (1993). National Education Association Video, Teacher TV Episode #15. West Haven, CT: National Education Association.

Weishew, N. L., and Peng, S. S. (1993). "Variables Predicting Students' Problem Behaviors." *Journal of Educational Research* 87:5–17.

Education Law and Policy

18

Beyond the Regulations
Maintaining the Prudent Parent Model

Duties and Responsibilities of Teaching

The idea of duty of care, based in Common Law,[1] is also emphasized in the statutory duties for teachers outlined in the Acts and Regulations that govern teaching. Ontario's *Education Act* and its attendant regulations specify the responsibilities that a teacher must undertake. In the realm of assuring student safety, each teacher under section 264 of the *Education Act* has the duty "to teach diligently and faithfully the classes or subjects assigned to the teacher and principal,". . ."to maintain, under the direction of the principal, proper order and discipline in the teacher's classroom and while on duty in the school and on the school ground."

Regulation 298, Section 20 further defines duties of the teacher regarding student safety and well-being. The teacher shall "be responsible for effective instruction, training and evaluation of the progress of the pupils in the subjects assigned to the teacher and for the management of the class or classes, and report to the principal the progress of pupils on request,". . ."carry out the supervisory duties and instructional program assigned to the teacher by the principal and supply such information related thereto as the principal may require". . ."ensure that all reasonable safety procedures are carried out in courses and activities for which the teacher is responsible,". . ."co-operate with the principal and other teachers to establish and maintain consistent disciplinary practices in the school."

---

[1] Yogis, J. A. (1990). Canadian Law Dictionary (2nd Edition). Toronto: Barrons, p. 44. Common Law has been explained by John Yogis as a "system of jurisprudence . . . that is based on judicial precedent rather than legislative enactment. Common Law depends for its authority upon the recognition given by the courts to principles, customs, and practices previously existing among the people. It is now recorded in the law reports that embodied judgments together with the reasons they assigned for their decisions."

Reprinted from *Orbit* 32, no. 2 (2001), by permission of Ontario Institute for Studies in Education.

Am I liable? Was I negligent?
How do I know if I'm negligent?
The standard of care that is expected of a teacher is first that of a careful and pru-
dent parent.

The principal of the school is also charged with certain duties to safeguard students' welfare. In the *Education Act,* section 265, the principal, in addition to his/her duties as a teacher, is "to maintain proper order and discipline,". . . "to give assiduous attention to the health and comfort of the pupils, . . . to the care of all teaching materials and other school property, and to the condition and appearance of the school buildings and grounds."

Duty of Care

Parents empower teachers to work with their children, and teachers, on being assigned to work with children, assume a duty of care. This special student-teacher relationship finds its basis in Common Law which clearly establishes that there is a duty of care that teachers owe to their students. Teachers are to be attentive and careful in situations where students are involved to ensure that students are not exposed to any unnecessary risk of harm. This duty of care is imposed on teachers because of the distinctive character of their work.

This article explorers "the prudent parent standard" which also governs the Acts and Regulations of the teaching profession. Citing examples from case law, the author acknowledges that the prudent parent model is no guarantee that accidents will not happen but not adhering to the standard will compromise students' safety and well-being and teachers, principals, and school boards may be found liable.

Regulation 298 section 11 outlines that the principal has responsibility for "the instruction and the discipline of pupils in the school" and "the organization and management of the school." Further, ". . . in addition to the duties under the Act and those assigned by the board, the principal of a school shall . . . provide for the supervision of pupils during the period of time during each school day when the school buildings and playgrounds are open to pupils," "provide for the supervision of and the conducting of any school activity authorized by the board,". . ."provide for instruction of pupils in the care of the school premises," "inspect the school premises at least weekly and report forthwith to the board."

The Doctrine of *In Loco Parentis*

While these duties and responsibilities are generally prescriptive, they are also open to interpretation. What constitutes conformity to these duties and regulations? To what degree is a teacher in compliance with these? And if a teacher is not adhering to the statutes, the question asked when an incident happens is: Am I liable? Was I negligent? How do I know if I'm negligent? The standard of care that is expected of a teacher is first that of a careful and prudent parent. This standard of care is dependent on a number of variables including the circumstances around the incident, the likelihood of risk, and usual teaching practices.

In addition to the regulations, the Court has, over the years, ruled on what is expected of a teacher. . .

Traditionally, *in loco parentis* allows teachers to act in the place of the parent. Although the concept has been and continues to be questioned and debated, it is still widely accepted today.[2] The *in loco parentis* doctrine as practised by a teacher does not equate the teacher with parent, with the teacher assuming the same prerogatives as the parent. The teacher has these privileges for the purpose of educating the child. The child responds to a person acting *in loco parentis* under Regulation 298 (Operation of Schools—General) section 23 1(c) Requirements for Pupils) which requires that "a pupil shall . . .accept such discipline as would be exercised by a kind, firm and judicious parent."

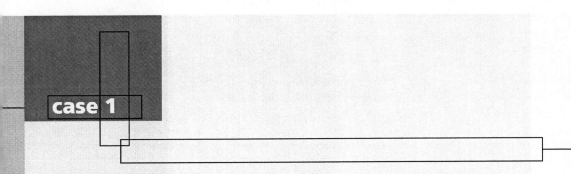

case 1

"The Ordinary Nature of Young Boys"

One of the first references of the prudent parent standard of care occurred in 1893 in *Williams v. Eady*.[3] In this instance, some boys found a bottle of phosphorus in a room and lit the chemical with a match, resulting in serious burns to one of the boys. The Court stated:

> ". . .the school master was bound to take such care of his boys as a careful father would take of his boys, and there could be not be a better definition of the duty of a schoolmaster. Then he was bound to take notice of the ordinary nature of young boys, their tendency to do mischievous acts, and their propensity to meddle with anything that came in their way."[4]

In this case, the Court found that the schoolmaster had not acted as a careful father and found him negligent, even though the schoolmaster had locked the chemical away and the boys had taken the key in a surreptitious manner.

---

[2]MacKay A. W. and Dickinson, G. M. (1998). *Beyond the "Careful Parent" Tort Liability in Education*, Toronto: Emond Montgomery Publications Limited. p. 9.
[3]Williams v. Eady (1893), 10 T.L.R. 41 (C.A.).
[4]Ibid., at 42.

"The Factors Affecting the Standard of Care"

In *Myers v. the Peel County Board of Education*[5] in 1981, a 15-year-old boy broke his neck in attempting his dismount from gymnastic rings. The teacher was not in the room where the student was practising his routine and, at the time of the accident, there were better quality gym mats that could have been used than those under the rings. Mr. Justice McIntyre of the Supreme Court of Canada explained the careful or prudent parent model as follows:

> "The standard of care to be exercised by school authorities in providing for the supervision and protection of students for whom they are responsible is that of the careful or prudent parent, described in Williams v. Eady. It has, no doubt, become somewhat qualified in modern times because of the greater variety of activities conducted in schools, with probably larger groups of students using more complicated and more dangerous equipment than formerly . . . It is not, however, a standard which can be applied in the same manner and to the same extent in every case. Its application will vary from case to case and will depend upon the number of students being supervised at any given time, the nature of the exercise or the activity in progress, the age and the degree of skill and training which the students may have received in connection with such activity, the nature and condition of the equipment in use at the time, the competency and capacity of the students involved, and a host of other matters which may be widely varied but which, in a given case, may affect the application of the prudent parent standard to the conduct of the school authority in the circumstances."[6]

Key Points

- The idea of duty of care is based in Common Law but it is also emphasized in the statutory duties for teachers outlined in the Acts and Regulations that govern education.
- Traditionally the *in loco parents* privilege allows teachers to act in the place of the parent for the *purpose of educating the child.*
- In determining if there has been a violation of the standard of care the Courts have ruled, over the years, on what is expected of the teacher: what would a firm, kind, and judicious parent do in similar circumstances?
- The standard of care is not the same in every case. It depends on the number of students being supervised; the nature of the activity in progress; the age and degree of skill the students may have developed; the nature and condition of the equipment in use; the competency of the students involved; and other factors ranging from student dress at the time of the incident to lighting.

---

[5]Myers v. Peel County Board of Education, (1981), 17 C.C.L.T. 269.
[6]Ibid., at 279.

The standard of care, Mr. Justice McIntyre concluded, is not the same in every case and depends upon the following:

a. *The number of students being supervised at any given time:* It stands to reason that the more students that there are in the activity, the less direct supervision each individual student will receive. Thus, adequate supervision must be provided.
b. *The nature of the exercise or activity in progress:* If the activity is judged to be dangerous or could cause harm to the student, then attentive supervision and progressive and precise instruction are required.
c. *The age and the degree of skill and training which the students may have received in connection with such activity:* The younger the students are, the more supervision, training, and direct instruction are required.
d. *The nature and condition of the equipment in use at the time:* If the equipment is in poor condition and/or unsuitable for the activity, the greater is the likelihood of injury.
e. *The competency and capacity of the students involved:* If the students do not understand what is expected of them, the greater is the risk of harm and injury.
f. *A host of other matters which may be widely varied:* Other factors could include student dress, attentiveness of the student to the activity, lighting, health of the student, etc.

In addition, Mr. Justice McIntyre chastised the teacher for not having "anticipated reckless behaviour from at least some of the boys"[7] since these were high school students who were given to work their gymnastic routines without spotters and tended to act carelessly at times.[8] In this case, foreseeability that an accident may happen demanded greater caution on the part of the teacher and the school authorities. However, the fact that students participate in higher risk activities is not a breach of the standard of care of itself.

In addition to the regulations, the Court, assuming its responsibility to determine if there has been a violation of the standard of care has, over the years, ruled on what is expected of a teacher, that is, what is reasonable, what would a firm, kind and judicious parent or careful and prudent parent do. In determining the standard of care, each case is viewed on its own merits and these benchmarks or standards are in use in today's schools along with the policies and procedures that school boards have developed.

> . . . not adhering to the standard of care and observing the duties will guarantee that the safety and well-being of students are compromised.

[7]Ibid., at 282.
[8]Ibid., at 282.

"Unforeseeable Dangers"

Working in chemistry laboratories can also be fraught with danger as the next scenario outlines. During a science class, one 15-year-old student sprayed another student with an acid. In this case, *Crouch v. Essex County Council,*[9] the Court found: that it was not foreseeable that the student would intentionally squirt another student with the acid since the teacher had explained the hazards of using chemicals; that the deportment of the students was generally appropriate; and that the teacher's classroom management was appropriate.[10] The teacher had anticipated that an accident could happen and took all reasonable measures to ensure that it would not, but could not predict the action of the offending student.

CONCLUSIONS

Given the number of children in schools and the nature of children to be active, there are many opportunities for accidents, even with close supervision. These accidents range from very minor to the worst case scenario. Maintaining the careful and prudent parent model and diligently exercising the duties of a teacher or principal cannot guarantee that nothing will happen. It should be emphasized that not adhering to the standard of care and observing the duties of a teacher will increase the likelihood that the safety and well-being of students is compromised.

Shirley Van Nuland is Assistant Professor at Nipissing University where she teaches Education and Schooling, and Religious Studies. She has been a principal and a teacher in the elementary and secondary school panels and has worked with the Ministry of Education as the Education Officer and Coordinate for the Freedom of information and Protection of Privacy (Acting) Her research interests are teachers' professional learnings and the impact of law on teachers Contact: Shirley@unipissing.ca

---

[9]Crouch v. Essex County Council, (1966), 64 L.G.R. 240.
[10]Brown, A.F. and Zuker, M.A. (1998). *Education Law* (2nd Ed.). Toronto: Carswell, Scarborough, 1994.

19

Implications of the Charter for School Discipline

by Austin J. Harte and Kent McDonald

The purpose of this article is to heighten educators' awareness of how Canada's Charter of Rights and Freedoms affects schools' ability to discipline. The authors identify ways in which educators may need to modify their techniques and policies for maintaining discipline.

There is a growing need for school officials, especially administrators, to be accurately informed about new legal issues associated with the development, administration, and enforcement of school rules and regulations. This need is a function of at least the following factors:

- An increase in student discipline problems,
- An erosion of the school's authority.
- A growing tendency for students and parents to see their rights and freedoms protected, especially since the 1982 entrenchment of the *Charter of Rights and Freedoms* within the *Canadian Constitution*.

Yet, Snelgrove and Warren's (1989) study of educator's knowledge of legal rights in schools showed that "educators' knowledge of the law seems to be far short of that required to function effectively in the litigious society in which they practice today" (p. 81).

The purpose of this article is to heighten educators' awareness of the impact of the *Charter of Rights and Freedoms* on student discipline policy. We show how the Charter affects schools' ability to discipline. And we show how educators need to modify their approaches to maintaining discipline so as to be consistent with *Charter* considerations and with the notion of due process. Although very few *Charter* cases in education have come before our courts, we agree that "school administrators should

Reprinted from *The Canadian School Executive* 15, no. 7 (1996).

undertake a full review of their rules and throw out old, discriminatory regulations which could be challenged under the *Charter of Rights and Freedoms*" (MacKay, 1986). As school boards and school administrators are the most likely targets of Charter challenges, it is incumbent upon district administrative personnel and school principals to ensure that current policies, procedures, and practices provide for due process. Violations may occur with respect to the content, administration, and enforcement of school rules.

Content of Rules

In the United States, students were recognized as having full constitutional rights through the historic case of Tinker *vs*. Des Moines Independent Community District (1969). Tinker *vs*. Des Moines established that students are "persons" under the Constitution and as such are possessed of fundamental rights which the state must respect. A subsequent case, Goss *vs*. Lopez (1975), established the right of students to procedural due process in discipline cases involving suspension. Prior to 1982, however, American precedent had little impact in Canada as fundamental rights were not constitutionally guaranteed. Canadian school boards and school had broad discretionary powers to make and enforce rules as they saw appropriate. And, if required, the courts almost always supported school officials. In the Saskatchewan case of Ward *vs*. Board of Blaine Lake School (1971), for example, the court held that the principal was engaged in administrative acts of the school when he expelled a student for breaching a school rule on length of hair. Because this was considered an administrative not a judicial act, the court ruled that no hearing was required.

Today, however, with the *Charter* firmly entrenched in our Constitution, the judiciary of Canada will have to decide if students will be given full constitutional rights as in the United States and, if so, how such rights will be balanced with the common law and statutory duties of educators to maintain standards of discipline.

Two sections of the *Charter* prove worthy of attention: Section 2 states that everyone has a fundamental freedom of religion, thought, belief, expression, peaceful assembly, and association. Section 15 (1) states that "Every individual is equal before and under the law and has the right to the equal protection and equal benefit of the law without discrimination based on race, national or ethnic origin, colour, religion, sex, age, or mental or physical disability."

> *A record of notification of parents, with a non-judgemental comment on their reaction, might also be included in the "discipline file"— this might prove worthwhile in the event of court action.*

It may be that the rights guaranteed under these Sections of the *Charter* may limit the scope of school rules, regulations, and practices as they now stand in many Canadian schools. For example, in the case of Zylberberg *vs*. Sudbury Board of Education (1988), Section 2 (a) of the *Charter*, guaranteeing freedom of conscience and religion, was used to successfully challenge a rule requiring prayer in a public school. And while freedom of expression in the school setting has yet to be tested in the courts, Section 2 brings into question the legitimacy of rules that restrict certain styles or articles of clothing, ban certain slogans and buttons, and prohibit certain publications or meetings in the school.

Likewise, discrimination in rules or regulations which restricts access to school programs or facilities on the basis of age or sex may be challenged under Section 15. Restrictions prohibiting boys from the choice of taking Home Economics, or which prevent girls from trying out for the school hockey team, must be seriously reconsidered. While there have not been any cases in Canada concerning discrimination in school sports based on sex, an out-of-school precedent appears worthy of examination. In the case of Blainey vs. Ontario Hockey Association (1986), a twelve year old girl claimed that her rights were infringed when a provision in the *Human Rights Code of Ontario* denied participation in a sport based on sex. The Ontario Court of Appeal agreed that Section 15 had been violated, and held that the girl could indeed try out for the team. Again, in the case of contact sports, American precedents might prove useful. In the case of Yellow Springs Exempted School District Board of Education *vs.* Ohio High School Athletic Association (1978), the court concluded that physically qualified girls cannot be denied the right to compete with boys in interscholastic contact sports.

In considering the legality of rules and regulations or in the defence against an alleged infringement under Sections 2 or 15 of the *Charter*, school administrators may be called to justify the rule under *Section 1* of the *Charter*. Section 1 states:

> The Canadian Charter of Rights and Freedoms *guarantees the rights and freedoms set out in it subject only to such reasonable limits proscribed by law as can be demonstrably justified in a free and democratic society.*

Hence, school officials may have to "demonstrably justify" a rule as reasonable in "a free and democratic society" and show that the rule, while infringing upon the *Charter*, was necessary and legitimate given the objectives it sought. As Paul Ebbs, a Halifax lawyer, maintains:

> If a principal must justify a rule under Section 1 *of the* Charter, *for the most part the courts will support the educator and the decisions or actions he or she has taken because the justice system realizes the educational process is essential to society and disrupting this is clearly wrong. I would be concerned, however, if the rule has been arbitrarily created with no educational or discipline basis.*

> (Personal communication, August, 1991)

Administration of Rules

Once the content of the student discipline policy is determined to be in accordance with the *Charter of Rights and Freedoms*, the next consideration facing school officials is fairness or due process. Section 7 of the *Charter* states:

> Everyone has the right to life, liberty, and security of the person and the right not to be derived thereof in accordance with the principles of fundamental justice.

The concept of due process would appear to be guaranteed by the phrase "the principles of fundamental justice."

The administration of school rules is usually based on regulations, prescribed in a school discipline policy manual, that are in accordance with district policy and provincial legislation. It is imperative that school rules are made known and available to students and parents, and that the language of school rules is clear and not open to charges of ambiguity and vagueness. MacKay and Sutherland (1987, p. 72) cite the Nova Scotia case of RE M.B. (1984) in which a teenage girl was placed in a private school after she was labeled unmanageable and removed from her high school:

> The court held that this placement violated Section 7 of the Charter because the girl was not provided with the dates, locations, and specific instances of her alleged

"unmanageability" to allow for a proper defence. It is a commonly held principle of fundamental justice that accused persons have the right to know the case against them. Most provinces in Canada have now legislated the procedures to be followed in dealing with suspending and expelling students and most allow students the opportunity to be heard.

For example, in Newfoundland, under the *Schools Act,* a principal has the authority to suspend students in accordance with the regulations or bylaws of his/her board. The Act does not guarantee the right of the student to be heard or to appeal. School boards, however, may set out regulations governing suspension, including the right of the student to appeal. For example, under a section entitled "Principles of due process - Suspensions (Revised 1990 03 06)", the Roman Catholic School Board for the Burin Peninsula provides for an appeal process for all suspensions.

While the Newfoundland *Schools Act* does not mandate an appeal process for suspension, it does require principals to give a student and his/her parents prior warning that his/her behaviour may result in expulsion. And when an expulsion does occur, the Act further provides that the Minister shall, upon the request of the parent or guardian, appoint a review board to carry out an investigation into the circumstances of the expulsion and to make a binding recommendation either upholding or reversing the expulsion.

In all disciplinary matters brought to the attention of school administrators, officials would be well advised to establish a disciplinary file on each student which records such information as the date and nature of the infraction, the names of teachers and other students involved, a brief description of the events, and a record of the disciplinary action taken. A record of notification of parents, with a non-judgemental comment on their reaction, might also be included—this might prove worthwhile in the event of further action. To ensure objectivity and fairness, as well as the perception of fair treatment, both students and teachers (depending on the seriousness of the infraction) should be required to provide a written account of the incident to be kept in the student's disciplinary file. Such a file, however, must be available to the student concerned and to his/her parents and/or their legal representatives.

The doctrine of in loco parentis endows school officials with a duty that is quite distinct from any delegation of parental authority — a statutory duty to maintain discipline in the school.

Apart from the obvious benefits of due process and legal liability, the existence of "a disciplinary file" in itself becomes a psychological deterrent to misbehaviour. Of course, policy must assure confidentiality of such files as well as a periodic "cleansing of the slate." It is important that students not be led to believe that every little incident will be held "in your file" for future use. On the contrary, efforts should be made to ensure that students and parents understand that such practice and procedures are for the protection of their right to due process and for the overall good of the school community.

While this degree of formality seems necessary to guarantee due process, such an approach to general disciplinary matters may become burdensome and time-consuming for school officials. Consequently, in the case of minor misbehaviours that call for less severe punishments (such as in-school suspensions or detention), a less formal opportunity for a student to "air her/his side of the story" seems sufficient to satisfy the due process requirement. Teachers should be encouraged, however, to maintain brief factual notes on such incidents, particularly if they are repetitive and involve particularly troublesome students. In the event that a matter is brought to the attention of administrators for disciplinary action, an investigation should follow, with the student given the opportunity to have "his/her side of the story" recorded. As one lawyer who is experienced in educational law notes:

Just because the teacher or principal grants a student a moment to explain his or her version of the alleged misconduct, it does not have to dictate the decision the teacher or principal makes. But it does help to see that the rights of the student are maintained.

(Woods, 1991)

Of course, in an instance where the continued presence of a student poses an immediate threat to others, or where a student causes a serious disruption to order and learning, school officials would be justified in removing the student without acknowledging a right to a hearing. As with many aspects of a school administrator's role, discretion and the wisdom of experience should rule the day.

Enforcement of School Rules

The acceptability of protocols for enforcing school rules is linked to Section 12 of the *Charter of Rights and Freedoms:* "Everyone has the right not to be subjected to any cruel and unusual treatment or punishment." This resembles the "cruel and unusual punishment" prohibition in the Eight Amendment of the *American Bill of Rights.* While the US Supreme Court has held that the cruel and unusual prohibition did not apply to students (being limited to criminal matters), there is reason to believe that Section 12 of the Canadian *Charter of Rights and Freedoms* may apply to school students. The reasons are that Section 12 neither refers to "fines and bails" which apply to criminal cases, nor uses of the term "treatment"—which lacks criminal connotation. Hence in Canada we must consider the relation between the effects of a punishment and the reasons for it. The effects of a punishment must not be disproportionate to the circumstances of the offence or goal to be accomplished by the punishment.

While it may be reasonable to think that this line of reasoning does not apply to minor disciplinary procedures (such as school detentions or reprimands), in the case of more serious punishments it is important for teachers and administrators to know the boundaries of appropriate discipline. Again, formal policies provide one avenue for guarding against accusations of "unfair treatment."

One area of particular concern is the use of corporal punishment. At present teachers are afforded some protection from criminal responsibility for administering corporal punishment. Hurlbert and Hurlbert (1990, p. 190) cite *Blackstone's Commentaries* on the law of England (1765):

He (the parent) may also delegate part of his parental responsibility, during his life, to the tutor or school master of his child, who is then in loco parentis, and has such a portion of power committed to his charge, viz. that of restraint and correction, as may be necessary to answer the purpose for which he is employed.

Manley-Casimir and Sussel (1986, p. 195) cite Wilson's (1978) Canadian elaboration of the *in loco parentis* doctrine:

The rights of the parent and the duties of the child are transferable to the role of the teacher and pupil respectively. It is said that the parent, by sending his child to school, delegates his disciplinary rights to the teacher. Moreover, because the teacher's power is seen as necessary for maintaining order in the classroom, and not simply for meting out parental punishment, the teacher can exercise the necessary discipline, even over the objections of the parent.

In addition to the authority delegated to teachers to maintain discipline through the doctrine of *in loco parentis,* school officials also owe a statutory duty to maintain discipline in the school system; a duty that is quite distinct from any parental delegation of authority. Also, Section 43 of the *Criminal Code of Canada* describes the extent to which correction of a child by force may be:

> *Every school teacher, parent, or person standing in the place of a parent is justified in using force by way of correction of pupil or child, as the case may be, who is under his care, if the force does not exceed what is reasonable under the circumstances.*

It is important to understand that this does not condone the use of corporal punishment to discipline students but simply recognizes the fact that there is protection for the teacher in the event that criminal charges are laid. All educators should recognize this and be cognizant of provincial and school board regulations governing the use of corporal punishment. While the banning of corporal punishment at the provincial level (as in British Columbia) or at the local level (as in the case of the Halifax School Board) does not affect a teacher's defence in a criminal case, its use may constitute a blatant breach of board policy—for which the teacher or administrator could be reprimanded or even fired.

CONCLUSION

In Canada's schools student discipline has become a more serious problem for educators for there is an increasing tendency for students and their parents to see their rights and freedoms as protected in law. The best approach for educators is preventive—to develop and implement a student discipline policy which, among other things, recognizes a student's right to due process, the dignity of the individual person, and the right of the teacher to teach. This will best serve the interests of all concerned. Educators need not become semi-trained lawyers but, as professionals, they should be familiar with the *Charter,* the *Young Offenders Act,* and the *Criminal Code* at federal level; the statutes and regulations that govern education at the provincial level; and the policies of their school districts.

While it may not be possible at this time to anticipate the full effect on student discipline policies of the *Charter of Rights and Freedoms,* educators should keep abreast of current and future challenges and decisions under the *Charter.* Rather than thinking of the *Charter* as inimical, educational leaders must view it as an opportunity to assess the validity and desirability of existing rules and as a means to improve the educational system for our children. Edward Broadbent, the former leader of the New Democratic Party of Canada, summarized succinctly the value of having a *Charter of Rights and Freedoms* in a school setting. In the 1981 House of Commons debate on the *Charter,* he argued:

> I would like this resolution, particularly the *Charter of Rights and Freedoms,* to hang on the wall of every classroom in every school in every region of Canada . . . because . . . constitutions are fundamentally about people; and people from childhood on must be encouraged to acquire a deep understanding of their own liberties as well as an even deeper appreciation of the liberties of others.

(Government of Canada, 1982)

REFERENCES

Ebbs, P. (1991). Personal interview.

Hurlbert, E.L., & Hurlbert, M.A. (1991). *School law under the Charter of Rights and Freedoms.* Calgary, AB: University of Calgary Press.

MacKay, A.W. (1984). *Education law in Canada.* Toronto, On: Emond-Montgomery.

MacKay, A.W. (1986). *The Chronicle Herald,* Halifax, February.

MacKay, A.W., &ampersand; Sutherland, L. (1988). Making and enforcing school rules in the wake of the Charter of Rights and Freedoms. In Lam, Y.L.J. (Ed.), *Canadian public education: Issues and prospects.* Calgary, AB: Detselig.

Manley-Casimir, M.E., & Sussel, T.A. (1986). *Courts in the classroom: Education and the Charter of Rights and Freedoms.* Calgary, AB: Detselig.

Proudfoot, A.J., & Hutchings, L. (1988). *Teacher beware: A legal primer for the classroom teacher.* Calgary, AB: Detselig.

Government of Canada. (1982). *The Charter of Rights and Freedoms: A guide for Canadians.* Ottawa, ON: Author.

Snelgrove, V.J., & Warren, P.J. (1989). *Legal rights in education: Educators' knowledge and opinions. A report to the Secretary of State, Ottawa.* St. John's, NF: Memorial University of Newfoundland.

Wood, M.J. (1991). Personal interview.

CASES CITED:

RE M.B. (1984), 65 N.S.R. (2d) 181 (N.S. Fam. Ct.).

Re: Blainey and the Ontario Hockey Association et al. (1986), 54 O.R. (2d) 513, 26 D.L.R. (4th) 728 (C.A.) leave to appeal refused (26 June 1986, S.C.C.).

Tinker v. Des Moines Independent Community School District (1969), 393 U.S. 503.

Ward v. Board of Blaine Lake (1971), 4 W.W.R. 161. (Sask., QB).

Yellow Springs Exempted School District of Education v. Ohio High School Athletic Association 43 F. Supp. 753 (S.D. 1978).

Zylberberg v. Sudbury Board of Education (1988), 52 D.L.R. (4th) 577.

Austin Harte passed away in March 1995. At the time he was Assistant Professor, Faculty of Education, Memorial University of Newfoundland, St. John's, NF, AIB 3X8. Tel.: 709-737-7550. Fax: 709-737-2345.

Kent McDonald is a graduate student at St. Francis Xavier University, Antigonish, Nova Scotia.

20

Canadian Charter of Rights and Freedoms, 1982

Whereas Canada is founded upon principles that recognize the supremacy of God and the rule of law:

Guarantee of Rights and Freedoms

Rights and freedoms in Canada

1. The Canadian Charter of Rights and Freedoms guarantees the rights and freedoms set out in it subject only to such reasonable limits prescribed by law as can be demonstrably justified in a free and democratic society.

Fundamental Freedoms

Fundamental freedoms

2. Everyone has the following fundamental freedoms:
   (a) freedom of conscience and religion;
   (b) freedom of thought, belief, opinion and expression, including freedom of the press and other media of communication;
   (c) freedom of peaceful assembly; and
   (d) freedom of association.

Democratic Rights

Democratic rights of citizens

3. Every citizen of Canada has the right to vote in an election of members of the House of Commons or of a legislative assembly and to be qualified for membership therein.

Maximum duration of legislative bodies

4. (1) No House of Commons and no legislative assembly shall continue for longer than five years from the date fixed for the return of the writs at a general election of its members.

Continuation in special circumstances

(2) In time of real or apprehended war, invasion or insurrection, a House of Commons may be continued by Parliament and a legislative assembly may be continued by the legislative beyond five years if such continuation is not opposed by the votes of more than one-third of the members of the House of Commons or the legislative assembly, as the case may be.

Annual sitting of legislative bodies

5. There shall be a sitting of Parliament and of each legislature at least once every twelve months.

Mobility Rights

Mobility of citizens

6. (1) Every citizen of Canada has the right to enter, remain in and leave Canada.

Rights to move and gain livelihood

(2) Every citizen of Canada and every person who has the status of a permanent resident of Canada has the right
   (a) to move to and take up residence in any province; and
   (b) to pursue the gaining of a livelihood in any province.

Limitation

(3) The rights specified in subsection (2) are subject to
   (a) any laws or practices of general application in force in a province other than those that discriminate among persons primarily on the basis of province of present or previous residence; and
   (b) any laws providing for reasonable residency requirements as a qualification for the receipt of publicly provided social services.

Affirmative action programs

(4) Subsections (2) and (3) do not preclude any law, program or activity that has as its object the amelioration in a province of conditions of individuals in that province who are socially or economically disadvantaged if the rate of employment in that province is below the rate of employment in Canada.

Legal Rights

Life, liberty and security of person

7. Everyone has the right to life, liberty and security of the person and the right not to be deprived thereof except in accordance with the principles of fundamental justice.

Search or seizure

8. Everyone has the right to be secure against unreasonable search or seizure.

Detention or imprisonment

9. Everyone has the right not to be arbitrarily detained or imprisoned.

Arrest or detention

10. Everyone has the right on arrest or detention
   (a) to be informed promptly of the reasons therefor,
   (b) to retain and instruct counsel without delay and to be informed of that right; and
   (c) to have the validity of the detention determined by way of *habeas corpus* and to be released if the detention is not lawful.

Proceedings in criminal and penal matters

11. Any person charged with an offence has the right
   (a) to be informed without unreasonable delay of the specific offence;
   (b) to be tried within a reasonable time;
   (c) not to be compelled to be a witness in proceedings against that person in respect of the offence;
   (d) to be presumed innocent until proven guilty according to law in a fair and public hearing by an independent and impartial tribunal;
   (e) not to be denied reasonable bail without just cause;
   (f) except in the case of an offence under military law tried before a military tribunal, to the benefit of trial by jury where the maximum punishment for the offence is imprisonment for five years or a more severe punishment;
   (g) not to be found guilty on account of any act or omission unless, at the time of the act or omission, it constituted an offence under Canadian or international law or was criminal according to the general principles of law recognized by the community of nations;
   (h) if finally acquitted of the offence, not to be tried for it again and, if finally found guilty and punished for the offence, not to be tried or punished for it again; and

(i) if found guilty of the offence and if the punishment for the offence has been varied between the time of commission and the time of sentencing, to the benefit of the lesser punishment.

Treatment or punishment

12. Everyone has the right not to be subjected to any cruel and unusual treatment or punishment.

Self-crimination

13. A witness who testifies in any proceedings has the right not to have any incriminating evidence so given used to incriminate that witness in any other proceedings, except in a prosecution for perjury or for the giving of contradictory evidence.

Interpreter

14. A party or witness in any proceedings who does not understand or speak the language in which the proceedings are conducted or who is deaf has the right to the assistance of an interpreter.

Equality Rights

Equality before and under law and equal protection and benefit of law

15. (1) Every individual is equal before and under the law and has the right to the equal protection and equal benefit of the law without discrimination and, in particular, without discrimination based on race, national or ethnic origin, colour, religion, sex, age or mental or physical disability.

(2) Subsection (1) does not preclude any law, program or activity that has as its object the amelioration of conditions of disadvantaged individuals or groups including those that are disadvantaged because of race, national or ethnic origin, colour, religion, sex, age or mental or physical disability.

Official Languages of Canada

Official languages of Canada

16. (1) English and French are the official languages of Canada and have equality of status and equal rights and privileges as to their use in all institutions of the Parliament and government of Canada.

Official languages of New Brunswick

(2) English and French are the official languages of New Brunswick and have equality of status and equal rights and privileges as to their use in all institutions of the legislature and government of New Brunswick.

Advancement of status and use

(3) Nothing in this Charter limits the authority of Parliament or a legislature to advance the equality of status or use of English and French.

Proceedings of Parliament

17. (1) Everyone has the right to use English or French in any debates and other proceedings of Parliament.

Proceedings of New Brunswick legislature

(2) Everyone has the right to use English or French in any debates and other proceedings of the legislature of New Brunswick.

Parliamentary statutes and records

18. (1) The statutes, records and journals of Parliament shall be printed and published in English and French and both language versions are equally authoritative.

New Brunswick statutes and records

(2) The statutes, records and journals of the legislature of New Brunswick shall be printed and published in English and French and both language versions are equally authoritative.

Proceedings in courts established by Parliament

19. (1) Either English or French may be used by any person in, or in any pleading in or process issuing from, any court established by Parliament.

Proceedings in New Brunswick courts

(2) Either English or French may be used by any person in, or in any pleading in or process issuing from, any court of New Brunswick.

Communications by public with federal institutions

20. (1) Any member of the public in Canada has the right to communicate with, and to receive available services from, any head or central office of an institution of the Parliament or government of Canada in English or French, and has the same right with respect to any other office of any such institution where

(a) there is a significant demand for communications with and services from that office in such language; or

Communications by public
with New Brunswick
institutions

(b) due to the nature of the office, it is reasonable that communications with and services from that office be available in both English and French.

(2) Any member of the public in New Brunswick has the right to communicate with, and to receive available services from, any office of an institution of the legislature or government of New Brunswick in English or French.

Continuation of existing
constitutional provisions

21. Nothing in sections 16 to 20 abrogates or derogates from any right, privilege or obligation with respect to the English and French languages, or either of them, that exists or is continued by virtue of any other provision of the Constitution of Canada.

Rights and privileges
preserved

22. Nothing in sections 16 to 20 abrogates or derogates from any legal or customary right or privilege acquired or enjoyed either before or after the coming into force of this Charter with respect to any language that is not English or French.

Minority Language Educational Rights

Language of instruction

23. (1) Citizens of Canada
(a) whose first language learned and still understood is that of the English or French linguistic minority population of the province in which they reside, or
(b) who have received their primary school instruction in Canada in English or French and reside in a province where the language in which they received that instruction is the language of the English or French linguistic minority population of the province, have the right to have their children receive primary and secondary school instruction in that language in that province.

Continuity of language
instruction

(2) Citizens of Canada of whom any child has received or is receiving primary or secondary school instruction in English or French in Canada, have the right to have all their children receive primary and secondary school instruction in the same language.

Application where
numbers warrant

(3) The right of citizens of Canada under subsections (1) and (2) to have their children receive primary and secondary school instruction in the language of the English or French linguistic minority population of a province
(a) applies wherever in the province the number of children of citizens who have such a right is sufficient to warrant the provision to them out of public funds of minority language instruction; and
(b) includes, where the number of those children so warrants, the right to have them receive that instruction in minority language educational facilities provided out of public funds.

Enforcement

Enforcement of guaranteed
rights and freedoms

24. (1) Anyone whose rights or freedoms, as guaranteed by this Charter, have been infringed or denied may apply to a court of competent jurisdiction to obtain such remedy as the court considers appropriate and just in the circumstances.

Exclusion of evidence
bringing administration
of justice into disrepute

(2) Where, in proceedings under subsection (1), a court concludes that evidence was obtained in a manner that infringed or denied any rights or freedoms guaranteed by this Charter, the evidence shall be excluded if it is established that, having regard to all the circumstances, the admission of it in the proceedings would bring the administration of justice into disrepute.

General

Aboriginal rights and freedoms not affected by Charter

25. The guarantee in this Charter of certain rights and freedoms shall not be construed so as to abrogate or derogate from any aboriginal, treaty or other rights or freedoms that pertain to the aboriginal peoples of Canada including

(a) any rights or freedoms that have been recognized by the Royal Proclamation of October 7, 1763; and

(b) any rights or freedoms that may be acquired by the aboriginal peoples of Canada by way of land claims settlement.

Other rights and freedoms not affected by Charter

26. The guarantee in this Charter of certain rights and freedoms shall not be construed as denying the existence of any other rights or freedoms that exist in Canada.

Multicultural heritage

27. This Charter shall be interpreted in a manner consistent with the preservation and enhancement of the multicultural heritage of Canadians.

Rights guaranteed equally to both sexes

28. Notwithstanding anything in this Charter, the rights and freedoms referred to in it are guaranteed equally to male and female persons.

Rights respecting certain schools preserved

29. Nothing in this Charter abrogates or derogates from any rights or privileges guaranteed by or under the Constitution of Canada in respect of denominational, separate or dissentient schools.

Application to territories and territorial authorities

30. A reference in this Charter to a province or to the legislative assembly or legislature of a province shall be deemed to include a reference to the Yukon Territory and the Northwest Territories, or to the appropriate legislative authority thereof, as the case may be.

Legislative powers and extended

31. Nothing in this Charter extends the legislative powers of any body or authority.

Application of Charter

Application of Charter

32. (1) This Charter applies

(a) to the Parliament and government of Canada in respect of all matters within the authority of Parliament including all matters relating to the Yukon Territory and Northwest Territories; and

(b) to the legislature and government of each province in respect of all matters within the authority of the legislature of each province.

Exception

(2) Notwithstanding subsection (1), section 15 shall not have effect until three years after this section comes into force.

Exception where express declaration

33. (1) Parliament or the legislature of a province may expressly declare in an Act of Parliament or of the legislature, as the case may be, that the Act or a provision thereof shall operate notwithstanding a provision included in section 2 or sections 7 to 15 of this Charter.

Operation of exception

(2) An Act or a provision of an Act in respect of which a declaration made under this section is in effect shall have such operation as it would have but for the provision of this Charter referred to in the declaration.

Five-year limitation

(3) A declaration made under subsection (1) shall cease to have effect five years after it comes into force or on such earlier date as may be specified in the declaration.

Re-enactment

(4) Parliament or a legislature of a province may re-enact a declaration made under subsection (1).

Five-year limitation

(5) Subsection (3) applies in respect of a re-enactment made under subsection (4).

Citation

Citation

34. This Part may be cited as the Canadian Charter of Rights and Freedoms.

21

School Attendance

18. Definition — In sections 21, 23, 26, 28 and 30, "guardian", in addition to having the meaning ascribed in section 1, includes any person who has received into his or her home a child of compulsory school age who is not the person's child but resides with the person or is in his or her care.

19. (1) **Closing of school or class by board** — A board may close or authorize the closing of a school or class for a temporary period where such closing appears unavoidable because of,

(a) failure of transportation arrangements; or

(b) inclement weather, fire, flood, the breakdown of the school heating plant, the failure of an essential utility or a similar emergency.

(2) **Same** — In case of strike by members of a teachers' bargaining unit or a lockout of those members, the board may close one or more schools if it is of the opinion that,

(a) the safety of pupils may be endangered during the strike or lockout;

(b) the school building or the equipment or supplies in the building may not be adequately protected during the strike or lockout; or

(c) the strike or lockout will substantially interfere with the operation of the school.

(3) **Teachers' salary** — A teacher is not entitled to be paid his or her salary for the days on which the school in which he or she is employed is closed under subsection (2).

(4) **Definition** — In this section,

"strike" and "lock-out" have the same meaning as in the *Labour Relations Act, 1995.* [S.O. 1997, c. 31, s. 10]

20. Closing of schools on civic holiday — Where the head of the council of a municipality in which a school is situated proclaims a school day as a civic holiday for the municipality, the board may, by resolution, close any of the schools under its jurisdiction on such day.

21. (1) **Compulsory attendance** — Unless excused under this section,

(a) every child who attains the age of six years on or before the first school day in September in any year shall attend an elementary or secondary school on every school day from the first school day in September in that year until the child attains the age of sixteen years; and

(b) every child who attains the age of six years after the first school day in September in any year shall attend an elementary or secondary school on every school day from the first school day in September in the next succeeding year until the last school day in June in the year in which the child attains the age of sixteen years.

(2) **When attendance excused** — A child is excused from attendance at school if,

(a) the child is receiving satisfactory instruction at home or elsewhere;

(b) the child is unable to attend school by reason of sickness or other unavoidable cause;

(c) transportation is not provided by a board for the child and there is no school that the child has a right to attend situated,

    (i) within 1.6 kilometres from the child's residence measured by the nearest road if the child has not attained the age of seven years on or before the first school day in September in the year in question, or

    (ii) within 3.2 kilometres from the child's residence measured by the nearest road if the child has attained the age of seven years but not the age of ten years on or before the first school day in September in the year in question, or

    (iii) within 4.8 kilometres from the child's residence measured by the nearest road if the child has attained the age of ten years on or before the first school day in September in the year in question;

(d) the child has obtained a secondary school graduation diploma or has completed a course that gives equivalent standing;

(e) the child is absent from school for the purpose of receiving instruction in music and the period of absence does not exceed one-half day in any week;

(f) the child is suspended, expelled or excluded from attendance at school under any Act or under the regulations;

(g) the child is absent on a day regarded as a holy day by the church or religious denomination to which the child belongs; or

(h) the child is absent or excused as authorized under this Act and the regulations.

(3) **Blind, deaf or mentally handicapped children** — The fact that a child is blind, deaf or mentally handicapped is not of itself an unavoidable cause under clause (2) (b).

(4) **Child under compulsory age** — Where a child under compulsory school age has been enrolled as a pupil in an elementary school, this section applies during the period for which the child is enrolled as if the child were of compulsory school age.

(5) **Duty of parent, etc.** — The parent or guardian of a child who is required to attend school under this section shall cause the child to attend school as required by this section.

22

Opening or Closing Exercises

(O. Reg. 435/00)

Application

1. The requirements set out in this Regulation apply with respect to the opening and closing exercises referred to in section 304 of the Act.

Pledge of Citizenship

2. (1) The principal may decide whether the opening or closing exercises at a school will include the recitation of the pledge of citizenship.

(2) The principal's decision about reciting the pledge of citizenship must be consistent with the policies and guidelines, if any, established by the board.

(3) Before making his or her decision about reciting the pledge of citizenship, the principal shall consult the school council.

(4) The principal shall review his or her decision about reciting the pledge of citizenship at the beginning of each school year and must consult with the school council.

3. The following is the pledge of citizenship:

> *I affirm that I will be faithful and bear true allegiance to Her Majesty Queen Elizabeth the Second, Queen of Canada, and to her heirs and successors, and that I will faithfully observe the laws of Canada and fulfill my duties as a Canadian citizen.*

Exemptions

4. A pupil is not required to sing *O Canada* or recite the pledge of citizenship in the following circumstances:
1. In the case of a pupil who is less than 18 years old, if the pupil's parent or guardian applies to the principal to be exempted from doing so.
2. In the case of a pupil who is at least 18 years old, if the pupil applies to the principal to be exempted from doing so.

Operation of Schools—General

(R.R.O. 1990, Reg. 298)

Amendments: O. Reg. 242/92; 95/96; 425/98; 436/00; 613/00; 492/01; 209/03; 191/04; 132/05.

1. In this Regulation,

"business studies" means the courses prescribed or developed under subsection 8 (1) of the Act and described in,

    (a) the document entitled "Business Studies - The Ontario Curriculum, Grades 9 and 10 - 1999", available on the Ministry of Education web site at www.edu .gov.on.ca, and

    (b) the document entitled "Business Studies - The Ontario Curriculum, Grades 11 and 12 - 2000", available on the Ministry of Education web site at www.edu .gov.on.ca;

"certificate of qualification" means a certificate of qualification granted under Ontario Regulation 184/97 made under the *Ontario College of Teachers Act, 1996*;

"division" means the primary division, the junior division, the intermediate division or the senior division;

"French as a second language" includes programs for English speaking pupils in which French is the language of instruction;

"general studies" means the courses prescribed or developed for the intermediate and senior divisions under subsection 8 (1) of the Act and described in the secondary curriculum documents available on the Ministry of Education web site at www.edu.gov.on.ca, excluding the courses described in,

    (a) the document entitled "Technological Education - The Ontario Curriculum, Grades 9 and 10 - 1999", other than the sections relating to Computer and Information Science, Grade 10, Open and Computer Engineering Technology, Grade 10, Open, and

    (b) the document entitled "Technological Education - The Ontario Curriculum, Grades 11 and 12 - 2000", other than Part B: Computer Studies;

"OSIS" [Repealed, O. Reg. 191/04, s. 1]

"parent" includes guardian;

"technological studies" means the courses prescribed or developed under subsection 8 (1) of the Act and described in,

    (a) the document entitled "Technological Education - The Ontario Curriculum, Grades 9 and 10 - 1999", other than the sections relating to Computer and Information Science, Grade 10, Open and Computer Engineering Technology, Grade 10, Open, available on the Ministry of Education web site at www.edu.gov.on.ca, and

    (b) the document entitled "Technological Education - The Ontario Curriculum, Grades 11 and 12 - 2000", other than Part B: Computer Studies, available on the Ministry of Education web site at www.edu.gov.on.ca.

[O. Reg. 191/04, s. 1]

Accommodation

2. (1) A board shall file with the Ministry plans for the erection of, addition to, or alteration of a school building together with details of the site thereof.

(2) It is a condition of the payment of a legislative grant in respect of capital cost that the plans and details referred to in subsection (1) be approved by the Minister.

Daily Sessions

3. (1) The length of the instructional program of each school day for pupils of compulsory school age shall be not less than five hours a day excluding recesses or scheduled intervals between classes.

(2) The instructional program on a school day shall begin not earlier than 8 a.m. and end not later than 5 p.m. except with the approval of the Minister.

(3) Despite subsection (1), a board may reduce the length of the instructional program on each school day to less than five hours a day for an exceptional pupil in a special education program.

(4) Every board may establish the length of the instructional program on each school day for pupils in junior kindergarten and kindergarten.

(5) Each pupil and each teacher shall have a scheduled interval for a lunch break.

(5.1) A pupil's interval for a lunch break shall be not less than forty consecutive minutes and need not coincide with the scheduled interval for the lunch break of any other pupil or any teacher.

(5.2) A teacher's interval for a lunch break shall be not less than forty consecutive minutes and need not coincide with the scheduled interval for the lunch break of any other teacher or any pupil.

(6) In the intermediate division and the senior division, a principal may, subject to the approval of the board, provide for recesses or intervals for pupils between periods.

(7) Every board shall determine the period of time during each school day when its school buildings and playgrounds shall be open to its pupils, but in every case the buildings and the playgrounds shall be open to pupils during the period beginning fifteen minutes before classes begin for the day and ending fifteen minutes after classes end for the day.

(8) There shall be a morning recess and an afternoon recess, each of which shall be not less than ten minutes and not more than fifteen minutes in length, for pupils in the primary and junior divisions.
[O.Reg. 492/01, s. 1]

Opening or Closing Exercises

4. (1) This section applies with respect to opening and closing exercises in public elementary schools and in public secondary schools.

(2) The opening or closing exercises may include the singing of *God Save The Queen* and may also include the following types of readings that impart social, moral or spiritual values and that are representative of Ontario's multicultural society:

1. Scriptural writings including prayers.
2. Secular writings.

(3) The opening or closing exercises may include a period of silence.

(4) In the following circumstances, a pupil is not required to participate in the opening or closing exercises described in this section:

1. In the case of a pupil who is less than 18 years old, if the pupil's parent or guardian applies to the principal of the school for an exemption from the exercises.
2. In the case of a pupil who is at least 18 years old, if the pupil applies to the principal for an exemption from the exercises.

[O. Reg. 436/00, s. 1]

Flag

5. (1) Every school shall fly both the National Flag of Canada and the Provincial Flag of Ontario on such occasions as the board directs.

(2) Every school shall display in the school the National Flag of Canada and the Provincial Flag of Ontario.

Emergency Procedures

6. (1) In addition to the drills established under the fire safety plan required under Regulation 454 of Revised Regulations of Ontario, 1990 (Fire Code), every board may provide for the holding of drills in respect of emergencies other than those occasioned by fire.

(2) Every principal, including the principal of an evening class or classes or of a class or classes conducted outside the school year, shall hold at least one emergency drill in the period during which the instruction is given.

(3) When a fire or emergency drill is held in a school building, every person in the building shall take part in the fire or emergency drill.

Textbooks

7. (1) The principal of a school, in consultation with the teachers concerned, shall select from the list of the textbooks approved by the Minister the textbooks for the use of pupils of the school, and the selection shall be subject to the approval of the board.

(2) Where no textbook for a course of study is included in the list of the textbooks approved by the Minister the principal of a school, in consultation with the teachers concerned, shall, where they consider a textbook to be required, select a suitable textbook and, subject to the approval of the board, such textbook may be introduced for use in the school.

(3) In the selection of textbooks under subsection (2), preference shall be given to books that which been written by Canadian authors and edited, printed and bound in Canada.

(4) Every board shall provide without charge for the use of each pupil enrolled in a day school operated by the board such textbooks selected under subsections (1) and (2) as relate to the courses in which the pupil is enrolled.

Elementary School Boards

8. (1) Where the area of jurisdiction of a district school area board, a Roman Catholic school authority, or a Protestant separate school board is not within a secondary school district, the board shall provide instruction that would enable its resident pupils to obtain sixteen credits towards a secondary school graduation diploma or an Ontario secondary school diploma.

(2) A board referred to in subsection (1) that offers courses of instruction during July or August or both in any year may provide instruction that would enable its resident pupils to obtain two credits in addition to the sixteen credits referred to in subsection (1).

(3) Where a board referred to in subsection (1) provides,

(a) daily transportation for its resident pupils; or

(b) reimbursement for board and lodging and for transportation once a week to and from the places of residence of its resident pupils, that it considers necessary to enable its resident pupils to attend a school operated by another board, the other board may provide such instruction as would enable such resident pupils to obtain the number of credits referred to in subsections (1) and (2).

(4) A Roman Catholic school authority, or a Protestant separate school board that has jurisdiction in a secondary school district may provide instruction for its resident pupils that would enable the pupils to obtain up to eighteen credits towards a secondary school graduation diploma or an Ontario secondary school diploma.

[O. Reg. 191/04, s. 2]

Qualifications for Principals and Vice-Principals

9. (1) The principal and vice-principal of a school having an enrolment greater than 125 shall each be a teacher who,

    (a) holds or is deemed to hold, under Ontario Regulation 184/97, made under the *Ontario College of Teachers Act, 1996,* principal's qualifications; or

    (b) holds a principal's certificate that is a qualification to be principal or vice-principal, as the case may be, in the type of school identified on the certificate, or is deemed under 50 of Ontario Regulation 184/97 made under the *Ontario College of Teachers Act, 1996* to hold such a certificate,

and, in the case of a school,

    (c) in which English is the language of instruction; or

    (d) that is established under Part XII of the Act and in which French is the language of instruction,

shall each be a person who is eligible to teach in such school under subsection 19 (11), (12) or (13), as the case may be.

(2) Despite subsection (1), where a teacher who does not hold the degree of Bachelor of Arts or Bachelor of Science from an Ontario university or a degree that the Minister considers equivalent thereto was, prior to the 1st day of September, 1961, employed by a board as principal or vice-principal of an elementary school that had an enrolment of 300 or more pupils, the teacher shall be deemed to be qualified as principal or vice-principal, as the case may be, of any elementary school operated by that board or its successor board.

(3) Despite subsection (1), where a teacher who does not hold the qualifications referred to in subsection (1),

    (a) was employed by a board prior to the 1st day of September, 1972 as principal of an elementary school that had an enrolment of 300 or more pupils and is employed by such board as principal of an elementary school on the 8th day of September, 1978;

    (b) was employed by a board on the 1st day of September, 1978 as vice-principal of an elementary school that had an enrolment on the last school day in April, 1978 of 300 or more pupils; or

    (c) was employed by a board on the 1st day of September, 1978 as principal or vice-principal of an elementary school that had an enrolment on the last school day in April, 1978 that was greater than 125 and less than 300,

such teacher shall be deemed to be qualified as principal or vice-principal, as the case may be, of any elementary school operated by that board or its successor board.

(4) A board may appoint a person who holds the qualifications required by subsection (1) as a supervising principal to supervise the administration of two or more elementary schools operated by the board and such person shall be subject to the authority of the appropriate supervisory officer.

(5) A supervising principal may be principal of only one school.

(6) Despite subsection (1), a teacher who, before the 1st day of September, 1970, held the necessary qualifications as principal of a secondary school continues to be qualified as principal or vice-principal of a secondary school.

[O. Reg. 191/04, s. 3]

10. [Repeated, O. Reg. 191/04, s. 4]

Duties of Principals

11. (1) The principal of a school, subject to the authority of the appropriate supervisory officer, is in charge of,

(a) the instruction and the discipline of pupils in the school; and

(b) the organization and management of the school.

(2) Where two or more schools operated by a board jointly occupy or use in common a school building or school grounds, the board shall designate which principal has authority over those parts of the building or grounds that the schools occupy or use in common.

(3) In addition to the duties under the Act and those assigned by the board, the principal of a school shall, except where the principal has arranged otherwise under subsection 26 (3),

(a) supervise the instruction in the school and advise and assist any teacher in cooperation with the teacher in charge of an organizational unit or program;

(b) assign duties to vice-principals and to teachers in charge of organizational units or programs;

(c) retain on file up-to-date copies of outlines of all courses of study that are taught in the school;

(d) upon request, make outlines of courses of study available for examination to a resident pupil of the board and to the parent of the pupil, where the pupil is a minor;

(e) provide for the supervision of pupils during the period of time during each school day when the school buildings and playgrounds are open to pupils;

(f) provide for the supervision of and the conducting of any school activity authorized by the board;

(g) where performance appraisals of members of the teaching staff are required under a collective agreement or a policy of the board, despite anything to the contrary in such collective agreement or board policy, conduct performance appraisals of members of the teaching staff;

(h) subject to the provisions of the policy of the board or the provisions of a collective agreement, as the case may be, in respect of reporting requirements for performance appraisals, report thereon in writing to the board or to the supervisory officer on request and give to each teacher so appraised a copy of the performance appraisal of the teacher;

(i) where the performance appraisals of members of the teaching staff are not required by board policy or under a collective agreement, report to the board or to the supervisory officer in writing on request on the effectiveness of members of the teaching staff and give to a teacher referred to in any such report a copy of the portion of the report that refers to the teacher;

(j) make recommendations to the board with respect to,

(i) the appointment and promotion of teachers, and

(ii) the demotion or dismissal of teachers whose work or attitude is unsatisfactory;

(k) provide for instruction of pupils in the care of the school premises;

(l) inspect the school premises at least weekly and report forthwith to the board,

(i) any repairs to the school that are required, in the opinion of the principal,

    (ii) any lack of attention on the part of the building maintenance staff of the school, and

    (iii) where a parent of a pupil has been requested to compensate the board for damage to or destruction, loss or misappropriation of school property by the pupil and the parent has not done so, that the parent of the pupil has not compensated the board;

(m) where it is proposed to administer a test of intelligence or personality to a pupil, inform the pupil and the parent of the pupil of the test and obtain the prior written permission for the test from the pupil or from the parent of the pupil, where the pupil is a minor;

(n) report promptly any neglect of duty or infraction of the school rules by a pupil to the parent or guardian of the pupil;

(o) promote and maintain close co-operation with residents, industry, business and other groups and agencies of the community;

(p) provide to the Minister or to a person designated by the Minister any information that may be required concerning the instructional program, operation or administration of the school and inform the appropriate supervisory officer of the request;

(q) assign suitable quarters for pupils to eat lunch.

(4) A principal shall only make a recommendation to the board under subclause (3)(j)(ii) after warning the teacher in writing, giving the teacher assistance and allowing the teacher a reasonable time to improve.

(5) A principal of a school,

(a) in which there is a French-language instructional unit as defined in subsection 1(1) of the Act, who does not hold qualifications to teach in the French language as required by subsection 19 (12) or is qualified to teach in such unit only under subsection 19 (13); or

(b) in which pupils receive instruction in the English language under subsection 290(5) or 291(4) of the Act, who does not hold qualifications to teach in the English language as required by subsection 19 (11) or is qualified to teach in each unit only under subsection 19 (13),

shall notify the appropriate supervisory officer in writing of the impracticability of the duty placed on the principal, having regard to the qualifications of the principal, to supervise the instruction, to conduct performance appraisals and to assist and advise the teachers referred to in the notice.

(6) Where arrangements are made under subsection 26 (3), the principal is relieved from compliance with clauses (3) (a), (g), (h) and (i) to the extent that such duties are performed by another qualified person or persons.

(7) The other qualified person or persons who perform the duties shall be responsible to the board for the performance of such duties.

(8) The outlines of the courses of study mentioned in clause (3) (c) shall be written and provided,

(a) in the French language in the case of courses of study provided in a French-language instructional unit operated under Part XII of the Act; and

(b) in both the English and French languages in the case of a course of study in a program established in the school under paragraph 25 of subsection 8 (1) of the Act.

(9) Where, after reasonable notice by the principal, a pupil who is an adult, or the parent of a pupil who is a minor, fails to provide the supplies required by the pupil for a course of study, the principal shall promptly notify the board.

(10) A principal shall transmit reports and recommendations to the board through the appropriate supervisory officer.

(11) A principal, subject to the approval of the appropriate supervisory officer, may arrange for home instruction to be provided for a pupil where,

(a) medical evidence that the pupil cannot attend school is provided to the principal; and

(b) the principal is satisfied that home instruction is required.

(12) The principal of a school shall provide for the prompt distribution to each member of the school council of any materials received by the principal from the Ministry that are identified by the Ministry as being for distribution to the members of school councils.

(12.1) The principal shall post any materials distributed to members of the school council under subsection (12) in the school in a location that is accessible to parents.

(13) In each school year, the principal of a school shall make the names of the members of the school council known to the parents of the pupils enrolled in the school, by publishing those names in a school newsletter or by such other means as is likely to bring the names to the attention of the parents.

(14) The principal shall meet the requirements of subsection (13) in each school year not later than 30 days following the election of parent members of the school council.

(15) The principal of a school shall promptly provide the names of the members of the school council to a supporter of the board that governs the school or to a parent of a pupil enrolled in the school, on the request of the supporter or the parent.

(16) The principal of a school shall attend every meeting of the school council, unless he or she is unable to do so by reason of illness or other cause beyond his or her control.

(17) The principal of a school shall act as a resource person to the school council and shall assist the council in obtaining information relevant to the functions of the council, including information relating to relevant legislation, regulations and policies.

(18) The principal of a school shall consider each recommendation made to the principal by the school council and shall advise the council of the action taken in response to the recommendation.

(19) In addition to his or her other obligations to solicit the views of the school council under the Act and the regulations, the principal of a school shall solicit the views of the school council with respect to the following matters:

1. The establishment or amendment of school policies and guidelines that relate to pupil achievement or to the accountability of the education system to parents, including,

   i. a local code of conduct established under subsection 303 (1) or (2) of the Act governing the behaviour of all persons in the school, and

   ii. school policies or guidelines related to policies and guidelines established by the board under subsection 302 (5) of the Act respecting appropriate dress for pupils in schools within the board's jurisdiction.

2. The development of implementation plans for new education initiatives that relate to pupil achievement or to the accountability of the education system to parents, including,

   i. implementation plans for a local code of conduct established under subsection 303 (1) or (2) of the Act governing the behaviour of all persons in the school, and

   ii. implementation plans for school policies or guidelines related to policies and guidelines established by the board under subsection 302 (5) of the Act respecting appropriate dress for pupils in schools within the board's jurisdiction.

3. School action plans for improvement, based on the Education Quality and Accountability Office's reports on the results of tests of pupils, and the communication of those plans to the public.

(20) Subsection (19) does not limit the matters on which the principal of a school may solicit the views of the school council.

[O. Reg. 425/98, s. 1; 613/00, s. 1; 191/04, s. 5]

Vice-Principals

12. (1) A board may appoint one or more vice-principals for a school.

(2) A vice-principal shall perform such duties as are assigned to the vice-principal by the principal.

(3) In the absence of the principal of a school, a vice-principal, where a vice-principal has been appointed for the school, shall be in charge of the school and shall perform the duties of the principal.

Principals, Vice-Principals and Teachers in Charge of Schools and Classes Established Under Part XII of the Act

13. (1) Where, under section 290 of the Act, more than two classes where French is the language of instruction are established in an elementary school that is not a French-language elementary school, the board that operates the school shall appoint one of the teachers of such classes or a teacher who holds the qualifications required to teach such classes to be responsible to the principal for the program of education in such classes.

(2) Where the enrolment in classes established under section 291 of the Act in a secondary school that is not a French-language secondary school is more than seventy-five but not more than 200 pupils, the board that operates the school shall appoint one of the teachers of such classes or a teacher who holds the qualifications required to teach such classes to be responsible to the principal for the program of education in such classes.

(3) Where, in a secondary school, the enrolment in the classes referred to in subsection (2) is more than 200 pupils, the board shall appoint for such school a vice-principal who is qualified to teach in such classes and who shall be responsible to the principal for the program of education in such classes.

(4) Despite subsections (1), (2) and (3), where a teacher who does not hold the qualifications referred to in such subsections was, on the 8th day of September, 1978, employed by the board as a teacher or vice-principal, as the case may be, to carry out the responsibility referred to in such subsections, the teacher shall be deemed to be qualified for such position in any elementary or secondary school, as the case may be, operated by that board or its successor board.

(5) Subsections (1) to (4) apply with necessary modifications to schools or classes for English-speaking pupils established under sections 290 and 291 of the Act.

[O. Reg. 191/04, s. 6]

Teachers in Charge of Organizational Units

14. (1) The organization of a secondary school may be by departments or other organizational units.

(2) The organization of an elementary school may be by divisions or other organizational units.

(3) A board may appoint for each organizational unit of an elementary or secondary school a teacher to direct and supervise, subject to the authority of the principal of the school, such organizational unit.

(4) A teacher appointed under subsection (3) may be appointed to direct and supervise more than one organizational unit.
[O. Reg. 95/96, s. 1]

15. [Repealed, O. Reg. 95/96, s. 1]

16. [Repealed, O. Reg. 95/96, s. 1]

Subject and Program Supervision and Co-ordination

17. (1) A board may, in respect of one or more subjects or programs in the schools under its jurisdiction, appoint a teacher to supervise or co-ordinate the subjects or programs or to act as a consultant for the teachers of the subjects or programs.

(2) A teacher appointed under subsection (1) shall hold specialist or honour specialist qualifications, if such are available, in one or more of the subjects or programs in respect of which the teacher is appointed.

(3) Despite subsection (1), a teacher who, on the 8th day of September, 1978, was employed by a board to supervise or co-ordinate a subject or program in its schools or to act as a consultant shall be deemed to be qualified for such position in the schools operated by that board or its successor board.

18. (1) Subject to the authority of the appropriate supervisory officer, a teacher appointed in a subject or program under section 17 shall assist teachers in that subject or program in maintaining proper standards and improving methods of instruction.

(2) A teacher appointed under section 17 in performing duties in a school is subject to the authority of the principal of that school.

Qualifications of Teachers

19. (1) Subject to subsection (3), no person shall be a teacher in a school unless he or she,

(a) holds or is deemed to hold a certificate of qualification of any kind or class provided for in Ontario Regulation 184/97 made under the *Ontario College of Teachers Act, 1996;* and

(b) subject to subsections (4), (5), (11) and (12), is assigned or appointed to teach according to a qualification recorded on the certificate of qualification.

(2) [Repealed, O. Reg. 132/05, s. 1]

(3) A person who does not have any of the qualifications referred to in subsection (2) but who holds a letter of eligibility referred to in section 14 of Ontario Regulation 184/97 made under the *Ontario College of Teachers Act, 1996* may be employed by a board as an occasional teacher,

(a) in classes where English is the language of instruction if the letter of eligibility is in Form 5 of Regulation 297 of the Revised Regulations of Ontario, 1990 as that regulation read immediately before it was revoked; or

(b) in classes where French is the language of instruction if the letter of eligibility is in Form 5a of Regulation 297 of the Revised Regulations of Ontario, 1990 as that regulation read immediately before it was revoked.

(4) Subject to subsections (6), (11), (12), (14) and (15), and with due regard for the safety and welfare of the pupils and the provision of the best possible program, a teacher whose certificate of qualification, indicates qualification in the primary division, the junior division, the intermediate division in general studies or the senior division in general studies may, by mutual agreement of the teacher and the principal of a school and with the approval of the appropriate supervisory officer, be assigned or appointed to teach in a division or a subject in general studies for which no qualification is recorded on the teacher's certificate of qualification.

(5) Subject to subsections (11), (12) and (15), and with due regard for the safety and welfare of the pupils and the provision of the best possible program, a teacher whose certificate of qualification, has entries indicating qualifications in technological studies may by mutual agreement of the teacher and the principal of a school, with the approval of the appropriate supervisory officer, be assigned or appointed to teach a subject in technological studies for which no qualification is recorded on the certificate of qualification.

(6) Subject to subsections (7), (8), (9) and (10), a teacher who does not hold an acceptable post-secondary degree as defined in subsection 1(1) of Ontario Regulation 184/97 made under the *Ontario College of Teachers Act, 1996* shall not be assigned or appointed to teach general studies in a secondary school, except that where the teacher is qualified to teach in the primary division, the junior division and the intermediate division of an elementary school and,

(a) on the 30th day of June, 1981 was teaching in a secondary school; or

(b) on or before the 2nd day of October, 1981 was assigned or appointed to teach general studies in a secondary school, and on the 30th day of June, 1982 was teaching in a secondary school,

the teacher may be assigned or appointed to teach general studies to pupils enrolled in a modified or basic level course by that board or its successor board.

(7) Despite subsection (1), a teacher who holds,

(a) a commercial-vocational qualification; or

(b) technological studies qualifications in any one or more of clerical practice, merchandising or warehousing,

may be assigned or appointed to teach the courses in business studies equivalent to the courses in business studies shown on the teacher's certificate of qualification.

(8) A teacher who holds qualifications in technological studies in sewing and dressmaking, or textiles and clothing, or home economics may be assigned or appointed to teach in a secondary school the clothing portion of the family studies course.

(9) A teacher who holds qualifications in technological studies in food and nutrition or home economics may be assigned or appointed to teach in a secondary school the food and nutrition portion of the family studies course.

(10) A teacher who holds qualifications in technological studies in vocational art, instrumental music or vocal music may be assigned or appointed to teach art, instrumental music or vocal music, as the case may be, in general studies in a secondary school.

(11) A teacher who has not received basic teacher education in the English language or who is not otherwise qualified under the regulations for such assignment or appointment shall not be assigned or appointed to teach in classes where English is the language of instruction.

(12) A teacher who has not received basic teacher education in the French language or who is not otherwise qualified under the regulations for such assignment or appointment shall not be assigned or appointed to teach in schools or classes established under Part XII of the Act where French is the language of instruction.

(13) Despite subsections (11) and (12), a teacher who holds qualifications to teach in the intermediate division and the senior division may be assigned or appointed to teach in either or both of such divisions in classes where English or French is the language of instruction.

(14) No teacher shall,

(a) be assigned, or appointed to teach, in any of grades 9, 10, 11 and 12 in any one school year for more than the time required for two courses that are recognized for credit in art, business studies, guidance including counselling, family studies, instrumental music, vocal music or physical education; or

(b) be placed in charge of,

    (i) a school library program,

    (ii) a guidance program, or

    (iii) special education; or

(c) be assigned or appointed to teach,

    (i) French as a second language,

    (ii) English as a second language,

    (iii) design and technology,

    (iv) subject to subsections (5) and (15), technological studies,

    (v) in a special education class,

    (vi) in a class for deaf, hard of hearing, blind or limited vision pupils, or

    (vii) as a resource or withdrawal teacher in special education programs,

unless,

(d) the teacher's certificate of qualification indicates qualifications in the subject or program to which the teacher is to be assigned or appointed or placed in charge; or

(e) the teacher is qualified for such assignment, appointment or placement under subsection (2) or (16) or deemed to be qualified therefor under subsection (17).

(15) On or after the 1st day of September, 1982, no teacher shall be assigned or appointed to teach courses in the senior division in technological studies at the General or Advanced levels unless the teacher's certificate of qualification indicates advanced level qualifications in the area of technological studies to which the teacher is to be assigned or appointed.

(16) [Repealed, O. Reg. 191/04, s. 7].

(17) A teacher who, on the 8th day of September, 1978, was employed by a board to teach,

(a) French as a second language or English as a second language in an elementary school or a secondary school; or

(b) industrial arts in an elementary school,

and is not qualified for such position under subsection (14), shall be deemed to be qualified for such position in the elementary schools or the secondary schools, as the case may be, that are operated by that board or its successor board.

(18) Where a teacher's certificate of qualification has entries indicating qualifications both in technological studies and in guidance, the teacher may be assigned or appointed to teach guidance and counselling in general studies in a secondary school.

(19) The provision of subsection (14) that no teacher shall be assigned or appointed to teach in a special education class or program unless the teacher holds qualifications in special education does not apply to the teaching of classes in general studies or technological studies in what was formerly designated a special vocational or occupational program until the 1st day of September, 1985.

(20) A teacher may be assigned or appointed to teach those courses that are equivalent to those courses that appear on the teacher's certificate of qualification.

[O. Reg. 242/92, s. 1; 191/04, s. 7, 132/05, s. 1]

Duties of Teachers

20. In addition to the duties assigned to the teacher under the Act and by the board, a teacher shall,

    (a) be responsible for effective instruction, training and evaluation of the progress of pupils in the subjects assigned to the teacher and for the management of the class or classes, and report to the principal on the progress of pupils on request;

    (b) carry out the supervisory duties and instructional program assigned to the teacher by the principal and supply such information related thereto as the principal may require;

    (c) where the board has appointed teachers under section 14 or 17, co-operate fully with such teachers and with the principal in all matters related to the instruction of pupils;

    (d) unless otherwise assigned by the principal, be present in the classroom or teaching area and ensure that the classroom or teaching area is ready for the reception of pupils at least fifteen minutes before the commencement of classes in the school in the morning and, where applicable, five minutes before the commencement of classes in the school in the afternoon;

    (e) assist the principal in maintaining close co-operation with the community;

    (f) prepare for use in the teacher's class or classes such teaching plans and outlines as are required by the principal and the appropriate supervisory officer and submit the plans and outlines to the principal or the appropriate supervisory officer, as the case may be, on request;

    (g) ensure that all reasonable safety procedures are carried out in courses and activities for which the teacher is responsible;

    (h) co-operate with the principal and other teachers to establish and maintain consistent disciplinary practices in the school.

    (i) ensure that report cards are fully and properly completed and processed in accordance with the guides known in English as Guide to the Provincial Report Card, Grades 1–8 and Guide to the Provincial Report Card, Grades 9–12, and in French as Guide d'utilisation du bulletin scolaire de l'Ontario de la 1ère à la 8$^\text{e}$ année and Guide du bulletin scolaire de l'Ontario de la 9$^\text{e}$ à la 12$^\text{e}$ année, as the case may be, both available electronically through a link in the document known in English as Ontario School Record (OSR) Guideline, 2000 and in French as Dossier scolaire de l'Ontario: Guide, 2000, online at www.edu.gov.on.ca/eng/document/curricul/osr/osr.html or www.edu.gov.on.ca/fre/document/curricul/osr/osrf.html;

    (j) co-operate and assist in the administration of tests under the *Education Quality and Accountability Office Act, 1996;*

    (k) participate in regular meetings with pupils' parents or guardians;

    (l) perform duties as assigned by the principal in relation to co-operative placements of pupils; and

    (m) perform duties normally associated with the graduation of pupils.

[O. Reg. 95/96, s. 2]

Appointment to Teach in the Case of an Emergency

21. (1) Where no teacher is available, a board may appoint, subject to section 22, a person who is not a teacher or a temporary teacher.

(2) A person appointed under subsection (1) shall be eighteen years of age or older and the holder of an Ontario secondary school diploma, a secondary school graduation diploma or a secondary school honour graduation diploma.

(3) An appointment under this section is valid for ten school days commencing with the day on which the person is appointed.

Cancelled and Suspended Certificates

22. (1) A board shall not appoint a person whose teaching certificate is cancelled or under suspension to teach under section 21 or in accordance with a Letter of Permission.

(2) A person whose teaching certificate is cancelled or under suspension ceases to hold teacher's qualifications during the period of cancellation or suspension and shall not be appointed as a teacher.

Requirements for Pupils

23. (1) A pupil shall,

(a) be diligent in attempting to master such studies as are part of the program in which the pupil is enrolled;

(b) exercise self-discipline;

(c) accept such discipline as would be exercised by a kind, firm and judicious parent;

(d) attend classes punctually and regularly;

(e) be courteous to fellow pupils and obedient and courteous to teachers;

(f) be clean in person and habits;

(g) take such tests and examinations as are required by or under the Act or as may be directed by the Minister; and

(h) show respect for school property.

(2) When a pupil returns to school after an absence, a parent of the pupil, or the pupil where the pupil is an adult, shall give the reason for the absence orally or in writing as the principal requires.

(3) A pupil may be excused by the principal from attendance at school temporarily at any time at the written request of a parent of the pupil or the pupil where the pupil is an adult.

(4) Every pupil is responsible for his or her conduct to the principal of the school that the pupil attends,

(a) on the school premises;

(b) on out-of-school activities that are part of the school program; and

(c) while travelling on a school bus that is owned by a board or on a bus or school bus that is under contract to a board.

Advertisements and Announcements

24. (1) No advertisement or announcement shall be placed in a school or on school property or distributed or announced to the pupils on school property without the consent of the board that operates the school except announcements of school activities.

(2) Subsection (1) does not apply to anything posted in the school in accordance with the regulations.

[O. Reg. 613/00, s. 2]

Canvassing and Fund-Raising

25. (1) It is the duty of a pupil to ensure that any canvassing or fund-raising activity on school property by the pupil is carried on only with the consent of the board that operates the school.

(2) No principal, vice-principal or teacher, without the prior approval of the board that operates the school at which they are employed, shall authorize any canvassing or fund-raising activity that involves the participation of one or more pupils attending the school.

Supervision

26. (1) The appropriate supervisory officer, in addition to the duties under the Act, may, during a visit to a school, assume any of the authority and responsibility of the principal of the school.

(2) Psychiatrists, psychologists, social workers and other professional support staff employed by a board shall perform, under the administrative supervision of the appropriate supervisory officer, such duties as are determined by the board and, where such persons are performing their duties in a school, they shall be subject to the administrative authority of the principal of that school.

(3) A supervisory officer who is notified under subsection 11 (5) shall forth-with notify the French-language education council or section, English-language education council or section or majority language section of the board, as the case requires, and arrange for,

(a) the provision of supervision of instruction;

(b) assistance and advice to the teachers in respect of whom the supervisory officer was given notice under subsection 11 (5); and

(c) the conducting of performance appraisals, where appropriate, of the teachers in respect of whom the supervisory officer was given notice under subsection 11 (5),

in the language in which the instruction is provided.

Religion In Schools

27. Sections 28 and 29 do not apply to a Roman Catholic board or to a Protestant separate school board.

[O. Reg. 191/04, s. 8]

28. (1) A board may provide in grades one to eight and in its secondary schools an optional program of education about religion.

(2) A program of education about religion shall,

(a) promote respect for the freedom of conscience and religion guaranteed by the *Canadian Charter of Rights and Freedoms;* and

(b) provide for the study of different religions and religious beliefs in Canada and the world, without giving primacy to, and without indoctrination in, any particular religion or religious belief.

(3) A program of education about religion shall not exceed sixty minutes of instruction per week in an elementary school.

29. (1) Subject to subsections (2) and (3), a board shall not permit any person to conduct religious exercises or to provide instruction that includes indoctrination in a particular religion or religious belief in a school.

(2) A board may enter into an agreement with a Roman Catholic board that permits the Roman Catholic board to use space and facilities to conduct religious exercises or provide religious instruction for the purposes of the Roman Catholic board.

(3) A board may permit a person to conduct religious exercises or to provide instruction that includes indoctrination in a particular religion or religious belief in a school if,

(a) the exercises are not conducted or the instruction is not provided by or under the auspices of the board;

(b) the exercises are conducted or the instruction is provided on a school day at a time that is before or after the school's instructional program, or on a day that is not a school day;

(c) no person is required by the board to attend the exercises or instruction; and

(d) the board provides space for the exercises or instruction on the same basis as it provides space for other community activities.

(4) A board that permits religious exercises or instruction under subsection (3) shall consider on an equitable basis all requests to conduct religious exercises or to provide instruction under subsection (3).

[O. Reg. 191/04, s. 9]

Special Education Programs and Services

30. A hearing-handicapped child who has attained the age of two years may be admitted to a special education program for the hearing-handicapped.

31. The maximum enrollment in a special education class shall depend upon the extent of the exceptionalities of the pupils in the class and the special education services that are available to the teacher, but in no case shall the enrolment in a self-contained class exceed,

(a) in a class for pupils who are emotionally disturbed or socially maladjusted, for pupils who have severe learning disabilities, or for pupils who are younger than compulsory school age and have impaired hearing, eight pupils;

(b) in a class for pupils who are blind, for pupils who are deaf, for pupils who have developmental disabilities, or for pupils with speech and language disorders, ten pupils;

(c) in a class for pupils who are hard of hearing, for pupils with limited vision, or for pupils with orthopaedic or other physical handicaps, twelve pupils;

(d) in a class for pupils who have mild intellectual disabilities, twelve pupils in the primary division and sixteen pupils in the junior and intermediate divisions;

(e) in an elementary school class for pupils who are gifted, twenty-five pupils;

(f) in a class for aphasic or autistic pupils, or for pupils with multiple handicaps for whom no one handicap is dominant, six pupils; and

(g) on and after the 1st day of September, 1982, in a class for exceptional pupils consisting of pupils with different exceptionalities, sixteen pupils.

[O. Reg. 191/04, s. 10]

23

Teachers' Contract

(R.R.O. 1990, Reg. 310)

Form of Contracts

1. (1) Every contract between a board and a permanent teacher shall be in Form 1.

(2) Every contract between a board and a probationary teacher shall be in Form 2.

(3) Except where otherwise provided under subsection 259 (5) or (6) of the Act, every contract between a board and a continuing education teacher shall be in Form 3.

Payment of Salaries

2. (1) Subject to subsection (4), a board shall pay the salary of a teacher under contract in Form 1 or Form 2 in the number of payments set out in the contract.

(2) Subject to subsection (4), a board shall pay the salary of a teacher under contract in Form 3 in the number of payments or on the dates set out in the contract.

(3) In the case of a contract in Form 1 or Form 2, the contract shall provide for not fewer than ten salary payments.

(4) Where during the term of a contract between a board and a teacher the salary of the teacher is changed by mutual agreement in writing between the board and the teacher, the contract shall be deemed to be varied accordingly.

Form 1

Education Act

Permanent Teacher's Contract

This Agreement made in duplicate this . . . . day of . . . ., 19 . . . ., between . . . . hereinafter called the "Board" and . . . . of () (the . . . . of . . . . in the County) () ((or as the case may be) of . . . .) () hereinafter called the "Teacher".

1. The Board agrees to employ the Teacher as a permanent teacher and the Teacher agrees to teach for the Board commencing the . . . . day of . . . ., 19 . . . . at a yearly salary of . . . . Dollars, subject to any changes in salary mutually agreed upon by the Teacher and the Board, payable in . . . . (not fewer than ten) payments, less any lawful deduction, in the following manner:
   i. Where there are ten payments, one-tenth on or before the last teaching day of each teaching month.

Form 2

Education Act

Probationary Teacher's Contract

This Agreement made in duplicate this . . . . day of . . . . 19 . . . ., between . . . . hereinafter called the "Board" and . . . . of () (the . . . . of . . . . in the County) () ((or as the case may be) of . . . .) () hereinafter called the "Teacher".

1. The Board agrees to employ the Teacher as a probationary teacher for a probationary period of . . . . years and the Teacher agrees to teach for the Board commencing the . . . . day of . . . ., 19 . . . . at a yearly salary of . . . . Dollars, subject to any changes in salary mutually agreed upon by the Teacher and the Board, payable in . . . . (not fewer than ten) payments, less any lawful deduction, in the following manner:
   i. Where there are ten payments, one-tenth on or before the last teaching day of each teaching month.
   ii. Where there are more than ten payments, at least one-twelfth on or before the last teaching day of each teaching month, any unpaid balance being payable on or before the last teaching day of June, or at the time of leaving the employ of the Board, whichever is the earlier.

2. This Agreement is subject to the Teacher's continuing to hold qualifications in accordance with the Acts and regulations administered by the Minister.

3. The Teacher agrees to be diligent and faithful in his or her duties during the period of employment, and to perform such duties and teach such subjects as the Board may assign under the Acts and regulations administered by the Minister.

4. Where the Teacher attends an educational conference for which the school has been legally closed and his or her attendance at it is certified by the supervisory officer concerned or by the chair of the conference, the Board agrees to make no deductions from the Teacher's salary for his or her absence during that attendance.

5. Where an Act of Ontario or a regulation thereunder authorizes the Teacher to be absent from school without loss of pay, the Board agrees that no deduction from his or her pay will be made for the period of absence so authorized.

6. Despite anything in this contract this Agreement may be terminated,
   (a) at any time by the mutual consent in writing of the Teacher and the Board;

(b) on the 31st day of December in any year of the Teacher's employment by either party giving written notice to the other on or before the last preceding 30th day of November; or

(c) on the 31st day of August in any year of the Teacher's employment by either party giving written notice to the other on or before the last preceding 31st day of May.

7. The Teacher agrees with the Board that if the Teacher enters into an agreement with another board he or she will within forty-eight hours notify the Board in writing of the termination of the Agreement unless the notice has already been given.

IN WITNESS WHEREOF the Teacher has signed and the Board has affixed hereto its corporate seal attested by its proper officers.

. . . .

. . .

. . . (signature of Teacher)

24

Teachers, Pupil Records and Education Numbers

*[S.O. 1996, c. 13, s. 10; 1997, c. 31, s. 116; subheading
and sub-subheading amended S.O. 1997, c. 31, s. 115]*

Contracts

261. Probationary period — The probationary period, if any, for teachers when they first become employed by a board shall not exceed two years.
[S.O. 1997, c. 31, s. 117]

262. Membership in Ontario College of Teachers — Except as otherwise provided in or under this Act, no person shall be employed in an elementary or secondary school to teach or to perform any duty for which membership in the College is required under this Act unless the person is a member of the Ontario College of Teachers.
[S.O. 1996, c. 12, s. 64]

263. Termination of contract where welfare of school involved — Despite the other provisions of this Part and despite any provision in a collective agreement, if any, when a teacher is employed by a board and a matter arises that in the opinion of the Minister adversely affects the welfare of the school in which the teacher is employed,

(a) the board or the teacher may, with the consent of the Minister, give the other party thirty days written notice of termination, and the teacher's employment is terminated at the expiration of thirty days from the date the notice is given; or

(b) the board may, with the consent of the Minister, give the teacher written notice of immediate termination together with one-tenth of the teacher's yearly salary in addition to the amount to which the teacher would otherwise be entitled, and, on doing so, the teacher's employment is terminated.
[S.O. 1997, c. 31, ss. 118, 119]

Duties

264. (1) **Duties of teacher** — It is the duty of a teacher and a temporary teacher,

(a) **teach** — to teach diligently and faithfully the classes or subjects assigned to the teacher by the principal;

(b) **learning** — to encourage the pupils in the pursuit of learning;

(c) **religion and morals** — to inculcate by precept and example respect for religion and the principles of Judaeo-Christian morality and the highest regard for truth, justice, loyalty, love of country, humanity, benevolence, sobriety, industry, frugality, purity, temperance and all other virtues;

(d) **co-operation** — to assist in developing co-operation and co-ordination of effort among the members of the staff of the school;

(e) **discipline** — to maintain, under the direction of the principal, proper order and discipline in the teacher's classroom and while on duty in the school and on the school ground;

(f) **language of instruction** — in instruction and in all communications with the pupils in regard to discipline and the management of the school,

   (i) to use the English language, except where it is impractical to do so by reason of the pupil not understanding English, and except in respect of instruction in a language other than English when such other language is being taught as one of the subjects in the course of study, or

   (ii) to use the French language in schools or classes in which French is the language of instruction except where it is impractical to do so by reason of the pupil not understanding French, and except in respect of instruction in a language other than French when such other language is being taught as one of the subjects in the course of study;

(g) **timetable** — to conduct the teacher's class in accordance with a timetable which shall be accessible to pupils and to the principal and supervisory officers;

(h) **professional activity days** — to participate in professional activity days as designated by the board under the regulations;

(i) **absence from school** — to notify such person as is designated by the board if the teacher is to be absent from school and the reason therefor;

(j) **school property** — to deliver the register, the school key and other school property in the teacher's possession to the board on demand, or when the teacher's agreement with the board has expired, or when for any reason the teacher's employment has ceased; and

(k) **textbooks** — to use and permit to be used as a textbook in a class that he or she teaches in an elementary or a secondary school,

   (i) in a subject area for which textbooks are approved by the Minister, only textbooks that are approved by the Minister, and

   (ii) in all subject areas, only textbooks that are approved by the board.

(l) **duties assigned** — to perform all duties assigned in accordance with this Act and the regulations.

(1.1) **Sign language** — Despite clause (1) (f), a teacher or temporary teacher y use American Sign Language or Quebec Sign Language in accordance with regulations.

(1.2) [Repealed, S.O. 2001, c. 14, Sch. A, s. 7]

(1.3) [Repealed, S.O. 2001, c. 14, Sch. A, s. 7]

(2) **Refusal to give up school property** — A teacher who refuses, on demand or order of the board that operates the school concerned, to deliver to the board any school property in the teacher's possession forfeits any claim that the teacher may have against the board.

(3) **Teachers, conferences** — Teachers may organize themselves for the purpose of conducting professional development conferences and seminars.
[S.O. 1993, c. 11, s. 36; 2000, c. 11, s. 17; 2003, c. 2, s. 20]

265. (1) **Duties of principal** — It is the duty of a principal of a school, in addition to the principal's duties as a teacher,

(a) **discipline** — to maintain proper order and discipline in the school;

(b) **co-operation** — to develop co-operation and co-ordination of effort among the members of the staff of the school;

(c) **register pupils and record attendance** — to register the pupils and to ensure that the attendance of pupils for every school day is recorded either in the register supplied by the Minister in accordance with the instructions contained therein or in such other manner as is approved by the Minister;

(d) **pupil records** — in accordance with this Act, the regulations and the guidelines issued by the Minister, to collect information for inclusion in a record in respect of each pupil enrolled in the school and to establish, maintain, retain, transfer and dispose of the record;

(e) **timetable** — to prepare a timetable, to conduct the school according to such timetable and the school year calendar or calendars applicable thereto, to make the calendar or calendars and the timetable accessible to the pupils, teachers and supervisory officers and to assign classes and subjects to the teachers;

(f) **examinations and reports** — to hold, subject to the approval of the appropriate supervisory officer, such examinations as the principal considers necessary for the promotion of pupils or for any other purpose and report as required by the board the progress of the pupil to his or her parent or guardian where the pupil is a minor and otherwise to the pupil;

(g) **promote pupils** — subject to revision by the appropriate supervisory officer, to promote such pupils as the principal considers proper and to issue to each such pupil a statement thereof;

(h) **textbooks** — to ensure that all textbooks used by pupils are those approved by the board and, in the case of subject areas for which the Minister approves textbooks, those approved by the Minister;

(i) **reports** — to furnish to the Ministry and to the appropriate supervisory officer any information that it may be in the principal's power to give respecting the condition of the school premises, the discipline of the school, the progress of the pupils and any other matter affecting the interests of the school, and to prepare such reports for the board as are required by the board;

(j) **care of pupils and property** — to give assiduous attention to the health and comfort of the pupils, to the cleanliness, temperature and ventilation of the school, to the care of all teaching materials and other school property, and to the condition and appearance of the school buildings and grounds;

(k) **report to M.O.H.** — to report promptly to the board and to the medical officer of health when the principal has reason to suspect the existence of any communicable disease in the school, and of the unsanitary condition of any part of the school building or the school grounds;

(l) **persons with communicable diseases** — to refuse admission to the school of any person who the principal believes is infected with or exposed to communicable diseases requiring an order under section 22 of the *Health Protection and Promotion Act* until furnished with a certificate of a medical officer of health or of a legally qualified medical practitioner approved by the medical officer of health that all danger from exposure to contact with such person has passed;

(m) **access to school or class** — subject to an appeal to the board, to refuse to admit to the school or classroom a person whose presence in the school or classroom would in the principal's judgment be detrimental to the physical or mental well-being of the pupils; and

(n) **visitor's book** — to maintain a visitor's book in the school when so determined by the board.

(2) **Co-instructional activities** — In addition, it is the duty of a principal, in accordance with the board plan to provide for co-instructional activities under subsection 170 (1), to develop and implement a school plan providing for co-instructional activities.

(3) **School council** — The principal shall consult the school council at least once in each school year respecting the school plan providing for co-instructional activities.

(4) [Repealed, S.O. 2001, c. 14, Sch. A, s. 8, in force July 1, 2001]
[S.O. 1991, c. 10, s. 6; 2000, c. 11, s. 18; 2001, c. 14, Sched, A, s. 8]

Pupil Records

266. (1) **Definition** — In this section, except in subsection (12), "record", in respect of a pupil, means a record under clause 265 (d).

(1) **Definition** — In this section, except in subsection (12), "record", in respect of a pupil, means a record under clause 265 (1) (d).
[S.O. 2000, c. 11, s. 19, to come into force on proclamation]

(2) **Pupil records privileged** — A record is privileged for the information and use of supervisory officers and the principal and teachers of the school for the improvement of instruction of the pupil, and such record,

(a) subject to subsections (2.1), (3) and (5), is not available to any other person; and

(b) except for the purposes of subsection (5) is not admissible in evidence for any purpose in any trial, inquest, inquiry, examination, hearing or other proceeding, except to prove the establishment, maintenance, retention or transfer of the record,

without the written permission of the parent or guardian of the pupil or, where the pupil is an adult, the written permission of the pupil.

(2.1) **Information to medical officer of health** — The principal of a school shall, upon request by the medical officer of health serving the area in which the school is located, give that medical officer of health the following information in respect of pupils enrolled in the school:

1. The pupil's name, address and telephone number.

2. The pupil's birthdate.

3. The name, address and telephone number of the pupil's parent or guardian.

(3) **Right of parent and pupil** — A pupil, and his or her parent or guardian where the pupil is a minor, is entitled to examine the record of such pupil.

(4) **Idem** — Where, in the opinion of a pupil who is an adult, or of the parent or guardian of a pupil who is a minor, information recorded upon the record of the pupil is,

(a) inaccurately recorded; or

(b) not conducive to the improvement of instruction of the pupil,

such pupil, parent or guardian, as the case may be, may, in writing, request the principal to correct the alleged inaccuracy in, or to remove the impugned information from, such record.

(5) **Reference where disagreement** — Where the principal refuses to comply with a request under subsection (4), the pupil, parent or guardian who made the request may, in writing, require the principal to refer the request to the appropriate supervisory officer who shall either require the principal to comply with the request or submit the record and the request to a person designated by the Minister, and such person shall hold a hearing at which the principal and the person who made the request are the parties to the proceeding, and the person so designated shall, after the hearing, decide the matter, and his or her decision is final and binding upon the parties to the proceeding.

(6) **Use re further education or employment** — Nothing in subsection (2) prohibits the use by the principal of the record in respect of a pupil to assist in the preparation of,

(a) a report required by this Act or the regulations; or

(b) a report,

(i) for an educational institution or for the pupil or former pupil, in respect of an application for further education, or

(ii) for the pupil or former pupil in respect of an application for employment,

where a written request is made by the former pupil, the pupil where he or she is an adult, or the parent or guardian of the pupil where the pupil is a minor.

(7) **Information for Minister or board** — Nothing in this section prevents the compilation and delivery of such information as may be required by the Minister or by the board.

(8) **No action re content** — No action shall be brought against any person in respect of the content of a record.

(9) **Testimony re content** — Except where the record has been introduced in evidence as provided in this section, no person shall be required in any trial or other proceeding to give evidence in respect of the content of a record.

(10) **Secrecy re contents** — Except as permitted under this section, every person shall preserve secrecy in respect of the content of a record that comes to the person's knowledge in the course of his or her duties or employment, and no such person shall communicate any such knowledge to any other person except,

(a) as may be required in the performance of his or her duties; or

(b) with the written consent of the parent or guardian of the pupil where the pupil is a minor; or

(c) with the written consent of the pupil where the pupil is an adult.

(11) **Definition** — For the purposes of this section, "guardian" includes a person, society or corporation who or that has custody of a pupil.

(12) **Application to former records** — This section, except subsections (3), (4) and (5), applies with necessary modifications to a record established and maintained in respect of a pupil or retained in respect of a former pupil prior to the 1st day of September, 1972.

(13) **Use of record in disciplinary cases** — Nothing in this section prevents the use of a record in respect of a pupil by the principal of the school attended by the pupil or the board that operates the school for the purposes of a disciplinary proceeding instituted by the principal in respect of conduct for which the pupil is responsible to the principal.

[S.O. 1991, c. 10, s. 7; 2000, c. 11, s. 19]

25

Child and Family Services Act

(R.S.O. 1990, c. C.11; sections 3, 28, 37, 72, 85, 106 and 207)

Amendments to reproduced sections: S.O. 1993, c. 27, Sch.; S.O. 1999, c. 2, ss. 9, 22, 30(1), 30(4) in force Mar. 31, 2000; 2004, c. 3, Sched. A, s. 78.

Editor's Note

The *Child and Family Services Act* (the CFSA) is large and complex legislation governing children's services in the Province of Ontario including child protection, voluntary services to families and children, adoption, rights of children in state care, youth justice services, children's mental health services and the governance of children's residential services throughout the province. The portions that follow govern counselling, duty to report and the definition of a child in need of protection, parental rights with respect to education, consent to medical treatment and the upbringing of children, and the constitution of the Child and Family Services Review Board. The Board is the tribunal empowered to hear appeals of expulsions imposed by school boards. The rules established by the Board for hearings before it, follow this Act.

. . .

Interpretation

3. (1) **Definitions** — In this Act,

. . .

"board" means the Child and Family Services Review Board continued under Part IX (Licensing).

. . .

Voluntary Access to Services

. . .

Consents

. . .

28. Counselling service: child twelve or older — A service provider may provide a counselling service to a child who is twelve years of age or older with the child's consent, and no other person's consent is required, but if the child is less than sixteen years of age the service provider shall discuss with the child at the earliest appropriate opportunity the desirability of involving the child's parent.

. . .

Part III

Child Protection

. . .

37. (2) Child in need of protection — A child is in need of protection where,

(a) the child has suffered physical harm, inflicted by the person having charge of the child or caused by or resulting from that person's,

    (i) failure to adequately care for, provide for, supervise or protect the child, or

    (ii) pattern of neglect in caring for, providing for, supervising or protecting the child;

(b) there is a risk that the child is likely to suffer physical harm inflicted by the person having charge of the child or caused by or resulting from that person's,

    (i) failure to adequately care for, provide for, supervise or protect the child, or

    (ii) pattern of neglect in caring for, providing for, supervising or protecting the child;

(c) the child has been sexually molested or sexually exploited, by the person having charge of the child or by another person where the person having charge of the child knows or should know of the possibility of sexual molestation or sexual exploitation and fails to protect the child;

(d) there is a risk that the child is likely to be sexually molested or sexually exploited as described in clause (c);

(e) the child requires medical treatment to cure, prevent or alleviate physical harm or suffering and the child's parent or the person having charge of the child does not provide, or refuses or is unavailable or unable to consent to, the treatment;

(f) the child has suffered emotional harm, demonstrated by serious,

    (i) anxiety,

    (ii) depression,

    (iii) withdrawal,

    (iv) self-destructive or aggressive behaviour, or

    (v) delayed development,

and there are reasonable grounds to believe that the emotional harm suffered by the child results from the actions, failure to act or pattern of neglect on the part of the child's parent or the person having charge of the child;

(f.1) the child has suffered emotional harm of the kind described in subclause (f) (i), (ii), (iii), (iv) or (v) and the child's parent or the person having charge of the child does not provide, or refuses or is unavailable or unable to consent to, services or treatment to remedy or alleviate the harm;

(g) there is a risk that the child is likely to suffer emotional harm of the kind described in subclause (f) (i), (ii), (iii), (iv) or (v) resulting from the actions, failure to act or pattern of neglect on the part of the child's parent or the person having charge of the child;

(g.1) there is a risk that the child is likely to suffer emotional harm of the kind described in subclause (f) (i), (ii), (iii), (iv) or (v) and that the child's parent or the person having charge of the child does not provide, or refuses or is unavailable or unable to consent to, services or treatment to prevent the harm;

(h) the child suffers from a mental, emotional or developmental condition that, if not remedied, could seriously impair the child's development and the child's parent or the person having charge of the child does not provide, or refuses or is unavailable or unable to consent to, treatment to remedy or alleviate the condition;

(i) the child has been abandoned, the child's parent has died or is unavailable to exercise his or her custodial rights over the child and has not made adequate provision for the child's care and custody, or the child is in a residential placement and the parent refuses or is unable or unwilling to resume the child's care and custody;

(j) the child is less than twelve years old and has killed or seriously injured another person or caused serious damage to another person's property, services or treatment are necessary to prevent a recurrence and the child's parent or the person having charge of the child does not provide, or refuses or is unavailable or unable to consent to, those services or treatment;

(k) the child is less than twelve years old and has on more than one occasion injured another person or caused loss or damage to another person's property, with the encouragement of the person having charge of the child or because of that person's failure or inability to supervise the child adequately; or

(l) the child's parent is unable to care for the child and the child is brought before the court with the parent's consent and, where the child is twelve years of age or older, with the child's consent, to be dealt with under this Part.

[S.O. 1999, c. 2, s. 9]

. . .

Duty to Report

72. (1) **Duty to report child in need of protection** — Despite the provisions of any other Act, if a person, including a person who performs professional or official duties with respect to children, has reasonable grounds to suspect one of the following, the person shall forthwith report the suspicion and the information on which it is based to a society:

1. The child has suffered physical harm, inflicted by the person having charge of the child or caused by or resulting from that person's,
   i. failure to adequately care for, provide for, supervise or protect the child, or
   ii. pattern of neglect in caring for, providing for, supervising or protecting the child.
2. There is a risk that the child is likely to suffer physical harm inflicted by the person having charge of the child or caused by or resulting from that person's,
   i. failure to adequately care for, provide for, supervise or protect the child, or
   ii. pattern of neglect in caring for, providing for, supervising or protecting the child.

3. The child has been sexually molested or sexually exploited, by the person having charge of the child or by another person where the person having charge of the child knows or should know of the possibility of sexual molestation or sexual exploitation and fails to protect the child.

4. There is a risk that the child is likely to be sexually molested or sexually exploited as described in paragraph 3.

5. The child requires medical treatment to cure, prevent or alleviate physical harm or suffering and the child's parent or the person having charge of the child does not provide, or refuses or is unavailable or unable to consent to, the treatment.

6. The child has suffered emotional harm, demonstrated by serious,
   i. anxiety,
   ii. depression,
   iii. withdrawal,
   iv. self-destructive or aggressive behaviour, or
   v. delayed development, and there are reasonable grounds to believe that the emotional harm suffered by the child results from the actions, failure to act or pattern of neglect on the part of the child's parent or the person having charge of the child.

7. The child has suffered emotional harm of the kind described in subparagraph i, ii, iii, iv or v of paragraph 6 and the child's parent or the person having charge of the child does not provide, or refuses or is unavailable or unable to consent to, services or treatment to remedy or alleviate the harm.

8. There is a risk that the child is likely to suffer emotional harm of the kind described in subparagraph i, ii, iii, iv or v of paragraph 6 resulting from the actions, failure to act or pattern of neglect on the part of the child's parent or the person having charge of the child.

9. There is a risk that the child is likely to suffer emotional harm of the kind described in subparagraph i, ii, iii, iv or v of paragraph 6 and that the child's parent or the person having charge of the child does not provide, or refuses or is unavailable or unable to consent to, services or treatment to prevent the harm.

10. The child suffers from a mental, emotional or developmental condition that, if not remedied, could seriously impair the child's development and the child's parent or the person having charge of the child does not provide, or refuses or is unavailable or unable to consent to, treatment to remedy or alleviate the condition.

11. The child has been abandoned, the child's parent has died or is unavailable to exercise his or her custodial rights over the child and has not made adequate provision for the child's care and custody, or the child is in a residential placement and the parent refuses or is unable or unwilling to resume the child's care and custody.

12. The child is less than 12 years old and has killed or seriously injured another person or caused serious damage to another person's property, services or treatment are necessary to prevent a recurrence and the child's parent or the person having charge of the child does not provide, or refuses or is unavailable or unable to consent to, those services or treatment.

13. The child is less than 12 years old and has on more than one occasion injured another person or caused loss or damage to another person's property, with the encouragement of the person having charge of the child or because of that person's failure or inability to supervise the child adequately.

(2) **On-going duty to report** — A person who has additional reasonable grounds to suspect one of the matters set out in subsection (1) shall make a further report under subsection (1) even if he or she has made previous reports with respect to the same child.

(3) **Person must report directly** — A person who has a duty to report a matter under subsection (1) or (2) shall make the report directly to the society and shall not rely on any other person to report on his or her behalf.

(4) **Offence** — A person referred to in subsection (5) is guilty of an offence if,

(a) he or she contravenes subsection (1) or (2) by not reporting a suspicion; and

(b) the information on which it was based was obtained in the course of his or her professional or official duties.

(5) **Same** — Subsection (4) applies to every person who performs professional or official duties with respect to children including,

(a) a health care professional, including a physician, nurse, dentist, pharmacist and psychologist,

(b) a teacher, school principal, social worker, family counsellor, priest, rabbi, member of the clergy, operator or employee of a day nursery and youth and recreation worker;

(c) a peace officer and a coroner;

(d) a solicitor; and

(e) a service provider and an employee of a service provider.

(6) **Same** — In clause (5) (b), "youth and recreation worker" does not include a volunteer.

(6.1) **Same** — A director, officer or employee of a corporation who authorizes, permits or concurs in a contravention of an offence under subsection (4) by an employee of the corporation is guilty of an offence.

(6.2) **Same** — A person convicted of an offence under subsection (4) or (6. 1) is liable to a fine of not more than $1,000.

(7) **Section overrides privilege** — This section applies although the information reported may be confidential or privileged, and no action for making the report shall be instituted against a person who acts in accordance with this section unless the person acts maliciously or without reasonable grounds for the suspicion.

(8) **Exception: solicitor client privilege** — Nothing in this section abrogates any privilege that may exist between a solicitor and his or her client.
[S.O. 1993, c. 27, Sch; 1999, c. 2, s. 22]

(9) **Conflict** — This section prevails despite anything in the *Personal Health Information Protection Act, 2004.*
[S.O. 2004, c, 3, Sched. A, s. 78]

. . .

Offences, Restraining Orders, Recovery on Child's Behalf

. . .

85. (1) **Offences** — A person who contravenes,

(a) an order for access made under subsection 58 (1);

(b) [Repealed, S.O. 1999, c. 2, s. 30]

(c) subsection 74 (5) (disclosure of information obtained by court order);

(d) subsection 75 (6) or (10) (confidentiality of child abuse register);

(e) an order made under subsection 76 (8) (amendment of society's records);

(f) subsection 79 (3) or (5) (leaving child unattended, etc.);

(g) a restraining order made under subsection 80 (1);

(h) section 82 (unauthorized placement);

(i) any provision of section 83 (interference with child, etc.); or

(j) clause 84 (a) or (b),

and a director, officer or employee of a corporation who authorizes, permits or concurs in such a contravention by the corporation is guilty of an offence and on conviction is liable to a fine of not more than $1,000 or, to imprisonment for a term of not more than one year, or to both.

(2) **Idem** — A person who contravenes subsection 79 (2) (child abuse), and a director, officer or employee of a corporation who authorizes, permits or concurs in such a contravention by the corporation is guilty of an offence and on conviction is liable to a fine of not more than $2,000 or to imprisonment for a term of not more than two years, or to both.

(3) **Idem** — A person who contravenes subsection 45 (8) or 76 (11) (publication of identifying information) or an order prohibiting publication made under clause 45 (7) (c) or subsection 45 (9), and a director, officer or employee of a corporation who authorizes, permits or concurs in such a contravention by the corporation, is guilty of an offence and on conviction is liable to a fine of not more than $10,000 or to imprisonment for a term of not more than three years, or to both.

[S.O. 1999, c. 2, s. 30]

26

Behaviour, Discipline and Safety

300. (1) **Definition** — In this Part,
"school premises" means, with respect to a school, the school buildings and premises.

(2) **Interpretation** — In this Part, where reference is made to a regulation or to a matter prescribed by regulation, it means a regulation to be made by the Minister under this Part.
[S.O. 2000, c. 12, s. 3]

301. (1) **Provincial code of conduct** — The Minister may establish a code of conduct governing the behaviour of all persons in schools.

(2) **Purposes** — The following are the purposes of the code of conduct:
1. To ensure that all members of the school community, especially people in positions of authority, are treated with respect and dignity.
2. To promote responsible citizenship by encouraging appropriate participation in the civic life of the school community.
3. To maintain an environment where conflict and difference can be addressed in a manner characterized by respect and civility.
4. To encourage the use of non-violent means to resolve conflict.
5. To promote the safety of people in the schools.
6. To discourage the use of alcohol and illegal drugs.

(3) **Notice** — Every board shall take such steps as the Minister directs to bring the code of conduct to the attention of pupils, parents and guardians of pupils and others who may be present in schools under the jurisdiction of the board.

(4) **Code is policy** — The code of conduct is a policy of the Minister.

(5) **Policies and guidelines governing conduct** — The Minister may establish additional policies and guidelines with respect to the conduct of persons in schools.

(6) **Same, governing discipline** — The Minister may establish policies and guidelines with respect to disciplining pupils, specifying, for example, the circumstances in

which a pupil is subject to discipline and the forms and the extent of discipline that may be imposed in particular circumstances.

(7) **Same, promoting safety** — The Minister may establish policies and guidelines to promote the safety of pupils.

(8) **Different policies, etc.** — The Minister may establish different policies and guidelines under this section for different circumstances, for different locations and for different classes of persons.

(9) **Duty of boards** — The Minister may require boards to comply with policies and guidelines established under this section.

(10) **Not regulations** — Policies and guidelines established under this section are not regulations within the meaning of the *Regulations Act*.
[S.O. 2000, c. 12, s. 3]

302. (1) **Boards' policies and guidelines governing conduct** — Every board shall establish policies and guidelines with respect to the conduct of persons in schools within the board's jurisdiction and the policies and guidelines must address such matters and include such requirements as the Minister may specify.

(2) **Same, governing discipline** — A board may establish policies and guidelines with respect to disciplining pupils, and the policies and guidelines must be consistent with this Part and with the policies and guidelines established by the Minister under section 301, and must address such matters and include such requirements as the Minister may specify.

(3) **Same, promoting safety** — If required to do so by the Minister, a board shall establish policies and guidelines to promote the safety of pupils, and the policies and guidelines must be consistent with those established by the Minister under section 301 and must address such matters and include such requirements as the Minister may specify.

(4) **Same, governing access to school premises** — A board may establish policies and guidelines governing access to school premises, and the policies and guidelines must be premises consistent with the regulations made under section 305 and must address such matters and include such requirements as the Minister may specify.

(5) **Same, governing appropriate dress** — If required to do so by the Minister, a board shall establish policies and guidelines respecting appropriate dress for pupils in schools within the board's jurisdiction, and the policies and guidelines must address such matters and include such requirements as the Minister may specify.

(6) **Same, procedural matters** — A board shall establish policies and guidelines governing a review or appeal of a decision to suspend a pupil and governing, with respect to expulsions, a principal's inquiry, an expulsion hearing and an appeal of a decision to expel a pupil, and the policies and guidelines must address such matters and include such requirements as the Minister may specify.

(7) **Different policies, etc.** — A board may establish different policies and guidelines under this section for different circumstances, for different locations and for different classes of persons.

(8) **Role of school councils** — When establishing policies and guidelines under this section, a board shall consider the views of school councils with respect to the contents of the policies and guidelines.

(9) **Periodic review** — The board shall periodically review its policies and guidelines established under this section and shall solicit the views of pupils, teachers, staff, volunteers working in the schools, parents and guardians, school councils and the public.

(10) **Not regulations** — Policies and guidelines established under this section are not regulations within the meaning of the *Regulations Act*.
[S.O. 2000, c. 12, s. 3]

303. (1) **Local codes of conduct** — A board may direct the principal of a school to establish a local code of conduct governing the behaviour of all persons in the school, and the local code must be consistent with the provincial code established under subsection 301 (1) and must address such matters and include such requirements as the board may specify.

(2) **Same, mandatory** — A board shall direct a principal to establish a local code of conduct if the board is required to do so by the Minister, and the local code must address such matters and include such requirements as the Minister may specify.

(3) **Role of school council** — When establishing or reviewing a local code of conduct, the principal shall consider the views of the school council with respect to its contents.

(4) **Not regulation** — A local code of conduct is not a regulation within the meaning of the *Regulations Act*.
[S.O. 2000, c. 12, s. 3]

304. (1) **Opening and closing exercises at schools** — Every board shall ensure that opening or closing exercises are held in each school under the board's jurisdiction, in accordance with the requirements set out in the regulations.

(2) **Same** — The opening or closing exercises must include the singing of *O Canada* and may include the recitation of a pledge of citizenship in the form set out in the regulations.

(3) **Exceptions** — A pupil is not required to participate in the opening or closing exercises in such circumstances as are prescribed by regulation.
[S.O. 2000, c. 12, s. 3]

305. (1) **Access to school premises** — The Minister may make regulations governing access to school premises, specifying classes of persons who are permitted to be on school premises and specifying the days and times at which different classes of persons are prohibited from being on school premises.

(2) **Prohibition** — No person shall enter or remain on school premises unless he or she is authorized by regulation to be there on that day or at that time.

(3) **Same, board policy** — A person shall not enter or remain on school premises if he or she is prohibited under a board policy from being there on that day or at that time.

(4) **Direction to leave** — The principal of a school may direct a person to leave the school premises if the principal believes that the person is prohibited by regulation or under a board policy from being there.

(5) **Offence** — Every person who contravenes subsection (2) is guilty of an offence.
[S.O. 2000, c. 12, s. 3]

306. (1) **Mandatory suspension of a pupil** — It is mandatory that a pupil be suspended from his or her school and from engaging in all school-related activities if the pupil commits any of the following infractions while he or she is at school or is engaged in a school-related activity:

1. Uttering a threat to inflict serious bodily harm on another person.
2. Possessing alcohol or illegal drugs.
3. Being under the influence of alcohol.
4. Swearing at a teacher or at another person in a position of authority.
5. Committing an act of vandalism that causes extensive damage to school property at the pupil's school or to property located on the premises of the pupil's school.
6. Engaging in another activity that, under a policy of the board, is one for which a suspension is mandatory.

(2) **Duration of mandatory suspension** — The minimum duration of a mandatory suspension is one school day and the maximum duration is 20 school days. The

minimum and maximum duration may be varied by regulation, and different standards may be established for different circumstances or different classes of persons.

(3) **Duties of teachers** — If a teacher observes a pupil committing an infraction that requires a mandatory suspension, the teacher shall suspend the pupil or refer the matter to the principal.

(4) **Duty to suspend, principal** — The principal has a duty to suspend a pupil who commits an infraction requiring a mandatory suspension, unless a teacher has already suspended the pupil for the infraction.

(5) **Mitigating factors** — Despite subsection (1), suspension of a pupil is not mandatory in such circumstances as may be prescribed by regulation.

(6) **Restriction on suspension by teacher** — A teacher cannot suspend a pupil under this section for a period longer than the minimum duration required by subsection (2).

(7) **Referral to principal** — If a teacher who suspends a pupil under this section is of the opinion that a longer suspension of the pupil is warranted, the teacher shall recommend to the principal that the suspension be extended.

(8) **Extension by principal** — Upon receiving a recommendation from a teacher to extend the suspension imposed on a pupil by the teacher, the principal may extend the suspension up to the maximum duration permitted by subsection (2).

(9) **Factors affecting duration of suspension** — In order to determine the duration of a mandatory suspension, the principal shall consider the pupil's history and such other factors as may be prescribed by regulation and the principal may consider such other matters as he or she considers appropriate.

(10) **Notice** — The teacher or principal who suspends a pupil under this section shall ensure that written notice of the mandatory suspension is given promptly to the pupil and, if the pupil is a minor, to the pupil's parent or guardian.

(11) **Policies and guidelines** — The Minister may issue policies and guidelines to boards to assist principals and teachers in interpreting and administering this section.

(12) **School-related activities** — A pupil who is suspended is not considered to be engaged in school-related activities by virtue of using services, taking a course or participating in a program to assist such pupils.

(13) **Definition** — In this section,
"mandatory suspension" means a suspension required by subsection (1).
[S.O. 2000, c. 12, s. 3]

307. (1) **Discretionary suspension of a pupil** — A pupil may be suspended if he or she engages in an activity that, under a policy of the board, is an activity for which suspension is discretionary.

(2) **Same** — A pupil may be suspended,

(a) from his or her school and from engaging in all school-related activities; or

(b) from one or more classes or one or more school-related activities or both.

(3) **Duration of discretionary suspension** — The minimum duration of a discretionary suspension is as specified by the board policy that authorizes the suspension and the maximum duration is 20 school days. The maximum duration may be varied by regulation, and different standards may be established for different circumstances or different classes of persons.

(4) **Authority to suspend, principal** — The principal may suspend a pupil who engages in an activity for which suspension is discretionary.

(5) **Authority of teachers** — If a teacher observes a pupil engaging in an activity for which suspension is discretionary, the teacher may suspend the pupil or refer the matter to the principal.

(6) **Restriction on suspension by teacher** — A teacher cannot suspend a pupil under this section for a period longer than the minimum duration described in subsection (3).

(7) **Other matters** — Subsections 306 (7) to (10) and 306 (12) apply, with necessary modifications, with respect to a discretionary suspension under this section.

(8) **Definition** — In this section,
"discretionary suspension" means a suspension authorized by subsection (1).
[S.O. 2000, c. 12, s. 3]

308. (1) **Review of suspension** — The following persons may request a review of a decision to suspend a pupil, other than a decision to suspend a pupil for one day or less:

1.   If the pupil is a minor, his or her parent or guardian.
2.   If the pupil is not a minor, the pupil.
3.   Such other persons as may be specified in a policy of the board.

(2) **The review process** — The review shall be conducted in accordance with the requirements established by board policy.

(3) **Same** — The review shall be conducted by the person specified in the board policy and, for the purposes of the review, the person has the powers and duties set out in the policy.

(4) **Appeal of suspension** — Following a review, the following persons may appeal a decision to suspend a pupil, other than a decision to suspend a pupil for one day or less:

1.   If the pupil is a minor, his or her parent or guardian.
2.   If the pupil is not a minor, the pupil.
3.   Such other persons as may be specified by board policy.

(5) **The appeal process** — An appeal under this section must be conducted in accordance with the requirements established by board policy.

(6) **Same** — The board shall hear and determine an appeal and, for that purpose, the board has the powers and duties set out in its policy. The decisions of the board are final.

(7) **Delegation by board** — The board may delegate its powers and duties under subsection (6) to a committee of the board, and may impose conditions and restrictions on the committee.
[S.O. 2000, c. 12, s. 3]

309. (1) **Mandatory expulsion of a student** — It is mandatory that a pupil be expelled if the pupil commits any of the following infractions while he or she is at school or is engaged in a school-related activity:

1.   Possessing a weapon, including possessing a firearm.
2.   Using a weapon to cause or to threaten bodily harm to another person.
3.   Committing physical assault on another person that causes bodily harm requiring treatment by a medical practitioner.
4.   Committing sexual assault.
5.   Trafficking in weapons or in illegal drugs.
6.   Committing robbery.
7.   Giving alcohol to a minor.
8.   Engaging in another activity that, under a policy of the board, is one for which expulsion is mandatory.

(2) **Duty to suspend pending expulsion, principal** — The principal shall suspend a pupil who the principal believes may have committed an infraction for which expulsion is mandatory.

(3) **Mitigating factors** — Despite subsection (1), expulsion of a pupil is not mandatory in such circumstances as may be prescribed by regulation.

(4) **Action following suspension** — If the principal suspends a pupil under subsection (2), the principal shall promptly refer the matter to the board or conduct an inquiry to determine whether the pupil has committed an infraction for which expulsion is mandatory.

(5) **Notice of suspension** — The principal shall ensure that written notice of the suspension under subsection (2) is given promptly to the pupil and, if the pupil is a minor, to the pupil's parent or guardian.

(6) **Conduct of inquiry** — The principal's inquiry shall be conducted in accordance with the requirements established by a policy of the board and the powers and duties of the principal are as specified by board policy.

(7) **Action following inquiry** — If, after the inquiry, the principal is satisfied that the pupil committed an infraction for which expulsion is mandatory, the principal shall,

(a) impose a limited expulsion as described in subsection (14) on the pupil; or

(b) refer the matter to the board for its determination.

(8) **Restriction on expulsion by principal** — The principal cannot expel a pupil if more than 20 school days have expired since the principal suspended the student under subsection (2), unless the parties to the inquiry agree upon a later deadline.

(9) **Hearing by board** — When a matter is referred to the board under subsection (4) or clause (7) (b), the board shall hold an expulsion hearing and, for that purpose, the board has the powers and duties specified by board policy.

(10) **Conduct of hearing** — The expulsion hearing shall be conducted in accordance with the requirements established by board policy.

(11) **Duty to expel, board** — If, after the expulsion hearing, the board is satisfied that the pupil committed an infraction for which expulsion is mandatory, the board shall impose a limited expulsion as described in subsection (14) or a full expulsion as described in subsection (16) on the pupil.

(12) **Restriction on expulsion by board** — The board cannot expel a pupil if more than 20 school days have expired since the principal suspended the pupil under subsection (2), unless the parties to the expulsion hearing agree upon a later deadline.

(13) **Delegation** — The board may delegate its duty to hold an expulsion hearing and its powers and duties under subsection (11) to a committee of the board, and may impose conditions and restrictions on the committee.

(14) **Limited expulsion** — A pupil who is subject to a limited expulsion is not entitled to attend the school the pupil was attending when he or she committed the infraction and is not entitled to engage in school-related activities of that school until the later of,

(a) the date specified by the principal or the board when expelling the pupil, which date cannot be more than one year after the date on which the principal suspended the pupil under subsection (2); and

(b) the date on which the pupil meets such requirements as may be established by the board for returning to school after being expelled.

(15) **Same** — A regulation may vary the limit described in clause (14) (a) and may specify a different limit for different circumstances or different classes of persons.

(16) **Full expulsion** — A pupil who is subject to a full expulsion is not entitled to attend any school in the province or to engage in school-related activities of any school in the province until he or she meets such requirements as may be established by regulation for returning to school after being expelled.

(17) **Effect on other rights** — A pupil's rights under sections 33, 36, 42 and 43 are inoperative during a full expulsion.

(18) **Minimum duration of mandatory expulsion** — The minimum duration of a mandatory expulsion is 21 school days and, for the purposes of this subsection,

the period of a pupil's suspension under subsection (2) shall be deemed to be a period of expulsion. The minimum duration may be varied by regulation, and a different standard may be established for different circumstances or different classes of persons.

(19) **Factors affecting type and duration of expulsion** — When considering the type and duration of expulsion that may be appropriate in particular circumstances, the principal or board shall consider the pupil's history and such other factors as may be prescribed by regulation and may consider such other matters as he, she or it considers appropriate.

(20) **Notice** — The principal or board that expels a pupil under this section shall ensure that written notice of the mandatory expulsion is given promptly to the pupil and, if the pupil is a minor, to the pupil's parent or guardian.

(21) **Policies and guidelines** — The Minister may issue policies and guidelines to boards to assist boards and principals in interpreting and administering this section.

(22) **School-related activities** — A pupil who is expelled is not considered to be engaged in school-related activities by virtue of using services to assist such pupils or taking a course or participating in a program that prepares the pupil to return to school. [S.O. 2000, c. 12, s. 3]

310. (1) **Discretionary expulsion of a pupil** — A pupil may be expelled if the pupil engages in an activity that, under a policy of the board, is one for which expulsion is discretionary.

(2) **Suspension pending expulsion, principal** — If the principal believes a pupil may have engaged in an activity for which expulsion is discretionary, the principal may suspend the pupil.

(3) **Other matters** — If the principal suspends a pupil under subsection (2), subsections 309 (4) to (20) and 309 (22) apply, with necessary modifications, with respect to an expulsion authorized by this section. [S.O. 2000, c. 12, s. 3]

311. (1) **Appeal of expulsion** — The following persons may appeal a decision to expel a pupil, including a decision under section 310 respecting the type and duration of the expulsion:

1. If the pupil is a minor, his or her parent or guardian.
2. If the pupil is not a minor, the pupil.
3. Such other persons as may be specified by a policy of the board.

(2) **The appeal process** — An appeal under this section must be conducted in accordance with the requirements established by board policy.

(3) **Same, expulsion by principal** — The board shall hear and determine an appeal from a decision of a principal to expel a pupil and, for that purpose, the board has the powers and duties set out in its policy. The decisions of the board are final.

(4) **Delegation by board** — The board may delegate its powers and duties under subsection (3) to a committee of the board, and may impose conditions and restrictions on the committee.

(5) **The appeal process, expulsion by board** — A person or entity designated by regulation shall hear and determine an appeal from a decision of a board to expel a pupil, and, for that purpose, the person or entity has the powers and duties set out in the regulations. The decisions of the person or entity are final.

(6) **Same** — For the purposes of subsection (5), the Minister may by regulation establish an entity to exercise the powers and perform the duties referred to in that subsection, and the Minister may determine the composition and the other powers and duties of the entity. [S.O. 2000, c. 12, s. 3]

312. (1) **Programs, etc., for suspended pupils** — The Minister may require boards to establish and maintain specified programs, courses and services for pupils who are suspended, and may impose different requirements for different circumstances, different locations or different classes of pupils.

(2) **Same, expelled pupils** — The Minister may require boards to establish and maintain specified programs, courses and services for pupils who are expelled and may authorize boards,

(a) to enter into agreements with other boards for the provision of the programs, courses and services;

(b) to retain others to provide the programs, courses and services; or

(c) to establish one or more corporations to provide the programs, courses and services.

(3) **Authorization** — The Minister may impose conditions and restrictions when authorizing a board to engage in an activity described in subsection (2).

(4) **Programs for expelled pupils** — The Minister may establish one or more programs for expelled pupils to prepare the pupils to return to school and may require boards to give specified information about the programs to expelled pupils.

(5) **Same** — The Minister may establish policies and guidelines respecting pupils' eligibility to participate in a program established under subsection (2) or (4) and respecting the criteria to be met for successful completion of the program.
[S.O. 2000, c. 12, s. 3]

313. (1) **Transition, suspension of a pupil** — This section applies with respect to a pupil who engages in an activity before section 306 comes into force that may result in his or her suspension under section 23 as it reads on the day the pupil engages in the activity.

(2) **Same** — Section 23, as it reads on the day the pupil engages in the activity, continues to apply after section 306 comes into force for the purpose of determining whether, and for how long, the pupil is to be suspended and for the purpose of determining any appeal relating to the suspension of the pupil.
[S.O. 2000, c. 12, s. 3]

314. (1) **Transition, expulsion of a pupil** — This section applies with respect to a pupil who engages in an activity before section 309 comes into force that may result in his or her expulsion under section 23 as it reads on the day the pupil engages in the activity.

(2) **Same** — Section 23, as it reads on the day the pupil engages in the activity, continues to apply after section 309 comes into force for the purpose of determining whether, from where and for how long the pupil is to be expelled and determining the criteria for the pupil's return to school.
[S.O. 2000, c. 12, s. 3]

315. (1) **Collection of personal information** — The Minister may collect and may by regulation require boards to collect such personal information as is specified by regulation from, or about, the classes of persons specified by regulation for the following purposes, and the Minister may specify or restrict the manner in which the information is to be collected:

1. To ensure the safety of pupils.

2. To administer programs, courses and services to pupils who are suspended or expelled and to determine whether an expelled pupil has successfully completed a program, course or service and as a result is eligible to return to school.

(2) **Disclosure** — A board or other person is authorized to disclose the personal information collected under subsection (1) to the Minister for the purposes described

in that subsection, and the Minister may disclose it to such persons or entities as may be prescribed by regulation for those purposes.

(3) **Definition** — In this section,

"personal information" has the same meaning as in section 38 of the *Freedom of Information and Protection of Privacy Act* and section 28 of the *Municipal Freedom of Information and Protection of Privacy Act.*

[S.O. 2000, c. 12, s. 3]

316. (1) **Regulations** — The Minister may make regulations,

(a) prescribing such matters as are required, or permitted, under this Part to be prescribed or to be done by regulation;

(b) specifying when, during a school day, a suspension of a pupil is permitted to begin and to end.

(2) **Classes** — A regulation under subsection (1) may impose different requirements on different classes of person, place or thing or in different circumstances.

(3) **Exceptions** — A regulation under subsection (1) may provide that one or more provisions of this Part or of the regulation does not apply to specified persons or in specified circumstances.

[S.O. 2000, c. 12, s. 3]

317. to 326. [Repealed, S.O. 1997, c. 31, s. 129]

27

Ontario Schools Code of Conduct

[Note: The *Safe Schools Act, 2000*, which provides for the establishment of a Code of Conduct, was given Royal Assent on June 13, 2000.]

Introduction

A school is a place that promotes responsibility, respect, civility and academic excellence in a safe learning and teaching environment.

All students, parents, teachers and staff have the right to be safe, and feel safe, in their school community. With this right comes the responsibility to be law-abiding citizens and to be accountable for actions that put at risk the safety of others or oneself.

The Ontario Code of Conduct sets clear provincial standards of behaviour. It specifies the mandatory consequences for student actions that do not comply with these standards.

The Provincial standards of behaviour apply not only to students, but also to all individuals involved in the publicly funded school system—parents or guardians, volunteers, teachers and other staff members—whether they are on school property, on school buses or at school-authorized events or activities.

Guiding Principles

- All participants involved in the publicly funded school system—students, parents or guardians, volunteers, teachers and other staff members—are included in this Code of Conduct whether they are on school property, on school buses or at school-authorized events or activities.
- All members of the school community are to be treated with respect and dignity, especially persons in positions of authority.

- Responsible citizenship involves appropriate participation in the civic life of the school community. Active and engaged citizens are aware of their rights, but more importantly, they accept responsibility for protecting their rights and the rights of others.
- Members of the school community are expected to use non-violent means to resolve conflict. Physically aggressive behavior is not a responsible way to interact with others.
- The possession, use or threatened use of any object to injure another person endangers the safety of oneself and others.
- Alcohol and illegal drugs are addictive and present a health hazard. Ontario schools will work cooperatively with police, drug and alcohol agencies to promote prevention strategies and, where necessary, respond to school members who are in possession of, or under the influence of, alcohol or illegal drugs.
- Insults, disrespect, and other hurtful acts disrupt learning and teaching in a school community. Members of the school community have a responsibility to maintain an environment where conflict and difference can be addressed in a manner characterized by respect and civility.

Roles and Responsibilities

School Boards provide direction to their schools that ensure opportunity, excellence and accountability in the education system. School boards:

- develop policies that set out how their schools will implement and enforce the Provincial Code of Conduct and all other rules that they develop as related to the provincial standards for respect, civility, responsible citizenship and physical safety;
- seek input from school councils and review these policies regularly with students, staff, parents or guardians, volunteers and the community;
- establish a process that clearly communicates the Provincial Code of Conduct to all parents, students and staff in a manner that ensures their commitment and support;
- ensure an effective intervention strategy and response to all infractions related to the standards for respect, civility, responsible citizenship and physical safety;
- provide opportunities for all staff to acquire the knowledge, skills and attitudes necessary to develop and maintain academic excellence and safe learning and teaching environments.

Principals, under the direction of their school board, take a leadership role in the daily operation of a school. They provide this leadership by:

- demonstrating care and commitment to academic excellence and a safe teaching and learning environment;
- holding everyone, under their authority, accountable for their behavior and actions;
- communicating regularly and meaningfully with all members of their school community.

Teachers and School staff, under the leadership of their principals, maintain order in the school and are expected to hold everyone to the highest standard of respectful and responsible behaviour. As role models, staff uphold these high standards when they:

- help students work to their full potential and develop their self-worth;
- communicate regularly and meaningfully with parents;

- maintain consistent standards of behaviour for all students;
- demonstrate respect for all students, staff and parents;
- prepare students for the full responsibilities of citizenship.

Students are to be treated with respect and dignity. In return, they must demonstrate respect for themselves, for others and for the responsibilities of citizenship through acceptable behaviour. Respect and responsibility are demonstrated when a student:

- comes to school prepared, on time and ready to learn;
- shows respect for themselves, for others and for those in authority;
- refrains from bringing anything to school that may compromise the safety of others;
- follows the established rules and takes responsibility for his or her own action.

Parents play an important role in the education of their children and have a responsibility to support the efforts of school staff in maintaining a safe and respectful learning environment for all students. Parents fulfill this responsibility when they:

- show an active interest in their child's school work and progress;
- communicate regularly with the school;
- help their child be neat, appropriately dressed and prepared for school;
- ensure that their child attends school regularly and on time;
- promptly report to the school their child's absence or late arrival;
- become familiar with the Code of Conduct and school rules;
- encourage and assist their child in following the rules of behaviour;
- assist school staff in dealing with disciplinary issues.

Police and community members are essential partners in making our schools and communities safer. Community members need to support and respect the rules of their local schools. Police investigate incidents in accordance with the protocol developed with the local school board. These protocols are based on a provincial model developed by the Ministry of the Solicitor General and the Ministry of Education.

Standards of Behaviour

Respect, Civility and Responsible Citizenship

All school members must:

- respect and comply with all applicable federal, provincial and municipal laws;
- demonstrate honesty and integrity;
- respect differences in people, their ideas and opinions;
- treat one another with dignity and respect at all times, and especially when there is disagreement;
- respect and treat others fairly, regardless of their race, ancestry, place of origin, colour, ethnic origin, citizenship, religion, gender, sexual orientation, age or disability;
- respect the rights of others;
- show proper care and regard for school property and the property of others;
- take appropriate measures to help those in need;
- respect persons who are in a position of authority;
- respect the need of others to work in an environment of learning and teaching.

Physical Safety

Weapons

All school members must:

- not be in possession of any weapon, including but not limited to firearms;
- not use any object to threaten or intimidate another person;
- not cause injury to any person with an object.

Alcohol and Drugs

All school members must:

- not be in possession of, or under the influence of, or provide others with, alcohol or illegal drugs.

Physical Aggression

All school members must:

- not inflict or encourage others to inflict bodily harm on another person;
- seek staff assistance, if necessary, to resolve conflict peacefully.

Mandatory Consequences

Police will be involved, as indicated by the police/school protocol, and the student will be immediately suspended and proceed to an expulsion hearing for the following:

- possession of a weapon, including, but not limited to firearms;
- trafficking in drugs or weapons;
- robbery;
- use of a weapon to cause bodily harm, or to threaten serious harm;
- physical assault causing bodily harm requiring professional medical treatment;
- sexual assault;
- providing alcohol to minors.

Immediate Suspension will be the minimum penalty faced by a student for:

- uttering a threat to inflict serious bodily harm;
- possession of illegal drugs;
- acts of vandalism causing extensive damage to school property or property located on school premises.

In these instances, police will be involved, as required, and conditions to return to school will be specified in accordance with school board policies.

A student will be immediately suspended for:

- swearing at a teacher, or other person in authority;
- being in possession of alcohol;
- being under the influence of alcohol.

28

School Year Calendar

(R.R.O. 1990, Reg. 304)

Amendments: O. Reg. 822/82; O. Reg. 91/98.

1. (1) In this Regulation,

"instructional day" means a school day that is designated as an instructional day on a school calendar and upon which day an instructional program that may include examinations is provided for each pupil whose program is governed by such calendar;

"professional activity" includes evaluation of the progress of pupils, consultation with parents, the counselling of pupils, curriculum and program evaluation and development, professional development of teachers and attendance at educational conferences;

"professional activity day" means a school day that is designated as a day for professional activities on a school calendar;

"school day" means a day that is within a school year and is not a school holiday;

"school year" means the period prescribed as such by or approved as such under this Regulation.

(2) A board may designate half a school day an instructional program and the remainder of the day for professional activities, but such a day constitutes a half-day in determining the number of instructional days in the school year.

[O. Reg. 822/82, s. 1]

[**Note:** The title of the regulation was amended by O. Reg. 91/98, s. 1.]

2. (1) Subject to section 5, the school year shall commence on or after the 1st day of September and end on or before the 30th day of June.

(2) [Repealed]

(3) [Repealed]

(3.1) Subject to section 5, every school year after the 1997–1998 school year shall include a minimum of 194 school days of which up to 4 days may be designated by the board as professional activity days and the remaining school days shall be instructional days.

(4) Subject to section 5, the following are school holidays:

1. Every Saturday and Sunday.
2. When the school is open during July, Canada Day.
3. Labour Day.
4. A day appointed by the Governor General or the Lieutenant Governor as a public holiday or for Thanksgiving.
5. A Christmas vacation consisting of fourteen consecutive days commencing on the Monday next following the Friday preceding the 21st day of December, but when the 21st day of December is a Thursday or a Friday, commencing on the Monday next following.
6. Five consecutive days commencing on the Monday next following the Friday preceding the 14th day of March.
7. Good Friday.
8. Easter Monday.
9. Victoria Day.

[O. Reg. 822/82, s. 2; O. Reg. 91/98, s. 2]

3. (1) [Repealed]

(2) [Repealed]

(3) Where a school has a policy of granting exemptions to pupils from the writing of examinations, such exemptions may be granted only from the final examinations in a course and only where at least one other set of examinations has been held.

(3.1) With respect to every school year after the 1997–1998 school year, a board may designate up to 10 instructional days as examination days.

(4) The teaching staff shall be in school during regular school hours on examination days and accessible to pupils, unless the board directs otherwise.

[O. Reg. 91/98, s. 3]

4. (1) In each year every board shall, except in respect of a school or class for which the board has submitted a proposed school calendar under section 5, prepare, adopt and submit to the Minister on or before the 1st day of May in respect of the school year next following, the school calendar or school calendars to be followed in the schools under its jurisdiction, and each such school calendar shall,

(a) state the school or schools in which the calendar is to be followed;

(b) conform to section 2; and

(c) identify each day of the school year as an instructional day, a professional activity day or a school holiday.

(2) In preparing a school calendar under subsection (1), the board shall ensure that some of the professional activity days are designated for the purposes of curriculum development, implementation and review.

(3) A school calendar submitted under subsection (1) shall be accompanied by a general outline of the activities to be conducted on the professional activity days identified on the calendar.

5. (1) For one or more schools under its jurisdiction a board may designate a school year and school holidays that are different from those prescribed in section 2 and, where a board does so, the board shall submit to the Minister on or before the first day of March a proposed school calendar for the school year next following in respect of such school or schools, identifying thereon each day of the school year as an instructional day, a professional activity day or a school holiday, and the board may, upon approval thereof by the Minister, implement such school calendar.

(2) Where the Minister informs a board that he or she does not approve the school calendar submitted under subsection (1), the board may amend its proposed school

calendar and submit to the Minister a revised school calendar and, upon approval thereof by the Minister, the board may implement the revised school calendar.

(3) Where a board has submitted a proposed school calendar under subsection (1) and the Minister has not approved on or before the 15th day of April such calendar or a revision thereof submitted under subsection (2), the board shall, on or before the 1st day of May, prepare, adopt and submit to the Minister a school calendar in accordance with section 4.

6. (1) Where in the opinion of the board it is desirable to alter the date of a professional activity day or an examination day on a school calendar that has been submitted under section 4 or subsection 5 (3) or approved and implemented under subsection 5(1) or (2), the board may alter the school calendar.

(2) Where, the board alters a school calendar under subsection (1), the board shall notify the parents concerned and the Minister of the altered date as far in advance as possible.

(3) The prior approval of the Minister is required for changes other than to the date of a professional activity day or an examination day.

(4) Where,

(a) a school or class is closed for a temporary period because of failure of transportation arrangements, inclement weather, fire, flood, a breakdown of the school heating plant or a similar emergency, or a school is closed under the *Health Protection and Promotion Act* or the *Education Act;* and

(b) the school calendar is not altered under subsection (1), the day on which the school or class is closed remains an instructional day or a professional activity day, as the case may be, as designated on the school calendar applicable to such school or class.

7. (1) Every board shall publish annually its school calendar or school calendars and ensure that copies thereof are available at the beginning of the school year for the information of parents and pupils.

(2) A school calendar or school calendars published under subsection (1) shall, in addition to the information required to be listed under subsection 4 (1), indicate in a general manner the activities to be conducted on professional activity days.

8. In each year, every board shall undertake an annual evaluation of the activities of the professional activity days of the previous year and retain such evaluations on file.

9. (1) A Remembrance Day service shall be held in every school on the 11th day of November or, when the 11th day of November is a Saturday or a Sunday, on the Friday preceding the 11th day of November.

(2) Subsection (1) does not apply where the school participates in a service of remembrance at a cenotaph or other location in the community.

Your Teaching Future

29

Education Issues
for the Twenty-First
Century

At the turn of the century, more and more educators are working in a world of intensifying and rapid change.... New technologies, greater cultural diversity, the skills called for in a changing economy, restructured approaches to administration and management, and a more sophisticated knowledge-base about teaching and learning, are all pulling students and their teachers in new directions.

—Mission Statement excerpt
International Centre for Educational Change
Ontario Institute for Studies in Education
University of Toronto

Taken from *Becoming a Teacher,* Second Canadian Edition, by Forrest W. Parkay, Beverly Hardcastle Stanford, John P. Vaillancourt, and Heather C. Stephens.

1. What knowledge and skills will prepare students for a global information age?

2. How can schools and teachers provide an outstanding education for all learners?

3. How can community-based partnerships address social problems that hinder students' learning?

4. How will the fledgling charter school movement affect equity and excellence in education?

5. What can teachers and schools learn from international education?

6. What is our vision for the future of education?

*H*ow will education change during the twenty-first century? What new school–community linkages will help schools meet the needs of all learners? In what ways will teachers' professional lives become more collaborative and oriented toward system-wide reform? How likely is it that, as a teacher, you will have experiences similar to the following?*

After a short drive through early-morning traffic less heavy than usual, you arrive at school in time for a 7:30 AM meeting of your school's Teacher Leadership Team (TLT), a group that makes curricular and instructional decisions for the school. The TLT also works directly with the school's Site-Based Council (SBC), which makes budget, personnel, and other policy decisions. SBC members include three teachers, the principal, five community members, and two professors from a nearby university.

Like most schools around the country, the changing demographics of the nation are reflected in an increasingly diverse student population at your school. About 15 percent of students are from families who live below the poverty line, and one in eight students is learning with English as a second language. According to a district survey, students represent 18 different language groups with Arabic being second to English as the most prevalent tongue. Overall, students at your school score in the top percentiles on provincial examinations; 50 percent of students go on to college, and 15 percent enrol in other forms of postsecondary programs.

With a few minutes before the meeting begins, you enter the classroom of another TLT member. Both of you were selected to be part of a nationwide network of teachers who will field test an interactive computer simulation developed by an instructional technology laboratory at a major university. Last week you both received the beta-test (trial) software, field-test guidelines, and registration materials for a four-day preparatory workshop to be held at the university. The university is paying for travel plus expenses, as well as providing a stipend.

"Well, did you have a chance to try out the software?" you ask upon entering the room. "I did last night, and it looks pretty impressive. I'm anxious to see what the kids think."

"I haven't had a chance yet; I've been preparing for this morning's TLT meeting," your friend says, pausing momentarily as she staples handouts arranged in neat stacks on top of her desk. Last spring she was elected to be one of the school's two curriculum coordinators. At today's TLT meeting, she and the other coordinator are presenting a model for school-wide curriculum integration. "What do we have to do as field testers?" she asks, continuing with her stapling task. "I just glanced at the field-test guidelines."

"Well, actually quite a lot, but I think it'll be interesting," you say. "The lab wants us to use the software every day for three weeks. Also, collect student performance data on a regular basis and samples of students' work. Plus, students will complete a survey at the beginning and at the end of the field test. That's about it ... oh, I forgot, they want us to do some student interviews ... there's a set of constructivist-oriented questions we're supposed to use. Basically, the lab wants us to develop a picture of students' problem-solving strategies as they work through the simulation."

"That does sound interesting," your friend says.

"Right. Well, I better get out of here and let you finish getting ready for the TLT meeting," you say.

Walking down the hallway to the conference room, you think about how satisfying it is to teach at your school. Teachers are hard-working and share a strong commitment to good teaching and to building a collegial professional community. Ample leadership opportunities, common planning periods, stimulating colleagues who are professionally involved, and solid support from the district and community are just a few of the factors that make working conditions at your school very positive.

Though no one has an educational crystal ball that can give a totally accurate glimpse of how the profession of teaching will evolve during the twenty-first century and how students will be taught, powerful forces are shaping schools and teaching in the directions just outlined. Moreover, thousands of teachers are collaborating and playing key leadership roles in shaping that future; and, today, hundreds of schools have professional communities identical to that described in the preceding scenario. We believe that the conditions under which teachers will work in this century will provide a dramatic contrast to those that many teachers experienced throughout much of the previous century. Isolation, lack of autonomy and self-governance, and few chances for professional growth are being replaced by collaboration, empowerment, stronger professionalism, and opportunities to provide leadership for educational change.

Figure 29.1

Educational priorities for the future

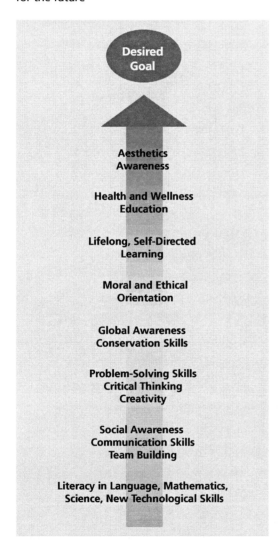

What Knowledge and Skills Will Prepare Students for a Global Information Age?

What knowledge and skills will students need to succeed in a global information age? Teachers in every generation have asked that question. At the beginning of the twenty-first century, the answer is confounded by conflicting theories, expectations, and values. One thing everyone agrees on, however, is that increasing cultural diversity in Canada and other countries and increasing global economic interdependence will call for communication and cooperation skills. People will need to be able to live together well and use environmental resources wisely. To equip students to do this, teachers will need to dedicate themselves to ensuring that all students develop knowledge, skills, attitudes, and values in nine key areas (see Figure 29.1). Though these nine areas of learning will not be all that students will need, learning in these areas will best enable them to meet the challenges of the future.

Literacy in Language, Mathematics, and Science

To solve the problems of the future, students will need to be able to write and speak clearly and succinctly. To access critical information from enormous data banks, they will need to be able to read complex material with a high degree of comprehension. Moreover, the continued development of "user-friendly" technologies such as voice-activated computers and reading machines will not reduce the need for high-level language arts literacy. In addition to strong skills in reading and writing, students will also need to be able to apply mathematical and scientific concepts to solve new problems. For example, they will need to be able to analyze unfamiliar situations, pose appropriate questions, use trial-and-error methods to gather and evaluate relevant data, and summarize results.

New Technology Skills

Students of the future will also need to attain high levels of skill in computer-based technologies. To teach students skills in accessing the vast stores of information that computers routinely handle today, our nation's schools will become more technologically rich and teachers more technologically sophisticated. No longer able to resist the "irresistible force" of Information Age technology (Mehlinger 1996), schools will join the larger society where "the computer is a symbol of the future and all that is good about it" (Morton 1996, 417). In such an environment, students will not only learn to use computers as "tools" to access information—they will use computers to communicate worldwide and to generate creative solutions to real-world problems.

Problem Solving, Critical Thinking, and Creativity

Students of the future will need to be able to think rather than to remember. Although the information that students learn in schools may become outdated or useless, the thinking processes they acquire will not. These processes focus on the ability to find, obtain, and use information resources for solving problems or taking advantage of opportunities. Students will need to learn how to cope with change, how to anticipate alternative future developments, how to think critically, and how to analyze and synthesize large amounts of complex data.

Forecasts about the future share one thing in common—they place a priority on creative thinking to solve future problems. The acquisition of structured bodies of knowledge, while important, is not sufficient preparation for the future. Students must learn to think creatively to solve unforeseen problems. Students who are stretched to develop their creativity today will become the adults who invent ways to solve tomorrow's problems.

Can creative thinking be taught? William J. J. Gordon (1968, 1971a, 1971b, 1975), who has devoted his career to the study of creativity, believes it can. Gordon developed synectics, a teaching method based on the thinking process that is designed to

What knowledge and skills for the twenty-first century does this learning activity support? What else will students need to know and be able to do in the future?

"teach" creativity through the use of metaphor and analogy. **Synectics** is based on the assumptions that (1) creativity is important; (2) creativity is not mysterious; (3) in all fields, creative invention draws from the same underlying intellectual processes; and (4) the creativity of individuals and groups is similar (Joyce, Weil, and Calhoun 2000).

Social Awareness, Communication Skills, and Team Building

Tomorrow's students must be able to communicate with people from diverse cultures. The ability to create a better world in the future, then, will surely depend on our willingness to celebrate our rich diversity through the kind of communication that leads to understanding, friendly social relations, and the building of cohesive teams. "[T]he classroom should be a laboratory for collaborative decision making and team building" (Uchida, Cetron, and McKenzie 1996, 8).

An important lesson for students will be to learn that poverty, discrimination, violence, crime, and unequal opportunities, wherever they occur, affect us all. To solve these and other social problems, students will need to become socially aware, politically active, and skilled in conflict resolution strategies.

Global Awareness and Conservation Skills

Tomorrow's students will need to recognize the interconnectedness they share with all countries and with all people. Our survival may depend on being able to participate intelligently in a global economy and respond intelligently to global threats to security, health, environmental quality, and other factors affecting the quality of human life. The curriculum of the future must emphasize cultural diversity, interdependence, respect for the views and values held by others, an orientation toward international cooperation for resolving global issues, and practical knowledge and skills on, for example, the conservation of natural energy resources.

Health and Wellness Education

With ever-increasing health care costs, the spread of diseases such as AIDS, increased risks of cancer, and longer life spans, it is imperative that students of the future acquire appropriate knowledge, skills, and attitudes in the area of health education. To live healthy lives, then, students of tomorrow will need consumer education to select from among an increasingly complex array of health care services. In addition, they will need to be able to make informed choices among alternatives for the prevention or treatment of problems relating to substance abuse, nutrition, fitness, and mental health. Sex education, still a matter for debate in some communities, seems more critical today than at any time in the past.

Moral and Ethical Orientation

The school culture and the curriculum reflect both national and community values. The traditional practice of using values-clarification activities in the classroom, however, has been criticized by some for promoting relativism at the expense of family values or religious doctrines. Yet, as we witness the effects of violence in schools, racial intolerance, sexual exploitation of children, drunk driving, white-collar crime, false advertising, unethical business practices, excessive litigation, and so on, many citizens are calling for schools to pay more attention to issues of public morality and ethical behaviour. "[T]o survive and prosper in the twenty-first century, students will need self-discipline, which entails an ethical code and the ability to set and assess progress toward their own goals" (Uchida, Cetron, and McKenzie 1996, 17). In response to harassment and intimidation that can lead to violence in the hallways, for example, many Canadian schools have implemented anger management programs similar to the Second Step program created by the Seattle-Based Committee for Children. According to a teacher at a school that begins the year with Second Step lessons for all students, "We have created a culture in our school that says we all recognize that some things just aren't accepted" (Gutloff 1999).

Aesthetic Awareness

Another challenge for teachers and schools is to encourage creativity and greater appreciation for the arts. Many observers of Canadian education point out that emotional, spiritual, aesthetic, and reflective, or meditative, dimensions of life receive less emphasis than analytical thinking and practical life skills. Although literature and drama are standard fare in curricula, for example, most students know little about music, painting, and sculpture. Public school students are rarely taught art history or principles of design or other criteria for evaluating creative works. As a result, students may lack the concepts and experiences that lead to an appreciation of beauty and the development of aesthetic judgment.

Lifelong Self-Directed Learning

The key educational priority that should guide teachers of the future is to create within each student the ability, and the desire, to continue self-directed learning throughout his or her life.

It has often been said that one of the primary purposes of schooling is for students to learn how to learn. In a world characterized by rapid social, technological, economic, and political changes, all persons must take responsibility for their own learning. Career changes will be the norm, and continuing education over a lifetime will be necessary.

How Can Schools and Teachers Provide an Outstanding Education for All Learners?

Although we don't know exactly how teaching will change during the twenty-first century, we do know that teachers will continue to have a professional and moral obligation to reach all learners, many of whom will be from environments that provide little support for education. Imagine, for example, that one of your students is Dolores, described in the following scenario.

> Fifteen-year-old Dolores and her twin brother, Frank, live with their mother in a housing project in a poor section of the city. Their mother divorced her third husband two years ago, after she learned that he had been sexually abusing Dolores. Since then, Dolores' mother has been struggling to make ends meet with her job as a custodian at a hospital. Two evenings a week, she goes to a neighbourhood centre to learn English. She hopes to become proficient enough in English to get a job as a secretary.

Dolores wishes her mother and Frank didn't fight so much. The fights usually revolve around Frank missing school and his drinking. Just last night, for example, Frank came home drunk and he and his mother got into another big fight. When she accused him of being involved in a street gang, Frank stormed out and went to spend the night at his cousin's apartment two blocks away.

At 6:30 that morning, Dolores awoke just as her mother left for work. The hinges on the apartment door, painted over by a careless maintenance worker, creaked loudly as she closed the door behind her. Dolores felt reassured by the sound of her mother locking the dead bolt—the apartment beneath them had been burglarized last week. Like Frank, she wasn't getting along well with her mother lately, so it would be nice to have the apartment to herself while she got ready for school.

Dolores got up slowly, stretched, and looked around the cluttered living room of the one-bedroom apartment. Her mother slept in the bedroom, and Frank, when he wasn't out all night or at his cousin's, slept on the other couch in the living room.

She had had trouble sleeping last night. Now that it was winter, the radiator next to the beige couch on which she slept clanked and hissed most of the night. Also, she was worried—two weeks ago a doctor at the neighbourhood clinic confirmed that she was pregnant. Yesterday, she finally got up enough courage to tell her boyfriend. He got angry with her and said he "wasn't gonna be no father."

Dolores knew she ought to be seeing a doctor, but she dreaded going to the clinic alone. Her mother took a day off from work—without pay—when she went two weeks ago. Right after that, her mother complained about missing work and said, "Don't expect me to take off from work every time you go to the clinic. You should have thought about that before you got in trouble."

Later that morning, Dolores is in your class, sitting in her usual spot in the middle of the back row. While your students work on an in-class writing assignment, you glance at Dolores and wonder why she hasn't been paying attention during the last few weeks like she usually does. At that moment, Dolores, wearing the same clothes she wore yesterday, stifles a yawn.

As you continue to move about the room, checking on students' progress and answering an occasional question, you wonder if you should talk with Dolores after class. You don't want to pry into her life outside of school, but you're worried about what might be causing her to act differently.

Although the family will continue to remain a prominent part of our culture, evidence indicates that many children, like Dolores and Frank, live in families that are under acute stress. Soaring numbers of runaway children and cases of child abuse suggest that the family is in trouble. In addition, teachers will continue to find that more and more of their students are from families that are smaller, have working mothers, have a single parent present, or have unrelated adults living in the home.

Equity for All Students

A dominant political force in the twenty-first century will be continued demands for equity in all sectors of Canadian life, particularly education. For example, the legalities of school funding laws will be challenged where inequities are perceived, and tax reform measures will be adopted to promote equitable school funding. Classroom teachers will continue to be held accountable for treating all students equitably.

In Chapter 5, you learned about the importance of preparing multicultural instructional materials and strategies to meet the learning needs of students from diverse cultural, ethnic, and linguistic backgrounds. In Chapter 6, you learned how to create an inclusive classroom to meet the needs of all students, regardless of their developmental levels, intelligences, abilities, or disabilities. In addition, you should create a learning environment in which high-achieving and low-achieving students are treated the same. Thomas Good and Jere Brophy (2000) reviewed the research in this area and found that several teacher behaviours indicated unequal treatment of students. The behaviours identified include waiting less time for them to answer questions, interacting with them less frequently, giving less feedback, calling on them less often, seating them farther way, failing to accept and use their ideas, smiling at them less often, making less eye contact, praising them less, demanding less, grading their tests differently, and rewarding inappropriate behaviours.

Effective teachers establish respectful relationships with *all* students; they listen to them; they give frequent feedback and opportunities to ask questions; and they demand higher-level performance. In their assessment of student's learning, they give special attention to the questions they ask of students. Research indicates that most questions teachers ask are **lower-order questions,** those that assess students' abilities to recall specific information. Effective teachers, however, also ask **higher-order questions** that demand more critical thinking and answers to questions such as, Why? What if ... ? In addition, to reach all learners and prepare them for the future, effective teachers provide students with active, authentic learning experiences.

Active, Authentic Learning

Since the 1970s, educational researchers have increased our understanding of the learning process. Though learning theorists and researchers disagree about a definition for *learning,* most agree that **learning** "occurs when experience causes a relatively permanent change in an individual's knowledge or behavior" (Woolfolk 1998, 204). Research into multiple intelligences and multicultural learning modes has broadened our understanding of this definition of learning. In addition, research in the fields of neurophysiology, neuropsychology, and cognitive science will continue to expand our understanding of how people think and learn.

Our growing understanding of learning indicates that all students learn best when they are actively involved in authentic activities that connect with the "real world." Small-group activities, cooperative learning arrangements, field trips, experiments, and integrated curricula are among the instructional methods you should incorporate into your professional repertoire.

How Can Community-Based Partnerships Address Social Problems That Hinder Students' Learning?

Earlier in this book, we examined social problems that affect schools and place students at risk of dropping out: poverty, family stress, substance abuse, violence and crime, teen pregnancy, HIV/AIDS, and suicide (see Chapter 5). We also looked at intervention programs schools have developed to ensure the optimum behavioural, social, and academic adjustment of at-risk children and adolescents to their school experiences: peer

An Exemplary School

The following case describes a prototypical exemplary urban elementary school, "Paul Robeson Elementary School," as compiled by Gloria Ladson-Billings, an award-winning researcher and author. Not a futuristic school, the school is an example for today—incorporating the best practices and perspectives that Ladson-Billings observed in eight classrooms that she studied over a two-year period. Consider Ladson-Billings' Robeson School as presented and then project it 20 years into the future. How might it be different and even better?

Paul Robeson Elementary School is located in a low-income predominantly ethnic community. More than merely a school, Robeson is a neighbourhood centre and gathering place that is open from 6:00 AM to 10:00 PM It includes a daycare centre, a preschool, a health clinic, and a job training centre. Local civic and church groups use the school as a meeting place. If one needs information about the community, the school is the likely place to locate it.

The banner across the main hallway of the school reads, "It takes a whole village to educate a child." Robeson's teaching staff is multicultural. The teaching staff has representatives from a variety of racial and ethnic backgrounds. However, every credentialed adult at Robeson, not just the teachers, teaches a class—the principal, the counsellor, the special teachers. This means that classes are relatively small—12 to 15 students. There are no "pull out" programs, such as those that require students to be taken out of their regular classrooms to receive remedial instruction while simultaneously depriving them of the instruction that is occurring in the regular class. There is no separate class for students evaluated as learning-disabled. Instead, students with learning disabilities are integrated into the regular classrooms and receive additional attention with the help of teachers' aides, the classroom teacher, and more advanced peers.

Robeson has one requirement—that its students be successful. The curriculum is rigorous and exciting. The student learning is organized around problems and issues. For example, one fourth-grade class is studying how cities develop. The students have studied cities in Europe, Africa, and Asia. They are studying their own city. They have taken trips to City Hall and have seen the city council in action. The mayor visited their classroom. In current events they read about the city news. Groups of students are working on solutions to problems specific to their city. The problems include the city's budget deficit, homelessness, the poor conditions of roads, and crime—particularly drug-related crime.

The students have read Carl Sandburg's poetry and they have studied architecture—buildings and bridges. They have studied geography and urban planning. They have written letters to the editor of a city newspaper about conditions in the city and in their neighbourhood. Each student is an "expert" in some aspect of cities. Together they are planning an exhibition that will be shown in the evening so that their parents and other community members can attend.

All students at Robeson Elementary participate in a community service program. The students in the primary grades usually participate as a class group. Community service activities include visiting a local nursing home, where students participate in the Adopt-a-Grandparent program. They also participate in neighbourhood cleanup days and recycling drives. The older students develop their own community service projects, which are approved by their teachers. They usually work in small groups or in pairs. Occasionally, an intermediate class will take on a project such as becoming readers at the local library, volunteering in the pediatric ward of the hospital, and planting and maintaining a community garden.

Parents play an important role at Robeson. Each household is assessed 20 h of volunteer service to the school. Some volunteer one hour a week in the classroom. Others participate in the school's Artists and Scholars in Residence program. Parents who participate in the local church choir offer their musical skills. Others share their cooking, sewing, knitting, woodworking, or athletic talents.

School governance at Robeson involves the principal, the teachers, the parents, and the students. The school council meets once a month to discuss the curriculum, instruction, personnel, and finances. The council members determine school policy and hiring and firing issues, and they constitute the school's disciplinary board.

One of Robeson's unique qualities is its residence program. By working with local social-service agencies Robeson obtained use of a renovated small apartment building nearby to house students whose family lives are in turmoil. Under the best circumstances students spend only a short time at the residence; in some unfortunate cases they spend the entire year there. By living in a centre in their own community, they do not have to leave Robeson or the neighbourhood they know. The residence is not for students with disciplinary problems. It is designed simply to alleviate family stresses.

As a testament to the success of Robeson Elementary School, its students score above the national norm on standardized tests, but Robeson does not make a fuss over its test score performance. The school community knows that in a caring, supportive environment where all of the children are made to feel special, test scores are but one of the marks of accomplishment that can be expected.

Questions

1. What features of this school are exemplary?

2. What societal problems are addressed by the school? How?

3. Do you agree with the school's perspective on test scores? Why or why not?

4. How would you add to this exemplary school to make it an ideal school for the year 2020?

5. Design your own ideal school, making it a rural, urban, suburban, or virtual school in the year 2020.

Source: Reprinted with permission from Gloria Ladson-Billings, The Dreamkeepers: Successful Teachers of African American Children. San Francisco, Jossey-Bass, 1994. Selection from pp. 140–42.

counselling, full-service schools, school-based inter-professional case management, compensatory education, and alternative schools and curricula. Here, we describe innovative, community-based partnerships that some schools have developed recently to prevent social problems from hindering students' learning.

The range of school-community partnerships found in today's schools is extensive. For example, as the "Interactive Organizational Model" in Figure 29.2 illustrates, Exeter High School in suburban Toronto has developed partnerships with 13 community organizations and more than 100 employers. Through Exeter's Partners in Learning program, business, industry, service clubs, and social service agencies make significant contributions to students' learning.

The Community As a Resource for Schools

To assist schools in addressing the social problems that impact students, many communities are acting in the spirit of a recommendation made by Ernest Boyer: "Perhaps the time has come to organize, in every community, not just a *school* board, but a *children's* board. The goal would be to integrate children's services and build, in every community, a friendly, supportive environment for children" (Boyer 1995, 169). In partnerships between communities and schools, individuals, civic organizations, or businesses select a school or are selected by a school to work together for the good of students. The ultimate goals of such projects are to provide students with better school experiences and to assist students at risk.

Civic Organizations

To develop additional sources of funding, many local school districts have established partnerships with community groups interested in improving educational opportunities in the schools. Some groups, such as the Lions Club, have actively supported a variety of school projects. Others adopt or sponsor schools and enrich their educational programs by providing funding, resources, or services.

Volunteer Mentor Programs

Mentorship is a trend in community-based partnerships today, especially with students at risk. Parents, business leaders, professionals, and peers volunteer to work with students in neighbourhood schools. Goals might include dropout prevention, high achievement, improved self-esteem, and healthy decision making. Troubleshooting on lifestyle issues often plays a role, especially in communities plagued by drug dealing, gang rivalry, casual violence, and crime. Mentors from organizations such as " Big Brothers and Big Sisters of Canada" also model success for participating children and adolescents.

Corporate-Education Partnerships

Business involvement in schools has taken many forms, including, for example, contributions of funds or materials needed by a school, release time for employees to visit classrooms, adopt-a-school programs, cash grants for pilot projects and teacher development, educational use of corporate facilities and expertise, employee participation, and student scholarship programs. Extending beyond advocacy, private sector efforts include job initiatives for disadvantaged youths, in-service programs for teachers, management training for school administrators, minority education and faculty development, and even construction of school buildings.

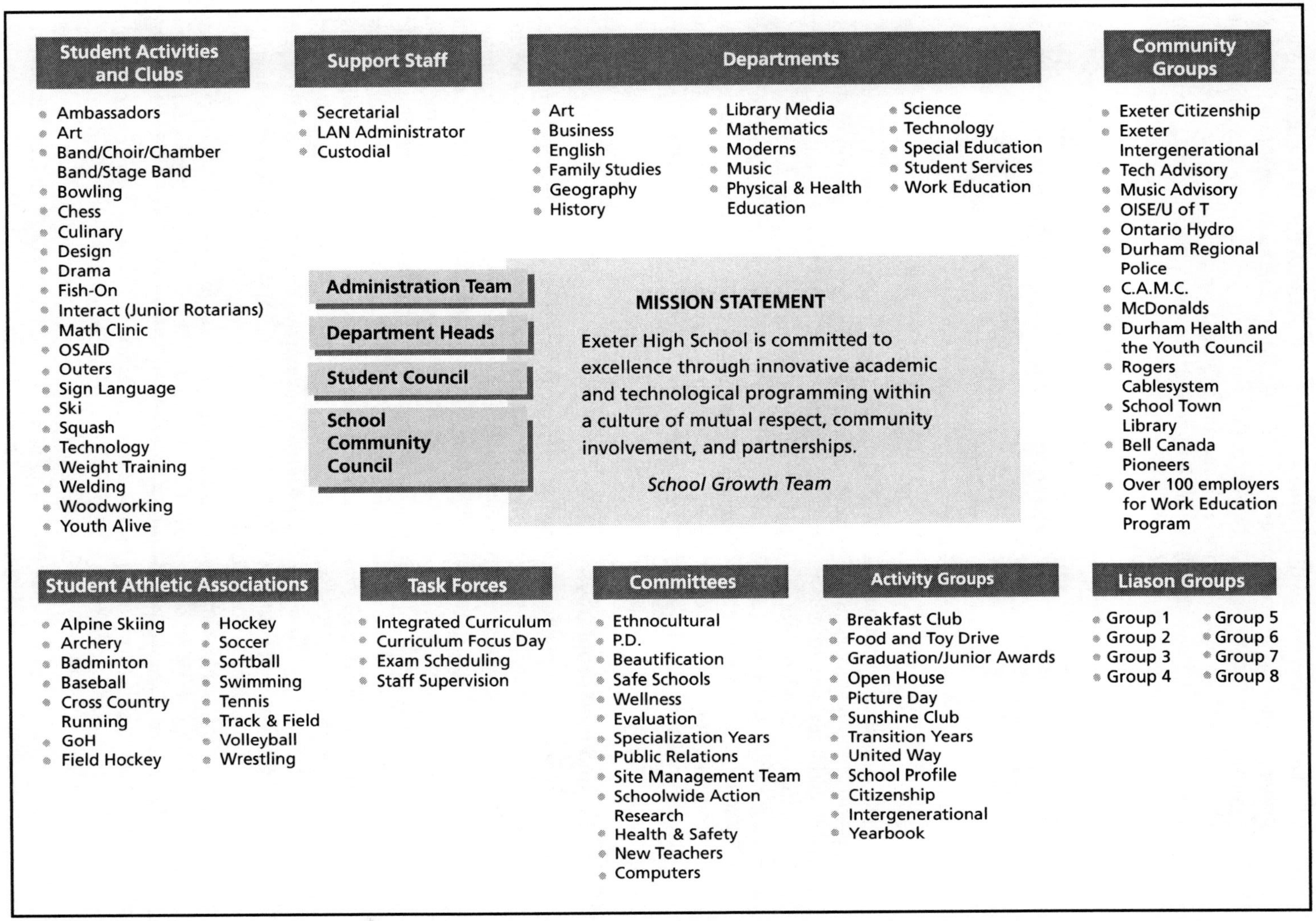

Student Activities and Clubs

- Ambassadors
- Art
- Band/Choir/Chamber
- Band/Stage Band
- Bowling
- Chess
- Culinary
- Design
- Drama
- Fish-On
- Interact (Junior Rotarians)
- Math Clinic
- OSAID
- Outers
- Sign Language
- Ski
- Squash
- Technology
- Weight Training
- Welding
- Woodworking
- Youth Alive

Support Staff

- Secretarial
- LAN Administrator
- Custodial

Departments

- Art
- Business
- English
- Family Studies
- Geography
- History
- Library Media
- Mathematics
- Moderns
- Music
- Physical & Health Education
- Science
- Technology
- Special Education
- Student Services
- Work Education

Community Groups

- Exeter Citizenship
- Exeter Intergenerational
- Tech Advisory
- Music Advisory
- OISE/U of T
- Ontario Hydro
- Durham Regional Police
- C.A.M.C.
- McDonalds
- Durham Health and the Youth Council
- Rogers Cablesystem
- School Town Library
- Bell Canada Pioneers
- Over 100 employers for Work Education Program

MISSION STATEMENT

Exeter High School is committed to excellence through innovative academic and technological programming within a culture of mutual respect, community involvement, and partnerships.

School Growth Team

Administration Team

Department Heads

Student Council

School Community Council

Student Athletic Associations

- Alpine Skiing
- Archery
- Badminton
- Baseball
- Cross Country Running
- GoH
- Field Hockey
- Hockey
- Soccer
- Softball
- Swimming
- Tennis
- Track & Field
- Volleyball
- Wrestling

Task Forces

- Integrated Curriculum
- Curriculum Focus Day
- Exam Scheduling
- Staff Supervision

Committees

- Ethnocultural
- P.D.
- Beautification
- Safe Schools
- Wellness
- Evaluation
- Specialization Years
- Public Relations
- Site Management Team
- Schoolwide Action Research
- Health & Safety
- New Teachers
- Computers

Activity Groups

- Breakfast Club
- Food and Toy Drive
- Graduation/Junior Awards
- Open House
- Picture Day
- Sunshine Club
- Transition Years
- United Way
- School Profile
- Citizenship
- Intergenerational
- Yearbook

Liason Groups

- Group 1
- Group 2
- Group 3
- Group 4
- Group 5
- Group 6
- Group 7
- Group 8

Figure 29.2

Exeter High School interactive organizational model

Source: Gordon Cawelti, *Portraits of Six Benchmark Schools: Diverse Approaches to Improving Student Achievement.* Arlington, VA: Educational Research Service, 1999, p. 32. Used with permission.

This involvement of the business community with education is not without its critics. Maude Barlow, in her article *The Assault on Canadian Schools* (1995, 1-8), points out, in the strongest of language, that the efforts of transnational corporations to infiltrate Canadian schools is a serious problem which must be addressed. She writes about the United States, where Burger King operates fully accredited high schools, as does its main competitor, McDonalds Corporation, and also of New Zealand, where "students are writing exams brought to them by Reebok and Coca Cola ... [with] the corporate logos on each exam." (Barlow 1995, 7) In addition to contributing more resources to education, chief executive officers of 99 Canadian corporations surveyed by the *Financial Post* "said they should be, and very soon would be, in the schools (Barlow 1995, 7).

Schools As Resources for Communities

The view that schools should serve as multipurpose resources *for* the community is a shift from the more traditional perspective of schools needing community support to meet the needs of students affected by social problems. By focusing not only on the development of children and youth, but on their families as well, schools ultimately enhance the ability of students to learn. As Ernest Boyer (1995, 168) puts it, "No arbitrary line can be drawn between the school and life outside. Every [school] should take the lead in organizing a *referral service*—a community safety net for children that links students and their families to support agencies in the region—to clinics, family support and counseling centers, and religious institutions."

Beyond the School Day

Many schools and school districts are serving their communities by providing educational and recreational programs before and after the traditional school day and during the summers. Increasingly, educational policymakers recognize that the traditional school year of approximately 190 days is not the best arrangement to meet students' learning needs. As the RCM Research Corporation, a nonprofit group that studies issues in educational change, points out: "Historically, time has been the glue that has bonded the traditions of our public school system—i.e., equal class periods, no school during summer months, 12 years of schooling, etc.,—and, as a result, the use of time has become sacrosanct, 'We have always done it this way!' How time is used by schools often has more to do with administrative convenience than it does with what is best educationally for the student" (RCM Research Corporation 1998). In 2003, for example, British Columbia considered having the regular school day extended in length while reducing the actual number of school days per week to four from the more customary five. In the late 1990s some Nova Scotia school districts also considered, but eventually rejected, a similar possibility.

Proposals for year-round schools and educationally oriented weekend and after-school programs address the educational and developmental needs of students impacted by social problems. While Canadian provinces and territories have yet to make substantive changes to the regular school year, examples of what might eventually take place can be found in the United States. There, according to the San Diego–based National Association for Year-Round Education, more than 2800 public schools now extend their calendars into the summer, and more than two million students go to school year-round. In Austin, Texas, for example, schools can participate in an Optional Extended Year (OEY) program that allows them to provide additional instruction in reading and mathematics to students at risk of being retained a grade. Schools participating in

OEY can choose from among four school day options: (1) extended day, (2) extended week, (3) intersession of year-round schools, and (4) summer school (Idol 1998; Washington 1998). Futurist Marvin Cetron predicts that, soon, "schools will educate and train both children and adults around the clock: the academic day will stretch to seven hours for children; adults will work a 32-hour week and prepare for their next job in the remaining time" (Uchida, Cetron, and McKenzie 1996, 35).

Programs that extend beyond the traditional school day also address the needs of parents and the requirements of the work world. Every day, thousands of elementary-age, "latchkey" children arrive home to an empty house. As one elementary teacher said, "Many of my students just hang around at the end of every day. They ask what they can do to help me. Often there's no one at home, and they're afraid to go home or spend time on the streets" (Boyer 1995, 165).

After-school educational and recreational programs are designed to (1) provide children with supervision at times when they might become involved in antisocial activities, (2) provide enrichment experiences to widen children's perspectives and increase their socialization, and (3) improve the academic achievement of children not achieving at their potential during regular school hours (Fashola 1999). Ernest Boyer argues that schools should adapt their schedules to those of the workplace so that parents can become more involved in their children's education, and that businesses, too, should give parents more flexible work schedules. Drawing on the model of Japan, Boyer suggests that the beginning of the school year could be a holiday to free parents to attend opening day ceremonies and celebrate the launching and continuation of education in the same way that we celebrate its ending.

Although some research indicates that extended school days and school calendars have a positive influence on achievement (Gandara and Fish 1994; Center for Research on Effective Schooling for Disadvantaged Students 1992), the Center for Research on the Education of Students Placed at Risk (CRESPAR) at Johns Hopkins University concluded that "there is no straightforward answer to the question of what works best in after-school programs" (Fashola 1999). According to CRESPAR, few studies of the effects of after-school programs on measures such as achievement or reduction of antisocial behaviour meet minimal standards for research design. Nevertheless, CRESPAR found that after-school programs with stronger evidence of effectiveness had four elements: training for staff, program structure, evaluation of program effectiveness, and planning that includes families and children (Fashola 1999).

Social Services

In response to the increasing number of at-risk and violence-prone children and youth, many schools are also providing an array of social services to students, their families, and their communities. The following comments by three female students highlight the acute need for support services for at-risk youth who can turn to aggression and violence in a futile attempt to bolster their fragile self-esteem and to cope with the pain in their lives. All three girls have been involved in violent altercations in and around their schools, and all three frequently use alcohol and illegal drugs.

Fifteen-year-old "Mary" has been physically abused by both her father and mother, and she was raped when she was 14. "Linda," also 15 years old, was sexually molested during a four-year period by a family acquaintance, and she endures constant physical and psychological abuse from her father. Fourteen-year-old "Jenny" is obsessed with death and suicide, and she aspires to join a gang.

> When you're smoking dope, you just break out laughing, you don't feel like punching people because it's just too hard. It takes too much.... You're mellow.... You just want to sit there and trip out on everybody.... It's even good for school work. When

I used to get stoned all the time last year, I remember, I used to sit in class and do my work because I didn't want the teacher to catch me, and this year I'm getting failing marks 'cause I'm not doing my work 'cause I'm never stoned (Mary).

I just know I got a lot of hatred.... And there's this one person [Jenny], and it just kinda happened after she mouthed me off, I was just like totally freaked with her and now I just want to slam her head into something. I wanna shoot her with a gun or something. I wanna kill her.... If I could get away with it I'd kill her. I wouldn't necessarily kill her, but I'd get her good. I just want to teach her a lesson. I'd beat the crap out of her. She's pissed me off so badly. I just want to give her two black eyes. Then I'd be fine. I'd have gotten the last word in (Linda).

I like fighting. It's exciting. I like the power of being able to beat up people. Like, if I fight them, and I'm winning, I feel good about myself, and I think of myself as tough.... I'm not scared of anybody, so that feels good. My friends are scared of a lot of people, and I go "Oh yeah, but I'm not scared of them.... All these people in grade eight at that junior high are scared of me, they don't even know me, and they're scared of me. It makes me feel powerful (Jenny) (Artz 1999, 127, 136, 157).

In Chapter 5, we looked at how some schools provide educational, medical, social and/or human services, and how the school-based inter-professional case management model uses case managers to deliver services to at-risk students and their families. Although many believe that schools should not provide such services, an increase in the number of at-risk students like Mary, Linda, and Jenny suggest that the trend is likely to continue, with more schools requiring a service agency "which brings together all of the community agencies concerned with children, coordinates the services, increases support, and prepares a report card on progress" (Boyer 1995, 169). More social initiatives such as parent support groups, infant nurseries, and programs for students with special needs, are likely to form a more prominent part of future Canadian schooling.

How Will the Fledgling Charter School Movement Affect Equity and Excellence in Education?

One of the most interesting experiments in Canadian education during the last decade has been the development of charter schools. While there are only ten such schools in Canada, all in Alberta, these schools present a new direction in educational reform. Charter schools offer a modern and flexible approach to the complex teaching environment of today. While held fully accountable to a publicly elected government body, they control their own budget, staffing, programs, and services, to better meet the needs of their students.

Charter schools are independent, innovative, outcome-based, public schools. "The charter school concept allows a group of teachers, parents, or others who share similar interests and views about education to organize and operate a school. Charters can be granted by a local school district or by the province. In effect, charter schools offer a model for restructuring that gives greater autonomy to individual schools and promotes school choice by increasing the range of options available to parents and students within the public schools system" (Wohlstetter and Anderson 1994, 486).

To open a charter school, an original charter (or agreement) is signed by the school's founders and a sponsor (usually the local school board). The charter specifies the learning outcomes that students will master before they continue their studies. Charter schools, which usually operate in the manner of autonomous school districts (a feature that distinguishes them from the alternative schools that many school districts operate), are public schools and must teach all students. If admission requests for a charter school exceed the number of available openings, students are selected by a draw.

Because charter schools are designed to promote the development of new teaching strategies that can be used at other public schools, they can prove to be an effective tool for promoting educational reform and the professionalization of teaching in the future. Moreover, charter schools give teachers unprecedented leadership opportunities and the ability to respond quickly to students' needs:

> [We had] the chance to create a school that takes into account the approaches we know will work. We listen to what the students want and need, because we ask them. And each day we ask ourselves if we are doing things the best way we can. We also have the flexibility to respond. We can change the curriculum to meet these needs as soon as we see them. Anywhere else it would take a year to change. It is much better than anything we have known in the traditional setting (North Central Regional Education Laboratory 1993, 3).

Murnane and Levy (1996) suggest that charter schools are "too new to have a track record," and they should not be seen as a "magic bullet" that will dramatically, and with little effort, improve students' achievement. In addition, they suggest four questions that observers should pose to determine whether individual charter schools promote both equity and excellence.

- Does the charter school commit itself to a goal, such as mastery of critical skills for all its students, or will it emphasize other goals?
- Does the charter school commit itself to serve a fair share of the most difficult-to-educate children, and does it have a strategy for attracting such children—or will it discourage applications from such children?
- Does the charter school's contract with the school district provide enough time and enough financial support for the school to persevere and learn from the mistakes that are inevitable in any ambitious new venture?
- Does the charter school commit itself to providing information about student achievement that will allow parents to make sound judgments about the quality of the education their children are receiving (Murnane and Levy 1996, 113)?

The United States and For-Profit Schools

Other than a short-lived experiment in Nova Scotia with Public-Private Partnership (P–3) schools, there are no for-profit schools in Canada. However, in the United States—which often provides us with a hint of future educational directions—one of the most controversial educational issues for the twenty-first century is the practice of turning the operation of public schools over to private, for-profit companies. Advocates of **privatization** believe privately operated schools are more efficient; they reduce costs and maximize "production"—that is, student achievement. Opponents, however, are concerned that profit, rather than increasing student achievement, is the real driving force behind **for-profit schools**. Critics of for-profit schools are also concerned that school districts may not be vigilant enough in monitoring the performance of private education companies.

Like Maude Barlow, Canadian essayist and novelist John Ralston Saul is very concerned about the possible privatization of our schools. In his article "In Defense of Public Education" (Saul 2002, 12) he states that "Our country has been built, from the very beginnings of its democratic system 150 years ago, upon a happy linkage between democracy and public education." He makes the additional comment that "if society and its leaders are not willing to fund the [educational] system, then we

highlights

How does Canada compare to other countries regarding the importance of information technology in the curriculum?

Students leaving school today, both in Canada and around the world, will compete for jobs in a global economy that is powerfully influenced by information technology. In many respects, the "coin of the realm" for the global economy of the twenty-first century will be neither raw materials nor labour but information. As a result, the place of information technology in the school curriculum is critical.

Figure 29.3 shows the percentage of the public in eleven OECD (Organization for Economic Co-operation and Development) countries who gave information technology and technical studies a rating of either "essential" or "very important" in the school curriculum. (Unfortunately, Canada was not included in this study, with the result that where Canadians stand on this issue stands is

only an estimate.) Information technology (eg., computing and database management) was viewed as relatively more important than technical studies (eg., metal shop and drafting) in all countries except Spain, where they were viewed as nearly the same. It is noteworthy that the United States public, more than the public in the other countries, views information technology as especially important. To what extent do you believe the *actual* emphasis on information technology in school curricula reflects the importance the Canadian public attaches to instruction in information technology? As a teacher, what role can you play in ensuring that your students acquire the information technology skills they will need for their future in a global economy?

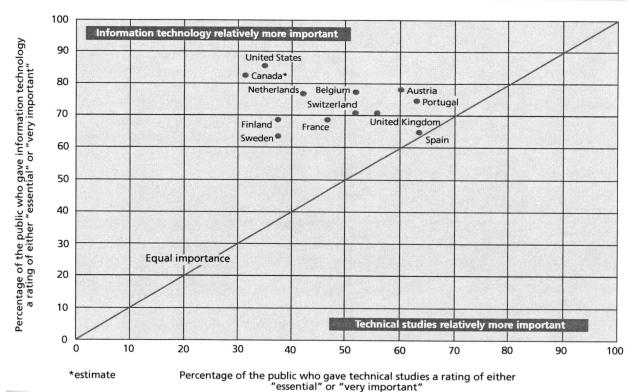

Figure 29.3

The importance of information technology and technical studies: An international perspective.

Source: Public Attitudes Toward Secondary Education: The United States in an International Context. Washington, DC: U.S. Department of Education, 1997.

Should Canada emulate the United States' for-profit school model?

Would businesses do a better job running public schools in Canada than the provincial, government-based system? Should businesses make a profit from schools? Should taxpayers contribute funds to schools that in turn give businesses profits? With the rise of privatization of education in the late 1990s, people were beginning to ask such questions.

With some now starting to refer to the education system as an "education industry," *The Economist,* a London publication, reported on privatization of US education (1999b), noting that

... the government says that the country spends a total of $625 billion a year on education—more than it devotes to pensions or defence [sic]—and predicts that spending per pupil will rise by 40% over the next decade. Private companies currently have only 13% of the market.... But International Data Corporation, a consultancy, reckons that this share will expand to 25% over the next two decades.

US businesses privatize schools in three ways: establishing for-profit charter schools, placing public schools under corporate management (for example, the Edison Schools), and providing supplementary services such as testing and coaching (for example, the Sylvan Learning Systems). The "education industry" covers schooling from preschool through college, with the former in particular regarded as a "boom area."

Teachers' unions and education scholars and writers expressed alarm over the expansion of privatization. Henry Giroux criticized its advocates:

They view education primarily as a commercial venture in which the only form of citizenship offered to young people is consumerism. Yet reducing public education to the ideological imperatives of corporate culture works against the critical social demands of educating citizens who can sustain and develop inclusive democratic identities, relations, and public spheres. (Giroux 1999)

Education researchers questioned the merit and ethics of commercializing education. In a study of eleven for-profit schools in western Michigan, Christy Lancaster Dykgraaf, and Shirley Kane Lewis concluded that the emergence of such schools was "cause for concern," adding, "Issues related to cost-cutting strategies, communication, and public ownership of the public schools deserve serious attention if these charter schools are to match the expectations and meet the needs of the constituencies they are intended to serve" (1998).

In April 1999, Henry Levin, Stanford education professor and leader of the Accelerated Schools Project, moved to Columbia University to head the new National Center for the Study of Privatization in Education. According to an *Education Week* issue paper (1999, July 29), Levin "hopes to conduct neutral research, without any political pull from conservatives or liberals, on the impact of privatization to advance the debate about vouchers, charter schools, and private companies in education."

While the experts are evaluating the matter, what do you think about the move toward privatization? Is this an effective way to improve education?

Yes, privatization is an effective way to improve education.

The country's poor record in student achievement compared to that in other countries makes it imperative to do something different. U.S. businesses and colleges complain about the inadequate skills and limited knowledge of high school graduates. What the country has been doing has not been working. Now the problem is too great to ignore. As the world news journal, *The Economist* (1999b), observes:

America spends more of its GDP on education than most countries, yet it gets mediocre results. Children in Asia and Europe often trounce their American counterparts in standardised [sic] scholastic tests. More than 40 percent of American ten-year-olds cannot pass a basic reading test; as many as 42 million adults are functionally illiterate. Part of the reason for this dismal performance is that close to half of the $6500 spent on each child is eaten up by "non-instructional services"—mostly administration.

The best solution is to combine business expertise with government regulation to spend education money more effectively. "Government's oversight function and its responsiveness to the needs of citizens can be retained while taking advantage of private enterprise's ability to be more efficient, reduce costs, and maximize production—in this case, student achievement," *Education Week* observed (1999, July 29).

Many believe that the competition that free enterprise provides will motivate schools to improve. Others believe privatization will bring fresh ideas to a weary education system. Michael R. Sandler, the chief executive officer for EduVentures, is quoted in a May 1999 *Education Week* article as saying, "The true agents of change for education reform in the twenty-first century are going to be the innovative for-profit enterprises built by education entrepreneurs" (Walsh 1999). And *The Economist* (1999, Jan. 16) reported that "Such schemes free education from the stifling grip of teaching unions and bureaucrats." With the freedom to innovate and the unique perspectives and know-how of business, for-profit charter schools and corporate management of public schools may breathe new life into education in the U.S.

No, privatization is not an effective way to improve education.

Most of the arguments against privatization fall into two broad areas—reductionism of education and alteration of the purpose of schools.

Privatization reduces education by narrowing the curriculum, standardizing the way it is taught, and devaluing the gifts of teachers. Because for-profit schools and management corporations need to demonstrate that they are effective, they must specify exactly what will be learned and then be able to prove that students have learned it. Accountability is the prime focus; and the narrower and more standardized the curriculum, the easier it is to assess. Curricula also become limited to that which can be tested. Lessons regarding attitudes, values, correct behaviour, creative expression, leadership, art, music, sports, speech, and drama all are difficult to assess. As a consequence they tend to be set aside or given limited focus so that teachers and students can prepare for tests on core curricula. Similarly, the instruction teachers provide is strictly prescribed to maximize the likelihood that test scores rise. Teachers' abilities to enrich school experiences and make learning meaningful are squelched by the standardization process and assessment focus.

More serious is privatization's impact on the direction and purpose of schools. Its focus on profit, integration of commercialism in curricula, and preparation of students as consumers is a far cry from the original purposes of schools—to prepare students to lead morally good lives and be good and informed citizens able to participate in a democratic government. Henry Giroux, a passionate voice against the corporatizing of U.S. education, writes that advocates of privatization are attempting to "transform public education from a public good, benefiting all students, to a private

good designed to expand the profits of investors, educate students as consumers, and train young people for the low-paying jobs of the new global marketplace" (Giroux 1999). He observes that these advocates critique U.S. education by viewing it separate from the social conditions in society:

Stripped of a language of social responsibility advocates of privatization reject the assumption that school failure might be better understood within the political, economic, and social dynamics of poverty, joblessness, sexism, race and class discrimination, unequal funding, or a diminished tax base.

Privatization of education serves the profit interests of businesses, not the good of students and the country. Citizens need to be wary.

Where do you stand on this issue?

1. Which are the best arguments on each side of this issue?

2. Where do you stand on this issue? Why do you hold this position?

3. What are the potential costs if either side has complete control of education?

4. Update yourself on this issue by following it on the web through Ebscohost or First Search. In First Search choose "all data bases" and then explore Wilson Select and PerAbs for full text articles.

Recommended Sources

AFT on the Issues (1999, July). Vouchers and the accountability dilemma.

Kane, S. and Dykgraaf, C. L. (1998, October). For-profit charter schools: What the public needs to know. *Educational Leadership, V. 56*(2), 51–53.

The Economist (1999a, January 16). A contract on schools: Why handing education over to companies can make sense.

The Economist (1999, January 16). Reading, writing and enrichment: Private money is pouring into American education—and transforming it.

Education Week on the Web (1999, July 29). Issue Paper: Privatization of public education.

Giroux, H. A. (1999, Winter). Schools for sale: public education, corporate culture, and the citizen-consumer. *The Educational Forum, 63*(2), 140–49.

Nathan, J. (1998, March). Heat and light in the charter school movement. *Phi Delta Kappan 79*(7), 499–505.

Pipho, C. (1999, February). The profit side of education. *Phi Delta Kappan, 80*(6), 421–22.

Walsh, M. (1999, May). Two reports offer bright outlook for education industry. *Education Week, 18*(36), 5.

collectively, and they specifically, must all take responsibility for the decline of our own children and the children of our fellow citizens" (Saul 2002, 12). Whether Canadian schools will succumb to the private sector's desire to become more deeply involved in education as a business initiative is an unsettled issue. For an examination of the arguments for and against for-profit schools, see the "where do you stand?" feature on pages 497–498.

What Can Teachers and Schools Learn from International Education?

The world has truly become smaller and more interconnected as telecommunications, cyberspace, and travel by jet bring diverse people and countries together. As we continue to move closer together, it is clear that education is crucial to the well-being of every country and to the world as a whole. "For teachers, on whom the quality of education ultimately depends, the challenges and opportunities the twenty-first century will bring are remarkably similar worldwide, and there is much the [we] can learn from other countries about the conditions that promote the ability of teachers and students to deal with that future" (Parkay and Oaks 1998). For example, an observation in a *Bangkok Post* editorial on the need to prepare Thai youth for a changing world echoes calls for educational improvement in Canada. "The country's policy planners [s]hould seriously review and revamp the national education system to effectively prepare our youths [for] the next century" (Sricharatchanya 1996, 15). Similarly, a community leader's comments about educating young substance abusers in Bangkok's Ban Don Muslim community could apply to youth in scores of Canadian communities: "We are in an age of cultural instability. Children are exposed to both good and bad things. [I]t's hard to resist the influences and attitudes from the outside world that are pulling at the children's feelings" (Rithdee 1996, 11). Lastly, the curriculum goals at Shiose Junior High School in Nishinomiya, Japan, are based on Japan's fifteenth Council for Education and would "fit" Canadian junior high schools as well; according to principal Akio Inoue (1996, 1), "Students will acquire the ability to survive in a changing society, that is, students will study, think and make judgments on their own initiative. It is also important that we provide a proper balance of knowledge, morality, and physical health, and that we nurture humanity and physical strength for that purpose." As a result of the universal challenges that confront educators, we are entering an era of increasing cross-national exchanges that focus on sharing resources, ideas, and expertise for the improvement of education worldwide.

Comparative Education

As the nations of the world continue to become more interdependent, educational policies and practices will be influenced increasingly by **comparative education,** the study of educational practices in other countries. Comparative education studies show how school systems in other countries work and how Canadian students compare with students in other countries on certain measures of schooling and achievement. In addition, research in comparative education enables professionals to share information about successful innovations internationally. Teachers can collaborate on global education projects and test change models that other countries have used to help match educational and societal needs and goals.

Table 29.1 and Table 29.2 contain the results of an international study by the Organization for Economic Cooperation and Development (OECD) on the reading, mathematical, and scientific literacy skills of students near the ends of their high school careers. This study, conducted in 2000, indicates wide disparities between developed and developing countries. While Canada as a whole ranks significantly above the OECD average in all three areas, within the area of literacy skills there are several provinces which are not rated as highly.

However, one must be careful when interpreting the results of cross-national studies of education achievement. David Berliner and Bruce Biddle (1995, 63) offer these cautions when interpreting such data.

- Few studies have yet focused on the unique values and strengths of each country's educational system.
- Many studies can be affected by sampling biases and inconsistent methods for gathering data.
- Many or most results of such studies are subject to differences in curricula—in opportunities to learn—in the countries studied.
- Aggregate results can be misleading because of the huge range of school quality in most countries—ranging from marvellous to terrible.

In a comparative study of Japanese education, Harry Wray (1999, 137) concludes that Japan's system of national examinations "reinforce[s] excessive conformity, passivity, standardization, anxiety, group consciousness, and controlled education." Wray goes on to say that "Excessive emphasis on passing entrance examinations plays a contributing role in killing most students' interest in studying and scholarship after entering a university, especially for those outside the science, engineering, and medical areas. Students exhausted by the dehumanizing methodology lose motivation and curiosity" (Wray 1999, 138). Additionally, provincial examinations have been criticized because they encourage students to take a narrow view of learning, and tend to emphasize lower-order thinking skills that can be assessed easily by pencil-and-paper measures. As one Japanese university student confided to Wray: "In elementary school we had many occasions to give our opinions; however, after we entered junior high school, we did not get such opportunities because all the studies are for high school entrance examinations, and all the studies in high school are for university entrance examinations. One who is considered 'intelligent' is one who can get good grades, not those who have their own opinions" (Wray 1999, 137).

Lessons from Other Countries

The previous comments about Japanese education aside, Canadian educators can learn a great deal from their colleagues around the world regarding what works and what doesn't work in other countries. When considering the possibility of adopting practices from other countries, however, it is important to remember that educational practices reflect the surrounding culture. When one country tries to adopt a method used elsewhere, a lack of support from the larger society may doom the new practice to failure. In addition, it is important to realize that the successes of another country's educational system may require sacrifices that are unacceptable to our way of life. Nevertheless, there are many practices in other countries that Canadian educators and policymakers might consider.

Table 29.1

Reading, mathematical, and scientific literacy

Mathematical Literacy

Countries	Mean	S.E	Range of possible rank order positions Upper	Lower
Countries statistically significantly above the OECD average				
Japan	557	(5.5)	1	3
Korea	547	(2.8)	2	3
New Zealand	537	(3.1)	4	8
Finland	536	(2.1)	4	7
Australia	533	(3.5)	4	9
Canada	533	(1.4)	5	8
Switzerland	529	(4.4)	4	10
United Kingdom	529	(2.5)	6	10
Belgium	520	(3.9)	9	15
France	517	(2.7)	10	15
Austria	515	(2.5)	10	16
Denmark	514	(2.4)	10	16
Iceland	514	(2.3)	11	16
Liechtenstein[2]	514	(7.0)	9	18
Sweden	510	(2.5)	13	17
Countries not statistically different from the OECD average				
Ireland	503	(2.7)	16	19
Norway	499	(2.8)	17	20
Czech Republic	498	(2.8)	17	20
United States	493	(7.6)	16	23
Countries statistically significantly below the OECD average				
Germany	490	(2.5)	20	22
Hungary	488	(4.0)	20	23
Russian Fed.[2]	478	(5.5)	21	25
Spain	476	(3.1)	23	25
Poland	470	(5.5)	23	26
Latvia[2]	463	(4.5)	25	28
Italy	457	(2.9)	26	28
Portugal	454	(4.1)	26	29
Greece	447	(5.6)	27	30
Luxembourg	446	(2.0)	29	30
Mexico	387	(3.4)	31	31
Brazil[2]	334	(3.7)	32	32
Netherlands[1]	—	—	1	4

Scientific Literacy

Countries	Mean	S.E	Range of possible rank order positions Upper	Lower
Countries statistically significantly above the OECD average				
Korea	552	(2.7)	1	2
Japan	550	(5.5)	1	2
Finland	538	(2.5)	3	4
United Kingdom	532	(2.7)	3	7
Canada	529	(1.6)	4	8
New Zealand	528	(2.4)	4	8
Australia	528	(3.5)	4	8
Austria	519	(2.5)	8	10
Ireland	513	(3.2)	9	12
Sweden	512	(2.5)	9	13
Czech Republic	511	(2.4)	10	13
Countries not statistically different from the OECD average				
France	500	(3.2)	13	18
Norway	500	(2.7)	13	18
United States	499	(7.3)	11	21
Hungary	496	(4.2)	13	21
Iceland	496	(2.2)	14	20
Belgium	496	(4.3)	13	21
Switzerland	496	(4.4)	13	21
Countries statistically significantly below the OECD average				
Spain	491	(3.0)	16	22
Germany	487	(2.4)	19	23
Poland	483	(5.1)	19	25
Denmark	481	(2.8)	21	25
Italy	478	(3.1)	22	25
Liechtenstein[2]	476	(7.1)	20	26
Greece	461	(4.9)	25	29
Russian Fed.[2]	460	(4.7)	26	29
Latvia[2]	460	(5.6)	25	29
Portugal	459	(4.0)	26	29
Luxembourg	443	(2.3)	30	30
Mexico	422	(3.2)	31	31
Brazil[2]	375	(3.3)	32	32
Netherlands[1]	—	—	3	14

Reading Literacy

Countries	Mean	S.E	Range of possible rank order positions Upper	Lower
Countries statistically significantly above the OECD average				
Finland	546	(2.6)	1	1
Canada	534	(1.6)	2	4
New Zealand	529	(2.8)	2	8
Australia	528	(3.5)	2	9
Ireland	527	(3.2)	3	9
Korea	525	(2.4)	4	9
United Kingdom	523	(2.6)	5	9
Japan	522	(5.2)	3	10
Sweden	516	(2.2)	9	11
Austria	507	(2.4)	11	16
Belgium	507	(3.6)	11	16
Iceland	507	(1.5)	11	15
Countries not statistically different from the OECD average				
Norway	505	(2.8)	11	16
France	505	(2.7)	11	16
United States	504	(7.0)	10	20
Denmark	497	(2.4)	16	19
Switzerland	494	(4.2)	16	21
Countries statistically significantly below the OECD average				
Spain	493	(2.7)	17	21
Czech Republic	492	(2.4)	17	21
Italy	487	(2.9)	19	24
Germany	484	(2.5)	21	25
Liechtenstein[2]	483	(4.1)	20	26
Hungary	480	(4.0)	21	26
Poland	479	(4.5)	21	27
Greece	474	(5.0)	23	28
Portugal	470	(4.5)	24	28
Russian Fed.[2]	462	(4.2)	27	29
Latvia[2]	458	(5.3)	27	29
Luxembourg	441	(1.6)	30	30
Mexico	422	(3.3)	31	31
Brazil[2]	396	(3.1)	32	32
Netherlands[1]	—	—	2	14

[1] Response rate is too low to ensure comparability (see Annex A3).

[2] Non-OECD country

Source: Reproduced with permission from the Organization for Economic Co-operation and Development.

Table 29.2

Reading literacy scores by province

Alberta	550
British Columbia	538
Ontario	533
Quebec	536
Manitoba	529
Saskatchewan	528
Nova Scotia	521
Prince Edward Island	517
Newfoundland	517
New Brunswick	501

Source: Organization for Economic Cooperation and Development (OECD), 2001.

Figure 29.4

Ratio of teacher salaries (starting and maximum) per-capita GDP, by education level and career point

Source: Organization for Economic Co-operation and Development, Center for Educational Research and Innovation, International Indicators, 2001.

Support for Teachers and Teaching

In many other countries, teachers and the profession of teaching receive a level of societal support that surpasses that experienced by teachers in Canada. For example, teachers in many countries are accorded greater respect than their Canadian counterparts; and, as Figure 29.4 shows, the salary range (as a ratio of per-capita Gross Domestic Product) for teachers in Japan, the UK, Italy, Germany, and the United States. While Canada was not included in this study, it is likely that the results for our country would roughly approximate those of the United States (Science and Engineering, March, 2003).

In addition, most Canadian teachers have about one hour or less per day for planning, and Canadian high school teachers teach about 30 classes a week, compared with 20 by teachers in Germany and fewer than 20 by Japanese teachers. While teachers from these latter two countries have over 15 h per week to work collaboratively on school-based endeavours, little such time is available to Canadian teachers. Among Western countries the number of contracted hours is quite variable. In Switzerland, the total number of in-class hours worked by elementary teachers during the school year is 1085; in Canada and United States, the contact hours are in the 950 range; while in Norway and Sweden, the average is approximately 650 h (OECD 1994, 60).

Other countries also invest their resources in hiring more teachers, who make up a statistically higher proportion of total staff than is the case in Canada. While exact

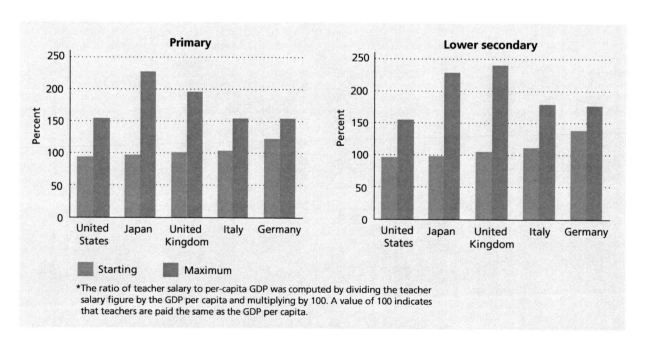

*The ratio of teacher salary to per-capita GDP was computed by dividing the teacher salary figure by the GDP per capita and multiplying by 100. A value of 100 indicates that teachers are paid the same as the GDP per capita.

data for the Canadian context are not available, in the United States (see Figure 29.5), where teaching loads are comparable, a 1996 study noted that "too many people and resources are allocated to activities outside of classrooms, sitting on the sidelines rather than the front lines of teaching and learning." Many countries also invest more resources in beginning-teacher support programs. They provide novice teachers with experiences that are, as the following practices indicate, more positive than those of their Canadian counterparts.

1. New teachers are viewed as professionals on a continuum, with increasing levels of experience and responsibility; novice teachers are not expected to do the same job as experienced teachers without significant support.
2. New teachers are nurtured and not left to flounder on their own; interaction with other teachers is maximized.
3. Teacher induction is a purposive and valued activity.
4. Schools possess a culture of shared responsibility and support, in which all or most of the school's staff contributes to the development and nurturing of the new teacher.
5. Assessment of new teachers is downplayed.

Parental Involvement

The powerful influence of parental involvement on students' achievement is well documented (Booth and Dunn 1996; Buzzell 1996; ERIC Clearinghouse 1993; Epstein 1992). Japan probably leads the world when it comes to parental involvement in education. Japanese mothers frequently go to great lengths to ensure that their children get the most out of the school's curriculum. The *kyoiku mama* (literally, education mother) will tutor her child, wait for hours in lines to register her child for periodic national exams, prepare healthy snacks for the child to eat while studying, forego television so her child can study in quiet, and ensure that her child arrives on time for calligraphy, piano, swimming, or martial arts lessons. Though few Canadian parents might wish to assume the role of the *kyoiku parent,* it seems clear that Canadian students would benefit from greater parental involvement.

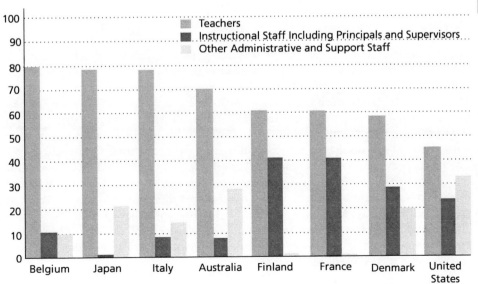

Figure 29.5

Comparisons of educational staff by function

Source: Organization for Economic Cooperation and Development (OECD), *Education at a Glance: OECD Indicators.* Paris, OECD, 1995, table, p. 31, pp. 176–77. Taken from National Commission on Teaching and America's Future, *What Matters Most: Teaching for America's Future.* New York, National Commission on Teaching and America's Future, p. 15.

Pressure to Excel

There have been many calls to make Canadian schooling more rigourous—a longer school calendar, longer school days, more homework, and harder examinations, for example, have all been proposed. These changes, it is assumed, would increase student achievement and find favour with the majority of the public that wants greater academic rigour in the schools. More often than not, Japan, Korea, and other Asian countries are held up as models for the direction Canadian education might emulate.

But should Canadian schools be patterned after schools in these countries? Several of those who have studied and experienced Asian schools are beginning to think not. For example, Paul George (1995), who studied the Japanese public school his son attended for two years, reports in *The Japanese Secondary School: A Closer Look* that large numbers of students, deprived of sleep from having attended *jukus* (cram schools) to do well on college entrance exams, waste time in school, having been told by their *juku* instructors not to pay attention to their teachers. Additionally, a teacher of English in rural Japan reports that 70 percent of students at her school attend *jukus* and frequently are awake past midnight (Bracy 1996). According to Gerald Bracey (1996, 128), if parents want their children to achieve at the level of Asian students, which is often only a few percentage points higher on standardized examinations, they must understand the sacrifices made by Asian students and their parents and be prepared to adhere to these guidelines:

1. [W]hen their children come home from public school, they should feed them and then ship them off to a private school or tutor until 10 PM; most youngsters, both elementary and secondary, will need to go to school all day on Sunday, too.
2. [They should] spend 20 to 30 percent of their income on [a]fter-school schools.
3. [W]hen their children turn four, they should take them on their knees and tell them, "You are big boys and girls now, so you need to start practicing for college entrance examinations" (Bracey 1996, 128).

In addition, Canadian students would need to realize that "if they sleep four hours a night, they will get into college, but if they sleep five hours a night, they won't; they must study instead" (Bracey 1996, 128).

What Is Our Vision for the Future of Education?

Imagine that it is the year 2020, and we are visiting Westside Elementary school, a school in a medium-sized city. All of the teachers at Westside are fully certified and have salaries which are on a par with those of other professionals with comparable education and training. About half of the 55 teachers at Westside have also earned advanced professional certification. These teachers are known as lead teachers and may earn as much as $85 000 per year. Westside has no principal; the school is run by an executive committee of five lead teachers elected by all teachers at the school. One of these lead teachers is elected to serve as committee chair for a two-year period. In addition, the school has several student interns and educational assistants who are assigned to lead teachers as part of their graduate-level teacher-preparation program. Finally, teachers are assisted by a diagnostician; hypermedia specialist; computer specialist; video specialist; social worker; school psychologist; four counsellors; special remediation teachers in reading, writing, mathematics, and oral communication; bilingual and ESL teachers; and special-needs teachers.

What vision of the school of the future does this photograph suggest? What might you add to the image to achieve a broader perspective on tomorrow's teachers and learners?

Westside Elementary operates many programs that illustrate the close ties the school has developed with parents, community agencies, and businesses. The school houses a daycare centre that provides after-school employment for several students from the nearby high school. On weekends and on Monday, Wednesday, and Friday evenings, the school is used for adult education and for various community group activities. Executives from three local businesses spend one day a month at the school visiting with classes and telling students about their work. Students from a nearby college participate in a tutoring program at Westside, and the college has several on-campus summer enrichment programs for Westside students.

Westside has a school-based health clinic that offers health care services and a counselling centre that provides individual and family counselling. In addition, from time to time Westside teachers and students participate in service-learning activities in the community. At the present time, for example, the Grade 5 classes are helping the city develop a new recycling program.

All the facilities at Westside—classrooms, library, multimedia learning centre, gymnasium, the cafeteria, and private offices for teachers—have been designed to create a teaching/learning environment free of all health and safety hazards. The cafeteria, for example, serves meals based on findings from nutrition research about the best foods and methods of cooking. The school is carpeted, and classrooms are soundproofed and well lit. Throughout, the walls are painted in soft pastels tastefully accented with potted plants, paintings, wall hangings, and large murals depicting life in different cultures.

The dress, language, and behaviours of teacher, students, and support personnel at Westside reflect a rich array of cultural backgrounds. In the cafeteria, for example, it is impossible not to hear several languages being spoken and to see at least a few students and teachers wearing non-Western clothing. From the displays of students' work on bulletin boards in hallways and in classrooms, to the international menu offered in the cafeteria, there is ample evidence that Westside is truly a multicultural school and that gender, race, and class biases have been eliminated.

Each teacher at Westside is a member of a teaching team and spends at least part of his or her teaching time working with other members of the team. Furthermore, teachers determine their schedules, and every effort is made to assign teachers according to their particular teaching expertise. Students attend Westside by choice for its excellent teachers; its curricular emphasis on problem solving, human relations, creative thinking, and critical thinking; and its programs for helping at-risk students achieve academic success.

Instruction at Westside is supplemented by the latest technologies. The school subscribes to several computer databases and cable television services, which teachers and students use regularly. The hypermedia learning centre has an extensive collection of CD-ROMs and computer software, much of it written by Westside teachers. The centre also has virtual-reality interactive videodisc systems, workstations equipped with the latest robotics, and an extensive lab with voice-activated computers. The computer-supported interactive multimedia in the centre use the CD-ROM format and the more advanced Integrated Services Digital Network (ISDN) delivery system based on the optical fiber.

Every classroom has a video camera, fax machine, hypermedia system, and telephone that, in addition to everyday use, are used frequently during satellite video teleconferences with business executives, artists, scientists, scholars, and students at schools in other states and countries. Westside Elementary's technological capabilities permit students to move their education beyond the classroom walls, as they determine much of how, when, where, and what they learn.

Tomorrow's Teacher

Teaching and the conditions under which teachers work may change in some fundamental and positive ways during the next two decades. Teaching will become increasingly professionalized, for example, through such changes as more lengthy and rigorous preservice training programs, salary increases that put teaching on a par with other professions requiring similar education, and greater teacher autonomy and an expanded role for teachers in educational policy making. There will be more male teachers who are African-Canadians, Arabic and Asian, or members of other ethnic and racial groups. There will be greater recognition for high-performing teachers and schools through such mechanisms as merit pay plans, master teacher programs, and career ladders. Tomorrow's teachers will achieve new and higher levels of specialization. The traditional teaching job will be divided into parts. Some of the new jobs may be the following:

- Learning diagnostician
- Researcher for software programs
- Courseware writer
- Curriculum designer
- Mental health diagnostician
- Evaluator of learning performances
- Evaluator of social skills
- Small-group learning facilitator
- Large-group learning facilitator
- Media-instruction producer
- Home-based instruction designer
- Home-based instruction monitor

Though we cannot claim to have handed you an educational crystal ball so that you can ready yourself for the future, we hope you have gained both knowledge and inspiration from our observations in this chapter. Certainly, visions of the future, such as the one of Westside Elementary, will not become a reality without a lot of dedication and hard work. The creation of schools like Westside will require commitment and vision on the part of professional teachers like you.

Professional Reflection — What does the future hold for your province or territory?

Predict the future of education in your province or territory in terms of the following list of innovations and trends. Rate each development according to whether it already exists in your state or when you think it will become common practice in the schools—within the next five or the next 15 years. If you don't know the status of a particular development in your province, find out. Add at least one new item representing a trend in your province that does not appear on the list. When you have finished rating the items, share your results with your classmates. What reasons or evidence will you give for your predictions?

Innovation//Trend	Now	Within 5 years	Within 15 years	Not likely
1. Alternative/authentic assessment of students' learning	___	___	___	___
2. Cross-age tutoring/mentoring	___	___	___	___
3. Peer counselling/peer coaching	___	___	___	___
4. Faculty teams/team teaching	___	___	___	___
5. Business–school partnerships	___	___	___	___
6. Community–school teaming	___	___	___	___
7. School-based clinics/counselling centres	___	___	___	___
8. Organized after-school programs	___	___	___	___
9. Year-round schools	___	___	___	___
10. School development	___	___	___	___
11. Equity in school funding	___	___	___	___
12. Open enrollment/school choice	___	___	___	___
13. Telephones in the classroom	___	___	___	___
14. Student computer networking	___	___	___	___
15. Video teleconferencing	___	___	___	___
16. Interactive multimedia/hypermedia	___	___	___	___
17. Multimedia distance learning	___	___	___	___
18. Sex education	___	___	___	___
19. AIDS education	___	___	___	___
20. Character education curricula	___	___	___	___
21. Globalism/multiculturalism	___	___	___	___

(continued)

Innovation//Trend	Now	Within 5 years	Within 15 years	Not likely
22. Aesthetics orientation	____	____	____	____
23. Alcohol and drug intervention	____	____	____	____
24. Reduction of gender bias	____	____	____	____
25. Reduction of racial/ethnic prejudice	____	____	____	____
26. Inclusion of students who have special needs	____	____	____	____
27. Teacher empowerment	____	____	____	____
28. Constructivist teaching approaches	____	____	____	____
29. Charter schools	____	____	____	____
30. Corporate-education partnerships	____	____	____	____
31. For-profit schools	____	____	____	____
32. _____	____	____	____	____
33. _____	____	____	____	____

SUMMARY

What Knowledge and Skills Will Prepare Students for a Global Information Age?

■ Conflicting theories, expectations, and values make it difficult to answer what students need to know and be able to do in the future; however, increasing cultural diversity and global economic interdependence call for communication and cooperation skills and wise use of environmental resources.

■ To meet the challenges of the future, students will need knowledge, skills, attitudes, and values in nine key areas: literacy in language, mathematics, and science; new technological skills; problem solving, critical thinking, and creativity; social awareness, communication skills, and team building; global awareness and conservation skills; health and wellness education; moral and ethical orientation; aesthetics awareness; and lifelong, self-directed learning.

How Can Schools and Teachers Provide an Outstanding Education for All Learners?

■ To reach all learners, teachers must understand how some families are under acute stress, how crime and violence impact students' lives, and how to develop multicultural curricula and instructional repertoires that develop the potentialities of students from varied backgrounds.

- In addition to preparing multicultural instructional materials and strategies for students from diverse cultural, ethnic, and linguistic backgrounds, teachers treat students equitably when they treat high- and low-achieving students the same. Research has identified several teacher behaviours that reflect inequitable treatment of low-achieving students: waiting less time for them to answer questions, interacting with them less frequently, giving them less feedback, calling on them less often, seating them farther away, failing to accept and use their ideas, smiling at them less often, making less eye contact, praising them less, demanding less, grading their tests differently, and rewarding inappropriate behaviours.

- Effective teachers establish positive relationships with all students by listening to them, giving frequent feedback and opportunities to ask questions, and demanding higher-level performance by asking higher-order questions that require more critical thinking.

- To reach all learners, teachers should provide them with active, authentic learning experiences.

How Can Community-Based Partnerships Address Social Problems That Hinder Students' Learning?

- Communities help schools address social problems that hinder students' learning by providing various kinds of support.

- Civic organizations raise money for schools, sponsor teams, recognize student achievement, award scholarships, sponsor volunteer mentor programs, and provide other resources and services to enrich students' learning.

- Corporate–education partnerships provide schools with resources, release time for employees to visit schools, scholarships, job initiatives for disadvantaged youth, in-service programs for teachers, and management training for school administrators.

- Schools serve as resources for their communities by providing educational and recreational programs before and after the school day, and by providing health and social services.

How Will the Fledgling Charter School Movement Affect Equity and Excellence in Education?

- Charter schools and U.S. for-profit schools, both part of the privatization movement, were developed in response to perceived inadequacies of the public schools.

- Charter schools are independent, innovative, outcome-based public schools started by a group of teachers, parents, or others who obtain a charter from a local school district, a province, or the federal government.

What Can Teachers and Schools Learn from International Education?

- The challenges and opportunities for teachers in the twenty-first century are remarkably similar worldwide, and teachers in different countries can learn much from one another. Comparative education, the study of educational practices in other countries, enables educators to collaborate internationally.

- A study conducted by the Organization for Economic Cooperation and Development (OECD) indicates that Canadian schools are among the best in the world.

- Education in many other countries is centralized and teachers follow a national curriculum. In Canada each province and territory is responsible for the education of its children.

- Many other countries tend to provide greater support for teachers and teaching and have greater parental involvement, two practices that would benefit Canadian education. However, pressure for students in other countries to excel is often extreme.

- Many other countries provide greater support for teachers and the teaching profession, have greater parental involvement, and take more steps to nurture beginning teachers.

What Is Our Vision for the Future of Education?

- It is not unrealistic to imagine that teachers in schools during the year 2020 will be well-paid, self-governing professionals who have developed specialized areas of expertise. This vision becomes more possible with each teacher who makes a commitment to its realization.

KEY TERMS AND CONCEPTS

charter schools	higher-order questions	privatization
comparative education	learning	movement
for-profit schools	lower-order questions	synectics

APPLICATIONS AND ACTIVITIES

Teacher's Journal

1. Write a scenario forecasting how the teaching profession will change during the next two decades.

2. Select one of the following areas and develop several forecasts for changes that will occur during the next two decades: energy, environment, food, the economy, governance, family structure, demographics, global relations, media, and technology. On what current data are your forecasts based? How might these changes affect teaching and learning?

3. Think about two children you know and project them into the future, twenty years from now. What skills are they likely to need? Which talents should help them? How can schools better promote the development of these skills and talents?

Teacher's Database

1. Begin at the web home pages for the Organization for Economic Cooperation and Development (OECD) and the Canadian Teachers' Federation (CTF) and gather information on educational systems in other countries. In what areas of the curriculum and at what levels is the achievement of Canadian students at or above the international average? What conclusions about the strengths and weaknesses of Canadian schools can you draw from your analysis of these data?

2. Explore the field of international education or comparative education and talk to teaching professionals in other countries online. For example, you might ask them what they see as the greatest challenge facing educators in their respective countries. Or, you might ask them about working conditions for teachers—that is, number of students taught, time for planning, professional responsibilities beyond the classroom, and so on.

Observations and Interviews

1. Interview the principal at a local or nearby school and ask him or her to describe what the school will be like in ten years. Now interview several teachers at the school. Compare the forecasts of the principal with those of the teachers. What might account for any differences you find?

2. Search for examples of school–community partnership arrangements in the local school district. Find out if these partnerships are progressing and propose a specific new one based on your knowledge of the community.

Professional Portfolio

1. Prepare a portfolio entry of instructional resources—curriculum guides, teaching tips, assessment strategies, relevant professional associations, books and articles, software, and online resources—related to one of the nine areas of learning students will need to meet the challenges of the future (i.e., literacy in language, mathematics, and science; new technological skills; problem solving, critical thinking, and creativity; social awareness, communication skills, and team building; global awareness and conservation skills; health and wellness education; moral and ethical orientation; aesthetics awareness; and lifelong, self-directed learning). For each entry include a brief annotation describing the materials, how you will use them, and where they may be obtained. After you have prepared this portfolio entry, meet with your classmates and exchange information.

Case Studies: Application and Practice

Case Study

1

Mr. Cal's Dilemma

Mr. Cal is a Science teacher with 22 years of experience and has taught in several departments at the same secondary school. He spoke of enjoying lower-level (e.g., workplace and college-bound) classes more than the advanced-level (university-bound) students. "I like teaching lower-level kids better than advanced-level kids. It's a little more work, but you get more satisfaction from it. Not everyone thinks the way I do."

Mr. Cal was shortly to meet a challenge that would cause him to reconsider his optimistic approach to teaching. Kumar, a student who had recently been released from a closed custody youth detention centre, was consistently creating disruptions in his Grade 10 science class. These incidents challenged Mr. Cal's role as a teacher but, to date, did not deflate his optimism about changing Kumar's negative attitude and behaviour. Mr. Cal found that "winning over" Kumar was a difficult task; however, he was still hopeful and up to the challenge. It was his willingness to tackle what some staff viewed as "lost causes" that earned him the respect of both students and teachers.

Mr. Cal's outlook on education was well-seasoned with diverse experiences from working with students like Kumar. In his experience, problem students eventually complied with his expectations of appropriate classroom behaviour.

One day, when the students were working on an experiment, Mr. Cal noticed that Kumar was not using the Bunsen burner properly. He approached Kumar and advised him about how he should be handling the burner. Kumar became verbally abusive, calling Mr. Cal an "asshole." The class was quite noisy, as the students were busy completing their own experiments. So, Mr. Cal turned and walked away hoping this incident would go unnoticed—perhaps Kumar was just having a bad day. At the end

Reprinted from *Education Methods: A Case Study Approach to Professional Development* (2006), John Wiley & Sons, Inc.

of the class, he asked the students to complete their lab reports as homework and bring them to the next class.

The next day at class, Mr. Cal moved from student to student checking their completed reports. When he came up to Kumar, he asked him about his failure to complete the lab report. Kumar exploded, pushed Mr. Cal aside, and stormed out of the classroom. This time, the whole class noticed Kumar's inappropriate behaviour. Their eyes were upon Mr. Cal, and every face wore a puzzled expression. What was Mr. Cal to do? Was this a teachable moment?

QUESTIONS

1. What errors, if any, has Mr. Cal made?

2. Detail what Mr. Cal should do immediately to address this situation with the class.

3. What should Mr. Cal do before meeting with Kumar?

Case Study

2

Riches Found in the Mind or Mine?

Mr. Yurri, a sixth-year teacher, teaches at a rural secondary school. Most of the parents are well-off and always willing to contribute financially to the school. Because of their shift-work schedules in the area mine, they are often prevented from other forms of school involvement. In fact, many of the children go home to an empty house. Most of Mr. Yurri's Grade 9 students are responsible for taking care of their other siblings and even getting the evening meal prepared.

One of Mr. Yurri's top students, Bill, frequently engaged in disruptive behaviour in the classroom. Further, though he was consistently successful academically, he usually came to school with his homework incomplete. The parent-teacher conference following first semester reports did not result in a plan of action to deal with this problem. Bill's parents indicated that they were not often home in the evening to monitor his homework completion and that Bill had to take care of their other children. Further, as Bill was 14 and responsible for his own actions, his parents considered it Bill's responsibility to complete his homework. The discussion about his homework concluded with Bill's parents commenting that his lack of attention to homework was obviously not an issue, since Mr. Yurri himself considered Bill's comprehension in class and his grades to be good. Bill's parents also pointed out that managing classroom behaviour was Mr. Yurri's responsibility as a professional teacher.

Mr. Yurri had to acknowledge that if he was to distract Bill from engaging in inappropriate behaviour in class, he would have to come up with a plan. He spent some time reflecting on what may be the cause of Bill's outbursts. It occurred to him that Bill might be simply seeking attention. Bill frequently made funny comments to create laughter in the classroom and engaged in verbal confrontations with his teacher. He had recently begun to refuse to participate in large and small group activities in

Reprinted from *Education Methods: A Case Study Approach to Professional Development* (2006), John Wiley & Sons, Inc.

class as well. Mr. Yurri realized that his use of nonverbal and verbal interventions and consistent consequences have had little effect in deterring Bill's problem behaviour. He felt that Bill was beginning to take control of the classroom as it seemed more and more difficult to redirect the class back on task after one of his outbursts.

In an attempt to better understand Bill's state of mind, Mr. Yurri asked Bill to talk to him about his future. Mr. Yurri said in a kind voice that he knew Bill was bright and could easily be successful in secondary school and college. He expressed his concern that Bill's disruptive behaviour in class and his failure to complete his homework might jeopardize his opportunities in the future. Surprisingly, Bill said to Mr. Yurri that as there were always employment opportunities at the mine, it was his intention to quit school at the end of Grade 10 and go to work at the mine, since it was unionized and offered great benefits and exceptional pay. Bill's dad and mom worked at the mine. They were doing fine, and so high school graduation was not really needed, he said.

Mr. Yurri decided to ask his principal and the school resource teacher to give him some ideas to deal with Bill. His concern was not only about managing Bill's in-class behaviour, but he also wanted to encourage him to continue and complete his education. The principal suggested that Mr. Yurri primarily needed to examine his current way of handling the problems that Bill created and that he should think about how to support the other students in the classroom in this situation. The resource teacher pointed out that Mr. Yurri's primary concern should be to make Bill realize how far he could go in the future with his own abilities combined with a good education. Mr. Yurri agreed with both their suggestions; however, neither the principal nor the resource teacher had come up with any concrete suggestions to deal with the immediate problems. He was still at a loss as to what he should actually do.

QUESTIONS

1. Brainstorm ways to deal with Bill in the classroom. Based on these ideas, create a behaviour management contract that moves from nonverbal cues through verbal cues to logical consequences for acting out. Good contracts include a date and a timeline, a review date, the student's name, expectations, and a reward. It should be simply written and no longer than one page.

2. In Bill's experience, going to work and making money is an achievable and appropriate goal. While recognizing that this may, indeed, be true, as a teacher, what creative ideas do you have to help Bill explore other options?

3. As good education requires a blending of the cognitive (creating learning) and the affective (creating motivation and influencing learning), it is important that Mr. Yurri try to help Bill by paying attention to his affective domain. How could Mr. Yurri influence and motivate Bill to be a good learner?

Case Study

3

The Spaghetti Strap Solution

Students have a keen awareness of fashion and how fashion can signify individuality. How should a school's code of conduct determine clothing standards so that teachers, parents, community, and students are in support of this policy?

As Marsha talked on the phone, she caught sight of John, one of the members of her teaching staff, standing nervously at the office door, running his finger along her nameplate. He then tapped lightly on the glass to get her attention. As she was ending the phone conversation, she motioned for John to enter. "Hmm," she thought to herself, "so unlike him to bypass the secretary. He's usually so meek that he'd be afraid to offend her." John sat and immediately began to fiddle with a tissue that he pulled off the box on her desk.

"Well, John," she said, placing the phone decisively on the cradle and trying to take on a friendly, yet formal air, "what can I do for you?"

"Well," muttered John in a low voice, "I wanted to talk to you about my math class."

"Uh-huh . . . concerning, what?" Marsha said, trying to draw him out.

However, John rose from the chair and went to the door. After looking around outside, he shut it and then came back and sat down, leaning over Marsha's desk. "Well, it's one of my students in Grade 8 . . ."

"Failing?" Marsha inquired.

"No, no, it's nothing like that. It's more to do with her, um, clothing . . ." John said in a worried tone.

As Marsha looked puzzled, John said, "As you know, we decided at our beginning-of-the-year staff meeting to implement some rules about how the students should dress."

Reprinted from *Education Methods: A Case Study Approach to Professional Development* (2006), John Wiley & Sons, Inc.

Marsha knew that she had not been very demanding when it came to implementing a dress code at the school, but some of the students' clothing was becoming increasingly outlandish. The staff had decided that no gang colours or emblems would be allowed, nor would caps be allowed in class. Halter tops and muscle shirts were also banned, as well as clothing with rude, racist, or suggestive words.

"But," continued John, "as the weather got warmer this spring, one of the students started to ignore the rules." Marsha motioned him to proceed. "Uh, she came to class one day wearing a top that exposed a lot of skin."

"Oh?" inquired Marsha, pressing for more details.

"Yes, she was wearing a top that bared her shoulders, and the whole thing was held up by just a few strings."

"You mean spaghetti straps?"

"Is that the name for it? I just thought it was some kind of halter top."

"Uh-huh," Marsha wanted John to get on with it. "So, did you try talking to her about this?"

"Well, I was a little hesitant to do so," said John. "It's a bit embarrassing discussing things like this with a teenager. But I convinced Sue, whose classroom is just across from mine, to have a chat with Jasmine— the girl with the spaghetti straps."

"Aha. So, how did that work out?"

"Well, not so good. Sue later told me that Jasmine said that it was hot and she had the right to wear clothes that helped her stay cool. The next thing I know, Jasmine is in my class wearing even skimpier clothing—a skirt several inches above her knees and a top with . . . uh . . . spaghetti-straps, that wasn't tucked into her skirt." John leaned in even further and spoke in almost a whisper. "She appears to have a piece of rhinestone in her navel."

That was it. Marsha had to do something. It was already 3:15, and she asked her secretary to immediately call Jasmine into her office before the school day ended. She was wearing clothing just as John had described. Jasmine presented the same argument to Marsha as well about wearing clothes that suited the warmer weather. Marsha countered by saying that there was a difference between clothing to keep cool and clothing to "be cool." Besides, she pointed out, the staff had decided on the dress code at the beginning of the year and made the rules clear about what was considered acceptable. She further explained to Jasmine that if she were to turn up at school wearing such clothes in the future, she would be required to cover up with a lab coat or something, or else she would be sent home to change into something more appropriate. Marsha hoped that she would not have to impose the ultimate penalty for refusal to comply—suspension. She just hated using this consequence, but rules were rules.

The day after this chat with Jasmine, Marsha returned to her school office from her hall rounds to face something she dreaded. There was a woman—a middle-aged version of Jasmine—sitting in the waiting area. She was wearing an almost identical spaghetti-strap halter top, with a cheesecloth skirt flowing to the top of her sandaled feet. Marsha noticed a small, twinkling nose ring on her right nostril and a tiny, artistically rendered tattoo of a dove in flight on her right arm.

The woman rose, slinging her hemp purse over her shoulder and thrusting her hand forward to grasp Marsha's. She said, "My name is Corrine. I'm Jasmine's mother. If you are the principal, we have a few things to discuss."

"Yes, come into my office. Please have a seat. What can I do for you?" said Marsha, figuring she was in for a long, hot morning.

Settling herself in the chair beside Marsha's desk, Corrine declared, "I'm pretty put out about how you're treating my daughter. I think this lab coat business is an insult."

Marsha, trying to keep her voice even and calming, began to explain the dress code that was agreed upon by the teachers at the beginning of the year and how Jasmine's outfits were contravening these rules.

"What a stupid rule," Corrine interjected and immediately stood up. "I understand the business about gang colours and rude words on t-shirts, but the rule against halter tops and muscle skirts is just ridiculous. It's such rules that start kids down the road of being ashamed of their bodies. Don't you think they should have the freedom to make up their own minds about what they wear, when the weather permits? And, quite frankly, I find it insulting that you teachers think you can make up rules about what our kids can and can't wear without even consulting us. Well, I'm her mother, and I say, let Jasmine have some liberty here to find her own path. She's beautiful and smart, not some little grey drone, and I won't let you turn her into one." With this, she gave Marsha's ecru pant suit a disdainful once-over and sat back in her chair.

Marsha smiled wryly, thinking about the brightly coloured butterfly tattoo on her own backside, as she tried to think of an appropriate response.

QUESTIONS

1. There are a number of factors at play here: school rules, parent and student rights, and community norms. Can you think of a response from Marsha that would satisfy the mother, herself, the student, the school's teaching staff, and the community?

2. Should one group's interests take precedence here? Why, or why not? Is there a way to balance the needs and interests of all?

3. How do communities make decisions about acceptable dress codes and codes of behaviour? What roles should teachers, parents, and students play?

4. In what ways did the adult members of the internal school community support one another in this situation? To what degree might this reflect the norms of school culture? To what degree does school culture encourage "group-think" or conformity?

5. Do you think your response to the situation would be different if the situation involved religious items (i.e., a turban or a hajib)? Why, or why not?

Case Study

4

The Hidden Guns

Lightening Bay was a mid-sized town whose population comprised mostly second and third-generation Canadians. As "The Bay" became increasingly attractive to retirees and less attractive to young families, the school population experienced low enrolments. The demographic change and low enrolment resulted in the system-wide amalgamation of schools.

Orilene and Alphonsious Billes had recently emigrated from Morocco to The Bay with their three children—Euger, Charity, and Jasmine. To ensure that their children would continue speaking their second language, they enrolled them in one of the French Immersion schools in the city for the upcoming school year starting in September. Euger was put in Grade 5 French Immersion and Charity and Jasmine, the twins, in Grade 4.

The parents were happy that their three children seemed to adjust quickly to their respective French Immersion classes during the first two weeks of school. The school's annual family corn roast was scheduled for the Thursday of the third week of September.

As the family was getting ready to attend the corn roast where they would meet the teachers and other families, Euger was chattering away to his younger sisters about the day's events at school. Orilene's ears perked up when she heard Euger say, "I don't know why Jordie and Dane keep making jokes about me on the school bus. What's so funny about drinking chocolate milk? I know they're only in Grade 3."

Charity retorted, "Yeah, I know. Some of the kids in our class think that it is funny to make jokes about Jasmine's and my brown skin. We just ignore them because there are lots of kids who are nice to us."

Reprinted from *Education Methods: A Case Study Approach to Professional Development* (2006), John Wiley & Sons, Inc.

Euger added, "Do you think that I should ignore Dane's and Jordie's comments to me on the bus coming home today? They're only Grade 3 kids."

"What did they say?" asked Jasmine.

"Well, Dane said that his dad has four guns at home under the bed to deal with people who look like me. Jordie said that they would be afraid to bring them to school."

Orilene could no longer contain herself. She interrupted their conversation. "What did you say about Dane's father? Did you say he had guns? Did you say he was coming after you?"

Exasperated, Euger said, "Mum, 8-year-old kids are not going to bring guns to school. That's stupid. They were just being silly, weren't they?"

Orilene had heard enough. She needed to act immediately. Racism raised its ugly head everywhere. At that moment, Alphonsious entered the room. She took him aside and relayed Euger's story. They decided that they would speak to the principal at the corn roast to express their concern. In addition, they decided that none of their children would be on the bus until the issue was resolved.

It was time to leave for the corn roast. The children eagerly got into the car excited about seeing their new friends and being at school for dinner. Once at the school, the children bounded off to find their friends. Orilene and Alphonsious sought out the principal. When they found him, they repeated Euger's story. The principal listened. At the end of the story, he said that he would speak with Euger and the boys the next day. He assured them that in The Bay, 8-year-old boys did not bring guns to school.

Orilene and Alphonsious were not satisfied. They were fearful that their son might be in danger.

After the corn roast, Alphonsious dropped the family off at home. He and Orilene had decided that he should go to the police and give them the information to see if they would do anything. Those 8-year-old boys most likely were repeating adults' comments that they had overheard, but the couple still felt uneasy about the whole situation.

The community liaison officer took notes and assured Alphonsious that he would look into the matter immediately. In the meantime, he suggested that Euger not speak or play with Dane or Jordie until the issue had been resolved.

The next day, when Orilene dropped the children off at school, she told Euger's teacher about what had occurred. She also informed her that they had gone to the police who had suggested that there be no contact between the boys until the issue had been resolved. Therefore, her children would not be taking the bus. She asked that the teacher inform the principal.

Orilene was most surprised when the teacher indicated that she knew nothing about the incident. The principal had not shared any information with her that morning. Furthermore the teacher was not aware of any racist comments occurring in her classroom and indicated that this must just be an isolated incident. Orilene was quite concerned that the school did not appear to be taking the issue more seriously.

Before lunch, Orilene received a call from the community police officer indicating that he had gone to visit Dane's home and had talked with Dane's dad. The father admitted to having four unregistered guns—they were antique hunting rifles—but he vehemently denied that he or his family were racist and was quite disturbed that his son would make such comments. He would speak to his son that evening about the seriousness of his comments. The officer also indicated that he had spoken with Jordie's family. They, too, could not believe that their son would say such things. They said that they would discuss this serious issue with Jordie. At this time, the officer was confident that the Billes family was in no danger and that Dane's and Jordie's family would make a sincere effort to deal with their children's inappropriate behaviour.

Orilene was quite relieved and hoped that everything would be okay at school. She heard nothing from the school that day. When she picked up her children after school, Euger said that the principal had talked with him and Dane and Jordie.

"What happened?" asked Orilene.

"Well. . .we talked about saying only nice things to people, and then Dane and Jordie said that they were sorry about what they said. Mr. Phelps wanted me to say sorry to them and I asked him why. He said I should say I'm sorry for making such a big issue about this."

QUESTIONS

1. If you were Euger's parents, would you feel satisfied with the way in which the school dealt with this issue? Explain.

2. From a teacher's perspective:
   a) Describe teaching/learning strategies that could be introduced to address racist issues in your class.
   b) Describe any board-mandated policies or programs that deal with racism or bullying.

3. If you were Mr. Phelps:
   a) Describe the steps you would take prior to having a meeting with Euger and the boys.
   b) Describe the steps you would take during and after the meeting with the boys.

4. From the principal's perspective, was it necessary for the parents to contact the police? Explain your position.

5. How would you decide that a comment or action is harmless teasing and when it is harassment or bullying?

6. Should the education environment be responsible for addressing all teasing activity? Explain your position.

Case Study

5

You're on Candid Camera

Mr. Himsworth, principal of Blythe High School, heard the lunch bell ring. He slowly got up from his desk moving a few papers toward the phone. They would be waiting for his attention after he completed his noon hour walkabout. On his way out, he stopped to give his secretary a heads-up about an expected phone call. As he and the secretary were talking, he glanced up to look through the office window. Mr. Himsworth saw a distinct flow of students rapidly moving toward the rear of the school. Immediately, his internal warning bells went off.

"Looks like a fight somewhere," he told the secretary. "Find the vice-principals and send them to the rear parking lot; that's where the students seem to be heading."

He reached for one of the walkie-talkies, strategically placed for easy access for such occurrences, and quickly exited the office. Instantly, he heard the excited murmur of students confirming his suspicion—there was going to be a fight between a student from his school and a student from a neighbouring school on the pathway adjacent to the rear parking lot.

This pathway led to an area outside school boundaries. A common belief among students was that if you fight off school property, you would not have to suffer the consequences of a school suspension.

As Mr. Himsworth exited the rear doors, he was amazed to see the number of students running through the parking lot and down the hill to the pathway. He stopped for a moment and called the office on the walkie-talkie asking for immediate staff back-up. He continued toward the crest of the hill. Once at the top of the hill, he could not believe his eyes. There were maybe 300 to 400 students on the hill and pathway, shouting and cheering as two students flailed at each other. There were students not

Reprinted from *Education Methods: A Case Study Approach to Professional Development* (2006), John Wiley & Sons, Inc.

only from his school but from the neighbouring school as well. Out of the corner of his eye, he noticed a student with a video camera recording the fight.

Mr. Himsworth raced toward the crowd hoping that his vice-principals and some teachers would soon be along. As soon as the students saw him moving toward the melee, the word was out and a number of them quickly dispersed.

"Okay now, break it up! Head back to your schools!" Mr. Himsworth called out as he moved toward the fight. The students reluctantly moved out of his way, and soon he was close to the fight. He continued to talk and encourage the students to disperse. Over his shoulder, he saw Mrs. Seaver, one of his vice-principals, hurrying to join him. He was right in the circle now and "commanded" the students to stop. Seeing a break in their contact, he stepped between the girls holding out his arms to keep them apart. Both were a mess, with scratch marks on their faces and necks, their hair dishevelled, and clothes partially ripped. He knew one of the students, but the other was not a student in his school. He started to talk quietly to them, encouraging them to follow him to the office.

Mrs. Seaver arrived and started to get the other students to move away from the area. More teachers appeared and did the same until all the students left. Mr. Himsworth led the two girls to his office. Meanwhile, Mrs. Seaver questioned several students who had been close to the fight. She asked them to return with her so that she could record their observations.

After talking with the two girls and calling the principal of the neighbouring school, Mr. Himsworth compared his notes with those that Mrs. Seaver had collected. They quickly realized that this was no ordinary fight. The two students hardly knew each other, but each had been told by different students that the other was "dissing" her and was going to fight her during lunch break. As the morning progressed, various students in both schools encouraged them to "beat the crap" out of the other. Once lunch time arrived, they were quite worked up and were "swept" along to the pathway. By this point in time, the girls truly felt that they had no choice but to fight to avenge their reputations. Their peers had convinced them that there was no alternative but to fight. There was no escape. One girl even said, "I thought that I'd better just fight and get it over with". The interviews with students also indicated that this was not the first time that students had been set up to fight. One student even commented that it would not surprise him to see this fight on the Internet. Mr. Himsworth remembered seeing the video camera and knew that it was a real possibility. This situation clearly required further investigation by him and the principal of the neighbouring school.

QUESTIONS

1. If the fight occurred off school property, should school consequences apply? Explain.

2. If this was an orchestrated fight:
    a) What would be a fair consequence for the students who were fighting?
    b) What would be a fair consequence for the students who orchestrated the fight?
    c) If you were one of the fighters, what would your reaction to the consequences be?
    d) If you were the student who recorded the fight, what would your reaction to the consequences be?
    e) In this case, do you think that the instigators should get a more severe or less severe consequence than the fighters? Why?

3. What types of proactive safe school programs could be offered at the respective schools that would encourage students to use alternative strategies to deal with rumours and peer pressure?

4. At what point should the police be involved in student altercations at schools?

5. If the student is correct and the fight appears on the Internet, what consequence should be given to the student(s) responsible for orchestrating this spectacle?

6. In the opinion of some, the student bystanders are also at fault for encouraging this fight.
   a) Why do young people flock to a fight and cheer it on?
   b) What aspects of "character/ moral fibre" need to be addressed to bring about change in the behaviour of the bystander?
   c) Should "character/values education" be part of a mandated curriculum?
   d) What are reasonable expectations for bystanders?

Case Study

6

A Morning in the Life of Ms. Teacher

"No two school days are ever alike," thought Ms. Teacher, even though she had taught Grade 4 for five years. It seemed as if the circumstances of the children and the school changed on a daily basis; however, the routines that she had established with the students so well early in the school year seemed to be working effectively and thus made the daily disruptions less tiresome. She thoroughly enjoyed the work she did and was satisfied with the progress of her students, which she had shared in the parent-teacher interviews last month.

As Ms. Teacher walked from the parking lot toward the school, she met Phyllis James, an aunt of one of her students. Phyllis volunteered in the Grade 2 class every Wednesday and asked Ms. Teacher how her niece, Joanne, was doing. Ms. Teacher responded, "Now that you mention it, I am concerned about Joanne. She seemed so interested in school at the beginning of the year; now she seems to be distant and not so attentive in class. When I broach the subject with her, she doesn't want to talk about what's bothering her."

"Oh," said Phyllis. "I guess you don't know. Joanne's parents are fighting a lot these days, and since we've had one marriage break-up in the family already, she may be worried that her parents are in the same situation. I'll mention your concerns to my sister and ask her to contact you."

"Thanks for the information. That's probably it. I'll wait to hear from her mother," said Ms. Teacher.

She went into the school, checked the yard duty schedule, and reminded herself that she was on for the morning recess in the junior yard. She wanted to set up her classroom for the day and began to photocopy the three chapters from *Charlotte's Web* that she needed for her Group 3 session. She could not understand what the hold up

Reprinted from *Education Methods: A Case Study Approach to Professional Development* (2006), John Wiley & Sons, Inc.

was in receiving copies of that book. She knew they had been ordered several months ago, and it was so frustrating waiting for them. "Honestly," she thought, "those folks in the board aren't doing their job properly."

She stopped at her mail box and picked up the minutes from the last school council meeting at which she had represented the junior teachers. The meeting discussions had centred on playground equipment and how the school could raise money for it. At her previous school, Ms. Teacher had been involved in a read-a-thon that had raised almost $10,000 for student activities. She decided to suggest that this school should also undertake a similar fundraiser, or that they could sell chocolate bars to raise the necessary funds. Both would get the students involved and send them into the community to get pledges or sell the chocolate bars. She really wished, though, that the principal would be more supportive whenever she made such suggestions. Mr. Principal was not usually very supportive of her proposals. "Oh well," she thought, "I know how he got his job!"

Her thoughts were interrupted by Jock Physed, who started to complain about Matt Six, the Grade 6 teacher, and his promise to help coach the boys' volleyball team. "Don't talk to me about Matt," she interrupted. "I needed help with my art show, and he was all talk about helping but no action. Matt's just like Mr. Principal—all talk and no action. My students and many others worked so hard to put on a wonderful exhibition, and when it came time to put up the exhibits, I had to do it with the help of a couple of Grade 8 students. But guess who wanted to take the credit?"

"I know what you mean about Mr. Principal," said Mr. Physed. "He promised me new equipment when I came here two years ago. I'm still waiting."

Soon the bell rang, and she had to rush to make it to her classroom on time. In the classroom, she saw several of the students standing around the rabbit cage. She had introduced a bunny as part of the science program, and the students had completed an impressive unit on the rabbit's development and growth. The students researched what food it ate and what else it required, carefully measured the feeds, weighed the rabbit periodically, and charted its growth. She was so proud of their hard work and the care that they showed. Caring for another living thing had changed the attitudes of some of the children, and they became attached to the rabbit.

But now, the expression on the children's faces told her that something was wrong. "Ms. Teacher, Ms. Teacher," they cried. "There's something wrong with Bud. He's not moving very much."

She took one look and knew that all was not well. She waited until all the students had come in and told them to take their seats. By now, the class had realized that Bud was sick; all of them were deeply upset and she knew she needed to do something. They looked expectantly at her for the problem to be fixed somehow.

"Take out your math books," she said. "I want you to begin to work on page 27 and continue until I come back. You know that Bud is not well, and I'm going to take him to the vet. I want you to work very quietly. If you can't do a question, go on to the next one, but I need you to be extremely quiet while I'm gone. If you finish that work, then you can take out your library book and read it. When morning announcements come on, I want you to stand at attention for the national anthem and then sit quietly until the announcements are finished. After that, get back to work. Remember, I'm counting on you to be quiet while I'm gone. Promise?" They all nodded in agreement, and Ms. Teacher picked up the rabbit cage and left.

Mr. Principal was making the morning rounds after the announcements and noted that Ms. Teacher's class was extremely quiet and concentrating on their work. He continued on to the other classes looking in on all of them. He must remember, he thought, to notify the parents that no one could bring peanut butter sandwiches or cookies to school any longer, as the Brown twins both had a violent allergic reaction two weeks ago. "Why hadn't Ms. Teacher told him about that?" he wondered. He would remember to ask her as he walked by her classroom again. "Wow, her students are really quiet," he thought.

QUESTIONS

1. What aspects of the legislation and the Standards of Practice governing teachers did Ms. Teacher follow? What aspects did she violate?

2. Every teacher wants to be considered "effective," proficient in planning and preparation, structuring the classroom environment, instruction, and professional responsibilities. Given the information provided about Ms. Teacher, is she, in your opinion, effective as a teacher? Defend your decision.

3. What advice would you give Ms. Teacher to encourage her to become an even better teacher?

4. For each incident in the case where you believe Ms. Teacher was wrong, write a script for her to improve her response to the situation.

Case Study

7

The Written and Spoken Word

Kyeong Park was an outstanding English teacher. She loved her subject and her students, and they, in turn, responded well to the challenges she presented. She often quoted John Stuart Mill's ideas—that there must be protection for expression of opposing views and that the individual, along with freely expressed opinions, must be protected from suppression. She supported all of the fundamental freedoms, even though the Supreme Court of Canada has affirmed that freedom of expression is one of the most important, if not the most important, right for a democratic society. The Canadian Charter of Rights and Freedoms s. 2 states: Everyone has the following fundamental freedoms:(a) freedom of conscience and religion; (b)freedom of thought, belief, opinion and expression, including freedom of the press and other media of communication; (c) freedom of peaceful assembly; and (d) freedom of association. Ms. Park worked diligently to ensure that these freedoms were respected in her classroom.

Chris, one of Ms. Park's students, found an outlet for his creative ideas in her class. She allowed him to freely write his poems, while other English teachers did not. However, even though she was very supportive of Chris's artistic endeavours, she was also firm that he should complete his other assignments for her course. She would discuss his poems with him after class and often critiqued his work applying higher standards than those for other students. He excelled under her tutelage, and was sure that he wanted to continue studying English.

One piece of Chris's writing, however, caused Kyeong some concern. In his second assignment, he had written about a gay character— "a queer," as Chris described him, who wanted to "do in" some students and one teacher. Chris had described the character's hostility in such detail that it chilled her when she read the assignment. She

Reprinted from *Education Methods: A Case Study Approach to Professional Development* (2006), John Wiley & Sons, Inc.

was highly perplexed by Chris's attitude as expressed in his writing. He was not an aggressive or antagonistic student, as far as she could tell, and was somewhat quiet, although he would answer in class and participate in discussions when called upon to do so. She quietly asked Chris to stay after class so she could talk with him.

But for now, the class would undertake a discussion of Shakespeare's "The Merchant of Venice." The work she assigned in the last class was to examine Shylock's rhetoric and how his speeches reflected his character.

Mario was the first to offer his view point: "The setting is in Venice, and I think I'll begin there. Since my family is originally from Venice, I know a little about that. Shylock does his 'I am a Jew' speech. He's working the sympathy angle. Oh woe is me! He's trying to place himself the same as everyone else. He's a moneylender, for heaven's sake, a banker, and you know how greedy they are! Shylock has the same qualities as all the other Jews: treacherous, sadistic, money loving, and power hungry. I think Mr. Kegs, our history teacher, is right. Jews are out to destroy Christianity and are responsible for all the evil in the world. And Shylock's speech shows this."

There was complete silence in the class after Mario's speech. Kyeong was stunned. Never had she heard a student sound so vehement in his condemnation of Shylock. She thought that this could not go unaddressed. At that moment, the bell rang to signal the end of class. When Mario walked past her, she told him that she would like to see him during lunch.

"Can't, Miss," he said. "Got a football meeting." And he kept on walking.

Kyeong could not go after him at that time, as Chris was waiting to meet with her.

"Chris, I really enjoy reading your work. You have good control of language and write in a clear style with an awareness of your readers. Your character development is so very realistic. It's as if I almost know the person," she said. He looked away at her last comment.

She continued, "I have a concern, though, about the subject matter. From your perspective, why do you think I'm concerned?"

Chris did not answer for a moment. "Well," he began hesitantly. "It's dealing with violence in a school setting."

"That's a concern to me, Chris. Anything else?" she pressed.

"No, I think that would be mainly it," he responded.

"That's part of it. You're writing in a school environment about a school environment, and that's a sensitive issue."

"But you're always telling us to make it real!" he interjected.

"Yes, I am, but your writing does need to be respectful of all. Certain issues, such as the one you're writing about, will make people uncomfortable, and while I don't object to someone's writing challenging others' ideas, I do expect it to be respectful. You're such an accomplished writer, and you're capable of using your writing voice in an effective way," Kyeong said.

When Chris did not respond to what she said, Kyeong continued, "Tell me about your main character."

QUESTIONS

1. What are the conflicts and dilemmas in this case? Investigate the aspects of each conflict and dilemma.

2. What aspects of the Canadian Charter of Rights and Freedoms are at issue in this case? Are the rights and freedoms of individuals violated in any situation? Explain.

3. What aspects of the duties of teachers and standards for the teaching profession are addressed in this case?

4. What does Kyeong do to preserve the self-esteem of both students?

5. Knowing that the word "gay" is often used in a derogatory manner, how would you address this issue with Chris, if at all? What questions would you develop to initiate the discussion?

6. Analyze the issue(s) from the perspectives of Kyeong, Chris, Mario, and the other students in the class.

7. How should Kyeong deal with the issue(s)? Why? What role, if any, should the school's principal or vice-principal take in any discussion or action? How quickly would you, as the teacher, respond to the issues? Why?

Case Study

8

A Student Teacher Faces the Challenges of the Classroom

Thinking Ahead

As you read this Case Study, reflect on the following questions and issues:

- Consider the teacher candidate's experience, skills, and knowledge. Examine the teacher candidate's preconceptions about the students, classroom management, and school community even before she encounters the principal dilemmas in the case.
- Consider the many contextual elements of the classroom that play a role in framing this case.
- Consider the teacher's ability to deal with classroom disruptions.
- What are the dilemmas that confront this neophyte? Are the problems that occur caused by teacher inexperience?

"I'll be away tomorrow, so you'll be working with a substitute teacher for the day," Mr. Harris, my mentor teacher, an experienced teacher with the ability to calmly manage even the most unconventional classes, informs me. As a teacher candidate, I am not as excited as my students are to spend the day with a substitute teacher. I have several burning questions that cannot be answered at this moment: "Who will the substitute teacher be? Will the class be manageable? How bad can they really be?" I am in the middle of my placement in a seventh-grade integrated learning disabled homeroom that has been designated, by the teachers, as the school's worst class. On a normal day, there are two regular teachers, an educational assistant, and I, the teacher candidate, in the class. I know that the students are aware of their negative reputation. In addition, the constant supervision by four adults, resembling police officers on a stakeout, is a constant reminder of their difference. With all of the attention that

Reprinted from *Cases for Teacher Development: Preparing for the Classroom* (2005), Sage Publications, Inc.

these students receive on a daily basis, a substitute teacher represents an opportunity to act out without suffering severe consequences. I actually feel tremendous excitement because I will be able to teach the class as if it is my own, and the substitute can sit back and watch. Tomorrow this class will be mine. I will be in charge.

The next day, when I meet the substitute teacher, a young female like myself, she introduces herself and very pleasantly remarks, "I'm not the type of substitute teacher who just sits back and does nothing, but I will try not to interfere with any of your plans." She seems very honest and friendly, but I am more concerned about the upcoming day, and I am ready to begin. The morning consists of geography and history classes as well as French. The French class is a much-needed prep for me. I find that it is difficult to begin the geography class due to the students' inability to focus. One child, Dennis, refuses to do any work. This is his regular behavior, and, as well, there is constant pervasive chatter that continues to irritate me. Miraculously, I am able to quiet down the class to deliver a brief lesson about the economy. The class even cooperates enough to hear the subsequent explanations of the textbook assignment. Now my confidence mounts, and I begin to think that this class is not as bad as their reputation with the other teachers that has been reported. I execute the history class lesson in the similarly successful method that I have established earlier, although amidst gossipy chatter, but I still can't envisage this class without four attentive adults in the room.

The school is an ethnically diverse kindergarten-to-eighth-grade inner-city school. In addition, most classes have as many as five English as a Second Language (ESL) students. This also presents its own challenge. Boy, am I ever relieved that the morning is over, and that I have completed two entire lessons. Hooray for me! I am definitely beginning to understand the stress and irritation that is predominant in teaching. More important, I am enjoying the challenge and am pleased with the present outcome.

After lunch, I am anticipating the students' increased energy because I have been warned of the bizarre mood swings that occur after the lunch hour. It was not long ago that I was the perpetrator of such hyperactive behavior! During the afternoon, the seventh- and eighth-grade students rotate from classroom to classroom, and I will be teaching guidance along with the very friendly substitute teacher. My lesson involves a survey and a small debate about issues of gender equity in the sports world. My first class is my homeroom class, with whom I have already established a rapport. I am preparing for a noisy class in which a lot of discussion will occur. For some reason unknown to me, I am finding it extremely difficult to take full command of the class. I am able to distribute the surveys, but the attentive behavior is slowly dissipating. Dennis is having a scientific debate with Steven across the room about whether or not a human brain will explode on Mars, a group of five girls is giggling, and nonstop conversations are relentlessly escalating in volume.

Earlier in the term, I had established a successful method that quieted the class, and now I am ready to use it. I ask the class for their attention and wait while keeping an eye on the clock. The students know that I mean business, and that I am not afraid to keep them late after school to complete any parts of the lesson that they have prevented me from presenting due to the incessant noise.

I am not quite sure of the substitute teacher's opinion of my teaching and classroom management methods, but I soon learn that she is not willing to wait for silence. She interjects, "You are all in the eighth grade and I think it's about time that you started acting like it! I can't believe how rude you all are!" She is obviously appalled by their lack of respect for me, but I also experience disrespect from her for the abrupt interruption of my silencing method. Her plea is successful for a moment. Then the noise returns. Insecurity briefly races through me: She must think that I'm an incompetent teacher, but she'll see that this method works with these students. Confidently, I continue with my classroom management strategy.

Finally, the substitute teacher, unable to control her irritation, storms next door to grab the class's special education teacher in desperation. This teacher is a large male who is feared by many students, both male and female.

At this moment I am not sure whether my face is red and burning or pale and cold; however, I know that I am both angry and in awe of the situation. I can't seem to understand the act of desperation that has just occurred. Why did she have to go and get him? I thought I had everything controlled. My authority—whatever authority remains—has been squashed. I am very embarrassed. I can't believe she decided that two young female teachers needed to be saved by a strong male figure. This is a far cry from my lesson on gender equity and the positive model I have attempted to establish as a strong, confident, and "in control" female: *we can hold our own ground.* Immediately, upon entering the classroom, the male teacher uses his powerful and domineering voice. He demands answers from the students: "What is going on in here? Why can't you cooperate with Ms. Elvin and Ms. Wright?"

Garit, one of the students who immigrated over 8 years ago, forcefully raises his hand and confidently answers the questions: "Sir, I feel that it's just much easier to respect male teachers than female teachers!"

My jaw drops. I think to myself, did I just hear that correctly? I thought that throughout the past 2 months I had created a community in the classroom that respected and valued both male and female students. I couldn't help but wonder, "Is this how my students see me?" Am I a powerless female when compared with dominant male teachers? I certainly think not!

I notice that I am frozen in my shoes in front of the class, unable to respond, and unsure of exactly how to approach the situation. How can I take action without challenging this student's belief, which may reflect deep cultural roots? How do I prevent other students from agreeing with Garit's point of view? Then the bell rings, but somehow, at this moment I do not feel that I am saved by the bell but rather interrupted.

Exploring The Case

A pre-service teaching candidate wrote this case.

Identification

Identify the key facts of this case. What factual events are central to understanding this situation? Identify the dilemmas and tensions in this case. Explore the main aspects of each dilemma and tension. Consider the dilemma from the various perspectives of the individuals involved in the case.

Analysis

Analyze the issue(s) from the viewpoints of the different people in the case. Analyze the situation by examining the benefits and risks of the teacher candidate's actions. How might the teacher plan for the next class after being "saved by the bell"?

Evaluation

Examine critically the teacher's strategies for handling the challenge(s). Does the teacher depicted fulfill, fall short of, or surpass your notion of the role of a teacher?

Alternative Solutions

Were there alternative solutions or strategies available to deal with the dilemma? Generate alternative solutions to the ones presented in the narrative. Take into consideration risks, benefits, and long- and short-term consequences of each proposed action.

Reflection

Does the teacher's concluding reflection provide a satisfying ending? What does her reference to being "saved by the bell" suggest?

Changing Opinions

Consider your thoughts and assumptions at the beginning of the chapter. Who or what has caused you to consider a new way of thinking? How strongly do you still feel about your previous assumptions?

Synthesis

Synthesize your understanding of this case into a statement. What is this a case of?

Case Study

9

Balancing the Needs of All Students in an Inclusive Classroom

Thinking Ahead

As you read this Case Study, reflect on the following questions and issues:

- Consider the teacher's attitudes, experience, and knowledge. How does the teacher prepare for this particular class? What difficulties does the teacher foresee?
- Consider the contextual elements of the school and the classroom that influence the dilemmas faced by the teacher.
- What strategies does the teacher use to balance the needs of all members of the class?
- What does the teacher do to remedy the situation?
- Consider the teacher's frustration. What professional issues are at stake here?

"This is going to be fun! Scott is in our class."

My ears prick up. This is an early warning sign of an interesting classroom challenge, which might have long-term classroom management implications.

It is the first day of school, our very first meeting—a class of 35 advanced-enriched students enrolled in the 10th-grade Contemporary Government and World Concerns course. I sense the dominant male energy in the room as they jostle for position, just going through the door. I have been teaching this history program at this school for many years. I know these students will be energetic, verbal, involved, talented, highly skilled, and outward looking. These teenagers are always fun and a real joy to teach. They can be intellectually engaged and are ready to participate in all forms of learning. They are eager for success, marks are important to them, and most are prepared to work hard and experiment with new ideas.

I teach in a large urban center in a school of 2,200. We liken ourselves to a small town. The school is ethnically diverse, and its specialized programs and facilities draw

Reprinted from *Cases for Teacher Development: Preparing for the Classroom* (2005), Sage Publications, Inc.

students from the whole city. The school atmosphere is conducive to the academic and personal development of every student. It is a vibrant, noisy, "happening" place, and the school prides itself on providing an inclusive atmosphere where every child has the opportunity to excel. Courses are offered at the general, advanced, and advanced-enriched levels. Students are invited into the advanced-enriched program based on their academic achievement, creativity, and task commitment.

All I truly know at this moment is that there are 30 boys and 5 girls in this class, including the unknown quantity: Scott.

I meet Scott, and I know that I am confronted with my classroom challenge. He immediately fills my personal space. He is "nose to nose" when he is on the offensive, but he quickly retreats when I step forward. His constant interruptions during attendance demonstrate a lack of understanding of basic classroom procedures and dynamics. Initially, the other students are quiet, but soon, they needle him, turn away, or quietly try to provoke him. They are aware of the triggers that will set him off: "Did you see the article about the lap dancers in the newspaper?" But really, almost anything sets him off.

Eyebrows raise, heads turn to smirk or giggle at his outlandish take on what most consider commonplace. Issues about smoking, drug use, and sexual practices and orientation intrigue Scott. Surprisingly, there is a strong religious overtone to his comments. "You'll go to hell and be punished forever for smoking," he intones, with more than a hint of moral indignation. His body language is peculiar as well. He can be abrupt and threatening. It is obvious that he has no comprehension about how to create positive peer relationships. He rants or mumbles.

What is it about Scott? His behavior is so different from the usually noisy, aggressive, disruptive student that I have encountered during my long teaching career.

I continue to ponder the best course of action for this unusual young man. The class is always on tenterhooks, waiting for my response to Scott. He is going to require a great deal of patience and all of my parenting skills to deal effectively with his particular situation. I have questions for Guidance, his vice principal, the head of the advanced-enriched department, and possibly the local school team.

After the first few weeks of term with Scott burrowing into any plans I make for the class, I am aware that I am going to have to rethink some of my teaching strategies. I have 100 Tenth-grade students, and our plan is to create and hold our own model government and model United Nations. I utilize collaborative teaching strategies to cover large areas of material because classroom management and good peer relationships are critical for student success.

This is the situation: I need to integrate Scott into the classroom. I need to find a "place" for him in my student activities where he can shine and not disrupt the learning around him. I need to spend less classroom time helping him to manage his behavior. He has the ability to distract all of us from the task at hand. When he is absent, the class breathes a collective sigh of relief. I observe that the classroom dynamics are weakening as more and more students amuse themselves by engaging Scott in silly, disruptive banter. Yet I feel a need to reach out and discuss Scott with the class, to openly gain their support, but I realize that the issue of confidentiality would be compromised.

I need to know about Scott.

There are no answers forthcoming. His medical records and his diagnosis are confidential. There is no interaction, no response from his parents. I never meet them. There is no opportunity to consult with all of his teachers simultaneously. There is little support from Guidance; his Guidance teacher is bound by parental requests for silence. The head of the advanced-enriched program and the vice principal will only say that he has been placed in the program because his parents fear for his physical safety within the general school environment. As the year progresses, there are hints from others that he may suffer from a form of autism known as Asperger's Syndrome. I begin to wonder whether or not I have the right to know about Scott. Is a family's need for privacy greater than my need to know?

We still have to manage the daily program. Regular classes are improving. Scott and I meet daily for lunch for a few weeks. We come to a mutual understanding about his classroom behavior. Scott and I have developed small signals for each other—time for me to teach, and time for Scott to raise issues of concern. These issues must come from the newspaper and may not be related to smoking, drugs, or sexual behavior. In a way, they are loosely linked to my history course content. The class attempts to listen and discuss political issues initiated by his comments or conjectures. Although Scott grasps the facts, he finds their interrelationships difficult to comprehend. The other students perceive the threads of history, how past and present intermingle, and this baffles and annoys Scott.

But Scott also needs time to back out of potentially nasty encounters with his neighboring students. We decide that he will sit slightly apart from the others. He needs to maintain the integrity of his own space. The signals we have agreed on have some success, but he often forgets them as the year progresses. All of us are constrained by the sudden changes of his behavior. Our expectations for the year are becoming limited.

Yet we have established a structure to our daily classroom routines where Scott is not able to always interrupt and totally divert my intentions for study, and the class is more amenable to organizing our classroom simulations. The model government and model United Nations are excellent tools for discussion and for individual and group research. We are able to include Scott in some of the group work, and the class is satisfied that they will be able to earn their own marks. I have decided that group mark will not be influenced by any of Scott's work. His classmates even find a special role for him in our model government as Party Whip. Scott feels powerful, accepted, and an integral component of the model government. We choose a very strong Speaker of the House, and I am voted in as Sergeant at Arms. Their sense of humor is still intact.

The year passes. We have struggled with each other, and the program has suffered. My department head is concerned about the retention rate for our senior elective enriched history programs. Scott has found a precarious acceptance in class. He achieves limited academic success. He passes on his own merit with some extra weighting for appropriate classroom behavior. He has managed to complete all of his assignments. His arguments are thin, but since these students are to be evaluated as advanced-level students, and since he can grasp and organize the factual material, he is able to achieve 51 percent. He is very disappointed. He does not understand how little he understands, and he is angry.

My patience has worn thin, and I am not pleased with the year. The rest of the class has not received the attention that I feel is their due. All of Scott's teachers are frustrated with the lack of support from the administration, frustrated with the loss of teaching time while they struggled to mold his behavior to suit their classroom needs. His privacy was maintained—but there was a cost.

In retrospect, Scott was an invaluable lesson to all of us.

Exploring The Case

A secondary school teacher with 28 years of experience wrote this case.

Identification

Identify the key facts of this case. What events are central to understanding this situation? Identify the dilemmas and tensions in this case. Explore the main aspects of each dilemma and tension.

Analysis

Analyze the issue(s) from the viewpoints of the different people in the case. What makes Scott's story unique? Consider the consequences of integrating a student like Scott with special needs into regular or special classes.

Evaluation

Examine critically the teacher's strategies for handling the challenge(s). Does the teacher depicted fulfill, fall short of, or surpass your notion of the role of a teacher?

Alternative Solutions

Were there alternative solutions or strategies available to deal with the teacher's dilemma? Generate alternative solutions to the ones presented in the narrative. Take into consideration risks, benefits, and long- and short-term consequences of each proposed action.

Reflection

At the conclusion of the case, the teacher ponders the role that Scott played in the lives of the other students. What new insight has been revealed? Has anything been resolved?

Changing Opinions

Consider your thoughts and assumptions at the beginning of the chapter. Who or what has caused you to consider a new way of thinking? How strongly do you still feel about your previous assumptions?

Synthesis

Synthesize your understanding of this case into a statement. What is this a case of?

Case Study

10

Developing Appropriate Boundaries
With a Troubled Student

Thinking Ahead

As you read this Case Study, reflect on the following issues:

- Consider the skills, attitudes, experience, and knowledge of the teacher.
- Consider the contextual issues.
- Identify the problems and pressures that are disturbing Mel.
- List the dilemmas the teacher must face regarding Mel.

There was an uneasy silence in the almost empty classroom. Mel looked downward before she spoke. "I need to talk." There was a tremor in her voice, and I knew that something important was to follow.

"I was wondering if you have this friend, and she's into drugs big-time, and she tells you she wants to get off them, what do you do? I don't know how to help her."

So typical of Mel. She was the type of kid who always thought of others first. I had known her for 5 years when she had come from outside the district to attend our school because it was a Gifted Center. Even in the first days of our ninth-grade English class, I could tell that her choice to join the gifted class was not an easy one. There was shyness about her, and I could see she felt awkward moving in her own skin. Growth spurts do that sometimes. But I knew she belonged here, in this class. I could see how much she loved to learn, and for the most part, it came easily to her. Now she was in the home stretch, her final semester of high school.

She was the type of kid who takes time to know. In fact, it was only when I taught her a second time in my 11th-grade Media class that I discovered her intense passion for horses. She was an accomplished rider who committed herself totally to the sport, winning local and provincial competitions. I also learned then that Mel, a high-

Reprinted from *Cases for Teacher Development: Preparing for the Classroom* (2005), Sage Publications, Inc.

performance individual, had no respect for failure—especially her own. The way she talked, I could picture Mel and her horse, groundless together. Riding simply spoke to who she was. I think that's why she loved writing, because no one need speak; yet at the same time, she could be connected to the unspoken rhythms in her own life.

"I think she wants help."

I told her I would get some information about drug programs in our community from the guidance office, and that I would get back to her.

Later, that same evening, a small surge pulsed from deep within me, grew like a wave, and pressed hard against my chest. I knew in an instant that the troubled teen that Mel had alluded to was, in fact, her. Questions flooded my mind. How should I broach the subject without jeopardizing her trust in me? If my hunch were true, what was my role to be?

The next morning I went directly to the head of guidance at our school. Joan was a strong advocate of students, especially for those with exceptionalities. We shared a natural rapport, and I respected Joan's judgment. I told her about the situation, while protecting the anonymity of the student. However, as I began to tell the story, I realized that I had come here as much for myself as for Mel. I needed a space to think out loud and examine my own lack of knowledge. I wasn't even aware of my legal responsibilities regarding disclosure, but Joan calmly reassured me that, from her perspective, the girl was in no immediate danger to herself or others.

But these were uncharted waters for me. I was not a trained counselor, and I realized I had assumed a significant role in Mel's story.

Upon reflection, I knew Mel trusted me and that the foundation of that trust had begun 5 years earlier in my ninth-grade English gifted class. I was proud that I always situated my students in the center of their own learning. We often ended our class discussions in literature by making connections to our own lives. We respected everyone's input and considered seriously the diverse voices that were encouraged in my class. All voices belonged, and so, when students would, over time, raise their concerns and explore their frustrations about being labeled "gifted," I would be part of that discussion.

Mel must have seen then that I honored the voices of my students by truly listening and affirming their struggles. How could I honor her voice now?

I had a clear sense that she had a place for me on this journey. I knew I was not interested in becoming a "professional pal," but what was an appropriate distance to serve her needs? As I talked, a picture began to form in my mind:

"What if I could serve as a bridge for her?"

A bridge to resources and a bridge back to her family.

Mel had grown up in a high-performance home. She was the gifted daughter of gifted parents. Her mom was an accomplished doctor and writer. Her dad was a professional engineer. Mel's older sister, Sarah, was developmentally delayed, and Mel grew up watching the quiet devotion of her parents to Sarah's special needs. Mel confided that she felt guilty for being the "smart one." She worked hard not to give her parents trouble. It was difficult to reconcile the two conflicting pictures of Mel—the good child and the drug user.

I was glad the next day that our graduating English class backed on to lunch, and there was a chance to talk. I circled the hard edges of exposing "her friend's" identity for a short time, and then I took the leap.

"Mel, I have this gut feeling that the person we are talking about is you."

Simply, she said, "Yes."

Since that day, I have often wondered about the way she hid herself inside the story. Perhaps it was a clever strategy to give her the chance to see if she indeed trusted me, and to determine if she really wanted help. In a curious way, I sensed that she needed to test me: the highly intuitive child checking on the teacher's own level of unspoken awareness. How difficult for Mel to expose for the very first time her own sense of failure to another adult.

Over time, I learned many things. She told me that she had been progressively smoking more dope each day for over 2 years. She smoked at home in the basement, and she smoked in the washrooms. Her friends readily accepted her into the group: "Mel was cool." They shared an unspoken habit, and closeness was measured by how often they smoked together. Support was defined by helping a friend get more weed. Belonging was tied to a single need. This was friendship at no cost.

I was relieved when Mel finally decided to tell Joan about her situation. This was a good sign because she was beginning to build a network of support inside the school. However, there was nothing calm about this journey.

That first week that she stopped taking drugs, she entered my classroom while I was teaching. Her face was pale. Her hands trembled.

"I can't do this," she whispered. "It's just too hard."

I was in the middle of teaching a class and directed her to Joan's office. After she left, I took a deep breath, returned to my room, and continued the lesson. But in front of my students, I was troubled by Mel's physical well-being.

Thank goodness for the solid support of colleagues. I hurried to see Joan that day. She reported that Mel was not sleeping well, and that she had stopped eating. Keeping her secret was becoming more and more difficult at home. We both agreed that Mel must talk to her mom as soon as possible.

That same week, Mel confided how easy it was to fabricate lies in order to trick her parents. I knew Mel trusted me because I spoke from the center of my conviction. Much later, she confessed that she liked that I challenged her.

"They think I'm at a friend's house when I'm really at a rave. They never suspect a thing."

"As a parent myself, Mel, I have to tell you that parents want what's best for their children. Up to this point, you've given them no cause to mistrust you."

"They've always trusted me. Given me the freedom to figure things out on my own."

"Why was that?"

"Because I could be trusted. They had confidence in me."

"And now you have lied to them for over 2 years, and see them as fools for not figuring it out? You said you trusted me. That's why you came to me in the first place. Mel, talk to your mom. Give your parents the chance to really support you—not just when things are going well, but when things are going badly."

One week later, she revealed the truth to her mom. Shortly after, I met with Mel and her mom at the mom's request. As soon as we shook hands, I observed that she was a high-energy woman who had a plan of action. She gave Mel the latest research on drugs and a crash course in the physiology of addiction. She put her in touch with a professional counselor, and for that I was thankful.

There was nothing easy in Mel's relationship with her mom. There was a strain in the mother's look, a detachment in her voice. She wanted so badly a clean solution to such a complex problem. When she told me that she always valued "an honest and open relationship with her daughter," I noticed that Mel immediately looked down. For me, the mother had a simple request: to be a connection in her daughter's school day, to listen, and to support.

Mel and I walked every day during my prep period, usually for about one-half hour. I think she felt freer to speak her mind when we walked side by side, never making eye contact, but going in one direction. Our walks continued for three months, leading up to graduation.

As I listened to Mel's story, I was reminded of the importance of understanding the special needs and backgrounds of students, particularly my gifted students. As I learned more about Mel's predicament, my attitude began to change.

I was troubled by my school's approach to gifted education. As early as eighth grade, secondary schools were actively recruiting these talented students.

Our principal had recently been promoted, and he saw his role as instilling pride in his school by "showcasing" the talents and accomplishments of the gifted students to the larger community. He blithely promoted our school's image of excellence on the backs of these students.

I have been teaching these gifted students for over 15 years now, and attitudes that stereotype them—the image of the dream class—doesn't change easily. Even yesterday in the staff room, a senior teacher told me that it must be nice to teach these students: "They show up every day, do what they're told, and teach themselves."

I was furious. I wanted to challenge her, but just wasn't up for it. I was too tired. My thoughts had returned to Mel, the gifted, Mel, the horsewoman, Mel, the troubled.

In all of my conversations with Mel, one moment stands out:

"Remember you said life is like sailing. You need to grab hold of the rigging, take charge of the boat. I think I know what you mean now."

"That's good to hear, Mel."

"Remember how I told you I felt I was in a fog."

"Yeah, I remember."

"Well, the fog is starting to rise."

"And what do you see?"

"I'm a long way from shore."

"You always were, Mel. But now, you finally know it for the first time."

And she began to cry.

Mel started to keep a journal and began to write more. She said that even William, her horse, knew that she was more connected to her "real self."

Even though Mel graduated clean that spring, I can't say that she has totally recovered. I hear from her in university, and she tells me that when stress gets bad, she finds her way back to drugs. Perhaps those currents will always pull her.

Since that time, however, I have tried to apply what I have learned. I gave a workshop last February at our professional development day, challenging the myths of teaching the gifted. I am currently leading the mentorship program at our school, and for next year, I have decided to form a staff gifted team to identify the specific learning needs of at-risk students.

Time locates timeliness.

There are moments in our teaching careers we don't choose. They choose us. And what of the role of the teacher beyond the mechanics of the classroom, the routines that organize our comings and goings? Sometimes we are forced to leave the safe harbor, to set sail for a short time with another, to nudge with our listening care, toward this simple wish—that we all may know our singular uniqueness and accept our place of belonging on this good earth. And groundless becomes grounded in this new understanding.

Exploring The Case

A secondary school teacher with 20 years of experience wrote this case.

Identification

Identify the key facts of this case. What events are central to understanding this situation? Identify the dilemmas and tensions in this case. Explore the main aspects of each dilemma and tension.

Analysis

Analyze the issue(s) from the viewpoints of the different people in the case. What is Mel's story? Does she represent the typical gifted student? As you begin to reread this case, consider whether or not the teacher depicted fulfills, falls short of, or surpasses your notion of the role of a teacher.

Evaluation

Examine critically the teacher's strategies for handling the challenge(s) with Mel. Does the teacher depicted fulfill, fall short of, or surpass your notion of the role of a teacher?

Alternative Solutions

Were there alternative solutions or strategies available to deal with the dilemma(s)? Generate alternative solutions to the ones presented in the narrative. Take into consideration risks, benefits, and long- and short-term consequences of each proposed action.

Reflection

The teacher is very philosophical at the end of the story, moving outward to thoughts on education and its place in the larger scheme of life. Has anything been resolved or learned through this experience with Mel?

Changing Opinions

Consider your thoughts and assumptions at the beginning of the chapter. Who or what has caused you to consider a new way of thinking? How strongly do you still feel about your previous assumptions?

Synthesis

Synthesize your understanding of this case into a statement. What is this a case of?